APPROACHING
POETRY
Perspectives and Responses

About the Authors

Peter Schakel is Peter C. and Emajean Cook Professor of English at Hope College, Holland, Michigan. He is author of *The Poetry of Jonathan Swift* (1978) and two books on C. S. Lewis—*Reading with the Heart: The Way into Narnia* (1979) and *Reason and Imagination in C. S. Lewis* (1984). He is also editor of *Critical Approaches to Teaching Swift* (1992) and *The Longing for a Form: Essays on the Fiction of C. S. Lewis* (1977), and coeditor with Charles A. Huttar of *Word and Story in C. S. Lewis* (1991) and *The Rhetoric of Vision: Essays on Charles Williams* (1996). He has published dozens of scholarly essays and reviews, given numerous popular and scholarly lectures, and presented many papers at professional meetings.

Jack Ridl is professor of English at Hope College, where he teaches courses in poetry writing and the nature of poetry. He has published four volumes of poetry, the most recent of which is *Poems from* The Same Ghost *and* Between (1993). He has published more than 150 poems in some fifty literary magazines, and his work has appeared in a half-dozen anthologies. Ridl has led numerous workshops in poetry for both students and teachers and been recognized for his teaching, including being named 1996 Michigan Professor of the Year by the Council for the Advancement and Support of Education.

APPROACHING POETRY
Perspectives and Responses

Peter Schakel

HOPE COLLEGE

Jack Ridl

HOPE COLLEGE

FOREWORD BY

Alberto Ríos

BEDFORD/ST. MARTIN'S
Boston ◆ New York

SPONSORING EDITOR: Meg Spilleth
MANAGING EDITOR: Patricia Mansfield Phelan
PROJECT EDITORS: Diana M. Puglisi, Harold Chester
PRODUCTION SUPERVISOR: Kurt Nelson
ART DIRECTOR: Lucy Krikorian
TEXT DESIGN: Anna George
COVER DESIGN: Lucy Krikorian
COVER PHOTO: © M. Gesinger

Library of Congress Catalog Card Number: 96-67028

Manufactured in the United States of America.

3   2   1   0
f   e   d   c

For information, write:
Bedford/St. Martin's
75 Arlington Street
Boston, MA 02116
(617-399-4000)

ISBN: 0-312-13281-6

Acknowledgments

Contents in Brief

APPENDIXES

Contents

8 Sounds   *118*

9 Rhythm and Meter   *131*

PART III: VANTAGE POINTS

11 Authors   *179*

APPENDIXES

Preface

Approaching Poetry: Perspectives and Responses is organized around two premises. The first is that an introduction to poetry needs to alleviate the trepidation with which many students approach poetry. It meets that need by its empathetic tone, its clear and careful explanations of technical material, and the reader-oriented approach that undergirds it. The second premise is that introductions to poetry are not and cannot be theory-free. *Approaching Poetry: Perspectives and Responses* begins, therefore, by explaining its underlying assumptions directly; it blends theoretical considerations into its introduction to the elements of poetry; and it offers alternative perspectives from which to approach and engage with a poem.

FEATURES

Focus on Readers Throughout the book there is an emphasis on the reader's response: to the elements of poetry as well as to poems themselves. The book's approach assumes that the particulars of a poem deserve attention for their own sake, as well as for the role they play in the poem. Students often are (have been taught to be) primarily concerned with *subject,* with "comprehension" of a poem. *Approaching Poetry* suggests asking initially not "What does this poem say?" or "What does this poem mean?" but "What engages me in this poem?" It encourages students to notice and talk about a variety of things in a poem, "subject" being but one of them. It presents diction, tone, imagery, figures, symbols, rhythm, and form as dynamic elements that readers can respond to and that open up a poem to a variety of ways of talking or writing about it. Thus some students may gravitate toward images, for example, while others may concentrate on rhythm or form. As they learn to discuss what engages them about that element, and hear what other students say about different elements, they will have gone a long way toward experiencing the richness and complexity of a poem.

Attention to Theory *Approaching Poetry* regards awareness of theoretical issues as essential to informed reading. Consideration of theory leads students to recognize the approaches they (and their instructors) employ, and provides them with tools and understanding for responding in a variety of ways to poetry—in the classroom, in conversation, in writing, and in their lives outside the classroom. The coverage of theory in this book stresses application, not abstraction. Because *Approaching Poetry: Perspectives and Responses* is intended as an introduction to poetry, not an introduction to theory, it does not try to provide a comprehensive survey of approaches. Theory must not overwhelm the poetry; but an introduction to poetry today, if it is to reflect contemporary studies and concerns, must recognize that people approach poetry from a variety of perspectives.

Diverse Selection of Poems The poems in the chapters and in the anthology together comprise a representative group of works by respected writers prior to 1950, and a generous selection from writers whose work has appeared since 1950, among them many women, authors from various cultures, and exciting writers often overlooked by introductory anthologies. The book, of course, cannot include selections by every poet whose work is valuable. Many poems that teachers and students will want to read are not here. What we tried to do is select poems that will be interesting and constructively challenging, that affirm a plurality of approaches and visions, and that may lead the reader to further exploration. We only wish there were more space.

Applications At the end of each chapter is a section called "Applications," offering suggestions for how students can put into practice the inquiry the chapter has initiated. We begin with "Suggestions for Writing." These fall roughly into two types. The first few prompts suggest ways students can synthesize what they've read by applying concepts to experiences outside of poetry. Prompts for writing about poems and poetry then follow. The "Suggestions As You Continue to Read Poetry" summarize key material in the chapter in terms of what students can do with the material once they have made it their own. We prefer to call these "suggestions" to indicate that they open up options for student response. We recognize that writing and reading are not the only ways students can apply what they are learning, and encourage teachers to invite other modes of application and response as well.

Flexible Approaches to Writing The emphasis in the appendix section "Responding on Paper" is on providing clear, specific guidelines and examples for critical essays. But just as recent theory has introduced new ideas about reading, so it has led to changes in ways of writing about literature. Students learn best in different ways and write best in different ways: this book both presents students with various possibilities that will engage their intellects and imaginations and encourages them to respond actively to poems.

World Wide Web Site *Approaching Poetry: Perspectives and Responses* has a page on the World Wide Web that offers information about web sites that feature poetry. An on-line Instructor's Manual is also available, with tips on teaching individual poems, additional possibilities for paper topics, and questions that can lead to ideas for class sessions. Available as well is an on-line discussion group for raising questions and sharing ideas about poems or problems encountered in teaching.

The aim of *Approaching Poetry: Perspectives and Responses* is freshness in both approach and illustrative examples, clarity in explanations (always remaining sensitive to where undergraduates are coming from), presented in an engaging style. Unifying the book and forming its underlying premise is an affirmation of the value of teaching *approaches* to literature, not just one approach (whether the one be formalism, feminism, Marxism, or whatever), in order to enrich conversations about individual works and the study not just of poetry but of literature as a whole.

ACKNOWLEDGMENTS

We thank all our colleagues in the English Department at Hope College for their help and encouragement on this project, particularly Jane Bach, John Cox, and Francis Fike for their comments and suggestions and Charles Huttar for his careful critiques of many of the chapters, which offered valuable suggestions and corrections and helped solve numerous problems. We also thank our students, who have stimulated our thinking about poetry and teaching, used the book in typescript, and improved it by their ideas and suggestions. We are indebted particularly to Andrew DeGraves and Kristin Knippenberg, who served as student assistants, and to Jonathan Schakel, who did excellent work for a year and a half on research, revisions, and permissions. Thanks as well to Anne Lucas, Patti Carlson, and Kristin Knippenberg for allowing us to include their writing.

We appreciate the help given us by colleagues elsewhere, especially Tom Andrews of Purdue University and Peter Connelly of Grinnell College for reading parts of the book and offering good counsel; Bill Sheidley of the University of Southern Colorado, who read and reread most of the book at various stages, and made numerous invaluable corrections and suggestions for improving its organization and presentation; and Naomi Shihab Nye and Alberto Ríos, who read and responded to the manuscript from their perspectives as exemplary poet/teachers. We are indebted to the reviewers of the manuscript—Jane Agee, The University at Albany–State University of New York; Jane Archer, Birmingham-Southern College; Tim Barnes, Portland Community College–Sylvania Campus; Betty Beckley, University of Maryland; Wendy Bishop, Florida State University; Malcolm Glass, Austin Peay State University; Janet Hubbs, Ocean County College; Lauren Marsh, University of Minnesota; Rev. Noel Mueller, St. Meinrad College; Kevin Murphy, Ithaca College; Sidney Poger, University of Vermont; Roger Weaver, Oregon State University—for the insights and encouragement they provided.

We are grateful also for support from Hope College, especially from Provost Jacob Nyenhuis, Dean Bobby Fong, and Dean William Reynolds, and for two summer Faculty Development Grants that made early work on the book possible. We owe more than we could possibly recount—though the list includes typing, organizing materials, problem solving, and various kinds of assistance in meeting deadlines—to Myra Kohsel, who held both the book and us together with her gifts of exceptional capability and patience.

We are very grateful for support from St. Martin's Press. Meg Spilleth believed in the project, kept us encouraged and disciplined, and saw the book through its editing stages with keen judgment, excellent ideas, and unfailing vision. Diana Puglisi and Harold Chester prepared the manuscript with meticulous attention to form and details, and coordinated production with great efficiency and effectiveness. We also thank Nancy Lyman for her confidence that this was a book worth doing and for guiding it through its earliest stages.

Finally, we thank our wives, Karen Schakel and Julie Ridl. Their enthusiasm, encouragement, ideas, and insights can be read between every line of the book.

Peter Schakel

Jack Ridl

Foreword

I did not read poems very much growing up, yet it was out of my growing up that poems came. In one form or another, I lived my poems—and that's something we don't account for very well in the classroom. We read poems, but we don't bring to that moment the life they have in them.

We don't, for example, assemble into the center of the classroom the things that are said in the poem: the fir tree, the marbles, the warm tears, the branding iron. We assume that the words for these things will do their work responsibly. But I don't know about that anymore. Words sometimes feel like our weakest hold on the world.

Yet they are a hold, nonetheless, perfect or imperfect, and weak as they may be they constitute one of our greatest strengths as human beings: language. And written language is a magic, the ability to speak to someone who is not with you in the room. Written language in this way is like an early telephone or telegraph, even an early television or radio.

But what about poetry? It is at once far more ancient than these technologies, yet constantly new. The stakes here are suddenly raised, because the point in poetry is not just to write a thing, but to write it well. And something done well, that is what makes art.

Some people say that poets work like the antennae of culture—they feel ahead for what's coming. In doing this, many poems that get written are "strange," but only because everything new is strange. It's part of the definition.

Another kind of work that poets do is to look backward, to remember. In doing this, many poems that get written are the opposite of strange, because everything old is known—or forgotten. Yet such poems, at their best, are neither "boring" nor "familiar." Going backward for me is something I always talk about. The farther back I can stretch, just like the farthest forward I can reach, is a kind of stretching that makes me stronger. It builds poetry muscles.

But perhaps the most difficult and best work that poets do is finding the edge in the middle, showing us what we already know, but showing it new. They offer up what's right in front of us in a way that surprises and engages. They show us what we know, but remember for us as well the delight of how we came to know it. They try to translate that understanding through language onto the page, not as simple words but as some*thing*.

In my own poetry, all three approaches work in concert, within a framework of details. I was born in Nogales, Arizona, on the border of Mexico. My father was from Tapachula, Chiapas, Mexico, and my mother from Warrington, Lancashire, England. I grew up around my father's family, but I look like my mother—which means I got to see two worlds from the beginning. I could even physically experience the difference growing up where I did: every day of my life I could stand with one foot in Mexico and one foot in the United States, both at the same time.

For all practical purposes my first language was more or less Spanish, though my mother's British English had its quiet share of my voice. Living in Arizona in the 1950s, I had no problem with this until the first grade. When we got to that first-grade classroom, my friends and I, we were told: you can't speak Spanish here.

That was crazy, of course, and we all raised our hands, saying *seguro que sí*—of course we can speak it! But no, they said, that's not what they meant. We were simply not to speak it, and some got swats, even for speaking Spanish on the playground. Our teachers were trying to help, but we learned far more than that basic lesson. Our equation was bigger than that classroom. Our parents had taught us that you got swatted for doing something bad. So, if we got swatted for speaking Spanish, then Spanish must be bad.

There was a bargain in this, though: what we saw when we got to the first-grade classroom was clay, blackboards, cubbyholes, fingerpaints, kickballs that weren't flat. And when we got home and looked around, we didn't see any of that stuff. We knew what we wanted. The decision was easy. And if learning English was going to get these things for us—well, we weren't dumb. We could play along.

But again we were learning something bigger than the classroom. We were smart enough to understand that if speaking Spanish was bad, then we must be bad kids. And since our parents still spoke Spanish, they had to be bad, too. This was easy enough for children to grasp; so, though of course we loved our parents, we learned to be ashamed, if only at school. We didn't say it that way, but it's the only word I've got. You can imagine what PTA meetings were like—we didn't have any. None of us ever took the notes home.

By junior high school and the beginning of high school, I could no longer speak Spanish—which is to say, I didn't want to; I was embarrassed, and I didn't practice. Not until my later years of high school and college did I relearn Spanish, but that is what I had to do, relearn. It was more than words, though; I discovered that my Spanish hadn't gone anywhere. It was still inside of me. What I had to do was not relearn the language itself, but rather relearn my attitude toward it. In doing this I was learning how to look at something in more than one way.

After all these years, however, this was the bonus, and the path that would lead me to poetry. In having to pay double and triple attention to language— first to forget, and then to relearn—I began to see earnestly how everything, every object, every idea, had at least two names, and that the process worked like a pair of binoculars. It showed me how, by using two lenses, one might see something more closely, and thereby understand it better.

I was relearning how to look at the world. A language implies, after all, a different set of ideas—different ways of looking. This took me from the one-dimensional to an approach with depth. Whether I knew this or not at the time I began teaching and writing, this is what my writing and my teaching are all about now—how to look at something better, how to look at something from many perspectives. And there is no shame in this.

While I had more than one language growing up, I feel it's inaccurate to say so easily that my first language was either Spanish or English. What I've come to realize is that my first language was the language of listening, of taking in. Today, I find myself in the middle of debates on things such as bilingualism, and am asked questions about whether I write in English or Spanish, or both. Somewhere along the line English and Spanish got all the billing. But it occurs to me that I still write in my *true* "first" language—again, that language of listening. I look for it, I smell for it, wherever it is. I follow it. We all share this primary language of listening, and in this way we are all bilingual.

As a younger writer, I used to look for language *only* in words, rather than in the things those words were. But when I was a boy, I "talked" to my grandmother in a different way: she would cook, and I would eat. The whole exchange was not about words at all, but it's how she and I talked best. It was poetry, but it was meatballs and mint, Spanish rice and lemons.

This language, this exchange, is about more than recognizing something from both sides. It's about first recognizing something inside all the words for it. That's what I want in my own poems, and it's what I want to find in the poems of others. I look for things that have a voice of their own and I try to listen before I speak. In this way, I try not to be simply a user, but a partner to those things in the world around and inside and beyond me. On their own terms, and in their own languages. This is how writing comes to me, and how I give it back.

But if I am a user, I would like to think that I do what my grandmother did for me, that I take what I know, what's happened to me or what I imagine, and from these experiences I make something that is the equal of bread at the kitchen table—that is, something that has value in the community. This includes the community of people in which I live, the community of ideas, and the community of the imagination, in all of which I have a real stake, and not just as a writer or a reader.

But how might we change our reading in profound ways and not simply cosmetic ones? How do we reach farther than we have, and farther than we can? How can a piece of writing itself be partner to this process? The reading and study of poetry is one good way of cultivating the many lives inside a moment, of understanding how to move, as I have, from wanting kickballs that weren't flat to knowing shame, from tasting Spanish rice to hearing in it my grandmother's voice.

This all has to do with what's *in* poems, but what about what's around poems? Or what about the poem itself, and the most obvious thing that jumps out at us when we look at poems: their form, their visual immediacy? And what about all those names for these forms, like "sonnets" and "sestinas," "haiku" and "kyrielles," *corridos* and "epithalamiums" and other intimidating names? Well, if poems have requisite forms or shapes or rules, and often they do, before you think about names like "sonnets" or "haiku," maybe the first thing to look for is simply what is familiar. What in the poem have you held in your hand? What in it have you tasted before?

You understand what I'm getting at here; as a reader, don't be afraid to look for yourself in the poems in this book. You'll never get a perfect reflection, but maybe that's why you picked up this book and not a mirror or a camera. The reflection will be you, if just some part; it will reflect what you want, or where you've been; it will be the opposite of you, or startlingly like you. You will find, however, something that matters.

But after you have found yourself in here, you must use that confidence and let it lead you. The familiar makes the leap to the unfamiliar possible. The binoculars come again to mind—how the putting together of two lenses brings something that is far away closer, allowing us to understand it better. The rest follows easily: understanding is knowledge, and knowledge is intrinsically valuable. Using the familiar—binoculars—to look at the unfamiliar is a valuable and brave enterprise. We may not always have binoculars, but it will not scare us when we find in their place such words as "sonnet," or "villanelle," which are also devices of examination that bring the unfamiliar into focus.

But let us raise this metaphor still one more level. I live in the desert, a landscape with its own form, its own rules and shape and language. When you look at this desert world, so much of it is so bright, you are forced to close your eyes. But when you close your eyes, you are resting, sleeping, even dreaming. Stepping out into the desert world, stepping out into light, then closing your eyes: in this moment—much as when you open this book—you are stepping into dream. But it is not dream alone.

You look at this world, if only for a moment, with your eyes and with your imagination both. That is what the desert is. You become a part of this place in that instant, complicit in its landscape, a partner to its vistas. You help to make up what you think you are seeing by *focusing,* with your eyes and your mind both.

One last thing about the desert—and it's awful. During brushfires, jackrabbits can get caught in the flames, no matter how fast they are. And when they're caught, their hair can catch on fire. Of course they run away from the flame, but you know what happens—they bring the fire with them. I think poetry is like that sometimes, catching us. This is not a perfect metaphor, by any means. I'm sorry for the rabbits. But the power of this moment, there's something in it that I recognize. I can see the picture in these words.

This book is called *Approaching Poetry.* I found *approach* defined simply as "come nearer to," which seems like the "stepping into" I describe when talking about the desert where I live. If after having read through this book you "come nearer to" poetry, you won't be sorry. You may catch on fire, though, so be warned. But it won't be like the jackrabbits. It may feel like it, but no flames will come from your hair. Not at first.

—Alberto Ríos

APPROACHING POETRY
Perspectives and Responses

Approaching Poetry

When you think of "poetry," what comes to mind? Something along these lines?

> Whose woods these are I think I know.
> His house is in the village, though;
> He will not see me stopping here
> To watch his woods fill up with snow.

—ROBERT FROST (see p. 326)

or

> How do I love thee? Let me count the ways.
> I love thee to the depth and breadth and height
> My soul can reach, when feeling out of sight
> For the ends of Being and ideal Grace.

—ELIZABETH BARRETT BROWNING
(see p. 245)

or

> I'm Nobody! Who are you?
> Are you—Nobody—Too?
> Then there's a pair of us?
> Don't tell! they'd advertise—you know!
>
> How dreary—to be—Somebody!
> How public—like a Frog—
> To tell one's name—the livelong June—
> To an admiring Bog!

—EMILY DICKINSON

There is common agreement that these are excellent and widely loved poems. But what about the ones on the following pages, which may not fit the traditional "look" of a poem? They illustrate how poems are printed in many books of poetry and poetry journals—each starting at the top of a page, with the white space surrounding it contributing to its aesthetic effect and inviting the reader to pause and reflect. Unfortunately, every poem in a textbook cannot be on its own page. But we urge you to try to visualize other poems this way, too, as you read them.

DISINTEGRATION
DISINTEGRATION
DISINTEGRATION
DISINTEGRATION
DISINTEGRATION

homage to my hips

these hips are big hips
they need space to
move around in.
they don't fit into little
petty places. these hips
are free hips.
they don't like to be held back.
these hips have never been enslaved,
they go where they want to go
they do what they want to do.
these hips are mighty hips.
these hips are magic hips.
i have known them
to put a spell on a man and
spin him like a top!

Questions My Son Asked Me, Answers I Never Gave Him

1. Do gorillas have birthdays?
   Yes. Like the rainbow, they happen.
   Like the air, they are not observed.

2. Do butterflies make a noise?
   The wire in the butterfly's tongue
   hums gold.
   Some men hear butterflies
   even in winter.

3. Are they part of our family?
   They forgot us, who forgot how to fly.

4. Who tied my navel? Did God tie it?
   God made the thread: O man, live forever!
   Man made the knot: enough is enough.

5. If I drop my tooth in the telephone
   will it go through the wires and bite someone's ear?
   I have seen earlobes pierced by a tooth of steel.
   It loves what lasts.
   It does not love flesh.
   It leaves a ring of gold in the wound.

6. If I stand on my head
   will the sleep in my eye roll up into my head?
   Does the dream know its own father?
   Can bread go back to the field of its birth?

7. Can I eat a star?
   Yes, with the mouth of time
   that enjoys everything.

8. Could we Xerox the moon?
   This is the first commandment:
   I am the moon, thy moon.
   Thou shalt have no other moons before thee.

9. Who invented water?
   The hands of the air, that wanted to wash each other.

10. What happens at the end of numbers?
    I see three men running toward a field.
    At the edge of the tall grass, they turn into light.

11. Do the years ever run out?
    God said, I will break time's heart.
    Time ran down like an old phonograph.
    It lay flat as a carpet.
    At rest on its threads, I am learning to fly.

The Deaf Dancing to Rock

The eardrums of the deaf are already broken; they like it loud. They dance away the pain of silence, of a world where people laugh and wince and smirk and burst into tears over words they don't understand. As they dance the world reaches out to them, from the floor, from the vibrating walls. Now they hear the ongoing drone of a star in its nearly endless fall through space; they hear seedlings break through the crust of the earth in split-second thumps, and in another part of the world, the thud of billions of leaves hitting the ground, apart and together, in the intricate rhythmic patterns we cannot hear. Their feet, knees, hips, enact the rhythms of the universe. Their waving arms signal the sea and pull its great waves ashore.

Drift

Imagine bouncing   bumping   humping over a cliff
the briskets heaving   the baskets hooping   the birds inside out
Imagine settling out of the high air
loops   beaks   tiny dolls with inch-long skirts

Then imagine rain   The draggle of it
glinting mud   drying paste
one doll's skirt over its head
the feathers stuck   their quills all whichways

and wind   winds

Silent Poem

backroad leafmold stonewall chipmunk
underbrush grapevine woodchuck shadblow

woodsmoke cowbarn honeysuckle woodpile
sawhorse bucksaw outhouse wellsweep

backdoor flagstone bulkhead buttermilk
candlestick ragrug firedog brownbread

hilltop outcrop cowbell buttercup
whetstone thunderstorm pitchfork steeplebush

gristmill millstone cornmeal waterwheel
watercress buckwheat firefly jewelweed

gravestone groundpine windbreak bedrock
weathercock snowfall starlight cockcrow

"Disintegration" is by Richard Kostalanetz (1970); "homage to my hips" is by Lucille Clifton (1980); "Questions My Son Asked Me, Answers I Never Gave Him" is by Nancy Willard (1982); "The Deaf Dancing to Rock" is by Lisel Mueller (1979); "Drift" is by Alberta Turner (1983); "Silent Poem" is by Robert Francis (1970). (The dates given indicate when a poem was first published in a book.) For a student response to "Drift," see pages 450 and 452.

WHAT, THEN, *IS* POETRY?

The works you just read certainly vary in subject and structure. How, then, can we tell if something is poetry? The nature of poetry has always been problematic, a mystery—one that has led poets, readers, critics, and scholars to fashion their own solutions and definitions:

> If I read a book [and] it makes my whole body so cold no fire ever can warm me I know *that* is poetry. If I feel physically as if the top of my head were taken off, I know *that* is poetry. These are the only way I know it. Is there any other way.
> —Emily Dickinson

> Choose one word and say it over
> and over, till it builds a fire inside your mouth.
> —Naomi Shihab Nye

> If a line of poetry strays into my memory, my skin bristles . . . [and] a shiver [goes] down [my] spine.
> —A. E. Housman

> Poetry is the orphan of silence. Maternal silence. That in you which belongs to the Universe. The mother's voice calls its name at dusk over the roofs of the world. Whoever hears it, turns towards his ancestral home.
> —Charles Simic

> [Poetry] looks in some fresh way for the energy in the moment, and tries to translate that through language onto the page—not as words, simply, but as something. . . . Poems show us what's right in front of us—in a way that surprises and engages.
> —Alberto Ríos

> A poem is a statement in language about a human experience; since language is conceptual in its nature, this statement will be more or less rational or at least apprehensible in rational terms. . . . Poetry is written in verse: verse is exceptionally rhythmical language. . . . Rhythm is expressive of emotion, and the language of verse makes possible a more precise rendition of emotion, a more precise relationship of emotion to rational content, than would otherwise be possible.
> —Yvor Winters

> Poetry is a composition of words set to music. Most other definitions of it are indefensible, or metaphysical.
> —Ezra Pound

Sources for the definitions listed above: Dickinson—*The Letters of Emily Dickinson,* ed. Thomas H. Johnson (Cambridge, Mass.: The Belknap Press, 1958), pp. 473–74; Nye—"How Palestinians Keep Warm," *Red Suitcase* (Brockport, N.Y.: BOA Editions, 1994), p. 26; Housman —*The Name and Nature of Poetry* (Cambridge: Cambridge University Press, 1933), p. 46; Simic—statement in *The New Naked Poetry,* eds. Stephen Berg and Robert Mezey (Indianapolis: Bobbs-Merrill, 1976), p. 406; Ríos—personal communication; Winters—*Forms of Discovery* ([Chicago]: Alan Swallow, 1967), p. xvii; Pound—"Vers Libre and Arnold Dolmetsch," *Literary Essays of Ezra Pound,* ed. T. S. Eliot ([Norfolk, Conn.]: New Directions, 1954), p. 437.

The essence of poetry remains elusive and open to a range of definitions. It seems to transcend or escape all attempts to pin it down. We hope this book will not remove the mystery, but preserve it. What the book will do is introduce you to the formal elements that make up a poem, in various combinations, and offer a variety of poems to read. The aim is that as you read you will discover the pleasures and values of poetry even if, or even though, poetry itself is inexplicable.

Poets have explored the mystery of poetry. A few years ago, Heather McHugh visited Italy with several other American poets. Near the end of their time there, some of the Americans went with a group of Italian poets from Rome to Fano, to see the city and meet with dignitaries. At dinner, on their last evening in Italy, they began, almost inevitably, to discuss the nature of poetry. McHugh, perhaps almost as inevitably, wrote a poem about the experience. As you read her account, catching (like the participants) more or less of the host's response to the question, reflect on what the last two lines suggest and how you react to them. At least at first, read the poem as if someone were telling you an anecdote or story about an experience. Sit back and just listen to the speaker, almost listening in a matter-of-fact manner. Don't try to "figure anything out." Just follow along. The poem looks long, but it's simply as long as almost any clearly told anecdote.

HEATHER MCHUGH (b. 1948)

What He Thought (1994)

for Fabbio Doplicher

We were supposed to do a job in Italy
and, full of our feeling for
ourselves (our sense of being
Poets from America) we went
from Rome to Fano, met   5
the mayor, mulled
a couple matters over (what's
cheap date, they asked us; what's
flat drink). Among Italian literati

we could recognize our counterparts: 10
the academic, the apologist,
the arrogant, the amorous,
the brazen and the glib—and there was one

administrator (the conservative), in suit
of regulation gray, who like a good tour guide   15
with measured pace and uninflected tone narrated
sights and histories the hired van hauled us past.
Of all, he was most politic and least poetic,
so it seemed. Our last few days in Rome

(when all but three of the New World Bards had flown)
I found a book of poems this
unprepossessing one had written: it was there
in the *pensione* room (a room he'd recommended)
where it must have been abandoned by
the German visitor (was there a bus of *them?*)
to whom he had inscribed and dated it a month before.
I couldn't read Italian, either, so I put the book
back into the wardrobe's dark. We last Americans

were due to leave tomorrow. For our parting evening then
our host chose something in a family restaurant, and there
we sat and chatted, sat and chewed,
till, sensible it was our last
big chance to be poetic, make
our mark, one of us asked

        "What's poetry?
Is it the fruits and vegetables and
marketplace of Campo dei Fiori, or
the statue there?" Because I was

the glib one, I identified the answer
instantly, I didn't have to think—"The truth
is both, it's both," I blurted out. But that
was easy. That was easiest to say. What followed
taught me something about difficulty,
for our underestimated host spoke out,
all of a sudden, with a rising passion, and he said:

The statue represents Giordano Bruno,
brought to be burned in the public square
because of his offense against
authority, which is to say
the Church. His crime was his belief
the universe does not revolve around
the human being: God is no
fixed point or central government, but rather is
poured in waves through all things. All things
move. "If God is not the soul itself, He is
the soul of the soul of the world." Such was
his heresy. The day they brought him
forth to die, they feared he might
incite the crowd (the man was famous
for his eloquence). And so his captors
placed upon his face
an iron mask, in which

he could not speak. That's
how they burned him. That is how
he died: without a word, in front   65
of everyone.
                    And poetry—
                                    (we'd all
put down our forks by now, to listen to
the man in gray; he went on   70
softly)—
                    poetry is what

he thought, but did not say.

Consider carefully what their host said about Giordano Bruno. What does it
suggest when the host says, "poetry is what / he thought, but did not say"?
What does it indicate about poetry? Where does it leave you in your thinking
about what poetry is?

> Poetry began when somebody wandered off a savanna or out of a cave and
> looked up at the sky with wonder and said, "Ah-h-h!" That was the first
> poem.
>
> —LUCILLE CLIFTON

READING POETRY

Reading poetry requires some adjustments to the usual approach we take
to reading. Here are a few broad guidelines that you may find useful:

- Remember to listen. Listen to the poem. It's you and the poem.
- Read slowly. Take your time. A poem isn't meant for speed-reading, any
  more than you would "speed listen" to your favorite CD.
- Read straight through the first time, getting a feel for the poem, without
  worrying about what you do not know.
- Read the poem several times, just as you listen to a song several times, get-
  ting to know it, feeling the life within it, each time discovering something
  new in it.
- Notice the title. Titles are not labels. They can sometimes offer an entry
  point, can be a part of the poem. They can set a tone or atmosphere,
  create a tension, even interact with the poem itself. (Some poems—
  Shakespeare's sonnets, for example, and poems by Emily Dickinson—
  have come to be known by their first lines, which are used in place of a
  title. This book follows that convention. Be aware that the first lines are
  not actual titles and should not be treated as such.)

- Work through the sentences, if the poem uses them, to get the subjects, verbs, objects, and other elements straight.
- Read the poem aloud at least once. Because sounds and rhythms are crucial parts of poetry, it helps to *hear* poems, not just "say them in your mind." Sometimes the sounds and rhythms bring out aspects you will not notice in silent reading. And you'll be enticed to slow down and may feel the words and rhythms, even the life in the poem, in your mouth. So, go off by yourself and read out loud (or read to someone who loves to listen).

> Poetry is like bread—everybody shares it.
>
> —CLARIBEL ALEGRÍA

WHAT POEMS DO

Reading poetry differs from reading a newspaper or a memo, or a book such as this one. You usually read these to find information or ideas. Many poems, of course, do convey information or ideas. But poems can also lead us to feel intensely, to experience deeply, and often to extend our understanding of experiences different from our own or to affirm our own ideas and experiences. Poems are also a rich complex of rhythm, diction, imagery, sound, tone, and other elements discussed in this book. We often respond first to a poem by asking ourselves, "What does it mean?" or "What does it say?" But even these may be limiting, as the following poem suggests.

WILLIAM STAFFORD (1914–1995)

Notice What This Poem Is Not Doing (1980)

The light along the hills in the morning
comes down slowly, naming the trees
white, then coasting the ground for stones to nominate.

Notice what this poem is not doing.

A house, a house, a barn, the old   5
quarry, where the river shrugs—
how much of this place is yours?

Notice what this poem is not doing.

Every person gone has taken a stone
to hold, and catch the sun. The carving   10
says, "Not here, but called away."

Notice what this poem is not doing.

The sun, the earth, the sky, all wait.
The crows and redbirds talk. The light
along the hills has come, has found you.

Notice what this poem has not done.

What do you think "this poem is not doing"? If you try to force out a single statement of what it is "about," you may end up frustrated. You might explore various possibilities for what it *is* doing—as well as what it is *not* doing.

Poems are complex—because experience is complex. It's complicated to clean a basement, plan a trip, organize a party. There's a lot to pay attention to. But that's also part of the fun, even the challenge. Among the many things poems do, there are three fairly common ones: poems can tell a story; they can embody feeling; and they can portray characters caught in conflict, just as prose fiction does. And many poems do all three.

> Poetry is an act of mischief.
> —THEODORE ROETHKE

Poetry is an act of mischief.

Poetry is an act of mischief.
Poetry is an act of mischief.

WHERE TO START

Many things are going on in any poem, try focusing on whatever engages you in it. In one poem you may be drawn to the imagery or rhythm; in another you may notice the language or concentrate on the sounds; or you may generally find yourself intrigued by the handling of the line endings. Try focusing first on whatever engages you in the poem. You do not need to have a grasp of the whole poem to be able to talk about things in it; paying attention to what is in a poem is one way of experiencing the poem, and as different people share what they notice, the variety of things brought up can combine to create a very full experiencing of it.

Although "Cherrylog Road" was published in 1963, the action takes us back even further, perhaps to the car-crazed decade of the 1950s, with its drive-in restaurants, drive-in movies, cruising, and backseat sexual trysts. Sexual encounters in cars were certainly common at the time the action of the poem takes place. But using the back seat of an abandoned car in a hot, dusty junkyard was uncommon enough to create a provocative, and humorous, story. Later, we will come back to the poem to consider its poetic elements. For now enjoy it just for the story. In fact, read it as a story.

Where to Start   **13**

JAMES DICKEY (b. 1923)

Cherrylog Road (1963)

Off Highway 106
At Cherrylog Road I entered
The '34 Ford without wheels,
Smothered in kudzu,
With a seat pulled out to run   5
Corn whiskey down from the hills,

And then from the other side
Crept into an Essex
With a rumble seat of red leather
And then out again, aboard   10
A blue Chevrolet, releasing
The rust from its other color,

Reared up on three building blocks.
None had the same body heat;
I changed with them inward, toward   15
The weedy heart of the junkyard,
For I knew that Doris Holbrook
Would escape from her father at noon

And would come from the farm
To seek parts owned by the sun   20
Among the abandoned chassis,
Sitting in each in turn
As I did, leaning forward
As in a wild stock-car race

In the parking lot of the dead.   25
Time after time, I climbed in
And out the other side, like
An envoy or movie star
Met at the station by crickets.
A radiator cap raised its head,   30

Become a real toad or a kingsnake
As I neared the hub of the yard,
Passing through many states,
Many lives, to reach
Some grandmother's long Pierce-Arrow   35
Sending platters of blindness forth

From its nickel hubcaps
And spilling its tender upholstery
On sleepy roaches,

The glass panel in between
Lady and colored driver
Not all the way broken out,

The back-seat phone
Still on its hook.
I got in as though to exclaim,
"Let us go to the orphan asylum,
John; I have some old toys
For children who say their prayers."

I popped with sweat as I thought
I heard Doris Holbrook scrape
Like a mouse in the southern-state sun
That was eating the paint in blisters
From a hundred car tops and hoods.
She was tapping like code,

Loosening the screws,
Carrying off headlights,
Sparkplugs, bumpers,
Cracked mirrors and gear-knobs,
Getting ready, already,
To go back with something to show

Other than her lips' new trembling
I would hold to me soon, soon,
Where I sat in the ripped back seat
Talking over the interphone,
Praying for Doris Holbrook
To come from her father's farm

And to get back there
With no trace of me on her face
To be seen by her red-haired father
Who would change, in the squalling barn,
Her back's pale skin with a strop,
Then lay for me

In a bootlegger's roasting car
With a string-triggered 12-gauge shotgun
To blast the breath from the air.
Not cut by the jagged windshields,
Through the acres of wrecks she came
With a wrench in her hand,

Through dust where the blacksnake dies
Of boredom, and the beetle knows
The compost has no more life.

Someone outside would have seen
The oldest car's door inexplicably
Close from within:

I held her and held her and held her,   85
Convoyed at terrific speed
By the stalled, dreaming traffic around us,
So the blacksnake, stiff
With inaction, curved back
Into life, and hunted the mouse   90

With deadly overexcitement,
The beetles reclaimed their field
As we clung, glued together,
With the hooks of the seat springs
Working through to catch us red-handed   95
Amidst the gray, breathless batting

That burst from the seat at our backs.
We left by separate doors
Into the changed, other bodies
Of cars, she down Cherrylog Road   100
And I to my motorcycle
Parked like the soul of the junkyard

Restored, a bicycle fleshed
With power, and tore off
Up Highway 106, continually   105
Drunk on the wind in my mouth,
Wringing the handlebar for speed,
Wild to be wreckage forever.

All three effects are there—a story, various feelings, and conflicts between char-
acters. These three effects have given names to three types of poetry (**narrative,
lyric,** and **dramatic**), though assigning a given poem to a given type is often ar-
bitrary or problematic. Some people describe the three as structures, rather
than types, and compare the structures to those of stories, songs, and plays.
Thus a narrative poem *moves* through a sequence of events, just as many sto-
ries do; a lyric poem *circles* or *hovers* around a subject, dwells on it, just as many
songs do; and a dramatic poem has a structure that includes a development of
intensity, often involving a confrontation of some sort, that reaches a climax
and is followed by rapidly falling action, just as many plays do.

• • •

For the poems below, notice which ones tell stories, which express emo-
tion by hovering around a subject, and which develop situations of conflict.
Which do more than one of these? What else does each of them do?

ANONYMOUS

There Is a Lady Sweet and Kind (1607)

There is a lady sweet and kind,
Was never face so pleased my mind;
I did but see her passing by,
And yet I love her till I die.

Her gesture, motion and her smiles,   5
Her wit, her voice, my heart beguiles,
Beguiles my heart, I know not why,
And yet I love her till I die.

Her free behavior, winning looks,
Will make a lawyer burn his books.   10
I touched her not, alas, not I,
And yet I love her till I die.

Had I her fast betwixt mine arms,
Judge you that think such sports were harms,
Were't any harm? No, no, fie, fie!   15
For I will love her till I die.

Should I remain confinèd there,
So long as Phoebus in his sphere,
I to request, she to deny,
Yet would I love her till I die.   20

Cupid is wingèd and doth range;
Her country so my love doth change,
But change she earth, or change she sky,
Yet will I love her till I die.

WILLIAM STAFFORD (1914–1995)

Traveling Through the Dark (1962)

Traveling through the dark I found a deer *— A stone in the path.*
dead on the edge of the Wilson River road.
It is usually best to roll them into the canyon: *— practicality, the hardened traveler*
that road is narrow; to swerve might make more dead.

By glow of the tail-light I stumbled back of the car   5
and stood by the heap, a doe, a recent killing;
she had stiffened already, almost cold.
I dragged her off; she was large in the belly.

My fingers touching her side brought me the reason—
her side was warm; her fawn lay there waiting, *— silent but alive*   10

alive, still, never to be born.
Beside that mountain road I hesitated.

The car aimed ahead its lowered parking lights;
under the hood purred the steady engine.
I stood in the glare of the warm exhaust turning red;
around our group I could hear the wilderness listen.

I thought hard for us all—my only swerving—,
then pushed her over the edge into the river.

*like fawn in the doe
- like blood;
soporific image
predicts a slow,
sleepy death

Again, a traveler
with an agenda.*

RUSSELL EDSON (b. 1935)

The Fall (1969)

There was a man who found two leaves and came indoors holding
them out saying to his parents that he was a tree.

To which they said then go into the yard and do not grow in the
living-room as your roots may ruin the carpet.

He said I was fooling I am not a tree and he dropped his leaves.

But his parents said look it is fall.

LANGSTON HUGHES (1902–1967)

Harlem (1951)

What happens to a dream deferred?

> Does it dry up
> like a raisin in the sun?
> Or fester like a sore—
> And then run?
> Does it stink like rotten meat?   5
> Or crust and sugar over—
> like a syrupy sweet?

> Maybe it just sags
> like a heavy load.   10

> *Or does it explode?*

EMILY BRONTË (1818–1848)

Riches I Hold in Light Esteem (1846)

Riches I hold in light esteem
And Love I laugh to scorn
And lust of Fame was but a dream
That vanished with the morn—

And if I pray, the only prayer   5
That moves my lips for me
Is—"Leave the heart that now I bear
And give me liberty."

Yes, as my swift days near their goal
'Tis all that I implore—   10
Through life and death, a chainless soul
With courage to endure!

GARY SOTO (b. 1952)

in the morning – a bold act of violence

The Morning They Shot Tony Lopez, Barber and Pusher Who Went Too Far, 1958 (1977)

When they entered through the back door, — *betrayal*
You were too slow in raising an arm — *too slow for what?*
Or thinking of your eyes refusing the light,
Or your new boots moored under the bed, — *trapped, motionless*
Or your wallet on the bureau, open   5
And choking with bills,
Or your pockets turned inside out, hanging breathless as tongues,
Or the vendor clearing his throat in the street,
Or your watch passed on to another's son,
Or the train to Los Banos,   10
The earth you would slip into like a shirt — *same chance of wearing a shirt as dying that day*
And drift through forever.
When they entered, and shot once,
You twisted the face your mother gave, *the Holy trinity...*
With the (three) short grunts that let you slide *Mother reverence.*   15
In the same blood you closed your eyes to.
grunting – mother or pusher?

APPLICATIONS[1] FOR CHAPTER 1

SUGGESTIONS FOR WRITING

1. One way to interact with poems is by writing in the book as you read—circling words, underlining phrases, jotting your reactions in the margins. Pages 449–50 say more about this and supply a sample.
2. Many readers keep journals as a way of recording their reactions to what they read. You might note things that engage you in several of the poems in this chapter; then, later, check to see if your responses have changed. On journal writing, see pages 451–52.
3. Pick one poem and record your response to it, or to parts of it, in your journal. Then go back to it after each chapter and add to your list, noticing how your responses grow and change.

[1] For information on these Applications, see preface, page xxii.

4. Many poems deal with grief or loss in one way or another. Why do you think this is so? Throughout the course, record in your journal poems of grief that you find particularly engaging and add a response that expresses what is striking or different about each one. You could also, or instead, do the same with another felt experience—ecstasy, for example.
5. If someone asks you what you like about a poem, how do you answer? Choose a poem and write a list of reasons. Keep the list to compare it with what you say at the end of the course.
6. Write a journal entry or short paper discussing the interplay between a poem and its title.
7. Write, in prose or as an experiment with writing poetry, your own homage to a body part or magical answers to either everyday or unusual questions.
8. Russell Edson in "The Fall" creates an outrageous proposition and then takes it seriously, tracing the consequences of doing so. Try doing that in prose or in a poem (perhaps a "poem in sentences," like his).
9. If you are asked to write a paper responding to this chapter, consider writing an essay evoking a happy or unhappy experience you had with poetry. For information on writing essays, see pages 454, 457–68.
10. Reflect on the social situations that such poems as "homage to my hips" and "Questions My Son . . ." evoke or depict, and write a paper discussing how one of these poems reflects and comments on its background in family or society.

SUGGESTIONS AS YOU CONTINUE TO READ POETRY

1. Be open to the great variety of types and styles of poetry.
2. Read slowly and attentively, read repeatedly, pay attention to titles and syntax, read aloud.
3. Recognize different things poems can *do*, not limiting your focus to what they "say" or are "about."
4. Notice particular aspects of a poem and be comfortable with the idea that you can talk and write about any of these parts as well as the whole.

Reading Responsively   2

In Chapter 1 you read poems, noticing how they can look on the page and how they can sound as you listen to them. That approach focuses on poems as written works, groupings of letters printed on pages. Another way to approach poetry is to focus on the reader. The reader, according to this approach, is a contributing factor in all elements and aspects of a poem, a necessary ingredient in processing and reacting to its forms and structures. This chapter will introduce that approach—or group of approaches, actually, since there are a number of reader-oriented approaches to literature, each with its own terminologies and details. What all have in common is their attention to the reader, the process of reading, and the effect of the work on the reader.

FOCUSING ON THE READER

To lead into this approach, let's look at Robert Frost's poem "'Out, Out—.'" Read it for the story, the narrative. Slow down. Don't speed read.

ROBERT FROST (1874–1963)
"Out, Out—" (1916)

The buzz saw snarled and rattled in the yard
And made dust and dropped stove-length sticks of wood,
Sweet-scented stuff when the breeze drew across it.
And from there those that lifted eyes could count
Five mountain ranges one behind the other   5
Under the sunset far into Vermont.
And the saw snarled and rattled, snarled and rattled,
As it ran light, or had to bear a load.
And nothing happened: day was all but done.
Call it a day, I wish they might have said   10
To please the boy by giving him the half hour

That a boy counts so much when saved from work.
His sister stood beside them in her apron
To tell them "Supper." At the word, the saw,
As if to prove saws knew what supper meant, 15
Leaped out at the boy's hand, or seemed to leap—
He must have given the hand. However it was,
Neither refused the meeting. But the hand!
The boy's first outcry was a rueful laugh,
As he swung toward them holding up the hand, 20
Half in appeal, but half as if to keep
The life from spilling. Then the boy saw all—
Since he was old enough to know, big boy
Doing a man's work, though a child at heart—
He saw all spoiled. "Don't let him cut my hand off— 25
The doctor, when he comes. Don't let him, sister!"
So. But the hand was gone already.
The doctor put him in the dark of ether.
He lay and puffed his lips out with his breath.
And then—the watcher at his pulse took fright. 30
No one believed. They listened at his heart.
Little—less—nothing!—and that ended it.
No more to build on there. And they, since they
Were not the one dead, turned to their affairs.

We would like you now to reflect, not on *what* the poem is about, but on *how* you were able to comprehend it—on the *process* involved in reading a poem (or anything else). That process is sequential: you make sense of the early part, then the middle, finally the end. You don't think about the process as it occurs, usually—you're eager to get to the end and see the whole picture. We want you to reflect on your reading process as you moved through the poem. To help you do so, we will follow a group of students reading the poem section by section and talking about how they figured out what is going on, step by step, and how they were affected as they went along.

We offer this fictional dialogue (based on an actual class session) for two reasons. First, to discuss each section "textbook style" would seem to be telling you what you *should* have seen. That is exactly *not* the point. The emphasis must be on what *did* you see; and on what did *you* see. The discussion emphasizes the ways readers engage with a text, often struggling with it and noticing different things about it. Second, the dialogue affirms the importance of conversation about the experiencing of literature to help clarify what is going on and to notice more about the poem. As you read what follows, think back to your first reading of the poem, to what you noticed and reacted to and to how your intellect and imagination brought the story to life in your mind.

"Out, Out—" (1916)

The buzz saw snarled and rattled in the yard
And made dust and dropped stove-length sticks of wood,
Sweet-scented stuff when the breeze drew across it.
And from there those that lifted eyes could count
Five mountain ranges one behind the other   5
Under the sunset far into Vermont.

H: I liked the vivid language.

Y: What do you mean by "vivid language"?

H: Well, the preciseness of the words fascinated me, appealed to me. We always *see* things in poems, but here I *heard* things right away. The sound of the saw—"snarl" and "rattle," they're the right sounds for one of those big circular saws.

B: And smells. The smell of the wood—"sweet-scented"; for me it's pine. Oh, and touch: the soft touch of the breeze on my face. Then there was sight, but after those others. For example, the beauty of the mountains at sunset.

S: The poem bothered me. I figured they were cutting the trees with no concern about them. And as for sounds, "stove-length sticks" grated my ears. But mostly I was turned off by the cutting down of the trees.

I: True. But they're getting ready for winter. After all, they need fuel and there's plenty of wood there. And it doesn't say they cut down living trees— maybe they're cleaning out dead trees and using them.

S: Okay, that may be true—but the lines still bothered me.

K: Yeah, I know what you mean. I remember going to my uncle's house when I was little and they would be cutting wood. I hated the noise of the chain saw. I'd get scared and run back to the house.

H: It says *the* buzz saw, as if we knew which buzz saw. *The* yard, as if we knew which yard. But we don't know. It's as if we came in on the middle of something.

Y: But don't most stories or poems start that way? You start out and try to form a picture. You can't be sure if it's right. Then you read further and the picture fills in. You go back and change what you first thought, if you have to.

T: I agree. And I like doing that. For me, it's a lovely, peaceful scene.

S: Really? You really think it is?

H: I agree, too, but that makes me wonder. When you read stories, lovely, peaceful beginnings often turn out bad. They actually make me nervous. So, I always feel on guard.

And the saw snarled and rattled, snarled and rattled,
As it ran light, or had to bear a load.
And nothing happened: day was all but done.

M: I hardly noticed "snarled" in line 1—it just sounded right. But in line 7, when it gets repeated twice, it feels different: like a mean dog . . .

J: Or some cornered animal, like a woodchuck or badger or something.

S: But it says "nothing happened." They were still cutting wood, weren't they? That's something, isn't it?

D: Maybe it means nothing unusual. It's a pretty, calm, ordinary scene.

H: Like I said before, it makes me think something will happen.

A: I want to go back to those sounds. I've been listening to them: the sound of the buzz saw rattling, but also the sounds in the words—*sn*arled, *r*att*l*ed; *d*ust, *d*ropped; *st*ove, *st*icks, *st*uff; *sc*ented, *wh*en; *sw*eet, *br*eeze; *th*ere, *th*ose, *th*at; *c*ould, *c*ount; *l*ight, *l*oad; *d*ay, *d*one. These all make the scene sound so lovely.

> Call it a day, I wish they might have said   10
> To please the boy by giving him the half hour
> That a boy counts so much when saved from work.
> His sister stood beside them in her apron
> To tell them "Supper."

Y: I know what it means about a half-hour saved from work. Like with my part-time job: if things are slow and the boss lets me leave early, it feels like I have so much more time in the evening.

K: Who's the "they"?

L: I don't know. I didn't pay attention. Maybe the great, faceless, anonymous bureaucrats?

C.J.: Whew!!

T: Maybe it's the adults he's working with?

L: Maybe we'll find out later.

H: Whoever it is, when the poem wishes they'd have let him quit early, I got nervous. It feels like something is going to happen *now*.

M: Did you notice the apron? The girl is in the kitchen helping "mommy," and the guy is out sawing wood with "daddy." I get furious at that.

A: Me too. Once in a while, you would think they'd at least reverse it.

> At the word, the saw,
> As if to prove saws knew what supper meant,   15
> Leaped out at the boy's hand, or seemed to leap—
> He must have given the hand. However it was,
> Neither refused the meeting. But the hand!
> The boy's first outcry was a rueful laugh,
> As he swung toward them holding up the hand,   20
> Half in appeal, but half as if to keep
> The life from spilling.

H: I knew it!

B: You were right—it really took me off guard, too. It was really peaceful and beautiful—then this!

H: You said it caught you off guard. But that's the way these things always happen, don't they? Isn't that the way you'd have felt if you'd have been there? You would've been surprised, shocked, right?

L: See, what makes it really awful is the saw "leaping," or seeming to leap—that's partly what I hate to think about. Like when somebody said the saw was like a mean dog.

S: I think it's awful, too. But what struck me is the way it says "life" instead of "blood"—losing too much blood could kill him.

C.J.: Did you notice he first thought it was funny? Gave a "loud laugh."

S: Wait, I don't think "rueful" is "loud." It's more like "sorrowful," isn't it?

Y: My psych book says that a laugh can be an ordinary reaction to a terrible shock. It's not a funny laugh; it just happens on its own. Wow, my psych major helped with a poem!

> Then the boy saw all—
> Since he was old enough to know, big boy
> Doing a man's work, though a child at heart—
> He saw all spoiled. "Don't let him cut my hand off—
> The doctor, when he comes. Don't let him, sister!"
> So. But the hand was gone already.
> The doctor put him in the dark of ether.

25

Y: What do you think it means when it says, "the boy saw all"?

B: It says below, "He saw all spoiled"—but "spoiled" isn't strong enough. Losing his hand *ruins* things: he can't play ball, can't play a guitar, can't do a lot of jobs.

M: When he asks his sister for help—those are the only lines spoken in the poem, so far. It touched me when I heard him make that plea.

Y: It actually gave me hope for a second—maybe it wasn't as bad as it seemed.

D: Yes, but then it's even sadder to read in the next line, "But the hand was gone already."

L: Is the "dark of ether" scary for you? It is for me. I've gone under myself and remember the feeling.

A: I'm still listening to the sounds. The *d* sounds give it a "thump" you can't miss: "The *d*octor put him in the *d*ark of ether." But I want to go on to the next lines.

> He lay and puffed his lips out with his breath.
> And then—the watcher at his pulse took fright.
> No one believed. They listened at his heart.
> Little—less—nothing!—and that ended it.

30

J: It is hard for *me* to believe this. That doesn't seem enough to kill him.

H: I think it was the shock.

C.J.: They didn't have medevac units and stuff back then—the doctor probably did the best he could.

Y: This poem's sad—it all happened so fast, and he was so young.

No more to build on there. And they, since they
Were not the one dead, turned to their affairs.

M: That's callous!

SEVERAL OTHERS: Sure is.

K: That's the way things are. They've got to go on getting ready for winter—not the same day, of course; the lines compress the time. But eventually you do have to put even a tragedy behind you. It's not healthy if you don't. Life goes on. You have to go on.

D: That may be true mentally, intellectually. But the lines first make you *feel* callousness. I think the compression does it. It really heightens the sense that they don't care very much.

Y: But we *do* react that way, don't we? About all tragedies—a family whose child is killed, victims of a big storm, people starving in Africa. At first we feel really bad, but soon we carry on with our lives.

H: What else can we do?

C.J.: What's the title mean?

B: It refers to the boy—his life has gone out, suddenly, like a light switched off.

S: Maybe the last lines fit, too—he is out of their lives, their memories.

M: I think there's something else about it. "Out, Out—" is a quotation, has quotation marks around it. From *Macbeth*—when Lady Macbeth feels like she still has blood on her hands and keeps rubbing them and saying, "Out, damned spot." The other people wash their hands of this affair and forget what happened, the way Lady Macbeth wanted to.

J: What you say makes sense, but it has only one "out." There's another place in *Macbeth*, after Lady Macbeth died and Macbeth is really despondent— he says, "Out, out, brief candle!"—which would fit the young boy's life being snuffed out, perfectly.

S: I saw *Macbeth* last summer. Then I came home and read it, I liked it so much. I noticed that passage. It goes on something about life being like a crazy person's talk—it doesn't make sense.[1]

D: That's what the poem makes me feel. So many things in life don't make sense—kids dying of AIDS, earthquakes, famines.

A: It's a depressing poem. I like stories to have a happy ending.

SEVERAL VOICES: Me, too! / Oh, come on! / That's not realistic.

Let's reflect on this discussion and on what it means to focus on the reader.

> Poetry is a conversation with the world; poetry is a conversation with the words on the page in which you allow those words to speak back to you; and poetry is a conversation with yourself.
>
> —NAOMI SHIHAB NYE

[1] For the passage from *Macbeth*, see page 478.

THE READING PROCESS

Reader-oriented criticism emphasizes the *nature* of reading. It assumes, as most reading specialists today do, that reading is not a mechanical decoding of marks on a page, the way a radio receives signals and emits sounds. Rather, reading is a sense-*making* activity. As we read we select from our memories definitions and pictures that make sense of the words and phrases we encounter; we anticipate what may be ahead; we revise our earlier anticipations in the light of what we find later. In the usual course of reading we grasp what words and phrases say, figure out the characters and situations involved, and fill in gaps instantaneously, without thinking about it. Focusing on the reading process involves paying attention to it, so we notice the activity itself, not just the end result. You would not want to do that all the time, any more than you would want to watch every football game in slow motion. But a lot can be learned when a team is watching a game film and the coach says, "Slow that down; see what you're doing there?" And a lot can be learned by slowing down the reading of a work and seeing what you're doing there.

Reader-oriented approaches assume that the reader's initial processing of the text, uninfluenced by what's ahead and what happens later, is vitally important. That's why the class discussion above went through the poem section by section, to emphasize the importance of paying attention to what is happening as you read a work for the first time. Later readings are important too, not only to confirm and correct the first reading, but also because the responses made in the course of the first reading become part of what we respond to in the second reading: we respond differently since we know what is ahead and how we responded before.

> More and more poetry is going to be what it used to be—a spoken thing. Poetry is an oral art.
>
> —ETHERIDGE KNIGHT

FILLING IN GAPS

In the process of reading, we also use our imaginations to fill in "gaps" left by the author, supplying information or explanations the author doesn't spell out, or leaves up to us. Of course, something always is left out; no work can include everything. So, if we reflect on "'Out, Out—,'" we may ask: How old was the boy? (Notice how you are left to fill in for yourself what "big boy . . . though a child at heart" means.) Why was he doing a man's work? Was helping out simply expected of children then? Or was his family asking too much of him? Was his family irresponsible in allowing him to work around dangerous machinery at that age, whatever age it was? To ask such questions is a natural part of reading. Our imaginations reach for what has been omitted, seek to supply missing details or connecting links.

Many reader-oriented approaches hold that what is left out is actually very much a part of the poem. Sometimes gaps indicate what is *not* important (what it is *not* doing): the fact that "'Out, Out—'" leaves the above questions unanswered seems to suggest that its interest does not lie in determining human responsibility (though that may not keep your mind from trying to, at least momentarily). Other times gaps signal things that may be very important, perhaps to put emphasis on a detail or bit of information by having the reader supply it, perhaps to suggest that the very process of working to fill the gap is crucial to the effect.

"TEXT" AND "POEM"

Focusing on the reader affirms reading as a personal and individual activity. As we read, we are constantly relating and connecting what we read to knowledge we already possess and experiences we have had, creating pictures and feelings by connecting words to things stored in our memories, and bringing our own attitudes and assumptions to bear as we take in the figures of speech. Obviously a poem can't mean just anything, any more than the sentence "It is going to snow" can mean "An elephant is doing math." There *is* a text; there *are* words and sentences on the page that we must look at and respond to. But *we* are filling the words with meaning—personal meaning. What we see and feel as we read is unique for each of us, as we saw when various readers in the discussion of "'Out, Out—'" indicated ways in which their previous experiences shaped what they saw and felt in reading the poem. Thus, for a reader-oriented approach, the actual **poem** (or story or play) is not an object, not a shape on the page, but *what is completed in the reader's mind*. The words on the page are called the **text**. There can be a text (the words of the writer, written or spoken) without a reader (we "read" a spoken text just as we do a written one); but there can't be a "poem" without a reader (or hearer) to complete what the writer began.

Since no two people have the same personality and the same experiences, the poems they actualize out of the same text will not be exactly identical: in a sense they are reading different works. Thus, the trees and the logs *you* see in "'Out, Out—'" may be similar to those *I* see, but we cannot assume they are the same—and we should not gloss over the difference by saying that it is what they have in common that really matters. That partly explains why it's enjoyable to talk to another person about a poem, to compare our similar (often) but differing (always) experiences with the work. Such conversations change and enrich the way we will read the work thereafter.

Thus, also, you the reader can reread the same text, but not the same poem. Your second reading is different because you know from the beginning what is ahead, so you see things differently: it is a "new poem." If a good bit of time has passed between readings, you also are a different person, bringing new knowledge, interests, and experiences to the process. The text does not change. However, as the reader changes and the context changes, the poem changes.

EFFECT AS MEANING

W. H. Auden said that poetry makes nothing happen. However, focusing on the reader directs attention to the *effect* a work does have. The effect is part of the "meaning experience" created by the interaction between text and reader. Reader-oriented critics tend not to search for the "theme" of a work to determine what it "is about"; they say it "is about" both what is experienced in the poem and how that experience affects the reader. "'Out, Out—'" enables you to experience the same surprise and shock the characters in the poem do, to be hit by the horror of a hand being severed, to sense what seems to be a lack of concern at the end, and to reflect on how such an event and reaction affect you—that complexity of response is part of the "meaning" of the poem.

Sometimes someone will say or write in a paper, "I'm using reader-oriented criticism, so the poem means whatever I believe it means" or "Since I'm using a reader-response approach, I'm focusing on what I feel about the story instead of what it means." Reader-oriented criticism is less concerned with *what* a work "means" or *what* a reader feels about a work than with the *process* through which the reader arrives at "meaning" or "feeling." And though reader-oriented approaches recognize and emphasize the individuality of reading, their purpose and intention is not to promote or justify personalized interpretations. Reader-oriented approaches should give you confidence as a reader that you can interact with poetry in an enjoyable and meaningful way, and should encourage you to learn more about the reading process itself.

> In one sense the efficacy of poetry is nil—no lyric has ever stopped a tank. In another sense, it is unlimited. . . . It does not propose to be instrumental or effective. Instead, in the rift between what is going to happen and whatever we would wish to happen, poetry holds attention for a space, functions not as distraction but as pure concentration, a focus where our power to concentrate is concentrated back on ourselves.
>
> —SEAMUS HEANEY

Thus far, this chapter has been doing a lot of the responding for you and hasn't yet given you much chance to respond yourself. Try approaching the following poem from the reader's perspective. As you read, focus on the process involved. Notice how you figure out what the poem is about. Pick out gaps and spaces and reflect on how your mind fills them. Watch for ways in which you are led to reassess your initial responses as the poem proceeds. Consider how your experiences and your culture shape the way you construe details in the poem.

SHARON OLDS (b. 1942)

The Victims (1984)

When Mother divorced you, we were glad. She took it and
took it, in silence, all those years and then
kicked you out, suddenly, and her
kids loved it. Then you were fired, and we
grinned inside, the way people grinned when   5
Nixon's helicopter lifted off the South
Lawn for the last time. We were tickled
to think of your office taken away,
your secretaries taken away,
your lunches with three double bourbons,   10
your pencils, your reams of paper. Would they take your
suits back, too, those dark
carcasses hung in your closet, and the black
noses of your shoes with their large pores?
She had taught us to take it, to hate you and take it   15
until we pricked with her for your
annihilation, Father. Now I
pass the bums in doorways, the white
slugs of their bodies gleaming through slits in their
suits of compressed silt, the stained   20
flippers of their hands, the underwater
fire of their eyes, ships gone down with the
lanterns lit, and I wonder who took it and
took it from them in silence until they had
given it all away and had nothing   25
left but this.

Reflect on your responses. For example, does your own life affect the degree to which you identified with "we" and the way you filled in "it" in line 1? Do your experiences make a difference in the way the details in lines 8–14 affect you? Do you think lines 5–7 have more impact for people who watched this event live, on TV, in 1974 than for those who didn't? Who are the victims? How do the details in the text affect your response? Did your feelings grow more intense, or change, or get muddled as you went through the text? Can you identify points in the text where your feelings turned? What are you left feeling at the end?

• • •

As you read the texts on the next few pages, note the patterns of your response. Reflect on how the reading process varies from text to text, and how your own experiences make it easier or more difficult to interact with a particular text.

TED KOOSER (b. 1939)

Flying at Night (1985)

Above us, stars. Beneath us, constellations.
Five billion miles away, a galaxy dies
like a snowflake falling on water. Below us,
some farmer, feeling the chill of that distant death,
snaps on his yard light, drawing his sheds and barn   5
back into the little system of his care.
All night, the cities, like shimmering novas,
tug with bright streets at lonely lights like his.

ANONYMOUS

Western Wind

Western wind, when will thou blow,
    The small rain down can rain?
Christ, if my love were in my arms
    And I in my bed again!

WALLACE STEVENS (1897–1955)

Anecdote of the Jar (1923)

I placed a jar in Tennessee,
And round it was, upon a hill.
It made the slovenly wilderness
Surround that hill.

The wilderness rose up to it,   5
And sprawled around, no longer wild.
The jar was round upon the ground
And tall and of a port in air.

It took dominion everywhere.
The jar was gray and bare.   10
It did not give of bird or bush,
Like nothing else in Tennessee.

WANDA COLEMAN (b. 1946)

At the Jazz Club He Comes on a Ghost (1983)

remember? we were here once. love was a new cut
of meat, the sweat of fresh blood. into each other's eyes
falling. a closeness of breath. a toast. two glasses. reflection
his knee courting mine. and i thought wrong. thought maybe

flesh time. widowed sheets. a memory of a half flushed toilet.   5
the smell of him lingers just at the edge of my nose. a pressed
carnation stains the paper of our lives. pages to lock away
in a chest of disquiet

where are they all now? the ones who listened so rapt to our
rhetoric? the spirits that mirrored my enthusiasm/lust for adventure?   10
the window that promised escape in case the smoke became too thick

a prayer catches me unaware. religiosity is something other than
dogma. the stink of our love losing potence between applications of
pine sol and i'm burning for him/bacon on a hot greasy grill

the singer sets a mood. what more can we do, we cemented in bond of   15
flesh, eager to get there, never tiring of the ritual: detergent and
bleach. the sun burning kisses on the tips of my fingers pressed against
safety glass. sometimes his touch comes through with the urgency of
a dying race: my heart beneath his shoe

we whispered overthrows, speculated on the egyptian book of the dead   20
soul train and liberation. whatever happened to the brown-eyed
me, a mini-skirted wound weeping soft red candle light? she
reappears occasionally behind motel doors, takes her
lover's wallet while he sleeps and steals away

Sir Thomas Wyatt the Elder (1503–1542)

They Flee from Me (1557)

They flee from me, that sometime did me seek,
With naked foot stalking in my chamber.
I have seen them, gentle, tame, and meek,
That now are wild, and do not remember
That sometime they put themselves in danger   5
To take bread at my hand; and now they range,
Busily seeking with a continual change.

Thanked be Fortune it hath been otherwise,
Twenty times better; but once in special,
In thin array, after a pleasant guise,   10
When her loose gown from her shoulders did fall,
And she me caught in her arms long and small,
And therewith all sweetly did me kiss
And softly said, "Dear heart, how like you this?"

It was no dream, I lay broad waking.   15
But all is turned, thorough my gentleness,

Into a strange fashion of forsaking;
And I have leave to go, of her goodness,
And she also to use newfangleness.
But since that I so kindly am served, 20
I fain would know what she hath deserved.

JIMMY SANTIAGO BACA (b. 1952)

Family Ties (1989)

Mountain barbecue.
They arrive, young cousins singly,
older aunts and uncles in twos and threes,
like trees. I play with a new generation
of children, my hands in streambed silt 5
of their lives, a scuba diver's hands, dusting
surface sand for buried treasure.
Freshly shaved and powdered faces
of uncles and aunts surround taco
and tamale tables. Mounted elk head on wall, 10
brass rearing horse cowboy clock
on fireplace mantle. Sons and daughters
converse round beer and whiskey table.
Tempers ignite on land grant issues.
Children scurry round my legs. 15
Old bow-legged men toss horseshoes on lawn,
other farmhands from Mexico sit on a bench,
broken lives repaired for this occasion.
I feel no love or family tie here. I rise
to go hiking, to find abandoned rock cabins 20
in the mountains. We come to a grass clearing,
my wife rolls her jeans up past ankles,
wades ice cold stream, and I barefooted,
carry a son in each arm and follow.
We cannot afford a place like this. 25
At the party again, I eat bean and chile
burrito, and after my third glass of rum,
we climb in the car and my wife drives
us home. My sons sleep in the back,
dream of the open clearing, 30
they are chasing each other with cattails
in the sunlit pasture, giggling,
as I stare out the window
at no trespassing signs white flashing past.

APPLICATIONS FOR CHAPTER 2

SUGGESTIONS FOR WRITING

1. Write a journal entry in which you explain the difference between how a poem affects you and what you feel about a poem. Try working from a particular text to show the distinction.
2. To experiment with the way a story changes as a reader changes, reread a poem or book you read when you were much younger. In a journal entry or essay, discuss how and why your experience of reading the text is different now from what it was when you were younger.
3. Choose one of the poems from pages 31–33 and try writing a poem like it as a response to it.
4. Go back to the discussion of "'Out, Out—'" at the beginning of the chapter and add your voice and responses to it.
5. Choose a poem from the anthology and write an imaginary class discussion about it.
6. If the material in this chapter has changed your way of responding to poetry, write about this in your journal, or in a letter to someone, or in an essay.

SUGGESTIONS AS YOU CONTINUE TO READ POETRY

1. Give attention, at least occasionally, to the process of reading—how you make sense of words and phrases, anticipate what is ahead, fill in gaps, go back to revise anticipations in light of what is encountered later, and are affected by prior experience in completing the text.
2. Remember the difference between "text" and "poem," and the importance of *effect* as part of meaning.

Words | 3

The old adage "Sticks and stones may break my bones, but words will never hurt me" isn't completely true. Words *can* hurt us; words can also help us. The point is, words definitely affect us. Obviously it is impossible to read a poem without reading the words. But reading words is not necessarily the same as noticing them. As you read a poem, try pausing for a moment to pay closer attention than you usually would to particular words. Poets seem often to live in words—their look, their sounds, their textures, the feelings clustered around them, what they evoke, their power. Poets roll words around on their tongues and in their minds, experimenting with different combinations of them, playing with them, listening to the results. They care about the meanings of words, and about the uses and abuses of those meanings. They discover new words or new definitions, and often they follow the ways in which the meanings and usages of words change over the years. Poet William Stafford said that we live in language events.

DENOTATION

A way to begin being attentive to language is to focus on what words mean—what their **denotations,** or dictionary definitions, are. That may seem obvious, but sometimes it takes some effort. It is usually easiest to understand the denotations of words in poems written in your own time and culture. Because they are connected to something you are familiar with, you can count on having a vocabulary pretty much in common with that of the poet. But even in these cases you occasionally may need to refer to a dictionary. When you read "Cherrylog Road" you may have needed to look up "kudzu" or "rumble seat" or "chassis" or "strop" in order to be able to understand the poem fully or to be able to imagine precisely what you read. With all that in mind, consider the following poem, doing your best to imagine it as you read:

RITA DOVE (b. 1952)

Silos (1989)

Like martial swans in spring paraded against the city's
shabby blue, they were always too white and
suddenly there.

They were never fingers, never xylophones, although once
a stranger said they put him in mind of Pan's pipes   5
and all the lost songs of Greece. But to the townspeople
they were like cigarettes, the smell chewy and bitter
like a field shorn of milkweed, or beer brewing, or
a fingernail scorched over a flame.

No, no, exclaimed the children. They're a fresh packet of chalk,   10
dreading math work.

They were masculine toys. They were tall wishes. They
were the ribs of the modern world.

In the second line, we hit the pronoun "they"—and our minds automatically
want to connect the pronoun with its antecedent. The only plural noun that
qualifies is the title word, "Silos." "Silos" is a familiar word—you probably
know at least one denotation for it. But the image that denotation forms in
your mind probably does not look like swans in spring, nor does it parade.
Since there is no other word for "they" to refer back to, we are left dangling.
When we read on, we find "they" occurring six more times, but what it refers
to is never stated. There remains only "silos." We are challenged to discover if
and how "they" and "silos" actually are connected.

What we have to guide us is a series of sentences stating what "they" are
like, and the title. That's it. In a work such as this one, it is usually helpful to
look for a pattern—for what key images or words have in common. You
might, for example, check the title word in a dictionary to see if there are other
definitions that may lead to a common connection. *Webster's College Dictionary*
(Random House) gives us this:

> **si·lo** (sī'lō), *n., pl.* **-los,** *v.,* **-loed, -lo·ing.** —*n.* **1.** a structure, typically cylindrical,
> in which fodder or forage is kept. **2.** a pit or underground space for storing
> grain, green feeds, etc. **3.** an underground installation constructed of concrete
> and steel, designed to house a ballistic missile. —*v.t.* **4.** to put into or preserve
> in a silo. [1825–1835; < Sp: place for storing grain, hay, etc., orig. subterranean;
> ulterior orig. uncert.]

When we compare these denotative possibilities with the poem, nothing espe-
cially connects with the first or second entry: farm silos aren't always white, they
would seem more like ribs of an earlier agrarian age than of the present techno-
logical age, and almost everyone associates them with hard work, not toys. But
entry three might connect with the second word of the poem, "martial":

> **mar·tial** (mär'shəl), *adj.* **1.** inclined or disposed to war; warlike. **2.** pertaining to
> or suitable for war or the armed forces: *martial music.* **3.** characteristic of or be-

fitting a warrior: *a martial stride*. [1325–75; ME < L *Mārtiālis* of, belonging to Mars = *Mārti-* (s. of *Mārs*) + *-ālis* -AL'] **—mar′tial·ism**, *n*. **—mar′tial·ist**, *n*. **—mar′tial·ly**, *adv.*

"They," perhaps, refers not to farm silos but to the ballistic missiles stored in military silos. The first line, then, might call up an image of May Day parades in the old U.S.S.R.: missile carriers moved slowly and gracefully like swans, and looked somewhat like them; using the poem's words, they appeared ironically inappropriate against the backdrop of "the city sky's / shabby blue."

A row of missiles has the shape of fingers or of a xylophone set on edge, though they lack the everyday usefulness of the former and the musical potential of the latter. An upright missile certainly could resemble a cigarette or a piece of chalk. Military weaponry has traditionally been more closely associated with men than with women; "wishes" connects the length of missiles with the high hopes people pinned on them; and "ribs of the modern world" suggests the importance placed on missiles in the years before the demise of the Soviet Union. Now the first and second dictionary entries might prove relevant, after all, in the contrast between the uses of grain stored in farm silos and weaponry stored in military silos, and in the fact that aboveground farm silos often have the same shape as missiles. Exploring the dictionary meanings—the denotations—of even fairly common words like "silo" can often prove helpful for understanding and responding to poems, and there is always more that can be explored—you might see what else there is to find

US Army Missile Command Historical Office

> A fascination with words, single words or groups of words, has been the origin of a number of my recent poems. . . .
>
> I became so fond of the strong character of solid compounds ("backroad," "stonewall," etc.) that I made a list purely for my pleasure. In time I wanted to make a poem out of these words, fitting them together like a patchwork quilt. In so doing I saw I could paint a picture of old-time New England, a picture moving from wildwood to dwelling, outdoors and in, then out and up to pasture and down to millstream.
>
> —ROBERT FRANCIS

about "silos" that can open up the poem still further, or perhaps in additional directions.

• • •

In Chapters 4 and 6 we urge you to let images be themselves first, rather than leapfrogging to a grander meaning than themselves. You may be asking, about now, "Why can't they just be silos?" They *are* just silos, but perhaps not the first kind of silos you thought of. The point is that we need to be open and flexible as we read, and not limit our attention to the first definitions that occur to us, or to the definitions we already know.

Denotation can pose a bigger problem when you read poems from the past or from a culture different from your own. You know you need to look up unfamiliar words. Much trickier are words that look familiar, but seem unusual in the context of the poem. In some cases, their meanings have changed or their previous meanings are no longer used. Consider these lines from Shakespeare's *Julius Caesar*. Portia asks Brutus what has been bothering him:

Is Brutus sick? And is it physical
To walk unbraced and suck up the humors
Of the dank morning?

(2.1.262)

Both "physical" and "humor" are familiar words, but none of our current uses seems to fit these lines. Looking in an ordinary desk dictionary won't help:

phys·i·cal (fiz′i kəl), *adj.* **1.** of or pertaining to the body. **2.** of or pertaining to that which is material: *the physical universe.* **3.** noting or pertaining to the properties of matter and energy other than those peculiar to living matter. **4.** carnal; sexual: *a physical attraction.* **5.** physically demonstrative. **6.** requiring, characterized by, or liking rough physical contact or strenuous physical activity. **7.** contained in or being computer hardware: *a physical disk drive; physical memory contained on a chip.* —*n.* **8.** PHYSICAL EXAMINATION.

hu·mor (hyoo′mər; *often* yoo′-), *n., v.,* **-mored, -moring.** —*n.* **1.** a comic, absurd, or incongruous quality causing amusement. **2.** the faculty of perceiving and expressing or appreciating what is amusing or comical: *a writer with humor and zest.* **3.** an instance of being or attempting to be comical or amusing; something humorous. **4.** comical writing or talk in general; comical books, skits, plays, etc. **5.** mental disposition or temperament. **6.** a temporary mood or frame of mind: *in a sulky humor today.* **7.** a capricious or freakish inclination; whim or caprice; odd trait. **8.** any animal or plant fluid, esp. one of the body fluids once regarded as determining a person's constitution: blood, phlegm, black bile, or yellow bile. —*v.t.* **9.** to comply with the humor or mood of in order to soothe, cheer up, etc.: *to humor a child.* **10.** to adapt or accommodate oneself to: *I'll humor your whim for now.* —**Idiom. 11. out of humor,** dissatisfied; cross. Also, *esp. Brit.,* **humour.**

More helpful would be the ⌐*Oxford English Dictionary,* often called the *OED*⌐. It is a historical dictionary, found in most libraries. It gives the meanings of words in earlier times as well as now and shows, through illustrative quotations, when each meaning was in use and, if it is no longer current, when that usage ceased. If you look up *physical* you will find about two columns of definitions and examples, divided into sections. Definitions in Section I involve natural science; these do not fit the line. Definitions in Section II deal with medical meanings; these seem more promising. When you reach definition 5b, lights should start to flash:

> **b.** Beneficial to health; curative, remedial; restorative to the body, good (*for one's health*). Also *fig. Obs.*
>
> **1447** BOKENHAM *Seyntys* (Roxb.) 13, I cowde as weel bothe forge and fyle As cowd Boyce in hys phisycal consolacyoun. **1601** SHAKS. *Jul. C.* II. i. 261 Is Brutus sicke? and is it Physicall To walke vnbraced, and sucke vp the humours Of the danke Morning? **1604** E. G[RIMSTONE] *D' Acosta's Hist. Indies* IV. xl. 318 They say moreover, that this wooll..is phisicall for other indispositions, as for the gowt. **1616** R. C. *Times' Whistle* v. 2212 With mediocrity..To take Tobacco thus were phisicall. **a1633** AUSTIN *Medit.* (1635) 113 A physicall Banket for our Soules.

In this case you can be sure you have found the right meaning because the line from *Julius Caesar* is quoted as an illustration of this definition. Usually you will not be that lucky; to be sure that a definition actually applies, check to see that examples from the time period of your poem are included under the definition.

If you look up *humor* (it will appear under the British spelling *humour*), the first entry will fit, and again the passage from *Julius Caesar* is cited:

> **humour, humor** ('hju:mə(r), 'ju:mə(r)), *sb.* Also 4 umour, -or, 4–6 humure, 5 –ore, 5–6 -oure. [a. AF. (h)umour, F. (h)umor,-ur, mod. F. *humeur* (= It. *umore,* Sp., Pg. *humor*):—L. *hūmōrem,* more properly *ūmōr-em* fluid, moisture.
>
> For the spelling cf. HONOUR; *humour* is now usual in Great Britain, *humor* in U.S. The English formations, *humoured, humourless, humoursome,* are here spelt like the sb. and vb.; but the derivatives formed on a Latin type, as *humoral, humorist, humorous,* are spelt *humor-* as in L. *humōrōsus,* etc. (This agrees with Johnson's use.) The pronunciation of the initial *h* is only of recent date, and is sometimes omitted, esp. in the senses under II: see H (the letter).]
>
> **I.** Physical senses.
>
> † **1.** Moisture; damp exhalation; vapour. *Obs.*
>
> **1382** WYCLIF *Jer.* xvii. 8 As a tree, that is ouer plauntide vp on watris, that at the humour [L. *ad humorem,* **1388** moisture] sendith his rootes.—*Ecclus.* xxxviii. 29 The humour [L. *vapor*] of the fyr brenneth his flesh. **c1420** *Pallad. on Husb.* 1. 790 That diche wol drie vp humours of thy londe. **1599** CHAPMAN *Hum. Dayes Myrth* Plays 1873 I. 52 The skie hangs full of humour and I thinke we shall haue raine. **1601** SHAKS. *Jul. C.* II. i. 262 To walke vnbraced, and sucke vp the humours Of the danke Morning. **1670** in *Evelyn's Mem.* (1857) III. 228 At Christmas last we could hardly find humour enough in the ground to plant. **1697** DRYDEN *Virg. Georg.* I. 129 Redundant Humours thro' the Pores expire.

Notice that the last example given is from 1697—this is the latest example that has been found in print of this usage. By then that meaning may already have disappeared from spoken language, or it may have lingered in speech a bit longer; in any case, it died out completely around 1697, so present-day dictionaries do not bother to include it (not even as an "archaic" usage). Try the method out by using the *OED* as you explore the following poem:

JOHN SKELTON (ca. 1460–1529)

Though Ye Suppose All Jeopardies Are Passed (ca. 1500)

Though ye suppose all jeopardies are passed,
    And all is done ye lookèd for before,
Ware yet, I rede you, of Fortune's double cast,
    For one false point she is wont to keep in store,
    And under the fell oft festered is the sore: 5
That when ye think all danger for to pass
Ware of the lizard lieth lurking in the grass.

> In looking for the accurate word, [the poet] comes upon a word which, in its meaning and sound, makes him say, "Aha! This is the word I need for this thing that I'm saying." At that moment that word becomes a natural part of his vocabulary. After all, the whole thing was once unknown territory to each of us.
>
> —DENISE LEVERTOV

CONNOTATION

As you pay closer attention to words themselves, you will notice that there is more connected to them than their dictionary definitions. Many have feelings and associated meanings that have become attached to them through repeated uses in various situations, experiences, and cultures. When the word is used, those secondary meanings, or **connotations,** are often evoked. Two words may have almost the same dictionary meaning, or denotation, but very different connotations; the feelings and associations a reader is likely to connect with them could in a certain situation make one suitable and the other unsuitable. For example, the words *courser* and *horse* have nearly the same denotations. To use *courser* in a poem to create a romantic, antique feel would be fitting; but to tell a friend you are going to the track to watch coursers race would probably come across as affected or pretty silly. As we use words, they must not only have the right dictionary meaning, but must also convey the appropriate emotions and implications. To catch the difference connotations make, try an experiment: look up *frigate, courser,* and *frugal;* then read the following poem by Emily Dickinson.

EMILY DICKINSON (1830–1886)

There Is No Frigate Like a Book (ca. 1873)[1]

There is no Frigate like a Book   *frigate - sailboat*
To take us Lands away
Nor any Coursers like a Page   *coursers - horses*
Of prancing Poetry—
This Traverse may the poorest take   5
Without oppress of Toll—
How frugal is the Chariot
That bears the Human soul.

Now try substituting *sailboat* for *frigate, racehorse* for *courser,* and *inexpensive* for *frugal;* reflect on the difference in the images and feelings the lines give you.

From the perspective of the "text," connotations are a fixed part of a word, as necessary to it and inseparable from it as its dictionary meanings are. To the extent that connotations are a part of the history of a word, it can be a fascinating challenge to learn those overtones and bring them to bear in one's reading, and to recognize when personal associations vary from the shared effect. Text-oriented critics might argue that such "objective" connotations are different from the personal associations a word or image may carry for an individual because of an experience connected with it ("*sailboats* always make me think of people who own them and how they got the money to buy them").

But reader-oriented ("poem"-oriented) critics would reply that personal associations cannot be so sharply separated from connotation and the way connotations affect us. Connotations were and are shaped by cultures and sets of beliefs, and to feel what "most readers" feel requires being able to share their context. For example, denotatively, the word *mother* means a woman who has borne a child; for her children *mother* often connotes tenderness, support, and caring. For people who were abused by their mothers, the word "mother" would not have the "common" connotation, and it could be difficult for them even to respond to it imaginatively. Viewing connotations as "objective" assumes a large degree of similarity of experience among readers, and in today's society diversity is so prevalent that a common effect in language is less usual than it was in the past. Our challenge is always to recognize that connotation is complex and problematic and is very important in determining how any of us as readers experience a poem. Try going back to "Silos" and look for both objective connotations (ones shaped by culture and history) and personal associations; consider how both affect your reading.

Most poets play with words, searching for the one that has exactly the right meaning, sound, and feeling, and then depend on the reader to weigh

---

[1] The dates given for poems usually indicate earliest publication in a book. When the date of composition is of interest or occurred long before publication, it will be given instead, in *italics.*

denotations and connotations carefully. As you read the following poem, pay particular attention to the words.

GWENDOLYN BROOKS (b. 1917)

The Bean Eaters (1960)

They eat beans mostly, this old yellow pair.
Dinner is a casual affair.
Plain chipware on a plain and creaking wood,
Tin flatware.

Two who are Mostly Good.   5
Two who have lived their day,
But keep on putting on their clothes
and putting things away.

And remembering . . .
Remembering, with twinklings and twinges,   10
As they lean over the beans in their rented back room that
     is full of beads and receipts and dolls and cloths,
     tobacco crumbs, vases and fringes.

The denotations of words in the poem are probably clear to you. You might look up "flatware" (utensils, such as knives, forks, and spoons); you might look for "chipware," though you are not likely to find it in a dictionary—it appears to be a term Brooks coined for beat-up china. You can probably figure it out, and most of the other words, from the context. More important to this poem, however, are the connotations of the words. What beans are, denotatively, is not the crucial thing; what we feel about them, what we associate them with, is. The feeling or association generated by a word depends, to some extent at least, on the background and experiences of the reader. Brooks probably expected that readers generally would feel that beans are inexpensive and ordinary. Given those connotations, it seems safe to conclude that this couple's eating beans *mostly* suggests that they are poor. "Yellow" may describe the color of their skin, but equally important are the feelings of age and fragility that for many people have come to be associated with the word. The facts of what chipware and tin flatware are do not solely create their effect as words in the poem—the way we feel about them as inexpensive, utilitarian products does.

Denotatively, "rented back room" simply states that the room they live in is not in the front of the building and that the building is owned by someone else. But the connotations are meaningful. Back rooms are cheaper (and less desirable) than front rooms. Presumably they are renting a room because they cannot afford to own a house, and a back room because they cannot afford even a front room. Finally, the things listed in the last line are more important to the couple—and to us—for the feelings they evoke than for what they are in and of themselves. This old pair lives more in the past than in the present, and memories cluster with "twinklings and twinges" around the objects that fill the room. Perhaps you have more—or other—connotations for the words in the poem. Bring them into the reading of it and discuss how they may differ from those we presented. What part does your background play in your response to the poem?

> The colonizers knew what they were doing when they tried to destroy tribal languages, and which, infuriatingly, they were successful at in many instances. Language is culture, a resonant life form itself that acts on the people and the people on it. The worldview, values, relationships of all kinds—everything, in fact, is addressed in and through a language. I'm always aware of the spectrum of other languages and modes of expression, including, for instance, cloud language, cricket singing talk, and the melodic whirr of hummingbirds.
>
> —JOY HARJO

Consider the effects of words in the following poem

ROBERT FROST (1874–1963)

The Road Not Taken (1916)

Two roads diverged in a yellow wood,
And sorry I could not travel both   *one life, one chance*
And be one traveler, long I stood.   *per life*
And looked down one as far as I could   *— no predictions*
To where it bent in the undergrowth;   5

Then took the other, as just as fair,   *— all paths are equal*
And having perhaps the better claim,
Because it was grassy and wanted wear;
Though as for that, the passing there
Had worn them really about the same,   10

And both that morning equally lay   *— all paths are equal*
In leaves no step had trodden black.
Oh, I kept the first for another day!   *— next life...*
Yet knowing how way leads on to way,
I doubted if I should ever come back.   *— all actions have*   15
                                              consequence
I shall be telling this with a sigh   *reincarnation*
Somewhere ages and ages hence:
Two roads diverged in a wood, and I—
I took the one less traveled by,
And that has made all the difference.   *— all actions have*   20
                                           consequence

Examine the poem for words that might be worth looking up, to see if the dictionary might enrich your understanding of their denotations, perhaps by noting their origins, as with *diverge,* for example.[2] Reread the poem, noticing words that have feelings or associations that seem as important as the dictionary definition. You could start with *roads* and *yellow wood* in line 1—do they ripple with associations for you? Talk about them with classmates. How about *fair* and *grassy* and *wanted wear* in stanza two? What do those words make you *feel* as you read them? Are there other words in that stanza that convey feelings for you? What about in stanzas three and four? The poem is about a person walking through a woods and needing to decide which path to follow. There are readers who find further suggestion in it than that. Do you? If so, what, and what gives rise to such suggestions? If not, what makes you hesitant? What, if anything, do connotations contribute?

IMAGINATIVE USES OF WORDS

When you were very young you probably made up words from time to time—maybe you gave them meanings based on what they sounded like. They were probably fun to feel roll around in your mouth and off your tongue. Words do involve sounds and sights as well as possibilities for meanings and feelings. Poets work with all of these elements. Occasionally a poet will concentrate mostly, or even only, on the sounds, or the sounds and pictures, the words create. Here's a famous example:

LEWIS CARROLL [CHARLES LUTWIDGE DODGSON] (1832–1898)

Jabberwocky (1871)

'Twas brillig, and the slithy toves
    Did gyre and gimble in the wabe:
All mimsy were the borogoves,
    And the mome raths outgrabe.

"Beware the Jabberwock, my son!   5
    The jaws that bite, the claws that catch!
Beware the Jubjub bird, and shun
    The frumious Bandersnatch!"

He took his vorpal sword in hand:
    Long time the manxome foe he sought—   10
So rested he by the Tumtum tree,
    And stood awhile in thought.

---

[2] Sometimes noting the origins, or "etymologies," of words, as we do occasionally in this text (see pages 82, 83, 85 and 88, for example) can clarify even a familiar word or make you able to picture it and remember it more readily.

And, as in uffish thought he stood,
    The Jabberwock, with eyes of flame,
Came whiffling through the tulgey wood,   15
    And burbled as it came!

One, two! One, two! And through and through
    The vorpal blade went snicker-snack!
He left it dead, and with its head
    He went galumphing back.   20

"And hast thou slain the Jabberwock?
    Come to my arms, my beamish boy!
O frabjous day! Callooh! Callay!"
    He chortled in his joy.

'Twas brillig, and the slithy toves   25
    Did gyre and gimble in the wabe:
All mimsy were the borogoves,
    And the mome raths outgrabe.

Martin Gardner in *The Annotated Alice*[3] examines the origins of the words
Carroll uses in "Jabberwocky." Many of them can be found in the *Oxford English
Dictionary*, either as main entries (*gyre*—turn or whirl around; *mome*—
blockhead, buffoon; *whiffling*—being evasive or variable; *calloo*—a species of
arctic duck) or as variant spellings (*slithy* for *sleathy*—slovenly; *gimble* for
gimbal—pivoted rings for holding things), though they do not seem to retain
their *OED* definitions. Others are combinations of existing words: *burbled* =
"burst" + "bubbled"; *galumphing* = "gallop" + "triumphant"; *chortled* =
"chuckle" + "snort." Still others are Carrollian inventions: *outgrabe, vorpal,
manxome*. Gardner comments, "Although the strange words have no precise
meaning, they chime with subtle overtones" (p. 192). Consider what this
poem reveals about the reading process, as our minds strain to make sense
out of a text, and about denotation and connotation, the way words can
evoke emotion even when they do not convey a precise dictionary meaning.

· · ·

Language works because its users have a common agreement that certain
sounds mean certain things. Some poets, however, experiment by breaking
that agreement: in their poems the words float free of the usual references and
take on new senses and connotations. Such poems ask you to let go of your
expectations of language, absorb the sounds and pictures created by the
words, perhaps catch the absurdities or fresh perceptions glimpsed in them. It
may add up to nothing; it may add up to more than we would ever expect.

[3] *The Annotated Alice: Alice's Adventures in Wonderland and Through the Looking Glass*, with an
introduction and notes by Martin Gardner (New York: World Publishing Company, 1960),
191–98.

The following poem illustrates such handling of language, and suggests why it is used:

EDWARD LUEDERS (b. 1923)

Your Poem, Man . . . (1969)

unless there's one thing seen
suddenly against another—a parsnip
sprouting for a President, or
hailstones melting in an ashtray—
nothing really happens. It takes   5
surprise and wild connections,
doesn't it? A walrus chewing
on a ballpoint pen. Two blue tail-
lights on Tyrannosaurus Rex. Green
cheese teeth. Maybe what we wanted   10
least. Or most. Some unexpected
pleats. Words that never knew
each other till right now. Plug us
into the wrong socket and see
what blows—or what lights up.   15
Try
    untried
        circuitry,
new
    fuses.   20
Tell it like it never really was,
man,
and maybe we can see it
like it is.

Here is an example of what Lueders means, by a poet who often stretches language in creating remarkably unusual perceptions.

JAMES TATE (b. 1943)

End of a Semester (1972)

I know I will never pass history,
though I can hear the death rattle of a party,
tears full of stickpins
and a tongue of hot wires.
Nobody remembers   5
what came out of the sea,

her nose broken;
nobody cared about the green diffused light   10
across her wrist.
Now, ten thousand Americans
die every minute

from an overdose of cough drops.   *alcohol poisoning...*
Does that make kissing a fetish?   *little innocuous things in*   15
Not if you still have   *large doses can be harmful...*
my childhood with you.
I can belch when I want to,
I can smoke a cigar

when I want to . . .   20
but I know
I will never get through history.
That cloud
is made of wood. *— inaccessible*

Much of what is in the poem is accessible: though the speaker cannot pass a course about things in the past (they are impenetrable, by eyes or hands), he does know what is going on in the present—the grief, the pains. People have little interest in Venus rising from the sea—but they do care about the way people die needlessly. What gets abused in it all is love, unless one can maintain the freedom and innocence one had as a child. The speaker can belch, smoke a cigar.

Read the poem again. The ideas above may be "easier to get" than the poem, but even if you can "summarize" the poem, that summary likely isn't as fresh, powerful, and fun as the poem with its surprising and wild connotations, its words plugged in at "wrong" places: for example, the way "tears full of stickpins" and "a tongue of hot wires" capture vividly how crying can be painful and words can be cutting. The poem wants us to "see it / like it is," as "Your Poem, Man . . ." put it, and these are the words, phrases, images, and sounds the poet needed to do so.

> As a writer, I entrust my life's work to language. It is my tool, and as with any tool you have to be constantly aware where it fails you and where you fail it.
>
> —MARGE PIERCY

SOME POEMS PARTLY ABOUT WORDS

Watch for what the following poems say about words, and for the effects created by the way words are used in them. Discuss them with a classmate, or be ready to discuss them in class.

MURIEL RUKEYSER (1913–1980)

Rune (1976)

The word in the bread feeds me,
The word in the moon leads me,
The word in the seed breeds me,
The word in the child needs me.

The word in the sand builds me,   5
The word in the fruit fills me,
The word in the body mills me,
The word in the war kills me.

The word in the man takes me,
The word in the storm shakes me,   10
The word in the work makes me,
The word in the woman rakes me,
The word in the word wakes me.

GARY MIRANDA (b. 1938)

Love Poem (1978)

A kind of slant—the way a ball will glance
off the end of a bat when you swing for the fence
and miss—that is, if you could watch that once
up close and in slow motion; or the chance
meanings, not even remotely intended, that dance   5
at the edge of words, like sparks. Bats bounce
just so off the edges of the dark at a moment's
notice, as swallows do off sunlight. Slants

like these have something to do with why "angle"
is one of my favorite words, whenever it chances   10
to be a verb; and with why the music I single
out tonight—eighteenth century dances—
made me think just now of you untangling
blueberries, carefully, from their dense branches.

HEATHER McHUGH (b. 1948)

Language Lesson, 1976 (1981)

When Americans say a man
takes liberties, they mean
he's gone too far. In Philadelphia

today a kid on a leash ordered
bicentennial burger,   5
hold the relish. Hold

is forget, in American.
On the courts of Philadelphia
the rich prepare

to serve, to fault.   10
The language is a game in which
love means nothing, doubletalk

means lie. I'm saying
doubletalk with me. I'm saying go
so far the customs are untold,   15

make nothing without words
and let me be
the one you never hold.

APPLICATIONS FOR CHAPTER 3

SUGGESTIONS FOR WRITING

1. Pay attention to your own use of language. Record in your journal specific examples of what you say. Examine these examples closely. Comment on what you discover: What characterizes your usage? When and why do you use denotation, connotation, imagery?
2. Write in your journal about an occasion when misunderstanding either the denotation or connotation of a word, or both, resulted in a problem for you.
3. Write in your journal about an occasion when words deeply affected you. Try turning some of those words into a poem.
4. Write a poem about words. Or try to write your own "Jabberwocky" poem.
5. Choose another sort of text—a letter from someone, an advertisement, or an editorial, for example—and discuss in your journal or in a paper how the denotations and connotations of the words are or are not being manipulated.

6. Find two poems on a similar subject. Look closely at the words used in both—are they familiar or unfamiliar? loaded with connotations or not? Write a paper in which you discuss differences of language in the two poems and the effects those differences create.

7. Write a paper that discusses words in one of the poems on pages 48–49, or "God's Grandeur" (p. 317), or "Snake-Back Solo 2" (p. 136), or a poem of your choice. Consider using a reader-oriented approach in doing so.

SUGGESTIONS AS YOU CONTINUE TO READ POETRY

1. Pay careful attention to denotations—the pertinent dictionary definition(s) of words in a poem.

2. Use a desk dictionary and specialized dictionaries (like the *Oxford English Dictionary*) for finding useful and sometimes surprising denotations.

3. Be open to the connotations of words in poetry—the feelings or associations that become connected with a word, individually or collectively, through repeated uses.

Images | 4

Our earliest knowledge of the world comes through our senses. Babies become acquainted with objects by looking at them, touching them, putting them in their mouths; and sight, hearing, smell, taste, and touch remain crucial sources of knowledge for us as adults as well. It's no wonder, then, that an important effect of a poet's words is to enable us to experience representations of sense impressions. Because so much primary human experience is sensory, it's understandable that poetry should rely heavily on images. Sense impressions send messages that create images in the brain. A large portion of the brain's work is processing data sent by the senses, sorting and storing it, connecting it with ideas and feelings, even rejecting and repressing some of it. Our imaginations use those images—recalling, rearranging, renewing them, turning them into dreams and fantasies.

IMAGING A POEM

In the following poem, Gary Snyder writes about the way words, including words in poems, become things (that is, images of things) in the mind. "Riprap" is a foundation or wall of stones thrown together irregularly. And images are a "foundation" for us, since they are the way we perceive the world around us. Snyder's poem invites you to think about the relationship between images as sensory perceptions of things and images as words that recall such sensory perceptions.

GARY SNYDER (b. 1930)

Riprap (1959)

Lay down these words
Before your mind like rocks.
    placed solid, by hands
In choice of place, set
Before the body of the mind
    in space and time: 5

Solidity of bark, leaf, or wall
          riprap of things:
Cobble of milky way,
          straying planets,   10
These poems, people,
          lost ponies with
Dragging saddles—
          and rocky sure-foot trails.
The worlds like an endless   15
          four-dimensional
Game of *Go*.
          ants and pebbles
In the thin loam, each rock a word
          a creek-washed stone   20
Granite: ingrained
          with torment of fire and weight
Crystal and sediment linked hot
          all change, in thoughts,
As well as things.   25

Words are rocks, rocks are words. Part of what the poem seems to be conveying is that in a four-dimensional world (line 16—including the mind as a dimension) they are equally real. Thus, just as the irregular mixture of solid things catalogued in the poem—bark, leaf, wall, stars, planets, people, ponies, ants, and pebbles—makes up the world we experience, that world is no more (or less) real than the words Snyder uses to depict them. Although not all poets would go as far in this direction as Snyder, many poets, like him, concentrate on images because of the way imagistic words bring sensory experience into a poem and through the poem connect us to the sensory world.

> The greatest poverty is not to live
> In a physical world.
>
> —WALLACE STEVENS
> From "Esthétique du Mal"

REALISTIC IMAGERY

Images in a poem—"literary images"—are words that appeal to one or more of the senses, words that enable us imaginatively to see, hear, taste, smell, touch, or feel what is being referred to. To help focus your mind on this element in poetry, go through a poem and circle such words, bringing them to the foreground, noticing them more clearly. "Realistic" images are ones that occur in frequent, mutually understood combinations, and enable us to participate imaginatively in familiar experiences. Think back to "Cherrylog Road." Its "realistic" imagery enables us imaginatively to picture the rusty, vine-covered cars in the junkyard, to hear the sounds as Doris removes auto parts to take home, and to feel the heat of the sun and the pressure of a seat spring pushing through a seat cover. In large part it is the images that carry us imaginatively to a junkyard in the South, several decades ago, and enable us to share for a few moments the experience of the speaker. Here again is the first stanza. Notice the words that enable you to see objects in your mind's eye:

> Off Highway 106
> At Cherrylog Road I entered
> The '34 Ford without wheels,
> Smothered in kudzu,
> With a seat pulled out to run   5
> Corn whiskey down from the hills.

The words on the page, however, are in one sense only potential images; the sights, sounds, smells, tastes, and sensations called up in your mind are the actualized images, the way you personally apprehend the word images in the poem. They may be sharp if you have seen Ford cars from the 1930s; they may be fuzzy and general if you have never seen kudzu. Focus on the images as you read the following poem:

WILLIAM CARLOS WILLIAMS (1883–1963)

The Red Wheelbarrow (1923)

so much depends
upon

a red wheel
barrow

glazed with rain   5
water

beside the white
chickens.

The actualizing of images is an individual process, dependent on our experiences. The wheelbarrow formed in *your* mind may be made of metal, while the one in *mine* is made of wood; you may have trouble visualizing it at all if you've never seen one, or a picture of one. Writers attempt to help us by supplying precise details. If I say to you, "Think of a dog," you may visualize a spaniel, poodle, mutt, or whatever. *Dog* is general. You make up the particular dog. However, if I say, "Do not imagine a collie," you cannot help visualizing one (provided that you know what a collie looks like).

Image forming is easiest with poems from familiar settings, in our own neighborhood or culture. It becomes more challenging with poems from different places or different cultures—but such poems can provide valuable and exciting opportunities to expand our range of knowledge and our imaginative experience. In the poem below, watch for sights, sounds, smells, tastes, and touch sensations that are familiar to you, and ones that are not.

GARRETT KAORU HONGO (b. 1951)

Yellow Light (1982)

One arm hooked around the frayed strap
of a tar-black, patent-leather purse,
the other cradling something for dinner:
fresh bunches of spinach from a J-Town *yaoya*,
sides of split Spanish mackerel from Alviso's,   5
maybe a loaf of Langendorf; she steps
off the hissing bus at Olympic and Fig,
begins the three-block climb up the hill,
passing gangs of schoolboys playing war,
Japs against Japs, Chicanas chalking sidewalks   10
with the holy double-yoked crosses of hopscotch,
and the Korean grocer's wife out for a stroll
around this neighborhood of Hawaiian apartments
just starting to steam with cooking
and the anger of young couples coming home   15
from work, yelling at kids, flicking on
TV sets for the Wednesday Night Fights.

If it were May, hydrangeas and jacaranda
flowers in the streetside trees would be
blooming through the smog of late spring.   20
Wisteria in Masuda's front yard would be
shaking out the long tresses of its purple hair.
Maybe mosquitoes, moths, a few orange butterflies
settling on the lattice of monkey flowers
tangled in chain-link fences by the trash.   25

But this is October, and Los Angeles
seethes like a billboard under twilight.
From used-car lots and the movie houses uptown,
long silver sticks of light probe the sky.
From the Miracle Mile, whole freeways away,   30
a brilliant fluorescence breaks out
and makes war with the dim squares
of yellow kitchen light winking on
in all the side streets of the Barrio.

She climbs up the two flights of flagstone   35
stairs to 201-B, the spikes of her high heels
clicking like kitchen knives on a cutting board,
props the groceries against the door,
fishes through memo pads, a compact,
empty packs of chewing gum, and finds her keys.   40

The moon then, cruising from behind
a screen of eucalyptus across the street,
covers everything, everything in sight,
in a heavy light like yellow onions.

Hongo's poem is packed with particular images that, combined, create a larger image of a Los Angeles neighborhood, with the sights and sounds and smells of an evening in early fall just as the moon emerges, casting a yellow glow over the entire scene. The details will trigger sharp images if you are familiar with the foods, shops, games, plants, and architecture in the poem; if you don't recognize Langendorf, jacaranda, or the Miracle Mile, forming those images will be difficult, though the overall effect of the poem can still be very evocative.

Images often show us what is present in the world of the poem, but they can also be used to evoke hypothetical sights—what the neighborhood would look like if the month were May instead of October, or what is going on in the mind of a speaker, as in these lines from "Cherrylog Road":

Praying for Doris Holbrook   65
To come from her father's farm

And to get back there
With no trace of me on her face
To be seen by her red-haired father
Who would change, in the squalling barn,   70
Her back's pale skin with a strop.

An image of screams from the barn and welts rising on Doris's back as her father whips her has formed in the speaker's mind. It may be in ours as well. But at this point the beating has occurred only in the speaker's mind. It may happen later, or it may not. The image formed in our minds can be just as sharp as the images of car bodies, and it may affect us more deeply than those images, but it's important to notice the difference between images of things that are "literally there" or "actually happen" and images created in the mind of a character—or created by a comparison:

I popped with sweat as I thought
I heard Doris Holbrook scrape
Like a mouse in the southern-state sun.

The sweat that breaks out and the scraping sound are "literally there" in the story. But the image of a mouse that may form in your mind is created by the comparison, not necessarily by the presence of mice in the junkyard. If the image of the junkyard formed in your mind has lots of mice running around, that part of your image is not supported by the details of the text. Comparisons and other figures of speech (covered in Chapter 6) can create vivid images, but it is wise to remember that images arise from different causes. Jumbling all images together could lead to confusion or misunderstanding.

In poetry, an image is, first, simply itself. Even a symbol (Chapter 7) grows from "an image that is exactly what it is." An image may suggest further meanings, but it doesn't "turn into" something else. It is *first* itself. Because imagery is so rich a part of poetry, one starting point in reading poems can be to look at—*and trust*—the literal, to realize, appreciate, and enjoy what images are and do themselves.

Some readers believe that all poetry is indirect and "symbolic"—even that it is a "code." They think that reading poetry means finding hidden meanings, as if poets think of meanings and then hide them. Such readers often distrust or overlook the literal and immediately search for "deeper meanings." The opening line of "The Red Wheelbarrow" seems to invite digging for deeper meaning—if "so much depends" on the objects mentioned, we had better figure out what they *really* mean. But the line more likely asserts the importance of images as themselves: so much depends on sensuously experiencing and respecting and realizing the value of things as themselves, on *really* using our senses, on experiencing the world with our senses alert and sensitive.

> To love objects is to love life.
> The pure shaft of a single granary on the prairie,
> The small pool of rain in the plank of a railway siding . . .
> —THEODORE ROETHKE
> From "Straw for the Fire"

NONREALISTIC IMAGERY

Poets can work with "realistic" imagery, picturing the way most people experience the world—but they can also create images that do not necessarily reflect the world as we see it, or that lead us to see it in new ways, or that create an altogether different world. We may be tempted to say they are "distorting reality." But we can never be sure that the way we see the world is the way the world really is. As the following poem shows, there are many ways of seeing.

MARK STRAND (b. 1934)

Eating Poetry (1968)

Ink runs from the corners of my mouth.
There is no happiness like mine.
I have been eating poetry.

The librarian does not believe what she sees.
Her eyes are sad   5
and she walks with her hands in her dress. *— the Master*

The poems are gone.
The light is dim. *— the dogs are hungry.*
The dogs are on the basement stairs and coming up *(dogs = independent thought)*
— unleashed mind.
Their eyeballs roll,
their blond legs burn like brush.   10
The poor librarian begins to stamp her feet and weep.

She does not understand.
When I get on my knees and lick her hand, *— Happy...*
she screams. *— Threatened that someone else*   15
is challenging her, on her intellectual
I am a new man. *level.*
I snarl at her and bark.
I romp with joy in the bookish dark.

scream— happy or scared? Either way, an outlet.

Think about what has happened to the speaker (the "I" in the poem): "Eating poetry" has changed him, made him different, a "new man." If you have ever "devoured" a book, you know it can be an exhilarating experience. But how do you convey that to someone else? Maybe a graphic drawing—ink dripping from some happy fiend's mouth—could make someone else see your experience like it really is. And think about the librarian. Librarians often say that they want people to read, to devour books—that books can change lives. But what if they saw people changed by reading—turned rabid, for instance? How would they react? Do they (and we) often feel more secure with books than with readers? If you were the librarian, would you perhaps feel threatened if people began being changed by books? Would it feel as though the library had actually become a place full of strange creatures that keep creeping up from below?

The poem, to use the words of "Your Poem, Man . . ." from Chapter 3, tries untried circuitry. It says things in ways they haven't been said before, makes new connections. It tells things the way they never were and never will be, and thus maybe enables us to see them the way they are.

> When you work at a poem long enough—if you just do that one poem and don't worry about anything else—then the imagery of one verse line exudes a sparkling fountain of energy that fills your spirit.
>
> —Jimmy Santiago Baca

What in the following poems enables you to see more clearly, or in a fresh way, or the way it "really is"? Pay particular attention to images, to the sensory experiences they connect you to and to their effects.

John Keats (1795–1821)

To Autumn (1820)

I

Season of mists and mellow fruitfulness,
   Close bosom-friend of the maturing sun;
Conspiring with him how to load and bless
   With fruit the vines that round the thatch-eves run;
To bend with apples the mossed cottage-trees,   5
   And fill all fruit with ripeness to the core;
     To swell the gourd, and plump the hazel shells
With a sweet kernel; to set budding more,
   And still more, later flowers for the bees,
     Until they think warm days will never cease,   10
     For Summer has o'er-brimmed their clammy cells.

II

Who hath not seen thee oft amid thy store?
   Sometimes whoever seeks abroad may find
Thee sitting careless on a granary floor,
   Thy hair soft-lifted by the winnowing wind;   15
Or on a half-reaped furrow sound asleep,
   Drowsed with the fume of poppies, while thy hook
     Spares the next swath and all its twinèd flowers:
And sometimes like a gleaner thou dost keep
   Steady thy laden head across a brook;   20
     Or by a cider-press, with patient look,
     Thou watchest the last oozings hours by hours.

III

Where are the songs of Spring? Aye, where are they?
   Think not of them, thou hast thy music too,—
While barrèd clouds bloom the soft-dying day,   25
   And touch the stubble-plains with rosy hue;

Then in a wailful choir the small gnats mourn
    Among the river sallows, borne aloft
        Or sinking as the light wind lives or dies;
And full-grown lambs loud bleat from hilly bourn;
    Hedge-crickets sing; and now with treble soft
        The red-breast whistles from a garden-croft;
        And gathering swallows twitter in the skies.

30

CATHY SONG (b. 1955)

Girl Powdering Her Neck (1983)

From a Ukiyo-e Print by Utamaro

The light is the inside
sheen of an oyster shell,
sponged with talc and vapor,
moisture from a bath.

A pair of slippers   5
are placed outside
the rice-paper doors.
She kneels at a low table
in the room,
her legs folded beneath her   10
as she sits on a buckwheat pillow.

Her hair is black
with hints of red,
the color of seaweed
spread over rocks.   15

Morning begins the ritual
wheel of the body,
the application of translucent skins.
She practices pleasure:
the pressure of three fingertips   20
applying powder.
Fingerprints of pollen
some other hand will trace.

The peach-dyed kimono
patterned with maple leaves   25
drifting across the silk,
falls from right to left
in a diagonal, revealing
the nape of her neck
and the curve of a shoulder   30
like the slope of a hill
set deep in snow in a country

of huge white solemn birds.
Her face appears in the mirror,
a reflection in a winter pond,   35
rising to meet itself.

She dips a corner of her sleeve
like a brush into water
to wipe the mirror;
she is about to paint herself.   40
The eyes narrow
in a moment of self-scrutiny.
The mouth parts
as if desiring to disturb
the placid plum face;   45
break the symmetry of silence.
But the berry-stained lips,

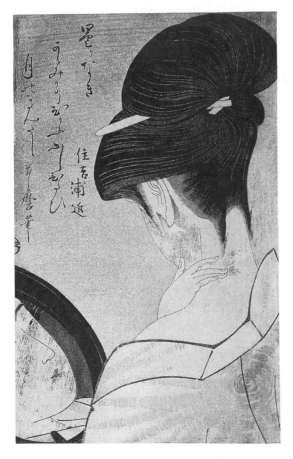

Kitagawa Utamaro (1753–1806). Girl Powdering Her Neck.
(Musée Guimet, Paris.)

stenciled into the mask of beauty,
do not speak.

Two chrysanthemums
touch in the middle of the lake
and drift apart.

50

ROBERT BLY (b. 1926)

Driving to Town Late to Mail a Letter (1962)

[handwritten: ordinary title — maybe an extraordin-ary story lies beneath.]

It is a cold and snowy night. The main street is deserted.
The only things moving are swirls of snow.
As I lift the mailbox door, I feel its cold iron.
There is a privacy I love in this snowy night.
Driving around, I will waste more time.

5

THEODORE ROETHKE (1908–1963)

Meditation at Oyster River (1964)

1

Over the low, barnacled, elephant-colored rocks,
Come the first tide-ripples, moving, almost without sound, toward me,
Running along the narrow furrows of the shore, the rows of dead clam
    shells;
Then a runnel behind me, creeping closer,
Alive with tiny striped fish, and young crabs climbing in and out of the
    water.

5

No sound from the bay. No violence.
Even the gulls quiet on the far rocks,
Silent, in the deepening light,
Their cat-mewing over,
Their child-whimpering.

10

At last one long undulant ripple,
Blue-black from where I am sitting,
Makes almost a wave over a barrier of small stones,
Slapping lightly against a sunken log.
I dabble my toes in the brackish foam sliding forward,

15

Then retire to a rock higher up on the cliff-side.
The wind slackens, light as a moth fanning a stone:
A twilight wind, light as a child's breath
Turning not a leaf, not a ripple.
The dew revives on the beach-grass;

20

The salt-soaked wood of a fire crackles;
A fish raven turns on its perch (a dead tree in the rivermouth),
Its wings catching a last glint of the reflected sunlight.

2

The self persists like a dying star,
In sleep, afraid. Death's face rises afresh,   25
Among the shy beasts, the deer at the salt-lick,
The doe with its sloped shoulders loping across the highway,
The young snake, poised in green leaves, waiting for its fly,
The hummingbird, whirring from quince-blossom to morning-glory—
With these I would be.   30
And with water: the waves coming forward, without cessation,
The waves, altered by sand-bars, beds of kelp, miscellaneous driftwood,
Topped by cross-winds, tugged at by sinuous undercurrents
The tide rustling in, sliding between the ridges of stone,
The tongues of water, creeping in, quietly.   35

3

In this hour,
In this first heaven of knowing,
The flesh takes on the pure poise of the spirit,
Acquires, for a time, the sandpiper's insouciance,
The hummingbird's surety, the kingfisher's cunning—   40
I shift on my rock, and I think:
Of the first trembling of a Michigan brook in April,
Over a lip of stone, the tiny rivulet;
And that wrist-thick cascade tumbling from a cleft rock,
Its spray holding a double rain-bow in early morning,   45
Small enough to be taken in, embraced, by two arms,—
Or the Tittebawasee, in the time between winter and spring,
When the ice melts along the edges in early afternoon.
And the midchannel begins cracking and heaving from the pressure
     beneath,
The ice piling high against the iron-bound spiles,   50
Gleaming, freezing hard again, creaking at midnight—
And I long for the blast of dynamite,
The sudden sucking roar as the culvert loosens its debris of branches
     and sticks,
Welter of tin cans, pails, old bird nests, a child's shoe riding a log,
As the piled ice breaks away from the battered spiles,   55
And the whole river begins to move forward, its bridges shaking.

4

Now, in this waning of light,
I rock with the motion of morning;
In the cradle of all that is,
I'm lulled into half-sleep   60
By the lapping of water,
Cries of the sandpiper.
Water's my will, and my way,

And the spirit runs, intermittently,
In and out of the small waves,   65
Runs with the intrepid shorebirds—
How graceful the small before danger!

In the first of the moon,
All's a scattering,
A shining.   70

The next poem presents some challenges different from those in the poems
above. Try following the "I" through his (or her?) dream, using your imagina-
tion to see the images. Don't interpret. Enter the experience of the images.
Then consider the title. An **elegy** is a poem lamenting the death of a particu-
lar person or any loss of significant proportions; traditionally, it is sustained
and formal, often ending in consolation for the loss. Does that definition help
give focus to what you are experiencing?

ROBERT HAYDEN (1913–1980)

Bone-Flower Elegy (1978)

In the dream I enter the house
          wander vast rooms that are
               catacombs midnight subway
                    cavernous ruined movie-palace
               where presences in vulture masks   5
                    play scenes of erotic violence
                         on a scaffold stage   I want
          to stay and watch but know somehow
I must not linger and come to the funeral
               chamber   in its icy nonlight see   10
                    a naked corpse
                         turning with sensual movements
                    on its coffin-bed
               I have wept for you many times
          I whisper but shrink from the arms   15
               that would embrace me
                    and treading water reach
          arched portals opening on a desert
groves of enormous nameless flowers
               twist up from firegold sand   20
          skull flowers flowers of sawtooth bone
               their leaves and petals interlock
                    caging me for you beastangel
                    raging toward me
               angelbeast shining come   25
                    to rend me and redeem

APPLICATIONS FOR CHAPTER 4

SUGGESTIONS FOR WRITING

1. In your journal, record some of the images that have an effect on you dur-
    ing a single day. Then try recording images that affected you strongly in
    the past (more than four years ago). Compare the two lists. Notice which
    (if any) still carry an impact.
2. In your journal, or in a paper, describe something using realistic imagery.
    Describe something using nonrealistic imagery. Discuss the similarities
    and differences in effect.
3. Write a poem consisting mostly of images. Do your best not to convey any
    ideas or feelings outright. Try to embody the experience entirely in im-
    ages.
4. Create some nonrealistic images. Then try re-creating an especially pow-
    erful experience you've had, using nonrealistic images to embody and
    evoke what it felt like.
5. Reread "Jabberwocky" (Ch. 3, p. 44–45). Focus, this time, not on sounds
    or words, but on images. Write a journal entry or paper on what images
    form in your mind, or on how images struggle to form, as you read the
    text.
6. Look for some realistic and nonrealistic images in artwork, in music
    videos, or in advertising. Write a paper on the importance of imagery, or
    the effect of imagery, in that medium. Or compare that handling of images
    with the use of images in a poem.
7. Write a paper that discusses the effect of the imagery in one of the poems
    on pages 58–63, in "Ode to a Nightingale" (p. 201), "Madonna of the
    Evening Flowers" (p. 326), "Spring and All" (p. 329), "Begotten of the
    Spleen" (p. 399), or a poem of your choice.
8. Write a paper discussing a poem's "cinematography." See the poem as
    film. Describe the crucial camera angles, shots, close-ups, pans, and so
    on. Help your reader see the poem as a film. Explain why you decided to
    film it as you did.

SUGGESTIONS AS YOU CONTINUE TO READ POETRY

1. Respond to images (that is, words representing sensory experience or ob-
    jects that can be known by one or more of the senses) in a text and sense
    images (as representations) in our minds.
2. Be open to both realistic imagery (images that correspond to what is
    commonly experienced in the world) and nonrealistic imagery (imagina-
    tive images or combinations of images that do not necessarily correspond
    to what is commonly experienced in the world).

Speaker, Tone, and Irony 5

"I just can't get her (or his) voice out of my head!" Have you ever heard that or said it yourself?

When you read most poems—even if you don't read them aloud—you hear a voice. Part of the experience of a poem is listening attentively to that voice.

AUTHOR AND SPEAKER

The voice you hear may be that of a character, or of the poet speaking directly, or of a "speaker" very similar to the poet, as in the following poem:

WALT WHITMAN (1819–1892)

When I Heard the Learn'd Astronomer (1865)

When I heard the learn'd astronomer,
When the proofs, the figures, were ranged in columns before me,
When I was shown the charts and diagrams, to add, divide, and mea-
    sure them,
When I sitting heard the astronomer where he lectured with much ap-
    plause in the lecture-room,
How soon unaccountable I became tired and sick,   5
Till rising and gliding out I wander'd off by myself,
In the mystical moist night-air, and from time to time,
Look'd up in perfect silence at the stars.

Walt Whitman claims that the "I" here is the author himself. He says in section 24 of his famous long poem *Song of Myself:* "Walt Whitman, a kosmos, of Manhattan the son, / Turbulent, fleshy, sensual, eating, drinking and breeding." Many poems seem very personal and direct. However, the "I" who "speaks" for the *poet* Walt Whitman is not necessarily equivalent to the *person* Walt Whitman; being a poet is only one aspect of his life and self. So it's wise to be sensitive about using a phrase like "the author says," even in cases where the "I" and the poet seem identical. Think of the variety of ways your own "I" shifts depending on whether you are talking with your boss, your roommate, or a younger sibling, or on what you are talking about, or on your mood.

The poet may use someone else's voice or may develop a character (or characters)—often called a **persona**—as speaker(s) in the poem, or the poet may express only part of his or her inner life, or attitudes she or he holds only part of the time, or attitudes he or she has never accepted. Even when the poet uses the first person, we must not assume that the "I" can be closely identified with the poet. "Cherrylog Road" may recount events that occurred in James Dickey's life and the "I" may be very close to himself; or he may have made up the story entirely, or based it on stories other people told him—in that case the "I" may be very different, in attitudes and values, from himself. We cannot tell from "Cherrylog Road" itself.

In the following poem the "I" seems to be the poet speaking directly, and perhaps it is.

A. E. HOUSMAN (1859–1935)

Loveliest of Trees, the Cherry Now (1896)

Loveliest of trees, the cherry now
Is hung with bloom along the bough,
And stands about the woodland ride
Wearing white for Eastertide.

Now, of my threescore years and ten,   5
Twenty will not come again,
And take from seventy springs a score,
It only leaves me fifty more.

And since to look at things in bloom
Fifty springs are little room,   10
About the woodlands I will go
To see the cherry hung with snow.

It's interesting, however, that Housman published the poem in a volume he originally intended to entitle *The Poems of Terence Hearsay*. That proposed title was a way for Housman to separate the poems from himself. Thus, the "I" in "Loveliest of Trees" supposedly is Terence, the same speaker who defends his poems against those who say to him, "Terence, this is stupid stuff" (see p. 319). "Hearsay" implies that the thoughts in the poems are not Housman's, but just things he overheard. So, even though Housman likely shared the love of natural beauty and the reflections on life the poem expresses, it is safer, and perhaps more precise and accurate, to refer to the "I" as a speaker, rather than as Housman.

> I am trying to listen to the poem to hear if there's any being inside the poem, and I'm hoping I can speak the poem so the audience can hear if there's any being in the poem. . . . [That being is] a voice that's prior to personality and yet every time I speak, my own personality, my own character, my own personal history mitigate the voice. Poetic speech is a way of sounding in order to hear that voice. And once you hear it, everything else is like dishwater.
>
> —LI-YOUNG LEE

Consider the "I" in the following poem. Is it, or does it seem to be, the poet?

THOMAS HARDY (1840–1928)

The Man He Killed (1902)

"Had he and I but met
    By some old ancient inn,
We should have sat us down to wet
    Right many a nipperkin!

"But ranged as infantry,   5
    And staring face to face,
I shot at him as he at me,
    And killed him in his place.

"I shot him dead because—
    Because he was my foe,   10
Just so: my foe of course he was;
    That's clear enough; although

"He thought he'd 'list, perhaps,
    Off-hand like—just as I—
Was out of work—had sold his traps—   15
    No other reason why.

"Yes; quaint and curious war is!
    You shoot a fellow down
You'd treat if met where any bar is,
    Or help to half-a-crown."   20

The poem recounts and reflects on a powerful occurrence, one that it may seem the poet must have experienced personally. However, Thomas Hardy never served in the military or participated in a battle. The "I" in the poem must be a speaker, a briefly sketched character Hardy invented. Look back over the poem for cues that the poem is employing a speaker. Then, list some characteristics of the speaker and some ways he is different from Hardy. Consider how the use of a speaker with those characteristics helps shape the effect, even the power, of the poem.

From a textual perspective, all that matters is the voice of the speaker. The poem, once written, is treated as distinct from its author. But many readers today regard such separation as artificial and inadequate. Even when a poem uses a speaker, part of the voice of the author's internalized world is there, too; we can listen for that, as well as hear the foregrounded voice or speaker in the poem. Even when the speaker of a poem is very different from the author, we can sense the author's voice as well, shaping and directing the speaker's voice. Consider that for "The Man He Killed"; how does Hardy's presence come through, despite—or because of—his use of a speaker?

> When I hear Miles [jazz genius Miles Davis] speak, I hear my father and many other African-American men of his generation. I grew up listening to them on street corners, in barbershops, ballparks and gymnasiums, and bucket-of-blood bars. It's a speaking style that I'm proud and grateful to have documented.
>
> —QUINCY TROUPE

LISTENING TO A VOICE

"I recognize that voice! It's Cathy's. I could listen to her tell stories all day."

"Identifying" a voice and "listening" to it involve two different approaches to voice. Details in the text reveal who is speaking and convey aspects of his, her, or its "voice." So we, as readers, concentrate on such details, and we ought to be able to agree on what the details are and what they reveal—to agree, for example, that the speaker in "Loveliest of Trees, the Cherry Now" is twenty years old, not fifty or seventy. Approached from another angle, each of us pieces those details together individually, responding to them on the basis of our own experiences, attitudes, cultures, and daily lives. The way the details strike you and the way you interpret and describe them will differ at least slightly from someone else's interpretation (a seventy-year-old's response to "Loveliest of Trees" will be different from that of a twenty-year-old). Such differences are inevitable and are to be relished as part of what reading is about. It's important to exercise some care, however, to ground our individual responses in the details given, to avoid "reading into" a poem something that is neither actually present nor implied in the text.

Listen for the "voice" in the following poems. Use the details in each poem to help describe what sort of person, or who specifically, is speaking, and what the occasion or situation is. Then reflect on how you might clarify the relation between speaker and author, speaker and reader, author and reader.

GERALD STERN (b. 1925)

The Dog (1987)

What I was doing with my white teeth exposed
like that on the side of the road I don't know,
and I don't know why I lay beside the sewer
so that lover of dead things could come back
with his pencil sharpened and his piece of white paper.   5
I was there for a good two hours whistling
dirges, shrieking a little, terrifying
hearts with my whimpering cries before I died
by pulling the one leg up and stiffening.
There is a look we have with the hair of the chin   10
curled in mid-air, there is a look with the belly
stopped in the midst of its greed. The lover of dead things
stoops to feel me, his hand is shaking. I know
his mouth is open and his glasses are slipping.
I think his pencil must be jerking and the terror   15
of smell—and sight—is overtaking him;
I know he has that terrified faraway look
that death brings—he is contemplating. I want him
to touch my forehead once and rub my muzzle
before he lifts me up and throws me into   20
that little valley. I hope he doesn't use
his shoe for fear of touching me; I know,
or used to know, the grasses down there; I think
I knew a hundred smells. I hope the dog's way
doesn't overtake him, one quick push,   25
barely that, and the mind freed, something else,
some other thing, to take its place. Great heart,
great human heart, keep loving me as you lift me,
give me your tears, great loving stranger, remember
the death of dogs, forgive the yapping, forgive   30
the shitting, let there be pity, give me your pity.
How could there be enough? I have given
my life for this, emotion has ruined me, oh lover,
I have exchanged my wildness—little tricks
with the mouth and feet, with the tail, my tongue is a parrot's,   35
I am a rampant horse, I am a lion,
I wait for the cookie, I snap my teeth—
as you have taught me, oh distant and brilliant and lonely.

James Wright (1927–1980)

Saint Judas (1959)

When I went out to kill myself, I caught
A pack of hoodlums beating up a man.
Running to spare his suffering, I forgot
My name, my number, how my day began,
How soldiers milled around the garden stone   5
And sang amusing songs; how all that day
Their javelins measured crowds; how I alone
Bargained the proper coins, and slipped away.

Banished from heaven, I found this victim beaten,
Stripped, kneed, and left to cry. Dropping my rope   10
Aside, I ran, ignored the uniforms:
Then I remembered bread my flesh had eaten,
The kiss that ate my flesh. Flayed without hope,
I held the man for nothing in my arms.

> Poetry allows the human soul to speak.
>
> —Carolyn Forché

TONE AND IRONY

You have probably felt the impact of tone, perhaps even saying something like, "I agree with what you say, but your tone is really turning me off." **Tone** in a poem is comparable to the "tone of voice" we invariably use when speaking. And it is powerful. To be a discerning and appreciative reader, we need not only to discern whose voice we are hearing, but also to listen for the tone (or tones) in which the voice expresses itself. Tone embodies or expresses a "stance," attitude, or feeling toward the subject, the listener, even the speaker. Sometimes we speak seriously, sometimes playfully; sometimes we exaggerate, sometimes we understate; sometimes we are ironic, sometimes straightforward; and even more often our tone is a complex mixture or blend. Our actions as well as our words can express tone—consider the difference between closing a door softly and slamming it.

Poems can have a single tone. More often, however, the tone is not simple and straightforward; it cannot be summed up in just a word or two. Usually two or more tones play off or with each other. "The Dog," for example, includes dark humor, when the dog calls his master (the poet) "that lover of dead things" and describes him as having his mouth open, his glasses slipping, and his pencil jerking as the terror of smell—and sight—overtake him. There is gentle satire as the poet (through the dog's voice) jokes about himself as someone preoccupied with writing and not very good at anything practical and down-to-earth. Some parts of the poem evoke sympathy, as when the dog describes itself lying by the side of the road for two hours before it dies; some parts are poignant, as when the dead dog longs to have its master "touch my forehead once and rub my muzzle / before he lifts me up and throws me into / that little valley." And the end turns provocatively serious, raising some probing questions about what "training" looks like from the dog's point of view. Each tone invites us imaginatively into the dog's consciousness to connect, even sympathize, with its experience.

Within a poem, we must be alert for indicators of tone, such as word choice, ways of phrasing, repetitions, overstatement, a particular figure of speech; it is important to watch for them—as we watch for them in listening to a friend—to avoid, for example, taking something as serious that is actually playful. You know how easily we misunderstand one another's tones. We need to be as careful to understand the speaker in a poem as we would be to understand a friend. But tone by its very nature involves the reader's response: tone is about emotions, and for tone to be effective, our emotions must become involved to some degree. Response, however, is individual: you may, for example, recognize all the tonal signals and yet not respond sympathetically to a poem (you may not, for example, have sympathized with the dog), and thus you may be perplexed by the poem or end up "not liking it." Here is a poem readers have regarded in different ways because of their own varied responses to the connotations and tones. After you read and think about it, compare your responses to it with those of a friend or of other students in your class.

THEODORE ROETHKE (1908–1963)

My Papa's Waltz (1948)

The whiskey on your breath
Could make a small boy dizzy;
But I hung on like death:
Such waltzing was not easy.

We romped until the pans   5
Slid from the kitchen shelf;
My mother's countenance
Could not unfrown itself.

The hand that held my wrist
Was battered on one knuckle;   10
At every step you missed
My right ear scraped a buckle.

You beat time on my head
With a palm caked hard by dirt,
Then waltzed me off to bed   15
Still clinging to your shirt.

Among tones, one of the more complex is **irony**, a way of speaking in which the writer or speaker creates a discrepancy, or gap, between what is said and what is meant. Irony appears in a variety of forms. There is **verbal irony**: what is said is pretty nearly the opposite of what is meant ("Lovely day out," when the weather actually is miserable). **Sarcasm,** one form of verbal irony, is direct, harsh, and cutting ("Oh, no, these are fine. I *prefer* my eggs thoroughly charred"). Word choice, or the sheer absurdity of what is said, or the way a word or phrase is enunciated, can signal that what is said is not to be taken in a straightforward way. We pick out those "signals" and process them (that is irony from the reader's perspective). If we happen to miss those signals, we misread the poem. Try out your ear for irony as you read the following poem, watching for the signals about tone mentioned above.

STEPHEN CRANE (1871–1900)

Do Not Weep, Maiden, for War Is Kind (1899)

Do not weep, maiden, for war is kind.
Because your lover threw wild hands toward the sky
And the affrighted steed ran on alone,
Do not weep.
War is kind.   5

    Hoarse, booming drums of the regiment,
    Little souls who thirst for fight,
    These men were born to drill and die.
    The unexplained glory flies above them,
    Great is the Battle-God, great, and his Kingdom—   10
    A field where a thousand corpses lie.

Do not weep, babe, for war is kind.
Because your father tumbled in the yellow trenches,
Raged at his breast, gulped and died,
Do not weep.   15
War is kind.

    Swift blazing flag of the regiment,
    Eagle with crest of red and gold,
    These men were born to drill and die.
    Point for them the virtue of slaughter,   20
    Make plain to them the excellence of killing
    And a field where a thousand corpses lie.

Mother whose heart hung humble as a button
On the bright splendid shroud of your son,
Do not weep.   25
War is kind.

We sense several signals that the poem is not straightforward. For one, the title phrase is patently untrue, and as it is repeated, after exaggeratedly "unkind" details and situations, we increasingly experience the opposite meaning. Do you find other signals? Some might argue that the poet could just as well have stated the point directly. But others would reply that the poem has more power and emphasis when we are the ones who realize the actual meaning. What would be gained by "telling it straight"? What would be lost? Does one outweigh the other for you?

Other types of irony include **dramatic irony**, in which you as the audience realize implications of words or acts that the characters do not perceive, and **situational irony**, in which an outcome turns out to be very different from what was expected or hoped for. Dramatic irony and situational irony mix in the following poem, as we can see implications in the mother's replies that she could not, and as the child happens to be in the right place at the wrong time.

⸙ DUDLEY RANDALL (b. 1914)

Ballad of Birmingham (1969)
(*On the bombing of a church in*
Birmingham, Alabama, 1963)

"Mother dear, may I go downtown
Instead of out to play,
And march the streets of Birmingham
In a Freedom March today?"

"No, baby, no, you may not go,   5
For the dogs are fierce and wild,
And clubs and hoses, guns and jails
Aren't good for a little child."

"But, mother, I won't be alone.
Other children will go with me,   10
And march the streets of Birmingham
To make our country free."

"No, baby, no, you may not go,
For I fear those guns will fire.
But you may go to church instead   15
And sing in the children's choir."

She has combed and brushed her night-dark hair,
And bathed rose petal sweet,
And drawn white gloves on her small brown hands,
And white shoes on her feet.   20

The mother smiled to know her child
Was in the sacred place,
But that smile was the last smile
To come upon her face.

For when she heard the explosion, 25
Her eyes grew wet and wild.
She raced through the streets of Birmingham
Calling for her child.

She clawed through bits of glass and brick,
Then lifted out a shoe. 30
"Oh, here's the shoe my baby wore,
But, baby, where are you?"

These categories sound neat and tidy. But in practice irony often is not so easy to describe precisely. Detecting it and dealing with it can require you to be especially alert, and flexible enough to shift your response when you realize its presence.

DOROTHY PARKER (1893–1967)

Résumé (1926)

Razors pain you;
Rivers are damp;
Acids stain you;
And drugs cause cramp.
Guns aren't lawful; 5
Nooses give;
Gas smells awful;
You might as well live.

Here the irony is not that the poem advocates suicide but says the opposite. The irony lies in indirection, as it offers unexpected and ultimately despairing reasons for avoiding suicide and continuing to live, and in the ambiguity of the title: the word *resume,* without accents, means to "go on again, after an interruption; to continue," all of which is appropriate to the poem. *Résumé,* with the accents, means a "summary," particularly "a brief account of personal qualifications and experience," as if the poem summarizes the speaker's experiences and qualifications in this area (the speaker has tried them all and *knows!*). Irony can entail humor—as in the title and development of this poem; often there is a serious edge to or point behind the humor.

There is one further complexity involving tone, one that takes us back to the author's voice being heard behind the dog's voice in Stern's poem. When a poem has a speaker, there may be two levels of tone, the speaker's tone toward the subject and the poem's tone toward the speaker. In the following poem, the speaker's tone is serious, but the tone of the poem is not. The setting is a famous cathedral in London during World War II. The organ is playing and presumably people are gathering for a religious service, as the speaker pours out her feelings in prayer.

JOHN BETJEMAN (1906–1984)

In Westminster Abbey (1940) *— after WWII, Depression*

Let me take this other glove off
    As the *vox humana*[1] swells,
And the beauteous fields of Eden
    Bask beneath the Abbey bells.
Here, where England's statesmen lie,   5
Listen to a lady's cry.

Gracious Lord, oh bomb the Germans.
    Spare their women for Thy Sake,
And if that is not too easy
    We will pardon Thy Mistake.   10
But, gracious Lord, whate'er shall be,
Don't let anyone bomb me. *her selfishness...*

Keep our Empire undismembered
    Guide our Forces by Thy Hand,
Gallant blacks from far Jamaica,   15
    Honduras and Togoland;   *— WWII taught her*
Protect them Lord in all their fights, *nothing at all*
And, even more, protect the whites.

Think of what our Nation stands for,
    Books from Boots'° and country lanes,   *a pharmacy chain*   20
Free speech, free passes, class distinction,
    Democracy and proper drains.°   *good plumbing*
Lord, put beneath Thy special care
One-eighty-nine Cadogan Square.

Although dear Lord I am a sinner,   25
    I have done no major crime;
Now I'll come to Evening Service
    Whensoever I have the time.
So, Lord, reserve for me a crown,
And do not let my shares go down.   30

I will labour for Thy Kingdom,
    Help our lads to win the war,
Send white feathers to the cowards
    Join the Women's Army Corps,
Then wash the Steps around Thy Throne   35
In the Eternal Safety Zone.

Now I feel a little better,
    What a treat to hear Thy Word,
Where the bones of leading statesmen,

---

[1] *An organ stop that resembles a human voice.*

Poet vs. Narrator
Ironic   serious voice

Have so often been interr'd.
And now, dear Lord, I cannot wait
Because I have a luncheon date. . .

Although the speaker's tone is serious, the poem's tone is ironic: what the speaker says, in her earnest, frightened appeal to God, reveals her hypocrisy, self-centeredness, and shallowness, which expose and undercut what she says.

• • •

Voice and tone are always key aspects of **dramatic monologues** like those in "In Westminster Abbey" and the poem below. In dramatic monologues, there is only one speaker, overheard in a dramatic moment, usually addressing another character or characters who do not speak. The speaker's words reveal what is going on in the scene and bring out significant aspects of the speaker's character. You can, therefore, figure out who is speaking, to whom (if anyone; perhaps to him- or herself), on what occasion, and the substance and tone of what he or she is saying.

This poem is set in Renaissance Italy. The speaker is a duke from Ferrara, a city in northern Italy. He is giving a guest a personal guided tour of his palace and pauses to show him a portrait of his previous wife (painted by a fictitious but supposedly famous painter, Frà [that is, "brother," or monk] Pandolf); we overhear what he says about the painting, and about her. From that we are left to figure out what he is like, what she was like, who the guest is, and why the Duke says what he does.

ROBERT BROWNING (1812–1889)

My Last Duchess (1842)
Ferrara

That's my last Duchess painted on the wall,
Looking as if she were alive. I call
That piece a wonder, now: Frà Pandolf's hands
Worked busily a day, and there she stands.
Will't please you sit and look at her? I said 5
"Frà Pandolf" by design, for never read
Strangers like you that pictured countenance,
The depth and passion of its earnest glance,
But to myself they turned (since none puts by
The curtain I have drawn for you, but I) 10
And seemed as they would ask me, if they durst,
How such a glance came there; so, not the first
Are you to turn and ask thus. Sir, 'twas not
Her husband's presence only, called that spot
Of joy into the Duchess' cheek: perhaps 15
Frà Pandolf chanced to say "Her mantle laps
Over my lady's wrist too much," or "Paint
Must never hope to reproduce the faint

Half-flush that dies along her throat:" such stuff
Was courtesy, she thought, and cause enough   20
For calling up that spot of joy. She had
A heart—how shall I say?—too soon made glad,
Too easily impressed; she liked whate'er
She looked on, and her looks went everywhere.
Sir, 'twas all one! My favour at her breast,   25
The dropping of the daylight in the West,
The bough of cherries some officious fool
Broke in the orchard for her, the white mule
She rode with round the terrace—all and each
Would draw from her alike the approving speech,   30
Or blush, at least. She thanked men,—good! but thanked
Somehow—I know not how—as if she ranked
My gift of a nine-hundred-years-old name
With anybody's gift. Who'd stoop to blame
This sort of trifling? Even had you skill   35
In speech—(which I have not)—to make your will
Quite clear to such an one, and say, "Just this
Or that in you disgusts me; here you miss,
Or there exceed the mark"—and if she let
Herself be lessoned so, nor plainly set   40
Her wits to yours, forsooth, and made excuse,
—E'en then would be some stooping; and I choose
Never to stoop. Oh sir, she smiled, no doubt,
Whene'er I passed her; but who passed without
Much the same smile? This grew; I gave commands;   45
Then all smiles stopped together. There she stands
As if alive. Will't please you rise? We'll meet
The company below, then. I repeat,
The Count your master's known munificence
Is ample warrant that no just pretence   50
Of mine for dowry will be disallowed;
Though his fair daughter's self, as I avowed
At starting, is my object. Nay, we'll go
Together down, sir. Notice Neptune, though,
Taming a sea-horse, thought a rarity,   55
Which Claus of Innsbruck cast in bronze for me!

Poems do not endure as objects but as presences. When you read anything
worth remembering, you liberate a human voice; you release into the
world again a companion spirit. Perpetual resurrection—
    I read poems to hear that voice. And I write to speak to those I have
heard.
                                                            —LOUISE GLÜCK

Pay attention especially to voice and tone as you read the following poems. The first two use "I." Is it safe to assume in them that the poet is the speaker? If not, why not? If so, how would you clarify what the poet/speaker is like? Notice what the speaker is talking about and what tone he or she seems to use. The other poem is told in third person: an unidentified voice relates things "Zimmer" has experienced. Where is the poet's voice in this poem? How can you tell? Experiment by substituting "I" for "Zimmer." How would the effect be different? Why, do you think, did the poet not use first person?

LINDA HOGAN (b. 1947)

Workday (1988)

I go to work
though there are those who were missing today
from their homes.
I ride the bus
and I do not think of children without food   5
or how my sisters are chained to prison beds.
Now I go to the University
and out for lunch
and listen to the higher-ups
tell me all they have read   10
about Indians
and how to analyze this poem.

I ride the bus home
and sit behind the driver.
We talk about the weather and not enough exercise.   15
I don't mention Victor Jara's mutilated hands
or men next door
in exile from life
or my own family's grief over the lost children.

When I get off the bus   20
I look back at the light in the windows
and the heads bent
and how the women are all alone
framed in the windows
and the men coming home.   25
Then I see them walking on the avenue,
the beautiful feet,
the perfect legs
even with their spider veins,
the broken knees   30

with pins in them,
the thighs with their cravings,

the pelvis
and small back with its soft down,
the shoulders   35
which bend forward and forward
and forward
to protect the heart from pain.

KENNETH FEARING (1902–1961)

Love, 20¢ the First Quarter Mile (1956) *a price on love*

All right, I may have lied to you, and about you, and made a few
    pronouncements a bit too sweeping, perhaps, and possibly
    forgotten to tag the bases here or there,
And damned your extravagance, and maligned your tastes, and
    libeled your relatives, and slandered a few of your friends,   5
O.K., *insincerity, apathy?*
Nevertheless, come back.

Come home. I will agree to forget the statements that you issued
    so copiously to the neighbors and the press,
And you will forget that figment of your imagination, the blonde   10
    from Detroit;
no real/compromise I will agree that your lady friend who lives above us is not crazy,
    bats, nutty as they come, but on the contrary rather bright,
And you will concede that poor old Steinberg is neither a drunk,
    nor a swindler, but simply a guy, on the eccentric side,   15
    trying to get along.
(Are you listening, you bitch, and have you got this straight?)

Because I forgive you, yes, for everything,
I forgive you for being beautiful and generous and wise,
I forgive you, to put it simply, for being alive, and pardon you, in   20
    short, for being you.

Because tonight you are in my hair and eyes,
And every street light that our taxi passes shows me you again,
    still you,
And because tonight all other nights are black, all other hours are   25
    cold and far away, and now, this minute, the stars are very
    near and bright.

Come back. We will have a celebration to end all celebrations.
We will invite the undertaker who lives beneath us, and a couple
    of the boys from the office, and some other friends, *a threat*   30
And Steinberg, who is off the wagon, by the way, and that insane
    woman who lives upstairs, and a few reporters, if anything
    should break.

PAUL ZIMMER (b. 1934)

The Eisenhower Years (1981)

Flunked out and laid-off,
Zimmer works for his father
At Zimmer's Shoes for Women.
The feet of old women awaken
From dreams, they groan and rub   5
Their hacked-up corns together.
At last they stand and walk in agony
Downtown to Zimmer's fitting stool
Where he talks to the feet,
Reassures and fits them with   10
Blissful ties in medium heels.

Home from work he checks the mail
For greetings from his draft board.
After supper he listens to Brubeck,
Lays out with a tumbler of Thunderbird,   15
Cigarettes and *From Here to Eternity*.

That evening he goes out to the bars,
Drinks three pitchers of Stroh's,
Ends up in the wee hours leaning
On a lamp post, his tie loosened,   20
Fedora pushed back on his head,
A Chesterfield stuck to his lips.

All of complacent America
Spreads around him in the night.
Nothing is moving in this void,   25
Only the feet of old women,
Twitching and shuffling in pain.
Zimmer sighs and takes a drag,
Exhales through his nostrils.
He knows nothing and feels little.   30
He has never been anywhere
And fears where he is going.

for my father

APPLICATIONS FOR CHAPTER 5

SUGGESTIONS FOR WRITING

1. Listen to a variety of voices during an average day. Choose a range of settings: class, dining room, bull session, working environment, the street, a bus, television personality. . . . Describe some of them in your journal.
2. Record in your journal ironies you see or hear during a given day. Comment on what you conclude from them or what they reveal.

3. Compare two poems on the same subject. Write in your journal or in a paper about the differences in tone between them.
4. In your journal or in a paper, discuss why the images in a poem of your choice are appropriate to the speaker.
5. For several poems, try casting a familiar actor in the speaker's role. Explain why you chose that particular actor to play that speaker.
6. Try writing a persona poem—it could have the voice of someone you know, or the voice of a character you invent, or the voice of a plant or animal, or the voice of an object.
7. Write an imaginary panel discussion or conversation on the particular irony or ironies in a poem.
8. Take a poem and change the diction (words) in order to alter the tone. Write a description of what you did and explain why the effect of the poem is different now.
9. Write a paper in which you trace shifts in tone in a poem, explaining how you discovered them and what effects these shifts create.
10. Write on voice and tone in "Love, 20¢ the First Quarter Mile," or in "Terence, This Is Stupid Stuff" (p. 335), or in "The Love Song of J. Alfred Prufrock" (p. 319), or in another poem of your choice.

SUGGESTIONS AS YOU CONTINUE TO READ POETRY

1. Notice the speaker—the characteristics of whoever is speaking in the poem.
2. Listen for voice (either the voice of the speaker or the voice behind the speaker, or both) and tone: the attitude toward the subject implied in a literary work—playful, serious, ironic, cheerful, pessimistic, sorrowful, etc.
3. Recognize irony—that is, an expression involving a discrepancy between appearance and reality, between what is said and what is intended—and discern the differences among the main ways irony is employed:

VERBAL IRONY: an expression involving a discrepancy between what is said and intended; saying the opposite of what is actually meant
DRAMATIC IRONY: a discrepancy between what is known by an audience and what is known by a speaker; usually the audience recognizes implications a character is not aware of
SITUATIONAL IRONY: a discrepancy between what is expected or what should be and what actually occurs [also called cosmic irony, or irony of fate]

6 Figures

When Romeo says, "But, soft, what light through yonder window breaks? / It is the east, and Juliet is the sun," the hearer or reader knows that Juliet is not actually the sun—Romeo is comparing her to, or identifying her with, the sun in a way that makes imaginative, though not logical, sense. He is using a **figure of speech**—that is, a departure from the standard or customary usage of words in order to achieve a special effect or meaning.

Greek and Roman rhetoricians identified and labeled hundreds of different figures of speech. You will probably find it valuable to know about and recognize approximately a dozen of these. Just as it is helpful when discussing a dance or a stereo system to be able to refer to an arabesque or an amplifier and assume your listener understands these terms, attaching the proper names to figures can be helpful in getting to know them and a useful, shared shorthand when talking about a poem. Equally or more important, however, is being able to explain what kind of imaginative *action* takes place as you encounter, experience, and respond to a figure. That will be the focus in this chapter.

COMPARING

In order to think, to understand something, we often find it helpful to relate it, or *compare* it, to something else: to help someone understand something unfamiliar (the taste of squid, for instance), you compare it to something familiar ("squid tastes like chicken"). That's a simple example of a figure. More complex examples involve unexpected and surprising comparisons ("poetry is like dancing on your own grave," for example). We use figurative language all the time: "I worked like a beaver," "tough as nails." In fact, much of language by its very nature is figurative. Almost all of the words we use, except ones that identify concrete objects or actions, such as *cup* or *kick*, involve figures. Often the figures go unnoticed. You are reading this section in order to comprehend it. *Comprehend,* in that context, is figurative: its root is the Latin word *hendere,* to grasp or hold with the thumb. That physical action has been extended imaginatively to include "grasping" or "taking hold of" an idea or concept.

We don't notice or react to most of the figures in everyday language because they have become either too familiar or stale from overuse. Some originally inventive figures (a riverbed, a table leg, a sawhorse) have been absorbed into the language to such an extent that, though they are still figures, we have ceased to think of them as figurative. And yet even these, when you look at them again as figures, may surprise you.

Figurative comparisons occur when we discover that two things we thought were entirely dissimilar actually have attributes in common. The comparison then slips past our perception of dissimilarities and stretches our ideas about "similarity" ("I've never experienced it that way before")—and makes us aware of their differences in a new way, as in the following lines of a poem by Julie Moulds:

JULIE MOULDS (b. 1962)

from Wedding Iva (1985)

When he held her
she became
white and armless
like a goddess
or a bowling pin.

[handwritten marginalia: • Comparing • Identifying • Substitution • Transferring]

[handwritten marginalia: 20]

The lines first make us see a similarity in a rather conventional way: the comparison to a goddess. However, when we look a bit more closely, we realize that the woman feels "armless" like a goddess and we begin to wonder about how she is being held. Our assumption that being compared to a goddess is a positive thing is brought into tension. Then the surprise of the last line, which shifts the comparison to a startlingly dissimilar object, a bowling pin, makes us see the embrace, the comparison to a goddess, and the way the woman feels in a way that challenges our common perceptions and gets us to consider their differences as we may never have done before. And it's fun.

Direct, explicit comparisons, using such signal words as *like, as, than,* or *similar to,* are called **similes** (from the Latin word for "similar")—as in these often-quoted lines by Robert Burns (see p. 307):

ROBERT BURNS (1759–1796)

from A Red, Red Rose (1796)

O my luve's like a red, red rose,
    That's newly sprung in June;
O my luve's like the melodie
    That's sweetly played in tune.

The poet supplies the figure as a formal component of the poem, and *we* get to carry out the comparing action. We first notice the figurative phrase, then make the imaginative leap required to see the similarity, exploring the range of comparisons, both those that immediately seem appropriate for the context (the woman loved by the speaker is like a melody in that she is sweet, harmonious, memorable) and those that intrude in seemingly inappropriate ways (a melody also is fleeting and evanescent).

Direct comparisons are usually the easiest figures to notice, because they carry the signal word with them. One catch may be separating figurative comparisons from literal ones. When the speaker in "My Last Duchess" says, "for never read / Strangers like you that pictured countenance" (Ch. 5, p. 76; ll. 6–7), he is using a literal, not a figurative, comparison, since the man being addressed is not different from other persons to whom the Duke has shown the portrait. The following poem includes both kinds of comparisons. As you read it, try to distinguish between them, and between images and figurative expressions; notice the extent to which the poet does the comparing and how you have to become involved in the experience of comparison.

DOROTHY LIVESAY (b. 1909)

Green Rain (1932)

I remember long veils of green rain
Feathered like the shawl of my grandmother—
Green from the half-green of the spring trees
Waving in the valley.

I remember the road   5
Like the one which leads to my grandmother's house,
A warm house, with green carpets,
Geraniums, a trilling canary
And shining horse-hair chairs;
And the silence, full of the rain's falling   10
Was like my grandmother's parlour
Alive with herself and her voice, rising and falling—
Rain and wind intermingled.

I remember on that day
I was thinking only of my love   15
And of my love's house.
But now I remember the day
As I remember my grandmother.
I remember the rain as the feathery fringe of her shawl.

IDENTIFYING

"All the world is like a stage." "All the world's a stage." Can you sense the difference? Widely used and basic to poetry, and to language generally, are **metaphors.** Shakespeare's Jaques asserted "All the world's a stage," in *As You Like It.* Our minds may supply a "like," without even thinking about it ("the world is *like* a stage," with people playing roles, making entrances and exits, and so on). The line, however, does not say that the world is *like* a stage, but that it *is* a stage. Common sense and logic assure us that the world is not part of a theater, yet the figure says it is. Here is magic, powerful magic: metaphors open our minds to see what they have not seen before. They break down barriers erected by logic and carry us into a realm in which, through the imagination, we encounter uncommon relationships—even, sometimes, new "realities" and ways of experiencing. The world is a stage, really.

The figurative action in metaphor involves *identifying* one thing with another that is dissimilar to it. The word *metaphor* is derived from the Greek *metaphora,* "carry (*phor*) across (*meta*)." Thus, in a metaphor, characteristics of one thing are "carried across" to another; metaphor calls attention to things usually perceived as unlike by treating them not as "like," as in simile, but as *identical.* The figure makes them, imaginatively, for a moment, the same. Missiles *are* "a fresh packet of chalk," says the poem "Silos" (Ch. 3, p. 36). That is, characteristics of pieces of chalk (slender white cylinders, capable of making marks on a surface) are carried across to the missiles in the military silos.

We said above that language is figurative by its nature. Even more basic is that our conceptual system itself is metaphorical in nature. It is not just that we understand new things by comparing them to familiar ones. Rather, comparisons are embedded in our very understandings. George Lakoff and Mark Johnson[1] use the example ARGUMENT IS WAR. This metaphor occurs in everyday language in a variety of expressions: "His criticisms were *right on target*"; "I've never *won* an argument with him"; "He *shot down* all my arguments." Their point is that this metaphor is not just a matter of language; the metaphor shapes our actions. We carry out arguments as a verbal battle, with attack and defense, winning or losing. The importance of the metaphor would become clearer if someone tried to substitute the metaphor ARGUMENT IS DANCE; there would be no sense of winning and losing, but a coordinated, mutually supportive, and interactive movement. We would probably respond, "But that isn't argument." Thus, the metaphor is intrinsic to the concept. The essence of metaphor, Lakoff and Johnson conclude, is understanding and experiencing one kind of thing in terms of another. "Our conventional ways of talking about arguments presuppose a metaphor we are hardly ever conscious of. The metaphor is not merely in the words we use—it is in our very concept of an argument" (pp. 4–5). Noticing and considering the metaphor involved allows for a fuller understanding of our concept of arguing, and might even result in a reconsideration of our attitude toward argument.

Poetry, too, is permeated with metaphor, and here, too, noticing and experiencing and responding to what metaphors make us realize is essential to understanding and appreciating many poems. Metaphors are easiest to recognize when an *is* or *are,* or some other linking word, is present to clarify the identifying action, as in "All the world's a stage." But in the line "I remember long veils of green rain" in the poem above, "of" connects the key term (rain) to the word describing it (veils); the metaphor both sharpens the image itself of rain (steady, heavy, so that the speaker could not see through it clearly) and

---

[1] *Metaphors We Live By* (Chicago: University of Chicago Press, 1980).

shapes the speaker's concept. The speaker's memory of the event has no existence apart from the one supplied it by the figure, so the figure is not only descriptive, but also conceptual, and veils (blurring but not totally obscuring) become intrinsic to the entire experience.

More difficult to recognize and explain are **implied** or **buried metaphors,** in which the *to be* verb is omitted and the comparison may be implied, or "buried," rather than stated directly. "A car thief is a dirty dog" is direct metaphor. "Some dirty dog stole my car" contains an implied metaphor: the key term (car thief) is implied and must be supplied by the reader to complete the equation involved. In "For peace comes dropping slow" (W. B. Yeats, "The Lake Isle of Innisfree"), we must supply what is implied by "dropping," which gives peace the physical texture of something that can fall and surround one in that place. The ending of "Harlem" (Ch. 1, p. 18) relies on a shift from similes in lines 2–10 to the implied metaphor of line 11—*"Or does it explode?"* The reader is forced to supply the object that describes dreams that are indefinitely delayed, and this greatly increases the power of the ending.

> On one level metaphor is naming, however provisional and temporary the name is. Metaphor has interested me more as a way of knowledge, a way of grasping something. I like to take a metaphor and look at it, then do something like what I do with idiomatic expressions—discover a kind of mythic structure, use the metaphor as a way to discover something about the nature of reality.
>
> —CHARLES SIMIC

As you read the following, take your time and watch for, experience, and explore the images, similes, and metaphors; reflect on how your response to and participation in the figurative actions are crucial to the creating of images and the shaping of concepts in the poem.

JEAN TOOMER (1894–1967)

Face (1923)

Hair—
silver-gray,
like streams of stars,
Brows—
recurved canoes
quivered by the ripples blown by pain,   5
Her eyes—
mist of tears
condensing on the flesh below

And her channeled muscles
are cluster grapes of sorrow
purple in the evening sun
nearly ripe for worms.

10

Personification is a special variant of metaphor.[2] By definition, personification involves treating something nonhuman as if it had human characteristics or acted in a human way. Sometimes abstract qualities are treated as if they were human: in Thomas Gray's phrase "Fair Science frowned," for example, science cannot literally frown; it is being treated as if it were a human being. In other cases concrete things are given human characteristics: in the phrase "Wearing white for Eastertide" from "Loveliest of Trees, the Cherry Now" (Ch. 5, p. 66), cherry trees do not actually wear clothes—they are being given, briefly, a human attribute. Difficulty can arise when personification is redefined (incorrectly) as treating something nonhuman in terms of anything alive rather than specifically human: "the mouth of time" in Nancy Willard's poem (Ch. 1, p. 4) is metaphor, not personification, since animals as well as humans have mouths; in personification, the traits involved must be uniquely human. Notice how personification in the following poem intensifies the experience both in and of the poem.

MARY OLIVER (b. 1935)

Sleeping in the Forest (1979)

I thought the earth
remembered me, she
took me back so tenderly, arranging
her dark skirts, her pockets
full of lichens and seeds. I slept   5
as never before, a stone
on the riverbed, nothing
between me and the white fire of the stars
but my thoughts, and they floated
light as moths among the branches   10
of the perfect trees. All night
I heard the small kingdoms breathing
around me, the insects, and the birds
who do their work in the darkness. All night
I rose and fell, as if in water, grappling   15
with a luminous doom. By morning
I had vanished at least a dozen times
into something better.

---

[2] A particular type of personification is **apostrophe,** that is, addressing someone not present or something ordinarily not spoken to as if present or capable of understanding, as when Macbeth says, "Time, thou anticipatest my dread exploits" (4.1.144).

> If the poet has made you see something in terms of something else—in a way that you would not ordinarily have thought of putting two things together—then you have learned to see something as if for the first time, and you will see in a fuller way. After all, what the poet tries to make you do is look freshly at the world.
>
> —LINDA PASTAN

SUBSTITUTION

"The White House announced today. . . ." The form of that announcement involves another type of figurative action, *substitution*. In this case, two things that initially seem unlike are neither compared nor identified; instead one thing replaces the other, calling the original to mind in a fresh way. Substituting the name of one thing for that of something closely associated with it is called **metonymy** (from the Latin *meta,* "other," and *onoma,* "name"). Like similes and metaphors, metonymies are used frequently in everyday speech and writing. When you hear a news reporter say, "The White House announced today . . . ," you've encountered a metonymy: the phrase "White House" invites you to visualize a familiar image closely related to the president that substitutes for the staff members who issued the announcement.

Metonymy, like metaphor, is a linguistic device and a means of conceptualizing. Lakoff and Johnson list several examples of categories of metonymy:

PRODUCER FOR PRODUCT: He's got *a Picasso* in his den.
OBJECT USED FOR USER: The *buses* are on strike.
CONTROLLER FOR CONTROLLED: *Nixon* bombed Hanoi.
INSTITUTION FOR PEOPLE RESPONSIBLE: *Exxon* has raised its prices again.
THE PLACE FOR THE INSTITUTION: *Wall Street* is in a panic.
THE PLACE FOR THE EVENT: *Watergate* changed our politics.
THE CONTAINER FOR THE CONTENTS: I ate *two bowls*.

Metonymies help us organize our thoughts and actions and grasp one thing in relation to another. Being aware of their presence can help us better understand our own underlying premises and assumptions as well as those of a culture.

Poets work to find fresh and striking metonymies. They can be used for imaging: the phrase "platters of blindness" ("Cherrylog Road," line 36) substitutes for "flash of light," vividly creating the effect, or experience, of the sun reflecting off chrome. Metonymies are also used for conceptualizing. In "Traveling through the Dark," Stafford writes: "around our group I could hear the wilderness listen" (line 16). A wilderness cannot hear, though the animals within it can; the substitution of "wilderness" for "animals" shapes the meaning, in that "wilderness" encompasses all natural things, plants as well as animals, even the environment as a whole; those parts of nature are listening not just to hear the fate of another victim of the vehicles that have invaded the wilderness, but also for the fate of the wilderness itself, threatened by humans.

A subset of metonymy is **synecdoche,** that is, substitution of a part of a thing for the whole of which it is a part.[3] *Synecdoche* is a Latin word meaning "receive together." When someone says to you, "Give me a hand," he or she actually wants help not just from your hands but from your whole self. Likewise, the familiar phrases "lend me your ears" or "many mouths to feed" or "new faces"[4] employ synecdoche. In the following poem, synecdoche reinforces or shapes a conceptualization of government or rulers:

DYLAN THOMAS (1914–1953)

The Hand That Signed the Paper Felled a City (1936)

The hand that signed the paper felled a city;
Five sovereign fingers taxed the breath,
Doubled the globe of dead and halved a country;
These five kings did a king to death.

The mighty hand leads to a sloping shoulder,   5
The finger joints are cramped with chalk;
A goose's quill has put an end to murder
That put an end to talk.

The hand that signed the treaty bred a fever,
And famine grew, and locusts came;   10
Great is the hand that holds dominion over
Man by a scribbled name.

The five kings count the dead but do not soften
The crusted wound nor stroke the brow;
A hand rules pity as a hand rules heaven;   15
Hands have no tears to flow.

---

[3] Synecdoche also includes, though less frequently, substitution of the whole for one of its parts. "Wilderness listen" could be explained as a whole-for-the-parts synecdoche instead of a metonymy.

[4] Lakoff and Johnson use this one to illustrate how a synecdoche can function in our conceptual system. The synecdoche THE FACE FOR THE PERSON occurs in such phrases as "She's just a *pretty face*" or "We need some *new faces* around here." The tradition of portrait painting or photography is based on that synecdoche. As Lakoff and Johnson put it, "If you ask me to show you a picture of my son and I show you a picture of his face, you will be satisfied. You will consider yourself to have seen a picture of him. But if I show you a picture of his body without his face, you will consider it strange and will not be satisfied. You might even ask, 'But what does he look like?' " (p. 37).

The hand substitutes for the whole king who signed papers initiating attacks on a rival city; the five fingers, a replacement for the hand, signed a death warrant to execute the defeated king and signed orders establishing absolutist rule over the conquered people. The danger of the concentration of enormous power in a single person, or a small group of persons, is reflected in the figure the poem employs as well as in what it says. The author sets forth the substitution, but the reader must complete and respond to it, and the reader's response, in kind and intensity, is likely to be quite different for a dictator, accustomed to signing death warrants for political opponents, for a citizen living in a country under a totalitarian ruler, and for a citizen of a democratic society.

Recognizing and interacting with metonymies and synecdoches can help you appreciate the way things can often have greater importance than they at first seem to. Robert Frost said, "If I must be classified as a poet, I might be called a Synecdochist, for I prefer the synecdoche in poetry," that figure of speech in which . . . "a little thing touches a larger thing."[5] Instead of starting with huge, complex themes and issues, Frost uses local, finite experiences as triggering subjects and lets his mind expand from there. "Think small," Richard Hugo advises young poets; "if you have a big mind, that will show itself."[6] In that light, you might look again at Frost's poem "The Road Not Taken" (Ch. 3, p. 43) and at several other poems from earlier chapters, such as Stafford's "Traveling Through the Dark" (Ch. 1, p. 17), Brooks's "The Bean Eaters" (Ch. 3, p. 42), Williams's "The Red Wheelbarrow" (Ch. 4, p. 53), and Hugo's "Driving Montana" (p. 362).

As you read the following poems, pause to reflect on the effects of various figures, including comparisons, identifications, and replacements, and on your experience in completing and responding to them.

EDWIN ARLINGTON ROBINSON (1869–1935)

Richard Cory (1897)

Whenever Richard Cory went down town,
We people on the pavement looked at him:
He was a gentleman from sole to crown,
Clean favored, and imperially slim.

And he was always quietly arrayed,   5
And he was always human when he talked;
But still he fluttered pulses when he said,
"Good-morning," and he glittered when he walked.

---

[5] See Louis Untermeyer, *From Another World* (New York: Harcourt, Brace and Company, 1939), p. 208, and Elizabeth Shepley Sergeant, *Robert Frost: The Trial by Existence* (New York: Holt, Rinehart and Winston, 1960), p. 325.

[6] *The Triggering Town: Lectures and Essays on Poetry and Writing* (New York: Norton, 1979), 7.

And he was rich—yes, richer than a king—
And admirably schooled in every grace: 10
In fine, we thought that he was everything
To make us wish that we were in his place.

So on we worked, and waited for the light,
And went without the meat, and cursed the bread;
And Richard Cory, one calm summer night,   15
Went home and put a bullet through his head.

VERN RUTSALA (b. 1934)

The Furniture Factory (1981)

Upstairs the sanders
rubbed fingernails
thin, hands shiny
and soft as a barber's—
men past forty   5
down on their luck.
Below, I worked in a haze
of fine dust
sifting down—
the lives of the sanders   10
sifting down, delicately
riding the cluttered
beams of light.
I pounded nails
on the line.   15
The wood swallowed hard
nailheads like coins
too thin to pick up.
During breaks I read—
You gonna be   20
a lawyer, Ace?—
then forgot the alphabet
as I hammered
afternoons flat.
My father worked there too   25
breathing the sanding
room's haze.
We ate quiet lunches together
in the car.
In July   30
he quit—hands
soft, thick fingernails
feathery at the tips.

TRANSFERRING

Still another figurative action involves *transferring*—that is, moving, or changing, a word from one situation to another. It occurs when a modifier (usually an adjective) that, in ordinary speech, would apply to one word shifts to modify another word, one that it does not logically fit. In "Cherrylog Road," for example, the speaker says Doris's father "would change, in the squalling barn, / Her back's pale skin with a strop." A barn itself cannot cry or scream loudly and violently; it is Doris, being whipped in the barn, who will be squalling, and the adjective shifts from her to the barn. This action, a variant on metonymy, is sometimes labeled **transferred epithet**, "epithet" being a term used to describe or characterize a person or thing. In "The Morning They Shot Tony Lopez" (Ch. 1, p. 19), "breathless" is transferred from the mouth of Tony Lopez's dead body to the pockets of his pants, turned inside out.

Often, but not always, this action involves a speaker's projecting his or her feelings onto something. In other words, the speaker ascribes his or her own feelings to someone or something else that does not, or perhaps cannot, have the same feelings. To say "it was a sad day when that happened" projects onto a day (which cannot logically be sad) our own feelings about the day. Notice how projection helps shape concept and effect in the following poem:

THEODORE ROETHKE (1908–1963)

Dolor (1948)

I have known the inexorable sadness of pencils,
Neat in their boxes, dolor of pad and paper-weight,
All the misery of manilla folders and mucilage,
Desolation in immaculate public places,
Lonely reception room, lavatory, switchboard,　　　　　　　　　5
The unalterable pathos of basin and pitcher,
Ritual of multigraph, paper-clip, comma,
Endless duplication of lives and objects.
And I have seen dust from the walls of institutions,
Finer than flour, alive, more dangerous than silica,　　　　　10
Sift, almost invisible, through long afternoons of tedium,
Dropping a fine film on nails and delicate eyebrows,
Glazing the pale hair, the duplicate grey standard faces.

· · ·

SOME OTHER FIGURATIVE ACTIONS

We will point out briefly a few other imaginative actions. Each works through adjustments to tone and so relies heavily on your interaction and response as a reader. First is the figurative movement from apparent contradiction to resolution, or **paradox**—that is, a statement that seems initially to be self-contradictory or absurd but that turns out to make good sense. Notice especially the first two lines of Shakespeare's Sonnet 138:

WILLIAM SHAKESPEARE (1564–1616)

When My Love Swears That She Is Made of Truth (1609)

When my love swears that she is made of truth
I do believe her, though I know she lies,
That she might think me some untutored youth,
Unlearnèd in the world's false subtleties.
Thus vainly thinking that she thinks me young,   5
Although she knows my days are past the best,
Simply I credit her false-speaking tongue;
On both sides thus is simple truth suppressed.
But wherefore says she not she is unjust?
And wherefore say not I that I am old?   10
O, love's best habit is in seeming trust,
And age in love loves not to have years told.
 Therefore I lie with her, and she with me,
 And in our faults by lies we flattered be.

The lines seem contradictory at first: how can she be "made of truth" if "she lies"? On reading further and reflecting on the lines, we find she is twisting truth, saying he is not really old and close to death, though he is, because he needs to hear that in order to face the future with hope and optimism. She expresses the truth of her love by the lies she tells in order to convince him that she still regards him as worthy of her love and loyalty.

In the following poem, notice the paradox as the speaker's inconstancy (he leaves the woman he loves) proves his constancy (being true to his honor as a soldier and citizen is evidence that he will be true and honorable in his relation to her as well):

RICHARD LOVELACE (1618–1657)

To Lucasta, Going to the Wars (1649)

Tell me not, Sweet, I am unkind,
 That from the nunnery
Of thy chaste breast and quiet mind
 To war and arms I fly.

True, a new mistress now I chase,   5
 The first foe in the field;
And with a stronger faith embrace
 A sword, a horse, a shield.

Yet this inconstancy is such
    As you too shall adore;
I could not love thee, Dear, so much,
    Loved I not honor more.

10

When you read Chapter 12, you will discover how important paradox is for the theory of New Criticism because of its ability to reconcile and unify.

Two additional figurative actions are to overstate and to understate. **Overstatement,** or **hyperbole** (from the Greek for "throwing beyond"), means to state something more strongly than is warranted, to exaggerate. Overstatement is often used to make a point emphatically. It is often used by lovers, as when Hamlet protests that he loved Ophelia much more than her brother did: "Forty thousand brothers / Could not with all their quantity of love / Make up my sum" (5.1.272–74), and when the lover in W. H. Auden's "As I Walked Out One Evening" declares the longevity of his affection:

W. H. AUDEN (1907–1973)
from *As I Walked Out One Evening* (1940)

"I'll love you, dear, I'll love you
    Till China and Africa meet,
And the river jumps over the mountain
    And the salmon sing in the street."

    Understatement, or **litotes** (from the Greek for "plain, meager"), phrases something in an unexpectedly restrained way. Paradoxically (there's that word again!), to deemphasize through understatement can be a way of emphasizing, of making people react with "there must be more to it than that." In *Romeo and Juliet,* after Mercutio is stabbed by Tybalt, Benvolio asks, "What, art thou hurt?" and Mercutio answers, "Ay, ay, a scratch, a scratch" (3.1.92). He is understating, for the wound is serious—he calls for a doctor in the next line, and he dies a few minutes later. The following poem seems understated throughout.

A. E. HOUSMAN (1859–1936)
With Rue My Heart Is Laden (1896)

With rue my heart is laden
    For golden friends I had,
For many a rose-lipt maiden
    And many a lightfoot lad.

By brooks too broad for leaping
    The lightfoot boys are laid;
The rose-lipt girls are sleeping
    In fields where roses fade.

5

The sorrow or loss the speaker *feels* seems stronger than what the poem *expresses:* "rue" means a rather mild regret; "grief" might have reflected his feelings more accurately. But he prefers to understate by choice of "rue," by the softness of the double rhymes in lines 1, 3, 5, and 7, by the simplicity of the meter and diction, and by restricting the poem to description. He *describes* what he misses and lets the reader fill in what he must be feeling, instead of dwelling on and emphasizing his emotions.

Finally, there is the figurative action of bringing together, often humorously, two or more different meanings of the same word, or different words that sound alike (the **pun**). Mercutio, just after the lines quoted above, quips "Ask for me tomorrow, and you shall find me a grave man" (*Romeo and Juliet* 3.1.96–97), which pulls together two meanings of "grave"—its meaning as an adjective (serious, solemn) and its meaning as a noun (a place to be buried). The following epigram relies on recognition of a pun involving two words that sound alike—the color red and the past tense of "read":

HILAIRE BELLOC (1870–1953)

On His Books (1923)

When I am dead, I hope it may be said,
"His sins were scarlet, but his books were read."

> In metaphor it is usually the force, the boldness of the comparison that carries you away from the object. Yet even the most modest metaphor carries with it the implication that all things are mutable, that all things are comparable. If there is no other idea in the metaphoric poem, there is that.
> —RICHARD WILBUR

Two final observations about figures. No sharp lines divide figures from one another: often a figure can be explained equally well in more than one way. "I could hear the wilderness listen" could be explained either as metonymy ("wilderness" being substituted for the creatures and the natural habitat in it), or perhaps as personification ("wilderness" given a humanlike ability to understand, not just hear). In this and most cases, applying labels to figures is a means to an end: it may help alert us to their presence, and it helps us talk about them and clarify the nature of the imaginative action we participate in as we read them.

Also, always keep in mind that figures of speech occur *within* poems, not *as* poems. Inexperienced readers of poetry sometimes attempt to treat entire poems as figures of speech. After reading a poem, they may say, "On the surface it's about a man finding a deer on the road, but what it's *really* about is our journey through life and the difficult decisions we face along the way," thus substituting

an abstract "meaning" for the concrete images of the poem. Because of such re-
ductions of his poems to neat thematic capsules, Robert Frost resisted when
readers tried to say that "Stopping by Woods on a Snowy Evening" (p. 326) is
"really about death." The poem is *really* about a horse-and-sleigh in a forest—
though through use of archetype and symbol (treated in the next chapter), it
may *also* (as opposed to "really") be about death. This book discusses images be-
fore it discusses figures because of the importance of grounding the experience
of poetry in images and of letting the action or description be, first, itself.

. . .

The following poem is an unusual love poem. How would you feel if the
poem were addressed to you? Why might the poet (or speaker? which?) have
chosen to say it this way? You will probably notice and interpret figures as you
work out what is being said; reread, this time focusing on the variety of fig-
ures. You should be able to find almost all the types discussed in the chapter.

JOHN FREDERICK NIMS (b. 1913)

Love Poem (1947)

(apostrophe?)

My clumsiest dear, whose hands shipwreck vases,
At whose quick touch all glasses chip and ring, *exaggeration*
Whose palms are bulls in china, burs in linen,
And have no cunning with any soft thing *more exaggeration...*

Except all ill-at-ease fidgeting people: 5
The refugee uncertain at the door
You make at home; deftly you steady
The drunk clambering on his undulant floor.

Unpredictable dear, the taxi drivers' terror,
Shrinking from far headlights pale as a dime; *simile*   10
Yet leaping before red apoplectic streetcars—
Misfit in any space. And never on time.

A wrench in clocks and the solar system. Only
With words and people and love you move at ease;
In traffic of wit expertly manoeuvre *she's clever*   15
And keep us, all devotion, at your knees.

Forgetting your coffee spreading on our flannel,
Your lipstick grinning on our coat, *personification of lipstick*
So gayly in love's unbreakable heaven
Our souls on glory of spilt bourbon float.   20

Be with me, darling, early and late. Smash glasses—
I will study wry music for your sake.
For should your hands drop white and empty
All the toys of the world would break.

As you read, and reread, the following poems, take time to focus especially on how figures of speech shape the concepts and create or evoke particular effects.

DENNIS BRUTUS (b. 1924)

Nightsong: City (1963)

Sleep well, my love, sleep well:
the harbour lights glaze over restless docks,
police cars cockroach through the tunnel streets;

[handwritten: simile] from the shanties creaking iron-sheets
violence like a bug-infested rag is tossed   5
and fear is immanent as sound in the wind-swung bell;
[handwritten: Personification]
the long day's anger pants from sand and rocks;
but for this breathing night at least,
my land, my love, sleep well.

[handwritten: Apostrophe! This poem is about the city not a lover...]

AUDRE LORDE (1934–1992)

Coal (1962; rev. 1992)

I   is the total black
being spoken
from the earth's inside.

There are many kinds of open
how a diamond comes   5
into a knot of flame
how sound comes into a word
colored
by who pays what for speaking.

Some words are open   10
diamonds on a glass window
singing out within the crash
of passing sun
other words are stapled wagers
in a perforated book   15
buy and sign and tear apart
and come whatever wills all chances
the stub remains
an ill-pulled tooth
with a ragged edge.   20

Some words live in my throat
breeding like adders
others

know sun
seeking like gypsies   25
over my tongue
to explode through my lips
simile —like young sparrows
bursting from shell.

Some words   30
bedevil me.

Love is a word, another kind of open.
As the diamond comes
into a knot of flame
I am Black   35
because I come from the earth's inside
take my word for jewel
in the open light.

ANITA ENDREZZE (b. 1952)

The Girl Who Loved the Sky (1988)

Outside the second grade room,
the jacaranda tree blossomed
into purple lanterns, the papery petals
drifted, darkening the windows.
Inside, the room smelled like glue.   5
The desks were made of yellowed wood,
the tops littered with eraser rubbings,
rulers, and big fat pencils.
Colored chalk meant special days.
The walls were covered with precise   10
bright tulips and charts with shiny stars
by certain names. There, I learned
how to make butter by shaking a jar
until the pale cream clotted
into one sweet mass. There, I learned   15
that numbers were fractious beasts
with dens like dim zeros. And there,
I met a blind girl who thought the sky
similes —tasted like cold metal when it rained
and whose eyes were always covered   20
with the bruised petals of her lids.

She loved the formless sky, defined
only by sounds, or the cool umbrellas
of clouds. On hot, still days
we listened to the sky falling   25

like chalk dust. We heard the noon
whistle of the pig-mash factory,
smelled the sourness of home-bound men.
I had no father; she had no eyes;
we were best friends. The other girls   30
drew shaky hop-scotch squares
on the dusty asphalt, talked about
pajama parties, weekend cook-outs,
and parents who bought sleek-finned cars.
Alone, we sat in the canvas swings,   35
our shoes digging into the sand, then pushing,
until we flew high over their heads,
our hands streaked with red rust
from the chains that kept us safe.

I was born blind, she said, an act of nature.   40
Sure, I thought, like birds born
without wings, trees without roots.
I didn't understand. The day she moved
I saw the world clearly; the sky
backed away from me like a departing father.   45
I sat under the jacaranda, catching
the petals in my palm, enclosing them
until my fist was another lantern
hiding a small and bitter flame.

LARRY LEVIS (1946–1996)

The Poem You Asked For (1972)

My poem would eat nothing. *personification (= p*)*
I tried giving it water
but it said no, *p**

worrying me.
Day after day,   5
I held it up to the light,

turning it over,
but it only pressed its lips *p**
more tightly together. *a human. quality (p*)*
It grew sullen, like a toad *– simile*   10
through with being teased. *buried metaphor?*
I offered it all my money,
                              substitution:
my clothes, my car with a full tank. *container for contents*
But the poem stared at the floor. *p**
Finally I cupped it in   15

my hands, and carried it gently
out into the soft air, into the
evening traffic, wondering how

to end things between us.
For now it had begun breathing,   20
putting on more and
more hard rings of flesh. — *the poem is animate here*
And the poem demanded the food, *pf*
it drank up all the water, *pf*

beat me and took my money, *pf*   25
tore the faded clothes *pf*
off my back,

said Shit, *pf*
and walked slowly away,
slicking its hair down. *pf*   30

Said it was going *pf*
over to your place.

APPLICATIONS FOR CHAPTER 6

SUGGESTIONS FOR WRITING

1. In your journal, collect figures of speech you encounter in your everyday
    experience (for example, in conversations, advertising, or the broadcast
    media). Discuss how they enrich what you hear. Which ones are no
    longer effective? Why?
2. Write a journal entry or an essay that discusses the use of figures, or of
    one type of figure, in "Love Poem," "Nightsong: City," "Coal," "The Girl
    Who Loved the Sky," or "The Poem You Asked For" above, or "The Vic-
    tims" (Ch. 2, p. 30) or "To Autumn" (Ch. 4, p. 58), or a poem of your
    choice from the anthology.
3. Choose a subject and write as many different figures for it as you can—for
    example:

    Love is _____

    Love is like _____

    Love _____

    Then you might write a journal entry or paper in which you discuss the
    varied effects different figures create.
4. Write a poem or poems in which you incorporate several figures.
5. Find a poem in which the figures are particularly striking to you. Write a
    paper in which you discuss what these figures suggest, what they help
    you realize, how they affect your perceptions.

6. Write an imaginary discussion between one person who sees poets as dangerous because of how they change our perceptions and one who sees them as constructive.
7. Watch and/or listen to several comedians. Write a paper discussing their uses of paradox, overstatement, understatement, and pun.
8. Write an imaginary panel discussion, interview, or short play in which the characters discuss the figures in a particular poem.
9. Write a paper in which you discuss the relationship in a poem between the speaker, the tone(s), and the figures.

SUGGESTIONS AS YOU CONTINUE TO READ POETRY

1. Notice the figures (if any) and the variety of imaginative actions they involve:

SIMILE: expression of a direct similarity, using such words as *like, as,* or *than,* between two things usually regarded as dissimilar

METAPHOR: treatment of two things usually thought to be dissimilar as if they were alike and had characteristics in common

PERSONIFICATION: treating something nonhuman as if it had human characteristics or acted in a human way

APOSTROPHE: addressing directly an absent person, an abstract quality, or a nonhuman entity as if present

METONYMY: substituting a thing closely related to something for the thing itself

SYNECDOCHE: substituting a part of something for the whole of it

TRANSFERRED EPITHET: transferring a modifier (adjective) that ought, strictly, to apply to one word to another word that it does not strictly fit

PARADOX: making sense of an apparent contradiction by examining it imaginatively in another light

OVERSTATEMENT: exaggerating; stating something more strongly than is warranted

UNDERSTATEMENT: stating something in a very restrained way

PUN: a play on words that are similar in sound but have very different meanings

2. Consider how the choice of a figure affects the concept being developed.
3. Carry out your role in completing the imaginative action that figurative language entails.

7 | Symbols

Not only do poems often help us see things in fresh and meaningful ways; they also can help us see deeply *into* and *beyond* things as well, especially through **symbols:** images or actions that suggest or mean something in addition to themselves. Someone sending a rose to a loved one sends an object that can be touched and smelled. But the recipient recognizes it as more than itself, knows it suggests love, concern, support, and so on, and responds to its symbolic implications. We are symbol-using creatures, capable of recognizing additional layers of meaning in a rose, a cross, a piñata, a flag, or in black marks on a page (words are the most widely used of symbols).

SYMBOLS

A **literary symbol** is an image or an action in a poem (or story or play) that can be seen, touched, smelled, heard, tasted, or experienced imaginatively, but that also conveys abstract meanings beyond itself. The following poem is about an actual rose, but it also uses that rose to embody ideas of love and fragility and the brevity of life.

EDMUND WALLER (1606–1687)

Song (1645)

> Go, lovely rose!
> Tell her that wastes her time and me
> That now she knows,
> When I resemble her to thee,
> How sweet and fair she seems to be.   5
>
> Tell her that's young,
> And shuns to have her graces spied,
> That hadst thou sprung

In deserts, where no men abide,
Thou must have uncommended died.   10

    Small is the worth
Of beauty from the light retired;
    Bid her come forth,
Suffer herself to be desired,
And not blush so to be admired.   15

    Then die! that she
The common fate of all things rare
    May read in thee;
How small a part of time they share
That are so wondrous sweet and fair!   20

The explanation given above of what *rose* symbolizes in the poem is inadequate—explanations of symbols usually are. We can suggest some of what a symbol gathers into itself, but ultimately there will always be more to a symbol than we can comprehend or communicate. In fact, that may be why one sends a rose in the first place.

To be effective, a symbol requires us to respond to, or participate in, its action. If the person receiving the rose does not recognize that the object means more than itself, its function as a symbol has not been completed. Similarly, if as readers we do not recognize literary symbols as such, they will not achieve their symbolic function. That raises a much discussed issue—if we respond to something as if it were a symbol, does that make it one? And is its symbolic meaning whatever we say it is? From a radically reader-oriented perspective, the answers would be "yes" to both questions. Symbolic meaning can be discovered in almost anything. It has been said that the world is a forest of symbols. From a strictly form-centered perspective, however, the answers to both questions would be "no." A "formalist" would reply that the thing must meet certain basic criteria that define *symbol*: that it is an object or an action, that it is prominent in the poem, and that the symbolic meaning must grow out of structural signals in the text, not be projected by a reader.

We would suggest that at least initially you assume that images and actions in a poem are just themselves, but that you watch for strong signals that they may be symbolic. The key signal to be alert for is *prominence*: objects or actions that are mentioned repeatedly, or described in detail, or appear in noticeable or strategic positions (at the beginning, at the end, in the title, at a crucial moment, in the climactic lines) may point toward a meaning beyond themselves. But the signals are not always structural. Another signal is a sense of an image's weightiness or significance: sometimes you may simply feel that an image or action differs from other images and actions, that it is beginning to embody an idea related to an area of major concern in the poem. In that case it could be safe to assume it is a symbol. Make sure, though, that you do not undermine the use of concrete images and figural imaginativeness by skipping their action in the poem and seeing them only as symbols. Your reading experience is always richer when you respond to images and figures on all levels.

> There are ways of knowing that don't necessarily presuppose experience, something we call symbolic geography, a symbiotic relation between the way we ascertain experience and the way we ascertain information. Information is full of symbolism that we have to manipulate.
>
> —MICHAEL HARPER

Symbols appear in several overlapping varieties. Think of some things you keep—a toy, a piece of clothing, a photo, a souvenir—that carry personal meanings for you although for others they are simply what they are. These are *private symbols*—objects that have come to have a special meaning, beyond themselves, for an individual because of experiences associated with them. It may be difficult, if not impossible, to convey their meaning to another person. In contrast are *traditional symbols,* which over the years or even centuries have come to have meanings widely attached to them. The rose, again for example, an object that is beautiful and delicate, has by tradition become a symbol of love.

There are also *conventional symbols,* such as a national flag, a swastika, a dove, a star of David, the juju, that are rippling with associations and meanings particular groups have agreed to give them. Traditional and conventional symbols bring into a literary work the clusters of meaning they already carry outside the poem. For us to respond to them according to our usual expectations depends on our background and experiences. The following poem relies on the conventional symbol of the cross and the meanings associated with it over the centuries.

WINIFRED WELLES (1893–1939)

Cruciform (1938)

Here, in the sand, where someone laid him down,
The one known human signature is clear.
Whether woman or man, white-skinned or brown,
Whether the outflung arms were so for fear
Or agony or weariness or shame,   5
Here, in one line athwart another line,
Is briefly written the one, mutual name,
A savior's or a thief's, or yours or mine.
Dunes sifted undersea long since have borne
This selfsame cross, small and anonymous;   10

Tan deserts that the wind has not yet worn
Will print this symbol. And not one of us
But then, or some day, could lie down and fit
Our desolate arms and bodies into it.

Other symbols—*contextual symbols,* like the whale in *Moby Dick*—derive their symbolic quality from the way they are developed and handled, from their role in a particular literary work. These may be powerful and full of meaning within their work, but may have no symbolic overtones outside the work, as in this poem.

JOHN BERRYMAN (1914–1972)

The Ball Poem (1950)

What is the boy now, who has lost his ball,
What, what is he to do? I saw it go
Merrily bouncing, down the street, and then
Merrily over—there it is in the water!
No use to say "O there are other balls":   5
An ultimate shaking grief fixes the boy
As he stands rigid, trembling, staring down
All his young days into the harbour where
His ball went. I would not intrude on him,
A dime, another ball, is worthless. Now   10
He senses first responsibility
In a world of possessions. People will take balls,
Balls will be lost always, little boy,
And no one buys a ball back. Money is external.
He is learning, well behind his desperate eyes,   15
The epistemology of loss, how to stand up
Knowing what every man must one day know
And most know many days, how to stand up
And gradually light returns to the street,
A whistle blows, the ball is out of sight,   20
Soon part of me will explore the deep and dark
Floor of the harbour . . I am everywhere,
I suffer and move, my mind and my heart move
With all that move me, under the water
Or whistling, I am not a little boy.   25

"Ball" initially is an image—the opening lines are simply about a boy losing a ball. As the poem proceeds, the ball, from the title on, increases in prominence: it is mentioned again and again, it becomes the focus of philosophical reflection. The ball begins to suggest more than just itself: what started out as a possession precious to the boy comes to symbolize all possessions and how, for the little boy—and for all of us—they will be lost, or outgrown, or taken away. It does not symbolize just one specific thing, but a wide range of possible things. Meanings generally radiate out from a symbol; trying to find a one-to-one equivalence between symbol and meaning ("the ball symbolizes childhood!") is reductive, cutting off the ripples of suggestiveness that are part of the richness of symbol. The grief the little boy experiences over his lost ball, and must learn to cope with, will be repeated, on a larger scale, for all of us, as other things are outgrown, or fall apart, or die, or are left behind, throughout our lives.

> Poetry gives us revelations, flashes, which illuminate those things which were mysterious to us.
>
> —Victor Hernández Cruz

· · ·

As you read the following poems, notice the images and ask yourself whether some, in one or more of the poems, seem through prominent position, or "weightiness," to gather further meaning into or around themselves. Be sure to distinguish this from figurativeness—one or more of the poems may rely more on figures than on symbols. Of course, they may include both. And some of the images will just be images.

WILLIAM MATTHEWS (b. 1942)

Blues for John Coltrane, Dead at 41 (1970)

Although my house floats on a lawn
as plush as a starlet's body
and my sons sleep easily,
I think of death's salmon breath
leaping back up the saxophone   5
with its wet kiss.

Hearing him dead,
I feel it in my feet
as if the house were rocked
by waves from a soundless speedboat   10
planing by, full throttle.

WILLIAM BLAKE (1757–1827)

Ah Sun-flower (1794)

Ah sun-flower! weary of time,
Who countest the steps of the Sun,

Seeking after that sweet golden clime
Where the traveller's journey is done;

Where the Youth pined away with desire,   5
And the pale Virgin shrouded in snow,
Arise from their graves and aspire,
Where my Sun-flower wishes to go.

COUNTEE CULLEN (1903–1946)

Incident (1925)

for Eric Walrond

A Once riding in old Baltimore,
  B   Heart-filled, head-filled with glee,
C I saw a Baltimorean
B   Keep looking straight at me.

A Now I was eight and very small,   5
B   And he was no whit bigger,
C And so I smiled, but he poked out
B   His tongue, and called me, "Nigger."

A I saw the whole of Baltimore
B   From (May until December;) *Fall from innocence*   10
C Of all the things that happened there
B   That's all that I remember.

EMILY DICKINSON (1830–1886)

I Heard a Fly Buzz (ca. 1862)

I heard a Fly buzz—when I died—
The Stillness in the Room
Was like the Stillness in the Air—
Between the Heaves of Storm—

The Eyes around—had wrung them dry—   5
And Breaths were gathering firm
For that last Onset—when the King
Be witnessed—in the Room—

I willed my Keepsakes—Signed away
What portion of me be   10
Assignable—and then it was
There interposed a Fly—

With Blue—uncertain stumbling Buzz—
Between the light—and me—
And then the Windows failed—and then   15
I could not see to see—

ARCHETYPES

Along with the symbols mentioned above is another category—universal symbols, or archetypes, that have widely accepted significance throughout the world or across cultures. Archetypes are original models or patterns from which later things are made. **Literary archetypes** are images used again and again in myths, folktales, fairy tales, religious writings, stories, and poems that reflect those original patterns. Defined broadly, literary archetypes are images, symbols, character types, and plot lines that have been used frequently enough in literature to be recognizable as an element of literary experience as a whole.

Here is a list of some archetypal symbols—a small sampling of all those that could be listed—to illustrate what you can look for (often they occur in contrasting pairs, reflecting ideal or desirable experience and unideal or undesirable experiences):

> city as a symbol of order or community (or as a symbol of artificialness and corruption, in contrast to the country and natural beauty)
> a *meal* or *feast* as a symbol of harmony and union
> a *lamb* or *sheep* as a symbol of gentleness, vulnerability
> a *wolf* or *tiger* as a symbol of the power and fearsomeness of nature
> a *garden* or *park* as a type of paradise
> a *forest* as natural beauty, or as a scary place, where one can be lost
> *fire* as brilliant and warm, or purifying, or destructive
> a *spring* or *fountain* as a symbol of purity and fertility
> the *sea* as a source of life, or as dangerous, leading to death
> *day* and *light* as symbols of life, growth, safety
> *night* or *darkness* as symbols of death or threat
> a *desert* or *wilderness* as a symbol of barrenness, emptiness
> a *river* as boundary between worlds, thus as death—but sometimes as fertility and source of life
> the *phases of the day*
> the seasons

Among the most basic of archetypal patterns are the cycles of nature, which have long been associated with human life:

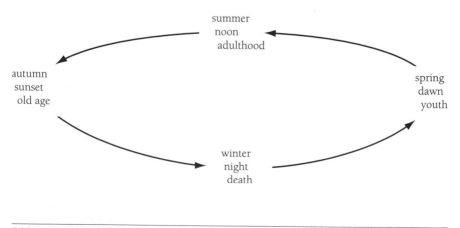

summer
noon
adulthood

autumn
sunset
old age

spring
dawn
youth

winter
night
death

This pattern has become deeply embedded in our consciousness, so that we speak of young people or novices as "green," or of postretirement as "the golden years," or of death as "sleep," without giving a thought to what lies behind them.

Archetypal symbols can add greatly to a poem's depth and range of implication. Consider the following poem.

GERARD MANLEY HOPKINS (1844–1889)

Spring and Fall (1918)

to a young child

Márgarét, áre you gríeving
Over Goldengrove unleaving?
Leáves, líke the things of man, you
With your fresh thoughts care for, can you?
Áh! ás the heart grows older   5
It will come to such sights colder
By and by, nor spare a sigh
Though worlds of wanwood leafmeal lie;
And yet you *will* weep and know why.
Now no matter, child, the name: 10
Sórrow's springs áre the same.
Nor mouth had, no nor mind, expressed
What heart heard of, ghost guessed:
It ís the blight man was born for,
It is Margaret you mourn for.   15

The poem is based on the archetypes in the title, of spring (archetype for birth and youth) and fall (archetype for the approach of death and for old age). The words of the poem are addressed to Margaret, who presumably at this point is too young to understand them. The speaker, noticing that Margaret is pensive as she watches bright yellow leaves falling in autumn ("Goldengrove unleaving"), speculates that she is responding from deep within to what autumn suggests. In her youth and innocence, she cares about the death of leaves—she doesn't yet differentiate things in nature from human concerns, but feels deeply about all things. As she gets older and has more experience with the world, she will become accustomed to nature's passing and will be less sensitive ("will come to such sights colder") and less caring: she will not sigh though piles ("worlds") of leaves ("wanwood"—woods looking "wan," or pale) are scattered on the ground ("leafmeal lie"—a wordplay on "piecemeal," or apart, separately). As the years go by she will feel less sympathy for nature, yet she will continue to feel sadness, for the same reason she does now. Now she is not aware of the ultimate source of sorrow (neither her mouth nor her mind expresses it consciously); but her heart, her spirit, unconsciously knows: the source of all sorrows is the presence of death in the world—the "blight." Thus, the still deeper cause, the subconscious source of Margaret's grief, is her own mortality: the falling of the leaves somehow gives her an unconscious sense that she too, eventually, will die. It is not just nature that she, young as she is, mourns for, but herself.

The poem uses archetypes and also models their effect. Young Margaret, watching leaves fall, senses what autumn is and means, and is moved deep within, at a depth that conscious thought (even if she were mature enough) cannot reach. The archetypes of the poem can move readers in a similar way: the juxtaposition of the images of the young girl and fall can move us deeply. Most of us have felt a sadness and nostalgia as summer ends and fall advances; the poem connects us to those feelings. The archetypes in the poem connect in many directions—with patterns in nature, in ourselves, and in the literature of many times and places. These patterns help us recognize—as the poem affirms—that the source of the sadness is universal; all of us grow older each year, and eventually all of us must face our own mortality.

> The earliest hominid being we can touch comes out in poetry. It's the way natural systems work.
>
> —GARY SNYDER

Take some time to think about how archetypes in the following poem deepen and universalize its implications.

WILLIAM SHAKESPEARE (1564–1616)

That Time of Year Thou Mayst in Me Behold (1609)

That time of year thou mayst in me behold
When yellow leaves, or none, or few, do hang
Upon those boughs which shake against the cold,
Bare ruined choirs, where late the sweet birds sang.
In me thou seest the twilight of such day   5
As after sunset fadeth in the west,
Which by and by black night doth take away,
Death's second self, that seals up all in rest.
In me thou seest the glowing of such fire
That on the ashes of his youth doth lie,   10
As the deathbed whereon it must expire,
Consumed with that which it was nourished by.
    This thou perceiv'st, which makes thy love more strong,
    To love that well which thou must leave ere long.

Just as images can have archetypal implications, character types and narrative motifs can also take on symbolic significance as archetypes. Among archetypal characters used through the centuries are the hero, the villain, the witch, the wanderer, the benevolent ruler, the tyrant, the trickster, and the keeper of wisdom. Motifs used throughout literature, and now rich with symbolic implications, are creation stories and temptation stories. Among the most frequently used symbolic motifs, especially in longer poems, is the *journey*. Throughout the centuries, journey as an archetype has suggested growth or advancement or maturing, especially through experience and education. Because, in that sense, all of us are on a journey of life, or through life, stories and poems involving journeys are often especially meaningful. Some of the most famous stories fall into this category—think of Odysseus (Ulysses), of the characters in *Roots,* of Lemuel Gulliver, of Huckleberry Finn. All are on journeys of maturation and education. Always on the journey there are *ordeals* to be faced and conquered. Sometimes the journey involves a *quest*—an expedition undertaken to find or obtain or achieve something (a lost city, a Holy Grail, or a rescue, for example). Thus Jason sails off to find a golden fleece and the Arthurian knights, Indiana Jones, and the Monty Python characters all search for the Holy Grail. Often the journey includes an *initiation,* a rite of passage from immaturity to adulthood, with many perils to be overcome, and involves temptations—the danger of being seduced to give up the quest, or the invitation to abandon the good and join the evil oppressors.

In "The Quest," W. H. Auden draws on typical archetypal elements, but treats them satirically—how, the poem asks, would a quest be undertaken today, in the modern world? Surely a huge organization would need to work for months investigating, planning, securing supplies; in the end it would be found that few people in the mid- (and late?) twentieth century have the vision and courage needed to be heroes and to go on quests. Here is its opening section.

W. H. AUDEN (1907–1973)

from *The Quest* (1940)

I

All had been ordered weeks before the start
From the best firms at such work; instruments
To take the measure of all queer events,
And drugs to move the bowels or the heart.

A watch, of course, to watch impatience fly,   5
Lamps for the dark and shades against the sun;
Foreboding, too, insisted on a gun,
And coloured beads to soothe a savage eye.

In theory they were sound on Expectation
Had there been situations to be in.   10
Unluckily they were their situation:

One should not give a poisoner medicine,
A conjurer fine apparatus, nor
A rifle to a melancholic bore.

Symbols are powerful—among the most evocative experiences for a reader. Though they cannot be reduced to a condensed meaning, they can condense the meaningfulness of an entire work into themselves. If read undiscerningly, they can turn poetry into a hunt for "hidden meaning," but when read with thoughtful common sense, they lend a rich, evocative, suggestive aura to a work and help us realize that meanings are not "hidden" but embodied and revealed, suggested, or evoked.

· · ·

Here is a poem that makes use of archetypes. If you are not familiar with the story of the three wise men who travel to Bethlehem to honor the Christ child, you may need to read Matthew 2:1–12 in the Bible in order to connect with the characters and events. Compare the perspective from which the story is told in Matthew with that in this poem, and be ready to discuss differences in effect. Pick out two or three archetypes and be ready to discuss their importance in the poem. By the way, lines 1–5 are enclosed within quotation marks because they are quoted almost unchanged from a sermon by Bishop Lancelot Andrewes on Christmas Day, 1622 (a little example of **found poetry**—rhythmic or even metrical phrases found in nonpoetic contexts, such as a newspaper, an advertisement, a conversation, or in this case a sermon).

T. S. ELIOT (1888–1965)

Journey of the Magi (1927)

"A cold coming we had of it,
Just the worst time of the year
For a journey, and such a long journey:
The ways deep and the weather sharp,
The very dead of winter." 5
And the camels galled, sore-footed, refractory,
Lying down in the melting snow.
There were times we regretted
The summer palaces on slopes, the terraces,
And the silken girls bringing sherbet. 10
Then the camel men cursing and grumbling
And running away, and wanting their liquor and women,
And the night-fires going out, and the lack of shelters,
And the cities hostile and the towns unfriendly
And the villages dirty and charging high prices: 15
A hard time we had of it.
At the end we preferred to travel all night,
Sleeping in snatches,
With the voices singing in our ears, saying
That this was all folly. 20

　　Then at dawn we came down to a temperate valley,
Wet, below the snow line, smelling of vegetation;

With a running stream and a water-mill beating the darkness,
And three trees on the low sky,
And an old white horse galloped away in the meadow.   25
Then we came to a tavern with vine-leaves over the lintel,
Six hands at an open door dicing for pieces of silver,
And feet kicking the empty wine-skins.
But there was no information, and so we continued
And arrived at evening, not a moment too soon   30
Finding the place; it was (you may say) satisfactory.

      All this was a long time ago, I remember,
And I would do it again, but set down
This set down
This: were we led all that way for   35
Birth or Death? There was a Birth, certainly,
We had evidence and no doubt. I had seen birth and death,
But had thought they were different; this Birth was
Hard and bitter agony for us, like Death, our death.
We returned to our places, these Kingdoms,   40
But no longer at ease here, in the old dispensation,
With an alien people clutching their gods.
I should be glad of another death.

In the following poems, watch for archetypes; if you find some, reflect on
how they are used and what they contribute.

THYLIAS MOSS (b. 1954)

Sunrise Comes to Second Avenue (1990)

Daylight announces
the start of a day six hours old.

We all have thankless
jobs to do. Consider

the devotion of fishes singing   5
hymns without voices.

The clock's hands searching
for the lost face, a place

for the Eucharist. The man
bedded down on the roadway,   10

the asphalt pope out of bread,
breath and blessings.

The streetcleaner
sweeping up confessions.

DAVID YOUNG (b. 1936)

The Portable Earth-Lamp (1988)

The planet on the desk, illuminated globe
we ordered for Bo's birthday,
sits in its Lucite crescent, a medicine ball
of Rand McNally plastic. A brown cord
runs from the South Pole toward a socket.   5

It's mostly a night-light for the boys
and it blanches their dreaming faces
a blue sphere patched with continents
mottled by deeps and patterned currents,
its capital cities bright white dots.   10

Our models: they're touching and absurd,
magical for both their truth and falsehood.

I like its shine at night. Moth-light.
I sleepwalk toward it, musing.
This globe's a bible, a bubble of myth-   15
light, a blue eye, a double
bowl: empty of all but its bulb and clever skin,
full of whatever we choose to lodge there.

I haven't been able to shake off all my grief,
my globe's cold poles and arid wastes,   20
the weight of death, disease and history.
But see how the oceans heave and shine,
see how the clouds and mountains glisten!

We float through space. Days pass.
Sometimes we know we are part of a crystal   25
where light is sorted and stored,
sharing an iridescence
cobbled and million-featured.

Oh, tiny beacon in the hurting dark.
Oh, soft blue glow.   30

One thing to watch for in poems based on myths is the way they adapt
and apply the ancient tales. The next poem is based on one of the oldest Greek
myths, about Demeter (her Roman name is Ceres), the goddess of crops and
harvest, and her daughter Persephone. Hades (Pluto), the god of the under-
world (the land of the dead), fell in love with Persephone and kidnapped her.
Demeter, searching desperately for her daughter, eventually learned what had
happened and appealed to Zeus (Jupiter), the supreme deity. He did not want
to offend Hades and refused to intervene. So Demeter wandered about the
earth, grieving and angry, and refused to let seeds germinate or crops grow.
Famine spread throughout the earth and the human race was threatened with

extinction. Zeus was forced to act. He sent messengers to plead with Demeter to allow Hades to marry Persephone, but Demeter refused. Having no other recourse, Zeus told Hades he must release Persephone. Hades pretended to agree, told Persephone she was free to leave, and offered her a pomegranate seed to eat. This was a trick, for anyone who eats food in the underworld must return there. The reunion of Demeter and Persephone was joyful until Demeter learned that Persephone had eaten the pomegranate seed and would have to return to the underworld. Demeter then refused to remove her curse upon the earth. Finally, Zeus arranged a compromise: that Persephone would spend a third of each year in the land of the dead with Hades (during that time, Demeter went into mourning and crops would not grow; it was winter on earth), but she would be with her mother for the other two-thirds of each year (during those months—spring and summer—Demeter was joyful and crops would grow and produce abundant harvests).

As you read the poem, watch for ways the speaker contemporizes the myth, applies it to various stages of her life, and identifies with different characters in it. Notice how seasons appear archetypally and how another ancient tale is woven in through allusions. Reflect on what it means that the speaker's daughter, like the speaker, will "enter" the myth.

EAVAN BOLAND (b. 1944)

The Pomegranate (1994)

The only legend I have ever loved is
The story of a daughter lost in hell.
And found and rescued there.
Love and blackmail are the gist of it.
Ceres and Persephone the names.   5
And the best thing about the legend is
I can enter it anywhere. And have.
As a child in exile in
A city of fogs and strange consonants,
I read it first and at first I was   10
An exiled child in the crackling dusk of
The underworld, the stars blighted. Later
I walked out in a summer twilight
Searching for my daughter at bedtime.
When she came running I was ready   15
To make any bargain to keep her.
I carried her back past whitebeams.
And wasps and honey-scented buddleias.
But I was Ceres then and I knew
Winter was in store for every leaf   20
On every tree on that road.
Was inescapable for each one we passed.
And for me.

It is winter
And the stars are hidden.   25
I climb the stairs and stand where I can see
My child asleep beside her teen magazines,
Her can of Coke, her plate of uncut fruit.
The pomegranate! How did I forget it?
She could have come home and been safe   30
And ended the story and all
Our heartbroken searching but she reached
Out a hand and plucked a pomegranate.
She put out her hand and pulled down
The French sound for apple and   35
The noise of stone and the proof
That even in the place of death,
At the heart of legend, in the midst
Of rocks full of unshed tears
Ready to be diamonds by the time   40
The story was told, a child can be
Hungry. I could warn her. There is still a chance.
The rain is cold. The road is flint-coloured.
The suburb has cars and cable television.
The veiled stars are above ground.   45
It is another world. But what else
Can a mother give her daughter but such
Beautiful rifts in time?
If I defer the grief I will diminish the gift.
The legend must be hers as well as mine.   50
She will enter it. As I have.
She will wake up. She will hold
The papery, flushed skin in her hand.
And to her lips. I will say nothing.

APPLICATIONS FOR CHAPTER 7

SUGGESTIONS FOR WRITING

1. In your journal, list some private symbols in your life. After each one, tell
    some of what it means or suggests.
2. Write a journal entry in which you list and describe or discuss some
    "mythic figures" in your life. For example, your uncle may be a saint; your
    worst enemy, a devil; a certain friend, a trickster; a parent, at times a god;
    and so on.
3. Reflect on some objects that have been memorable in your life. Choose
    one that seems particularly meaningful. Try writing a poem in which that
    object becomes a central image and takes on a symbolic effect.
4. Write a poem in which a person or persons appear mythic and participate
    in archetypal actions.

5. Write a paper in which you help someone recognize the symbol or symbols in a poem.
6. Write an imaginary argument between (1) a person who finds symbols everywhere in a particular poem and one who is skeptical about such; (2) a person who believes that looking for symbols wrecks the reading of a particular poem and one who feels it enriches it; or (3) two people who disagree on the meanings of a symbol or symbols in a particular poem.
7. Robert Frost's "Stopping by Woods" (p. 326) is often seen as a synecdoche, on the one hand, or as symbolic, on the other. Write an imaginary panel discussion in which you have different speakers argue for the figurative and the symbolic.
8. See if you can discern the presence of myth and archetype in a favorite television show. Write a paper explaining how they add depth and dimension to it, or comparing the show's handling of these elements to that in a favorite poem.
9. Retell a fable, fairy tale, or myth in your own way. Consider why you changed it as you did.

SUGGESTIONS AS YOU CONTINUE TO READ POETRY

1. Remember the difference between an image (a word representing an object that can be known by one or more of the senses) and a symbol (an image that also embodies an idea).
2. Allow images to be just images.
3. Watch for formal devices or signals commonly used for pointing at symbols (such as objects or actions mentioned repeatedly, described in detail, and/or placed in noticeable positions), use them to perceive when a poem is using symbols, and respond to and engage with the symbolic effects they create.
4. Notice archetypes (repeatedly used images and symbols recognizable as elements of literary experience as a whole) in a poem and be open to their effect.

8 | Sounds

Remember how when you were a kid you often made sounds that went along with what you were playing: the sound of a car or a gun or a ball going through a hoop or a jet plane? Or maybe there were some words you just loved to say over and over because of how they sounded. Sound is one of the great pleasures of life, and of poetry—combinations of sounds as well as the sounds of individual words, repeating or contrasting syllable sounds, vowel sounds, consonant sounds. Fine poets have "good ears" and experiment with sounds, building them into the structure of poems. We as readers get to participate in the effect of sounds by hearing and responding to them. To experience the full effect of poetry we need not only to hear words, but also to listen for the individual sounds of the syllables, vowels, and consonants that form the words. In the quality of their sounds, in their repetitions, in their connections, in their contrasts, a kind of verbal "music" is created.

SOUNDS AND MEANING

Each vowel and consonant has its own quality, its own character; these have been categorized according to where and how in the mouth they are formed. Vowels are classified as front, central, or back, and high, middle, or low. Consonants are grouped as liquids (*r, l*), nasals (*m, n, ng*), fricatives (*h, f, c, th, s, z, sh*), and stops (*p, b, t, d, k, g*), according to the place in and shape of the mouth as they are formed. Learning more about sounds themselves could help you enjoy and explain why certain sound combinations work the way they do: notice, for example, the difference in the way your mouth moves and reshapes itself as you read two lines from Alexander Pope's *An Essay on Criticism:* "Soft is the strain when Zephyr gently blows" and "The hoarse, rough verse shou'd like the Torrent roar."

The sounds in a poem generally seem to fit the meanings being expressed—that is what Pope was illustrating in the lines above. Attempts have been made to associate individual vowel and consonant sounds with specific feelings or meanings: high vowels, for example, with excitement; low vowels with power or gloominess; the nasal consonants (*m, n, ng*) with warm, positive associations (*mother*); *sn* with usually unpleasant things (*snake, sneer*); and *st* with strong, stable, energetic things. Those attempts have been countered with claims that meanings are being read into the sounds, rather than the sounds shaping meaning. In either case, something meaningful and interesting is being created or elicited by sound.

Beyond the notion that vowels and consonants can be associated with a feeling or meaning is the concept of **onomatopoeia**, the use of words whose pronunciation suggests their meaning. Samuel Johnson, in the eighteenth century, described it this way: "Every language has some words framed to exhibit the noises which they express, as *thump, rattle, growl, hiss.*" Onomatopoeia, at its best, involves not just individual words, but entire passages that carry their meaning in their sounds. Listen to these lines from "The Princess" by Alfred, Lord Tennyson: "The moan of doves in immemorial elms, / And murmuring of innumerable bees."

Read again "I Heard a Fly Buzz," concentrating this time on the sounds in it. Do you think they enhance the sense, or not? What might you use to support your response?

EMILY DICKINSON (1830–1886)

I Heard a Fly Buzz (ca. 1862)

I heard a Fly buzz—when I died—
The Stillness in the Room
Was like the Stillness in the Air—
Between the Heaves of Storm—

The Eyes around—had wrung them dry—   5
And Breaths were gathering firm
For that last Onset—when the King
Be witnessed—in the Room—

I willed my Keepsakes—Signed away
What portion of me be   10
Assignable—and then it was
There interposed a Fly—

With Blue—uncertain stumbling Buzz—
Between the light—and me—
And then the Windows failed—and then
I could not see to see—

15

ALLITERATION, CONSONANCE, ASSONANCE
(sounds) (words)

Amplifying the effect of the vowel and consonant sounds in a poem is the *repetition* of such sounds. **Alliteration** is the repetition of identical consonant sounds in words relatively near one another (in the same line or adjacent lines, usually). Alliteration is most common at the beginnings of words or syllables, especially stressed syllables ("green as grass"), but can involve consonants within words and syllables as well (golden baggage). The sound is what matters, not the spelling ("Call the kid in the center"). Alliteration can add musicality to poetry, and can contribute to meaning by strengthening connections between words, directing emphasis to particular words, and making phrases more memorable. Notice the alliteration, and how it contributes to sound and meaning, in "The Dark Forest":

EDWARD THOMAS (1878–1917)

The Dark Forest (1916)

Dark is the forest and deep, and overhead
Hang stars like seeds of light
In vain, though not since they were sown was bred
Anything more bright.

And evermore mighty multitudes ride   5
About, nor enter in;
Of the other multitudes that dwell inside
Never yet was one seen.

The forest foxglove is purple, the marguerite
Outside is gold and white,   10
Nor can those that pluck either blossom greet
The others, day or night.

A variant on alliteration is **consonance**, the use of words whose consonant sounds are the same but whose vowels are different. In perfect examples, all the consonants are alike—*live, love; chitter, chatter; reader, rider;* or, in Romeo's words, "I'll look to like, if looking liking move" (*Romeo and Juliet* 1.4.98). But words in which the consonants following the main vowels are identical also are considered consonance—*dive, love; swatter, chitter; sound, bond*. The following poem, about the challenges a traveler must confront if she or he is to go on a journey, relies heavily on consonance, as well as on alliteration. Listen for such sounds as you read the poem and then reflect on what they contribute as you go through it again.

W. H. AUDEN (1907–1973)
The Three Companions (1934)

"O where are you going?" said reader to rider, *consonance*
"That valley is fatal when furnaces burn, *assonance*
Yonder is the midden whose odours will madden,
That gap is the grave where the tall return."

"O do you imagine," said fearer to farer,   5
"That dusk will delay on your path to the pass,
Your diligent looking discover the lacking
Your footsteps feel from granite to grass?"

"O what was that bird," said horror to hearer,
"Did you see that shape in the twisted trees?   10
Behind you swiftly the figure comes softly,
The spot on your skin is a shocking disease."

"Out of this house"—said rider to reader.
"Yours never will"—said farer to fearer,
"They're looking for you"—said hearer to horror,   15
As he left them there, as he left them there.

Assonance is the repetition of identical vowel sounds in words whose consonants differ. It too can be initial within a line or perhaps adjacent lines (*Under* the *umbrella*), though internal is more usual (*tree* by *leaf*, *tree* and *treat*). Its strongest effect is a subtle musical quality that often reinforces the tone of a poem, adds gradations to its feel, and contributes to meaning by making connections and adding emphasis. Listen for the assonance in this poem, then reread it, thinking about its effects.

do you?

MARTÍN ESPADA (b. 1957)
The Saint Vincent de Paul Food Pantry Stomp (1990)
Madison, Wisconsin, 1980

Waiting for the carton of food
given with Christian suspicion
even to agency-certified charity cases
like me,
thin and brittle   5
as uncooked linguini,

anticipating the factory-damaged cans
of tomato soup, beets, three-bean salad
in a welfare cornucopia,
I spotted a squashed dollar bill   10
on the floor, and with
a Saint Vincent de Paul food pantry stomp
pinned it under my sneaker,
tied my laces meticulously,
and stuffed the bill in my sock   15
like a smuggler of diamonds,
all beneath the plaster statue wingspan
of Saint Vinnie,
who was unaware
of the dance   20
named in his honor
by a maraca shaker
in the salsa band
of the unemployed.

> I was born with the gift of being able to hear the music in the language and
> see the nobility in the people, that is, all the language and all the people.
> —LUCILLE CLIFTON

RHYME

A fairly noticeable type of sound repetition involves combining assonance
with consonance in the familiar combination called **rhyme,** the repetition of
the accented vowel sound and the sounds that follow it in a word, as in the
italicized words in the following poem.

WILLIAM BLAKE (1757–1827)

from *To See a World in a Grain of Sand* (ca. 1803)

To see a world in a grain of *sand*
And a heaven in a wild *flower,*
Hold infinity in the palm of your *hand*
And eternity in an *hour.*

Rhyme leads to various effects: it can give emphasis to important words; it can
create a type of connection or bonding; it can strengthen organization and
unity; it can contain meaning; it can provide a sense of completion, or termi-

nation, to lines, stanzas, and whole poems; and it can create a certain pleasure in its musicality and expectation. Sometimes, as Mekeel McBride indicates, it can trigger a whole poem:

MEKEEL MCBRIDE (b. 1950)
from *A Blessing* (1983)

From what sometimes seems an arbitrary   10
form or discipline often come two words
that rhyme and in the rhyming fully marry
the world of spoons and sheets and common birds
to another world that we have always known
where the waterfall of dawn does not drown   15
even the haloed gnat; where we are shown
how to find and hold the pale day moon, round
and blessed in the silver lake of a coffee spoon.

If well written, and well read, rhyme does not distract us from the rest of the poem, but blends with other aspects in a satisfying, pleasing way. When a poem is read aloud, an effective reader is able to emphasize rhyming words enough so that a listener can hear the echoes of sound, without having them "steal the show."

Rhyme is described according to several categories—exact or approximate; end or internal; single or double:

- In **exact rhyme** the vowel and the consonant sounds following it are the same: *bright* and *night, art* and *heart, ache* and *fake* (throughout this section, the *sound* matters, not the spelling). **Approximate rhyme** (also called **slant rhyme, near rhyme**, or **partial rhyme**) is consonance occurring at the ends of lines; that is, words with identical final consonant sounds but different vowel sounds: *gate* and *mat, set, pit; all* and *stole, will, hale.*

- **End rhyme** involves rhyming words that occur at the ends of lines; in **internal rhyme,** two or more words within a line, or within lines near each other, rhyme with each other, or words within lines rhyme with words at the ends.

- **Single rhyme** is rhyme involving only the final, stressed syllable in a line: *west* and *vest, away* and *today.* In **double rhyme** the accented, rhyming syllable is followed by one or more identical, unstressed syllables: *thrilling* and *killing, marry* and *tarry.*[1]

---

[1] In older books you may find single rhyme referred to as **masculine rhyme** (because it was considered "strong" and "forceful") and double rhyme as **feminine rhyme** (because it was regarded as "weaker" than single rhyme). These labels generally are no longer used because of their sexist overtones.

Unless otherwise specified, *rhyme* used alone means *exact, end, single rhyme*.

The pattern of end rhymes in a poem or stanza—that is, its recurring sequence—is called its **rhyme scheme**. The pattern is usually described by assigning a letter to each word-sound, with the same word-sounds having the same letter:

WILLIAM WORDSWORTH (1770–1850)

My Heart Leaps Up (1802)

My heart leaps up when I behold	*a*
A rainbow in the sky:	*b*
So was it when my life began;	*c*
So is it now I am a man;	*c*
So be it when I shall grow old,	*a*
Or let me die!	*b*
The Child is father of the Man;	*c*
And I could wish my days to be	*d*
Bound each to each by natural piety.	*d*

5

For poems in stanzas, the pattern is usually the same for each stanza. In that case you need to mark the rhyme scheme only once. Thus *abcb* is the rhyme scheme for "The Three Companions" (p. 121); there is no need to do *abcb defe ghih jklk*.

> If I had to give up rhyme, I'd have to give up being a poet. I have many students who say to me that rhyme is insincere, but for me it is not a question of sincerity. The rhymes are all there, all packed inside my head. It's a question of letting them all out a little at a time. Rhyme provides so much of an underbeat to the language of the poem, so much a measurement to the tension of the poem that I would be very hard put to write a deeply felt poem without it.
>
> —MAXINE KUMIN

For practice, mark the rhyme scheme, and label the different kinds of rhyme, in the following stanza:

PERCY BYSSHE SHELLEY (1792–1822)

from The Cloud (1820)

I bring fresh showers for the thirsting flowers,
    From the seas and the streams;
I bear light shade for the leaves when laid
    In their noonday dreams.

From my wings are shaken the dews that waken   5
    The sweet buds every one,
When rocked to rest on their mother's breast,
    As she dances about the sun.
I wield the flail of the lashing hail,
    And whiten the green plains under,   10
And then again I dissolve it in rain,
    And laugh as I pass in thunder.

A larger type of repetition with effects similar to those of rhyme is the use of a **refrain,** in which one or more identical or nearly identical lines is repeated throughout a poem. The refrain may come as the final line of a stanza, or as a block of lines between stanzas or sections of a poem. See, for example, "Lord Randal" (p. 295).

· · ·

As you read the following poems, focus especially on the variety of sounds created in them. Read the poems aloud, or ask a friend to read them to you. The first one celebrates the delights that childhood should include and explores the loss of innocence as one grows older. Lots of things appear within it that are worth attention, such as the handling of the speaker, the use of images, figures, and symbols, and the handling of rhythm and form (to anticipate Chapters 9 and 10). You might decide to write about one or more of those aspects in your journal or in a paper. You might want to write about how you respond to its subject and techniques. Its use of sound is also intriguing and contributes to most readers' responses. Listen for sounds as you read (and reread) it. Then consider and be ready to discuss what sound adds to its effect.

DYLAN THOMAS (1914–1953)

Fern Hill (1946)

Now as I was young and easy under the apple boughs
About the lilting house and happy as the grass was green,
    The night above the dingle starry,
      Time let me hail and climb
    Golden in the heydays of his eyes,   5
And honoured among wagons I was prince of the apple towns
And once below a time I lordly had the trees and leaves
      Trail with daisies and barley
    Down the rivers of the windfall light.

And as I was green and carefree, famous among the barns
About the happy yard and singing as the farm was home,   10
    In the sun that is young once only,
      Time let me play and be

Golden in the mercy of his means,
And green and golden I was huntsman and herdsman, the calves   15
Sang to my horn, the foxes on the hills barked clear and cold,
        And the sabbath rang slowly
    In the pebbles of the holy streams.

All the sun long it was running, it was lovely, the hay
Fields high as the house, the tunes from the chimneys, it was air   20
        And playing, lovely and watery
            And fire green as grass.
        And nightly under the simple stars
As I rode to sleep the owls were bearing the farm away,
All the moon long I heard, blessed among stables, the nightjars   25
        Flying with the ricks, and the horses
            Flashing into the dark.

And then to awake, and the farm, like a wanderer white
With the dew, come back, the cock on his shoulder: it was all
        Shining, it was Adam and maiden,   30
            The sky gathered again
        And the sun grew round that very day.
So it must have been after the birth of the simple light
In the first, spinning place, the spellbound horses walking warm
        Out of the whinnying green stable   35
            On to the fields of praise.

And honoured among foxes and pheasants by the gay house
Under the new made clouds and happy as the heart was long,
        In the sun born over and over,
            I ran my heedless ways,   40
        My wishes raced through the house high hay
And nothing I cared, at my sky blue trades, that time allows
In all his tuneful turning so few and such morning songs
        Before the children green and golden
            Follow him out of grace,   45

Nothing I cared, in the lamb white days, that time would take me
Up to the swallow thronged loft by the shadow of my hand,
        In the moon that is always rising,
            Nor that riding to sleep
        I should hear him fly with the high fields   50
And wake to the farm forever fled from the childless land.
Oh as I was young and easy in the mercy of his means,
        Time held me green and dying
    Though I sang in my chains like the sea.

The next four poems use sound for a variety of effects. Listen to their sounds, and consider how sound helps shape your response to each of them.

ALBERTO RÍOS (b. 1952)

Fixing Tires (1990)

Your rough hands, pins:
On me they make
The tin rasp my father used
Patching the bad
Tires of the round-back   5
Chevy, that fast, hard,
Repeat scrape making
Everything smooth
By its unevenness,
Smooth for the honey   10
Solvent to which we lit
A match and watched
It burn,
That fire making a seal
Sticky and, we could see,   15
Firm. This skin
You show me now,
The skin thrilling makes,
Up against my cheek,
This rubbing   20
Along all my lips,
It is the rasp
And strong enough.

JAMES JOYCE (1882–1941)

On the Beach at Fontana (1927)
Trieste, 1914

Wind whines and whines the shingle,
The crazy pierstakes groan;
A senile sea numbers each single
Slimesilvered stone.

From whining wind and colder   5
Grey sea I wrap him warm
And touch his trembling fineboned shoulder
And boyish arm.

Around us fear, descending
Darkness of fear above
And in my heart how deep unending
Ache of love!

10

ALICE FULTON (b. 1952) *(a sestina)*

You Can't Rhumboogie in a Ball and Chain (1983)

for Janis Joplin

You called the blues' loose black belly lover
and in Port Arthur they called you pig-face.
The way you chugged booze straight, without a glass,
your brass-assed language, slingbacks with jeweled heel,
proclaimed you no kin to their muzzled blood.
No Chiclet-toothed Baptist boyfriend for you.

Strung-out, street hustling showed men wouldn't buy you.
Once you clung to the legs of a lover,
let him drag you till your knees turned to blood,
mouth hardened to a thin scar on your face,
cracked under songs, screams, never left to heal.
Little Girl Blue, soul pressed against the glass.

That voice rasping like you'd guzzled fiberglass,
stronger than the four armed men behind you.
But a pale horse lured you, docile, to heel:
warm snow flanks pillowed you like a lover.
Men feared the black holes in your body and face,
knew what they put in would return as blood.

Craving fast food, cars, garish as fresh blood,
diners with flies and doughnuts under glass,
Formica bars and a surfer's gold face,
in nameless motels, after sign-off, you
let TV's blank bright stare play lover,
lay still, convinced its cobalt rays could heal.

Your songs that sound ground under some stud's heel,
swallowed and coughed up in a voice like blood:
translation unavailable, lover!
No prince could shoe you in unyielding glass,
stories of exploding pumpkins bored you
who flaunted tattooed breast and hungry face.

That night needing a sweet-legged sugar's face,
a hot, sky-eyed Southern comfort to heal
the hurt of senior proms for all but you,
plain Janis Lyn, self-hatred laced your blood.

5

10

15

20

25

30

In every stanza there are the words face, heal (heel), blood, glass = sestina

128 ENTRY POINTS • Sounds

You knew they worshiped drained works, emptied glass,
legend's last gangbang the wildest lover.   35

Like clerks we face your image in the glass,
suggest lovers, as accessories, heels.
"It's your shade, this blood dress," we say. "It's you."

SUSAN HOWE (b. 1937)

from *Speeches at the Barriers* (1983)

2.

Right or ruth
rent

to the winds shall be thrown

words being wind or web

What (pine-cone wheat-ear   35
sea-shell) what

volume of secrets to teach
Socrates

Banks of wild bees in story
sing in no wood so on   40

cornstalk and cornsheaf

prodigal benevolence
wealth washed up by the sea

What I find
signal seen by my eye   45

This winter falls froward
forever

sound and suggestion speared
open

Free will in blind duel   50

sees in secret houses in sand

each day's last purpose
each day's firm progress

schoolgirls sleeping
schoolboys sleeping and stemmed   55

I will dream you
Draw you

dawn and horses of the sun
dawn galloped in greek before flame

fugitive dialogue of masterwork 60

APPLICATIONS FOR CHAPTER 8

SUGGESTIONS FOR WRITING

1. Find a poem in which the sounds of words are intricately connected, creating a poem tightly stitched together by sounds. In your journal, record as many different "sound linkings" as you can or have time for. You could also write a paper discussing the intricacy of sounds in the poem.
2. Listen to a radio news program. Write a journal entry discussing how reporters use sound to evoke a sense of place, or to convey additional information about a person or an event.
3. The composer John Cage challenged our notions about music by saying that any sound qualifies as music. As you go about your day, listen for sounds going on around you. Record them in your journal as a list of images.
4. Try to remember the sounds you heard or loved to say as a child. Record them in your journal. Write a poem that incorporates these sounds.
5. Help someone who says she or he has a "tin ear" to hear and appreciate the musicality of a particular poem.
6. Listen to a poem in a language you do not understand. In your journal, write about its musicality and risk saying what you think the sounds convey.
7. Find a poem and change several of the words to create new sounds. Note how this may alter the meaning, at least slightly. Write a journal entry or paper about the relationship between sound and meaning.
8. Write your own "Jabberwocky" poem, a poem that evokes a response based on the sounds of words rather than on dictionary definitions. You may mix words from the dictionary with those you invent.
9. Write a paper discussing sounds in one of the poems on pp. 125–130; in "To Autumn" (Ch. 4, p. 58); or in "Naming of Parts" (p. 351); or in another poem of your choice.
10. Reread "Jabberwocky" (Ch. 3, p. 44) and write a paper in which you discuss what the sounds evoke.

SUGGESTIONS AS YOU CONTINUE TO READ POETRY

1. Listen for patterns of sound, such as alliteration, assonance, and consonance.
2. Watch for the pattern of rhyme (if any) in a stanza or poem, and notice the "rhyme scheme" (*abab,* etc.).

Rhythm and Meter   9

"It don't mean a thing if it ain't got that swing," as the famous Duke Ellington song put it.

When we think of rhythms in our lives, we usually recognize those that are regular: sunrise/sunset, the change of seasons, waves on the shore, even the routines in our lives—holiday visits, days to take out the trash, final exam week, income tax time. And of course, there's that old standby, the beats of our heart; however, even that can become problematic, sometimes turning into what is called an irregular heartbeat. We live, in fact, with many irregular rhythms: the rhythms of the city, the stutter step of a basketball player, the anxious cadence of our speech under stress and uncertainty, people dropping by unexpectedly, and the infamous pop quiz.

RHYTHM

Rhythm in poetry, the patterned "movement" of the poem created by words and their arrangement, taps into the varied rhythms of life. Rhythm can be difficult to describe. So, because there is no set of precise descriptive labels, we turn to metaphorical language. We say that rhythm can be fast or slow, syncopated or disjointed, smooth or halting, graceful or rough, deliberate or frenzied, or a mixture of any or all of these, or others. What shapes the rhythm or rhythms are such things as:

- **line length:** Short lines can (but don't always) quicken rhythm; long lines can draw it out.
- **line endings:** Lines that lack punctuation at the end and "run on" into the next line (**run-on lines**) tend toward a faster, smoother pace from line to line; lines with punctuation at the end, especially periods and semicolons (**end-stopped lines**), often slow down. Lines broken at unexpected or irregular places create a jolt and break up rhythmic flow; line breaks at expected or "natural" places can create a gentle shift carrying the rhythm along smoothly.
- **pauses** (or lack of them) within lines: Pauses, called **caesuras** and usually indicated by punctuation, tend to break up the flow of a line, slow it

down a bit, perhaps make it "jagged" or "halting"; lack of pauses can propel a line and make it either smooth and graceful or hurried, even frenetic.

- **spaces:** Leaving gaps within, at the beginning or end of, or between lines can slow up movement, even stop it altogether, or indicate which words to group together; crowding things together can speed up a rhythm.
- **word choice** and **combinations of sounds:** Those easy to say together can create a steady, smooth, harmonious pace in a line; those hard to say can make it "jagged" or "harsh" or "tired." Both uses can create a sense of "calm" or even "dreaminess," just as there are times when we are calm or dreamy in either pleasant or stressful situations. It is important to realize that different rhythms may be appropriate for the same experience.

Being aware of and alert to such structures can help you notice, feel, and respond to the life of rhythm with more confidence—and it can be fun.

Because rhythm is not fixed, your involvement is crucial. Rhythm is based on formal structures, but *you* as reader participate by interacting sensitively with these structures, "interpreting" (or "performing") them. How long a word is to be "held," or how much stress is to be put on a syllable, or how short a short line is and how long a long line is, and how much pause there is in a pause, are effects you get to create, or decide on. When you think about it, humor and a poem have this in common: along with a particularly insightful or sensitive perspective, each relies on an intuitively precise sense of timing. How is it that one person can tell a joke and another cannot? Timing. Why can one person, as writer or reader, evoke the rhythms, either consistent or varied, that make a poem work? Timing. A sense of rhythm, a sense of timing: without these, the joke and the poem fall flat.

Notice the rhythms in the following poem, as the gaps, divisions into lines, groupings of lines, and combinations of words and sounds lead you to speed up, slow down, pause, and adjust your timing.

E. E. CUMMINGS (1894–1962)

in Just- (1923)

in Just-
spring   when the world is mud-
luscious the little
lame balloonman

whistles   far   and wee   5

and eddieandbill come
running from marbles and
piracies and it's
spring

when the world is puddle-wonderful   10

the queer
old balloonman whistles
far   and   wee
and bettyandisbel come dancing

from hop-scotch and jump-rope and   15

it's
spring
and
   the
                                                                       20
      goat-footed

balloonMan   whistles
far
and
wee

> Changing a rhythm might cause you to discover what something really
> meant. There's a certain magic to it. . . . By diverting your attention from
> certain things, the rhythm might clear a way for other things to occur. The
> pattern might produce a chance discovery.
>
> —JOHN HOLLANDER

Sense the rhythms in the following poems. Try describing what the vari-
ous rhythms evoke or reinforce or embody or suggest and how those things
are appropriate for what each poem is dealing with.

WALT WHITMAN (1819–1892)

from *When Lilacs Last in the Dooryard Bloomed* (1865)

Coffin that passes through lanes and streets,
Through day and night with the great cloud darkening the land,
With the pomp of the inloop'd flags with the cities draped in black,   35
With the show of the States themselves as of crape-veil'd women standing,
With processions long and winding and the flambeaus of the night,
With the countless torches lit, with the silent sea of faces and the
     unbared heads,
With the waiting depot, the arriving coffin, and the sombre faces,
With dirges through the night, with the thousand voices rising strong
     and solemn,   40

With all the mournful voices of the dirges pour'd around the coffin,
The dim-lit churches and the shuddering organs—where amid these you
    journey,
With the tolling bells' perpetual clang,
Here, coffin that slowly passes,
I give you my sprig of lilac.   45

                    [*mourning the death of Abraham Lincoln*]

LINDA PASTAN (b. 1932)

love poem (1988)

I want to write you
a love poem as headlong
as our creek
after thaw
when we stand   5
on its dangerous
banks and watch it carry
with it every twig
every dry leaf and branch
in its path   10
every scruple
when we see it
so swollen
with runoff
that even as we watch   15
we must grab
each other
and step back
we must grab each
other or   20
get our shoes
soaked we must
grab each other

JOY HARJO (b. 1951)

She Had Some Horses (1983)

She had some horses.

She had horses who were bodies of sand.
She had horses who were maps drawn of blood.
She had horses who were skins of ocean water.
She had horses who were the blue air of sky.   5
She had horses who were fur and teeth.

She had horses who were clay and would break.
She had horses who were splintered red cliff.

She had some horses.

She had horses with long, pointed breasts.   10
She had horses with full, brown thighs.
She had horses who laughed too much.
She had horses who threw rocks at glass houses.
She had horses who licked razor blades.

She had some horses.   15

She had horses who danced in their mothers' arms.
She had horses who thought they were the sun and their
bodies shone and burned like stars.
She had horses who waltzed nightly on the moon.
She had horses who were much too shy, and kept quiet   20
in stalls of their own making.

She had some horses.

She had horses who liked Creek Stomp Dance songs.
She had horses who cried in their beer.
She had horses who spit at male queens who made   25
them afraid of themselves.
She had horses who said they weren't afraid.
She had horses who lied.
She had horses who told the truth, who were stripped
bare of their tongues.
                                                                30
She had some horses.

She had horses who called themselves, "horse."
She had horses who called themselves, "spirit," and kept
their voices secret and to themselves.
She had horses who had no names.   35
She had horses who had books of names.

She had some horses.

She had horses who whispered in the dark, who were afraid to speak.
She had horses who screamed out of fear of the silence, who
carried knives to protect themselves from ghosts.   40
She had horses who waited for destruction.
She had horses who waited for resurrection.

She had some horses.

She had horses who got down on their knees for any saviour.
She had horses who thought their high price had saved them.   45
She had horses who tried to save her, who climbed in her
bed at night and prayed as they raped her.

She had some horses.

She had some horses she loved.
She had some horses she hated.   50

These were the same horses.

QUINCY TROUPE (b. 1943)

Snake-Back Solo 2 (1979)

for Louis Armstrong, Steve Cannon, Miles Davis & Eugene Redmond

with the music up high, boogalooin
bass down way way low
up & under, eye come slidin on in, mojoin
on in, spacin on in on a riff full of rain
riffin on in full of rain & pain   5
spacin on in on a sound
like coltrane

& my metaphor is a blues
hot pain dealin blues, is a blues
axin guitar voices, whiskey broken, niggah   10
deep in the heart, is a blues in a glass filled with rain
is a blues in the dark
slurred voices of straight bourbon
is a blues, dagger stuck off in the heart
of night, moanin like bessie smith   15
is a blues filling up, glooming under
the wings of darkness, is a blues
is a blues, a blues

& looking through the heart
a dream can become a raindrop window to see through   20
can become a window, to see through this moment
to see yourself hanging around the dark
to see through this moment
& see yourself as a river catching rain there
feeding time there with your movement   25
to wash time clean as a window
to see through to the other side
while outside windows, flames trigger
the deep explosion, time steals rivers that move on
& stay where they are, inside yourself, moving   30
soon there will be daylight
breaking the darkness
to point the way home, soon there will be
voices breaking music, to come on home by
down & up river, breaking the darkness   35
to come on home by, stroking with the music

swimming up river
the sound of louie armstrong
swinging up river, carrying river boats
upstream, on the back of his honky-tonk jazz rhythms 40
licks of vibratos climbing up from new orleans, close heat & rain
swimming up river, up the river of mud & rain
satchmo breaking the darkness, his cornet speaking
flames bouncing off the river's back
at sunset, snake river's back, big muddy, mississippi 45
up from naw leans, to east st. louis, illinois
cross river from st. louis
to come on home by, up river now
the music swims, breaking silence to land
in miles dewey davis's horn, then leap off again 50
& fly up in space to create
new music in time with place
to create new music in time with this place
to pass it on, pass it on
pass it on, into space 55

where eye catch it now, inside myself
inside this poem eye am (w)riting here
where eye am soloing, now
soloing of rivers catching rains & dreams & sunsets
solo of trane tracks screaming through the night, stark 60
a dagger in the heart
solo of bird spreading wings for the wind
to lift up by, solo of miles, pied piper, prince of darkness
river rain voice now, eye solo at the root of the flower
leaning against promises of shadows 65
solo of bones leering beneath the river's snake-back
solo of trees cut down by double-bladed axes
river rain voice now eye solo
of the human condition, solo of the matrix
mojoin new blues, river rain voice 70
now, eye solo   solo
solo now to become the wings & eyes of an owl
to see through this darkness, eye solo now
to become a simple skybreak shattering darkness
to become lightning's jagged-sword-like thunder 75
eye solo now to become, to become
eye solo now to become

with the music up high
up way, way high, boogalooin bass down
way, way low 80
up & under, eye come slidin on in, mojoin on in
spacin on in on a poetic riff full of rain

river riff full of rain & trains & dreams
lookin through ajax clean windows
eye come slidin on through   85
these blues metaphors
riffin on in through rain & pain
ridin on a tongue of poetic flame
leanin & glidin, eye solo   solo
loopin & flyin eye solo now   solo   90

> I think it is absurd to feel that free verse—which has only been with us in
> America for a little over a hundred years—has definitely "replaced" mea-
> sure and rhyme and other traditional instruments. Precisely because
> trimeter, for example, doesn't mean anything, there's no reason why it
> shouldn't be put to good use now and tomorrow. It's not inherently dated,
> and, in ways one really needn't go into, meter, rhyme and the like are, or
> can be, serviceable for people who know how to handle them well.
>
> —RICHARD WILBUR

METER

When poems have a regular beat, it becomes an important part of the
poem's rhythm. Sensing that beat, and hearing it, are skills that almost any
reader of poetry can develop. A beat arises from the contrast of louder
("stressed" or "accented") and softer ("unstressed," "unaccented") syllables.
Poetry that has a steady beat, or measured pulse, is said to have **meter,** a reg-
ularized beat created by a repeating pattern of accents, or of syllables, or of
both. The most widely used type of meter (called **accentual-syllabic**) takes
into account both the number of stresses and the number of syllables per
line.[1] If you're unsure about syllables and accents for a particular word, check
a dictionary: it divides words into syllables and indicates where the stress is
put.

The basis of accentual-syllabic meter is the repetition of metrical "feet."
Feet are two- or three-syllable units of (usually) one stressed and one or two

---

[1] Two other types of metrical verse are used, though less frequently than accentual-syllabic.
In **syllabic verse** the number of syllables in lines is regular—all lines in the poem have the same
number of syllables (as in Sylvia Plath's "Metaphors," p. 388), or all first lines of stanzas the same
number, all second lines the same, etc. (see Dylan Thomas's "Fern Hill," Ch. 8, p. 125)—while
the stressed syllables are random in number and placement.

In **accentual verse** the number of stressed syllables per line is regular (all lines having the
same number, or the corresponding lines of stanzas having the same number), while the num-
ber of unstressed syllables in lines varies randomly. Gerard Manley Hopkins developed a unique
variety of accentual verse he called **sprung rhythm;** see one of Hopkins's poems for an example:
"Spring and Fall" (Ch. 7, p. 109), or "God's Grandeur" (p. 317), or "Inversnaid" (p. 317).

---

unstressed syllables. As these combinations of stressed plus unstressed syllables (*da DA,* or *da da DA*) are repeated, a regular pattern or beat becomes established (*da DA da DA da DA,* or *da da DA da da DA*) in your ear; you unconsciously expect to continue to hear it and notice variations from the "norm."

These feet have been given names. The *da DA* feet are **iambs,** and create **iambic** meter. Listen for it in this line:

i AM bic ME ter GOES like THIS.

Now try it in this stanza, from "The Man He Killed" (Ch. 5, p. 67):

> "Had HE and I but MET
> By SOME old ANcient INN,
> We SHOULD have SAT us DOWN to WET
> Right MAny a NIPperKIN!"

Iambic is by far the most frequently used foot; others are often used for variation in mostly iambic poems (like the "ny a NIP" in the fourth line), though sometimes they are found as the dominant foot in an entire poem.

The inversion of the iambic foot is the **trochee** (*DA da*), which forms a **trochaic** meter (again, *listen* for it):

TRO chees PUT the AC cent FIRST.

In this stanza from "In Westminster Abbey" (Ch. 5, p. 75), watch how the stresses fall on syllables that accentuate the speaker's self-centeredness:

> GRAcious LORD, oh BOMB the GERmans.
> SPARE their WOmen FOR thy SAKE,
> AND if THAT is NOT too EAsy
> WE will PARdon THY misTAKE.
> But, GRAcious LORD, whatE'ER shall BE,
> DON'T let ANyONE bomb ME.

10

Notice the switch to iambs in line 5; such **substitutions** (the use of a different kind of foot in place of the one normally demanded by the meter) add variety, emphasize the dominant foot by variation from it, and often fit with a switch in meaning. Stresses are never equally strong; that is one way of attaining rhythmic variety even in lines that are metrically regular. Thus, in the last line, AN and ME get more stress than DON'T and ONE. Some syllables (FOR in the second line, AND in line 3) are given a light stress mainly because we expect, from the pattern established, that they *should* be stressed.

Two other types of feet add an unstressed syllable to the feet described above. an **anapest** adds one to an iamb (*da da DA*—to help remember the labels, notice that these two begin with vowels); a **dactyl** adds one to a trochee

(*DA da da*—these two begin with consonants).[2] One other important foot, the **spondee,** has two stressed syllables (*DA DA*), with no unstressed syllables. Many other feet have been given names, but knowing these five (iamb, trochee, anapest, dactyl, spondee) will enable you to describe the basic meter and variations from it in most poems—and describing them can help you hear them more clearly.

The meter in a poem can be highlighted and clarified through a process called **scansion.** To scan a poem involves marking its stressed syllables—whether the stress is heavy or light—with an accent mark [ˊ], and its unstressed syllables with a curved line [ˇ], and using a vertical line to indicate the way it divides up into feet. (You need not try to distinguish stronger from weaker stresses—only syllables that receive at least *some* stress from those that receive *none*.)

ĭam|bĭc mé|tĕr goés|lĭke thís.[3]

You can then describe (or label) the type of foot used most often in the line, and the line length—that is, the number of feet in each line. Names derived from Greek roots are used for line lengths:

monometer = a line with one foot
dimeter = a line with two feet
trimeter = a line with three feet
tetrameter = a line with four feet
pentameter = a line with five feet
hexameter = a line with six feet (etc.)

The line scanned above ("Iambic meter goes like this") would be described as iambic tetrameter. The description identifies the predominant foot (here, iamb) and line length (four feet) in a poem—that is, the ones used the majority of the time in the poem, despite (often) a great many variations.

The ideal way to scan a poem is to listen for where you stress syllables—but to read with a natural emphasis, not a singsong regularity. Where *you* stress syllables is important: scansion is *not* a mechanical process; it involves

---

[2] Iambic and anapestic are called **rising meters** since they step "up" from unstressed to stressed syllables; trochaic and dactylic are called **falling meters,** since they step "down."

[3] In dividing lines into feet, begin by looking for the method that yields the most identical groupings of twos or threes, since most feet in a poem will be the same; then figure out the exceptions.

Notice that dividing lines into feet may involve dividing up words—feet work primarily with syllables, not words.

However, in a line like "Evening traffic homeward burns" (from Yvor Winters's "Before Disaster"), which could be scanned as either iambic or trochaic, trochaic seems preferable because it keeps the words together ("Évenĭng | tráffĭc | hómewărd | búrns" rather than "Ĕvé|nĭng tráf|fĭc home|wărd búrns").

your interpretation. Scansions reflect the way poems actually are read and so will differ slightly from one reader to another. Practice hearing the stresses as a recurring background beat, somewhat like the bass guitar or drums, but not emphasized: concentrate on the words, as you feel the beat.

You can, however, use logic to do a rough but generally adequate scansion. First, start with multisyllabic words—use a dictionary, if necessary, to put ′ on the accented syllables, ˘ on the unaccented ones. Then put stress marks on important shorter words (most nouns and verbs, for example). Helping words (such as *a, an, to*) are rarely stressed and can safely be given ˘ marks. Just examining a poem thoughtfully will show where at least three-fourths of the stressed or unstressed syllables fall. The remainder can be sounded out, or figured out: for example, in ˘ ˘ ? ˘ ˘, the ? will almost surely be stressed: five unstressed syllables in a row would be very unusual. After such an analysis, read the poem aloud to test how well the stress pattern you identified matches what you hear.

What does all this attention to form, all this analysis and description, gain you? Some people say very little; some say a lot. It can help you hear more clearly the regular beat in a metrical poem, and the irregular alterations in it. Poems written in meter will usually have a dominant foot, that is, one used the majority—probably a large majority—of the time. Once you get accustomed to the meter, your ear becomes attuned to that foot, begins to expect it, and notices when a different foot is substituted and alters the "sameness": such substitution is an important means of controlling emphasis as well as adding variety. In the following lines the meter seems overly regular and the stresses (and emphasis) do not necessarily fall on key words; the end result is that the meter doesn't provide much help to support and reinforce the meaning:

LUELLA CLARK

If You Love Me (19th cent.)   *trochaic*

If you love me, tell me not;
Let me read it in your thought;
Let me feel it in the way
That you say me yea and nay;
Let me see it in your eye   5
When you greet or pass me by;
Let me hear it in the tone
Meant for me and me alone.

In the stanza below, in contrast, the metrical substitutions control emphasis and make the sound natural, not artificially "poetic." Lines 1, 3, 5, and 6 are in regular iambic feet (to establish the prevailing "beat"), but line 2 begins with a spondee (Long fields), line 4 ends with a spondee (runs by), and lines 7 and 8 lack the opening, unstressed syllable; unlike the opening six lines, they begin with a stressed syllable and are seven syllables in length instead of eight.

ALFRED, LORD TENNYSON (1809–1892)

from *The Lady of Shalott* (1832)

On either side the river lie
Long fields of barley and of rye,
That clothe the wold and meet the sky;
And through the field the road runs by
    To many-towered Camelot;
And up and down the people go,
Gazing where the lilies blow
Round an island there below,
    The island of Shalott.

5

> More and more [since the 1950s] I began to think in terms of rhythmical units and not in terms of meter even when I'm writing in a fixed meter. In any case, even with a reformer's regard for meter, the meter is always being played off against rhetorical considerations, word lengths, syllable weight, and so on. It is not a metronome.
>
> —ROBERT PENN WARREN

For practice, try scanning the following lines—that is, mark the stressed syllables with ´ and the unstressed syllables with ˘, and use | to divide lines into feet. Try first to do it by hearing the beat; if that doesn't work, figure it out logically, following the steps we suggested above.

SAMUEL TAYLOR COLERIDGE (1772–1834)

Metrical Feet (1806)

Lesson for a Boy

Trochee trips from long to short;
From long to long in solemn sort
Slow Spondee stalks; strong foot! yet ill able
Ever to come up with Dactyl trisyllable.
Iambics march from short to long—
With a leap and a bound the swift Anapests throng.

5

To illustrate further, we will consider what scansion might add to our understanding, enjoyment, and appreciation of the following poem.

EMILY DICKINSON (1830–1886)

I Like to See It Lap the Miles (ca. 1862)

I like to see it lap the Miles—
And lick the Valleys up—
And stop to feed itself at Tanks—
And then—prodigious step (?)

Around a Pile of Mountains—   5
And supercilious peer
In Shanties—by the sides of Roads—
And then a Quarry pare

To fit its Ribs
And crawl between   10
Complaining all the while
In horrid—hooting stanza—
Then chase itself down Hill—

And neigh like Boanerges—
Then—punctual as a Star   15
Stop—docile and omnipotent
At its own stable door— (?)

In a way, this poem resembles a riddle—it forces the reader to supply the implied antecedent to the pronoun "it." The answer would have been obvious to most readers in Emily Dickinson's day, and perhaps it was to you as you read it too; but cultural changes (especially the replacement of rail systems with freeways) make the riddle less obvious for many readers today. Because trains are not as much a part of our visual imagery as they were during the last century, we may be tempted to read "neigh" and "stable" as literal, rather than as parts of an extended implied metaphor. Scanning the poem can help us clarify why meter is an important aspect of this imaginative depiction of a train. Listen to the beat as you read it again, aloud, or as someone else reads it. Try scanning it yourself first, then compare your reading with ours.

The poem starts with a stanza of regular iambic feet, alternating lines of tetrameter and trimeter.

> Ĭ líke | tŏ sée | ĭt láp | thĕ Míles—
> Ănd líck | thĕ Vál|lĕys úp—
> Ănd stóp | tŏ feéd | ĭtsélf | ăt Tánks—

Not only is the meter regular, but the rhythm is steady as well; the short, simple words can be read at an even pace, with no internal punctuation interrupting or slowing them down; the dashes at the ends of lines 1 and 2 give just enough pause for a breath to keep the pace in the following line. Meter and rhythm together echo the repetitive, predictable clickity-clack sound that train wheels seem to make as they pass over the cracks between the rails.

In line 4 the meter remains regular ("Ănd thén—| prŏdi̖|giŏus stép") but the rhythm slows down, because the dash creates a pause and because the multisyllabic word "prodigious" takes longer to say than short monosyllabic words like "stop to feed." Stanzas 1 and 2 have no end punctuation; in fact, the entire poem is made up of one sentence. We usually pause briefly at the end of a line even when there is no punctuation, and we pause a bit longer at the end of a stanza that lacks end punctuation. That too slows the rhythm—just as, we find in the next line, the speed of the train decreases as it curls around mountains. (We may even sense the effect of having our eyes "step around" the end of the first stanza into the beginning of the second, in imitation of the train.)

Scansion can alert us to another way of slowing the rhythm, in line 5. The pattern established in the first stanza leads us to expect that first and third lines will have eight syllables—four iambic feet. When you read line 5, your ear should sense a difference, something unexpected. Here's an example of the tension between "expected" meter and "heard" meter. Scanning the line ("Ăroúnd | ă Píle | ŏf Móun|taĭns—") reveals that the difference is that it has only seven syllables, and lacks the final stressed syllable all the other lines have. We tend to linger a bit on the end of that line, slowing the rhythmic pace, partly because of the dash but partly out of respect for the syllable that isn't there but that our ear expects and feels should be there.

The next three lines reestablish the "expected" pattern of iambic trimeter, tetrameter, trimeter, at a steady pace, but slower than lines 1–3, slower largely because the combinations of sounds cannot be said rapidly: "Ănd sú| pĕrci̖l|liŏus péer / Ĭn Shán|tiĕs—bý | thĕ sides | ŏf Roáds— / Ănd thén | ă Quár|rў pa̖re."

Just as we become reaccustomed to the "expected" pattern, we are jolted out of it again. Stanza 3 has five lines instead of the usual four and it begins with two lines of only four syllables—two iambic feet—instead of the expected eight syllables, four feet:

Tŏ fít | ĭts Ribs
Ănd cráwl | bĕtwéen
Cŏmpláin|ĭng áll | thĕ while
Ĭn hór|rĭd—hóot|ĭng stán|ză—

10

Scanning the lines helps us notice that the "unexpected" line still fits the "pattern": lines 9 and 10 are just an expected tetrameter line divided into two. With a playfulness typical of her, almost as a poetic joke, Dickinson has the stanza become visually narrower as the train peels along the edge of a quarry, fitting its metal "ribs" into the tight space. Line 9 is made tight by the sound of the "fit its" in the middle. As the train slows down for the narrow curves, the poem's rhythm does too, because of the pauses at the ends of the short lines 9 and 10, the long, slow *craaawwll* sound in the middle of line 10, and the length of words and the sound combinations of "Complaining" and "horrid—hooting."

The poem, like the train, hesitates at the end of line 12, which like line 5 lacks the final stressed syllable, then speeds up in regular meter as the train thunders downhill[4]—

Thĕn cháse | ĭtseĺf | dŏwn Híll—

Aňd neígh | lĭke Bó|ănér|gĕs—

only to pause sharply at the missing eighth syllable in line 14.

Scansion clarifies a final playful, but metrically effective, touch. After line 15 slows down, "Thĕn—puńc|tŭaĺ ás | ă Stár," because of the dash and the extra syllable (though some readers may slur "púnc|tŭal" into two syllables, and keep the meter regular), line 16 again does the unexpected: thus far, each line has begun with an unstressed syllable and an iambic foot, and our ears begin to expect that. This line jolts our ear, pulls us up short, by a metrical substitution—a spondee instead of an iamb: "Stóp—dóc|ĭle ańd | ŏmńi|pŏteńt / Ăt ĭts | ŏwn stá|ble doór." The substitution puts strong emphasis on "Stop," and that, together with the dash following it, interrupts the rhythm—stops us—as the train, now quiet though still powerful, stops at the end of its journey.

In this case it seems that Dickinson may have deliberately decided how meter would fit the shape and effects of the poem. However, poets who use meter do not always count syllables and decide, consciously, that it is time for a substitution or to leave off a final stressed syllable. Their ears are attuned to meters and they "hear" whether a line "sounds appropriate" or "right," or whether they need to make further changes. Looking back they may be able to figure out (perhaps by scanning the line) what made it sound better, what made it "work." Scanning—and attention to meter generally—can be retrospective, part of the process of figuring out why what was done proved effective, or it can be part of the creative process. (If you would like an additional discussion of scansion, working with a slightly more complicated passage, go to Appendix B at the back of the book.)

More space in this chapter has been given to meter than to rhythm. That reflects the technical detail that is required to explain meter, not necessarily its comparative significance. Rhythm is the more inclusive and more predominant element. Meter, a category of rhythm, is important, in the end, not just for itself, but for what it contributes to a poem's order, rhythm, effect, and emphasis.

• • •

To help get accustomed to interpreting meter, scan the italicized lines of the following poems and label the prevailing metrical foot and line length.

---

[4] Boanerges ("sons of thunder") is the name Jesus gave to his disciples James and John, the sons of Zebedee. See Mark 3:17.

Compare your results with those of others who scan the poems; talk about differences and listen to the way others read the lines to help you decide which way or ways of reading them you end up preferring.

ROBERT FROST (1874–1963)

Nothing Gold Can Stay (1923)

Nature's first green is gold,
Her hardest hue to hold.
Her early leaf's a flower;
But only so an hour.
Then leaf subsides to leaf.   5
So Eden sank to grief,
So dawn goes down to day.
Nothing gold can stay.

WILLIAM BLAKE (1757–1827)

Introduction to Songs of Innocence (1789)

Piping down the valleys wild,
Piping songs of pleasant glee,
On a cloud I saw a child,
And he laughing said to me:

"Pipe a song about a Lamb."   5
So I piped with merry cheer.
"Piper, pipe that song again."
So I piped; he wept to hear.

"Drop thy pipe, thy happy pipe;
Sing thy songs of happy cheer."   10
So I sung the same again
While he wept with joy to hear.

"Piper, sit thee down and write
In a book that all may read."
So he vanished from my sight,   15
And I plucked a hollow reed,

And I made a rural pen,
And I stained the water clear,
And I wrote my happy songs
Every child may joy to hear.   20

ROBERT BROWNING (1812–1889)

from *How They Brought the Good News from Ghent to Aix* (1845)

I sprang to the stirrup, and Joris, and he;
I galloped, Dirck galloped, we galloped all three;
"Good speed!" cried the watch, as the gate-bolts undrew;
"Speed!" echoed the wall to us galloping through;
Behind shut the postern, the lights sank to rest,   5
And into the midnight we galloped abreast.

THOMAS HARDY (1840–1928)

from *The Voice* (1914)

Woman much missed, how you *call to me, call to me,*
Saying that now you are not as you were
When you had changed from the one who was all to me,
But as at first, when our day was fair.

Both rhythm and meter influence the following "prayer poem" by John Donne. In it the speaker begs God to enter and transform his (or her?) life, but says God will have to take the initiative, will even have to use force to get in, because the speaker has built up such a strong resistance to receiving God. It's a good poem for examining figures: watch as each quatrain (four-line section) develops a different metaphor for the way the speaker wants God to proceed. After reading it for ideas and figures, read it again and listen to the rhythm(s). Then look for ways the meter and rhythm interact and why their interaction is appropriate for what the poem is doing.

JOHN DONNE (1572–1631)

Batter My Heart, Three-Personed God (1633)

Batter my heart, three-personed God, for you
As yet but knock, breathe, shine, and seek to mend;
That I may rise and stand, o'erthrow me, and bend
Your force to break, blow, burn, and make me new.
I, like an usurped town, to another due,   5
Labor to admit you, but oh, to no end;
Reason, your viceroy in me, me should defend,
But is captived, and proves weak or untrue.
Yet dearly I love you, and would be lovèd fain,
But am betrothed unto your enemy;   10

Divorce me, untie or break that knot again,
Take me to you, imprison me, for I,
Except you enthrall me, never shall be free,
Nor ever chaste, except you ravish me.

Listen for the rhythm in e. e. cummings's "Buffalo Bill's." To help focus on
the methods he used in the poem and their effect, you might compare the way
it could have been written—in six lines, using conventional punctuation, in a
loose iambic pentameter—with the way he did write it.

Buffalo Bill's defunct, who used to ride
A water-smooth silver stallion and break
One, two, three, four, five pigeons, just like that.
Jesus, he was a handsome man.
And what I want to know is,   5
How do you like your blue-eyed boy, Mister Death?

E. E. CUMMINGS (1894–1962)

Buffalo Bill's (1923)

Buffalo Bill 's
defunct
            who used to
            ride a watersmooth-silver
                                    stallion   5
and break onetwothreefourfive pigeonsjustlikethat
                                            Jesus

he was a handsome man
                        and what i want to know is
how do you like your blueeyed boy   10
Mister Death

Notice how meter interacts with rhythm in the following poems. Con-
sider how such interactions may help shape the readings of each poem. Have
several of your classmates read the poem. If the readings vary, discuss the dif-
ferences in terms of emphasis, possible meaning, and implication.

LUCILLE CLIFTON (b. 1936)

good times (1969)

my daddy has paid the rent
and the insurance man is gone
and the lights is back on
and my uncle brud has hit

for one dollar straight   5
and they is good times
good times
good times

my mama has made bread
and grampaw has come   10
and everybody is drunk
and dancing in the kitchen
and singing in the kitchen
oh these is good times
good times   15
good times

oh children think about the
good times

Robert Hayden (1913–1980)

Those Winter Sundays (1962)

Sundays too my father got up early
and put his clothes on in the blueblack cold,
then with cracked hands that ached
from labor in the weekday weather made
banked fires blaze. No one ever thanked him.   5

I'd wake and hear the cold splintering, breaking.
When the rooms were warm, he'd call,
and slowly I would rise and dress,
fearing the chronic angers of that house,

Speaking indifferently to him,   10
who had driven out the cold
and polished my good shoes as well.
What did I know, what did I know
of love's austere and lonely offices?

Francis Fike (b. 1933)

Doves (1989)

Doves before dawn begin their morning moan
As darkness mixes slowly with the light,
Each calling to assert a private zone
For which the caller paid the price of fight,
And hopes by calling not to hold alone.   5

Alone, I lie here hearing the gentle calls,
Some near, some far, and wait, myself, for dawn.

The light increases on the bedroom walls
As robins wake, and one, that rules the lawn
Joins sparrow, doves, and wren in madrigals.   10

When young, I dreamed and asked about the sounds—
Musical moans mysteriously around us—
Trail-voices, perhaps, of distant elfin hounds?
Iroquois voices, ghostly and piteous?
Calls of the uncle, whom the quicksand drowns?   15

"Doves" was my grandfather's only reply.
City-benumbed, I then began to hear
Fresh truth in sound, began to verify,
In all which might have generated fear,
Reality on which I might rely.   20

And this is now reality: the sun,
Probing, has found your pillow empty there
This morning as for days now I have done,
Lying by empty space at which I stare,
Thinking of loss never to be undone,   25

Watching the sun illuminate a wall,
Musing on birds and men and on their loves
(Which, whether birds or men, can still enthrall).
Thus, since you cannot answer if I call,
I delegate the dawn to mourning doves.   30

APPLICATIONS FOR CHAPTER 9

SUGGESTIONS FOR WRITING

1. In your journal, record examples of meter and rhythm that you discover in your daily life. What do these reveal?
2. Listen to a poem in a language you do not understand. In your journal, write about its rhythm and what you think it conveys. Then ask someone who knows the language what it really means and see if you were right.
3. Fill in the following sentence: I got up this morning and _____, then I _____, and then I _____. Now break it into rhythmic units, writing each unit as a line of poetry. Do this three different ways. In your journal reflect on the aesthetic decisions a writer has to make and the effects of breaking lines at different places.
4. Write a poem in which the rhythms and/or meter embody what the poem is about. For example, what rhythms would you use for a basketball poem, or a poem about a wild party, or one about paddling a canoe on a quiet lake?
5. Write a poem using one or more of the feet and line lengths discussed in this chapter.

6. Rewrite a nonmetrical work as metrical and/or a metrical work as nonmetrical. What did doing so reveal?
7. Help someone who says she or he has no sense of rhythm to hear and appreciate the rhythm or rhythms in a particular poem.
8. Write a paper similar to the example in this chapter about "I Like to See It Lap the Miles," explaining the role of meter and/or rhythm in the poem you choose to discuss—for example, one of the poems on pages 148–50, or "I Heard a Fly Buzz" (Ch. 7, p. 107), or "That Time of Year" (Ch. 7, p. 110), or "Ulysses" (p. 313).
9. In a paper discuss the relationship between rhythm/meter and speaker/tone in a poem of your choice.
10. Write an imaginary conversation between two, three, or more people discussing a variety of rythmic/metrical readings of a poem. Have them disagree and agree, always explaining why they do.

SUGGESTIONS AS YOU CONTINUE TO READ POETRY

1. Sense and engage with the rhythms of poems.
2. Note formal structures that affect rhythm (such as line length, line endings, pauses, word choice, combinations of sound).
3. Distinguish poems written in meter (like Donne's "Batter My Heart") from nonmetrical ones (like Pastan's "love poem").
4. Listen for the recurring beat in metrical poems—for such traditional meters as iambic (˘´), trochaic (´˘), anapestic (˘˘´), dactylic (´˘˘), and spondaic (´´), and such line lengths as trimeter (a line with three metrical feet), tetrameter (four feet), pentameter (five feet), and hexameter (six feet).

10   Form

Driving through a town or a neighborhood, you see a variety of housing. Inside, lives are going on, and we may wonder about them. We might also wonder if the buildings say anything about those lives or have an impact on the residents. Poems are somewhat like that. Form is usually the first thing you notice when you approach a poem. But sometimes when we're inside a poem looing at all that's going on, we forget what first caught our eye, the form around all the life within. This chapter will add to your experience and understanding of form and give you some ways to begin thinking about what form may mean, embody, express, or reveal. **Form** in poetry occurs as inner association and as external shape: (1) the artistic design, structure, or pattern that arranges, organizes, or connects the various elements in a work, and (2) the shape of the poem on the page.

Every poem has form. Obvious enough. Sometimes poets start out with a form in mind, but probably more often, they start out with an image or feeling or experience or idea or sense of expectancy, or a few words or lines to explore or work with—and they let the poem find the form it "needs." What it needs may be a form that emerges or evolves as a result of creating the poem, or an original form that the poet somewhat consciously develops, or an "inherited" form like a sonnet. Charles Simic echoed that when he said there are three kinds of poets: "those who write without thinking, those who think while writing, and those who think before writing."

Form, like the other elements of poetry, can be considered from the perspective of both the text and the reader. From the textual perspective, we ask such questions as: How would you describe the structuring of the poem? Is it a traditional or nontraditional structure? Is the form appropriate to what the poem is doing? Does the form itself carry any significance or meaning within the poem? From a reader's perspective, we raise other questions: Is the form aesthetically pleasing? How does the form engage you in the reading process? How does the form affect your reading? This chapter will consider both perspectives.

> Though life may be painful, there is a joy and a power in writing, even when you're dealing with something that is hard to live through day by day. You're trying to understand what you're living through by using the tools of words and images and the beautiful inner structure of language.
>
> –SANDRA MCPHERSON

INNER ARRANGEMENT

The first aspect of inner form is the arrangement of the life within the poem: the ideas, images, and events. The variety of such arrangements is endless, and we don't pretend to cover all the possibilities. But we will list some, as suggestions to help you notice and respond to inner arrangements. Most of the examples are from previous chapters. You might choose from among them the poems you were drawn to initially and read them again, this time paying attention to the *ways* things are arranged inside them.

Narrative

Perhaps the most basic of arrangements is narrative, as a poet recounts an event as a sequence of actions and details. Such an inner arrangement is used in "Cherrylog Road" (Ch. 1, p. 14), for example, and in " 'Out, Out—' " (Ch. 2, p. 21) and in Jimmy Santiago Baca's "Family Ties" (Ch. 2, p. 33), along with many others. Narrative, remember, has a beginning, middle, and end (but not necessarily in that order!).

Logical Pattern

Materials can be arranged in a logical pattern of development. This could be in the form of an argument, like the three-part argument you will find in "To His Coy Mistress" (Ch. 12, p. 231). Or it could be a pattern of logical alternations, as in John Frederick Nims's "Love Poem" (Ch. 6, p. 96), which alternates stanzas between the woman's physical clumsiness and her personal sensitivity. Or it could be the repeated attempts made by the speaker in Li-Young Lee's "Visions and Interpretations," at the end of this chapter, to grasp and express a particular experience.

Question–Answer

Poems can raise a question (explicitly or implicitly) and work toward an answer (which also can be stated or implied). Emily Dickinson's "I'm Nobody! Who Are You?" (Ch. 1, p. 1) raises a deep, perennial question and explores it playfully, but seriously. Langston Hughes's "Harlem" (Ch. 1, p. 18) is a series of questions with an implied answer phrased as a final question. And Nancy Willard's "Questions My Son Asked Me, Answers I Never Gave Him" (Ch. 1, p. 4) raises even more questions in the answers.

> I think as I'm getting older things are getting more complicated, and I
> need to find forms by which to contain the incredibly paradoxical sensa-
> tion of aging.
>
> —JORIE GRAHAM

Problem–Solution

Some poems raise or suggest a problem and develop or imply a solution.
Dorothy Parker's "Résumé" (Ch. 5, p. 74) explores (playfully? or not?) the prob-
lem (without exactly stating it) of the disadvantages attending various methods
of committing suicide. Other poems that discuss problems include William
Stafford's "Traveling Through the Dark" (Ch. 1, p. 17) and John Donne's "Batter
My Heart, Three-Personed God" (Ch. 9, p. 147). A variant on the problem-
solution arrangement is a poem where the reader must figure out the subject
and the structure provides possibilities and direction. Rita Dove's "Silos" (Ch. 3,
p. 36) might be thought of as such a poem; so might Sylvia Plath's "Metaphors"
(p. 388).

Meditative Movement

Some poems are arranged as meditations, often moving from a reflection on
a physical place or object to personal or spiritual perceptions—Robert Frost's
"The Road Not Taken" (Ch. 3, p. 43), John Keats's "To Autumn" (Ch. 4, p. 58),
Thylias Moss's "Sunrise Comes to Second Avenue" (Ch. 7, p. 113), David Young's
"The Portable Earth-Lamp" (Ch. 7, p. 114), Mark Doty's "Tiara" (p. 262), and
Leslie Marmon Silko's "Prayer to the Pacific" (later in this chapter—p. 171) are
among many possible examples. Or a poem can take the form of a meditation on
an event or experience, as in Wanda Coleman's "At the Jazz Club He Comes on a
Ghost" (Ch. 2, p. 31), Thomas Hardy's "The Man He Killed" (Ch. 5, p. 67), and
Anita Endrezze's "The Girl Who Loved the Sky" (Ch. 6, p. 98).

Statement–Counterstatement

A poem also can be arranged by framing a statement, then making a
counterstatement, and sometimes moving to a resolution of the contrary po-
sitions. Two such examples are Robert Frost's "Fire and Ice" (p. 325) and John
Milton's "When I Consider How My Light Is Spent" (p. 304).

Description

Another alternative is a descriptive approach, in whatever order focuses
attention most effectively. Poems using this approach are often unified by the
way specific images connect throughout the poem, much like a tapestry. See,
among many examples, Garrett Kaoru Hongo's "Yellow Light" (Ch. 4, p. 54),
Cathy Song's "Girl Powdering Her Neck" (Ch. 4, p. 59), Dorothy Livesay's
"Green Rain" (Ch. 6, p. 84), and Jean Toomer's "Face" (Ch. 6, p. 86).

Conversation

Some poems are written in a conversational voice (albeit heightened), arranged to create a sense of the natural flow of talking about something, as in John Betjeman's "In Westminster Abbey" (Ch. 5, p. 75), Linda Hogan's "Workday" (Ch. 5, p. 78), Kenneth Fearing's "Love, 20¢ the First Quarter Mile" (Ch. 5, p. 79), or Quincy Troupe's "Snake-Back Solo 2" (Ch. 9, p. 136). A variant of this would be a poem in the form of a letter or a message on a postcard (Margaret Atwood's "Postcard"—Ch. 13, p. 251).

Association

Poems arranged through association move from word or image or idea or other element to another word, image, idea, or other element connected to it on the basis of a relationship. They are sometimes constructed in the manner of a collage. See, for example, Robert Francis's "Silent Poem" (Ch. 1, p. 7), Gary Snyder's "Riprap" (Ch. 4, p. 51), or James Tate's "The Wheelchair Butterfly" (p. 409).

Lists (or Catalogs)

We all make lists. It may be the most common use of form, laying out a series of details, often referred to as a **catalog**. Lists were used to particularly strong effect by Walt Whitman—see, for example, his "When Lilacs Last in the Dooryard Bloomed" (Ch. 9, p. 133). Lists can add range, rhythm, intensity, and texture. For whole poems structured as catalogs, see Gary Soto's "The Morning They Shot Tony Lopez, Barber and Pusher Who Went Too Far, 1958" (Ch. 1, p. 19), Muriel Rukeyser's "Rune" (Ch. 3, p. 48), and Theodore Roethke's "Dolor" (Ch. 6, p. 92). Catalogs also can structure parts of a poem, as in James Dickey's "Cherrylog Road" (Ch. 1, p. 14), Dorothy Livesay's "Green Rain" (Ch. 6, p. 84), and Naomi Shihab Nye's "Catalogue Army" (p. 427).

Combinations of the Above

Almost any of the structures described above can be used with another or with others to create fresh and interesting combinations. See what combinations you can find in, for example, Heather McHugh's "What He Thought" (Ch. 1, p. 9), T. S. Eliot's "Journey of the Magi" (Ch. 7, p. 112), Dylan Thomas's "Fern Hill" (Ch. 8, p. 125), and Nikki Giovanni's "Nikki-Rosa" (p. 410) .

Parallelism and Juxtaposition

Other sets of organizational devices can be used as parts of the structures described above, or as ways to arrange an entire poem. We will discuss two, parallelism and juxtaposition.

A professor we know once called a student and heard the following on the answering machine: "Hi! I'm either in or I'm not. I'm either busy or I'm not. I'm either studying or I'm not. Leave a message." The professor replied, after the beep: "You're either passing my course or you're not." **Parallelism** is a basic aesthetic device in poetry, emphasizing similarities in content and organizing sounds and rhythms through repetition of words, phrases, and patterns of stress and pronunciation.[1] It is a verbal arrangement in which elements of equal weight within phrases, sentences, or paragraphs are expressed in a similar grammatical order and structure. Parallelism can appear within a line or pair of lines ("And he was always quietly arrayed, / And he was always human when he talked"—Edwin Arlington Robinson, "Richard Cory" [Ch. 6, p. 90]) or, more noticeably, as a series of parallel items, as in Lucille Clifton's "homage to my hips" (Ch. 1, p. 3) or Langston Hughes's "Harlem" (Ch. 1, p. 18). Parallel items can be used as the organizing principle of an entire poem, especially list or catalog poems—as in Dorothy Parker's "Résumé" (Ch. 5, p. 74), Joy Harjo's "She Had Some Horses" (Ch. 9, p. 134, and Gwendolyn Brooks's "We Real Cool" (later in this chapter—p. 159).

It is natural for parallelism to pair similar things, but it can also be used to highlight oppositions. The term **antithesis** is used for contrasting ideas expressed in balanced parallel structures. Joy Harjo's lines "She had some horses she loved. / She had some horses she hated" (Ch. 9, p. 136) illustrate antithesis. So do the final two lines from Sir John Denham's "Cooper's Hill" quoted later in this chapter, describing the flow of a river: "Though deep, yet clear, though gentle, yet not dull, / Strong without rage, without o'er-flowing, full."

A related term, but broader than antithesis, is **juxtaposition,** placing things side by side or close together for comparison or contrast or to create something new from the union, without making them grammatically parallel. Poets regularly juxtapose words, phrases, ideas, tones, and rhythms. The speaker in Shakespeare's Sonnet 130 juxtaposes the actual attributes of the woman he loves with the idealized qualities other poets claim for their loves:

My mistress' eyes are nothing like the sun;
Coral is far more red than her lips' red;
If snow be white, why then her breasts are dun;
If hairs be wires, black wires grow on her head.

Robert Browning's "My Last Duchess" (Ch. 5, p. 76) juxtaposes the speaker's self-image against the way his values and attitudes strike the reader. "Richard Cory" juxtaposes what Cory's life seemed to the citizens of his town—rich, handsome, happy—with the reality of his life, whatever it was that led him to suicide. Charles Simic juxtaposes Christian imagery with images of the Holocaust in "Begotten of the Spleen" (p. 399), James Tate juxtaposes images throughout "The Wheelchair Butterfly" (p. 409), and Victor Hernández Cruz's "Problems with Hurricanes" (p. 421) juxtaposes honorable death (drowning in a storm or being hurled by the wind against a mountain) with the danger of dying dishonorably from being smashed by a mango, banana, or plantain in a hurricane. Looking for juxtapositions, or contrasts, can in fact be a good start-

---

[1] Northrop Frye et al., *The Harper Handbook to Literature* (New York: Harper and Row, 1985), 336.

156   ENTRY POINTS • Form

ing point in trying to "get hold" of a poem. Juxtaposition will not always be present, but it often is, and it will usually have the effect of placing you between the juxtaposed items, so that you must work through the oppositions, reconciling them, being left with an inherent tension or reaching to the wonderful strangeness of what is created. In any case, juxtaposition will often lead you to a fresh perception because of the "untried circuitry" of the combination (with this in mind, reread Edward Lueders's "Your Poem, Man . . ."—Ch. 3, p. 46).

The following poem is arranged as a list of things a person living in the city will be cut off from, and it also depends on juxtaposition, as it places life in the city and life within nature side by side, evoking the impact of the contrasts between them. In this case the city side of the contrast is implied, mentioned only in the title—no details are given. We are left to complete the juxtaposition and its effect.

CHERYL SAVAGEAU (b. 1950)

Bones—A City Poem (1989)

forget the great blue heron flying low
   over the marsh, its footprints
   still fresh in the sand

forget the taste of wild mushrooms
   and where to find them   5

forget lichen-covered pines
   and iceland moss

forget shaking wild rice into your canoe

forget the one-legged duck
   and the eggs of the snapping turtle   10
   laid in the bank

forget the frog found in the belly of a bass

forget the cove testing its breath
   against the autumn morning

forget the down-filled nest   15
   and the snake swimming at midday

forget the bullhead lilies
   and the whiskers
   of the pout

forget walking on black ice   20
   beneath the sky hunter's bow

forget the living waters
   of Quinsigamond

forget how to find the Pole star and why

forget the eyes of the red fox 25
   the hornets that made their home
   in the skull of a cow

forget waking to hear the call of the loon

forget that raccoons are younger brothers
   to the bear 30

forget that you are walking
   on the bones of your grandmothers

EXTERNAL SHAPE

Lines

Perhaps the most apparent aspect of the external shape of a poem involves its division into **lines**. Not all poems are separated into lines: **prose poems** are one notable exception. The prose poem works with all the elements of poetry except line. It is often written in common paragraph form. According to poet David Young the prose poem is "a distilling and mimicking of the normal ways of prose. From that perspective, interesting possibilities start to suggest themselves: life histories reduced to paragraphs, essays the size of postcards, novels in nutshells."[2] This hybrid form draws together the variant associations we make with both prose and poetry as well as what informs each, creating new possibilities from the challenges presented by the fusion of genres. For varieties of prose poems, see for example Lisel Mueller, "The Deaf Dancing to Rock" (Ch. 1, p. 5) and Russell Edson, "The Fall" (Ch. 1, p. 18).

However, most poems are written in lines. Each line can create a rhythm—what Ezra Pound called "the musical phrase." Lines also offer additional opportunities for emphasis. In prose (like that in this book), the length of the line is controlled by the margins. Poets, however, can control the beginnings and ends of lines—positions that can confer added attention and emphasis. And lines can interplay with sentences, becoming units of rhythm discovered or decided on within a sentence. Lineation invites you to read line by line, feeling the musicality with each; and you also read "past" the lines in order to follow the syntax of the sentences. This superimposing of lines on sentences can also direct our attention to words that might otherwise get passed over. Sometimes this is humorous:

J. V. CUNNINGHAM (1911–1985)

Here Lies My Wife (1959)

Here lies my wife. Eternal peace
Be to us both with her decease.

---

[2] From a note on the back cover of his collection of prose poems, *Work Lights* (1977).

---

158 **ENTRY POINTS** • **Form**

Sometimes it has a serious effect:

GWENDOLYN BROOKS (b. 1917)

We Real Cool (1960)

> The Pool Players.
> Seven at the Golden Shovel.

We real cool. We
Left school. We

Lurk late. We
Strike straight. We

Sing sin. We   5
Thin gin. We

Jazz June. We
Die soon.

In the first poem, the pause after "peace" emphasizes it and heightens the surprise in the unexpected "Be to us both" (note the alliteration) instead of the expected "Be to her." The unusual line breaks in the second poem create anticipation and a jazzlike rhythm, enable us to emphasize both the subjects and predicates of the sentences, and lead to the isolated and unsettling last line. You can see and feel the importance and effect of line breaks by rewriting the poem so that the sentences and lines correspond. Try it and see how the poem changes when the lines change.

Part of the pleasure for us as readers is that we can respond to the rhythms of lines, can notice and feel how certain words get emphasized by their position in the line, can appreciate the interplay between line and sentence, and can recognize and experience the role of each line in the life of a poem. Notice, feel, and then think about the rhythm and emphasis in the lines in these two poems by Langston Hughes:

LANGSTON HUGHES (1902–1967)

Dream Variations (1926)

To fling my arms wide
In some place of the sun,
To whirl and to dance
Till the white day is done.
Then rest at cool evening   5
Beneath a tall tree
While night comes on gently,

Dark like me—
That is my dream!

To fling my arms wide   10
In the face of the sun,
Dance! Whirl! Whirl!
Till the quick day is done.
Rest at pale evening . . .
A tall, slim tree . . .   15
Night coming tenderly
        Black like me.

The Negro Speaks of Rivers (1926)

I've known rivers:
I've known rivers ancient as the world and older than the flow of
        human blood in human veins.

My soul has grown deep like the rivers.

I bathed in the Euphrates when dawns were young.
I built my hut near the Congo and it lulled me to sleep.   5
I looked upon the Nile and raised the pyramids above it.
I heard the singing of the Mississippi when Abe Lincoln went down to
        New Orleans, and I've seen its muddy bosom turn all golden in
        the sunset.

I've known rivers:
Ancient, dusky rivers.

My soul has grown deep like the rivers.   10

> Lines have reason for being. They are entities and one line after the other builds the form. So you're always working in a formal condition. I write free verse, as there's no repetition of a particular line length or pattern of repetition, but it is all formal.
>
> —CHARLES WRIGHT

Stanzas

Another thing to watch for in external shape is the presence of stanzas. A **stanza** is a division of a poem into sections, either according to form—a repeated grouping having the same number of lines and the same arrangement of line lengths, meter, and rhyme—or according to thought, creating irregular units comparable to paragraphs in prose. The word *stanza* derives from the Italian word for "room." We could say, following up on our previous architectural metaphor, that stanzas are "rooms" into which a building (the poem) is divided, with all the rooms often looking pretty much alike.

Stanza shapes can be **invented**, that is, individually created, unique to a particular poem. The poet may plan out such a stanza form before beginning to write, or create it in the process of writing. In the following poem, pay attention to the stanza form:

ROBERT HERRICK (1591–1674)

To Daffodils (1648)

Fair daffodils, we weep to see
   You haste away so soon;
As yet the early-rising sun
   Has not attained his noon.
      Stay, stay,   5
   Until the hasting day
      Has run
But to the evensong;
And, having prayed together, we
   Will go with you along.   10

We have short time to stay, as you;
   We have as short a spring;
As quick a growth to meet decay,
   As you or anything.
      We die,   15
As your hours do, and dry
      Away,
Like to the summer's rain;
Or as the pearls of morning's dew,
   Ne'er to be found again.   20

Probably no other poem in existence has stanzas just like these. Perhaps the first stanza found its own form, without conscious attention to its shape, initially. But at some point Herrick must have begun thinking about the form, and making the other stanza fit the form the first one had "found."

Many stanza patterns, however, are not invented but inherited; they have been handed down through the centuries, from one generation of poets to another, often with a prescribed meter and sometimes with a set rhyme scheme. The most frequently used, in the past and today, are four-line stanzas, called **quatrains**. A frequently used variety is the **ballad stanza**, a four-line stanza rhyming *abcb* with four feet in the first and third lines, three in the second and fourth. Other well-known inherited types include:

- **terza rima:** three-line stanzas, interlinked by rhymes: *aba bcb cdc ded efe,* etc., a form made famous by Dante Alighieri's use of it in *The Divine Comedy* (see Percy Bysshe Shelley, "Ode to the West Wind," p. 310)
- **Chaucerian stanza** (also called **rhyme royal,** since King James of Scotland once used it): seven lines rhyming *ababbcc* (see Sir Thomas Wyatt, "They Flee from Me," p. 32).
- **Spenserian stanza:** nine lines, eight of ten syllables and the ninth of twelve, rhyming *ababbcbcc* (none in this text; for an example, see John Keats, "The Eve of St. Agnes").
- **ottava rima:** eight iambic pentameter lines, rhyming *abababcc* (none in this text; see, for example, Lord Byron's *Don Juan*).

In addition to inherited stanza patterns, patterns for whole poems can be inherited. An inherited form provides a sort of blueprint for a poem: the size and dimensions are predetermined, and the poet (like a builder) must shape, arrange, and connect materials to fit the pattern. The poet may plan from the beginning to use an inherited form—may set out to do a poem in a preset pattern, like a sestina or a sonnet. Perhaps such a poet wants to participate in a centuries-old poetic tradition, or wants to revitalize an inherited form, wants to embody meaning within the form, or wants to meet the challenge of working within restraints (the opportunities offered by a prescribed form can lead one's imagination to come up with something it likely would not have without the "pressure" of the form). Or the poet may think about an inherited form while writing—may start with a subject or images but no particular form in mind, and then discover that an effective way the poem can develop is as a sonnet, or a sestina, or couplets: the material "needs" or may even "demand" that form, or the form may be the perfect "fit" for that poem. Think again of a building and of how some buildings seem just right for the lives inside.

Recognizing such forms can help you to experience form as meaningful. You can better appreciate the way a poem you are reading belongs to a tradition and the way the tradition influences and adds to the poem. Some inherited forms have been used more frequently than others in British and American literature, and so it may be helpful to remember them—we will discuss those in this chapter.

> Obviously it is the poem that is or is not the only possible justification for any form, however theory runs. The poem is or it is not the answer to "why that form?" The consideration of the evolution of forms, strict or open, belongs largely to history and to method. The visitation that is going to be a poem finds the form it needs in spite of both.
>
> —W. S. MERWIN

Sonnets

The inherited form you are likely to encounter most frequently is the sonnet. These fourteen-line poems originally were lyrical love poems, but came to be used also for meditations on death and nature, and are now open to all subjects. In English they are usually written in iambic pentameter and most often in one of two rhyme schemes. The **Italian** (or **Petrarchan**) **sonnet** is composed of an **octave** (an eight-line unit), rhyming *abbaabba,* and a **sestet** (a six-line unit), often rhyming *cdecde* or *cdcdcd,* though variations are frequent. The octave usually develops an idea or question or problem; then the poem pauses, or "turns," and the sestet completes the idea, answers the question, or resolves the difficulty, as in the following sonnet by William Wordsworth. The opening eight lines describe the impression a divinely beautiful evening makes on him, and the closing six lines suggest that the child walking beside him is less impressed than he because she experiences that closeness to nature, and the divine, all the time.

WILLIAM WORDSWORTH (1770–1850)

It Is a Beauteous Evening, Calm and Free (1807)

It is a beauteous evening, calm and free, *a*
The holy time is quiet as a Nun *b*
Breathless with adoration; the broad sun *b*
Is sinking down in its tranquility; *a*
The gentleness of heaven broods o'er the Sea: *a*   5
Listen! the mighty Being is awake, *b*
And doth with his eternal motion make *b*
A sound like thunder—everlastingly. *a*
Dear Child! dear Girl! that walkest with me here, *c*
If thou appear untouched by solemn thought, *d*   10
Thy nature is not therefore less divine: *e*
Thou liest in Abraham's bosom° all the year, *c*   *heaven (see Luke 16:22)*
And worship'st at the Temple's inner shrine, *d*
God being with thee when we know it not. *e*

The **English** (or **Shakespearean**) **sonnet** is formed of three quatrains (typically rhyming *abab cdcd efef*) and a couplet (two rhyming lines). Usually the subject is introduced in the first quatrain, expanded in the second, and expanded still further in the third; the couplet adds a logical, pithy conclusion or gives a surprising twist. Thus Shakespeare, in lines 1–4 of the following poem, states his point about the steadfastness of true love; he reinforces the point by comparing true love to the pole star in lines 5–8, then amplifies it still further in lines 9–12 by asserting that love remains constant despite the passing of time and physical beauty. Lines 13–14 give a pithy conclusion: if he is wrong, he never wrote any poems—the existence of the poem, thus, is proof of its own argument.

WILLIAM SHAKESPEARE (1564–1616)

Let Me Not to the Marriage of True Minds (1609)

Let me not to the marriage of true minds *a*
Admit impediments. Love is not love *b*
Which alters when it alteration finds, *a*
Or bends with the remover to remove. *b*
O, no, it is an ever-fixèd mark *c*   5
That looks on tempests and is never shaken; *d*
It is the star to every wandering bark, *c*
Whose worth's unknown, although his height be taken. *d*
Love's not Time's fool, though rosy lips and cheeks *e*
Within his bending sickle's compass come; *f*   10
Love alters not with his brief hours and weeks, *e*
But bears it out even to the edge of doom. *f*
    If this be error and upon me proved, *g*
    I never writ, nor no man ever loved. *g*

The precision of structure, meter, and rhyme in a sonnet represents through form a sense of reason and order. This same structure, however, can take on alternative meanings. For example, that very same form—representing control—can be juxtaposed with a subject that may be chaotic or wild or imprisoned or struggling to be free. Or that form can be used to protest against restriction, repression, or oppression. The point is that there are many exciting possibilities for the meaning of form. Take a look here at Claude McKay's "America" and consider what possibilities exist in the relationship between the life inside the poem and the form around it.

CLAUDE MCKAY (1890–1948)

America (1922)

Although she feeds me bread of bitterness, *a*
And sinks into my throat her tiger's tooth, *b*
Stealing my breath of life, I will confess *a*
I love this cultured hell that tests my youth! *b*
Her vigor flows like tides into my blood, *c*   5
Giving me strength erect against her hate. *d*
Her bigness sweeps my being like a flood. *c*
Yet as a rebel fronts a king in state, *d*
I stand within her walls with not a shred *e*
Of terror, malice, not a word of jeer. *f*   10

Darkly I gaze into the days ahead,
And see her might and granite wonders there,
Beneath the touch of Time's unerring hand,
Like priceless treasures sinking in the sand.

Haiku, Sestina, Villanelle

Three other familiar inherited patterns for whole poems are the haiku, the sestina, and the villanelle. **Haiku** has often been defined as a poem in three lines, the first and third having five syllables and the second seven. However, because Japanese, the haiku's original language, is a tonal, not a syllabic, language, a better definition might be one given to us by George Ralph: "a 'poem which can be said in one breath,' often related to nature and juxtaposing two images to evoke an immediate sensory experience." Haiku appears minimal, yet it reaches wide into experience both internal and external. It is usually constructed by an initial attentiveness to a particular sensory image, which then is added to in the second line, followed by a shift in sense experience that both stays connected to the initial experience and shifts our perception so that we have a sudden and quickening realization, the "ah hah!"

GEORGE RALPH (b. 1934)

Darkness of the Rose (1987)

darkness of the rose
hearing
the bee enter

Hanging from the Eaves (1986)

hanging from the eaves
on this frosty evening
a new winter moon

Sestinas and villanelles are part of a tradition of repetition in which repeated words or phrases take on a magical quality as they reappear, shifting in meaning and effect, at times mesmerizing us much the way a chant does, and revealing the power of context—how the very same thing can change in meaning, impact, or character (like a trickster) because the context changes. A **sestina** consists of six six-line stanzas and a three-line concluding stanza (or "envoy"). The six end-words of the first stanza must be used as the end-words of the other five stanzas, in a specified pattern:

The first line ends with the end-word from the last line of the previous stanza
The second line ends with that of the first line of the previous stanza

The third line—that of the previous fifth line
The fourth line—that of the previous second line
The fifth line—that of the previous fourth line
The sixth line—that of the previous third line

Traditionally, the three lines of the *envoy* use as end-words those of lines 5, 3, and 1 from the first stanza, usually in that order, or 1, 3, 5, and include the other three end-words within the lines. In addition to the following example, see Alice Fulton's "You Can't Rhumboogie in a Ball and Chain" (Ch. 8, p. 128).

ELIZABETH BISHOP (1911–1979)

Sestina (1965)

September rain falls on the house.
In the failing light, the old grandmother
sits in the kitchen with the child
beside the Little Marvel Stove,
reading the jokes from the almanac,   5
laughing and talking to hide her tears.

She thinks that her equinoctial tears
and the rain that beats on the roof of the house
were both foretold by the almanac,
but only known to a grandmother.   10
The iron kettle sings on the stove.
She cuts some bread and says to the child,

It's time for tea now; but the child
is watching the teakettle's small hard tears
dance like mad on the hot black stove,   15
the way the rain must dance on the house.
Tidying up, the old grandmother
hangs up the clever almanac

on its string. Birdlike, the almanac
hovers half open above the child,   20
hovers above the old grandmother
and her teacup full of dark brown tears.
She shivers and says she thinks the house
feels chilly, and puts more wood in the stove.

It was to be, says the Marvel Stove.   25
I know what I know, says the almanac.
With crayons the child draws a rigid house
and a winding pathway. Then the child
puts in a man with buttons like tears
and shows it proudly to the grandmother.   30

But secretly, while the grandmother
busies herself about the stove,
the little moons fall down like tears
from between the pages of the almanac
into the flower bed the child   35
has carefully placed in the front of the house.

Time to plant tears, says the almanac.
The grandmother sings to the marvellous stove
and the child draws another inscrutable house.

A **villanelle** is a nineteen-line poem divided into five tercets (three-line stan-
zas or groupings) and a final four-line stanza, rhyming *aba aba aba aba aba
abaa.* Line 1 is repeated to form lines 6, 12, and 18; line 3 is repeated to form
lines 9, 15, and 19. Sometimes, as in the poem below, lines are repeated with
variations. (For an additional example of the villanelle, see Dylan Thomas's
"Do Not Go Gentle into That Good Night," p. 350.)

JOHN YAU (b. 1950)

Chinese Villanelle (1979)

I have been with you, and I have thought of you
Once the air was dry and drenched with light
I was like a lute filling the room with description

We watched glum clouds reject their shape
We dawdled near a fountain, and listened   5
I have been with you, and I have thought of you

Like a river worthy of its gown
And like a mountain worthy of its insolence . . .
Why am I like a lute left with only description

How does one cut an axe handle with an axe   10
What shall I do to tell you all my thoughts
When I have been with you, and thought of you

A pelican sits on a dam, while a duck
Folds its wings again; the song does not melt
I remember you looking at me without description   15

Perhaps a king's business is never finished,
Though "perhaps" implies a different beginning
I have been with you, and I have thought of you
Now I am a lute filled with this wandering description

Blank Verse

There are also inherited patterns for **nonstanzaic** verse. These specify line lengths and sometimes sequences of rhyme, but without any specific separation into similar groupings of lines. The best-known pattern is **blank verse** (unrhymed iambic pentameter), the most widely used verse form of English poetry. Shakespeare's plays, Milton's *Paradise Lost* and *Paradise Regained,* Wordsworth's *Prelude,* and countless other long poems were composed in blank verse because it is well suited to narrative and dialogue.

JOHN MILTON (1608–1674)

from *Paradise Lost*, Book 9 (1667)

> He ended, and his words, replete with guile,
> Into her heart too easy entrance won:
> Fixed on the fruit she gazed, which to behold
> Might tempt alone, and in her ears the sound
> Yet rung of his persuasive words, impregned
> With reason, to her seeming, and with truth.

735

Iambic is often considered the "natural" meter of English—when we talk or write, we often fall into loose iambics that can be divided into groups about ten syllables long. Many say that is the primary reason it is so widely used.

Couplets

Couplets (two lines rhyming) can be grouped into stanzas, but often are strung out in extended, nonstanzaic passages. They provide a simple pattern, like blank verse, but because of the rhyme, the emphasis is different. In seventeenth- and eighteenth-century England, the **heroic couplet** (couplets in iambic pentameter with a full stop, usually at the end of the second line) was widely used for short and long poems. The following lines are from Sir John Denham's poem "Cooper's Hill." In them he describes the river Thames and compares it to his own poetic style. The first six lines illustrate the way heroic couplets can be used for narrative verse, as the thought runs on from couplet to couplet. The final couplet is famous for the way it exemplifies the tight, balanced, antithetical form heroic couplets can take in reflective and argumentative poems.

SIR JOHN DENHAM (1615–1669)

from *Cooper's Hill* (1668)

> My eye, descending from the hill, surveys
> Where Thames amongst the wanton valleys strays.
> Thames, the most loved of all the ocean's sons

160

By his old sire, to his embraces runs,
Hasting to pay his tribute to the sea
Like mortal life to meet eternity. . . .
O could I flow like thee, and make thy stream
My great example, as it is my theme!   190
Though deep, yet clear, though gentle, yet not dull,
Strong without rage, without o'er-flowing, full.

Concrete Poems

External shape is particularly evident in **shaped poems** or **concrete poems**—poems that are given a recognizable form. When George Herbert wanted his poem of praise to rise like a lark's song, he gave it the shape of two birds (or are they angels? or butterflies? or psyches [souls]?):

GEORGE HERBERT (1593–1633)

Easter-wings[3] (1633)

Lord, who createdst man in wealth and store,
Though foolishly he lost the same,
Decaying more and more
Till he became
Most poor: 5
          With thee
          O let me rise
     As larks, harmoniously,
And sing this day thy victories: 10
Then shall the fall further the flight in me.

My tender age in sorrow did begin:
And still with sicknesses and shame
Thou didst so punish sin,
That I became
Most thin.   15
          With thee
          Let me combine,
          And feel thy victory;
For, if I imp my wing on thine,
Affliction shall advance the flight in me.   20

Concrete poetry is a blend of verbal and visual arts, in which your eye and ear simultaneously interact, as in poems like "Disintegration" (Ch. 1, p. 2) and "Forsythia" on the next page.

---

[3] Originally the stanzas were printed on facing pages, the left page to be read first, then the right. For the sake of the meter, we have amended line 18 by deleting "this day" (apparently copied by mistake from line 9).

Mary Ellen Solt (b. 1920)

Forsythia (1966)

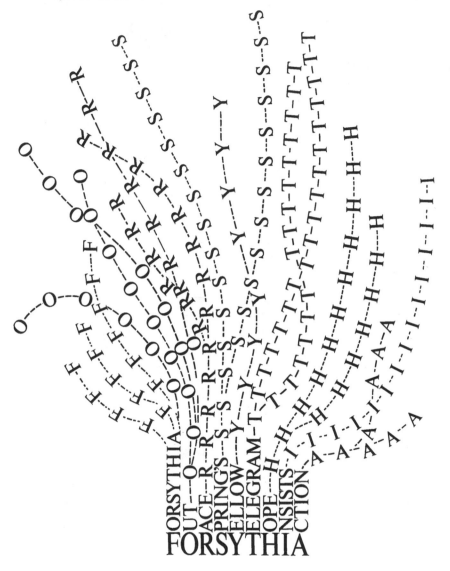

Open Form

Despite considerable recent interest in shaped and concrete poetry, many twentieth-century poets work without deliberate preplanning of a poem's form. In poet Charles Simic's terms, they write without deliberately thinking about form. Instead, they allow the entire poem to "find" its own shape. The poem may emerge from the poet's imagination and skillful intuition in the form it needs, or the form may develop in the process of writing and revising.

In either case the poet's attention is focused primarily on other things—on images, sounds, rhythms—and the poet allows forms to develop, consciously shaping them as they are discovered or letting them be the result of attention to line, rhythm, and so forth. Such poems have traditionally been called **free verse,** because they are free of predetermined metrical and stanzaic patterns. The term *free verse* can be misleading, however, if it is interpreted to mean "formless" or "arbitrary." The term **open form** has come to be widely used instead of "free verse," and we will use it in this book. Either term is usually acceptable. Just remember that no matter how "free" a poem appears, it *does have form.* Every poem does.

Open form poetry often relies on such formal principles as lines, spaces, juxtapositions, rhythms, timing, indentations of different sizes, and gaps. Consider formal structures and their effects in this poem about stories of the ancestors of Native Americans arriving on the West Coast.

LESLIE MARMON SILKO (b. 1948)

Prayer to the Pacific (1981)

I traveled to the ocean
        distant
                from my southwest land of sandrock
                to the moving blue water
        Big as the myth of origin.   5

Pale
pale water in the yellow-white light of
                sun   floating west
                      to China
              where ocean herself was born.   10
Clouds that blow across the sand are wet.

Squat in the wet sand and speak to the Ocean:
        I return to you   turquoise   the red coral you sent us,
                sister spirit of Earth.
Four round stones in my pocket   I carry back the ocean   15
                to suck and to taste.

Thirty thousand years ago
            Indians came riding across the ocean
            carried by giant sea turtles.

Waves were high that day   20
          great sea turtles waded   slowly out
                  from the gray sundown sea.

Grandfather Turtle rolled in the sand   four times
                         and disappeared
                                      swimming into the sun.   25

And so   from that time
                  immemorial,
                            as the old people say,
       rain clouds drift from the west
                            gift from the ocean.   30

Green leaves in the wind
Wet earth on my feet
                  swallowing raindrops
                               clear from China.

Open form poems may also adhere to the more usual use of the left margin, as
the following poem illustrates:

SIMON J. ORTIZ (b. 1941)

Speaking (1976)

I take him outside
under the trees,
have him stand on the ground.
We listen to the crickets,
cicadas, million years old sound.   5
Ants come by us.
I tell them,
"This is he, my son.
This boy is looking at you.
I am speaking for him."   10

The crickets, cicadas,
the ants, the millions of years
are watching us,
hearing us.
My son murmurs infant words,   15
speaking, small laughter
bubbles from him.
Tree leaves tremble.
They listen to this boy
speaking for me.   20

The lines and arrangement seem to have emerged as the poem emerged, the
sentences breaking into units of emphasis and rhythm. There is a wholeness

and unity, however, in the connections and in the patterns of repetition, parallel elements, and contrast.

For the beginning poet, writing in open form may look easier than writing in inherited forms. However, each approach requires an ability to work with the elements of poetry. Each is challenging when one is aware of the complexities of writing any poem well. Each is easy only if done carelessly.

Consider the formal features in the following poems from the perspective of form (How would you describe the structuring of the poem? Is it an inherited or nontraditional structure? In what ways is the form appropriate for the poem? Does the form itself carry any significance within the poem?) as well as from a reader's perspective (Is the form aesthetically dynamic? How does the form engage you in the reading process? How does the form affect your reading?).

LAWRENCE FERLINGHETTI (b. 1919)

Constantly Risking Absurdity (1958)

Constantly risking absurdity
           and death
    whenever he performs
        above the heads
            of his audience   5
  the poet like an acrobat
        climbs on rime
         to a high wire of his own making
and balancing on eyebeams
        above a sea of faces   10
    paces his way
       to the other side of day
  performing entrechats
       and sleight-of-foot tricks
and other high theatrics   15
       and all without mistaking
   any thing
      for what it may not be

  For he's the super realist
       who must perforce perceive   20
    taut truth
      before the taking of each stance or step
  in his supposed advance
       toward that still higher perch
where Beauty stands and waits   25
      with gravity
       to start her death-defying leap

                And he
                        a little charleychaplin man
                                    who may or may not catch   30
                        her fair eternal form
                                    spreadeagled in the empty air
                        of existence

LI-YOUNG LEE (b. 1957)

Visions and Interpretations (1986)

Because this graveyard is a hill,
I must climb up to see my dead,
stopping once midway to rest
beside this tree.

It was here, between the anticipation   5
of exhaustion, and exhaustion,
between vale and peak,
my father came down to me

and we climbed arm in arm to the top.
He cradled the bouquet I'd brought,   10
and I, a good son, never mentioned his grave,
erect like a door behind him.

And it was here, one summer day, I sat down
to read an old book. When I looked up
from the noon-lit page, I saw a vision   15
of a world about to come, and a world about to go.

Truth is, I've not seen my father
since he died, and, no, the dead
do not walk arm in arm with me.

If I carry flowers to them, I do so without their help,   20
the blossoms not always bright, torch-like,
but often heavy as sodden newspaper.

Truth is, I came here with my son one day,
and we rested against this tree,
and I fell asleep, and dreamed   25

a dream which, upon my boy waking me, I told.
Neither of us understood.
Then we went up.

Even this is not accurate.
Let me begin again: 30

Between two griefs, a tree.
Between my hands, white chrysanthemums, yellow chrysanthemums.

The old book I finished reading
I've since read again and again.

And what was far grows near,
and what is near grows more dear,

and all of my visions and interpretations
depend on what I see,

and between my eyes is always
the rain, the migrant rain.

One way to consider the effect of form is to consider the differences that changes in form make. May Swenson first published "The Shape of Death" in *The Nation,* August 27, 1955, a decade after the mushroom-shaped clouds marked the bombing of Hiroshima and Nagasaki in August 1945 and had become a symbol for the fear of nuclear war. She reprinted the poem in 1963 in *To Mix with Time: New and Selected Poems,* with some changes in wording and form.

MAY SWENSON (1913–1989)

The Shape of Death (1963)

What does love look like? We know
the shape of death. Death is a cloud
immense and awesome. At first a lid
is lifted from the eye of light:
there is a clap of sound, a white blossom   5

belches from the jaw of fright,
a pillared cloud churns from white to gray
like a monstrous brain that bursts and burns,
then turns sickly black, spilling away,
filling the whole sky with ashes of dread;   10

thickly it wraps, between the clean sea
and the moon, the earth's green head.
Trapped in its cocoon, its choking breath
we know the shape of death:
Death is a cloud.   15

What does love look like?
Is it a particle, a star—
invisible entirely, beyond the microscope and Palomar?
A dimension unimagined, past the length of hope?
Is it a climate far and fair that we shall never dare   20

discover? What is its color, and its alchemy?
Is it a jewel in the earth—can it be dug?

Or dredged from the sea? Can it be bought?
Can it be sown and harvested?
Is it a shy beast to be caught?   25

Death is a cloud,
immense, a clap of sound.
Love is little and not loud.
It nests within each cell, and it
cannot be split.   30

It is a ray, a seed, a note, a word,
a secret motion of our air and blood.
It is not alien, it is near—
our very skin—
a sheath to keep us pure of fear.   35

When she reprinted it again in *Iconographs* in 1970, it looked like this:

MAY SWENSON (1913–1989)

The Shape of Death (1970)

What does love look like?   We know the shape of death.
Death is a cloud, immense   and awesome. At first a
lid is lifted from the   eye of light. There is a
clap of sound. A white   blossom belches from the
jaw of fright. A   pillared cloud churns from
white to gray, like a   monstrous brain that bursts
and burns—then turns   sickly black, spilling
away, filling the whole   sky with ashes of dread.
Thickly it wraps, between   the clean seas and the
moon, the earth's green   head. Trapped in its
cocoon, its choking   breath, we know the shape
of death. Death is a   cloud. What does love look

like? Is it a particle,   a star, invisible entirely,
beyond the microscope and   Palomar? A dimension past
the length of hope? Is   it a climate far and fair,
that we shall never dare   discover? What is its
color, and its alchemy?   Is it a jewel in the earth,
can it be dug? Or   dredged from the sea? Can
it be bought? Can it be   sown and harvested? Is it
a shy beast to be caught?   Death is a cloud—immense
a clap of sound. Love is   little and not loud. It
nests within each cell,   and it cannot be split. It
is a ray, a seed, a note,   a word, a secret motion of
our air and blood. It is   not alien—it is near—
our very skin, a sheath   to keep us pure of fear.

She noted that it was "rearranged for this volume." She hoped to make the mind "re-member" the elements by dismembering them and creating a poem meant to be seen as well as read and heard.[4] Compare these two versions, and reflect on the difference the form makes in your experiencing of the poem.

APPLICATIONS FOR CHAPTER 10

SUGGESTIONS FOR WRITING

1. Reread some poems you found interesting, from the anthology or elsewhere, and write in your journal brief descriptions of their inner arrangements (you might start with our list of arrangements on pp. 153–55, but try adding other descriptions to the list).
2. Choose a poem and change its lineation. Then write in your journal about what you discovered from these changes.
3. Pick out a poem from this chapter or from the anthology in which you sense that form plays a vital role. Write a journal entry or a paper discussing that role.
4. Try writing a sestina, villanelle, or sonnet (Elizabethan or Italian) in contemporary diction. Then write a short description of what it was like trying to do this.
5. Be on the lookout for "found poetry," that is, prose containing elements of poetry (especially rhythm and meter), which can be accentuated by changes in line, positional emphasis, space, and so on. Write in your journal about what this revealed about form.
6. Try writing an open form poem. Then write a paper about how you knew what to put in and what to leave out and how you decided on line length, space, gaps; and so on.
7. One person considers inherited forms stifling. Another thinks of open form poetry as decadent and undisciplined. Write a paper discussing how you might try to dispute their ideas. Or write a conversation between yourself and either of them, or both.
8. Find a poem with striking juxtapositions. Write a paper about what these juxtapositions create, what their effects are.
9. Pick a sonnet that seems surprising to see in that form—for example, Gary Miranda's "Love Poem" (Ch. 3, p. 48) or James Wright's "Saint Judas" (Ch. 5, p. 70). Write a paper describing how the poem adapts or changes traditional sonnet conventions and discussing the appropriateness and effectiveness of the form to the content.
10. Write a paper relating the role of form in poetry to the role of form in another art, or in a sport, or in social behaviors, or in city planning and nature, or in another area you appreciate.
11. Write an imaginary class discussion in which participants discuss a variety of ways of reading the structural elements of a particular poem. Be

---

[4] *Iconographs* (New York: Charles Scribner's Sons, 1970), pp. 5, 86. This version was used again in *New and Selected Things Taking Place* (Boston: Little, Brown and Company, 1978).

---

sure to choose a poem that contains a number of such elements, giving the participants a variety of possible responses.

SUGGESTIONS AS YOU CONTINUE TO READ POETRY

1. Recognize the inner structures poetry relies on, such as narrative, logical development, catalog, parallelism, and juxtaposition.
2. Consider the effect of such external structures as the line and the stanza.
3. Appreciate the kind of creativity and imaginativeness that writing poetry in inherited forms (such as the English Sonnet, Italian sonnet, ballad stanza, blank verse, and couplet) entails.
4. Appreciate the kind of creativity and craft that open form poetry displays, with its unity of pattern (visual, verbal, rhythmic, and so on).
5. Notice the role form plays in a poem and the effect it has on your experience of reading the poem.

Authors | 11

Chapters 3–10 discuss various entry points one can use in approaching poems. Such approaches are always made from a vantage point. As we said in the preface, you always approach something from somewhere. A well-known literary scholar and theorist, M. H. Abrams, listed three such vantage points—as you approach literature, your primary concern can be with the author, or with the text, or with the reader. We will add a fourth—your primary concern can also be with the way literature shapes and is shaped by its cultural context.

This chapter and the next three will consider the implications of looking from each of these vantage points, what each specially emphasizes and how each is specially useful. These chapters can help you become more conscious of, sharpen, and refine your own approach to reading. They can also help you to become more aware of other approaches to reading and thus to be a more flexible reader yourself—and to understand why two readers of the same text can arrive at quite different readings. The chapters are arranged chronologically, from vantage points that received emphasis earlier to those that have arisen more recently.

The study of English literature began in the 1800s. Until then, students studied the Greek and Roman classics and read literature in English for enjoyment. The approach taken in the 1800s and the early 1900s was called *philology*, or the scientific study of language and literature. Philological scholarship included detailed study of the language and textual accuracy of a work and examination of its sources, historical context and influences, and biographical background.

Though linguistic, textual, and source studies of philology are important, most readers are more immediately interested in biographical and historical backgrounds. One of the pleasures of reading poetry can be to learn about the life and times of authors and to see how their poems illuminate and are illuminated by the world and experiences that surrounded them. Poets themselves acknowledge that interest when they give readings from their works: often they introduce poems by briefly describing the occasions or experiences the poems grew out of. Publishers have acknowledged it by publishing biographical encyclopedias of literary figures. This book acknowledges it by including brief biographies of the authors included in the text. This chapter will look at ways that interest in authors can illuminate poems and will discuss some of the practical and theoretical issues this vantage point raises.

"OLD HISTORICISM"

Many readers find literature rich and rewarding because of the way it can give detailed and particular depictions of life in earlier times. We are taken, imaginatively, into the experiences of people, enabled to see and feel things almost as they did. One vantage point from which to look at literature, then, is historical. This approach puts emphasis on a work as a reflection of life during its author's times or the times depicted in the work.

We have called this approach "**old historicism**" in contrast to the theorized "new historicism" described in Chapter 14. "Old historicism" is untheorized. It seeks to determine the truth about what really happened and to present an objective, factual description of events and a narrative relating these events to one another. It is likely to view history as linear and progressive. It does not wonder whether the truth about the past can be objectively known, or self-consciously discuss how the theory of history it employs influences the account it develops.

Read this sonnet by John Milton, written in 1655:

JOHN MILTON (1608–1674)

On the Late Massacre in Piedmont (1655)

Avenge, O Lord, thy slaughtered saints, whose bones
    Lie scattered on the Alpine mountains cold,
    Even them who kept thy truth so pure of old
    When all our fathers worshiped stocks and stones,
Forget not: in thy book record their groans   5
    Who were thy sheep and in their ancient fold
    Slain by the bloody Piedmontese that rolled
    Mother with infant down the rocks. Their moans
The vales redoubled to the hills, and they
    To Heaven. Their martyred blood and ashes sow   10
    O'er all th' Italian fields where still doth sway
The triple tyrant: that from these may grow
    A hundredfold, who having learnt thy way
    Early may fly the Babylonian woe.

You can get the general sense of the poem even without knowing its historical background, but some details help clarify it. A religious sect, the Waldenses, formed in the twelfth century, settled in the Alps of southern France and northern Italy. Their beliefs were similar to Protestantism as it developed in the sixteenth century, especially in their aversion to the images ("stocks and stones") associated at the time with Roman Catholicism. The Dukes of Savoy had granted the Waldenses religious tolerance within designated areas. They moved outside those areas and in 1655 an army forced them to withdraw. On April 24, 1655, the army went into the areas where toleration had been granted and massacred and mutilated more than 1,700 Waldensian men, women, and children. Protestant governments and individuals throughout Europe protested, and Milton, as Secretary for Foreign Tongues in the English Council of State at the time, wrote several official letters, as well as this poem. Milton was a deeply committed Protestant, who strongly feared and opposed the power and influence of Catholicism. This historical knowledge and knowledge of the author's background not only clarifies references, but also illuminates the religious tensions of the time. "The triple tyrant" is the Pope, with his three-tiered crown. Protestants in the seventeenth century, like Christians in New Testament times, often referred to Rome as Babylon; the pagan enemy of God's people in the Old Testament assumed the stature of archetype.

Knowledge of the author and historical setting also can help clarify why a poem says what it does; and one way to learn about an author is to consider other writings by the same person. A striking thing about Milton's sonnet is that it begins by calling upon God to avenge the Waldenses (echoing Luke 18:7—"And shall not God avenge his own elect, which cry day and night unto him"[1]), but then moves from vengeance to celebration of the faithfulness of those who died. The poem does not ask God to slaughter the Piedmontese, in contrast to the response of the English government, which threatened armed intervention. Milton himself, though he held a government post, had become disillusioned about such solutions. He had joined the revolutionary cause from a belief in religious freedom, but already in the mid-1640s, as he looked at the results of the 1642–46 Civil War, he saw oppression reemerging, though from different oppressors. "New Presbyter is but old Priest writ large," ends one of his sonnets. Another bemoans "all this waste of wealth and loss of blood." A line in *Paradise Lost,* almost two decades later, reflects a similar sense of the limited potential in armed conflict: "War wearied hath performed what war can do." Milton, instead, asks that the sufferings of the martyrs be credited in their favor in the heavenly judgment books, and presumably debited against the tyrannical Piedmontese. And he asks that the martyrdom of the Waldenses might lead many Catholics to convert to Protestantism: that their blood and ashes may be like seeds scattered all across Italy, yielding—not armed men to fight back, as in the Greek myth of Cadmus—but a rich harvest of converts who will flee from the "woe" ultimately to fall upon the Catholic Church.

Thus, historical and biographical data are helpful first for understanding details in the poem, and then for understanding why Milton calls for a spiritual victory over the Piedmontese instead of urging military retribution against them.

[1] One of many verbal echoes of the Bible used throughout the poem. See *Milton's Sonnets,* ed. E. A. J. Honigmann (New York: St. Martin's Press, 1966), 162–68.

BIOGRAPHICAL CRITICISM

Knowing something about Milton's life and beliefs enriches the experience of reading his poem. That is frequently the case with literature. Readers seek knowledge of authors, even when it doesn't affect their understanding of a work. Consider an example from ancient Greece. Epics are usually told by a narrator, with the author invisible and sometimes unknown. In the classic Greek epic *The Odyssey,* however, a single sentence with no effect on the overall plot has long fascinated readers. It occurs as lords and princes of Phaiacia gather for a feast at the palace of King Alcinoös in honor of the recently arrived visitor, Odysseus. As the court minstrel is ushered in, the following is said about him: "This man was the Muse's darling, but she had given him evil mixed with good: she took away the sight of his eyes, but she gave him the lovely gift of song."[2] Readers have long wondered if the author was writing himself into his story. From this arose the tradition of Homer, the blind poet. Almost nothing is known about the writer of *The Odyssey,* and if we did know more it might have little effect on our understanding and appreciation of the work, but readers for centuries have hungered to know more.

A similar fascination with biographical issues involves Shakespeare, particularly with reference to his sonnets. Sonnets flourished during the early to mid-1590s, when Shakespeare was emerging as a writer in London. From around 1591 until 1597, all the important poets wrote sonnet sequences, or series of connected or related sonnets. Shakespeare wrote some too: 154 sonnets are credited to him. They were finally published in 1609, apparently without Shakespeare's permission. Because of the circumstances of their publication, the sonnets have raised numerous questions and puzzles, which probably will never receive answers that will satisfy everyone. To whom are the sonnets addressed? Are they in the order Shakespeare intended for them? Do they tell a connected story? Do they reveal things about Shakespeare's life? Why did he not publish them earlier?

Sonnets 127–152 are addressed to a dark-haired woman. Who is she? Was she a real person or someone he imagined? If she was real, did they have an affair? Sonnet 131 makes us eager to know more:

WILLIAM SHAKESPEARE (1564–1616)
Thou Art As Tyrannous, So As Thou Art (1609)

Thou art as tyrannous, so as thou art,
As those whose beauties proudly make them cruel;
For well thou know'st to my dear doting heart
Thou art the fairest and most precious jewel.
Yet, in good faith, some say that thee behold   5
Thy face hath not the power to make love groan;
To say they err I dare not be so bold,
Although I swear it to myself alone.

---

[2] *The Odyssey,* trans. W. H. D. Rouse (New York: New American Library, 1937), 89.

And, to be sure that is not false I swear,
A thousand groans, but thinking on thy face,   10
One on another's neck, do witness bear
Thy black is fairest in my judgment's place.
    In nothing art thou black save in thy deeds,
    And thence this slander, as I think, proceeds.

The first 126 sonnets seem to be addressed to a friend, an aristocrat, young, handsome—though, again, we do not know if he was a real person or, if so, who he was. Sonnets 40–42 describe a love triangle in which the speaker and his friend are caught: "Thou dost love her because thou know'st I love her, / And for my sake even so doth she abuse me, / Suff'ring my friend for my sake to approve her." The speaker is unhappy, but doesn't want to lose either her or his friend. Can we assume this woman is the same as the dark-haired mistress? Was Shakespeare writing out of real-life experiences, or making up the conventional material of sonnet sequences? Why does he address his friend as "sweet boy" (Sonnet 108), "my lovely boy" (Sonnet 126)? Do these and other expressions of closeness in his relationship to his friend indicate homosexual or bisexual tendencies? Many answers to such questions have been offered—often with great passion and conviction—but they leave many other people unconvinced, and universally accepted answers probably never will be found. So, in reading Shakespeare's sonnets, we can look at them individually as beautifully crafted and often deeply meaningful works, but also, if we wish, as pieces in a fascinating biographical puzzle to which we will never find all the pieces.

More biographical information is available for many recent poets than for Homer or Shakespeare, but the information does not always lead to a common understanding. T. S. Eliot carefully collected and preserved data about himself as a help to eventual biographers; but information must be interpreted, and the portrait of Eliot that emerges from different biographers varies accordingly. We are left with puzzles that affect our understanding of what he wrote.

Read the following poem, by a poet from our century whose life has attracted a great deal of interest:

Edge (1965)

The woman is perfected.
Her dead

Body wears the smile of accomplishment,
The illusion of a Greek necessity

Flows in the scrolls of her toga,   5
Her bare

Feet seem to be saying:
We have come so far, it is over.

Each dead child coiled, a white serpent,
One at each little

breast Pitcher of milk, now empty.
She has folded

Them back into her body as petals
Of a rose close when the garden

Stiffens and odors bleed
From the sweet, deep throats of the night flower.

The moon has nothing to be sad about,
Staring from her hood of bone.

She is used to this sort of thing.
Her blacks crackle and drag.

10

15

20

What do you assume about the writer, based solely on this poem? Are these assumptions fair? Remember that the voice of a poem's narrator is not necessarily that of the "poet" as private citizen.

The poem was written by Sylvia Plath. You may already know some things about her life, perhaps from reading her novel *The Bell Jar* (1963), a slightly fictionalized account of parts of her own life. She grew up in a middle-class family in Boston and showed early promise as a writer, getting stories and poems published in magazines like *Seventeen* while she was in high school. She won a scholarship to prestigious Smith College in 1950 and earned high grades, honors, and prizes there. In 1953 she was chosen as one of twelve "guest editors" at *Mademoiselle* magazine and spent a month working in New York. Upon her return home, she suffered a serious breakdown and attempted suicide. After being institutionalized for a year, she returned to Smith College for her senior year in 1954, again was very successful, graduated *summa cum laude,* and won a Fulbright Scholarship to study at Cambridge University. She worked toward a degree in English literature there and met poet Ted Hughes. They were married in 1956. Both continued to write; Plath taught for a year at Smith; and they had two children. In 1962 their marriage broke up. Plath, then living in London with the children, wrote many of the powerful poems for which she is well known. But from her letters and poems, it appears she was approaching a breakdown, like that in 1953. On February 11, 1963, she committed suicide by gassing herself in the oven of her kitchen stove. "Edge" was written six days before she died. Read it again and compare the experience of reading it now with the experience of reading it before, as a way of testing for yourself whether a biographical approach has something valuable to offer you, and what sorts of things it offers.

Reading poems in biographical context can in many cases be illuminating. For example, Li-Young Lee has received much attention for his poems concerning his father. Lee's father was personal physician to Mao Tse-tung but fell out of favor and later became a political prisoner under Sukarno. He escaped, and the family, including Li-Young, became political refugees, eventually coming to the United States, where the father became a Presbyterian minister. You might look at Lee's work in his collections *Rose* and *The City in Which I Love You* and see if this information plays a role in your reading of it.

At the end of this chapter we have included groups of poems by three authors—John Keats, Rita Dove, and Gary Soto—with brief biographical sketches of their lives. Read one or more of the sets and consider how the backgrounds and lives of the authors influence or inform their poems.

> I believe I have a mission, and that I have many stories to tell on many levels—on a personal level, on the familial level, and on the historical–social level.
>
> —MARILYN CHIN

PSYCHOANALYTICAL CRITICISM

A good deal of biographical criticism began, around the middle of our century, to turn in a psychoanalytical direction. This was a result of the growing interest, at the time, in the parent of psychoanalysis, Sigmund Freud (1856–1939), an Austrian physician who sought a scientific understanding of the mind and mental illness. His methods and conclusions were revolutionary and controversial, and have been and continue to be challenged on many grounds. The field of psychoanalysis has now moved far beyond Freud—so far, in fact, that he is not given much attention in psychology courses today. Yet he is of great importance historically, as one of the most influential thinkers of the twentieth century, and his work has had a great impact on twentieth-century literature and twentieth-century approaches to literature.

A short summary of Freud's thought is needed before we can consider its effect on literature. Crucial to its early phase is Freud's realization of a dynamic tension between the conscious and the unconscious in mental activity. This was a radical shift. Pre-Freudian belief held that one could *know* oneself and *control* oneself. The idea that there are parts of the self knowable only through analysis is almost universally accepted now, but it was strikingly new when Freud advanced it. He described three areas of consciousness, each of which can contain causes for human behavior. First is the *conscious* level, the things we are aware of. Second is the *preconscious* level, feelings and sensations we are not presently aware of, but can bring to the surface if we reflect on them. Third is the *unconscious* level, the realm of things we are not aware of, though they influence us greatly. Of the three levels, the unconscious is by far the largest. Comparison to an iceberg may help clarify this: the conscious and preconscious are like the tiny tip of an iceberg extending above the waterline; the unconscious is like the rest of the iceberg, perhaps ninety percent of it, which is out of sight below the surface of the water.

In his second phase, Freud replaced the conscious and unconscious with the very different and now familiar concepts of the *id, ego,* and *superego.* The id is a reservoir of psychic energy, drives, and conflicts. It demands instant gratification of its needs and desires—for food, relieving ourselves, sexual gratification. But instant satisfaction is not always possible, and when satisfaction must be postponed, unpleasant tensions build up within us and cause inner conflict. We are often unaware that such tensions and conflicts exert an influence on our lives and actions. The ego (rational, controlled, partially conscious) is concerned first with pleasure, through the elimination of inner tensions and conflicts, but also with self-preservation, which requires that urges and needs be dealt with in a practical, realistic way: the id tells us we need to eat, and the ego *wants* to concur, but the ego, balancing the id's desire with the restraint imposed by the superego (the rules and taboos internalized through parental and societal influences) tells us to wait until lunchtime.

In a third phase of his work, Freud focused on the development of the ego in children. Although his biological approach to the stages of the early development of children is generally discredited now, evidences of it can be found in the literature of this century. Also important for literary study is another controversial theory, one presently under intense scrutiny, that of *repression.* This theory holds that memories (that is, bundles of psychic energy) of situations with painful or threatening or guilt-laden associations are unconsciously pushed out of consciousness and sealed off so we will not have to deal with them consciously. For example, someone who has been abused as a child may repress the experience and build strong barriers against it. When such matters are repressed, the pent-up energy has an effect on the personality—the repressed memory of abuse may interfere with the person's relationships. It will take something of great force to break through the barrier; but only when it has been broken through can the person be freed from the pain and its effects.

To illustrate how all this could prove useful to a reader, we will apply it to a poet discussed above, Sylvia Plath. Using her poem "Daddy," we will suggest first that a psychoanalytic reading can contribute toward a richer appreciation of the poem, then how it can help explore the relation of the poem to the author.

Sylvia Plath (1932–1963)

Daddy (1962)

You do not do, you do not do
Any more, black shoe
In which I have lived like a foot
For thirty years, poor and white,
Barely daring to breathe or Achoo.   5

Daddy, I have had to kill you.
You died before I had time—
Marble-heavy, a bag full of God,
Ghastly statue with one grey toe
Big as a Frisco seal   10

And a head in the freakish Atlantic
Where it pours bean green over blue
In the waters off beautiful Nauset.
I used to pray to recover you.
Ach, du.°   *Oh, you (German)*   15

In the German tongue, in the Polish town
Scraped flat by the roller
Of wars, wars, wars.
But the name of the town is common.
My Polack friend   20

Says there are a dozen or two.
So I never could tell where you
Put your foot, your root,
I never could talk to you.
The tongue stuck in my jaw.   25

It stuck in a barb wire snare.
Ich, ich, ich, ich,°   *I (German)*
I could hardly speak.
I thought every German was you.
And the language obscene   30

An engine, an engine
Chuffing me off like a Jew.
A Jew to Dachau, Auschwitz, Belsen.
I began to talk like a Jew.
I think I may well be a Jew.   35

The snows of the Tyrol, the clear beer of Vienna
Are not very pure or true.
With my gipsy ancestress and my weird luck
And my Taroc pack and my Taroc pack
I may be a bit of a Jew.   40

I have always been scared of you,
With your Luftwaffe, your gobbledygoo.
And your neat mustache
And your Aryan eye, bright blue.
Panzer-man, panzer-man, O You—   45

Not God but a swastika
So black no sky could squeak through.
Every woman adores a Fascist,
The boot in the face, the brute
Brute heart of a brute like you.   50

You stand at the blackboard, daddy,
In the picture I have of you,
A cleft in your chin instead of your foot
But no less a devil for that, no not
Any less the black man who   55

Bit my pretty red heart in two.
I was ten when they buried you.
At twenty I tried to die
And get back, back, back to you.
I thought even the bones would do.   60

But they pulled me out of the sack,
And they stuck me together with glue.
And then I knew what to do.
I made a model of you,
A man in black with a Meinkampf look   65

And a love of the rack and the screw.
And I said I do, I do.
So daddy, I'm finally through.
The black telephone's off at the root,
The voices just can't worm through.   70

If I've killed one man, I've killed two—
The vampire who said he was you
And drank my blood for a year,
Seven years, if you want to know.
Daddy, you can lie back now.   75

There's a stake in your fat black heart
And the villagers never liked you.
They are dancing and stamping on you.
They always *knew* it was you.
Daddy, daddy, you bastard, I'm through.   80

    First, consider the speaker and her situation within the poem. Plath was
well aware of Freud's works and ideas, and she herself indicated that psycho-
analytic concepts were a part of the poem as she understood it. Introducing
the poem in a poetry reading for BBC radio, Plath said,

> The poem is spoken by a girl with an Electra complex. Her father died while she thought he was God. Her case is complicated by the fact that her father was also a Nazi and her mother very possibly part Jewish. In the daughter the two strains marry and paralyze each other—she has to act out the awful little allegory once over before she is free of it.[3]

It can be helpful to listen to what authors say about their own work and their conscious intentions; however, their unconscious is at work not only in the creation of the poem, but also in controlling what they say about it. What they say, therefore, must be considered carefully.

Plath's reference to the "Electra complex" relates to Freud's ideas (very controversial, then and now) about sexual development in children. Freud held that part of the normal emotional development of a child includes an unconscious wish to replace the parent of the child's sex in the affection of the parent of the opposite sex. Freud developed this theory primarily in masculine terms: initially a little boy loves his nurturing mother though he identifies with his father, and these two feelings exist comfortably side by side. When the sexual urge increases, at around four or five years of age, the boy's love for his mother grows into a sexual desire for her and he begins to see the father as a rival and an obstacle; hostility and desire to get rid of the father emerge. (This is called the *Oedipus complex:* Oedipus in Greek mythology—the fullest account appears in Sophocles' play *Oedipus the King*—killed his father and married his mother.) These feelings create a dilemma for the boy. If he pursues his desire for his mother, he fears, unconsciously, that his father may be angered and may harm him, specifically by removing his penis (*castration anxiety*). This anxiety, ironically, provides the way out of the dilemma. Because of that fear, the boy gives up his incestuous desire for his mother and increases his identification with his father, assuming that eventually he will attain a similar authority and power role himself.

Freud also posited a corresponding process in a girl, called the *Electra complex*. It rests on the most controversial and most widely rejected and ridiculed of Freud's ideas, his belief (a product, some claim, of Freud's own hang-ups about women and masculinity) that girls initially see themselves as little men and that they experience "penis envy" when they find out they are not. The Electra complex involves a reversal of the boy's experience (Electra, in Aeschylus's play *The Libation Bearers,* helped her brother Orestes kill their mother to avenge their mother's role in the killing of her husband, their father). When a little girl discovers she does not have a penis, Freud argued, she holds her mother responsible and turns against her in hostility. In the unconscious, the wish for a penis continues, but is replaced by the wish to bear a child for the father. Thus the girl becomes a rival to the mother for the father's love.

The speaker in "Daddy," as a child, entered the stage of desiring her father—viewing him as everything, idolizing him (Electra complex). To pass

---

[3] Quoted by A. Alvarez in *The Art of Sylvia Plath: A Symposium,* ed. Charles Newman (Bloomington: Indiana University Press, 1970), 65.

beyond this stage in sexual development, she needed to separate from her father (to give up, or "kill" [line 6], her incestuous desire for him). Before she was able to, however, he died (line 7). Thus the speaker is caught in a situation of conflict, anxiety, and guilt: because her father is dead, she is unable to complete the natural process of separation from him and achieve a mature daughter–father relationship with him; but the desire to have such a separation (to "kill" him) creates a sense of guilt—did she *cause* his death by desiring it?—from which she now cannot escape. Thus her father, both during his life (as an authoritarian figure) and after his death, exerted a confining influence on her life—she is trapped (stanza one) inside her fixated relationship with him, imaged as the "black shoe" that later emerges as the boot that represents Nazi oppression and male dominance over women (lines 48–50).

The speaker's anxiety and guilt are increased by the fact that her father was a German and a Nazi, while her mother was part Jewish. Thus, her unresolved attachment to her father identifies her with behaviors she finds repulsive: the oppression of Jews, the extermination of Jews in the death camps (line 33), the underlying violence of the Nazi movement. Her unconscious desire for her father is imaged as a universal love for the force his politics endorsed: "Every woman adores a Fascist / The boot in the face, the brute / Brute heart of a brute like you" (lines 48–50). She feels simultaneous attraction and revulsion, sees her father simultaneously as god and as devil (lines 8, 54).

The speaker sees her mother both as rival and as a representative of a victimized race. She identifies with the oppressed race: "I think I may well be a Jew" (line 35). This leaves the speaker with a deep sense of guilt, torn between desire for her father and sympathy for the people he is oppressing. Her attempted suicide (line 58), she says, was an effort to be united with her father; it could equally be an effort to escape the tension and conflict her feelings about her father and her sense of guilt impose upon her.

The attempt at suicide proving unsuccessful (lines 61–62), she got married (line 67) and viewed the marriage as a fulfillment of her desire to unite with her father (she identifies husband with father—line 64—including the brutality and oppression she claimed to love—lines 65–66). But the marriage did not work out, so the speaker broke it off—"killed" it, "killed" her husband and in the process "killed" her father (lines 6, 71). By ending her marriage, the speaker gains freedom from her father as well as her husband. The father-husband vampire finally is dead, and the speaker is released from the guilt, confinement, and tensions of her unresolved attachment to him/them: "Daddy, daddy, you bastard, I'm through" (line 80).

How does all this relate to Sylvia Plath, the author? We must not simply, automatically ascribe conflicts and tensions in the work directly to the author. Literary works are not equivalent to dreams, as some of Freud's statements imply; they are not necessarily direct expressions of the author's unconscious wishes or fears. To some extent the unconscious is influencing the work, but authors do have some degree of control over their imaginations as well. You must be careful, therefore, not to use details of a work simplistically to psychoanalyze the author. If you start outside an author's works, by examining the author's life from other sources, that can in some cases supply useful supporting information.

Still, literary works are written by human beings and do, even must, reflect something of the authors' lives and experiences. Let's compare some details about the speaker in "Daddy" with some details about Plath's own life. The speaker's father was born in Poland (line 16); so was Plath's father—in Grábow. The speaker's father apparently was a teacher (line 51); Plath's father taught biology and German at Boston University. The speaker's father died when she was ten (line 57); Plath's father died when she was eight. The speaker attempted suicide later (line 58); so did Plath. The speaker married a few years after that (line 64–67); Plath married British poet Ted Hughes in 1956. The speaker's marriage lasted seven years (line 74) and apparently has ended (line 71); Plath and Hughes separated in the seventh year of their marriage. The speaker is thirty years old (line 4); so was Sylvia Plath when she wrote the poem on October 12, 1962, the day after Ted Hughes moved out.

Plath and the speaker are not identical. Plath's father and mother were German immigrants; her father was not a Nazi and there is no evidence that the ancestry of either included Jews (as Plath says the speaker's did). But many would say that the voice of Sylvia Plath *can* be heard through and around the speaker's voice (see again the section on Author and Speaker in Chapter 5). The speaker's need to, and inability to, separate from her father coincides with Plath's own need to do so. The speaker projects onto her father the guilt Plath seems to have felt over Nazi atrocities because of her own German ancestry, and she herself identifies with the Jews in an effort to alleviate that guilt. In a poem written as Plath's separation from Ted Hughes was becoming final, the speaker looks back on her marriage as an effort to achieve a relationship with her father, and identifies her husband with her father. Plath herself said that her actual father was not to be confused with the cruel, destructive Daddy, "the masculine principle gone mad."[4] In the poem, the speaker seems to initiate the break with her husband, thus also achieving the separation from her father that was prevented by her father's death. In real life, it was Hughes who took the initiative, reenacting what the father did twenty years earlier. Thus, although Plath does not kill her father/husband through divorce (as *in* the poem), she could be said to do so *by means of* the poem. A psychoanalytical reading could suggest that the poem serves as Plath's ritual "killing" of father and husband, the violent imagery becoming the means of, as well as the reason for, her rejection of and separation from them. The poem itself could become a vehicle to and declaration of freedom and wholeness.

---

[4] Richard Ellmann and Robert O'Clair, *The Norton Anthology of Modern Poetry*, 2nd ed. (New York: W. W. Norton, 1988), 1417.

Here are three more poems by Plath. Read them first to understand and enjoy them; then see if you sense psychoanalytic implications in them.

SYLVIA PLATH (1932–1963)

The Colossus (1959)

I shall never get you put together entirely,
Pieced, glued, and properly jointed.
Mule-bray, pig-grunt and bawdy cackles
Proceed from your great lips.
It's worse than a barnyard.   5

Perhaps you consider yourself an oracle,
Mouthpiece of the dead, or of some god or other.
Thirty years now I have labored
To dredge the silt from your throat.
I am none the wiser.   10

Scaling little ladders with gluepots and pails of lysol
I crawl like an ant in mourning
Over the weedy acres of your brow
To mend the immense skull plates and clear
The bald, white tumuli of your eyes.   15

A blue sky out of the Oresteia
Arches above us. O father, all by yourself
You are pithy and historical as the Roman Forum.
I open my lunch on a hill of black cypress.
Your fluted bones and acanthine hair are littered   20

In their old anarchy to the horizon-line.
It would take more than a lightning-stroke
To create such a ruin.
Nights, I squat in the cornucopia
Of your left ear, out of the wind,   25

Counting the red stars and those of plum-color.
The sun rises under the pillar of your tongue.
My hours are married to shadow.
No longer do I listen for the scrape of a keel
On the blank stones of the landing.   30

Tulips (1961)

The tulips are too excitable, it is winter here.
Look how white everything is, how quiet, how snowed-in.
I am learning peacefulness, lying by myself quietly
As the light lies on these white walls, this bed, these hands.
I am nobody; I have nothing to do with explosions.   5
I have given my name and my day-clothes up to the nurses
And my history to the anaesthetist and my body to surgeons.

They have propped my head between the pillow and the sheet-cuff
Like an eye between two white lids that will not shut.
Stupid pupil, it has to take everything in.   10
The nurses pass and pass, they are no trouble,
They pass the way gulls pass inland in their white caps,
Doing things with their hands, one just the same as another,
So it is impossible to tell how many there are.

My body is a pebble to them, they tend it as water   15
Tends to the pebbles it must run over, smoothing them gently.
They bring me numbness in their bright needles, they bring me sleep.
Now I have lost myself I am sick of baggage—
My patent leather overnight case like a black pillbox,
My husband and child smiling out of the family photo;   20
Their smiles catch onto my skin, little smiling hooks.

I have let things slip, a thirty-year-old cargo boat
Stubbornly hanging on to my name and address.
They have swabbed me clear of my loving associations.
Scared and bare on the green plastic-pillowed trolley   25
I watched my tea-set, my bureaus of linen, my books
Sink out of sight, and the water went over my head.
I am a nun now, I have never been so pure.

I didn't want any flowers, I only wanted
To lie with my hands turned up and be utterly empty.   30
How free it is, you have no idea how free—
The peacefulness is so big it dazes you,
And it asks nothing, a name tag, a few trinkets.

It is what the dead close on, finally; I imagine them
Shutting their mouths on it, like a Communion tablet.   35

The tulips are too red in the first place, they hurt me.
Even through the gift paper I could hear them breathe
Lightly, through their white swaddlings, like an awful baby.
Their redness talks to my wound, it corresponds.
They are subtle: they seem to float, though they weigh me down,   40
Upsetting me with their sudden tongues and their colour,
A dozen red lead sinkers round my neck.

Nobody watched me before, now I am watched.
The tulips turn to me, and the window behind me
Where once a day the light slowly widens and slowly thins,   45
And I see myself, flat, ridiculous, a cut-paper shadow
Between the eye of the sun and the eyes of the tulips,
And I have no face, I have wanted to efface myself.
The vivid tulips eat my oxygen.

Before they came the air was calm enough,   50
Coming and going, breath by breath, without any fuss.
Then the tulips filled it up like a loud noise.
Now the air snags and eddies round them the way a river
Snags and eddies round a sunken rust-red engine.
They concentrate my attention, that was happy   55
Playing and resting without committing itself.

The walls, also, seem to be warming themselves.
The tulips should be behind bars like dangerous animals;
They are opening like the mouth of some great African cat,
And I am aware of my heart: it opens and closes   60
Its bowl of red blooms out of sheer love of me.
The water I taste is warm and salt, like the sea,
And comes from a country far away as health.

Nick and the Candlestick (1962)

I am a miner. The light burns blue.
Waxy stalactites
Drip and thicken, tears

The earthen womb
Exudes from its dead boredom.   5
Black bat airs

Wrap me, raggy shawls,
Cold homicides.
They weld to me like plums.

Old cave of calcium   10
Icicles, old echoer.
Even the newts are white,

Those holy Joes.
And the fish, the fish—
Christ! they are panes of ice,   15

A vice of knives,
A piranha
Religion, drinking

Its first communion out of my live toes.
The candle   20
Gulps and recovers its small altitude,

Its yellows hearten.
O love, how did you get here?
O embryo

Remembering, even in sleep,   25
Your crossed position.
The blood blooms clean

In you, ruby.
The pain
You wake to is not yours.   30

Love, love,
I have hung our cave with roses,
With soft rugs—

The last of Victoriana.
Let the stars   35
Plummet to their dark address,

Let the mercuric
Atoms that cripple drip
Into the terrible well,

You are the one   40
Solid the spaces lean on, envious.
You are the baby in the barn.

· · ·

When a subject permeates society the way Freud's thought did and seems so widely influential, it is natural that poets would think of writing poems about it. Here are a few.

GAVIN EWART (b. 1916)

Psychoanalysis (1950)

How can one tell what Love may be about
In his uncharted waters, where the mines
Entice the summer swimmers as they shout
And fishermen reel in tremendous lines?

The marker buoys bob lightly in slow motion   5
And near the ports the fish are known by schools—
But not the monsters of the deeper ocean
Or those unclassified in the rock pools.

With clarity and elegance of style
Cartographers trace maps—till one forgets   10
That in the teeming sea, mile after mile,
The biggest fish are still outside the nets.

ALTA (b. 1942)

Penus Envy (1970)

penus envy, they call it
think how handy to have a thing
that poked out; you could just shove
it in any body, whang whang & come,
wouldn't have to give a shit.   5
you *know* you'd come!
wouldn't have to love that person,
trust that person.
whang, whang & come.
if you couldn't get relief for free,   10
pay a little $, whang whang & come.
you wouldn't have to keep, or abort,
wouldn't have to care about the kid.
wouldn't fear sexual violation.
penus envy, they call it.   15
the man is sick in his heart.
that's what I call it.

CHARLES SIMIC (b. 1938)

"Everybody knows the story about me and Dr. Freud" (1989)

"Everybody knows the story about me and Dr. Freud," says my
grandfather.
"We were in love with the same pair of black shoes in the window
of the same shoe store. The store, unfortunately, was always closed.

There'd be a sign: DEATH IN THE FAMILY or BACK AFTER LUNCH, but no mat-
ter how long I waited, no one would come to open.

"Once I caught Dr. Freud there shamelessly admiring the shoes. We
glared at each other before going our separate ways, never to meet again."

Schooling made me the quiet queen of yeses and nos, the little professor
of right and wrong. Today I struggle with that legacy—the academic
knack for revising the mess of the real world out (since the real world will
not fall on only one hand or the other) and the trouble of real love, too
(neither all nor nothing, my pet bailiwicks, but more importantly, more
negotiably, some some). The trouble with mind, says Bierce, is it only has
itself to know itself with. Raised on brain waves, making odes to diodes,
deriving my sense of consequence from sequence, stuck on time, I plowed
myself a rut of thought it's hard to climb from (etymology of delirium):
the rut of easy twos, exclusive twos, marked by beginning and end, im-
press of poet and priest, though the world be one and numberless.

–HEATHER McHUGH

Read one or more of the following biographical sketches and sets of po-
ems by John Keats, Rita Dove, and Gary Soto. Consider how aspects of their
lives and experiences appear in their poems. The work of Dove and Soto has
been called fictionalized autobiography. Consider what that term suggests
about truth and fact as you apply it to these works. How can truth be found
in "fictionalized autobiography"? Watch also for stylistic and thematic con-
nections among works by the same author, for ways one poem can illuminate
another poem and, perhaps, help readers get to know the author better.

JOHN KEATS (1795–1821)

*John Keats was born in London in 1795. His father was a stableman at a livery sta-
ble who married his employer's daughter and inherited the business. Keats was taken
out of school at age fifteen by his guardian and forced to study medicine. As soon as
he qualified for medical practice, in 1815, he abandoned medicine for poetry. His de-
velopment as a poet was astounding. He began writing poetry in 1813, when he was
eighteen; his early poetry was conventional and ordinary. In 1816 he suddenly found
his voice, in the sonnet "On First Looking into Chapman's Homer," and he went on
to write impressive long poems over the next few years. In 1818 Keats's brother died
of tuberculosis (as their mother had in 1809); he himself became ill after a long
walking tour in a cold, damp summer; and he fell madly in love with a pretty, viva-
cious young woman named Fanny Brawne, whom he could not marry because of his
poverty, illness, and devotion to poetry. In the midst of such stress and emotional tur-
moil, only five years after he began writing poetry, his masterpieces began to pour
out: between January and September 1819 he wrote his great odes, a number of son-*

---

nets, and several longer lyric poems, all of sensuous, lyrical beauty and emotional resonance, reflecting his delight in life as well as his awareness of life's brevity and difficulty. In February 1820 he began coughing up blood and his health failed rapidly; he went to Italy in the autumn, in the hope that the warmer climate would improve his health, but he died there on February 23, 1821.

On First Looking into Chapman's Homer (1816)

Much have I travell'd in the realms of gold, *a*
    And many goodly states and kingdoms seen; *b*
    Round many western islands have I been *b*
Which bards in fealty to Apollo hold. *a*
Oft of one wide expanse had I been told *a*   5
    That deep-brow'd Homer ruled as his demesne; *b*
    Yet did I never breathe its pure serene *b*
Till I heard Chapman speak out loud and bold. *a*
Then felt I like some watcher of the skies *c*
    When a new planet swims into his ken; *d*   10
Or like stout Cortez when with eagle eyes *c*
    He star'd at the Pacific—and all his men *d*
Look'd at each other with a wild surmise— *c*
    Silent, upon a peak in Darien. *d*

from Sleep and Poetry (1816)

    O for ten years, that I may overwhelm
Myself in poesy; so I may do the deed
That my own soul has to itself decreed.[2]
Then will I pass the countries that I see
In long perspective, and continually
Taste their pure fountains. First the realm I'll pass   100
Of Flora, and old Pan: sleep in the grass,
Feed upon apples red, and strawberries,
And choose each pleasure that my fancy sees;
Catch the white-handed nymphs in shady places,
To woo sweet kisses from averted faces,—   105

[1] Keats, who knew no Greek, read Homer through the night with his friend Charles Cowden Clarke in George Chapman's vigorous translation (pub. 1598–1616), and wrote this sonnet the next morning. (It was, of course, Balboa, not Cortez, who discovered the Pacific in 1513.)

[2] The young Keats sets out a plan for his writing career, beginning—as Virgil, Spenser, and Milton did—with idyllic pastoral poetry (lines 101–121) and moving, within ten years, to a nobler vein of poetry dealing with "the agonies, the strife / Of human hearts" (lines 122–25). He then describes a vision of the chariot of poesy (lines 125–54).

Play with their fingers, touch their shoulders white
Into a pretty shrinking with a bite
As hard as lips can make it: till agreed,
A lovely tale of human life we'll read.   110
And one will teach a tame dove how it best
May fan the cool air gently o'er my rest;
Another, bending o'er her nimble tread,
Will set a green robe floating round her head,
And still will dance with ever varied ease,   115
Smiling upon the flowers and the trees:
Another will entice me on, and on
Through almond blossoms and rich cinnamon;
Till in the bosom of a leafy world
We rest in silence, like two gems upcurl'd   120
In the recesses of a pearly shell.

    And can I ever bid these joys farewell?
Yes, I must pass them for a nobler life,
Where I may find the agonies, the strife
Of human hearts: for lo! I see afar,   125
O'ersailing the blue cragginess, a car
And steeds with streamy manes—the charioteer
Looks out upon the winds with glorious fear:
And now the numerous tramplings quiver lightly
Along a huge cloud's ridge; and now with sprightly   130
Wheel downward come they into fresher skies,
Tipt round with silver from the sun's bright eyes.
Still downward with capacious whirl they glide;
And now I see them on the green-hill's side
In breezy rest among the nodding stalks.   135
The charioteer with wond'rous gesture talks
To the trees and mountains; and there soon appear
Shapes of delight, of mystery, and fear,
Passing along before a dusky space
Made by some mighty oaks: as they would chase   140
Some ever-fleeting music on they sweep.
Lo! how they murmur, laugh, and smile, and weep:
Some with upholden hand and mouth severe;
Some with their faces muffled to the ear
Between their arms; some, clear in youthful bloom,   145
Go glad and smilingly athwart the gloom;
Some looking back, and some with upward gaze;
Yes, thousands in a thousand different ways
Flit onward—now a lovely wreath of girls
Dancing their sleek hair into tangled curls;   150
And now broad wings. Most awfully intent,
The driver of those steeds is forward bent,

And seems to listen: O that I might know
All that he writes with such a hurrying glow.

    The visions all are fled—the car is fled   155
Into the light of heaven, and in their stead
A sense of real things comes doubly strong,
And, like a muddy stream, would bear along
My soul to nothingness: but I will strive
Against all doubtings, and will keep alive   160
The thought of that same chariot, and the strange
Journey it went.

from *Endymion: A Poetic Romance* (1817)

From *Book 1*

A thing of beauty is a joy for ever:
Its loveliness increases; it will never
Pass into nothingness; but still will keep
A bower quiet for us, and a sleep
Full of sweet dreams, and health, and quiet breathing.   5
Therefore, on every morrow, are we wreathing
A flowery band to bind us to the earth,
Spite of despondence, of the inhuman dearth
Of noble natures, of the gloomy days,
Of all the unhealthy and o'er-darkened ways   10
Made for our searching: yes, in spite of all,
Some shape of beauty moves away the pall
From our dark spirits. Such the sun, the moon,
Trees old, and young sprouting a shady boon
For simple sheep; and such are daffodils   15
With the green world they live in; and clear rills
That for themselves a cooling covert make
'Gainst the hot season; the mid forest brake,
Rich with a sprinkling of fair musk-rose blooms:
And such too is the grandeur of the dooms   20
We have imagined for the mighty dead;
All lovely tales that we have heard or read:
An endless fountain of immortal drink,
Pouring unto us from the heaven's brink.

    Nor do we merely feel these essences   25
For one short hour; no, even as the trees
That whisper round a temple become soon
Dear as the temple's self, so does the moon,
The passion poesy, glories infinite,
Haunt us till they become a cheering light   30
Unto our souls, and bound to us so fast,

That, whether there be shine, or gloom o'ercast,
They alway must be with us, or we die.

When I Have Fears That I May Cease to Be (1818)

When I have fears that I may cease to be
    Before my pen has glean'd my teeming brain,
Before high piled books, in charactry,
    Hold like rich garners the full ripen'd grain;
When I behold, upon the night's starr'd face,   5
    Huge cloudy symbols of a high romance,
And think that I may never live to trace
    Their shadows, with the magic hand of chance;
And when I feel, fair creature of an hour,
    That I shall never look upon thee more,   10
Never have relish in the fairy power
    Of unreflecting love;—then on the shore
Of the wide world I stand alone, and think
Till love and fame to nothingness do sink.

Ode to a Nightingale (1819)

I

My heart aches, and a drowsy numbness pains
    My sense, as though of hemlock I had drunk,
Or emptied some dull opiate to the drains
    One minute past, and Lethe-wards had sunk:
'Tis not through envy of thy happy lot,   5
    But being too happy in thine happiness,—
        That thou, light-winged Dryad of the trees,
            In some melodious plot
    Of beechen green, and shadows numberless,
        Singest of summer in full-throated ease.   10

II

O, for a draught of vintage! that hath been
    Cool'd a long age in the deep-delved earth,
Tasting of Flora and the country green,
    Dance, and Provençal song, and sunburnt mirth!
O for a beaker full of the warm South,   15
    Full of the true, the blushful Hippocrene,
        With beaded bubbles winking at the brim,
            And purple-stained mouth;
    That I might drink, and leave the world unseen,
        And with thee fade away into the forest dim: 20

III

Fade far away, dissolve, and quite forget
    What thou among the leaves hast never known,
The weariness, the fever, and the fret
    Here, where men sit and hear each other groan;
Where palsy shakes a few, sad, last gray hairs,   25
    Where youth grows pale, and spectre-thin, and dies;
        Where but to think is to be full of sorrow
            And leaden-eyed despairs,
        Where Beauty cannot keep her lustrous eyes,
            Or new Love pine at them beyond to-morrow.   30

IV

Away! away! for I will fly to thee,
    Not charioted by Bacchus and his pards,
But on the viewless wings of Poesy,
    Though the dull brain perplexes and retards:
Already with thee! tender is the night,   35
    And haply the Queen-Moon is on her throne,
        Cluster'd around by all her starry Fays;
            But here there is no light,
Save what from heaven is with the breezes blown
        Through verdurous glooms and winding mossy ways.   40

V

I cannot see what flowers are at my feet,
    Nor what soft incense hangs upon the boughs,
But, in embalmed darkness, guess each sweet
    Wherewith the seasonable month endows
The grass, the thicket, and the fruit-tree wild;   45
    White hawthorn, and the pastoral eglantine;
        Fast fading violets cover'd up in leaves;
            And mid-May's eldest child,
    The coming musk-rose, full of dewy wine,
        The murmurous haunt of flies on summer eves.   50

VI

Darkling I listen; and, for many a time
    I have been half in love with easeful Death,
Call'd him soft names in many a mused rhyme,
    To take into the air my quiet breath;
Now more than ever seems it rich to die,   55
    To cease upon the midnight with no pain,
        While thou art pouring forth thy soul abroad
            In such an ecstasy!
    Still wouldst thou sing, and I have ears in vain—
    To thy high requiem become a sod.   60

VII

Thou wast not born for death, immortal Bird!
    No hungry generations tread thee down;
The voice I hear this passing night was heard
    In ancient days by emperor and clown:
Perhaps the self-same song that found a path   65
        Through the sad heart of Ruth, when, sick for home,
          She stood in tears amid the alien corn;
            The same that oft-times hath
        Charm'd magic casements, opening on the foam
          Of perilous seas, in faery lands forlorn.   70

VIII

Forlorn! the very word is like a bell
    To toll me back from thee to my sole self!
Adieu! the fancy cannot cheat so well
    As she is fam'd to do, deceiving elf.
Adieu! adieu! thy plaintive anthem fades   75
        Past the near meadows, over the still stream,
          Up the hill-side; and now 'tis buried deep
            In the next valley-glades:
        Was it a vision, or a waking dream?
          Fled is that music:—Do I wake or sleep?   80

Ode on a Grecian Urn (1819)

I

Thou still unravished bride of quietness,
    Thou foster child of silence and slow time,
Sylvan historian, who canst thus express
    A flowery tale more sweetly than our rhyme:
What leaf-fringed legend haunts about thy shape   5
        Of deities or mortals, or of both,
          In Tempe or the dales of Arcady?
        What men or gods are these? What maidens loth?
What mad pursuit? What struggle to escape?
        What pipes and timbrels? What wild ecstasy?   10

II

Heard melodies are sweet, but those unheard
    Are sweeter; therefore, ye soft pipes, play on;
Not to the sensual ear, but, more endeared,
    Pipe to the spirit ditties of no tone:
Fair youth, beneath the trees, thou canst not leave   15
        Thy song, nor ever can those trees be bare;
          Bold lover, never, never canst thou kiss,

Though winning near the goal—yet, do not grieve;
    She cannot fade, though thou hast not thy bliss,
Forever wilt thou love, and she be fair!   20

III

Ah, happy, happy boughs! that cannot shed
    Your leaves, nor ever bid the spring adieu;
And, happy melodist, unwearièd,
    Forever piping songs forever new;
More happy love! more happy, happy love!   25
    Forever warm and still to be enjoyed,
        Forever panting, and forever young;
All breathing human passion far above,
    That leaves a heart high-sorrowful and cloyed,
        A burning forehead, and a parching tongue.   30

IV

Who are these coming to the sacrifice?
    To what green altar, O mysterious priest,
Lead'st thou that heifer lowing at the skies,
    And all her silken flanks with garlands dressed?
What little town by river or sea shore,   35
    Or mountain-built with peaceful citadel,
        Is emptied of this folk, this pious morn?
And, little town, thy streets forevermore
    Will silent be; and not a soul to tell
        Why thou art desolate, can e'er return.   40

V

O Attic shape! Fair attitude! with brede
    Of marble men and maidens overwrought,
With forest branches and the trodden weed;
    Thou, silent form, dost tease us out of thought
As doth eternity: Cold Pastoral!   45
    When old age shall this generation waste,
        Thou shalt remain, in midst of other woe
Than ours, a friend to man, to whom thou say'st,
"Beauty is truth, truth beauty,"—that is all
        Ye know on earth, and all ye need to know.   50

RITA DOVE (b. 1952)

In 1993 Rita Dove was appointed United States Poet Laureate and Consultant in Poetry at the Library of Congress, making her the youngest person—and the first African American—to receive this highest official honor in American letters. She held the position for two years. Dove was born in Akron, Ohio, in 1952; her father was the first research chemist to break the race barrier in the tire industry. In 1970 she was invited to the White House as a Presidential Scholar, one of the two best high school graduates in the state of Ohio (and 100 most outstanding high school graduates in the United States) that year. She then attended Miami University in Oxford, Ohio, as a National Achievement Scholar. Dove graduated summa cum laude with a degree in English in 1973 and studied for a year on a Fulbright Scholarship at Universität Tübingen in Germany. She then joined the University of Iowa Writers Workshop, where she earned her Master of Fine Arts degree in 1977. She was awarded the Pulitzer Prize for poetry in 1987 for Thomas and Beulah, a book-length sequence loosely based on the lives of her grandparents. She has taught at Tuskegee Institute and Arizona State University and now is on the faculty of the University of Virginia. She has published seven collections of poetry, a verse drama, a collection of short stories, a novel, Through the Ivory Gate, and The Poet's World, her laureate lectures. Dove's poetry often grows out of personal experience and out of her extended family history. She transforms autobiography and family memories into works that become their own lyrical myths. The first poem below is from The Yellow House on the Corner; the second is from Museum; the others are from Thomas and Beulah.

Adolescence—III (1980)

With Dad gone, Mom and I worked
The dusky rows of tomatoes.
As they glowed orange in sunlight
And rotted in shadow, I too
Grew orange and softer, swelling out   5
Starched cotton slips.

The texture of twilight made me think of
Lengths of Dotted Swiss. In my room
I wrapped scarred knees in dresses
That once went to big-band dances;   10
I baptized my earlobes with rosewater.
Along the window-sill, the lipstick stubs
Glittered in their steel shells.

Looking out at the rows of clay
And chicken manure, I dreamed how it would happen: 15
He would meet me by the blue spruce,
A carnation over his heart, saying,
"I have come for you, Madam;
I have loved you in my dreams."
At his touch, the scabs would fall away.   20
Over his shoulder, I see my father coming toward us:
He carries his tears in a bowl,
And blood hangs in the pine-soaked air.

Anti-Father *(1983)*

Contrary to
tales you told us

summer nights when
the air conditioner

broke—the stars   5
are not far

apart. Rather
they draw

closer together
with years.   10

And houses
shrivel, un-lost,

and porches sag;
neighbors phone

to report cracks   15
in the cellar floor,

roots of the willow
coming up. Stars

speak to a child.
The past   20

is silent. . . .
Just between

me and you,
woman to man,

outer space is   25
inconceivably

intimate.

The Event *(1986)*

Ever since they'd left the Tennessee ridge
with nothing to boast of
but good looks and a mandolin,

the two Negroes leaning
on the rail of a riverboat   5
were inseparable: Lem plucked

to Thomas' silver falsetto.
But the night was hot and they were drunk.
They spat where the wheel

churned mud and moonlight,   10
they called to the tarantulas
down among the bananas

to come out and dance.
You're so fine and mighty; let's see
what you can do, said Thomas, pointing   15

to a tree-capped island.
Lem stripped, spoke easy: *Them's chestnuts,*
I believe. Dove

quick as a gasp. Thomas, dry
on deck, saw the green crown shake   20
as the island slipped

under, dissolved
in the thickening stream.
At his feet

a stinking circle of rags,   25
the half-shell mandolin.
Where the wheel turned the water

gently shirred.

Jiving (1986)

Heading North, straw hat
cocked on the back of his head,

tight curls gleaming
with brilliantine, he didn't stop

until the nights of chaw   5
and river-bright

had retreated, somehow
into another's life. He landed

in Akron, Ohio
1921,   10

on the dingy beach
of a man-made lake.

Since what he'd been through
he was always jiving, gold hoop

from the right ear jiggling
and a glass stud, bright blue

15

in his left. The young ladies
saying *He sure plays*

that tater bug
like the devil!

20

sighing their sighs
and dimpling.

Courtship (1986)

1.

Fine evening may I have
the pleasure . . .
up and down the block
waiting—for what? A
magnolia breeze, someone
to trot out the stars?

5

But she won't set a foot
in his turtledove Nash,
it wasn't proper.
Her pleated skirt fans
softly, a circlet of arrows.

10

King of the Crawfish
in his yellow scarf,
mandolin belly pressed tight
to his hounds-tooth vest—
his wrist flicks for the pleats
all in a row, sighing . . .

15

2.

. . . so he wraps the yellow silk
still warm from his throat
around her shoulders. (He made
good money; he could buy another.)
A gnat flies
in his eye and she thinks
he's crying.

20

Then the parlor festooned
like a ship and Thomas
twirling his hat in his hands
wondering how did I get here.

25

China pugs guarding a fringed settee
where a father, half-Cherokee,
smokes and frowns.
I'll give her a good life—
what was he doing,
selling all for a song?
His heart fluttering shut
then slowly opening.

30

35

The Satisfaction Coal Company (1986)

1.

What to do with a day.
Leaf through *Jet*. Watch T.V.
Freezing on the porch
but he goes anyhow, snow too high
for a walk, the ice treacherous.
Inside, the gas heater takes care of itself;
he doesn't even notice being warm.

Everyone says he looks great.
Across the street a drunk stands smiling
at something carved in a tree.
The new neighbor with the floating hips
scoots out to get the mail
and waves once, brightly,
storm door clipping her heel on the way in.

5

10

2.

Twice a week he had taken the bus down Glendale hill
to the corner of Market. Slipped through
the alley by the canal and let himself in.
Started to sweep
with terrible care, like a woman
brushing shine into her hair,
same motion, same lullaby.
No curtains—the cop on the beat
stopped outside once in the hour
to swing his billy club and glare.

It was better on Saturdays
when the children came along:
he mopped while they emptied
ashtrays, clang of glass on metal
then a dry scutter. Next they counted
nailheads studding the leather cushions.
Thirty-four! they shouted,

15

20

25

30

209

RitaRita Dove   **209**

that was the year and
they found it mighty amusing.

But during the week he noticed more—
lights when they gushed or dimmed
at the Portage Hotel, the 10:32
picking up speed past the B & O switchyard,
floorboards trembling and the explosive
kachook kachook kachook kachook
and the oiled rails ticking underneath.

                    3.
They were poor then but everyone had been poor.
He hadn't minded the sweeping,
just the thought of it—like now
when people ask him what he's thinking
and he says *I'm listening*.

Those nights walking home alone,
the bucket of coal scraps banging his knee,
he'd hear a roaring furnace
with its dry, familiar heat. Now the nights
take care of themselves—as for the days,
there is the canary's sweet curdled song,
the wino smiling through his dribble.
Past the hill, past the gorge
choked with wild sumac in summer,
the corner has been upgraded.
Still, he'd like to go down there someday
to stand for a while, and get warm.

Weathering Out (1986)

She liked mornings the best—Thomas gone
to look for work, her coffee flushed with milk,

outside autumn trees blowsy and dripping.
Past the seventh month she couldn't see her feet

so she floated from room to room, houseshoes flapping,
navigating corners in wonder. When she leaned

against a door jamb to yawn, she disappeared entirely.

Last week they had taken a bus at dawn
to the new airdock. The hangar slid open in segments

and the zeppelin nosed forward in its silver envelope.
The men walked it out gingerly, like a poodle,

then tied it to a mast and went back inside.
Beulah felt just that large and placid, a lake;

she glistened from cocoa butter smoothed in
when Thomas returned every evening nearly   15

in tears. He'd lean an ear on her belly
and say: *Little fellow's really talking,*

though to her it was more the *pok-pok-pok*
of a fingernail tapping a thick cream lampshade.

Sometimes during the night she woke and found him   20
asleep there and the child sleeping, too.

The coffee was good but too little. Outside
everything shivered in tinfoil—only the clover

between the cobblestones hung stubbornly on,
green as an afterthought. . . .   25

Sunday Greens (1986)

She wants to hear
wine pouring.
She wants to taste
change. She wants
pride to roar through   5
the kitchen till it shines
like straw, she wants

lean to replace
tradition. Ham knocks
in the pot, nothing   10
but bones, each
with its bracelet
of flesh.

The house stinks
like a zoo in summer,   15
while upstairs
her man sleeps on.
Robe slung over
her arm and
the cradled hymnal,   20

she pauses, remembers
her mother in a slip
lost in blues,
and those collards,
wild-eared,   25
singing.

GARY SOTO (b. 1952)

Gary Soto grew up in Fresno, California, where he was born in 1952. He earned his B.A. degree from California State University (Fresno) and his M.F.A. degree from the University of California at Irvine. He has received many awards, including a Guggenheim fellowship, the American Book Award from the Before Columbus Foundation, and the 1993 Andrew Carnegie medal for video excellence, and he was a finalist for the National Book Award in 1995. His first book, The Elements of San Joaquin, *won the 1976 United States Award from the International Poetry Forum. A prolific author, he has published eight collections of poetry, four essay collections, two works of fiction, and numerous children's books. His works have sold close to a million copies. Soto worked his way through college doing jobs like picking grapes and chopping beets and cotton. Much of his poetry comes out of and reflects his working background, that of migrant workers and tenant farmers in the fields of the central valley of California. Soto's language comes from earthy, gritty, raw everyday American speech. He takes readers to the center of the struggle for identity in late twentieth-century America. The first five poems below were first published in* The Elements of San Joaquin; *"Mexicans Begin Jogging" in* Where Sparrows Work Hard; *and "Envying the Children of San Francisco" in* Black Hair. *We have reprinted them from* New and Selected Poems *(1995).*

The Elements of San Joaquin (1977; rev. 1995)

for César Chávez

FIELD

The wind sprays pale dirt into my mouth
The small, almost invisible scars
On my hands.

The pores in my throat and elbows
Have taken in a seed of dirt of their own.   5

After a day in the grape fields near Rolinda
A fine silt, washed by sweat,
Has settled into the lines
On my wrists and palms.

Already I am becoming the valley,   10
A soil that sprouts nothing.
For any of us.

WIND

A dry wind over the valley
Peeled mountains, grain by grain,
To small slopes, loose dirt   15
Where red ants tunnel.

The wind strokes
The skulls and spines of cattle
To white dust, to nothing,

Covers the spiked tracks of beetles,   20
Of tumbleweed, of sparrows
That pecked the ground for insects.

Evenings, when I am in the yard weeding,
The wind picks up the breath of my armpits
Like dust, swirls it   25
Miles away

And drops it
On the ear of a rabid dog,
And I take on another life.

     WIND

When you got up this morning the sun   30
Blazed an hour in the sky,

A lizard hid
Under the curled leaves of manzanita
And winked its dark lids.

Later, the sky grayed,   35
And the cold wind you breathed
Was moving under your skin and already far
From the small hives of your lungs.

     STARS

At dusk the first stars appear.
Not one eager finger points toward them.   40
A little later the stars spread with the night
And an orange moon rises
To lead them, like a shepherd, toward dawn.

     SUN

In June the sun is a bonnet of light
Coming up,   45
Little by little,
From behind a skyline of pine.

The pastures sway with fiddle-neck,
Tassels of foxtail.

At Piedra   50
A couple fish on the river's edge,
Their shadows deep against the water.
Above, in the stubbled slopes,

Cows climb down
As the heat rises   55
In a mist of blond locusts,
Returning to the valley.

    RAIN

When autumn rains flatten sycamore leaves,
The tiny volcanos of dirt
Ants raised around their holes,   60
I should be out of work.

My silverware and stack of plates will go unused
Like the old, my two good slacks
Will smother under a growth of lint
And smell of the old dust   65
That rises
When the closet door opens or closes.

The skin of my belly will tighten like a belt
And there will be no reason for pockets.

    HARVEST

East of the sun's slant, in the vineyard that never failed,   70
A wind crossed my face, moving the dust
And a portion of my voice a step closer to a new year.

The sky went black in the ninth hour of rolling trays,
And in the distance ropes of rain dropped to pull me
From the thick harvest that was not mine.   75

    FOG

If you go to your window
You will notice a fog drifting in.

The sun is no stronger than a flashlight.
Not all the sweaters
Hung in closets all summer   80
Could soak up this mist. The fog:
A mouth nibbling everything to its origin,
Pomegranate trees, stolen bicycles,

The string of lights at a used-car lot,
A Pontiac with scorched valves.   85

In Fresno the fog is passing
The young thief prying a window screen,
Graying my hair that falls
And goes unfound, my fingerprints
Slowly growing a fur of dust—   90

One hundred years from now
There should be no reason to believe
I lived.

DAYBREAK

In this moment when the light starts up
In the east and rubs   95
The horizon until it catches fire,

We enter the fields to hoe,
Row after row, among the small flags of onion,
Waving off the dragonflies
That ladder the air.   100

And tears the onions raise
Do not begin in your eyes but in ours,
In the salt blown
From one blister into another;

They begin in knowing   105
You will never waken to bear
The hour timed to a heart beat,
The wind pressing us closer to the ground.

When the season ends,
And the onions are unplugged from their sleep,   110
We won't forget what you failed to see,
And nothing will heal
Under the rain's broken fingers.

Summer (1977)

Once again, tell me, what was it like?
There was a windowsill of flies.
It meant the moon pulled its own weight
And the black sky cleared itself
Like a sneeze.   5

What about the farm worker?
He had no bedroom. He had a warehouse
Of heat, a swamp cooler
That turned no faster than a raffle cage.

And the farms?   10
There were groves
Of fig trees that went unpicked.
The fruit wrinkled and flattened
Like the elbows
Of an old woman.   15

What about the Projects in the Eastside?
I can't really say. Maybe a child
Burned his first book of matches.
Maybe the burn is disappearing
Under the first layer   20
Of skin.

And next summer?
It will be the same. Boredom,
In early June, will settle
On the eyelash shading your pupil from dust,   25
On the shoulder you look over
To find the sun rising
From the Sierras.

Field Poem (1977; rev. 1995)

When the foreman whistled
My brother and I
Shouldered our hoes,
Leaving the field.
We returned to the bus   5
Speaking
In broken English, in broken Spanish
The restaurant food,
The tickets to a dance
We wouldn't buy with our pay.   10

From the smashed bus window,
I saw the leaves of cotton plants
Like small hands waving good-bye.

Hoeing (1977)

During March while hoeing long rows
Of cotton
Dirt lifted in the air
Entering my nostrils
And eyes   5
The yellow under my fingernails

The hoe swung
Across my shadow   chopping weeds
And thick caterpillars
That shriveled   10
Into rings
And went where the wind went

When the sun was on the left
And against my face
Sweat   the sea   15
That is still within me
Rose and fell from my chin
Touching land
For the first time

History (1977; rev. 1995)

Grandma lit the stove.
Morning sunlight
Lengthened in spears
Across the linoleum floor.
Wrapped in a shawl,   5
Her eyes small
With sleep,
She sliced *papas,*
Pounded chiles
With a stone   10
Brought from Guadalajara.

                              After
Grandpa left for work,
She hosed down
The walk her sons paved   15
And in the shade
Of a chinaberry,
Unearthed her
Secret cigar box
Of bright coins   20
And bills, counted them
In English,
Then in Spanish,
And buried them elsewhere.
Later, back   25
From the market,
Where no one saw her,
She pulled out
Pepper and beet, spines
Of asparagus   30
From her blouse,
Tiny chocolates
From under a paisley bandana,
And smiled.

That was the fifties 35
And Grandma in her fifties
A face streaked
From cutting grapes
And boxing plums.
I remember her insides 40
Were washed of tapeworm,
Her arms swelled into knobs
Of small growths—
Her second son
Dropped from a ladder 45
And was dust.
And yet I do not know
The sorrows
That sent her praying
In the dark of a closet, 50
The tear that fell
At night
When she touched loose skin
Of belly and breasts.
I do not know why 55
Her face shines
Or what goes beyond this shine,
Only the stories
That pulled her
From Taxco to San Joaquin, 60
Delano to Westside,
The places
In which we all begin.

Mexicans Begin Jogging (1981)

At the factory I worked
In the fleck of rubber, under the press
Of an oven yellow with flame,
Until the border patrol opened
Their vans and my boss waved for us to run. 5
"Over the fence, Soto," he shouted,
And I shouted that I was American.
"No time for lies," he said, and pressed
A dollar in my palm, hurrying me
Through the back door. 10

Since I was on his time, I ran
And became the wag to a short tail of Mexicans—
Ran past the amazed crowds that lined
The street and blurred like photographs, in rain.

I ran from that industrial road to the soft   15
Houses where people paled at the turn of an autumn sky.
What could I do but yell *vivas*
To baseball, milkshakes, and those sociologists
Who would clock me
As I jog into the next century   20
On the power of a great, silly grin.

Envying the Children of San Francisco (1985)

At a city square
Children laugh in the red
Sweaters of Catholics,
As they walk home between trucks
And sunlight angled off buildings that end in points.   5
I'm holding an apple, among shoppers
Clutching bags big enough to sleep in,
And the air is warm for October—
Torn pieces of paper
Scuttling like roaches, a burst at a time.   10

The children are blond,
Shiny, and careful at the lights—
The sister with her brother's hand.
They cross looking
At their watches, and I cross too.   15
I want to know where
They're going, what door they'll push
Open and call home—
The TV coming on,
Milk, a cookie for each hand.   20

As a kid I wanted to live
In the city, in a building that rose above it all,
The gray streets burst open, a rattle
Of jackhammers. I wanted to
Stare down from the eighteenth floor, and let things go—   25
My homework for one, a paper plane
With a half-drawn heart and a girl's name.
I wanted to say that I ate
And slept, ate and slept in a building
That faced other buildings, a sliver of sea   30
Blue in the distance.
I wanted to hear voices
Behind walls, the *click-click* of a poodle
Strolling to his bowl—a violin like fingers
Running down a blackboard.   35

I wanted to warm my hands at a teakettle
And comb my hair in an elevator, my mouth
Still rolling with cereal, as I started off
For school, a row of pens in my shirt pocket.
Back home at the window   40
I wanted it to be December—
Flags and honking cars,
A Santa Claus with his pot, a single red
Balloon let go and racing skyward,
And the tiny mothers who would come around   45
Buildings, disappear, and come around again,
Hugging bags for all they were worth to children.

APPLICATIONS FOR CHAPTER 11

SUGGESTIONS FOR WRITING

1. Select a favorite poem from an earlier chapter. Do some reading on the author's life, background, and times. Explore in your journal what this information adds to your earlier understanding and appreciation of the poem. You might then use this information and these thoughts as the basis for an essay or a research paper.

2. Select one of the authors at the end of this chapter—John Keats, Rita Dove, or Gary Soto. Do some research into his or her historical and social background. Reread the poetry included in this chapter and record in your journal observations about how that background influenced the poems. You might use this as the basis of an essay or extend it into a research paper.

3. Watch, for a day or two, for evidences of the presence of psychoanalytic influences anywhere around you—casual use of its terminology, allusions in cartoons or by comedians or in TV shows, and so on. Record them in your journal.

4. Watch a TV show or movie that uses a repressed experience or emotion as the basis of the plot, and write a paper explaining it and its effect on you.

5. Look again at the poems by Rita Dove. Do some research into the history of your own family and write a poem depicting one or more of the people you learned about.

6. Look again at the poems by Gary Soto. Write your own poem based on an event from your past. Record in your journal what informs your poem, both those things that appear in the poem and those that do not.

7. Do some additional reading in works by Sylvia Plath—*The Bell Jar* as well as additional poems—and in biographical material about her. Write an essay or research paper exploring the relationship between her life and her works.

8. Find an essay or book that employs a psychoanalytic approach to a poet's life or works. Write a journal entry discussing the way the approach is handled, whether it seems valuable, and why you like or dislike what it does.

1. Keep in mind the values and methods involved in the use of biographical and historical context as a way of approaching poetry.
2. Be alert for ways that Freud's ideas—the unconscious; the id, ego, and superego; the Oedipus complex; and defenses—and psychoanalytic methods might prove helpful in understanding the relationship between an author and his or her works.

12 | Texts

Is There a Text in This Class? More than a decade ago, a book with that intriguing title appeared[1]—a title that grew out of students' inquiries about whether they would be required to buy a book for a course. But for author Stanley Fish, the question raised the broader issue of what *text* means in literature.[2] All theoretical approaches to literature must at some point come to grips with the issue of how they regard texts. Approaches that focus on biography or history (Chapter 11) are less interested in the text (assumed to be equivalent to the words on the page) for itself than as a source of information regarding an author or an era. Reader-oriented theories (Chapters 2 and 13) are less interested in the text than in the reader, who brings a work to life by "performing" (actively reading) the text, which is viewed as analogous to a musical score—less important for itself than for the performance it allows to emerge.

In this chapter we will look at two approaches in which "text" is important for itself. All critical approaches develop in a context—as a response to, extension of, or reaction against existing approaches. To understand the approaches discussed in this chapter, we will need to give attention to what they were reacting against. The earlier of the two approaches, New Criticism, developed in the late 1930s and early 1940s in part as a reaction against prevalent modes of biographical and historical criticism that used works of literature as purveyors of information rather than valuing them for their own sake. Critics began taking texts themselves very seriously as self-contained works of art and looking at them closely. The other approach, deconstruction, emerged several decades later as a reaction against the excesses of a movement called structuralism. This chapter will illustrate what close attention to texts

---

[1] Stanley Fish, *Is There a Text in This Class? The Authority of Interpretive Communities* (Cambridge, Mass.: Harvard University Press, 1980).

[2] Alongside this use of *text,* the word is also used more broadly. Its etymology (from the same root as *textile*) reminds us that it is a product that has been made—words woven together. Many modern authors speak of nonverbal "texts"—for example, fashions (and individual choices) in footwear or hairstyle are a text that may be read; so is the structure of institutions in a society, or the seating arrangement in an office or classroom.

can contribute to your experience of poetry, as it examines these two varieties of textual criticism with their very different assumptions and emphases.

NEW CRITICISM

The text-centered approach most influential over the past half century is called **New Criticism,** or "Formalism." It originated in the 1930s and for over forty years it dominated the study of literature. The term *text* was not used then as it is now; New Critics simply referred to the printed or written work as "the poem" or "the story" or "the play." They knew that the work was more than the black marks on the page, just as a song is more than notes and words on a page. But in practice they combined what critics today refer to as "the text" (the notes and words) and "the poem" (the song). The words on the page represented a stable, objective text that all skilled readers could experience in pretty much the same way. The innovation that New Criticism introduced was to treat that text as an independent, integrated, unified work of art, and to focus attention on the elements that constitute it, examining them through the method of "close reading," sometimes called "explication."

The shift to focusing on the text was motivated in part by a desire to pay more attention to the aesthetic dimension inherent in a work of literary art. But primarily the focus on the text grew out of a desire to affirm and clarify literature as a form of knowledge. To illustrate the methods and value of New Criticism, we will use it to approach "Cherrylog Road," and then we will discuss its theory of knowledge.

Focusing on Form

To clarify this approach we will lead you through a partial reading of "Cherrylog Road" as a New Critic would approach it. As you participate with us, see if you can sense what this approach emphasizes. But first reread the poem (pp. 14–16) to get it fresh in your mind, this time paying particular attention to formal details—the kinds of things covered in Chapters 3–10.

New Critical readings often begin by looking at speaker and situation. In "Cherrylog Road" the speaker has arranged a romantic assignation in an ironically unromantic place, an abandoned junkyard. Such a secretive meeting creates a sense of tension (Will the young woman show up? Will they be discovered?) and of course excitement. It's important also to notice that the assignation took place in the past. The speaker uses past-tense verbs ("I entered," "I changed," and so on) and thus is looking back on an earlier experience, but the act of remembering makes it a new experience as well.

How old the speaker was when the events occurred is not made clear in the poem; he was old enough to drive a motorcycle, but young enough to play make-believe games: as he moves from car to car, he pretends to be a stock-car driver, then a movie star, then a rich older lady. His imagination runs free. That same imagination appears with anxious undertones as he thinks of himself being caught in a gangster-movie scene and gunned down from a speeding car by an enraged father. How old he is when he tells the story and how much time has passed are also not specified, and probably don't matter. What does matter is that he is looking back—nostalgically? a bit ruefully?—from perhaps a number of years later, even a decade or two later, on an afternoon he remembers, and the poem invites us to reflect on what was memorable about it.

New Critical readings pay close attention to imagery—sensory details which enable the reader to identify with the situation and experiences of a poem—and to figurative language. "Cherrylog Road," appropriately, is filled with automobile imagery: the makes of cars that fill the junkyard (Ford, Essex, Chevrolet, Pierce-Arrow) and the parts they are made of, from radiator caps, headlights, spark plugs, bumpers, mirrors, and gear-knobs to rumble seats, interphones, windshields, and seat springs. Although the cars were once filled with life (the speaker passes "through many states, / Many lives" as he goes from car to car), they now have "died"—the junkyard is, figuratively, "the parking lot of the dead." The sun now owns the cars and is metaphorically "eating" their paint. The junkyard is hot, dusty, and except for some crickets, a toad or kingsnake, some sleepy roaches, and some beetles, lifeless—even "the compost has no more life." The blacksnake "dies / Of boredom."

Into the junkyard, that place of death and decay, come the speaker and Doris, vibrant, passionate, and full of life. They enter the oldest car. The speaker "held her and held her and held her," while paradoxically escorted "at terrific speed / By the stalled dreaming traffic." As they cling, "glued together," the speaker and Doris bring life to this place of death, and by their example bring living things to life as well:

> So the blacksnake, stiff
> With inaction, curved back
> Into life, and hunted the mouse   90
>
> With deadly overexcitement.

This sudden enlivening is extended from the couple to the junkyard, as is conveyed by a series of figures of speech: "The hooks of the seat springs / Working through to catch us redhanded / Amidst the gray, breathless batting / That burst from the seat at our backs." For the personified seat springs to catch them red-handed is a reminder of the speaker's fear that Doris's father would discover them and "blast the breath from the air" with a string-triggered 12-gauge shotgun. The gray batting of course can't breathe, but to say that it is "breathless" is a transferred epithet projecting onto the batting their own breathless excitement. An additional transfer, a key one, follows:

> We left by separate doors
> Into the changed, other bodies
> Of cars.   100

The cars have not changed: the two people have. The feeling that things look different to them because of their new experiences is conveyed by projecting the change onto the cars.

The poem captures in imagery and narration what seems to have been the speaker's and Doris's first sexual experience together. The poem, presented from the male speaker's viewpoint, can say little of Doris's response: there is only the reference before they meet to "her lips' new trembling," a trembling not just of her lips but, through synecdoche, of her whole being. All of this, of course, may be a projection of the narrator's own eagerness or expectations, but the poem does imply that both are eager and excited. His response is more explicit. In still another transfer, he feels "fleshed / With power," as when he rides his motorcycle, metaphorically "drunk" not from wind but from sex, excitement. In the final lines the car imagery reaches its fullest effect as the speaker identifies with the cars—he is "Wild to be wreckage forever."

In addition to paying attention to speaker, imagery, and figures, a New Critical reading includes attention to the verse style. As you focus on the verse style of "Cherrylog Road" you'll notice that it is written in six-line stanzas without meter or uniform line length. Rhythm seems crucial, because the varied rhythms reflect the changing emotional experiences within the poem. Instead of writing in stanzas, Dickey could have allowed the poem to evolve without any spaces, or with spaces only between sentences (after lines 13, 25, 29, 44, 48, 53, 75, 81, and 97). Short lines tend toward a rapid rhythm, and without stanza divisions these would have been even faster. The stanzas add a sort of "metric" element to the rhythm, a brief pause at regular intervals.

If you are watching sentences as well as lines, you may notice that the opening thirteen-line sentence is made up of short phrases, often corresponding with lines; we tend to hesitate at the ends of the lines and read deliberately, with an anxious, even suspenseful, feeling of waiting. Lines 15–25 are made up of an eleven-line clause in which phrases carry over from line to line, with little punctuation; in them, the speaker is thinking about Doris Holbrook, and the formal elements may have the effect of helping evoke and embody his growing excitement.

The rhythm seems to speed up in the twenty-two-line sentence beginning at line 54. This sentence not only conveys the speaker's excitement, as he rushes from topic to topic without a pause, but it also leads us to read faster and faster, first through a headlong catalog of details, then through long pell-mell clauses. A similar effect occurs in the thirteen-line clause describing the sexual experience and the eleven-line sentence summing up the speaker's response. The rhythm, reinforced by alliteration, becomes even more rapid and intense:

> Through the acres of wrecks she came
> With a *wrench* in *her hand*,
>
> Through dust where the blacksnake dies
> Of *boredom*, and the *beetle knows*
> The compost has no more life.

80

The rhythm seems to draw us into the action. Even if we have not had this kind of sexual experience, we can share what the experience meant to the speaker.

As the now older speaker reflects back on and describes his experience, he brings out its tensions and conflicts (death versus life, parents versus children) and—consciously, do you think? or unconsciously?—some of its ironies, paradoxes, and juxtapositions: of a potentially life-causing episode occurring dramatically in a dead and decaying setting; of the "terrific speed" (echoed in the poem's rhythm) the couple brought to a place of inaction; of a young man who aspires to be "wreckage" forever. New Criticism seeks to enrich the experience of reading poems by helping readers appreciate the effectiveness of details and touches they might otherwise not notice, and to show that all facets of the poem, as a work of art, work together.

The New Critical Approach

It might be helpful to summarize briefly the assumptions behind the approach we have just been using. It begins by looking closely at various aspects of the poem, to determine how they contribute to the development of the poem's meaning and technique. It pays particular attention to tension, or conflict, which it regards as especially revealing. It assumes that a poem, as a work of art, has an artistic wholeness and integrity. All aspects, therefore—the choice of topic, the dramatic action, the character traits, the tone, the images, the figures, the sounds and rhythms—should, according to New Criticism, work together in a unified and coherent way. And all of them should contribute to conveying the *theme* of the poem (that is, the central "point" of the poem, an "idea" conveyed through experience rather than stated, one that can speak to everyone). If the poem contains a universal theme, conveyed in a complex and subtle manner, enriched by irony and paradox, with a resolution of all tensions, thematic and artistic, at the end, it would, according to New Critical means of evaluation, be an excellent poem.

The New Critics never developed an organized critical system, but running through most of their criticism are a number of common assumptions or principles. These became so well known that for several decades they served almost as "givens" for much of the study and criticism of all types of literature.

Multiple Readings. A New Critic reads a poem repeatedly. For New Criticism, your first reading of a work is less important than later ones, because you do not yet know the whole poem and cannot see how things early in the poem tie in with things further along. As you reread, again and again, you begin to see connections and to grasp the way large and small features relate to each other.

Ideal Reader. New Criticism treats reading as nonproblematic. The process of reading is taken for granted: one just *reads*. This is so partly because most New Critics assume that excellent poetry is written for an "ideal reader." This ideal reader is skilled at recognizing the elements of poetry, is attentive in picking out tones and nuances, is widely read and thus able to recognize literary echoes and allusions, and is knowledgeable about almost everything poets bring into their works. Even though the "ideal reader" may in fact be a composite of many readers—a synthesis of discussions or essays by several or many readers contributing different knowledge and insights—New Criticism implies that any individual reader should strive to do what its "ideal reader" can do. Thus it aims to illustrate how a skilled reader should approach a poem—what a reader should notice in and get from a poem—and to teach others how to be "better" readers themselves.

Emphasis on the Work Itself. For New Criticism, the poem is not dependent on its author or its reader. It is a freestanding work of art, just as a drama, once it is staged, has an existence of its own separate from its author and its audience. What the author *intended* is not relevant, and cannot really be known for sure, even if the author tries to explain. What matters is what the poem *actually* says and does, not what the poet hoped to say or do—the result, not the intention, counts. Nor is response to the poem important for New Criticism. Such emphasis on the text, rather than on intent or effect, was intended to counter the "nonscientific" practices of previous impressionists and historicists; although the New Critics were reacting against the popular adulation of science pervasive at the time, they did want the practices followed by critics to have more of the rigor and discipline the sciences have. Impressions are subjective, and using literature for historical evidence can be arbitrary; New Criticism sought a more objective and organized approach, focusing on the work itself, with its artistry and "theme," as perceived by an "ideal reader"—not on the reaction it creates in an individual, and thus subjective, actual reader.

Attention to Speaker and Conflict. New Critics tend to approach poems as miniature dramas. Two key things a New Critic looks for are clarified by this fact. First is identification of a speaker, or **persona,** in a poem. In a drama, the playwright creates characters who speak for themselves in a created, dramatic situation; one does not (or should not) confuse Macbeth with Shakespeare. So, too, for New Critics, the poet creates an independent speaker who speaks in a minidramatic situation. A second thing one looks for is "conflict" or "tension" in the poem. As conflicts and tensions between characters lie at the heart of a play's action, so for New Criticism "conflicts" or "tensions" or "problems" identify the key issues being dealt with in a poem. A key thing for New Criticism is the resolution of conflicts and tensions, which occurs often through the use of irony or paradox.

Emphasis on Structure and Unity. The central critical concept of New Criticism is structural unity. Earlier critical approaches treated literary works as collections of separable parts (beautiful or meaningful sections would be pulled out and memorized), not as unified wholes. For New Criticism, formal unity is crucial: in critic Cleanth Brooks's words, "The primary concern of criticism is with the problem of unity—the kind of whole which the literary work forms or fails to form, and the relation of the various parts to each other in building up this whole."[3] It is not, however, an interest in form for its own sake, or in form apart from content. The unity sought is ultimately unity of meaning; but meaning, for New Critics, cannot be separated from form. The full meaning of a poem cannot be summarized or paraphrased or expressed in

[3] "The Formalist Critics," *Kenyon Review* 13 (1951): 72.

any other way than the way in which the poem says it. The meaning is contained within the poem, and what the poem says and the way it says it are inseparable. Thus, a New Critic focuses on the structure, the movement of thought or action, the arrangement of parts and details, and the relationships among all of them. As the New Critic considers each of these, she or he always looks for unifying links, especially by discussing metaphors as ways of unifying dissimilar things, and by discussing ironies and paradoxes as ways in which conflicts, tensions, and apparent contradictions can be resolved.

Close Reading. As a central methodological tool, New Criticism borrowed from France a method of teaching literature called *explication de texte.* The word *explicate* comes from Latin roots meaning "to unfold, to give an account of" and means to explain in detail. A key method of New Criticism is to explain the interconnections and "ambiguities" (multiple meanings) within a poem through a detailed, close analysis of its language—the meanings, relationships, and complexities of its words, images, figures, and symbols. New Criticism can be especially useful when it is applied to poems that are rich in verbal subtleties and intricacies. However, a New Critic will put possible subtleties to the test of coherence with the critic's emerging view of the work as a whole. For example, you might notice in "Cherrylog Road" that the words "Pierce-Arrow" have connotations of sharpness, perhaps violence or aggression, and you might even imagine a poem where the poet would do something with these ideas. But, because you do not find anything else in "Cherrylog Road" that draws you in that direction, you decide that dwelling on that possible interpretation of the words would destroy the poem's unity, and thus you drop the idea.

Universality. New Criticism tends to look in literature for issues of significance to all people, in all times—issues of life and relationships, of worth and purpose, issues such as love, aging, death, faith, and doubt. Neither the poet nor the critic is to preach, or to supply answers, but literature does enable the reader to enter the experiences of other people—gaining a special kind of imaginative knowledge, perhaps being affected by what is valued, thought about, felt, and acted upon in the poem, and being reassured by a sense of the shared nature of such experiences.

Evaluation. New Criticism moves, as a final step, toward evaluation of a poem—of its value or success—judged, of course, by the New Critical standards of complexity, unity, verbal subtlety and intricacy, and universal significance. Books outlining New Critical methods often culminate in discussions of "Bad Poetry and Good" and "Knowing Excellence." The implied conclusion is that the reader should learn to discriminate bad from better, and to like the better and not be satisfied with the bad.

The Underlying Theory of Knowledge

To scholars of the humanities in the years between the two world wars and in the immediate postwar period, the methods and attitudes of the sciences and social sciences seemed pervasive. The sciences, according to the founders of New Criticism, dehumanized nature, and even people, through experimental methods—dissecting, analyzing in dispassionate ways. Yet society tended to respect and value the sciences more than it did literature and the arts (and the humanities generally) because the sciences dealt with facts, "reality," and logic. New Critical theory was an attempt to correct that imbalance and enhance the status of literature and the arts. Central to its position was a set of ideas about knowledge and the world that stood in direct contrast to the scientific views it criticized. The foundation of New Critical theory is its claim that poetry has its own kind of knowledge—experiential knowledge conveyed imaginatively, and that this knowledge is superior to the abstract, impersonal knowledge of science. According to Cleanth Brooks and Robert Penn Warren in the preface to the third edition of *Understanding Poetry,*

> Poetry gives us knowledge. It is a knowledge of ourselves in relation to the world of experience, and to that world considered, not statistically, but in terms of human purposes and values. . . . It embodies the human effort to arrive . . . at meaning. . . . Poetry—like all the arts—involves this kind of experiential knowledge.[4]

It is a view of knowledge as "realization," as full awareness in the sense in which we can say, "You don't really know what it is like until you have lived through it."[5] Thus, for New Criticism, images are of enormous importance: the language of poetry is concrete; it deals in details, in particulars—literature does not talk *about* reality but uses images to re-create or evoke or embody reality.

Also of vital importance to the theory underlying New Criticism is its stress on the integrity of works of art in and of themselves. The scientific approach, New Critics believed, had led to fragmentation and "dissociation" in society and even within individuals. In the face of such disintegration, New Criticism emphasized wholeness and unity. Such, they held, were the pervasive "themes" of literature: literature offers a hope of wholeness, of a "unified sensibility" combining intellect and feeling, of redemption from the disintegration—the division, specialization, and alienation—that science had inflicted on the modern world.

For the New Critic, it is vital to show respect for poems in and of themselves: "As science more and more completely reduces the world to its types and forms," the poet and critic John Crowe Ransom has written, "art, replying, must invest it again with body." Critics must "approach the object [work of art or object in nature] as such, and in humility"[6] (Ransom, p. 124), not imposing their own programs on it, as they felt science did all too often.

Recently the critical pendulum has swung the other way and New Critics have come under attack for being overly analytical, for treating literature impersonally as mere object. Such attacks are ironic, when New Criticism is con-

---

[4] New York: Holt, Rinehart, 1960, xiii.
[5] René Wellek, "The New Criticism: Pro and Contra," *Critical Inquiry* 4 (1978): 619.
[6] *The World's Body* (Port Washington, N.Y.: Kennikat Press, 1938), 198.

sidered in historical context. Actually its theory opposed analysis and reduction of things to objects, and aimed, instead, to increase the humaneness and concern for art and values in society. It is in that context that New Critics put emphasis on the literary work as an object—not a lifeless object, or one killed by dissection, or one isolated from reality, but one full of life, whose vital richness is to be enjoyed and enhanced by respectful attention.

> Forty years ago, when I was in school, we used to think of poems as self-contained objects, detachable from their time and even their authors, as a piece of gold jewelry from King Tut's tomb might be set beside a pre-Columbian Mexican necklace and a contemporary comb from Japan. There would be differences in pattern, of course, but beyond those differences an excellence in design and execution would be unmistakable, separating those pieces from the careless stuff you might dig up in Woolworth's.
>
> —Conrad Hilberry

Now try this approach yourself. If you want to read another example first, you might go to a student's reading of "Saint Pumpkin" by Nancy Willard, done primarily from a New Critical approach, in Appendix B, "Responding on Paper."

Some poems are better suited to New Critical readings than others. Poems with a complex style—poems that are rich in ambiguity and verbal complexity—work better than ones with a more straightforward style, or ones without closure. Here are some poems you could practice on. The first was written in England in the mid-1600s, one of many short, intricately woven poems from that era that the founders of New Criticism especially liked. A word of caution: don't assume that the word "mistress" necessarily has the same meaning we give it today when we say a man has a mistress. The *OED* (remember it? See Chapter 3, page 39, if you need a reminder) offers alternative definitions, which you might consider (including "a woman who has command over a man's heart; a woman who is loved and courted by a man; a sweetheart"). Some of the style and language may seem a bit difficult initially, because the poem was written over 300 years ago, but the subject of the poem is still current—a man trying to convince a woman to have sex with him. See if a New Critical approach, giving attention to speaker, conflict, images, figures, rhythm, sound, structure, unity, and universality, may enrich your reading of the poem.

ANDREW MARVELL (1621–1678)

To His Coy Mistress (ca. 1650)

Had we but world enough, and time,
This coyness, lady, were no crime.
We would sit down, and think which way
To walk, and pass our long love's day.
Thou by the Indian Ganges' side   5
Shouldst rubies find; I by the tide
Of Humber would complain. I would
Love you ten years before the Flood,
And you should, if you please, refuse
Till the conversion of the Jews.   10
My vegetable love should grow
Vaster than empires, and more slow;
An hundred years should go to praise
Thine eyes, and on thy forehead gaze;
Two hundred to adore each breast,   15
But thirty thousand to the rest;
An age at least to every part,
And the last age should show your heart.
For, lady, you deserve this state,
Nor would I love at lower rate.   20
      But at my back I always hear
Time's wingèd chariot hurrying near;
And yonder all before us lie
Deserts of vast eternity.
Thy beauty shall no more be found,   25
Nor, in thy marble vault, shall sound
My echoing song; then worms shall try
That long-preserved virginity,
And your quaint honour turn to dust,
And into ashes all my lust: 30
The grave's a fine and private place,
But none, I think, do there embrace.
      Now therefore, while the youthful hue
Sits on thy skin like morning dew,
And while thy willing soul transpires   35
At every pore with instant fires,
Now let us sport us while we may,
And now, like amorous birds of prey,
Rather at once our time devour
Than languish in his slow-chapped power.   40

Let us roll all our strength and all
Our sweetness up into one ball,
And tear our pleasures with rough strife
Thorough the iron gates of life;
Thus, though we cannot make our sun   45
Stand still, yet we will make him run.

RICHARD WILBUR (b. 1921)

Year's End (1950)

Now winter downs the dying of the year,
And night is all a settlement of snow;
From the soft street the rooms of houses show
A gathered light, a shapen atmosphere,
Like frozen-over lakes whose ice is thin   5
And still allows some stirring down within.

I've known the wind by water banks to shake
The late leaves down, which frozen where they fell
And held in ice as dancers in a spell
Fluttered all winter long into a lake;   10
Graved on the dark in gestures of descent,
They seemed their own most perfect monument.

There was perfection in the death of ferns
Which laid their fragile cheeks against the stone
A million years. Great mammoths overthrown   15
Composedly have made their long sojourns,
Like palaces of patience, in the gray
And changeless lands of ice. And at Pompeii

The little dog lay curled and did not rise
But slept the deeper as the ashes rose   20
And found the people incomplete, and froze
The random hands, the loose unready eyes
Of men expecting yet another sun
To do the shapely thing they had not done.

These sudden ends of time must give us pause.   25
We fray into the future, rarely wrought
Save in the tapestries of afterthought.
More time, more time. Barrages of applause
Come muffled from a buried radio.
The New-year bells are wrangling with the snow.   30

ROBERTA HILL WHITEMAN (b. 1947)

The White Land (1984)

When Orion straddled his apex of sky,
over the white land we lingered loving.
The River Eridanus flickered, foretelling
tropical waves and birds arrayed
in feathers of sunset, but we didn't waste   5
that prickling dark.

Not a dog barked our arrival before dawn.
Only in sleep did I drift vagabond
and suffer the patterns that constantly state
time has no time. Fate is a warlord.   10
That morning I listened to your long breath
for decades.

That morning you said bears
fell over the white land. Leaving their lair
in thick polar fur, they roused our joy   15
by leaving no footprint. Fat ones fell headlong,
but most of them danced, then without quarrel,
balanced on branches.

I couldn't breathe in the roar of that plane,
flying me back to a wooded horizon.   20
Regular rhythms bridge my uneven sleep.
What if the wind in the white land keeps you?
The dishwater's luminous; a truck
grinds down the street.

THE TEXT AND PSYCHOANALYTIC CRITICISM

A New Critic, like a biographical critic, can make use of psychoanalytic criticism. But the interest for the New Critic shifts from using it as a way of better understanding the author to using it as a way of better understanding the text and the characters depicted in the text. Read this poem and jot down some of the questions that are in your mind when you finish:

DAVID RAY (b. 1932)

Greens (1965)

A boy stoops, picking greens with his mother—
This is the scene in the great elm-shadows.
A pail stands by her feet, her dress conceals
Her chill knees, made bitter by the tall man

Who now lifts a glass, she thinks, with his friends,   5
Or worse, seeks a younger love in the town
While she with her fading muslin aprons
And her dented tin pail seeks greens, always
Greens, and wins, with her intermittent sighs,
Sympathy, love forever from the boy.   10
He does not know, this sharp-boned boy who bends
To his mother, that he has been seduced
Already, that he has known anguish, bliss
Of sex—as much as he will ever know.
He does not know, here in the bees' shadow,   15
He has become the tall and angry man,
The husband wounding the woman who bends,
Sighs and is ecstatic in her clutching
Of sons—bending, dark of brow, by her pail,
Stooped, brushing back the long, complaining strands   20
Of her hair. She is now too proud to weep,
But not to read the law, to reap greens, greens
Forever in her small, pathetic pail.

If you began in reader-response fashion, you perhaps started by wondering who the boy is, how old he is, why he is helping his mother, who "the tall man" is, and why he is angry. We do not receive specific answers to such questions, but if we pay close attention to the text it seems pretty clear that the man is the woman's husband, the father of the boy, and that the marital relationship is badly strained: she is "bitter" and has been "wounded" while he is off drinking or seeking "a younger love." But the poem deals more with the relationship between mother and son than with that between wife and husband, and that too should raise questions. Why that focus? And why does she react the way she does? Why does she win "with her intermittent sighs, / Sympathy, love forever from the boy"? The next few lines sound incestuous: "He does not know, this sharp-boned boy who bends / To his mother, that he has been seduced / Already." Are the lines in fact incestuous? In what sense has he "become the tall and angry man"?

Answering such questions requires that we look below the surface of the description, deeper into the situation of the woman and her son, even into emotions and motives they themselves are not conscious of. When line 12 says that the boy has been seduced, the context makes it seem to be an emotional, rather than a physical, seduction. Emotionally seduced how? And why does he not know? The woman, as she realizes she is losing her husband, begins to compensate. For social and cultural reasons, probably, she cannot, like her husband, develop a new relationship with an adult to replace the one she is losing. Instead, probably without realizing it, she transfers her need for affection to her son (or sons, line 19 suggests). Her sadness and sighs are evident to the boy; line 20 indicates that she has been complaining about her situation, probably in his hearing. The mother thus uses his pity to win his allegiance, his support, his "Sympathy, love forever." He does not realize that his feelings are being manipulated, that he is being "seduced" into an unhealthy kind of "love."

With his mother dependent on him and on his affection, he will never be free of her, of "her clutching / Of sons." Thus he has become his father, "has become the tall and angry man," as substitute for his father in his mother's life. Because he is emotionally "married" to his mother, he will have difficulty establishing a satisfactory sexual relationship with another adult. He, like his father, will feel anger, and will probably lash out at his mother. Unlike his father, however, he will be unable to escape her (or the guilt he will feel if eventually he does try to break away by leaving her). The "greens" of the title moves from an image (denotatively "the leaves and stems of certain plants, such as spinach, kale, or lettuce, eaten as a vegetable") to a symbol—a symbol of the hope she continually, sadly, pathetically seeks by clutching onto her boys.

The poem explores feelings, actions, needs, motives, and responses that lie below the conscious awareness of the boy and the mother. Engaging with the poem requires that we begin to analyze and speculate about what is going on below the surface—that we do a psychological analysis of the characters described in the work. In doing so from a textual vantage point, we have not raised any questions about the author; for New Critics, whether the poem has a biographical basis or not is immaterial. Whatever his motivation or the source of his materials or ideas may have been, the poet has created a work of art that now has an existence independent of him. It is on the poem as an artistic work that we must concentrate. From a strict New Criticism perspective, the author in a sense disappears, or ceases to be an issue of interest or concern.

DECONSTRUCTION

Throughout our discussion of New Criticism, the focus was on the unity and wholeness of a literary work. As you experimented with that approach, you may have felt some inner resistance. It's fine for New Critics to want stability, wholeness, unity, coherence, but that's not necessarily the way life is; the way we read poems should be able to reflect that, too. That indeed is the assumption of the approach to which we turn next.

Structuralism

The approach as a whole is called "poststructuralism." Getting into it requires that we begin with a brief digression, to summarize what it grew out of: another approach—a nontextual approach—called **structuralism.** Just as New Criticism reacted against the increasing emphasis in society on science, structuralism was, in part, a reaction against the "humanistic," "unscientific" basis of New Criticism. New Criticism, with its textual emphasis, concentrates on specific works; it doesn't step back and see the big picture. It asks how an individual poem or story works, but not how poetry or narrative as a whole works. For structuralists, this would be like studying an individual plant or animal, but not being concerned about the systems by which plants and animals function. Structuralists want literary studies, using the same approach as biology or chemistry or physics, to deal with the overall picture—with the "structure" of literature as a whole, of which individual works are only examples.

As a basis for this science, structuralists turned to linguistics. In the late 1800s, French linguist Ferdinand de Saussure developed a new approach to the study of language. He made a distinction between *langue* (the language system) and *parole* (specific things people say). He made *langue* the object of linguistic study; linguists look at *parole* only to find examples from which to discover the system of rules, the grammar, that governs the whole system of language. He also eliminated from his approach the assumption that words are symbols corresponding to things in the world. He held that words are "signs," made up of two parts: the "signifier" (the mark on the page) and the "signified" (the "thought" that occurs when the mark is made). The connection between signifier and signified is arbitrary: a sign communicates because users of the sign agree about what it means, not because of a "natural" connection between a sign and a thing. Thus many societies agree that a red traffic light signals "stop" and a green one signals "go"—but it could have been the other way around, or other colors could have been used.

In terms of an overall system, then, red lights and green lights do not signify something because of anything inherent in themselves, but only (Saussure's key point) through *difference*. A system creates opposites and contrasts: traffic-light "red" is "not-green" and "green" is "not-red."[7] We recognize *dog*, linguistically, because it is different from *frog*, and *log*, and *dung*. And we are able to recognize difference because of the underlying system of *binary oppositions*: we recognize *phonemes*, the smallest elements in the language system, as distinct units of sound—not meaningful in their own right, but different from other sounds. Such bipartite structures become important factors in our systems of knowing, generally.

At the heart of structuralism is a *scientific* ambition to discover the codes, the rules, the systems, that underlie all human social and cultural practices (Selden, p. 69), including those of literature. Structuralists seek "to establish a model of the system of literature itself"; as Saussure turned linguistics into a "science," so literary structuralists seek "to establish for literary studies a basis that is as scientific as possible."[8] Structuralist studies identify the basic units (by analogy, the "phonemes") of the system of literary expression, and then lay out the "grammar" of its "syntactical" system. All of this has implications regarding "author" and "reader." The author of a work is of no importance for structuralists. To them, an individual work is a recombination of "literary phonemes" according to "literary syntax"; literature is made of earlier litera-

---

[7] The example is from Raman Selden, *A Reader's Guide to Contemporary Literary Theory* (Lexington: University Press of Kentucky, 1985), 54. Selden provides clear summaries of structuralism and other theoretical approaches, and helpful bibliographies, for those who want to read further in this area.

[8] Robert Scholes, *Structuralism in Literature: An Introduction* (New Haven, Conn.: Yale University Press, 1974), 10.

ture; every text arises from what was "already written." The individual person who does the writing is not important; the important thing is to look at the rules and conventions *that led the individual* to put things together as he or she did. The interest in readers, for structuralists, is in *how* readers are able to negotiate codes and conventions and make literary sense. For this approach, the reader is not "free," any more than the author is: the structures in the text determine the response the reader will make. That raises the question of what the reader needs to bring in order to respond to the structures: Who is "the reader"? Although different labels are used—from "superreader" to "virtual reader" to "ideal reader" to "real reader"—structuralists always have to assume a reader who is informed, to some extent at least, about the conventions she or he is involved in "decoding."

Poststructuralism

Structuralism as an approach and a philosophy attained widespread influence and, in Europe, became intellectually and politically oppressive. Carried to its extreme, structuralism claims that all actions are predetermined: structures and conventions force all human actions in unalterable directions. A reaction set in against its claims, influenced especially by French philosophers Jacques Derrida and Michel Foucault and French critic Roland Barthes. The reaction is referred to broadly as **poststructuralism,** though we will concentrate mostly on one variety of it, **deconstruction.** At the heart of poststructuralism is rejection of the stability of signification that is implied by the effort to develop structuralism as a science. Saussure separated the signifier and the signified and said that the theoretical relation between them is arbitrary, but he allowed in practice for the possibility that some signifiers and signifieds could form unified signs and thus create a stability of meaning and concept. Poststructuralists, as Selden puts it, pry apart the two parts of the sign; they assert the total separation of signified and signifier and thus the complete instability of meaning.

You might want to protest at this point that meanings *are* stable: they are in the dictionary. You look up a word and its meaning is written down. But look again at what you just said (or at what we said you might want to say): when you look up a word in a dictionary, you actually find what its *meanings are*. The signifier *deck*, for example, has a whole range of possible signifieds:

deck (dek), *n., v.,* **decked, deck·ing.** —*n.* **1. a.** a floorlike surface wholly or partially occupying one level of a hull, superstructure, or deckhouse of a vessel. **b.** the space between such a surface and the next such surface above. **2.** a platform, surface, or level suggesting the deck of a ship. **3.** an open, unroofed porch or platform extending from a house or other building. **4.** the roadway of a bridge. **5.** a pack of playing cards. **6.** a cassette deck or tape deck. **7.** *Slang.* a small packet of a narcotic, esp. heroin. —*v.t.* **8.** to clothe or array in something dressy or festive (often fol. by *out*): *all decked out for the party.* **9.** to furnish with a deck. **10.** *Informal.* to knock down; floor. —*Idiom.* **11. clear the decks, a.** to prepare for combat, as by removing all unnecessary gear. **b.** to prepare for some activity or work. **12. hit the deck, a.** to fall or drop to the floor or ground. **b.** to get out of bed. **13. on deck, a.** present and ready to act or work. **b.** *Baseball.* next at bat. [1425–75; late ME *dekke* material for covering < MD *dec* covering, roof; cf. THATCH]

Poststructuralists assert, in reply to structuralists, that meaning is not determined just by difference (*deck* is different from *duck*). In determining what *deck* means in a particular usage, *context*—the parts of the sentence or paragraph surrounding the word—also is important. And ascertaining context often involves time—one cannot tell what meaning a word has until one has gone past it and determined the context. The phrase "the cleanup man is on deck" could lead into "waiting his turn at bat" or "polishing the brass railings." The meaning of both "cleanup man" and "deck" is in flux, or is "suspended" or "deferred," until one reads on to the end of the sentence. At the heart of poststructuralism is this sense of fluidity between words and meanings, between signifier and signified. The act of reading, therefore, must be responsive to such *flux* and *imprecision;* the reader must expect doubleness, contradiction, and discrepancy ("the cleanup man rubs a handful of dirt on his bat") and must adjust to them, treat them playfully, jostle meanings out of them, rather than attempting to force resolution and coherent unity on them.

In the following poem, "The Base Stealer," watch how meaning depends on context. The title by itself does not make clear whether to read "base" as an adjective (morally low, contemptible) or as part of a compound noun (someone who steals bases); and even if you were sure that it was the latter, "base" could mean that what is being stolen is "the bottom support on which a thing rests or stands" or "the foundation on which something rests" or "any of the four corners on a baseball diamond." Until you get *into the poem* and the *context* clarifies, you cannot be sure.

ROBERT FRANCIS (1901–1987)

The Base Stealer (1960)

Poised between going on and back, pulled
Both ways taut like a tightrope-walker,
Fingertips pointing the opposites,
Now bouncing tiptoe like a dropped ball
Or a kid skipping rope, come on, come on,   5
Running a scattering of steps sidewise,
How he teeters, skitters, tingles, teases,
Taunts them, hovers like an ecstatic bird,
He's only flirting, crowd him, crowd him,
Delicate, delicate, delicate, delicate—now!   10

An important part of the doubleness and playfulness of language involves the *traces* all words carry with them from uses in other contexts. The dictionary definition of "on deck" is "present and ready to act or work." Etymologically "deck" means a cover or roof, like a thatched roof on a cottage. The deck of a ship is the cover over the lower part, and "all hands on deck" means that the entire crew is to go up to the deck area ready to help as needed. Deconstruction holds that a word's etymology and earlier uses carry over into later uses—which takes us back to Chapter 3 and the importance of using dictionaries to get to know words thoroughly. In some cases the "trace" a word carries with it can be strikingly different from its primary meaning in a particular context. The alternative "traces" often create a playful situation—batter as sailor, swabber of decks, cleaning the bases. The meanings play off against one another, begging to be resolved but incapable of resolution. That may frequently be the outcome of deconstructive readings, and it may seem somewhat frustrating, even unsettling. However, it also may open up interdependencies, issues, and relationships that have gone unattended, leading to both a challenging reading and an alternative vision.

Look at "The Base Stealer" again. If you decide that baseball is its primary focus, think about whether traces of the other possibilities carry over and interact with the "primary" meaning and perhaps create additional meanings.

Elements and Procedures of Deconstruction

Any definition of **deconstruction** is inadequate—the theory is too encompassing and diverse for tidy definition. *Webster's College Dictionary* (Random House) describes it as "a theory of textual analysis positing that a text has no stable reference and questioning assumptions about the ability of language to represent reality." In practice, deconstruction is textual in approach. Deconstructive readings pay close attention to the text of a poem—as close as, or even closer than, New Criticism does. Watch deconstruction in action as we discuss the following poem; then we will explain and discuss the process briefly. Archibald MacLeish's "Ars Poetica" (or, The Art of Poetry; the phrase comes from the title of a theoretical work by the Latin poet Horace) is a famous manifesto for "imagist" poetry, a school of writers who wanted poetry to rely as much as possible on images.

ARCHIBALD MACLEISH (1892–1982)

Ars Poetica (1926)

A poem should be palpable and mute
As a globed fruit,

Dumb
As old medallions to the thumb,

Silent as the sleeve-worn stone   5
Of casement ledges where the moss has grown—

A poem should be wordless
As the flight of birds.
                              *

A poem should be motionless in time
As the moon climbs,   10

Leaving, as the moon releases
Twig by twig the night-entangled trees,

Leaving, as the moon behind the winter leaves,
Memory by memory the mind—

A poem should be motionless in time   15
As the moon climbs.
                    *

A poem should be equal to:
Not true.

For all the history of grief
An empty doorway and a maple leaf.   20

For love
The leaning grasses and two lights above the sea—

A poem should not mean
But be.

Initially, and taken at face value, the poem seems clear. It makes us want to agree strongly that poems "should not mean / But be." Upon a closer look, however, we may conclude that the poem does not *do* what it *says:* though it asserts *being,* it relies on *meaning.*

Before exploring that contradiction, some background may be useful. The surface meaning of the poem rests on an attitude toward "writing" deeply ingrained in Western thought. From at least as far back as Socrates, Western thought has been suspicious of "putting things into words" (that is, of "writing" in its broadest sense, to include thinking and speaking in words as well as putting words on paper). What we "put into words," the traditional attitude holds, is an inadequate reflection of "pure," unverbalized reason. "Putting an idea into words" is a step away from the "pure idea" (which supposedly exists before a mind converts it into words); saying words aloud is a further step away, and writing them down is a further step yet. The written word is secondary, an imitation of the spoken word; it does not require the presence of the writer, and it can be recopied or printed, and thus interpreted and reinterpreted, and possibly distorted in the process.

A close look at "Ars Poetica" suggests that such an attitude toward "writing" lies behind the poem. What the imagist craves is a poem free of words: "A poem should be wordless / As the flight of birds." At the heart of the poem is a binary opposition, words versus actual existence, with actual existence being preferred, or "privileged," over words.

That priority is accorded on the assumption that objects and existence are more "objective" and stable than words, because words need to be "interpreted" and existence doesn't: it simply "is." In words, the closest things to objects are images that call to mind external reality. Thus a poem consisting of pure images would be the ideal: it would simply show us "things," and the "things" would create an experience or emotion without the artificial intervention of reading. But presenting "things" in themselves does not in fact escape the problem. Even if we were presented with "An empty doorway and a maple leaf" without words, as physical objects or visual images of them, we would need to "read" them. We do not read just words and books; we "read" everything—people, and situations, and objects. The old saying "I can read you like a book" says more than its originator probably suspected. "Everything is a text," even ourselves.

In the binary pair "words/objects," then, the two are not just opposite to each other, in a stable relationship, with the latter being more important than the former. Words and objects are similar as well as different: objects, like words, must be "interpreted"—there is no escape from "reading." In fact, looked at this "new" way, the hierarchy reverses itself—words give us a truer image of "reality" than objects, because words acknowledge up front that their significance is created by a reader. But words have a kind of doubleness—they look outward and inward at the same time; they both represent and express. Thus, "reading" is also "writing" (again, in its broadest sense): the reader "composes" the "real poem," "constructs" what "An empty doorway and a maple leaf" convey. "Ars Poetica" exemplifies an unstable relationship. Language, in its characteristic playfulness and its doubleness, breaks down the opposition between reader and writer and identifies them with each other.

New Criticism would seek a way to resolve these contradictions, perhaps by celebrating MacLeish's cleverness in asserting through words that images are better than words and by demonstrating, ironically, that images in poetry are made up of words. Deconstruction says the discrepancy should not be so readily argued away. It is, in fact, a signal that something different is going on here from what MacLeish presumably thought he was conveying. The poem makes us aware of the role of *the reader* in the "art of poetry" (to translate the poem's title). The reader, as well as the poet, "writes" the poem. The poet, as well as the reader, must "read" the things he or she experiences. What the poem actually "says," therefore, goes far beyond its surface statements. Its ironies and contradictions (whether intended or not by the author) become part of what it "is about," when the reader "teases" out all its complexity and contradictoriness.

Deconstruction represents a challenge not just to established linguistic assumptions but also to the logical principles on which the thinking of the Western world since Socrates has been based. Fundamental to Western logic, for example, is the law of noncontradiction; that is, "A" is not the same as "not A." That law necessarily makes "A" and "not A" into a pair, different from and opposing each other. Such binary oppositions are basic to structuralism (p. 236) but, more than that, have become deeply embedded in Western thought: as we try to define words by differentiation, so we also try to understand things by thinking of them in pairs that differentiate them. For example.

conscious / unconscious
being / nonbeing
reality / image
reason / intuition
right / wrong
thing / sign
speech / writing

Western thinking, from the Greeks on, has favored (or privileged) the left side of this list over the right side. Such privileging reflects the classical, or Hellenic (Greek), influence on Western philosophy, with its love of order, clarity, reason, and logic. A key aspect of deconstruction is to challenge that impulse to divide and stratify. According to deconstructionists, things are not always separate and opposed; they can be different without being opposed and they can be interdependent and interactive. Light and dark illustrate such complementarity: they are different but also interdependent, since each exists because of the other. Difference alone is inadequate. We know each by relation to its opposite. Here is the heart of deconstruction as a critical approach.

> Modality is always about relationships. It is also about energy, true only unto itself, which means that a mode is perceived in a noncomparative context. The Cartesian analogical way of looking at the world will not do for modality. A mode is true only unto itself and can be understood only inside the modality. So that when one gets into a heavy schizophrenic method of analysis, that is, discursive thought, the Western orientation of division between denotation–connotation, body–soul, life–spirit, soul–body, mind–heart—that is a way of misunderstanding what modality is. Modality is always about unity. The point that I want to make is oneness, unity.
>
> —MICHAEL S. HARPER

The discussion of "Ars Poetica" illustrates the way a "deconstructive critic" might read the poem. Earlier in this chapter, in discussing New Criticism, we laid out a series of steps you could follow in order to do a New Critical reading. We can't do the same here, because deconstruction is not a critical *method,* the way New Criticism is. Rather, it is a philosophical approach, a way of thinking. We can suggest, however, a few elements that are common to most deconstructive readings. One is looking very closely at language, being alert to traces and doubleness, and being open to playfulness, as illustrated in our brief discussion of "The Base Stealer." Another common element is picking out key binary oppositions, identifying which term in those oppositions is being privileged (given preference), and showing how such privileging imposes an interpretive template on the subject being examined. Another element of deconstruction is watching for inconsistencies in the apparent unity and stability of the poem, as exposed by gaps (comparing what is privileged and what is passed over, or "marginalized") and by inconsistencies created by figurative language. A final typical element is displacement: not just inverting the hierarchy but destabilizing it and then moving it to a larger and more encompassing context. Thus, after exposing the hierarchy of objects and experience over words and reading in "Ars Poetica," a deconstructive reading must not just reverse the hierarchy, but must displace the oppositions into a new context, showing that experience is reading, that there is no escape from interpretation to "pure experiencing" of objects.

The Self-Referentiality of Texts

The dictionary definition on page 239 says that deconstruction questions assumptions about the ability of language to represent reality. The point here can be clarified by contrast with New Criticism. New Criticism views literature as "imaging" or "reflecting" reality outside itself; that is the basis of its theory of knowledge. Just as things in the world are held to be real and to "possess" their own significance, so New Criticism believes that meaning, a meaning that most people can agree on, is present in the literary work as an integral part of it.

For deconstruction a literary work does not *reflect* reality; rather, works *create* their own reality. "Meaning" is not *present* in the work, but is an *absence*, filled by the reader in the act of reading. "Presence" and "absence" are central considerations in deconstruction. One reason for the traditional privileging of speaking over writing is that the voice gives an illusion of presence—the presence of another speaker or even of oneself. To quote Terry Eagleton, "My spoken words seem immediately present to my consciousness, and my voice becomes their intimate, spontaneous medium. In writing, by contrast, my meanings threaten to escape from my control."[9] As deconstruction asserts the absence of presence, it simultaneously undermines the "presence" of "self" as an independent, self-possessed being able to create meanings and to control language in order to express them fully.

Deconstruction has proved controversial in part because of its direct challenge to "first principles," or "objectivism." Western philosophy, in addition to being "phonocentric" (speech-centered), has also been "logocentric" (word-centered), relying on a belief in a *logos*, in—as Eagleton puts it—some ultimate "word," presence, essence, truth, or reality that will act as the foundation of all our thought, language, and experience. Various possibilities have been held to be the "transcendental signifier"—God, the Idea, the World Spirit, the Self. Eagleton explains that a consequence of the theory of language on which deconstruction rests—the impossibility of stability and fixity, the impossibility of unqualified "presence"—is that any such transcendental meaning is a fiction. There is nothing knowable outside the signifying system upon which the system can rest. Any attempt to hold to an external, transcendental meaning can be deconstructed, can be shown to be "the products of a particular system of meaning, rather than what props it up from the outside" (Eagleton,

---

[9] *Literary Theory: An Introduction* (Minneapolis: University of Minnesota Press, 1983), 130.

p. 133). In literary terms, one cannot go outside the text—to the author's intentions, or to the text's referentiality to the outside world—to determine its signification. The text is "self-referential": only by looking closely at it, at its full range of interplay and implication, can we determine its signification.

. . .

Try deconstructing one or more of the following poems. You might begin by looking closely at the language, watching for doubleness and traces of meanings from other contexts. Then you might identify and list binary oppositions. Ask yourself: Are oppositions important in the poem? Is one member of a binary set preferred over the other? What is suggested in the preference? Are contradictions exposed by focusing on the oppositions? Do the contradictions point toward complementarity where the poem assumed opposition? Are underlying contradictions present in the choice of figurative language? If so, does any or all of this destabilize what might at first seem a unified and coherent meaning? How might the oppositions be displaced into a larger context?

In the first poem, for example, the central binary opposition seems to be honor/love. Look for other oppositions in the poem that relate to this one. Consider which side of the opposition is privileged in the poem. As you look over your list of binary pairs, do you find incompatibilities or contradictions? Consider the use of binary oppositions as an argumentative method in the poem—as one side of an implied binary opposition: What has been left out, or marginalized? Does that suggest other contradictions or incompatibilities? What is suggested by the choices of figures (such as war as a mistress)? Look up words (like "unkind," "chaste," "embrace," "inconstancy," "honor") and watch for traces. Do you sense a destabilization of the argument developed in the poem? If so, how might the oppositions and argument be displaced into a different context?

RICHARD LOVELACE (1618–1657)

To Lucasta, Going to the Wars (1649)

Tell me not, Sweet, I am unkind,
    That from the nunnery
Of thy chaste breast and quiet mind
    To war and arms I fly.

True, a new mistress now I chase,   5
    The first foe in the field;
And with a stronger faith embrace
    A sword, a horse, a shield.

Yet this inconstancy is such
    As you too shall adore;   10
I could not love thee, Dear, so much,
    Loved I not honor more.

WILLIAM WORDSWORTH (1770–1850)

She Was a Phantom of Delight (1807)

She was a phantom of delight
When first she gleamed upon my sight;
A lovely apparition, sent
To be a moment's ornament;
Her eyes as stars of twilight fair;   5
Like twilight's, too, her dusky hair;
But all things else about her drawn
From May-time and the cheerful dawn;
A dancing shape, an image gay,
To haunt, to startle, and way-lay.   10

I saw her upon nearer view,
A spirit, yet a woman too!
Her household motions light and free,
And steps of virgin-liberty;
A countenance in which did meet   15
Sweet records, promises as sweet;
A creature not too bright or good
For human nature's daily food;
For transient sorrows, simple wiles,
Praise, blame, love, kisses, tears, and smiles.   20

And now I see with eye serene
The very pulse of the machine;
A being breathing thoughtful breath,
A traveler between life and death;
The reason firm, the temperate will,   25
Endurance, foresight, strength, and skill;
A perfect woman, nobly planned,
To warn, to comfort, and command;
And yet a spirit still, and bright
With something of angelic light.   30

ELIZABETH BARRETT BROWNING (1806–1861)

How Do I Love Thee? Let Me Count the Ways (1850)

How do I love thee? Let me count the ways.
I love thee to the depth and breadth and height
My soul can reach, when feeling out of sight
For the ends of Being and ideal Grace.
I love thee to the level of everyday's   5
Most quiet need, by sun and candlelight.
I love thee freely, as men strive for Right;

I love thee purely, as they turn from Praise.
I love thee with the passion put to use
In my old griefs, and with my childhood's faith.   10
I love thee with a love I seemed to lose
With my lost saints—I love thee with the breath,
Smiles, tears, of all my life!—and, if God choose,
I shall but love thee better after death.

JOSEPHINE MILES (1911–1985)

On Inhabiting an Orange (1935)

All our roads go nowhere.
Maps are curled
To keep the pavement definitely
On the world.

All our footsteps, set to make   5
Metric advance,
Lapse into arcs in deference
To circumstance.

All our journeys nearing Space
Skirt it with care,   10
Shying at the distances
Present in air.

Blithely travel-stained and worn,
Erect and sure,
All our travelers go forth,   15
Making down the roads of Earth
Endless detour.

APPLICATIONS FOR CHAPTER 12

SUGGESTIONS FOR WRITING

1. In your journal, record several issues concerning texts that you see as be-
   ing involved as you shape your personal approach to literature. Include
   your reactions to New Criticism and deconstruction.
2. In your journal, describe your initial reactions to the approaches de-
   scribed in this chapter, and give your reflections on which approaches at
   this point you regard as more congenial and helpful. Come back to this
   entry after discussing the chapter in class, and then a week or two from
   now, to reevaluate what you said.
3. Choose a poem from pages 231–33 or from the anthology, and write a pa-
   per discussing it from a New Critical perspective. Some poems work bet-
   ter than others for this sort of reading. Think through your choice of

poem carefully—perhaps check it with your instructor—before you begin writing.

4. Apply New Criticism to something outside literature—a painting or sculpture, a piece of music, a TV sitcom, a commercial. How does it work? What does it help you consider?

5. The discussion of "Ars Poetica" and its attitude toward writing takes us back to the discussion in Chapter 1 about what poetry is. Reread Heather McHugh's "What He Thought" (p. 9). Does it mean more to you now, in the light of what you have experienced in reading poetry and what you read about deconstruction in this chapter? What does "That is how / he died; without a word" and "poetry is what / he thought, but did not say" suggest to you now? Write a journal entry or short paper exploring it.

6. Write a paper doing a deconstructive reading of one of the poems on pages 244–46.

7. Try deconstructing something other than a poem—a television show, an advertisement, a test, your campus, a letter. Write a paper on what you discovered.

8. Create a dialogue in which a New Critic and a deconstructionist discuss the same poem, and compare their differing ways of approaching it.

SUGGESTIONS AS YOU CONTINUE TO READ POETRY

1. Be alert to ways that New Critical methods (such as thinking of a poem as a self-contained work of art, looking closely at the poetic elements in it, noticing conflicts and tensions, and being alert to irony and paradox as ways of resolving them and thus attaining unity and coherence) can open up a particular poem.

2. Be alert for ways that psychoanalytic methods and insights might prove helpful in understanding characters and actions in a poem.

3. Watch for binary oppositions and test them (and figurative language) for contradictions and inconsistencies; try displacing oppositions into a larger context and playfully "teasing" out the richness and complexity of the poem.

13 | Readers

The primary emphasis in the opening sections of this book was on the role of readers—on their participation in all elements and aspects of poetry as a necessary ingredient in processing and reacting to its forms and structures. Because Chapter 2 explained the methods and procedures typical of reader-oriented approaches, in this chapter we will focus on the theory behind such procedures, to explain some variations in outlook among different reader-oriented approaches, and to discuss some practical problems they raise. There are, in fact, many varieties of **reader-response** criticism, with different theories and terminologies. What they have in common is their attention to the process of reading—to how readers make meaning.

The roots of reader-response criticism go back to the 1930s, when it developed as a reaction to historical and biographical approaches that gave little consideration to the role of the reader. A comparative literature professor, Louise Rosenblatt, began developing a reader-response theory just about the time New Criticism was emerging. However, New Criticism became better known and more widely accepted, and it dominated the field for several decades, while Rosenblatt's work was neglected. Interest in the reader re-emerged in the 1960s, as a reaction against New Criticism's emphasis on the text and its neglect of the reader, and has become popular and influential, especially as a classroom approach.

THE NATURE OF "THE READER"

One theoretical issue with which reader-oriented approaches must deal involves the question of what is meant by "the reader." Throughout Chapters 2–10, we tried to assume, as reader of this book and of the poems in it, an actual reader—you, most likely a first- or second-year college student in an introductory poetry course. But reading theorists say it isn't quite that simple. Who is the "you" that is reading this book? Is it the same "you" as the one who likes to watch movies? or the one who goes rollerblading? Of course, it is; yet, in a sense, it isn't. Many reading theorists assume that the person doing the reading is not an "actual reader" but what Wolfgang Iser termed an **implied reader.**[1]

The concept of implied readers grew out of the acceptance of the idea of "implied authors." That is, anyone who writes involves only part of her or his person in a particular piece of writing: as you write a history paper, some parts of you feed into the paper (your ability to sift through data, your critical acumen, your skill in organizing and writing clear, direct prose), while many other parts don't get in at all: your love of desserts, your musical ability, your skill as a driver. Someone searching in your paper for evidences of its author will find aspects of you, but not the whole you. The parts of you that appear in that paper are its "implied author"—that is, as much of the "actual author" as went into that work. The implied author is a verbal construct: it exists only in a written work, not outside it, and only in *that* work, for the implied author of anything else you write will be different—at least slightly, perhaps greatly different.

So, a story or poem has an "actual author" (the whole person who wrote it) and an "implied author" (the aspects of the actual author that gave rise to the work). Ordinarily one won't notice the implied author: we simply know that she or he must be there in order for the work to have been written. There can also be a "characterized author"—that is, a character created in the work who claims to be the one who wrote the work. To cite a familiar example outside of poetry, in *The Catcher in the Rye,* there is the actual author (J. D. Salinger), an implied author (the aspects of Salinger that went into this work), and Holden Caulfield, a character who claims to be writing it himself. Distinguishing these different authorial roles can be a valuable step toward a better understanding of the process of writing and the formation of a work as an independent object.

Reader-response theorists began asking whether the same thing can be found at the reader end of the work, and they found that indeed it can. There is the "actual reader," of course—the one who holds the book and whose eyes see the words on the page or who hears the words read or recited. As there can be a "characterized author," there can also be a "characterized reader," someone addressed in the text as "you" or as "dear reader." But there is also an "implied reader." At no time is the whole of the actual reader occupied in the reading process—as you read this book, many sides of you do not get involved. Within the text that you are now reading are constructs that draw out from your whole being those parts needed for processing it—your common sense, your imagination, your aesthetic appreciation, your feelings, for example, but not your skills in calculus, accounting, or video games. A text, thus, implies a reader: stories, drama, and poetry imply a reader willing and able to use her or his imagination, to accept figures figuratively, and so on; a book on philosophy implies a reader willing and able to think abstractly and to reason

---

[1] *The Implied Reader: Patterns of Communication in Prose Fiction from Bunyan to Beckett* (Baltimore: Johns Hopkins University Press, 1974). See also Iser's *The Act of Reading: A Theory of Aesthetic Response* (Baltimore: Johns Hopkins University Press, 1978).

and argue. Only as much of you gets involved in a text as is required to relate to the "reader" implied in the text. As Jonathan Culler put it, to read is to "play the role of a reader."[2] Built into any text, this view holds, are cues as to how you are to fill the role of reader in it, how you must adjust (or what parts of you must get involved) to relate to it well.

If "implied reader" is a role, you can refuse to play the role—or you may be unable to fill it—for imaginative, intellectual, aesthetic, or moral reasons. Fantasy stories imply readers willing to go, imaginatively, to a new world where sights, creatures, and physical laws may be entirely different from those in our world. Some people refuse to play that role, feeling that such unrealistic work is nonsense, and thus don't like to read fantasy. They cannot become the reader a fantasy work implies. Many people lack training and background in philosophy and thus are not able, intellectually, to fill the role of implied reader in philosophical texts. People who have had no exposure to surrealistic poetry or abstract art may be bewildered and turned off because they don't know how even to start filling, aesthetically and imaginatively, the role of reader. And readers may resist morally or just practically the positions developed in a work: they may fight off the persuasive techniques employed by the writers of an ad instead of going out and buying the product; or they may find the views expressed in a novel written by a Nazi or a Ku Klux Klan supporter so repellent that they are utterly unable to read the work in the spirit of the implied reader.

An implied reader is not the same as an "intended reader": intended readers are actual readers whom the actual author had in mind as her or his audience and who may, or may not, end up actually reading the work. One way to get at the difference between "implied" and "intended" readers is to think about advertisements in magazines (TV commercials would work, too). Advertisements and commercials, like all writing, have implied readers (or hearers)—that is, people who play the role the implied author anticipated and who respond with, "Yes, I do deserve those jeans. They may be expensive, but I'm going to buy a pair tomorrow." Advertisements also have intended readers: companies spend big money to identify what age group is most likely to buy expensive jeans and what magazines people in that age group read (or what programs they watch), and they pitch their ads at those groups. They hope that among those intended readers (and others outside the intended group as well) many will identify with the implied reader and will respond in the desired way.

The implied reader concept can be helpful for examining your engagement in the reading process. Let's go back to Robert Frost's poem " 'Out, Out—' " and take a minute to construct its implied reader. As the imaginary class in Chapter 2 read the poem, the implied reader would be open to imaginative constructions of events, receptive to telling such accounts in poetry, and able to appreciate the effects of sound, figures, and tone that the poem

---

[2] *On Deconstruction: Theory and Criticism after Structuralism* (Ithaca, N.Y.: Cornell University Press, 1982), 67.

employs. The implied reader would also seem sympathetic with the situation of the boy, at least slightly disturbed at the reaction of the people around him, but mostly uncertain about the kind of world in which such things happen— the implied reader is rather grim and depressed, because such events occur all the time in the world and he or she can't understand why, can't find meaning and purpose in such a world. Let's assume for the moment that you agree that this is essentially the response the implied author expected. If your own view of life is similar to that, you'll have no difficulty filling the role of the implied reader and responding favorably to the poem. But maybe you're more opti- mistic than that and believe that life makes sense despite the tragedies in it. You may, even so, be able imaginatively to identify with the implied reader and thus respond to the poem even though it doesn't express your own per- sonal views. Or you may not be able to identify with the implied reader at all—may resist the poem, be unable to enter and respond to it effectively (though apart from this concept you'd be inclined to say you just "don't like" the poem). The concept of "implied reader" is valuable, then, in helping us understand why we can read some things better than other things, and what we might do to become better readers of the latter.

The following poem offers a model of actual author, characterized author, and implied author, and actual reader, characterized reader, and implied reader. Start by identifying the "I" and "you" and the situation in the poem. Then consider your role and position. How do you relate to the "you"? If the "I" isn't writing to you, perhaps you aren't meant to be reading someone else's mail. Or is someone other than the "I" of the poem writing to you? Be ready to discuss the possible usefulness of these concepts in understanding how the poem works and achieves its effects.

MARGARET ATWOOD (b. 1939)

Postcard (1981)

I'm thinking about you. What else can I say?
The palm trees on the reverse
are a delusion; so is the pink sand.
What we have are the usual
fractured coke bottles and the smell   5
of backed-up drains, too sweet,
like a mango on the verge
of rot, which we have also.
The air clear sweat, mosquitoes
& their tracks; birds, blue & elusive.   10

Time comes in waves here, a sickness, one
day after the other rolling on;
I move up, it's called
awake, then down into the uneasy
nights but never   15

forward. The roosters crow
for hours before dawn, and a prodded
child howls & howls
on the pocked road to school.
In the hold with the baggage   20
there are two prisoners,
their heads shaved by bayonets, & ten crates
of queasy chicks. Each spring
there's a race of cripples, from the store
to the church. This is the sort of junk   25
I carry with me; and a clipping
about democracy from the local paper.

Outside the window
they're building the damn hotel,
nail by nail, someone's   30
crumbling dream. A universe that includes you
can't be all bad, but
does it? At this distance
you're a mirage, a glossy image
fixed in the posture   35
of the last time I saw you.
Turn you over, there's the place
for the address. Wish you were
here. Love comes
in waves like the ocean, a sickness which goes on   40
& on, a hollow cave
in the head, filling & pounding, a kicked ear.

THE READER AND THE TEXT

Just as the nature of the reader is an issue in reader-response theory, so is
the nature of the text. The issue boils down to this: Is the text—the words on
the page—"objective" or "subjective" in nature? For New Criticism, the nature
of texts was not problematic. New Critics regard texts as "objective": that is,
the text has integrity as an *object*—something that can be (to bring in etymol-
ogy) "thrown down" before or presented to the mind; its structures and mean-
ing exist independently of the mind that apprehends them and can be
understood in essentially the same way by all adequately skillful readers.
Thus, New Critics can examine the text closely, call attention to the structures
in it, and discuss the meaning or meanings it contains.

But texts can also be regarded as "subjective" (etymologically, "placed be-
neath" the mind, as a subject is beneath his or her monarch). From a subjec-
tive viewpoint, the text's only independent existence is as ink marks on paper,
which have no validity outside the way a reader fills them with meaning. The
"real text" exists in the mind of the reader, and that text will differ from reader

to reader, and no external standard exists by which some "real meaning" can be ascertained.

Reader-response critics have not always given conscious attention to their theory of texts, but looking at their work makes it clear that the positions taken differ greatly from one critic to another. In the early stages of reader-response criticism, emphasis was placed on the author's strategies and the way structures in the text guide the reader's response. This approach agrees with other varieties of reader-response criticism that meaning is not in the text but in the experience of the reader's interaction with the text; however, it sees that interaction as controlled by formal structures included in the text. The text itself, then, establishes limits on the reader—the proper response is objectively determined by the text.

This can be illustrated by returning to our discussion of " 'Out, Out—' " in Chapter 2. It would have taken only a slight shift to put the focus of our discussion more strongly on the text and on how structures in it shape or guide responses, and make certain responses almost inevitable. Thus, the calm, peaceful opening of " 'Out, Out—' " sets up the shock as the boy's hand is suddenly cut off; the compression of time at the end is deliberately designed to heighten the sense of unconcern. The meaning of the poem lies in our experiences of horror at the accident and death, anger at the apparent callousness of those around the boy, and frustration about a world full of awful things we cannot understand, but the poem predetermines those experiences through the structure and techniques in the text.

The attention in Chapter 2 to gaps in texts and to the ways readers fill them is adapted from a text-oriented reader-response approach popularized by Wolfgang Iser in *The Implied Reader* and *The Act of Reading*. For Iser the reader is constantly anticipating what is to come and then adjusting and reevaluating expectations. The gaps, or vacancies, or "indeterminacies" in the text direct and constrain the reader in the process of achieving a consistent and comprehensible meaning. Thus, the text is a stable and "objective" entity, and the reader has to pay close attention to the text to notice and follow the cues it supplies.

Another well-known example of text-based reader-response criticism appears in Stanley Fish's book *Surprised by Sin,* a study of John Milton's *Paradise Lost.*[3] Fish argues that Milton constructs the text in such a way that the reader unconsciously responds favorably to seductive aspects of Satan's arguments—is taken in by them. Thus, readers undergo a "fall" themselves, just as Adam and Eve did, and the reader's fall is the crucial one for the poem—the meaning of the work lies in the experience it creates. But the text remains an objective, stable entity, guiding—through the author's strategies—the way the reader experiences the poem. Fish, in his later work, moved away from such an objectivist view of the text, but its principle—that readers' responses are guided and determined by structures and conven-

---

[3] *Surprised by Sin: The Reader in* Paradise Lost (New York: St. Martin's Press, 1967).

tions within the text—continues to be fundamental for some other reader-response theorists.

As you read the following poem (or after you read it), consider the process by which you attempt to form a coherent meaning. Watch how you fill in gaps and figure out indeterminate sections. Think of the words and the gaps as structures in the text that shape and guide your interpretation, and be ready to discuss how that affects the way you think about the reading process.

LINDA HOGAN (b. 1947)

The Rainy Season (1985)

The women are walking to town
beneath black umbrellas
and the roofs are leaking.
Oh, let them be,
let the buckled wood give way this once   5
and the mildew rot the plaster,
the way it happens with age
when a single thought of loneliness
is enough to bring collapse.

See, here they come,   10
the witches are downstairs
undermining the foundations.
The skeletal clothes hanger
has unwound from its life at last,
hidden in a dark coat   15
thrown over its shoulders.
Nothing is concealed,
not silver moths
falling out the empty sleeves
or the old cat with shining fur   20
covering his bony spine,
that string of knots
for keeping track of this mouse
and that.

Even the mice have their days of woe.   25
In the field and in the world
there are unknown sorrows.
Every day collapses
despite the women
walking to town with black umbrellas   30
holding up the sky.

> All of us, I suspect, were drawn in childhood to fictional worlds more no-
> ble than the ones we lived in, worlds where good and evil were clear dis-
> tinctions, and the motivations of people were comprehensible—as they
> never were in "real" life. Perhaps we keep trying to reproduce such worlds
> through our art. But before books, there was my mother's voice singing
> and saying poems, my grandfather's voice telling stories while he held me
> on his lap. Do we try in our writing somehow to recover that early sense
> of the connection between wonderful language and somebody loving us?
>
> –ALICIA OSTRIKER

THE QUESTION OF LIMITS

For text-based approaches, the text itself, as an objective entity, sets lim-
its on the reader. A poem cannot mean just anything the reader says it does:
the reader must be able to provide evidence from within the text to support
the way he or she interprets it. In moving along the spectrum, away from an
objective view of texts toward a subjective view, the issue of limits emerges as
a problem. If the text exists only in readers' minds, it can no longer place lim-
its on the reader. A question that must be faced by reader-response approaches
that are not text-oriented is whether there are any limits on the reader. Does a
text mean anything the reader says it does? Some approaches hold that limits
do exist, without giving up subjectivity of the text.

One such approach grows out of recognition that reading occurs within
"interpretive communities." Interpretive communities in their broadest sense
are groups of readers in a common situation or with shared assumptions
about how literary works are actualized, or with shared agreement about how
literary conventions are used in approaching a text. The community provides
a context within which individual experiencing of a work can be assessed. A
class is an interpretive community. So are the readers of a professional journal,
and so are a group of scholars who specialize in a given area of literature. The
role of such a group is not to arrive at a single "best" reading, or to judge
which among several is the "right" one or which are "better" than others.
Rather, by its endorsements and discouragements, each interpretive commu-
nity indicates which readings go too far for that community, which ones it re-
gards as *unacceptable*. The judgments made are collective. Thus neither the
individual reader nor the text is authoritative. Authority lies in the group. A
text, then, can "mean" many things, but not just anything.

Paying attention to interpretive communities can help clarify why read-
ers arrive at similar—and different—readings of the same work. To be a
reader is inevitably to be in an interpretive community: most readers belong
to more than one, belong to different communities in different situations or
at different times of their lives or even as they read different works. Members
of the same community will construct works in similar ways, while those in
different communities will construct them in different ways. This answers

two questions—first, why do different readers come up with similar (not identical) readings? Because they belong to the same interpretive community and thus employ similar strategies in constructing the work. Second, why can the same reader come up with different readings of the same text or different ways to read different texts? Partly because he or she changes as a person, as explained in Chapter 2, but also because he or she can belong to more than one interpretive community at the same time and can change communities over time.

It is interpretive communities, in this view, not texts or readers, that create stability in reading texts. Even within the same community there will be variances in readings, because texts are not objective and different readers enact them in individual ways; but constraints do exist. Those constraints, however, are not *in* the text, but grow out of the strategies, assumptions, and conventions of the community.

Be attentive to the reading process and to your responses as you read the following poem. As you discuss it in class, notice how your "community" helps clarify it and defines boundaries for interpreting it. Talk about those limits and their value, and about how other groups might set them differently.

JEAN VALENTINE (b. 1934)

December 21st (1979)

How will I think of you
"God-with-us"
a name: a word

and trees paths stars this earth
how will I think of them   5

and the dead I love   and all absent friends
here-with-me

and table: hand: white coffee mug:
a northern still life:

and you   10
without a body

quietness

and the infant's red-brown mouth   a star
at the star of a girl's nipple . . .

READER, TEXT, AND PSYCHOANALYSIS

As we approach the subjective end of the textual spectrum, we find ourselves returning to psychoanalytic criticism yet again and then to poststructuralism. In Chapters 11 and 12 we found that psychoanalytic criticism can be helpful in achieving a better understanding of both authors and texts. It can also be helpful for understanding the reader's experience. The interest here is in real readers, not ideal or implied readers, and in what engagement with a text *reveals about the reader*. We will discuss here two well-known and influential approaches.

Norman Holland, a leading exponent of psychoanalytic criticism for almost three decades, has developed a theory based on a variant of psychoanalysis called "identity theory." While Freudian psychoanalysis concentrates on the id (on the unconscious and dealing with neuroses growing from it), identity theory, influenced by psychologists Erik Erikson and Heinz Lichtenstein, focuses on the ego, or the "self," and the development through it of personal identity.

Identity theory holds that development of an individual's self follows an "identity theme" that runs through his or her behavior—a central, unifying pattern that represents the unchanging essence of the person, permeating his or her millions of ego choices. Reading, then, as Holland explains it, is guided by an individual's identity theme. He calls his approach "transactive criticism"—that is, the reader bargains with the text to get out of it what the reader seeks. In the process of reading, we read ourselves into the text before us: "Each reader re-creates the work in terms of his [or her] own identity theme."[4] That is, as we read, we shape the work so that it will slip through our defensive and adaptive strategies for coping with the world and form from it the kind of fantasy we find pleasure in. "Each of us will find in the literary work the kind of thing we characteristically wish or fear the most" (Holland, p. 817). As an aspect of our identity, each of us has developed a characteristic pattern of defenses, expectations, fantasies, and transformations (Holland terms this DEFT). New experiences are filtered through these in order to assimilate them and make them fit in with our core identity. As we read we "transact" with the text (the marks on the page) to construct a work that pleases or satisfies us. The process of doing so reveals things about ourselves; our reading reflects our own anxieties, hopes, tensions.

The work of David Bleich[5] moves in a similar direction. Bleich, however, puts even more emphasis on the reader, less on the text (Holland has become more subjective in his view of the text, from pressure by Bleich, but he still ascribes some degree of authority to the text; Bleich does not). Bleich's method (like Holland's, but more so) is fundamentally a classroom methodology; he asks his students to write "response statements" answering three questions: What did you make of this? (perception). What did you feel as you read it? (affect). What personal associations did you make as you read it? (association). He is interested primarily in what a reader (student) *feels* about a text, rather than what the reader *thinks* about it; feeling comes first, and thinking—especially as articulated "interpretation" of a text—freezes, and perhaps falsifies, the personal perceptions, feelings, and associations that constitute the basic response. The approaches of Holland and Bleich can be discussed as a variant

---

[4] Norman N. Holland, "UNITY IDENTITY TEXT SELF," *PMLA* 90 (1975): 818.

[5] *Subjective Criticism* (Baltimore: Johns Hopkins University Press, 1978).

of reader-response criticism. But their psychological emphasis sets them apart from other reader-response approaches.

The published studies of Holland and Bleich appear as case studies. They have a group of students or other readers respond to a text. Then they examine the responses, comparing them to one another and sometimes to the readers' psychological profiles. Both are more interested in the responses and what the responses say about the reader than they are in the literary texts, and they use the responses as a means of reaching a better understanding of the reader.

Try Bleich's approach on one of the poems below. Read the poem and write a response giving your perception of it, what you felt as you read it, and the personal associations you made with it as you read. Be ready to compare your response with those of other students in the class and to discuss with them how things in your backgrounds may help account for differences in your responses.

RUSSELL EDSON (b. 1935)

A Performance at Hog Theater (1976)

There was once a hog theater where hogs performed as men, had men been hogs.

One hog said, I will be a hog in a field which has found a mouse which is being eaten by the same hog which is in the field and which has found the mouse, which I am performing as my contribution to the performer's art.

Oh let's just be hogs, cried an old hog.

And so the hogs streamed out of the theater crying, only hogs, only hogs . . .

ROBERT CREELEY (b. 1926)

The Language (1967)

Locate *I*
love you some-
where in

teeth and
eyes, bite
it but

take care not
to hurt, you
want so

5

much so   10
little. Words
say everything.

I
love you
again,   15

then what
is emptiness
for. To

fill, fill.
I heard words   20
and words full

of holes
aching. Speech
is a mouth.

> Poems should attempt to speak the unspoken, and so allow others to speak.
> —ANN LAUTERBACH

THE DEATH OF THE AUTHOR

Although we placed deconstruction in Chapter 12, "Texts," because it is
so concerned with close examination of texts, poststructuralism does in-
clude an emphasis on the reader. Underlying and sustaining that emphasis
is a reconsideration of authorship. Poststructuralists deemphasize what we
referred to above as the "actual author" in favor of the "implied author" or
"inscripted author." They would say that the kind of attention to authors we
described in Chapter 11 is unwarranted. The writing is the important thing,
not the historical person who did the writing. Writing creates its own voice
and destroys the voice of the historical author behind it as well as its point
of origin. Roland Barthes summarized the point in an essay with the arrest-
ing title "The Death of the Author"[6]—in which some readers at the time
might have noted an interesting parallel to the "death of God" theology then
current.

Barthes acknowledges that the sway of the author remains powerful: al-
though New Critics claimed to focus on autonomous works of art and not on

[6] *Image Music Text*, essays selected and translated by Stephen Heath (New York: Hill and
Wang, 1977), 142–48.

authors, in fact, Barthes argues, they were solidifying the sense of poems as created works, the creations of individuals whose godlike presence in the background conveys a sense of authority, a sense of the existence of an objective meaning for which we should be searching. Barthes cites in reply Mallarmé's dictum that it is language that speaks, not the author. "To write is, through a prerequisite impersonality . . . to reach that point where only language acts, 'performs,' and not 'me' " (p. 143). Writing is made of writing, and a text is the location where various previous writings are brought together and intersect. How then can an individual person claim "ownership" of what has been thus drawn together, not "created"?

The important thing is not the individual who brought the writings together, but the reader who fills the intersection with meaning. "A text is made of multiple writings, drawn from many cultures and entering into mutual relations of dialogue, parody, contestation, but there is one place where this multiplicity is focused and that place is the reader, not, as was hitherto said, the author" (p. 148). The death of the author liberates the reader from the earlier sense of an author's voice in control of the text. That elimination of the author and of authority over the text, and the shift of emphasis to the reader, is central to the radical subjectivity at the heart of the poststructuralist movement.

• • •

Be aware of the process involved as you read the following poems. Use them to reflect on and then to discuss issues and questions raised in reader-oriented approaches.

YUSEF KOMUNYAKAA (b. 1947)

Facing It (1988)

My black face fades,
hiding inside the black granite.
I said I wouldn't,
dammit: No tears.
I'm stone. I'm flesh.   5
My clouded reflection eyes me
like a bird of prey, the profile of night
slanted against morning. I turn
this way—the stone lets me go.
I turn that way—I'm inside   10
the Vietnam Veterans Memorial
again, depending on the light
to make a difference.
I go down the 58,022 names,
half-expecting to find   15
my own in letters like smoke.

I touch the name Andrew Johnson;
I see the booby trap's white flash.
Names shimmer on a woman's blouse
but when she walks away   20
the names stay on the wall.
Brushstrokes flash, a red bird's
wings cutting across my stare.
The sky. A plane in the sky.
A white vet's image floats   25
closer to me, then his pale eyes
look through mine. I'm a window.
He's lost his right arm
inside the stone. In the black mirror
a woman's trying to erase names: 30
No, she's brushing a boy's hair.

LEE UPTON (b. 1953)

Photographs (1984)

This is the one in which I look
demented, something about
the way the eyes focus.
It's like staring at someone else.
How many times have I caught myself   5
in a department store mirror
and thought I was another woman?
Once I even smiled back, absentminded.
And if my mind was absent,
perhaps it's here   10

in this photograph of me at five.
I would hate to look after that child.
Gerard took a look and said
You must have been a Real Child.
A child's child.   15
And here is a photograph of my mother
dressed like a Southern belle in a floppy
blue hat, letting us know she wants
to be beautiful.

Here are several of my father   20
hiding behind a newspaper.
Here he's ducking into the garage.
Here his arms collide with his face.
The same with my sister during her permanent
wave, head abuzz in pink curlers.   25

But my favorite is the home movie
where everyone tries to escape.
Lana wheels me in a wheelbarrow—fast.
Next we try to hide behind each other.
I put the hem of her dress over my head.   30
She shouts silently to the lens, *Go away!*
My mother buries her face in the dog.
My father runs around the side of the house.
It's almost like looking at someone else's family,
wanting to tell them,   35
Why can't you act natural?

MARK DOTY (b. 1953)

Tiara (1991)

Peter died in a paper tiara
cut from a book of princess paper dolls;
he loved royalty, sashes

and jewels. I don't know,
he said, when he woke in the hospice,   5
I was watching the Bette Davis film festival

on Channel 57 and then—
At the wake, the tension broke
when someone guessed

the casket closed because   10
he was *in there in a big wig
and heels,* and someone said,

*You know he's always late,
he probably isn't here yet—
he's still fixing his makeup.*   15

And someone said he asked for it.
Asked for it—
when all he did was go down

into the salt tide
of wanting as much as he wanted,   20
giving himself over so drunk

or stoned it almost didn't matter who,
though they were beautiful,
stampeding into him in the simple,

ravishing music of their hurry.   25
I think heaven is perfect stasis
poised over the realms of desire,

where dreaming and waking men lie
on the grass while wet horses
roam among them, huge fragments   30

of the music we die into
in the body's paradise.
Sometimes we wake not knowing

how we came to lie here,
or who has crowned us with these temporary,   35
precious stones. And given

the world's perfectly turned shoulders,
the deep hollows blued by longing,
given the irreplaceable silk

of horses rippling in orchards,   40
fruit thundering and chiming down,
given the ordinary marvels of form

and gravity, what could he do,
what could any of us ever do
but ask for it?   45

MEDBH McGUCKIAN (b. 1950)

Lighthouse with Dead Leaves (1988)

I was dissecting the brain of a child when I cut
My less than agile finger.
(One should keep aside
A pair of loose, black, cotton gloves
For shaking hands with children.)   5

When the blood ran to its sleeping places,
What dreams returned or were allowed to grow?
As if a ship that opened her planks
To the carpentry of the sea,
Became a thinking fog in which   10
All wounds began to glow,
And lighthouses sprang to mind.

Dead leaves and water, maybe he recollected
Walking two miles in the rain to wave goodbye,
And walking into the sky.   15
Like an outswollen shoe
That fits inside another, or
Swans that but appear
To be dancing to music,

So his love-nest is creeping over me,   20
Is keeping me amused
Till I am three girls or the same girl
Leading him, a figure no longer
Dreamt about, nor dreaming,
But partner to me like a ruptured seed.   25

I have locked my bedroom door from the inside,
And do not expect it to be mutilated.
My garb is chosen for a dry journey,
Sleep will be a line of trees searching for this stable
I would have left to rot if I'd been able.   30

APPLICATIONS FOR CHAPTER 13

SUGGESTIONS FOR WRITING

1. Reread journal entries you wrote for Chapter 2. Write a new journal entry
    discussing whether your understanding of a reader-oriented approach
    and your ability to focus on the role of the reader have grown, and if
    so, how.
2. At the end of Chapter 1 we suggested that you record in your journal a se-
    ries of responses to a particular poem as you moved through this book. If
    you did so, go back and read those responses. Then, write a journal entry
    assessing your growth as a reader of poetry. This could also become the
    basis of a reflective paper.
3. Select a poem from this chapter or from the anthology. Read it and write
    in your journal a response giving your perception of it, what you felt as
    you read it, and the personal associations you made with it as you read.
    This could be used as the basis for a paper discussing the experience you
    brought to the poem and your experience as you read it.
4. Arrange for some members of your class to join you in some firsthand
    research that could lead to a paper for each participant, or a group pa-
    per or presentation. All of you read the same poem and write down
    your perceptions of it, what you felt as you read it, and the personal as-
    sociations you made with it as you read. Then spend some time com-
    paring responses and discussing how things in your backgrounds may
    help account for differences in your responses. Take notes as the group
    talks, and record your evaluations of the whole process in your journal.
    Use your written responses, notes, and journal entry as the basis for a
    paper exploring personal experience in the reading process, and per-
    haps the relation of an interpretive community to individual response
    in reading.

1. Keep in mind the reading *process*—making sense of words and phrases, anticipating what is ahead, filling gaps, going back to revise anticipations in the light of what is encountered later, being affected by prior experience in completing the text, and so on—and the importance of your experience (what you bring to reading and your experience while reading) in that process.
2. Think about how your responses would be received by your interpretive community.

14 | Culture

However important "ideal readers" may be to literary theory, poems are written and read by real people, living in and influenced by particular social and cultural situations. Considering the way poems are influenced by their cultural context, and in turn influence their culture, is yet another way literature can be approached. Of the many strands of cultural criticism, this chapter will introduce you to the older variety of cultural criticism, to some varieties of contemporary cultural studies, including New Historicism and Marxist criticism, and to feminist criticism and gender studies.

CULTURAL CRITICISM

It has long—perhaps always—been clear that literature relates to the cultures that produce and consume it. Literature has always been regarded as a vehicle for preservation of the stories on which a culture is built and for instruction in the attitudes and behaviors the culture finds acceptable and unacceptable, as well as for enjoyment. The Roman poet, satirist, and theorist Horace voiced what was probably even then a commonplace, that literature should both *please* and *instruct*.

But the relation of literature to life assumed a particular emphasis in England in the mid-1800s, voiced most articulately by poet and critic Matthew Arnold. Arnold was deeply distressed by what he called the "barbarianism"— the lack of interest in ideas—of the upper classes in England; by the "philistinism" (lack of intelligence and taste) of the middle classes; and by the lack of interest among the lower classes in anything save "beer, gin, and fun." Through **cultural criticism** he attempted to improve society by challenging it to a commitment to "high culture" (his term again), "the knowledge of the best that has been thought and said in the world."

Culture, in this view, becomes a norm, or standard, for people to aspire to, and it has a unifying effect if they can be induced to strive toward the same values in aesthetics and morality. In Arnold's thinking, literature is central to culture: he echoed Horace's dictum, rephrasing it to say that the significance and appeal of literature is the way it offers readers "sweetness and light." His mission was to draw people out of a narrow, self-satisfied provincialism by inducing them to read widely and to appreciate a literary work "as in itself it really is." Arnold put so much emphasis on culture, especially literature, because he believed it could fill the role religion previously had filled, of offering society a source of moral values and an instrument for social unity and stability. For Arnold, education was the method for spreading this new religion. Through literature—especially the classics—the middle classes would be enabled to share some of the advantages the upper classes have always had available to them through their access to education.

Arnold's model of cultural criticism was strongly influential for over a century and continues to shape thinking today. It clearly affected New Criticism: both focus on the literary work as an object, endeavor to see the object "as it really is," take poetry and all of literature seriously, hold that literature should have universal themes, and evaluate works and concentrate on those that are best. Educators in the United States for decades used literature as an avenue for assimilating people into mainstream "American culture," with the aim of helping them rise to the middle class. And cultural criticism critiqued literature to assess what was worthy of attention and would contribute most to cultural development and to the unifying, socializing effect a common culture helps achieve.

The following poem by Arnold can be used to illustrate cultural criticism as he understood and practiced it. The speaker of the poem is at Dover, looking at the cliffs nearby and across the English Channel toward France and listening to the sound of the waves crashing onto the beach. The poem was written in the aftermath of armed revolutions in 1848 in all European countries except England—revolutions caused by social and economic disparities among different classes, and accompanied by a decline in the common religion that for centuries had helped sustain European social structure. Watch for references to religious decline, to the loss of common faith, and to what Arnold suggests as a replacement for it. Consider how the poem is a product of its culture, how it was influenced by the author's social and educational background (education in the classics was mostly the heritage of the upper classes in Arnold's day). Consider also what Arnold seemed to want to achieve through the poem, how it serves as a kind of cultural criticism. And reflect on how you might apply Arnold's kind of cultural criticism as an approach today —how the poem could be viewed as a way of speaking to society today and of raising standards to enhance the appreciation of "high culture."

MATTHEW ARNOLD (1822–1888)

Dover Beach (ca. 1851)

The sea is calm tonight.
The tide is full, the moon lies fair
Upon the straits; on the French coast the light
Gleams and is gone; the cliffs of England stand,
Glimmering and vast, out in the tranquil bay.   5

Come to the window, sweet is the night-air!
Only, from the long line of spray
Where the sea meets the moon-blanched land,
Listen! you hear the grating roar
Of pebbles which the waves draw back, and fling,   10
At their return, up the high strand,
Begin, and cease, and then again begin,
With tremulous cadence slow, and bring
The eternal note of sadness in.

Sophocles long ago   15
Heard it on the Aegean, and it brought
Into his mind the turbid ebb and flow
Of human misery; we
Find also in the sound a thought,
Hearing it by this distant northern sea.   20

The Sea of Faith
Was once, too, at the full, and round earth's shore
Lay like the folds of a bright girdle furled.
But now I only hear
Its melancholy, long, withdrawing roar,   25
Retreating, to the breath
Of the night-wind, down the vast edges drear
And naked shingles of the world.

Ah, love, let us be true
To one another! for the world, which seems   30
To lie before us like a land of dreams,
So various, so beautiful, so new,
Hath really neither joy, nor love, nor light,
Nor certitude, nor peace, nor help for pain;
And we are here as on a darkling plain   35
Swept with confused alarms of struggle and flight,
Where ignorant armies clash by night.

CULTURAL STUDIES

Cultural studies today means something quite different from the Arnoldian variety of cultural criticism. It regards Arnold's desire for objectivity, his effort "to see the object as in itself it really is," as futile: the object is always mediated through the viewer and it is impossible for any of us to see objects as they really are. Many people also dispute Arnold's claim to universality: they hold that what he put forward as universal standards and values actually are those of white educated males in Britain's upper economic class. And they tend to regard the Arnoldian emphasis on "high culture" as elitist, as implying that only the educated upper classes produce significant cultural achievements. They assert that cultural achievements of worth have been produced by people from a variety of social, economic, and ethnic backgrounds, past as well as present, and that criticism should enable us to appreciate all of it instead of rejecting much of it as lacking seriousness or universality.

> I think of myself as making poems that other poets haven't provided for me, & for the existence of which I feel a deep need.
>
> I look for new forms & possibilities, but also for ways of presenting in my own language the oldest possibilities of poetry going back to the primitive & archaic cultures that have been opening up to us over the last hundred years.
>
> —JEROME ROTHENBERG

In contrast to earlier cultural criticism, which focused attention on elements that helped promote cultural unity in a society, the cultural studies approach holds that we cannot assume a single, central culture, but rather that we find "inescapable cultural difference, division, and dissonance."[1] Cultural studies is inclusive, rather than exclusive as the Arnoldian tradition was. It is inclusive ethnically, with a strong multicultural emphasis, and inclusive in regard to subject matter—not limited to the literature of "high culture," but extending also to popular culture: comic books as well as novels, television sitcoms as well as drama, MTV as well as public television, pop songs as well as poetry, graffiti as well as paintings. It does not stress evaluation, the way the Arnoldian tradition did and New Criticism still does. The emphasis in cultural studies is on how people *relate to* all levels of art, rather than on their aesthetic standards and on getting them to recognize and appreciate "the best" poetry, music, or art.

Cultural studies rejects the older notion of a "canon" of the best works of art, which all educated persons should know and study. Its interest in the canon would be centered, instead, on the very *existence* of a canon. It would ask *why* such an idea developed. What does its development, and the definitions of "good taste" it presupposes, tell us about social, economic, educational, and political issues and situations that prevailed when it began to emerge, and as it was sustained? What kinds of power were used, and by whom, to put the canon in place and to keep it in place? And cultural studies would investigate the *effect* the existence of such a canon had on society, education, and the development of the arts.

---

[1] Gerald Graff and Bruce Robbins, "Cultural Criticism," in *Redrawing the Boundaries: The Transformation of English and American Literary Studies,* ed. Stephen Greenblatt and Giles Gunn (New York: Modern Language Association, 1992), 433. See also Ross C. Murfin, ed., *"The Heart of Darkness"* by Joseph Conrad, 2d ed., Case Studies in Contemporary Criticism (Boston: Bedford Books of St. Martin's Press, 1996), 258–71. We are indebted to his work in several sections of this chapter.

> I am reminded of a small example used in every Spanish class about a central cultural difference between English speakers and Spanish speakers. In English, one says, *I dropped the glass,* should such a thing happen. It is an "I"-centered instance, rugged individualism in its smallest moment. In Spanish, one says, *"Se me cayó el vaso,"* which means, "The glass, it fell from me." This is a different world view, a way of accommodating the world, of living with it instead of changing it. Which is the better view is not the point, but I do think that our notions of the West as representing rugged individualism may, in fact, be faulty. There's a messy middle, something in between. I think that's the language of this place. It's a rugged pluralism.
>
> —ALBERTO RÍOS

Cultural studies does not think in terms of a single, static, universal culture, which needs to be preserved, but of a set of dynamic, interactive, always-changing *cultures,* and it thinks of art not as something that can be separated from the rest of culture and treated by itself, in isolation (the way New Criticism and deconstruction tend to), but as something that must be viewed as integral to these interactive, always-changing cultures. Cultural studies views the poem itself ("the object" that cultural criticism wanted to focus on) as worth studying not so much for its intrinsic value, as for the light it sheds—by what it says and by what it leaves unsaid—on aspects of its culture. The text is a springboard for extratextual inquiries.[2] Thus cultural studies tends toward interdisciplinary approaches and seeks to view works in relation to other works (literary works, especially ones outside the traditional canon, but also journals, memoirs, and diaries of ordinary people, church records, medical reports, architectural drawings, and so on); to social and economic conditions that affected them; to the way they were shaped by those who held power (including editors, publishers, and reviewers, for example) or the way they reinforced forces or conditions of power, intentionally or not.

The following poem is of a kind that was not included in the New Criticism–oriented poetry books of forty or fifty years ago. Consider why it wasn't, and what that suggests about the literary/critical/educational culture of earlier times. The poem is about cultural difference and the difficulties it can pose. Look up Lorna Dee Cervantes in the Biographical Sketches section at the back of the book for an indication of her social and cultural background. Think about the cultural situation of the speaker and what the poem says from within that context. Consider also what the poem says about the culture of the young white man who asked the question and how the speaker's words might affect him, and others like him.

---

[2] It is interesting to see that cultural studies, thus, takes us back to Chapter 11, to the situation New Criticism sought to "correct": *using* the text for purposes extrinsic to it.

LORNA DEE CERVANTES (b. 1954)

Poem for the Young White Man Who Asked Me How I, an Intelligent, Well-Read Person Could Believe in the War Between Races (1981)

In my land there are no distinctions.
The barbed wire politics of oppression
have been torn down long ago. The only reminder
of past battles, lost or won, is a slight
rutting in the fertile fields.   5

In my land
people write poems about love,
full of nothing but contented childlike syllables.
Everyone reads Russian short stories and weeps.
There are no boundaries.   10
There is no hunger, no
complicated famine or greed.

I am not a revolutionary.
I don't even like political poems.
Do you think I can believe in a war between races?   15
I can deny it. I can forget about it
when I'm safe,
living on my own continent of harmony
and home, but I am not
there.   20

I believe in revolution
because everywhere the crosses are burning,
sharp-shooting goose-steppers round every corner,
there are snipers in the schools . . .
(I know you don't believe this.   25
You think this is nothing
but faddish exaggeration. But they
are not shooting at you.)

I'm marked by the color of my skin.
The bullets are discrete and designed to kill slowly.   30
They are aiming at my children.
These are facts.
Let me show you my wounds: my stumbling mind, my
"excuse me" tongue, and this
nagging preoccupation   35
with the feeling of not being good enough.

These bullets bury deeper than logic.
Racism is not intellectual.
I can not reason these scars away.

Outside my door
there is a real enemy
who hates me.   40

I am a poet
who yearns to dance on rooftops,
to whisper delicate lines about joy   45
and the blessings of human understanding.
I try. I go to my land, my tower of words and
bolt the door, but the typewriter doesn't fade out
the sounds of blasting and muffled outrage.
My own days bring me slaps on the face.   50
Every day I am deluged with reminders
that this is not
my land

and this is my land.

I do not believe in the war between races   55

but in this country
there is war.

> There's poetry in the language I speak. There's poetry, therefore, in my cul-
> ture, and in this place.
>
> —SEKOU SUNDIATA

New Historicism

One influential variety of cultural studies, **New Historicism,** grew out of
a sense that both New Criticism and poststructuralist theories like decon-
struction, through their neglect of the social and cultural milieu in which a
poem came to be written, were leaving out something important and valuable.
By focusing almost wholly on what occurs within a text, New Critics and de-
constructionists cut themselves off from the ways historical context can clar-
ify and illuminate a work. In particular, they lose referentiality. Despite many
differences among themselves, the varieties of historicist critics have in com-
mon a belief in referentiality—the idea that works of literature are influenced
by, and influence, the external world.

The developers of what came to be called New Historicism, such as
Louis Montrose and Stephen Greenblatt, did not simply return to the "old
historicism" discussed in Chapter 11, with its emphasis on facts and
events, its selective focus on the kinds of events that get recorded in offi-
cial documents, and its explanations in terms of causes and effects and of
development toward an end. They start from a very different viewpoint:

that it is virtually impossible to reconstruct the past. We have stories about the past, not objective facts and events existing independently; the stories are constructed by historians, reflecting the historians' assumptions and purposes and the choices they inevitably make about what to include, what to emphasize, what to omit. French philosophical historian Michel Foucault was particularly important in reminding us that all historians are "situated." It is difficult for them to recognize their own cultural practices and assumptions, and even more difficult to get outside them and enter those of another age.

The work of New Historicists is influenced by deconstruction and reader-response criticism, with their emphasis on subjectivity, and by cultural studies generally, with its attention to the myriad forces that shape events and motivations, rather than concentrating on economic and political forces, as the old historicism did. Like other types of cultural studies, it is open to other disciplines. It views history as a social science, closer to anthropology than to traditional historical studies. It attempts to elucidate how art is shaped by, and shapes, social, historical, and economic conditions, and how art is affected by politics and has political effects itself.

To illustrate how New Historicism might approach a text, Brook Thomas selects a poem closely associated with New Criticism, Keats's "Ode on a Grecian Urn" (it would be helpful before you proceed to read or reread the poem—p. 203). The poem was a central text in Cleanth Brooks's famous book of New Critical essays, *The Well Wrought Urn.*[3] Brooks examines the text closely, arguing that, if one views the *poem as a whole,* in terms of its dramatic unity, the final idea, " 'Beauty is truth, truth beauty'—that is all / Ye know on earth, and all ye need to know," is a dramatically appropriate thought for the personified urn to express. He carefully insists this is not a philosophical generalization, but "a consciously riddling paradox, put in the mouth of a particular character, and modified by the total context of the poem" (p. 154). The lines have "the validity of myth"—the urn as a sylvan historian properly ignores names, dates, and special circumstances, in order to achieve an insight into essential truth. Brooks likewise ignores historical context and influences in order (like the urn) to take a few details and order them so that we better appreciate the beauty of the poem and its own impact as myth.

Thomas, in contrast, suggests that the poem can raise the directly historical question of how much our sense of the past depends on art, and the consequences of that dependency. Art, the poem indicates, "both keeps alive a sense of beauty in a world of change *and* gives us a sense of the felt life of the past. But in its search for a realm in which truth and beauty coexist, art risks freezing the 'real' world and becoming a 'cold pastoral,' cut off from the very felt life it records" (pp. 515–16). This dramatized conflict can confront readers with "both art's power to keep the past alive and its tendency to distort it" (p. 516).

---

[3] Brook Thomas, "The Historical Necessity for—and Difficulties with—New Historical Analysis in Introductory Literature Courses," *College English* 49 (1987): 509–22; Cleanth Brooks, *The Well Wrought Urn: Studies in the Structure of Poetry* (New York: Harcourt, Brace, 1947), Ch. 8.

For Thomas it is important to place the poem in historical context (asking how economic and political conditions of early-nineteenth-century England shaped Keats's image of ancient Greece) and to situate the urn in the poem historically. This fits Greenblatt's tendency to start with analysis of a particular object or event, then to connect that object or event to the poem so that readers come to see "the event as a social text and the literary text as a social event."[4] Thomas asks first where Keats might have seen such an urn. The answer—in a museum—leads into a discussion of the rise of the art museum in eighteenth- and nineteenth-century Europe, as cultural artifacts from the past were placed in museums to be contemplated as art, isolated from their social setting. "In Keats' poem an urn that once had a practical social function now sparks aesthetic contemplation about the nature of truth, beauty, and the past," and reflecting on how the urn assumed a purely aesthetic function in a society that was becoming increasingly practical helps clarify "how our modern notion of art has been defined in response to the social order" ("The Historical Necessity," p. 518).

The urn's presence in a museum also raises political issues. The display of a Grecian urn in an English museum can lead to reflections on the political implications of a cultural heritage. The English in the nineteenth century, although they sympathized with the struggle for liberation in Greece, nevertheless took cultural treasures out of the country and put them on display in London. Thomas makes his point by quoting Marxist critic Walter Benjamin's warning that many of the cultural treasures we love have origins that should create great uneasiness within us: "They owe their existence not only to the efforts of the great minds and talents [of the artists] who created them, but also to the anonymous toil of their contemporaries [who quarried the marble, did the grunt work, etc.]. There is no document of civilization which is not at the same time a document of barbarism."[5] Thomas thus treats Keats's poem "as a social text, one that in telling us about the society that produced it also tells us about the society we inhabit today" ("The Historical Necessity," p. 519), and that should lead to reflection not just on present attitudes toward museums in the United States, but also on the implications of the way Keats's English poem has become a museum-type artifact in American culture today.

Marxist Criticism

Many, though definitely not all, varieties of cultural studies are influenced by **Marxist criticism.** Cultural studies is deeply concerned with *power,* particularly the indirect, unobvious, often ignored or unconscious kinds of power that underlie most societies. We will use a poem by William Blake to illustrate. After reading it, reflect on the kinds of power wielded in the chimney sweep's story.

[4] Brook Thomas, "The New Literary Historicism," *A Companion to American Thought*, ed. Richard Wightman Fox and James T. Klappenberg (New York: Blackwell, 1995), 490.

[5] Benjamin, "Theses on the Philosophy of History," *Illuminations*, trans. Harry Zohn (New York: Schocken, 1969), 256.

WILLIAM BLAKE (1757–1827)

The Chimney Sweeper (1789)

When my mother died I was very young,
And my father sold me while yet my tongue
Could scarcely cry " 'weep! 'weep! 'weep! 'weep!"
So your chimneys I sweep, and in soot I sleep.

There's little Tom Dacre, who cried when his head   5
That curled like a lamb's back, was shaved; so I said,
"Hush, Tom! never mind it, for when your head's bare,
You know that the soot cannot spoil your white hair."

And so he was quiet, and that very night,
As Tom was asleeping, he had such a sight!   10
That thousands of sweepers, Dick, Joe, Ned, and Jack,
Were all of them locked up in coffins of black;

And by came an Angel who had a bright key,
And he opened the coffins and set them all free.
Then down a green plain, leaping, laughing, they run,   15
And wash in a river, and shine in the Sun.

Then naked and white, all their bags left behind,
They rise upon clouds, and sport in the wind;
And the Angel told Tom, if he'd be a good boy,
He'd have God for his father, and never want joy.   20

And so Tom awoke, and we rose in the dark,
And got with our bags and our brushes to work.
Though the morning was cold, Tom was happy and warm;
So if all do their duty, they need not fear harm.

In the eighteenth century, small boys, sometimes as young as four years old, were used to clean chimneys by climbing up the flues and brushing the soot into bags. The boys were often sold into service by their parents or guardians, and were treated badly by their masters. Horrendous working conditions led to disease, injury, and deformity.

Many types of power come to bear on the situation. There is the power parents have over their children—a power so complete that they can even sell them, or rather their services; the children may technically not be slaves, but the effect is nearly the same. And a variety of forces have power over the parents—landlords, employers, businesspersons, the government. Situations of need and opportunity for profit grow out of and create economic power relations. Another, perhaps less immediately obvious, kind of power relation appears in Tom's dream when the angel tells him "if he'd be a good boy / He'd have God for his father, and never want [i.e., lack] joy." The words in Tom's dream are surely ones he heard when he was awake, perhaps from his employer or in church. Blake is exposing and challenging the way religion can be and has been used to validate and continue economic and human exploitation.

A cultural studies approach might study the social, economic, political, and religious context of the poem, in late-eighteenth-century London, and might compare Blake's poem with similar descriptions—in literature, diaries, pamphlets, art, and so on—in order to understand and appreciate more fully the problems and thinking of the time. It might go on to use all that as a basis for commenting on the continuing exploitation of child laborers in various nations today and on the economic structures and forces that allow it to continue. And in doing so, it might include a Marxist critique.

Although there has been, in recent decades, a widespread reaction against anything associated with Karl Marx, Marxist approaches to literature have been, and continue to be, influential within literary study, and they can furnish illuminating ways to approach a text. At the least, a student of literature needs to be conversant with the foundations of and procedures used in Marxist criticism.

Marxist criticism pushes beyond the sort of cultural readings we did above to analyze the influence of *ideology,* that is, the beliefs, values, and ways of thinking through which human beings perceive what they believe to be reality and carry out their roles in society. According to Marxist theory the ideology of an era (Marx called it the "superstructure") is determined by the contemporary socioeconomic system (the "base") and reflects the beliefs, values, and interests of the dominant class in it. Ideology includes everything that shapes the individual's mental picture of life experience—not what life really is, but the way it is perceived. This ideology may seem to people at the time just the natural, inevitable way of seeing and explaining things, but, Marxists claim, it seems that way only because ideology quietly, subtly works to legitimize and maintain the position, power, and economic interests of the ruling class, and, for the working classes, to cover up the reality of their exploitation. Ideology helps preserve the status quo by making what is artificial and oppressive seem natural and inevitable. According to Marxists, it must be exposed and overcome if people are to gain relief from their oppressors.

Marxist criticism is historical criticism, and as such is interested in the social context a work arises out of and the factors that have shaped it: it views literary works as *products,* and examines the economic and ideological forces that shape them. It is materialist criticism, which assumes that changes in society must be accounted for in social and physical factors and conditions, not in values attributed to people's minds or souls. It is social criticism, concerned with the social function of literature, and it is committed criticism, which aims not just at illumination but at involvement and action, seeking to change the lives and values of readers. It stands in many ways in opposition to formalist approaches, like New Criticism, which separate literature from its historical context, focus on its aesthetic qualities, and assume the existence of universal, transcendent truths and symbols. It does not, for the most part, engage in readings of individual works, as formalist approaches do; its orientation tends to be external, relating literature to culture, rather than internal, examining the work as a piece of art. Marxist criticism, therefore, is deeply involved with the relation of literature to ideology and reality, and with readers' awareness of the difference between them.

In some cases Marxist criticism affirms and clarifies works that transcend the ideology of their culture sufficiently to reflect "objective reality," at least partially. That would be true for Blake's "The Chimney Sweeper." More often, however, it confronts works that are in harmony with their dominant culture; its procedure in such cases is to read works "against the grain" in order to expose the ideology in them. The metaphor comes from carpentry: it is easiest to plane a board by pushing "with the grain"; the plane moves easily and produces smooth, pleasing results. It can glide over irregularities and inconsistencies in the wood. Pushing "against the grain" is harder and can cause rough edges. To apply the metaphor to reading, it is easiest and most "natural" to read a work "with the grain"—that is, to accept and follow the conventions and signals that correspond with the ideology behind it. Reading with the grain allows the reader to glide over problems and leads to smooth, reassuring results, compatible with what the dominant culture approves. It is harder to read "against the grain," to resist the conventions and ideology, to challenge and question them instead of accepting and following them. The values of the culture created by the upper classes inevitably creep into the literature they write, and in the capitalist system, Marxists believe, the production of literature rests mainly in the hands of the upper classes—they have the leisure to write and they have access to the means of publication. Therefore, deliberately or not, literary works become means of reinforcing and extending the influence of the culture's ideology. The role of a Marxist approach to literature is to expose that ideology, to bring what is hidden into the open, and to make readers see its ideological effect.

The function of ideology, in the Marxist view, is to "repress" revolutionary ideas or tendencies, to push them into the "political unconscious" (Marxist critic Fredric Jameson's term).[6] As ideology works itself into a text, things must be omitted: "In order to say anything, there are other things *which must not be said.*"[7] As a result, gaps and contradictions occur, and generally go unnoticed. Like psychoanalysts, Marxist critics tend to focus on the text's "unconscious," on what is unspoken and repressed, and bring it into "consciousness."

Look again at "Dover Beach" and think about what is not said in it. The speaker is concerned about the decline of values, taste, and commitment in his society. He refers to the world as a "land of dreams." The speaker is a member of the well-to-do class, the bourgeoisie—he is well educated, can talk about Greek authors, and has the leisure to reflect on national and international concerns. He seems totally unconscious of the fact that while the world is a "land of dreams" for those who have money and power, it exploits those who do not. The loss of faith and certitude he senses may worry him (or members of his social class) because these are things that help placate the masses—because they

---

[6] *The Political Unconscious: Narrative as a Socially Symbolic Act* (Ithaca, N.Y.: Cornell University Press, 1981).

[7] Pierre Machery, quoted in Raman Selden, *A Reader's Guide to Contemporary Literary Theory* (Lexington: University Press of Kentucky, 1985), 41.

distract the masses from the reality of their economic exploitation. In saying nothing about the masses, the poem actually says a great deal. It leaves gaps, which we might not see ordinarily. The Marxist critic notices them and brings them, and the social realities behind them, to our attention.

As you read the following poems, which come out of different times and cultural contexts, watch for what they say, and what they do not say, about power relations (who has and does not have power of various kinds—social, economic, political, sexual, racial) that are important in their situations. Ask yourself if they would respond well to a Marxist critique. Consider ways they seem to be influenced by (or products of) their culture and ways they seem to be responding to and commenting on that culture. Be ready to discuss what you see in them from a social or cultural perspective.

WILLIAM BLAKE (1757–1827)

London (1794)

I wander through each chartered street,
Near where the chartered Thames does flow,
And mark in every face I meet
Marks of weakness, marks of woe.

In every cry of every man,   5
In every Infant's cry of fear,
In every voice, in every ban,
The mind-forged manacles I hear.

How the Chimney-sweeper's cry
Every black'ning church appalls;   10
And the hapless soldier's sigh
Runs in blood down Palace walls.

But most through midnight streets I hear
How the youthful Harlot's curse
Blasts the new-born Infant's tear,   15
And blights with plagues the Marriage hearse.

FELICIA HEMANS (1793–1835)

The Homes of England (1825?)

"Where's the coward that would not dare
To fight for such a land?"
          —Marmion [by Sir Walter Scott]

The stately Homes of England,
     How beautiful they stand!
Amidst their tall ancestral trees,
     O'er all the pleasant land.

The deer across their greensward bound,   5
    Through shade and sunny gleam,
And the swan glides past them with the sound
    Of some rejoicing stream.

The merry Homes of England!
    Around their hearths by night,   10
What gladsome looks of household love
    Meet in the ruddy light!
There woman's voice flows forth in song,
    Or childhood's tale is told,
Or lips move tunefully along   15
    Some glorious page of old.

The blessed Homes of England!
    How softly on their bowers
Is laid the holy quietness
    That breathes from Sabbath hours!   20
Solemn, yet sweet, the church-bell's chime
    Floats through their woods at morn;
All other sounds, in that still time,
    Of breeze and leaf are born.

The Cottage Homes of England!   25
    By thousands on her plains,
They are smiling o'er the silvery brooks,
    And round the hamlet fanes.°   churches
Through glowing orchards forth they peep,
    Each from its nook of leaves,   30
And fearless there the lowly sleep,
    As the bird beneath their eaves.

The free, fair Homes of England!
    Long, long, in hut and hall,
May hearts of native proof be rear'd   35
    To guard each hallow'd wall!
And green for ever be the groves,
    And bright the flowery sod,
Where first the child's glad spirit loves
    Its country and its God!   40

JAMES WELCH (b. 1940)

Christmas Comes to Moccasin Flat (1976)

Christmas comes like this: Wise men
unhurried, candles bought on credit (poor price
for calves), warriors face down in wine sleep.
Winds cheat to pull heat from smoke.

Friends sit in chinked cabins, stare out   5
plastic windows and wait for commodities.
Charlie Blackbird, twenty miles from church
and bar, stabs his fire with flint.

When drunks drain radiators for love
or need, chiefs eat snow and talk of change,   10
an urge to laugh pounding their ribs.
Elk play games in high country.

Medicine Woman, clay pipe and twist tobacco,
calls each blizzard by name and predicts
five o'clock by spitting at her television.   15
Children lean into her breath to beg a story:

Something about honor and passion,
warriors back with meat and song,
a peculiar evening star, quick vision of birth.
Blackbird feeds his fire. Outside, a quick 30 below.   20

FEMINIST CRITICISM

The importance and influence of power relations is particularly evident in **feminist criticism.** Prior to 1970, especially during the period in which New Criticism was in vogue, literary standards and agendas were male-dominated. A large majority of college and university teachers and scholars were male; all of the founders of New Criticism were male; most of the poets studied and approved of by New Criticism were male. Cleanth Brooks and Robert Penn Warren's landmark New Critical textbook *Understanding Poetry* (1938) included poems by 89 men and 5 women (11 poems are anonymous). Of poems included, 220 were by men, 8 by women (one an example of a "bad" poem). In the original edition of a very influential formalist textbook on poetry, Laurence Perrine's *Sound and Sense* (1956), 107 male, but only 10 female, poets were represented (169 poems by men, 18 by women).

The tendency of male critics to favor works by men was reinforced by the theoretical position of New Criticism. New Criticism looked in literature for universal themes—themes it assumed would apply equally to men and women of all classes, cultures, and times. The shapers of New Criticism, however, did not seem aware of the extent to which their own backgrounds and presuppositions defined those "universal" issues: the issues were ones raised by well-educated, upper-class, conservative men. Just as their method of reading sought to unify and integrate aspects of literary works, so the themes they found in the works involved social unity and integration. Issues of importance to marginal groups—women, people of color, the lower classes—did not fit the mold and were overlooked (only one poem by an African American author—Countee Cullen's "Incident"—appears in the original *Sound and Sense,* none in *Understanding Poetry*).

Against this background arose a feminist protest movement. Pivotal in its development was Kate Millett's *Sexual Politics* (1970), which began to raise the consciousness of women to the fact that all avenues of power in Western culture were under male control. Literature was no exception. Men set the criteria for deciding what was good literature and which authors would be approved and anthologized. Men, therefore, had the power to determine who would be read, who would receive attention and achieve fame. Feminist criticism reacted against this power and its effects initially in two principal directions. First was reappraisal of works by men, to examine how they looked when read "against the grain," that is, from a feminine point of view. Second was systematic exploration of what many women had quietly been arguing—that excellent female writers, past and current, were being neglected, in part because men were not open to their approaches, styles, subjects, and perceptions.

Feminist criticism can be fused with a variety of critical approaches. Thus there can be feminist-reader-response, feminist-deconstructive criticism, and so on. Feminist criticism, in addition to indicating some things to *do* with a work of literature, points out issues to be aware of in a work. Its aim is to heighten awareness, to effect changes in attitudes and behavior, to correct injustices, and to improve society and individual situations. Not all readers are or will be committed to the feminist cause. Still, all readers, even men and women without such commitment, should become familiar with works by women and with feminist criticism of works by men and women, in order to gain greater understanding of and sensitivity to literature and concerns of deep significance to persons who represent at least half of the population.

Becoming a Resisting Reader

Feminist criticism began with rereadings and reappraisals of works in our literary heritage, particularly works by men, to expose the masculine biases (the patriarchal ideology) inherent in them, evident especially in the treatment of women: their absence, or stereotyping, or reduction to objects. The "universal" reader implied in most New Critical studies, though intended to be gender-neutral, was, in fact, male. Feminist critics began to ask what happens to a work when it is read instead from a consciously feminine perspective. The first act of a feminist reader, according to critic Judith Fetterly, is to become a "resisting reader" rather than an assenting reader[8]—that is, to question and challenge the assumptions of the poem about roles, power, and values instead of just accepting them as givens.

Think again about "Cherrylog Road." When we examined it from a New Critical perspective in Chapter 12, we focused on its use of narrative, images, and figures and its exploration of a universal theme—the movement from innocence to experience that is common to youth. A feminist perspective regards "universality" with suspicion and challenges it; by resisting such a reading, we open up a different set of concerns. Central to them is the handling of Doris Holbrook: What is the attitude in the poem toward the female character in-

[8] *The Resisting Reader: A Feminist Approach to American Fiction* (Bloomington: Indiana University Press, 1978).

volved? Does the speaker treat her as a real person? Does the poem? Is the speaker (or the poem) sensitive toward her feelings and situation?

Such questions bring to our attention what an assenting reader might pass over, that is, the specifically male orientation of this experience. It is told, of course, from a male perspective, looking back on a past event, one probably many years past. As the speaker looks back, he feels nostalgia over a significant rite of passage, but there is a tinge of humor and irony, particularly because the setting for any romantic beauty and tenderness the experience may contain is a junkyard. A resisting reader would point out that the humor and irony carry over, reductively, to the memories of Doris. She inevitably becomes associated with the cars, reducing her to an object. That is reinforced by the speaker's use of her full name three times—his saying "Doris Holbrook" the second and third times suggests a lack of intimacy and familiarity with her. The experience is more important than she is.

The excitement is heightened by the danger involved: they risk discovery. A resisting reader would notice that this excitement comes at the woman's expense. The dangers the speaker faces are imaginary: he would not in fact be assassinated gangland style by a shotgun blast from a passing car, in the imaginary scene his male fantasies create. Clearly, a double standard is operating: he had no need to *escape* from his father as she did from hers; and although her father would indeed be angry if they were caught, that anger would be vented on Doris, not on the speaker. Doris faces actual risks—a literal stropping, which the speaker does acknowledge, and possible pregnancy, which he does not.

We know nothing of the effect of this experience on Doris, since everything is told from the speaker's male perspective—even "her lips' new trembling" and "changed, other bodies" are projected on her by him. But we do know the effect on him: the emphasis throughout is on power—from the "wild stock-car race" early in the poem to the "bicycle fleshed / With power" at the end. The poem clearly reflects a "phallocentric" world, one where fathers and boyfriends hold power, and a "phallocentric" theme, celebrating the "attainment of manhood" with little regard for or concern about the woman involved.

• • •

Reflect now on the way we proceeded. We began by examining the attitude toward women contained in the work. That is usually the first step in a resisting reading, and many would say it is the key one. Pay attention not only to what is said, but also to what is not said. Even works in which no women are present may convey an attitude toward women: What does their absence say? How does the fact that no women are present shape and color the situation? Watch also for details that (perhaps unintentionally or unconsciously) demean women, or treat subjects in a way that is potentially insulting to women. Reread, for example, "Batter My Heart, Three-Personed God" (Ch. 9, p. 147). The speaker (we will assume it is a man) is uttering an anguished prayer asking God to take control of his life. He wants to be a servant of God, but his selfish desires interfere; so he asks God to overcome his resistance and enable him to be a faithful Christian. Although the speaker seems to be male, in his metaphors he portrays himself as female in relation to a masculine God, which is consistent with New Testament imagery of the Church as the "bride of Christ." For Donne the metaphors of battering and rape surely were meant as a fresh, striking, powerful way of expressing the need he felt for God's intervention in his life. For many readers today, however, those metaphors would come across as evidence that many men, in Donne's day as today, regard physical force against women less seriously than women do.

Feminist critics pay particular attention to stereotypes of women. One of the students in the discussion of " 'Out, Out—' " in Chapter 2 complained about role stereotypes: "The girl is in the kitchen helping 'mommy,' and the guy is out sawing wood with 'daddy.' I get furious at that." Depictions of women in literature and culture traditionally have embodied two additional stereotypes—the opposite archetypes of Mary and Eve, madonna and temptress: the quiet, obedient, idealized "good mother" and the beautiful, seductive, dangerous "bad woman." Both stereotypes are unjust and potentially harmful. Both narrow women to a single and simplistic definition and treat them as "other." Note, for example, how the stereotypes interact in "My Last Duchess" (Ch. 5, p. 76), as the duke desires his own version of a madonna as wife, but believes his last duchess was in fact a temptress ("she liked whate'er / She looked on, and her looks went everywhere"). Stereotypes have played a significant role in shaping the cultural constructs that characterize images of "woman" today. A central strategy of a feminist critic must be to look for and point out such stereotypes in literary works, and to discuss their effects or potential effects.

As you read the following poem, ask yourself about the conception of women, and of the relationship between men and women, that is implicit or expressed in it.

ROBERT HERRICK (1591–1674)

Delight in Disorder (1648)

A sweet disorder in the dress
Kindles in clothes a wantonness.
A lawn about the shoulders thrown
Into a fine distraction;
An erring lace, which here and there   5
Enthralls the crimson stomacher;
A cuff neglectful, and thereby
Ribbons to flow confusedly;
A winning wave, deserving note,
In the tempestuous petticoat;   10
A careless shoestring, in whose tie
I see a wild civility;
Do more bewitch me than when art
Is too precise in every part.

Reclaiming the Feminine Tradition

From a reappraisal of works by men, feminist criticism moved on to the study of literature written by women—what Elaine Showalter has termed "gynocriticism." This involves, on the one hand, reexamination of well-known women authors, ones long accepted into the tradition, and on the other hand, even more significantly, the discovery or rediscovery of many neglected or forgotten women writers, past and present. The result has been an opening up of the literary canon, to include works dealing with imagery and issues that earlier criticism, because it privileged universality over particularity, would have excluded (since they supposedly appealed to or involved only half the population). It has also led to the creation of an alternative canon, a body of women's writings from past and present. An important result of such attention to the literary tradition of women has been to provide a sense of ancestry for women writers and readers today. Their literary "mothers" offer models of how to write about the concerns of women, and provide authorization to do so.

The following poem, for example, describes the situation faced by a woman writer in the late seventeenth century. As you read it, reflect on ways her situation was similar to and/or different from what women encounter today.

ANNE FINCH, COUNTESS OF WINCHILSEA (1661–1720)

The Introduction (1689)

Did I my lines intend for public view,	
How many censures° would their faults pursue,	*criticisms*
Some would, because such words they do affect,	
Cry they're insipid, empty, uncorrect.	
And many have attained, dull and untaught,	5
The name of wit,° only by finding fault.	*perceptive person*
True judges might condemn their want° of wit,	*lack*
And all might say, they're by a woman writ.	
Alas! a woman that attempts the pen,	
Such an intruder on the rights of men,	10
Such a presumptuous creature, is esteemed,	
The° fault can by no virtue be redeemed.	*That the*

They tell us we mistake our sex and way;
Good breeding, fashion, dancing, dressing, play
Are the accomplishments we should desire;   15
To write, or read, or think, or to inquire
Would cloud our beauty, and exhaust our time,
And interrupt the conquests° of our prime;°   *(amorous)/best years*
Whilst the dull manage of a servile house°   *household with servants*
Is held by some our utmost art, and use.   20
    Sure 'twas not ever thus, nor are we told
Fables° of women that excelled of old;   *accounts*
To whom, by the diffusive° hand of Heaven   *scattering*
Some share of wit and poetry was given.

• • •

How are we fallen, fallen by mistaken rules?
And education's, more than nature's fools,
Debarred from all improvements of the mind,
And to be dull, expected and designed;°   *shaped, formed*
And if someone would soar above the rest,   55
With warmer fancy° and ambition pressed,   *desire*
So strong th' opposing faction still appears,
The hopes to thrive can ne'er outweigh the fears.
Be cautioned then my Muse, and still retired;
Nor be despised, aiming to be admired;   60
Conscious of wants, still with contracted wing,
To some few friends and to thy sorrows sing;
For groves of laurel° thou wert never meant;   *leaves worn as a*
Be dark enough thy shades, and be thou   *mark of distinction*
    there content.

Because customs regarding relationships between the sexes often favor
men and suppress women, difficulties between men and women frequently
were, and continue to be, the subject of poems by women. Following are three
poems from different time periods relating situations and problems faced by
women. Discuss with others in your class the different forms and approaches
used to explore those situations. Men and women often respond differently to
these issues, and to works dealing with them. Watch as the discussion pro-
ceeds to see if that happens in your class.

CHARLOTTE MEW (1870–1928)

The Farmer's Bride (1916)

Three Summers since I chose a maid,
Too young maybe—but more's to do
At harvest-time than bide and woo.
    When us was wed she turned afraid

Of love and me and all things human;   5
Like the shut of a winter's day
Her smile went out, and 'twadn't a woman—
          More like a little frightened fay.
               One night, in the Fall, she runned away.

"Out 'mong the sheep, her be," they said,   10
Should properly have been abed;
But sure enough she wadn't there
Lying awake with her wide brown stare.
So over seven-acre field and up-along across the down
We chased her, flying like a hare   15
Before our lanterns. To Church-Town
          All in a shiver and a scare
We caught her, fetched her home at last
          And turned the key upon her, fast.

She does the work about the house   20
As well as most, but like a mouse:
          Happy enough to chat and play
          With birds and rabbits and such as they,
          So long as men-folk keep away.

"Not near, not near!" her eyes beseech   25
When one of us comes within reach.
          The women say that beasts in stall
          Look round like children at her call.
          I've hardly heard her speak at all.

Shy as a leveret, swift as he,   30
Straight and slight as a young larch tree,
Sweet as the first wild violets, she,
To her wild self. But what to me?

The short days shorten and the oaks are brown,
          The blue smoke rises to the low grey sky,   35
One leaf in the still air falls slowly down,
          A magpie's spotted feathers lie
On the black earth spread white with rime,
The berries redden up to Christmas-time.
          What's Christmas-time without there be   40
          Some other in the house than we!

          She sleeps up in the attic there
          Alone, poor maid. 'Tis but a stair
Betwixt us. Oh! my God! the down,
The soft young down of her, the brown,   45
The brown of her—her eyes, her hair, her hair!

CAROLYN KIZER (b. 1925)

Bitch (1984)

Now, when he and I meet, after all these years,
I say to the bitch inside me, don't start growling.
He isn't a trespasser anymore,
Just an old acquaintance tipping his hat.
My voice says, "Nice to see you,"   5
As the bitch starts to bark hysterically.
He isn't an enemy now,
Where are your manners, I say, as I say,
"How are the children? They must be growing up."
At a kind word from him, a look like the old days,   10
The bitch changes her tone: she begins to whimper.
She wants to snuggle up to him, to cringe.
Down, girl! Keep your distance
Or I'll give you a taste of the choke-chain.
"Fine, I'm just fine," I tell him.   15
She slobbers and grovels.
After all, I am her mistress. She is basically loyal.
It's just that she remembers how she came running
Each evening, when she heard his step;
How she lay at his feet and looked up adoringly   20
Though he was absorbed in his paper;
Or, bored with her devotion, ordered her to the kitchen
Until he was ready to play.
But the small careless kindnesses
When he'd had a good day, or a couple of drinks,   25
Come back to her now, seem more important
Than the casual cruelties, the ultimate dismissal.
"It's nice to know you are doing so well," I say.
He couldn't have taken you with him;
You were too demonstrative, too clumsy,   30
Not like the well-groomed pets of his new friends.
"Give my regards to your wife," I say. You gag
As I drag you off by the scruff,
Saying, "Goodbye! Goodbye! Nice to have seen you again."

JO CARSON (b. 1946)

I Cannot Remember All the Times . . . (1989)

I cannot remember all the times he hit me.
I might could count black eyes,
how many times I said I ran into doors
or fell down or stepped into the path

of any flying object except his fist.   5
Once I got a black eye playing softball.
The rest were him. Seven, eight.
I can name what of me he broke:
my nose, my arm, and four ribs
in the course of six years' marriage.   10
The ribs were after I said divorce
and in spite of a peace bond.
I spent the night in the hospital.
He did not even spend a night in jail.
The sheriff I helped elect does not   15
apply the law to family business.
He always swore he never meant to do it.
I do believe he never planned.
It was always just the day,
the way I looked at him afraid.   20
Maybe the first time he did not mean to do it,
maybe the broken ribs were for good luck.

I want to post this in ladies rooms,
write it on the tags of women's underwear,
write it on coupons to go in Tampax packages   25
because my ex-husband will want to marry again
and there is no tattoo where he can't see it
to tell the next woman who might fall in love with him.
After six months, maybe a year,
he will start with a slap you can brush off.   30
Leave when he slaps you.
When he begins to call you cunt and whore
and threatens to kill you if you try to go
it will almost be like teasing but it is not.
Keep two sets of car keys for yourself.   35
Take your children with you when you go.
If he is throwing things, he is drinking.
If he is drunk enough he cannot catch you.
A punch in the breast hurts worse than a punch in the jaw.
A hit with an object does more damage than a hit with a fist   40
unless he is so drunk he picks up a broom instead of a poker.
If you pick up the poker, he will try to get it.
If he gets it, he will hit you with it.
He probably will not kill you because you will pass out
and then, he is all the sudden sorry and he stops.   45
When he says he will not hit you again
as he drives you to the hospital,
both of you in tears and you in pain,
you have stayed much too long already.
Tell the people at the hospital the truth   50

no matter how much you think you love him.
Do not say you fell down stairs
no matter how much he swears he loves you.
He does love you, he loves you hurt
and he will hit you again.

As women writers from the past have become better known over the last two decades, interest in reclaiming the tradition has shifted from finding forgotten authors to examining such issues as the relation of women as writers to literary form. This discussion has focused less on poetry than on the novel—on the way women became prominent novelists during the nineteenth century and through this achieved respect as literary artists in the twentieth century. It raises the question of why women found levels of success in the novel that they did not find in poetry or drama. Was it because initially men did not take the novel seriously, viewing it as an extension of romance fiction and concentrating on genres traditionally more highly respected, leaving its development to women? Was it that women recognized in the novel a mode without a long history of restrictive male authorities, a new form that they could mold to their own sensibilities—a form amenable to, even developing out of, forms long familiar to women, like the diary, the journal, and letters? Is it related to a general feminization of culture beginning in the latter part of the eighteenth century? Feminist critics also explore the affinity of women writers for popular fiction—utopian writing, detective fiction, science fiction—and the particularly problematic issue, for feminists, of the popularity of romantic fiction among women writers and readers.[9]

Feminist Cultural Criticism

One criticism of early varieties of feminist criticism is that much of it treats *woman* as a universal category, not recognizing differences among women—differences of race, economic and social class, and national origin—that contribute to their identity. Contemporary feminists such as Gayatri Spivak say that while all women are female, they are something else as well (such as working class or upper class, heterosexual or lesbian, African American or living in a postcolonial nation), and the something else is important to consider. Such an approach has led feminists to feel affinities with all those who are considered "the Other," or who are marginalized on the basis of race, ethnicity, class, or social background. Cultural feminists explore the way many factors—not just sex—contribute to disempowerment of various kinds.

Consider "Cherrylog Road" yet again, from a cultural viewpoint. The kudzu covering the junked cars and the allusions to Prohibition ("run / corn whiskey") locates the poem in the southern United States, perhaps the mid-South, since the whiskey is brought down from the hills. The classism of

[9] See Mary Eagleton, ed., *Feminist Literary Theory: A Reader,* 2d ed. (Oxford, England: Blackwell, 1996), 137–43, for a brief overview and bibliographical footnotes.

southern society is reflected in the references to the long Pierce-Arrow in which a white lady is giving directions on the interphone to her driver. The action of the poem suggests parallel, though subtle, class differences, and along with them the oppression of women typical in paternalistic attitudes. Doris Holbrook is from a lower-class ("redneck") level of society: her family lives on a farm and needs ways to supplement its income (thus, although her father would not approve of her going to the junkyard for a sexual encounter, he is willing to have her go to steal auto parts). The speaker appears to be from a higher social stratum: he does not need to steal auto parts; though a young man, he owns a motorcycle; it is not coincidental that she *walks down* Cherrylog Road, while he *rides up* Highway 106.

Doris must *escape* from her father: she is his "prisoner," his property; society has given him, as a father, the right to approve or disapprove of her sexual activities—presumably to disapprove of any until after her marriage, to a man of whom he approves. Although Doris "escapes" from her father and commits an act both of defiance and of *self*-possession, she clearly is not free. She must return to her father, so the escape is only temporary—and the price of the temporary escape may prove fearsome. Cultural conventions make her an object possessed by her father, but also an object used by the speaker. He leaves his class (whose women, cultural convention dictates, are to be reserved for marriage) and uses a woman from a lower class (someone he does not even seem to know well) as a casual sex partner. When cultural context and ideologies are ignored, the poem can seem to be about a sexual experience between two equal partners. When cultural aspects are considered, however, the exploitation of a woman—and, by extension, of all women—is implied in the poem.

GENDER STUDIES

The protest movement that began as feminist criticism has in large part moved on to the more inclusive area of **gender studies,** although opinion concerning the use of the two terms is mixed and divided. Gender studies focuses on the idea that gender is socially constructed, on the way attitudes toward masculinity and femininity are rooted in deeply but uncritically held beliefs of a society. Most varieties of gender studies assume a difference between the terms *sex* and *gender*. *Sex* refers to the physical characteristics of men and women biologically; *gender* refers to traits designated "masculine" and "feminine." One is born biologically male or female, but one *acquires* a "gender" (society's conceptions of "woman" and "man"). In Simone de Beauvoir's words, "One is not born a woman, one becomes one."[10] Inequality of the sexes, for example, is not a universal truth—not a biological or divine mandate—but is constructed by patriarchy to serve the interests of male supremacy.[11]

---

[10] *The Second Sex* (1949), trans. H. M. Parshley (New York: Vintage, 1974), 301.

[11] Gayle Greene and Coppélia Kahn, eds., *Making a Difference: Feminist Literary Criticism* (London: Methuen, 1985), 1, 3.

Gender studies shows that such distinctions in the West have traditionally been shaped through the use of binary oppositions: masculine/feminine, father/mother, son/daughter, brother/sister, active/passive, reason/emotion, intelligent/sensitive. Western cultures typically privilege the left side of these pairings over the right side. The effect of such thinking is to divide sexual identity into two camps, to relegate women to a lower status than men, and to limit socially legitimized sex to heterosexuality. Gender criticism includes *all* "the critical ramifications of sexual oppression,"[12] such as gay, lesbian, and queer studies. Just as early feminist critics called attention to the way women have traditionally been forced to read from a masculine perspective, so gay, lesbian, and queer studies have called attention to the way texts are traditionally read from a heterosexual viewpoint. Many readers almost automatically assume that a relationship described in a poem will be heterosexual, even when that is not indicated directly (would you have assumed a heterosexual relationship when you read Amy Lowell's "Madonna of the Evening Flowers"?). It is not always a safe assumption (it is not in this case). Lesbian and gay critics have produced revisionist rereadings—often provocative and illuminating, sometimes highly controversial—of many texts; one example is Adrienne Rich's study of Emily Dickinson's poetry from a lesbian perspective.[13]

The following poem retells a fairy tale in a new setting. Watch for indications of awareness of gender (masculine and feminine) as culturally constructed, of attempts to escape traditional constraints, of ways and reasons those attempts were frustrated. Consider how the poem might speak differently to women reading it in different contexts and situations. Reflect on how satisfactory you find the way in which the issues and the situation were resolved, or not resolved.

OLGA BROUMAS (b. 1949)

Cinderella (1977)

> . . . the joy that isn't shared
> I heard, dies young.
> —*Anne Sexton, 1928–1974*

Apart from my sisters, estranged
from my mother, I am a woman alone
in a house of men
who secretly
call themselves princes, alone   5
with me usually, under cover of dark. I am the one allowed in

to the royal chambers, whose small foot conveniently
fills the slipper of glass. The woman writer, the lady

[12] Jonathan Culler, *On Deconstruction: Theory and Criticism after Structuralism* (Ithaca, N.Y.: Cornell University Press, 1982), 56.

[13] Rich, "Vesuvius at Home: The Power of Emily Dickinson," *On Lies, Secrets, and Silence: Selected Prose 1966–1978* (New York: Norton, 1979), 151–83.

umpire, the madam chairman, anyone's wife.
I know what I know.   10
And I once was glad

of the chance to use it, even alone
in a strange castle, doing overtime on my own, cracking
the royal code. The princes spoke
in their fathers' language, were eager to praise me   15
my nimble tongue. I am a woman in a state of siege, alone

as one piece of laundry, strung on a windy clothesline a
mile long. A woman co-opted by promises: the lure
of a job, the ruse of a choice, a woman forced
to bear witness, falsely   20
against my kind, as each
other sister was judged inadequate, bitchy, incompetent,
jealous, too thin, too fat. I know what I know.
What sweet bread I make

for myself in this prosperous house   25
is dirty, what good soup I boil turns
in my mouth to mud. Give
me my ashes. A cold stove, a cinder-block pillow, wet
canvas shoes in my sisters', my sisters' hut. Or I swear

I'll die young   30
like those favored before me, hand-picked each one
for her joyful heart.

APPLICATIONS FOR CHAPTER 14

SUGGESTIONS FOR WRITING

1. Select two or three poems and for a week write down in your journal
   other media you discover that deal with the same subjects, ideas, themes,
   and issues. Jot down notes about similarities and differences in approach
   and handling.
2. Rating systems are now in effect for cultural forms like movies and
   recordings, and perhaps soon will be for television, but not for poetry. In
   your journal, explain why poetry doesn't have such a system, and what
   that says about the public's relation to other cultural forms and to poetry.
3. Write a paper in which you compare the way a poem handled an idea or
   theme with the way a television soap opera, television sitcom, movie, song,
   stand-up comedian, country singer, or rock 'n' roll group handled it.
4. Write a journal entry expressing what your attitude toward Marxism was
   before reading this chapter and why you held the positions you did. Note
   in the entry whether your attitudes changed as a result of reading the
   chapter, and if so, in what ways.

5. Write a poem or story about present-day equivalents to Blake's chimney sweeps.
6. Write a paper discussing "My Last Duchess" (Ch. 5, p. 76), William Blake's "London" (p. 278), Wendy Rose's "Loo-Wit" (p. 417), or another poem or group of poems, from a Marxist position.
7. Write a journal entry expressing what your attitude toward feminism was before reading this chapter and why you thought as you did. Note in the entry whether your attitudes changed as a result of reading the chapter, and if so, in what ways.
8. Choose several advertisements, song lyrics, television shows, or athletic events and apply a feminist theory to any of them. What do you discover? Write a paper discussing this process and what it revealed.
9. In a poem, story, or essay relate the events of "Cherrylog Road" from Doris's point of view.
10. Reread "My Papa's Waltz" (Ch. 5, p. 71). Did you assume the speaker was male or female? Read it again, reversing that assumption. Write on the differences that makes in the effect of the poem.
11. Reread "My Last Duchess" (Ch. 5, p. 76). Reflect on the situation from the late duchess's point of view and on how the values and attitudes of the duke embody masculine viewpoints.
12. The speaker in Alfred, Lord Tennyson's dramatic monologue "Ulysses" (p. 313) is Ulysses (the Roman name for Odysseus), hero of Homer's epic *The Odyssey*, which tells the story of Odysseus's adventures and tribulations on his voyage back to his home, after he and the other Greek heroes had defeated Troy. It took Odysseus ten years to reach Ithaca, the small, rocky island of which he was king, where his wife (Penelope) and son (Telemachus) had been waiting for him. Upon his return he defeated the suitors who had been trying to marry the faithful Penelope, and he resumed the kingship and his old ways of life. Here Homer's story ends, but in Canto 26 of the *Inferno* the great medieval Italian poet Dante extended the story: Odysseus eventually became restless and dissatisfied with the settled life of a small, calm, quiet island, after all his adventures, and he decided to return to the sea and sail west, through the Strait of Gibraltar, into the unknown sea, and seek whatever adventures he might find there. Tennyson's poem amplifies the speech delivered in Dante's poem, as Ulysses challenges his men to accompany him on this new voyage. It has long been praised as epitomizing the optimistic, adventurous spirit of the nineteenth century, with its attitude that humans are capable of more than they have dreamt of and should strive to be all that they can be. Read it first in that nineteenth-century, heroic vein, and then "against the grain," watching for what feminist critics might notice in it. Write a response in your journal, and/or a paper on what you find.
13. One area of interest to gynocriticism is seeking to identify subject matters characteristic of women writers—such as home and family, or pregnancy and childbirth, or awareness of their own bodies, or relations between mothers and daughters or between women. Find several such poems in

the anthology and write responses to them in your journal; they might, later, make good topics for papers.

14. As the anthology demonstrates, poems by women deal with a huge range of topics, situations, and concerns. One frequent topic, shared obviously by men, is love. Describe and respond briefly in your journal to the variety of stances and attitudes expressed in the poems by Anne Bradstreet, "To My Dear and Loving Husband" (p. 304), Aphra Behn, "On Her Loving Two Equally" (p. 304), Amy Lowell, "Madonna of the Evening Flowers" (p. 326), Kamala Das, "In Love" (p. 391), Ai, "Why Can't I Leave You" (p. 416), and Louise Erdrich, "A Love Medicine" (p. 430).

SUGGESTIONS AS YOU CONTINUE TO READ POETRY

1. Keep in mind the potential value of viewing literature from a social, political, or cultural perspective.
2. Consider the potential value of reading a poem "against the grain," paying attention to Marxist concerns as you do so.
3. Consider the potential value of reading a poem "against the grain" by paying attention to feminist or gender issues as you read.

For twenty years I've lived in New York City on a block with two "heroin hotels"—a lot of middle-of-the-night screaming, cop cars, loud radios, and over the years occasional singing, laughter, and gunshots. So I'm often hearing sounds of suffering, and seeing its signs. Deep down, I have a fear that poetry is useless, I guess I mean *my* poetry is useless, a self-indulgent activity—that it's obvious I should, instead, be holding infants in a hospital orphanage, or working at a food kitchen for the homeless. Other times I feel extremely lucky to be able to spend time on what I adore doing and need to do. But it's obvious that a worker at a shelter for battered women, or a tutor in a ghetto, is a more useful member of society.

And yet my wild hope is that poetry somehow, secretly, matters as much as anything.

—SHARON OLDS

An Anthology of Poems
for Further Reading

ANONYMOUS
Lord Randal

1

"O where ha' you been, Lord Randal, my son?
And where ha' you been, my handsome young man?"
"I ha' been at the greenwood; mother, mak my bed soon,
For I'm wearied wi' huntin', and fain wad* lie down."

2

"And wha° met ye there, Lord Randal, my son?   *who*   5
And wha met you there, my handsome young man?"
"O I met wi' my true-love; mother, mak my bed soon,
For I'm wearied wi' huntin', and fain wad lie down."

3

"And what did she give you, Lord Randal, my son?
And what did she give you, my handsome young man?"   10
"Eels fried in a pan; mother, mak my bed soon,
For I'm wearied wi' huntin', and fain wad lie down."

4

"And wha gat your leavin's, Lord Randal, my son?
And wha gat your leavin's, my handsome young man?"
"My hawks and my hounds; mother, mak my bed soon,   15
For I'm wearied wi' huntin', and fain wad lie down."

5

"And what becam of them, Lord Randal, my son?
And what becam of them, my handsome young man?"

*Gladly would.

"They stretched their legs out and died; mother, mak my bed soon,
For I'm wearied wi' huntin', and fain wad lie down."   20

6

"O I fear you are poisoned, Lord Randal, my son!
I fear you are poisoned, my handsome young man!"
"O yes, I am poisoned; mother, mak my bed soon,
For I'm sick at the heart, and I fain wad lie down."

7

"What d' ye leave to your mother, Lord Randal, my son?   25
What d' ye leave to your mother, my handsome young man?"
"Four and twenty milk kye;° mother, mak my bed soon,   *cows*
For I'm sick at the heart, and I fain wad lie down."

8

"What d' ye leave to your sister, Lord Randal, my son?
What d' ye leave to your sister, my handsome young man?"   30
"My gold and my silver; mother, mak my bed soon,
For I'm sick at the heart, and I fain wad lie down."

9

"What d' ye leave to your brother, Lord Randal, my son?
What d' ye leave to your brother, my handsome young man?"
"My houses and my lands; mother, mak my bed soon,   35
For I'm sick at the heart, and I fain wad lie down."

10

"What d' ye leave to your true-love, Lord Randal, my son?
What d' ye leave to your true-love, my handsome young man?"
"I leave her hell and fire; mother, mak my bed soon,
For I'm sick at the heart, and I fain wad lie down."   40

ANONYMOUS

Sir Patrick Spens

The king sits in Dumferling town,
    Drinking the blude-reid° wine;   *blood-red*
"O whar will I get guid sailor,
    To sail this ship of mine?"

Up and spak an eldern° knicht,°   *elderly/knight*   5
    Sat at the king's richt° knee: *right*
"Sir Patrick Spens is the best sailor
    That sails upon the sea."

The king has written a braid° letter   *broad (clear)*
    And signed it wi' his hand,   10
And sent it to Sir Patrick Spens,
    Was walking on the sand.

The first line that Sir Patrick read,
　　A loud lauch° lauched he;　　　　　　　　　　*laugh*
The next line that Sir Patrick read,　　　　　　　　　　　　　15
　　The tear blinded his ee.°　　　　　　　　　　*eye*

"O wha° is this has done this deed,　　　　　　*who*
　　This ill deed done to me,
To send me out this time o' the year,
　　To sail upon the sea?　　　　　　　　　　　　　　　20

"Mak haste, mak haste, my mirry men all,
　　Our guid ship sails the morn."
"O say na° sae,° my master dear,　　　　　　*not/so*
　　For I fear a deadly storm.

"Late, late yestre'en I saw the new moon　　　　　　　　　25
　　Wi' the auld moon in hir arm,
And I fear, I fear, my dear master,
　　That we will come to harm."

O our Scots nobles were richt laith°　　　　*loath*
　　To weet° their cork-heeled shoon,°　　*wet/shoes*　　30
But lang or° a' the play were played　　　*before*
　　Their hats they swam aboon.°　　　　*above*

O lang, lang may their ladies sit,
　　Wi' their fans into their hand,
Or ere they see Sir Patrick Spens　　　　　　　　　　　35
　　Come sailing to the land.

O lang, lang may the ladies stand
　　Wi' their gold kems° in their hair,　　　*combs*
Waiting for their ain° dear lords,　　　　*own*
　　For they'll see them na mair.°　　　　*more*　　40

Half o'er, half o'er to Aberdour
　　It's fifty fadom° deep,　　　　　　　　*fathoms*
And there lies guid Sir Patrick Spens
　　Wi' the Scots lords at his feet.

QUEEN ELIZABETH I (1533–1603)

When I Was Fair and Young (ca. 1585)

When I was fair and young, and favor graced me,
　　Of many was I sought, their mistress for to be;
But I did scorn them all, and answered them therefore,
　　"Go, go, go seek some otherwhere,
　　　　Importune me no more!"　　　　　　　　　　　　5

How many weeping eyes I made to pine with woe,
  How many sighing hearts, I have no skill to show;
Yet I the prouder grew, and answered them therefore,
  "Go, go, go seek some otherwhere,
    Importune me no more!"   10

Then spake fair Venus' son,° that proud victorious boy,   *Cupid*
  And said: "Fine dame, since that you be so coy,
I will so pluck your plumes that you shall say no more,
  'Go, go, go seek some otherwhere,
    Importune me no more!' "   15

When he had spake these words, such change grew in my breast
  That neither night nor day since that, I could take any rest.
Then lo! I did repent that I had said before,
  "Go, go, go seek some otherwhere,
    Importune me no more!"   20

EDMUND SPENSER (ca. 1552–1599)

One Day I Wrote Her Name Upon the Strand (1595)

One day I wrote her name upon the strand,
But came the waves and washèd it away:
Again I wrote it with a second hand,
But came the tide, and made my pains his prey.
"Vain man," said she, "that dost in vain assay,   5
A mortal thing so to immortalize,
For I myself shall like to this decay,
And eek° my name be wipèd out likewise."   *also*
"Not so," quod° I, "let baser things devise,   *quoth*
To die in dust, but you shall live by fame: 10
My verse your virtues rare shall eternize,
And in the heavens write your glorious name.
Where whenas death shall all the world subdue,
Our love shall live, and later life renew."

SIR PHILIP SIDNEY (1554–1586)

Loving in Truth, and Fain in Verse My Love to Show (1582)

Loving in truth, and fain in verse my love to show,
That the dear she might take some pleasure of my pain,
Pleasure might cause her read, reading might make her know,
Knowledge might pity win, and pity grace obtain,
  I sought fit words to paint the blackest face of woe: 5
Studying inventions fine, her wits to entertain,
Oft turning others' leaves, to see if thence would flow
Some fresh and fruitful showers upon my sunburned brain.

But words came halting forth, wanting° Invention's stay*;   *lacking*
Invention, Nature's child, fled step-dame Study's blows,   10
And others' feet still seemed but strangers in my way.
Thus great with child to speak, and helpless in my throes,
    Biting my truant pen, beating myself for spite,
    "Fool," said my Muse to me, "look in thy heart and write."

MARY (SIDNEY) HERBERT, COUNTESS OF PEMBROKE (1562–1621)

Psalm 100 Jubilate Deo (*ca. 1595*)

O all you lands, the treasures of your joy
    In merry shout upon the Lord bestow:
Your service cheerfully on him employ,
    With triumph song into his presence go.
Know first that he is God; and after know   5
    This God did us, not we ourselves create:
We are his flock, for us his feedings grow:
    We are his folk, and he upholds our state.
With thankfulness O enter then his gate:
    Make through each porch of his your praises ring,   10
All good, all grace, of his high name relate,
    He of all grace and goodness is the spring.
Time in no terms his mercy comprehends,
From age to age his truth itself extends.

CHRISTOPHER MARLOWE (1564–1593)

The Passionate Shepherd to His Love (1599)

Come live with me and be my love,
And we will all the pleasures prove
That valleys, groves, hills, and fields,
Woods, or steepy mountain yields.

And we will sit upon the rocks,   5
Seeing the shepherds feed their flocks,
By shallow rivers, to whose falls
Melodious birds sing madrigals.

And I will make thee beds of roses
And a thousand fragrant posies,   10
A cap of flowers, and a kirtle
Embroidered all with leaves of myrtle.

A gown made of the finest wool
Which from our pretty lambs we pull,
Fair lined slippers for the cold,   15
With buckles of the purest gold.

*support

A belt of straw and ivy buds,
With coral clasps and amber studs,
And if these pleasures may thee move,
Come live with me, and be my love.   20

The shepherd swains shall dance and sing
For thy delight each May morning.
If these delights thy mind may move,
Then live with me and be my love.

THOMAS CAMPION (1567–1620)

When Thou Must Home (1601)

When thou must home to shades of underground,
And there arrived, a new admirèd guest,
The beauteous spirits do engirt thee round,
White Iope,° blithe Helen, and the rest,   *Cassiopeia*
To hear the stories of thy finished love   5
From that smooth tongue whose music hell can move,

Then wilt thou speak of banqueting delights,
Of masques and revels which sweet youth did make,
Of tourneys and great challenges of knights,
And all these triumphs for thy beauty's sake;   10
When thou hast told these honors done to thee,
Then tell, Oh tell, how thou didst murther me.

JOHN DONNE (1572–1631)

The Sun Rising (1633)

            Busy old fool, unruly sun,
              Why dost thou thus
Through windows and through curtains call on us?
Must to thy motions lovers' seasons run?
            Saucy pedantic wretch, go chide   5
            Late schoolboys and sour prentices,
      Go tell court huntsmen that the King will ride,
      Call country ants to harvest offices;°   *autumn chores*
Love, all alike, no season knows nor clime,
Nor hours, days, months, which are the rags of time.   10

            Thy beams, so reverend and strong
              Why shouldst thou think?
I could eclipse and cloud them with a wink,
But that I would not lose her sight so long;
            If her eyes have not blinded thine,   15
            Look, and tomorrow late, tell me,
      Whether both th' Indias* of spice and mine

---

* East India, a source of spices, and the West Indies, a source of gold (mines).

Be where thou leftst them, or lie here with me.
Ask for those kings whom thou saw'st yesterday,
And thou shalt hear, All here in one bed lay.   20

      She is all states,° and all princes I,   *all nations*
      Nothing else is.
Princes do but play us; compared to this,
All honor's mimic, all wealth alchemy.
      Thou, sun, art half as happy as we,   25
      In that the world's contracted thus;
      Thine age asks ease, and since thy duties be
      To warm the world, that's done in warming us.
Shine here to us, and thou art everywhere;
This bed thy center is, these walls thy sphere.   30

JOHN DONNE (1572–1631)

A Valediction: Forbidding Mourning (1633)

As virtuous men pass mildly away,
    And whisper to their souls to go,
Whilst some of their sad friends do say
    The breath goes now, and some say, No;

So let us melt, and make no noise,   5
    No tear-floods, nor sigh-tempests move;
'Twere profanation of our joys
    To tell the laity our love.

Moving of th' earth brings harms and fears,
    Men reckon what it did and meant;   10
But trepidation of the spheres,
    Though greater far, is innocent.

Dull sublunary lovers' love
    (Whose soul is sense) cannot admit
Absence, because it doth remove   15
    Those things which elemented it.

But we, by a love so much refined
    That our selves know not what it is,
Inter-assurèd of the mind,
    Care less, eyes, lips, and hands to miss.   20

Our two souls therefore, which are one,
    Though I must go, endure not yet
A breach, but an expansion,
    Like gold to airy thinness beat.

If they be two, they are two so   25
    As stiff twin compasses are two;
Thy soul, the fixed foot, makes no show
    To move, but doth, if th' other do.

And though it in the center sit,
    Yet when the other far doth roam,
It leans and hearkens after it,
    And grows erect, as that comes home.   30

Such wilt thou be to me, who must,
    Like th' other foot, obliquely run;
Thy firmness makes my circle just,   35
    And makes me end where I begun.

BEN JONSON (1573–1637)

On My First Son (1616)

Farewell, thou child of my right hand, and joy;
My sin was too much hope of thee, loved boy:
Seven years thou'wert lent to me, and I thee pay,
Exacted by thy fate, on the just day.
O could I lose all father now! for why   5
Will man lament the state he should envý,
To have so soon 'scaped world's and flesh's rage,
And, if no other misery, yet age?
Rest in soft peace, and asked, say, "Here doth lie
Ben Jonson his best piece of poetry."   10
For whose sake henceforth all his vows be such
As what he loves may never like too much.

LADY MARY WROTH (1587?–1651?)

Am I Thus Conquered? (1621)

Am I thus conquered? Have I lost the powers
    That* to withstand, which joys† to ruin me?
    Must I be still while it my strength devours,
    And captive leads me prisoner, bound, unfree?
Love first shall leave men's fant'sies to them free,   5
    Desire shall quench Love's flames, spring hate sweet showers,
    Love shall loose all his darts, have sight, and see
    His shame, and wishings hinder happy hours.
Why should we not Love's purblind charms resist?
    Must we be servile, doing what he list?‡   10
    No, seek some host to harbor thee: I fly
Thy babish tricks, and freedom do profess.
    But O my hurt makes my lost heart confess
    I love, and must: So farewell liberty.

*I.e., love.

†Delights.

‡Pleases.

Robert Herrick (1591–1674)

To the Virgins, to Make Much of Time (1648)

Gather ye rosebuds while ye may,
    Old time is still a-flying;
And this same flower that smiles today
    Tomorrow will be dying.

The glorious lamp of heaven, the sun, 5
    The higher he's a-getting,
The sooner will his race be run,
    And nearer he's to setting.

That age is best which is the first,
    When youth and blood are warmer; 10
But being spent, the worse, and worst
    Times still succeed the former.

Then be not coy, but use your time,
    And while ye may, go marry;
For having lost but once your prime, 15
    You may forever tarry.

Thomas Carew (1595–1640)

The Spring (1640)

Now that the winter's gone, the earth hath lost
Her snow-white robes, and now no more the frost
Candies the grass, or casts an icy cream
Upon the silver lake or crystal stream;
But the warm sun thaws the benumbèd earth 5
And makes it tender, gives a sacred birth
To the dead swallow, wakes in hollow tree
The drowsy cuckoo and the humble bee.
Now do a choir of chirping minstrels bring
In triumph to the world the youthful spring. 10
The valleys, hills, and woods in rich array
Welcome the coming of the long'd-for May.
Now all things smile: only my love doth lour,
Nor hath the scalding noonday sun the power
To melt that marble ice which still doth hold 15
Her heart congeal'd, and makes her pity cold.
The ox, which lately did for shelter fly
Into the stall, doth now securely lie
In open fields; and love no more is made
By the fireside, but in the cooler shade: 20
Amyntas* now doth with his Chloris* sleep

*Traditional names for pastoral swains and nymphs.

Under a sycamore, and all things keep
Time with the season. Only she doth carry
June in her eyes, in her heart January.

JOHN MILTON (1608–1674)

When I Consider How My Light Is Spent (1652?)

When I consider how my light is spent*
    Ere half my days, in this dark world and wide,
    And that one talent which is death to hide
    Lodged with me useless, though my soul more bent
To serve therewith my Maker, and present   5
    My true account, lest he returning chide;
    "Doth God exact day-labor, light denied?"
    I fondly ask; but Patience to prevent
That murmur, soon replies, "God doth not need
    Either man's work or his own gifts; who best   10
    Bear his mild yoke, they serve him best. His state
Is kingly. Thousands at his bidding speed
    And post o'er land and ocean without rest:
    They also serve who only stand and wait."

ANNE BRADSTREET (1612?–1672)

To My Dear and Loving Husband (1678)

If ever two were one, then surely we.
If ever man were loved by wife, then thee;
If ever wife was happy in a man,
Compare with me ye women if you can.
I prize thy love more than whole mines of gold,   5
Or all the riches that the East doth hold.
My love is such that rivers cannot quench,
Nor ought but love from thee give recompense.
Thy love is such I can no way repay;
The heavens reward thee manifold, I pray.   10
Then while we live, in love let's so persever,
That when we live no more we may live ever.

APHRA BEHN (1640–1689)

On Her Loving Two Equally (1684)

I

How strong does my passion flow,
Divided equally twixt two?

---

* Milton went blind in 1652. Line 3 alludes to Matthew 25:14–30.

Damon* had ne'er subdued my heart
Had not Alexis* took his part;
Nor could Alexis powerful prove,   5
Without my Damon's aid, to gain my love.

II

When my Alexis present is,
Then I for Damon sigh and mourn;
But when Alexis I do miss,
Damon gains nothing but my scorn.   10
But if it chance they both are by,
For both alike I languish, sigh, and die.

III

Cure then, thou mighty wingèd god,
This restless fever in my blood;
One golden-pointed dart take back: 15
But which, O Cupid, wilt thou take?
If Damon's, all my hopes are crossed;
Or that of my Alexis, I am lost.

JONATHAN SWIFT (1667–1745)

A Description of the Morning (1709)

Now hardly here and there a hackney-coach
Appearing, showed the ruddy morn's approach.
Now Betty from her master's bed had flown,
And softly stole to discompose her own;
The slip-shod 'prentice from his master's door   5
Had pared the dirt and sprinkled round the floor.
Now Moll had whirled her mop with dext'rous airs,
Prepared to scrub the entry and the stairs.
The youth with broomy stumps° began to trace   *worn broom*
The kennel-edge,° where wheels had worn the place.   *gutter*   10
The small-coal man° was heard with cadence deep,   *coal vendor*
Till drowned in shriller notes of chimney-sweep:
Duns at his lordship's gate began to meet;
And brickdust Moll† had screamed through half the street
The turnkey now his flock returning sees,   15
Duly let out a-nights to steal for fees:
The watchful bailiffs take their silent stands,
And schoolboys lag with satchels in their hands.

* Traditional names in poetry.
† Woman selling powdered brick.

ALEXANDER POPE (1688–1744)

Epigram. Engraved on the Collar of a Dog Which I Gave to His Royal Highness (1738)

I am his Highness' dog at Kew;*
Pray tell me Sir, whose dog are you?

WILLIAM BLAKE (1757–1827)

The Lamb (1789)

    Little Lamb, who made thee?
    Dost thou know who made thee?
Gave thee life & bid thee feed,
By the stream & o'er the mead;
Gave thee clothing of delight,   5
Softest clothing wooly bright;
Gave thee such a tender voice,
Making all the vales rejoice!
    Little Lamb who made thee?
    Dost thou know who made thee?   10

    Little Lamb I'll tell thee,
    Little Lamb I'll tell thee!
He is callèd by thy name,
For he calls himself a Lamb:
He is meek & he is mild,   15
He became a little child:
I a child & thou a lamb,
We are callèd by his name.
    Little Lamb God bless thee.
    Little Lamb God bless thee.   20

WILLIAM BLAKE (1757–1827)

The Tyger (1794)

Tyger, Tyger, burning bright
In the forests of the night,
What immortal hand or eye
Could frame thy fearful symmetry?

In what distant deeps or skies   5
Burnt the fire of thine eyes?
On what wings dare he aspire?
What the hand, dare seize the fire?

And what shoulder, & what art,
Could twist the sinews of thy heart?   10

*A royal estate in the London borough of Richmond.

And when thy heart began to beat,
What dread hand? & what dread feet?

What the hammer? what the chain?
In what furnace was thy brain?
What the anvil? what dread grasp   15
Dare its deadly terrors clasp?

When the stars threw down their spears
And water'd heaven with their tears,
Did he smile his work to see?
Did he who made the Lamb make thee?   20

Tyger, Tyger, burning bright
In the forests of the night,
What immortal hand or eye
Dare frame thy fearful symmetry?

WILLIAM BLAKE (1757–1827)

The Garden of Love (1794)

I went to the Garden of Love,
And saw what I never had seen:
A Chapel was built in the midst,
Where I used to play on the green.

And the gates of this Chapel were shut,   5
And "Thou shalt not" writ over the door;
So I turn'd to the Garden of Love,
That so many sweet flowers bore,

And I saw it was filled with graves,
And tomb-stones where flowers should be: 10
And Priests in black gowns were walking their rounds,
And binding with briars my joys & desires.

ROBERT BURNS (1759–1796)

A Red, Red Rose (1796)

O my luve's like a red, red rose,
    That's newly sprung in June;
O my luve's like the melodie
    That's sweetly played in tune.

As fair art thou, my bonnie lass,   5
    So deep in luve am I;
And I will luve thee still, my dear,
    Till a' the seas gang dry.

Till a' the seas gang dry, my dear,
    And the rocks melt wi' the sun: 10

O I will love thee still, my dear,
    While the sands o' life shall run.

And fare thee weel, my only luve,
    And fare thee weel awhile!
And I will come again, my luve,   15
    Though it were ten thousand mile.

WILLIAM WORDSWORTH (1770–1850)

I Wandered Lonely as a Cloud (1804)

I wandered lonely as a cloud
That floats on high o'er vales and hills,
When all at once I saw a crowd,
A host, of golden daffodils;
Beside the lake, beneath the trees,   5
Fluttering and dancing in the breeze.

Continuous as the stars that shine
And twinkle on the milky way,
They stretched in never-ending line
Along the margin of a bay: 10
Ten thousand saw I at a glance,
Tossing their heads in sprightly dance.

The waves beside them danced; but they
Outdid the sparkling waves in glee:
A poet could not but be gay,   15
In such a jocund company:
I gazed—and gazed—but little thought
What wealth the show to me had brought:

For oft, when on my couch I lie
In vacant or in pensive mood,   20
They flash upon that inward eye
Which is the bliss of solitude;
And then my heart with pleasure fills,
And dances with the daffodils.

SAMUEL TAYLOR COLERIDGE (1772–1834)

Kubla Khan (ca. 1797–98)

Or, a Vision in a Dream. A Fragment*

In Xanadu did Kubla Khan
A stately pleasure dome decree:
Where Alph, the sacred river, ran
Through caverns measureless to man

Down to a sunless sea.
So twice five miles of fertile ground
With walls and towers were girdled round:
And there were gardens bright with sinuous rills,
Where blossomed many an incense-bearing tree;
And here were forests ancient as the hills,
Enfolding sunny spots of greenery.

But oh! that deep romantic chasm which slanted
Down the green hill athwart a cedarn cover!
A savage place! as holy and enchanted
As e'er beneath a waning moon was haunted
By woman wailing for her demon lover!
And from this chasm, with ceaseless turmoil seething,
As if this earth in fast thick pants were breathing,
A mighty fountain momently was forced:
Amid whose swift half-intermitted burst
Huge fragments vaulted like rebounding hail,
Or chaffy grain beneath the thresher's flail:
And 'mid these dancing rocks at once and ever
It flung up momently the sacred river
Five miles meandering with a mazy motion
Through wood and dale the sacred river ran,
Then reached the caverns measureless to man,
And sank in tumult to a lifeless ocean:
And 'mid this tumult Kubla heard from far
Ancestral voices prophesying war!
    The shadow of the dome of pleasure
    Floated midway on the waves;
    Where was heard the mingled measure
    From the fountain and the caves.
It was a miracle of rare device,
A sunny pleasure dome with caves of ice!

    A damsel with a dulcimer
    In a vision once I saw:
    It was an Abyssinian maid,
    And on her dulcimer she played,
    Singing of Mount Abora.
    Could I revive within me
    Her symphony and song,
    To such a deep delight 'twould win me,
That with music loud and long,
I would build that dome in air,

* Coleridge stated in a preface that this poem composed itself in his mind during an opium dream; that he began writing it down immediately upon waking but was interrupted by a caller; and that when he returned to his room an hour later he could not complete it.

That sunny dome! those caves of ice!
And all who heard should see them there,
And all should cry, Beware! Beware!
His flashing eyes, his floating hair!   50
Weave a circle round him thrice,
And close your eyes with holy dread,
For he on honey-dew hath fed,
And drunk the milk of Paradise.

GEORGE GORDON, LORD BYRON (1788–1824)

She Walks in Beauty (1815)

1.

She walks in beauty, like the night
    Of cloudless climes and starry skies;
And all that's best of dark and bright
    Meet in her aspect and her eyes:
Thus mellowed to that tender light   5
    Which heaven to gaudy day denies.

2.

One shade the more, one ray the less,
    Had half impaired the nameless grace
Which waves in every raven tress,
    Or softly lightens o'er her face;   10
Where thoughts serenely sweet express
    How pure, how dear their dwelling place.

3.

And on that cheek, and o'er that brow,
    So soft, so calm, yet eloquent,
The smiles that win, the tints that glow,   15
    But tell of days in goodness spent,
A mind at peace with all below,
    A heart whose love is innocent!

PERCY BYSSHE SHELLEY (1792–1822)

Ode to the West Wind (1820)

1

O wild West Wind, thou breath of Autumn's being,
Thou, from whose unseen presence the leaves dead
Are driven, like ghosts from an enchanter fleeing,

Yellow, and black, and pale, and hectic red,
Pestilence-stricken multitudes: O thou,   5
Who chariotest to their dark wintry bed

The wingèd seeds, where they lie cold and low,
Each like a corpse within its grave, until
Thine azure sister of the Spring shall blow

Her clarion o'er the dreaming earth, and fill   10
(Driving sweet buds like flocks to feed in air)
With living hues and odors plain and hill:

Wild Spirit, which art moving everywhere;
Destroyer and preserver; hear, oh, hear!

2

Thou on whose stream, mid the steep sky's commotion,   15
Loose clouds like earth's decaying leaves are shed,
Shook from the tangled boughs of Heaven and Ocean,

Angels of rain and lightning: there are spread
On the blue surface of thine airy surge,
Like the bright hair uplifted from the head   20

Of some fierce Maenad, even from the dim verge
Of the horizon to the zenith's height,
The locks of the approaching storm. Thou dirge

Of the dying year, to which this closing night
Will be the dome of a vast sepulcher,   25
Vaulted with all thy congregated might

Of vapors, from whose solid atmosphere
Black rain, and fire, and hail will burst: oh, hear!

3

Thou who didst waken from his summer dreams
The blue Mediterranean, where he lay,   30
Lulled by the coil of his crystàlline streams,

Beside a pumice isle in Baiae's bay,*
And saw in sleep old palaces and towers
Quivering within the wave's intenser day,

All overgrown with azure moss and flowers   35
So sweet, the sense faints picturing them! Thou
For whose path the Atlantic's level powers

Cleave themselves into chasms, while far below
The sea-blooms and the oozy woods which wear
The sapless foliage of the ocean, know   40

Thy voice, and suddenly grow gray with fear,
And tremble and despoil themselves: oh, hear!

* Near Naples, Italy.

4

If I were a dead leaf thou mightest bear;
If I were a swift cloud to fly with thee;
A wave to pant beneath thy power, and share   45

The impulse of thy strength, only less free
Than thou, O uncontrollable! If even
I were as in my boyhood, and could be

The comrade of thy wanderings over Heaven,
As then, when to outstrip thy skyey speed   50
Scarce seemed a vision; I would ne'er have striven

As thus with thee in prayer in my sore need.
Oh, lift me as a wave, a leaf, a cloud!
I fall upon the thorns of life! I bleed!

A heavy weight of hours has chained and bowed   55
One too like thee: tameless, and swift, and proud.

5

Make me thy lyre, even as the forest is:
What if my leaves are falling like its own!
The tumult of thy mighty harmonies

Will take from both a deep, autumnal tone,   60
Sweet though in sadness. Be thou, Spirit fierce,
My spirit! Be thou me, impetuous one!

Drive my dead thoughts over the universe
Like withered leaves to quicken a new birth!
And, by the incantation of this verse,   65

Scatter, as from an unextinguished hearth
Ashes and sparks, my words among mankind!
Be through my lips to unawakened earth

The trumpet of a prophecy! O Wind,
If Winter comes, can Spring be far behind?   70

ALFRED, LORD TENNYSON (1809–1892)

The Splendor Falls on Castle Walls (1850)

The splendor falls on castle walls
    And snowy summits old in story;
The long light shakes across the lakes,
    And the wild cataract leaps in glory.
Blow, bugle, blow, set the wild echoes flying,   5
Blow, bugle; answer, echoes, dying, dying, dying.

O, hark, O, hear! how thin and clear,
    And thinner, clearer, farther going!
O, sweet and far from cliff and scar
    The horns of Elfland faintly blowing!   10
Blow, let us hear the purple glens replying,
Blow, bugle; answer, echoes, dying, dying, dying.

O love, they die in yon rich sky,
    They faint on hill or field or river;
Our echoes roll from soul to soul,   15
    And grow for ever and for ever.
Blow, bugle, blow, set the wild echoes flying,
And answer, echoes, answer, dying, dying, dying.

ALFRED, LORD TENNYSON (1809–1892)

Ulysses* (1833)

    It little profits that an idle king,
By this still hearth, among these barren crags,
Matched with an agèd wife, I mete and dole
Unequal laws unto a savage race,
That hoard, and sleep, and feed, and know not me.   5
    I cannot rest from travel; I will drink
Life to the lees. All times I have enjoyed
Greatly, have suffered greatly, both with those
That loved me, and alone; on shore, and when
Through scudding drifts the rainy Hyades   10
Vexed the dim sea. I am become a name;
For always roaming with a hungry heart
Much have I seen and known—cities of men
And manners, climates, councils, governments,
Myself not least, but honored of them all—   15
And drunk delight of battle with my peers,
Far on the ringing plains of windy Troy.
I am a part of all that I have met;
Yet all experience is an arch wherethrough
Gleams that untraveled world whose margin fades   20
Forever and forever when I move.
How dull it is to pause, to make an end,
To rust unburnished, not to shine in use!
As though to breathe were life! Life piled on life
Were all too little, and of one to me   25
Little remains; but every hour is saved

* For background, see p. 293.

From that eternal silence, something more,
A bringer of new things; and vile it were
For some three suns to store and hoard myself,
And this gray spirit yearning in desire
To follow knowledge like a sinking star,
Beyond the utmost bound of human thought.

    This is my son, mine own Telemachus,
To whom I leave the scepter and the isle—
Well-loved of me, discerning to fulfill
This labor, by slow prudence to make mild
A rugged people, and through soft degrees
Subdue them to the useful and the good.
Most blameless is he, centered in the sphere
Of common duties, decent not to fail
In offices of tenderness, and pay
Meet adoration to my household gods,
When I am gone. He works his work, I mine.

    There lies the port; the vessel puffs her sail;
There gloom the dark, broad seas. My mariners,
Souls that have toiled, and wrought, and thought with me—
That ever with a frolic welcome took
The thunder and the sunshine, and opposed
Free hearts, free foreheads—you and I are old;
Old age hath yet his honor and his toil.
Death closes all; but something ere the end,
Some work of noble note, may yet be done,
Not unbecoming men that strove with Gods.
The lights begin to twinkle from the rocks;
The long day wanes; the slow moon climbs; the deep
Moans round with many voices. Come, my friends,
'Tis not too late to seek a newer world.
Push off, and sitting well in order smite
The sounding furrows; for my purpose holds
To sail beyond the sunset, and the baths
Of all the western stars, until I die.
It may be that the gulfs will wash us down;
It may be we shall touch the Happy Isles,
And see the great Achilles, whom we knew.
Though much is taken, much abides; and though
We are not now that strength which in old days
Moved earth and heaven, that which we are, we are—
One equal temper of heroic hearts,
Made weak by time and fate, but strong in will
To strive, to seek, to find, and not to yield.

30

35

40

45

50

55

60

65

70

ROBERT BROWNING (1812–1889)

Home-Thoughts, From Abroad (1845)

1

Oh, to be in England
Now that April's there,
And whoever wakes in England
Sees, some morning, unaware,
That the lowest boughs and the brushwood sheaf   5
Round the elm-tree bole are in tiny leaf,
While the chaffinch sings on the orchard bough
In England—now!

2

And after April, when May follows,
And the whitethroat builds, and all the swallows!   10
Hark, where my blossomed pear-tree in the hedge
Leans to the field and scatters on the clover
Blossoms and dewdrops—at the bent spray's edge—
That's the wise thrush; he sings each song twice over,
Lest you should think he never could recapture   15
The first fine careless rapture!
And though the fields look rough with hoary dew
All will be gay when noontide wakes anew
The buttercups, the little children's dower
—Far brighter than this gaudy melon-flower!   20

ARTHUR HUGH CLOUGH (1819–1861)

The Latest Decalogue* (1862)

Thou shalt have one God only; who
Would be at the expense of two?
No graven images may be
Worshipped, except the currency:
Swear not at all; for for thy curse   5
Thine enemy is none the worse:
At church on Sunday to attend
Will serve to keep the world thy friend:
Honour thy parents; that is, all
From whom advancement may befall: 10
Thou shalt not kill; but needst not strive
Officiously to keep alive:
Do not adultery commit;
Advantage rarely comes of it:

* For the poem's context, see Exodus 20:1–7 and Matthew 22:35–40.

Thou shalt not steal; an empty feat, 15
When it's so lucrative to cheat:
Bear not false witness; let the lie
Have time on its own wings to fly:
Thou shalt not covet; but tradition
Approves all forms of competition. 20

The sum of all is, thou shalt love,
If any body, God above:
At any rate shall never labour
More than thyself to love thy neighbour.

EMILY DICKINSON (1830–1886)

Because I Could Not Stop for Death (ca. 1863)

Because I could not stop for Death—
He kindly stopped for me—
The Carriage held but just Ourselves—
And Immortality.

We slowly drove—He knew no haste 5
And I had put away
My labor and my leisure too,
For His Civility—

We passed the School, where Children strove
At Recess—in the Ring— 10
We passed the Fields of Gazing Grain—
We passed the Setting Sun—

Or rather—He passed Us—
The Dews drew quivering and chill—
For only Gossamer, my Gown— 15
My Tippet—only Tulle—

We paused before a House that seemed
A Swelling of the Ground—
The Roof was scarcely visible—
The Cornice—in the Ground— 20

Since then—'tis Centuries—and yet
Feels shorter than the Day
I first surmised the Horses' Heads
Were toward Eternity—

CHRISTINA ROSSETTI (1830–1894)

Song (1862)

When I am dead, my dearest,
    Sing no sad songs for me;

Plant thou no roses at my head,
    Nor shady cypress tree:
Be the green grass above me
    With showers and dewdrops wet;   5
And if thou wilt, remember,
    And if thou wilt, forget.

I shall not see the shadows,
    I shall not feel the rain;   10
I shall not hear the nightingale
    Sing on, as if in pain:
And dreaming through the twilight
    That doth not rise nor set,
Haply I may remember,
    And haply may forget.

GERARD MANLEY HOPKINS (1844–1889)

God's Grandeur (1877)

The world is charged with the grandeur of God. _a_
    It will flame out, like shining from shook foil;* _b_
    It gathers to a greatness, like the ooze of oil° _b_
Crushed. Why do men then now not reck his rod? _a_
Generátions have trod, have trod, have trod; _a_
    And all is seared with trade; bleared, smeared, with toil; _b_
    And wears man's smudge and shares man's smell: the soil _b_
Is bare now, nor can foot feel, being shod. _a_
Ánd, for° all this, náture is never spent; _c_
    There lives the dearest freshness deep down things; _d_
And though the last lights off the black West went _c_
    Oh, morning, at the brown brink eastward, springs— _d_
Because the Holy Ghost óver the bent _c_
    World broods with warm breast and with ah! bright wings. _d_

GERARD MANLEY HOPKINS (1844–1889)

Inversnaid† (1881)

This dárksome búrn,° hórseback brówn,   _stream_
His rollrock highroad roaring down,
In coop° and in comb° the fleece of his foam   _hollow/crest_
Flutes and low to the lake falls home.

---

* Shaken gold foil.

† A town in the Scottish Highlands.

A windpuff-bónnet of fáwn-fróth   5
Turns and twindles over the broth
Of a póol so pítchblack, féll-frówning,
It rounds and rounds Despair to drowning.

Degged° with dew, dappled with dew   *sprinkled*
Are the groins of the braes° that the brook treads   *deep banks in a valley*
    through,   10
Wiry heathpacks,° flitches° of fern,   *clumps of heather/bunches*
And the beadbonny ash* that sits over the burn.

What would the world be, once bereft
Of wet and of wildness? Let them be left,
O let them be left, wildness and wet;   15
Long live the weeds and the wilderness yet.

A. E. HOUSMAN (1859–1936)

To an Athlete Dying Young (1896)

The time you won your town the race
We chaired you through the market-place;
Man and boy stood cheering by,
And home we brought you shoulder-high.

To-day, the road all runners come,   5
Shoulder-high we bring you home,
And set you at your threshold down,
Townsman of a stiller town.

Smart lad, to slip betimes away
From fields where glory does not stay   10
And early though the laurel grows
It withers quicker than the rose.

Eyes the shady night has shut
Cannot see the record cut,°   *broken*
And silence sounds no worse than cheers   15
After earth has stopped the ears:

Now you will not swell the rout
Of lads that wore their honours out,
Runners whom renown outran
And the name died before the man.   20

So set, before its echoes fade,
The fleet foot on the sill of shade,
And hold to the low lintel up
The still-defended challenge-cup.

*Ash trees clustered like pretty beads.

And round that early-laurelled head   25
Will flock to gaze the strengthless dead,
And find unwithered on its curls
The garland briefer than a girl's.

A. E. HOUSMAN (1859–1936)

*"Terence, This Is Stupid Stuff . . ."** (1896)

"Terence, this is stupid stuff:
You eat your victuals fast enough;
There can't be much amiss, 'tis clear,
To see the rate you drink your beer.
But oh, good Lord, the verse you make,   5
It gives a chap the belly-ache.
The cow, the old cow, she is dead;
It sleeps well, the horned head:
We poor lads, 'tis our turn now
To hear such tunes as killed the cow.   10
Pretty friendship 'tis to rhyme
Your friends to death before their time
Moping melancholy mad:
Come, pipe a tune to dance to, lad."

Why, if 'tis dancing you would be,   15
There's brisker pipes than poetry.
Say, for what were hop-yards meant,
Or why was Burton° built on Trent?°   *famous brewing town/river in England*
Oh many a peer of England brews
Livelier liquor than the Muse,   20
And malt does more than Milton can
To justify God's ways to man.[†]
Ale, man, ale's the stuff to drink
For fellows whom it hurts to think:
Look into the pewter pot   25
To see the world as the world's not.
And faith, 'tis pleasant till 'tis past:
The mischief is that 'twill not last.
Oh I have been to Ludlow° fair   *market town in Shropshire*
And left my necktie God knows where,   30
And carried half-way home, or near,
Pints and quarts of Ludlow beer:
Then the world seemed none so bad,
And I myself a sterling lad;
And down in lovely muck I've lain,   35
Happy till I woke again.

* See page 66.
[†] See *Paradise Lost* 1.26.

Then I saw the morning sky:
Heigho, the tale was all a lie;
The world, it was the old world yet,
I was I, my things were wet,   40
And nothing now remained to do
But begin the game anew.

     Therefore, since the world has still
Much good, but much less good than ill,
And while the sun and moon endure   45
Luck's a chance, but trouble's sure,
I'd face it as a wise man would,
And train for ill and not for good.
'Tis true, the stuff I bring for sale
Is not so brisk a brew as ale: 50
Out of a stem that scored° the hand   *cut*
I wrung it in a weary land.
But take it: if the smack is sour,
The better for the embittered hour;
It should do good to heart and head   55
When your soul is in my soul's stead;
And I will friend you, if I may,
In the dark and cloudy day.

     There was a king reigned in the East:
There, when kings will sit to feast,   60
They get their fill before they think
With poisoned meat and poisoned drink.
He gathered all that springs to birth
From the many-venomed earth;
First a little, thence to more,   65
He sampled all her killing store;
And easy, smiling, seasoned sound,
Sate the king when healths went round.
They put arsenic in his meat
And stared aghast to watch him eat;   70
They poured strychnine in his cup
And shook to see him drink it up:
They shook, they stared as white's their shirt:
Them it was their poison hurt.
—I tell the tale that I heard told.   75
Mithridates,* he died old.

MARY ELIZABETH COLERIDGE (1861–1907)

The Other Side of a Mirror (1882)

I sat before my glass one day,
    And conjured up a vision bare,

---

* King of Pontus, first century B.C.E.

Unlike the aspects glad and gay,
　　That erst were found reflected there—
The vision of a woman, wild
　　With more than womanly despair.　　　　　　　　　5

Her hair stood back on either side
　　A face bereft of loveliness.
It had no envy now to hide
　　What once no man on earth could guess.　　　　　10
It formed the thorny aureole
　　Of hard unsanctified distress.

Her lips were open—not a sound
　　Came through the parted lines of red.
Whate'er it was, the hideous wound　　　　　　　　15
　　In silence and in secret bled.
No sigh relieved her speechless woe,
　　She had no voice to speak her dread.

And in her lurid eyes there shone
　　The dying flame of life's desire,　　　　　　　　20
Made mad because its hope was gone,
　　And kindled at the leaping fire
Of jealousy, and fierce revenge,
　　And strength that could not change nor tire.

Shade of a shadow in the glass,　　　　　　　　　25
　　O set the crystal surface free!
Pass—as the fairer visions pass—
　　Nor ever more return, to be
The ghost of a distracted hour,
　　That heard me whisper, "I am she!"　　　　　　30

WILLIAM BUTLER YEATS (1865–1939)

Adam's Curse* (1903)

We sat together at one summer's end,
That beautiful mild woman, your close friend,
And you and I, and talked of poetry.
I said, "A line will take us hours maybe;
Yet if it does not seem a moment's thought,　　　　5
Our stitching and unstitching has been naught.
Better go down upon your marrow-bones
And scrub a kitchen pavement, or break stones
Like an old pauper, in all kinds of weather;
For to articulate sweet sounds together　　　　　10
Is to work harder than all these, and yet
Be thought an idler by the noisy set
Of bankers, schoolmasters, and clergymen

* See Genesis 3:17–19.

The martyrs call the world."
                              And thereupon   15
That beautiful mild woman for whose sake
There's many a one shall find out all heartache
On finding that her voice is sweet and low
Replied, "To be born woman is to know—
Although they do not talk of it at school—   20
That we must labour to be beautiful."

I said, "It's certain there is no fine thing
Since Adam's fall but needs much labouring.
There have been lovers who thought love should be
So much compounded of high courtesy   25
That they would sigh and quote with learned looks
Precedents out of beautiful old books;
Yet now it seems an idle trade enough."

We sat grown quiet at the name of love;
We saw the last embers of daylight die,   30
And in the trembling blue-green of the sky
A moon, worn as if it had been a shell
Washed by time's waters as they rose and fell
About the stars and broke in days and years.

I had a thought for no one's but your ears: 35
That you were beautiful, and that I strove
To love you in the old high way of love;
That it had all seemed happy, and yet we'd grown
As weary-hearted as that hollow moon.

WILLIAM BUTLER YEATS (1865–1939)

The Wild Swans at Coole* (1916)

The trees are in their autumn beauty,
The woodland paths are dry,
Under the October twilight the water
Mirrors a still sky;
Upon the brimming water among the stones   5
Are nine-and-fifty swans.

The nineteenth autumn has come upon me
Since I first made my count;
I saw, before I had well finished,
All suddenly mount   10
And scatter wheeling in great broken rings
Upon their clamorous wings.

* Coole Park, country estate of Lady Gregory, an Irish writer and promoter of Irish literature.

I have looked upon those brilliant creatures,
And now my heart is sore.
All's changed since I, hearing at twilight,   15
The first time on this shore,
The bell-beat of their wings above my head,
Trod with a lighter tread.

Unwearied still, lover by lover,
They paddle in the cold   20
Companionable streams or climb the air;
Their hearts have not grown old;
Passion or conquest, wander where they will,
Attend upon them still.

But now they drift on the still water,   25
Mysterious, beautiful;
Among what rushes will they build,
By what lake's edge or pool
Delight men's eyes when I awake some day
To find they have flown away?   30

WILLIAM BUTLER YEATS (1865–1939)

The Second Coming* (1919)

Turning and turning in the widening gyre
The falcon cannot hear the falconer;
Things fall apart; the centre cannot hold;
Mere anarchy is loosed upon the world,
The blood-dimmed tide is loosed, and everywhere   5
The ceremony of innocence is drowned;
The best lack all conviction, while the worst
Are full of passionate intensity.

Surely some revelation is at hand;
Surely the Second Coming is at hand.   10
The Second Coming! Hardly are those words out
When a vast image out of *Spiritus Mundi*†
Troubles my sight: somewhere in sands of the desert
A shape with lion body and the head of a man,

---

* The title alludes to Matthew 24:3–44, on the return of Christ at the end of the age. Yeats viewed history as a series of 2000-year cycles (imaged as gyres, cone-shaped motions). The birth of Christ in Bethlehem brought to an end the cycle that ran from the Babylonians through the Greeks and Romans. The approach of the year 2000, then, anticipated for Yeats the end of the Christian era. Yeats wrote this poem shortly after the Russian Revolution of 1917, which may have confirmed his sense of imminent change and of a new beginning of an unpredictable nature (Yeats expected the new era to be violent and despotic).

† *Spiritus mundi* means "the spirit of the universe." Yeats believed in a Great Memory, a universal storehouse of symbolic images from the past. Individuals, drawing on it for images, are put in touch with the soul of the universe.

A gaze blank and pitiless as the sun,   15
Is moving its slow thighs, while all about it
Reel shadows of the indignant desert birds.
The darkness drops again; but now I know
That twenty centuries of stony sleep
Were vexed to nightmare by a rocking cradle,   20
And what rough beast, its hour come round at last,
Slouches towards Bethlehem to be born?

WILLIAM BUTLER YEATS (1865–1939)

Leda and the Swan* (1924)

A sudden blow: the great wings beating still
Above the staggering girl, her thighs caressed
By the dark webs, her nape caught in his bill,
He holds her helpless breast upon his breast.

How can those terrified vague fingers push   5
The feathered glory from her loosening thighs?
And how can body, laid in that white rush,
But feel the strange heart beating where it lies?

A shudder in the loins engenders there
The broken wall, the burning roof and tower   10
And Agamemnon dead.
                              Being so caught up,
So mastered by the brute blood of the air,
Did she put on his knowledge with his power
Before the indifferent beak could let her drop?   15

ROBERT FROST (1874–1963)

After Apple-Picking (1914)

My long two-pointed ladder's sticking through a tree
Toward heaven still,
And there's a barrel that I didn't fill
Beside it, and there may be two or three
Apples I didn't pick upon some bough.   5
But I am done with apple-picking now.
Essence of winter sleep is on the night,
The scent of apples: I am drowsing off.

---

* In Greek mythology, Leda was seduced (or raped) by Zeus; she gave birth to Helen, whose abduction by Paris gave rise to the Trojan War (referred to in line 10). The Greek forces were headed by Agamemnon, who was killed upon his return by his wife Clytemnestra, daughter of Leda by her husband, Tyndareus. Yeats regarded Zeus's visit as a "violent annunciation" of the founding of Greek civilization, with parallels to the annunciation to Mary (Luke 1:26–38) of the coming of the Christian age.

I cannot rub the strangeness from my sight
I got from looking through a pane of glass   10
I skimmed this morning from the drinking trough
And held against the world of hoary grass.
It melted, and I let it fall and break.
But I was well
Upon my way to sleep before it fell,   15
And I could tell
What form my dreaming was about to take.
Magnified apples appear and disappear,
Stem end and blossom end,
And every fleck of russet showing clear.   20
My instep arch not only keeps the ache,
It keeps the pressure of a ladder-round.
I feel the ladder sway as the boughs bend.
And I keep hearing from the cellar bin
The rumbling sound   25
Of load on load of apples coming in.
For I have had too much
Of apple-picking: I am overtired
Of the great harvest I myself desired.
There were ten thousand thousand fruit to touch,   30
Cherish in hand, lift down, and not let fall.
For all
That struck the earth,
No matter if not bruised or spiked with stubble,
Went surely to the cider-apple heap   35
As of no worth.
One can see what will trouble
This sleep of mine, whatever sleep it is.
Were he not gone,
The woodchuck could say whether it's like his   40
Long sleep, as I describe its coming on,
Or just some human sleep.

ROBERT FROST (1874–1963)

Fire and Ice (1923)

Some say the world will end in fire,
Some say in ice.
From what I've tasted of desire
I hold with those who favor fire.
But if it had to perish twice,   5
I think I know enough of hate
To say that for destruction ice
Is also great
And would suffice.

ROBERT FROST (1874–1963)

Stopping by Woods on a Snowy Evening (1923)

Whose woods these are I think I know.
His house is in the village, though;
He will not see me stopping here
To watch his woods fill up with snow.

My little horse must think it queer   5
To stop without a farmhouse near
Between the woods and frozen lake
The darkest evening of the year.

He gives his harness bells a shake
To ask if there is some mistake.   10
The only other sound's the sweep
Of easy wind and downy flake.

The woods are lovely, dark, and deep,
But I have promises to keep,
And miles to go before I sleep,   15
And miles to go before I sleep.

AMY LOWELL (1874–1925)

Madonna of the Evening Flowers (1919)

All day long I have been working,
Now I am tired.
I call: "Where are you?"
But there is only the oak-tree rustling in the wind.
The house is very quiet,   5
The sun shines in on your books,
On your scissors and thimble just put down,
But you are not there.
Suddenly I am lonely:
Where are you?   10
I go about searching.

Then I see you,
Standing under a spire of pale blue larkspur,
With a basket of roses on your arm.
You are cool, like silver,   15
And you smile.
I think the Canterbury bells* are playing little tunes.

You tell me that the peonies need spraying,
That the columbines have overrun all bounds,

*A cultivated variety of bellflower or bluebell, taking its name from Canterbury Cathedral in England.

That the pyrus japonica should be cut back and rounded.   20
You tell me these things.
But I look at you, heart of silver,
White heart-flame of polished silver,
Burning beneath the blue steeples of the larkspur,
And I long to kneel instantly at your feet,   25
While all about us peal the loud, sweet *Te Deums** of the Canterbury
    bells.

GERTRUDE STEIN (1874–1946)

Susie Asado (1913)

Sweet sweet sweet sweet sweet tea.
    Susie Asado.
Sweet sweet sweet sweet sweet tea.
    Susie Asado.
Susie Asado which is a told tray sure.   5
A lean on the shoe this means slips slips hers.
When the ancient light grey is clean it is yellow, it is a silver seller.
This is a please this is a please there are the saids to jelly. These are
the wets these say the sets to leave a crown to Incy.
Incy is short for incubus.   10
    A pot. A pot is a beginning of a rare bit of trees. Trees tremble, the
old vats are in bobbles, bobbles which shade and shove and render
clean, render clean must.
    Drink pups.
    Drink pups drink pups lease a sash hold, see it shine and a bobolink   15
has pins. It shows a nail.
    What is a nail. A nail is unison.
Sweet sweet sweet sweet sweet tea.

WALLACE STEVENS (1879–1955)

Final Soliloquy of the Interior Paramour (1954)

Light the first light of evening, as in a room
In which we rest and, for small reason, think
The world imagined is the ultimate good.

This is, therefore, the intensest rendezvous.
It is in that thought that we collect ourselves,   5
Out of all the indifferences, into one thing:

Within a single thing, a single shawl
Wrapped tightly round us, since we are poor, a warmth,
A light, a power, the miraculous influence.

*Te deum laudamus (we praise thee, God) is an ancient Latin hymn.

Here, now, we forget each other and ourselves.
We feel the obscurity of an order, a whole,
A knowledge, that which arranged the rendezvous.
10

Within its vital boundary, in the mind.
We say God and the imagination are one . . .
How high that highest candle lights the dark.
15

Out of this same light, out of the central mind,
We make a dwelling in the evening air,
In which being there together is enough.

MINA LOY (1883–1966)

The Widow's Jazz (1931)

1.

The white flesh quakes to the negro soul
Chicago!   Chicago!

An uninterpretable wail
stirs in a tangle of pale snakes

to the lethargic ecstasy of steps
backing into primeval goal
5

White man quit his actin' wise
colored folk hab de moon in dere eyes

Haunted by wind instruments
in groves of grace
10

the maiden saplings
slant to the oboes

and shampooed gigolos
prowl to the sobbing taboos.

An electric clown
crashes the furtive cargoes of the floor.
15

The pruned contours
dissolve
in the brazen shallows of dissonance
revolving mimes
of the encroaching Eros
in adolescence
20

The black brute-angels
in their human gloves
bellow through a monstrous growth of metal trunks
25

and impish musics
crumble the ecstatic loaf
before a swooning flock of doves.

2.

Cravan
colossal absentee   30
the substitute dark
rolls to the incandescent memory

of love's survivor
on this rich suttee

seared by the flames of sound   35
the widowed urn
holds impotently
your murdered laughter

Husband
how secretly you cuckold me with death   40

while this cajoling jazz
blows with its tropic breath

among the echoes of the flesh
a synthesis
of racial caress   45

The seraph and the ass
in this unerring esperanto
of the earth
converse
of everlit delight   50

as my desire
receded
to the distance of the dead

searches
the opaque silence   55
of unpeopled space.

WILLIAM CARLOS WILLIAMS (1883–1963)

Spring and All (1923)

By the road to the contagious hospital
under the surge of the blue

mottled clouds driven from the
northeast—a cold wind. Beyond, the
waste of broad, muddy fields   5
brown with dried weeds, standing and fallen

patches of standing water
the scattering of tall trees

All along the road the reddish
purplish, forked, upstanding, twiggy   10
stuff of bushes and small trees
with dead, brown leaves under them
leafless vines—

Lifeless in appearance, sluggish
dazed spring approaches—   15

They enter the new world naked,
cold, uncertain of all
save that they enter. All about them
the cold, familiar wind—

Now the grass, tomorrow   20
the stiff curl of wildcarrot leaf

One by one objects are defined—
It quickens: clarity, outline of leaf

But now the stark dignity of
entrance—Still, the profound change   25
has come upon them: rooted, they
grip down and begin to awaken

EZRA POUND (1885–1972)

In a Station of the Metro (1916)

The apparition of these faces in the crowd;
Petals on a wet, black bough.

H. D. [HILDA DOOLITTLE] (1886–1961)

Garden (1916)

I

You are clear
O rose, cut in rock,
hard as the descent of hail.

I could scrape the colour
from the petals
like spilt dye from a rock.

If I could break you
I could break a tree.
If I could stir
I could break a tree—
I could break you.

                    II
O wind, rend open the heat,
cut apart the heat,
rend it to tatters.

Fruit cannot drop
through this thick air—
fruit cannot fall into heat
that presses up and blunts
the points of pears
and rounds the grapes.

Cut the heat—
plough through it,
turning it on either side
of your path.

MARIANNE MOORE (1887–1972)

The Steeple-Jack (1935; rev. 1961)

Dürer would have seen a reason for living
        in a town like this, with eight stranded whales
to look at; with the sweet sea air coming into your house
on a fine day, from water etched
        with waves as formal as the scales
on a fish.

One by one in two's and three's, the seagulls keep
        flying back and forth over the town clock,
or sailing around the lighthouse without moving their wings—
rising steadily with a slight
        quiver of the body—or flock
mewing where

a sea the purple of the peacock's neck is
        paled to greenish azure as Dürer changed
the pine green of the Tyrol to peacock blue and guinea
gray. You can see a twenty-five-
        pound lobster; and fish nets arranged
to dry. The

whirlwind fife-and-drum of the storm bends the salt
        marsh grass, disturbs stars in the sky and the   20
star on the steeple; it is a privilege to see so
much confusion. Disguised by what
        might seem the opposite, the sea-
side flowers and

trees are favored by the fog so that you have   25
        the tropics at first hand: the trumpet-vine,
fox-glove, giant snap-dragon, a salpiglossis that has
spots and stripes; morning-glories, gourds,
        or moon-vines trained on fishing-twine
at the back door;   30

cat-tails, flags, blueberries and spiderwort,
        striped grass, lichens, sunflowers, asters, daisies—
yellow and crab-claw ragged sailors with green bracts—toad-plant,
petunias, ferns; pink lilies, blue
        ones, tigers; poppies; black sweet-peas.   35
The climate

is not right for the banyan, frangipani, or
        jack-fruit trees; or for exotic serpent
life. Ring lizard and snake-skin for the foot, if you see fit;
but here they've cats, not cobras, to   40
        keep down the rats. The diffident
little newt

with white pin-dots on black horizontal spaced-
        out bands lives here; yet there is nothing that
ambition can buy or take away. The college student   45
named Ambrose sits on the hillside
        with his not-native books and hat
and sees boats

at sea progress white and rigid as if in
        a groove. Liking an elegance of which   50
the source is not bravado, he knows by heart the antique
sugar-bowl shaped summer-house of
        interlacing slats, and the pitch
of the church

spire, not true, from which a man in scarlet lets   55
        down a rope as a spider spins a thread;
he might be part of a novel, but on the sidewalk a
sign says C. J. Poole, Steeple-Jack,
        in black and white; and one in red
and white says   60

Danger. The church portico has four fluted
        columns, each a single piece of stone, made

modester by white-wash. This would be a fit haven for
waifs, children, animals, prisoners,
     and presidents who have repaid   65
sin-driven

senators by not thinking about them. The
     place has a school-house, a post-office in a
store, fish-houses, hen-houses, a three-masted
     schooner on   70
the stocks. The hero, the student,
     the steeple-jack, each in his way,
is at home.

It could not be dangerous to be living
     in a town like this, of simple people,   75
who have a steeple-jack placing danger-signs by the church
while he is gilding the solid-
     pointed star, which on a steeple
stands for hope.

EDITH SITWELL (1887–1964)

Lullaby (1942)

Though the world has slipped and gone,
Sounds my loud discordant cry
Like the steel birds' song on high:
"Still one thing is left—the Bone!"
Then out danced the Babioun.°   *baboon*   5

She sat in the hollow of the sea—
A socket whence the eye's put out—
She sang to the child a lullaby
(The steel birds' nest was thereabout).

"Do, do, do, do—   10
Thy mother's hied to the vaster race:
The Pterodactyl made its nest
And laid a steel egg in her breast—
Under the Judas-colored sun.
She'll work no more, nor dance, nor moan,   15
And I am come to take her place
Do, do.

There's nothing left but earth's low bed—
(The Pterodactyl fouls its nest):
But steel wings fan thee to thy rest,   20
And wingless truth and larvae lie
And eyeless hope and handless fear—

All these for thee as toys are spread,
Do—do—

Red is the bed of Poland, Spain,   25
And thy mother's breast, who has grown wise
In that fouled nest. If she could rise.
Give birth again,
In wolfish pelt she'd hide thy bones
To shield thee from the world's long cold,   30
And down on all fours shouldst thou crawl
For thus from no height canst thou fall—
Do, do.

She'd give no hands: there's nought to hold
And nought to make: there's dust to sift,   35
But no food for the hands to lift.
Do, do.

Heed my ragged lullaby,
Fear not living, fear not chance;
All is equal—blindness, sight,   40
There is no depth, there is no height:
Do, do.

The Judas-colored sun is gone,
And with the Ape thou art alone—
Do,
      Do."   45

ROBINSON JEFFERS (1887–1962)

Hurt Hawks (1928)

I

The broken pillar of the wing jags from the clotted shoulder,
The wing trails like a banner in defeat,
No more to use the sky forever but live with famine
And pain a few days: cat nor coyote
Will shorten the week of waiting for death, there is game without talons.   5
He stands under the oak-bush and waits
The lame feet of salvation; at night he remembers freedom
And flies in a dream, the dawns ruin it.
He is strong and pain is worse to the strong, incapacity is worse.
The curs of the day come and torment him   10
At distance, no one but death the redeemer will humble that head,
The intrepid readiness, the terrible eyes.
The wild God of the world is sometimes merciful to those
That ask mercy, not often to the arrogant.

You do not know him, you communal people, or you have forgotten
    him;   15
Intemperate and savage, the hawk remembers him;
Beautiful and wild, the hawks, and men that are dying, remember him.

II

I'd sooner, except the penalties, kill a man than a hawk; but the great
    redtail
Had nothing left but unable misery
From the bone too shattered for mending, the wing that trailed under
    his talons when he moved.   20
We had fed him six weeks, I gave him freedom,
He wandered over the foreland hill and returned in the evening, asking
    for death,
Not like a beggar, still eyed with the old
Implacable arrogance. I gave him the lead gift in the twilight.
    What fell was relaxed,   25
Owl-downy, soft feminine feathers; but what
Soared: the fierce rush: the night-herons by the flooded river cried fear
    at its rising
Before it was quite unsheathed from reality.

T. S. ELIOT (1888–1965)

The Love Song of J. Alfred Prufrock (1917)

S'io credesse che mia risposta fosse
A persona che mai tornasse al mondo,
Questa fiamma staria senza piu scosse.
Ma perciocche giammai di questo fondo
Non torno vivo alcun, s'i'odo il vero,
*Senza tema d'infamia ti rispondo.**

Let us go then, you and I,
When the evening is spread out against the sky
Like a patient etherised upon a table;
Let us go, through certain half-deserted streets,
The muttering retreats   5
Of restless nights in one-night cheap hotels
And sawdust restaurants with oyster-shells:
Streets that follow like a tedious argument
Of insidious intent
To lead you to an overwhelming question . . .   10

* "If I thought that my answer were being made to someone who would ever return to earth, this flame would remain without further movement; but since no one has ever returned alive from this depth, if what I hear is true, I answer you without fear of infamy" (Dante, *Inferno* 27.61–66). Dante encounters Guido de Montefeltro in the eighth circle of hell, where souls are trapped within flames (tongues of fire) as punishment for giving evil counsel. Guido tells Dante details about his evil life only because he assumes Dante is on his way to an even deeper circle in hell and will never return to earth and be able to repeat what he has heard.

Oh, do not ask, "What is it?"
Let us go and make our visit.

    In the room the women come and go
Talking of Michelangelo.

    The yellow fog that rubs its back upon the window-panes,   15
The yellow smoke that rubs its muzzle on the window-panes
Licked its tongue into the corners of the evening,
Lingered upon the pools that stand in drains,
Let fall upon its back the soot that falls from chimneys,
Slipped by the terrace, made a sudden leap,   20
And seeing that it was a soft October night,
Curled once about the house, and fell asleep.

    And indeed there will be time
For the yellow smoke that slides along the street,
Rubbing its back upon the window-panes;   25
There will be time, there will be time
To prepare a face to meet the faces that you meet;
There will be time to murder and create,
And time for all the works and days of hands
That lift and drop a question on your plate;   30
Time for you and time for me,
And time yet for a hundred indecisions,
And for a hundred visions and revisions,
Before the taking of a toast and tea.

    In the room the women come and go   35
Talking of Michelangelo.

    And indeed there will be time
To wonder, "Do I dare?" and, "Do I dare?"
Time to turn back and descend the stair,
With a bald spot in the middle of my hair—   40
[They will say: "How his hair is growing thin!"]
My morning coat, my collar mounting firmly to the chin,
My necktie rich and modest, but asserted by a simple pin—
[They will say: "But how his arms and legs are thin!"]
Do I dare   45
Disturb the universe?
In a minute there is time
For decisions and revisions which a minute will reverse.

    For I have known them all already, known them all:—
Have known the evenings, mornings, afternoons,   50
I have measured out my life with coffee spoons;
I know the voices dying with a dying fall
Beneath the music from a farther room.
    So how should I presume?

And I have known the eyes already, known them all—   55
The eyes that fix you in a formulated phrase,
And when I am formulated, sprawling on a pin,
When I am pinned and wriggling on the wall,
Then how should I begin
To spit out all the butt-ends of my days and ways?   60
    And how should I presume?

    And I have known the arms already, known them all—
Arms that are braceleted and white and bare
[But in the lamplight, downed with light brown hair!]
Is it perfume from a dress   65
That makes me so digress?
Arms that lie along a table, or wrap about a shawl.
    And should I then presume?
    And how should I begin?

      •   •   •   •   •

Shall I say, I have gone at dusk through narrow streets   70
And watched the smoke that rises from the pipes
Of lonely men in shirt-sleeves, leaning out of windows? . . .

    I should have been a pair of ragged claws
Scuttling across the floors of silent seas.

      •   •   •   •   •

And the afternoon, the evening, sleeps so peacefully!   75
Smoothed by long fingers,
Asleep . . . tired . . . or it malingers,
Stretched on the floor, here beside you and me.
Should I, after tea and cakes and ices,
Have the strength to force the moment to its crisis?   80
But though I have wept and fasted, wept and prayed,
Though I have seen my head [grown slightly bald] brought in upon a
    platter,
I am no prophet—and here's no great matter;
I have seen the moment of my greatness flicker,
And I have seen the eternal Footman hold my coat, and snicker,   85
And in short, I was afraid.

    And would it have been worth it, after all,
After the cups, the marmalade, the tea,
Among the porcelain, among some talk of you and me,
Would it have been worth while,   90
To have bitten off the matter with a smile,
To have squeezed the universe into a ball
To roll it toward some overwhelming question,
To say: "I am Lazarus, come from the dead,
Come back to tell you all, I shall tell you all"—   95
If one, settling a pillow by her head,

Should say: "That is not what I meant at all.
That is not it, at all."

And would it have been worth it, after all,
Would it have been worth while,   100
After the sunsets and the dooryards and the sprinkled streets,
After the novels, after the teacups, after the skirts that trail along the
    floor—
And this, and so much more?—
It is impossible to say just what I mean!
But as if a magic lantern threw the nerves in patterns on a screen: 105
Would it have been worth while
If one, settling a pillow or throwing off a shawl,
And turning toward the window, should say:
    "That is not it at all,
    That is not what I meant, at all."   110

· · · · ·

No! I am not Prince Hamlet, nor was meant to be;
Am an attendant lord, one that will do
To swell a progress, start a scene or two,
Advise the prince; no doubt, an easy tool,
Deferential, glad to be of use,   115
Politic, cautious, and meticulous;
Full of high sentence, but a bit obtuse;
At times, indeed, almost ridiculous—
Almost, at times, the Fool.

    I grow old . . . I grow old . . .   120
I shall wear the bottoms of my trousers rolled.

    Shall I part my hair behind? Do I dare to eat a peach?
I shall wear white flannel trousers, and walk upon the beach.
I have heard the mermaids singing, each to each.

    I do not think that they will sing to me.   125

    I have seen them riding seaward on the waves
Combing the white hair of the waves blown back
When the wind blows the water white and black.

    We have lingered in the chambers of the sea
By sea-girls wreathed with seaweed red and brown   130
Till human voices wake us, and we drown.

T. S. Eliot (1888–1965)

Preludes (1917)

I

The winter evening settles down
With smell of steaks in passageways.

Six o'clock.
The burnt-out ends of smoky days.
And now a gusty shower wraps   5
The grimy scraps
Of withered leaves about your feet
And newspapers from vacant lots;
The showers beat
On broken blinds and chimney-pots,   10
And at the corner of the street
A lonely cab-horse steams and stamps.
And then the lighting of the lamps.

II

The morning comes to consciousness
Of faint stale smells of beer   15
From the sawdust-trampled street
With all its muddy feet that press
To early coffee-stands.
With the other masquerades
That time resumes,   20
One thinks of all the hands
That are raising dingy shades
In a thousand furnished rooms.

III

You tossed a blanket from the bed,
You lay upon your back, and waited;   25
You dozed, and watched the night revealing
The thousand sordid images
Of which your soul was constituted;
They flickered against the ceiling.
And when all the world came back   30
And the light crept up between the shutters
And you heard the sparrows in the gutters,
You had such a vision of the street
As the street hardly understands;
Sitting along the bed's edge, where   35
You curled the papers from your hair,
Or clasped the yellow soles of feet
In the palms of both soiled hands.

IV

His soul stretched tight across the skies
That fade behind a city block,   40
Or trampled by insistent feet
At four and five and six o'clock;
And short square fingers stuffing pipes,
And evening newspapers, and eyes

Assured of certain certainties,   45
The conscience of a blackened street
Impatient to assume the world.

　　　I am moved by fancies that are curled
Around these images, and cling:
The notion of some infinitely gentle   50
Infinitely suffering thing.

　　　Wipe your hand across your mouth, and laugh;
The worlds revolve like ancient women
Gathering fuel in vacant lots.

JOHN CROWE RANSOM (1888–1974)

Bells for John Whiteside's Daughter (1924)

There was such speed in her little body,
And such lightness in her footfall,
It is no wonder her brown study
Astonishes us all.

Her wars were bruited in our high window.   5
We looked among orchard trees and beyond
Where she took arms against her shadow,
Or harried unto the pond

The lazy geese, like a snow cloud
Dripping their snow on the green grass,   10
Tricking and stopping, sleepy and proud,
Who cried in goose, Alas,

For the tireless heart within the little
Lady with rod that made them rise
From their noon apple-dreams and scuttle   15
Goose-fashion under the skies!

But now go the bells, and we are ready,
In one house we are sternly stopped
To say we are vexed at her brown study,
Lying so primly propped.   20

EDNA ST. VINCENT MILLAY (1892–1950)

Wild Swans (1921)

I looked in my heart while the wild swans went over.
And what did I see I had not seen before?
Only a question less or a question more;
Nothing to match the flight of wild birds flying.
Tiresome heart, forever living and dying,   5
House without air, I leave you and lock your door.

Wild swans, come over the town, come over
The town again, trailing your legs and crying!

WILFRED OWEN (1893–1918)

Dulce et Decorum Est (1920)

Bent double, like old beggars under sacks,
Knock-kneed, coughing like hags, we cursed through sludge,
Till on the haunting flares we turned our backs
And towards our distant rest began to trudge.
Men marched asleep. Many had lost their boots   5
But limped on, blood-shod. All went lame; all blind;
Drunk with fatigue; deaf even to the hoots
Of tired, outstripped Five-Nines* that dropped behind.

Gas! GAS! Quick, boys!—An ecstasy of fumbling,
Fitting the clumsy helmets just in time;   10
But someone still was yelling out and stumbling
And flound'ring like a man in fire or lime . . .
Dim, through the misty panes° and thick green light,   *of a gas mask*
As under a green sea, I saw him drowning.

In all my dreams, before my helpless sight,   15
He plunges at me, guttering, choking, drowning.

If in some smothering dreams you too could pace
Behind the wagon that we flung him in,
And watch the white eyes writhing in his face,
His hanging face, like a devil's sick of sin;   20
If you could hear, at every jolt, the blood
Come gargling from the froth-corrupted lungs,
Obscene as cancer, bitter as the cud
Of vile, incurable sores on innocent tongues,—
My friend, you would not tell with such high zest   25
To children ardent for some desperate glory,
The old Lie: Dulce et decorum est
Pro patria mori.†

YVOR WINTERS (1900–1968)

At the San Francisco Airport (1960)

to my daughter, 1954

This is the terminal: the light
Gives perfect vision, false and hard;
The metal glitters, deep and bright.

---

* 5.9-inch caliber shells.

† It is sweet and fitting / to die for one's country. (Horace, *Odes,* 3.12.13)

Great planes are waiting in the yard—
They are already in the night.   5

And you are here beside me, small,
Contained and fragile, and intent
On things that I but half recall—
Yet going whither you are bent.
I am the past, and that is all.   10

But you and I in part are one:
The frightened brain, the nervous will,
The knowledge of what must be done,
The passion to acquire the skill
To face that which you dare not shun.   15

The rain of matter upon sense
Destroys me momently. The score:
There comes what will come. The expense
Is what one thought, and something more—
One's being and intelligence.   20

This is the terminal, the break.
Beyond this point, on lines of air,
You take the way that you must take;
And I remain in light and stare—
In light, and nothing else, awake.   25

LANGSTON HUGHES (1902–1967)

Theme for English B (1951)

The instructor said,

> *Go home and write*
> *a page tonight.*
> *And let that page come out of you—*
> *Then, it will be true.*   5

I wonder if it's that simple?
I am twenty-two, colored, born in Winston-Salem.
I went to school there, then Durham, then here
to this college on the hill above Harlem.
I am the only colored student in my class.   10
The steps from the hill lead down into Harlem,
through a park, then I cross St. Nicholas,
Eighth Avenue, Seventh, and I come to the Y,
the Harlem Branch Y, where I take the elevator
up to my room, sit down, and write this page: 15

It's not easy to know what is true for you or me
at twenty-two, my age. But I guess I'm what

I feel and see and hear, Harlem, I hear you:
hear you, hear me—we two—you, me, talk on this page.
(I hear New York, too.) Me—who?   20
Well, I like to eat, sleep, drink, and be in love.
I like to work, read, learn, and understand life.
I like a pipe for a Christmas present,
or records—Bessie,* bop, or Bach.
I guess being colored doesn't make me *not* like   25
the same things other folks like who are other races.
So will my page be colored that I write?
Being me, it will not be white.
But it will be
a part of you, instructor.   30
You are white—
yet a part of me, as I am a part of you.
That's American.
Sometimes perhaps you don't want to be a part of me.
Nor do I often want to be a part of you.   35
But we are, that's true!
As I learn from you,
I guess you learn from me—
although you're older—and white—
and somewhat more free.   40

This is my page for English B.

LORINE NIEDECKER (1903–1970)

Will You Write Me a Christmas Poem? (ca. 1935)

Will I!

The mad stimulus of Gay Gaunt Day
meet to put holly on a tree
and trim green bells
and trim green bells

Now candles come to faces.   5
You are wrong to-day
you are wrong to-day,
my dear. My dear—

One translucent morning
in the damp development of winter,   10
one fog to move a city backward—
Backward, backwards, backward!

You see the objects and the movable fingers,
Candy dripping from branches,

* Bessie Smith, early blues singer.

Horoscopes of summer   15
and you don't have Christmas ultimately—
Ultima Thule* ultimately!

Spreads and whimpets
Good to the cherry drops,
Whom for a splendor   20
Whom for a splendor

I'm going off the paper I'm going off the pap-

Send two birds out
Send two birds out
And carol them in,   25
Cookies go round.

What a scandal is Christmas,
What a scandle Christmas is
a red stick-up
to a lily.   30

You flagellate my woes, you flagellate,
I interpret yours,
holly is a care divine
        holly is a care divine

and where are we all from here.   35
Drink for there is nothing else to do
but pray,
And where are we?

Throw out the ribbons
and tie your people in   40
All spans dissever
once the New Year opens
and snow derides
a doorway,
it spasms dissever   45

All spans dissever,
wherefore we, for instance, recuperate
no grief to modulate
no grief to modulate

The Christian cacophony   50
one word to another,
sound of gilt trailing the world

* For ancient travelers, the farthest point north.

slippers to presume,
postludes, homiclea, sweet tenses
imbecile and corrupt,— 55
     failing the whirled, trailing the whirlled

This great eventual heyday
to plenty the hour thereof,
fidelius.
Heyday! Hey-day! Hey-day! 60

I fade the color of my wine
that an afternoon might live
foiled with shine and brittle
I fade the color of my wine

Harmony in Egypt, 65
representative birthday.
Christ what a destiny
What a destiny's Christ's, Christ!

LOUIS ZUKOFSKY (1904–1978)

from "A" 15 (1978)

An
  hinny
by
  stallion
out of 5
  she-ass

He neigh ha lie low h'who y'he gall mood
So roar cruel hire
Lo to achieve an eye leer rot off
Mass th'lo low o loam echo 10
How deal me many coeval yammer
Naked on face of white rock—sea.
Then I said: Liveforever my nest
Is arable hymn
Shore she root to water 15
Dew anew to branch.

Wind: Yahweh at Iyyob°   *Job*
Mien His roar "Why yammer
Measly make short hates oh
By milling bleat doubt? 20
Eye sore gnaw key heaver haul its core
Weigh as I lug where hide any?
If you—had you towed beside the roots?

How goad Him—you'd do it by now—
My sum My made day a key to daw?   25
O Me not there allheal—a cave.

All mouth deny hot bough?
O Me you're raw—Heaven pinned Dawn stars
Brine I heard choir and weigh by care—
Why your ear would call by now Elohim: 30
Where was soak—bid lot tie in hum—
How would you have known to hum
How would you all oats rose snow lay
Assáy how'd a rock light rollick ore
Had the rush in you curb, ah bay,   35
Bay the shophar yammer *heigh horse*"

Wind: Yahweh at Iyyob "Why yammer,"
Wind: Iyyob at Yahweh, "Why yammer
How cold the mouth achieved echo."
Wind: Yahweh at Iyyob "Why yammer   40
Ha neigh now behēmoth and share I see see your make
Giddy pair—stones—whose rages go
Weigh raw all gay where how spill lay who"
Wind: Iyyob
"Rain without sun hated? *hurt no one*   45
In two we shadow, how hide any."

The traffic below,
sound of it a wind
eleven stories
below: *The Parkway*   50
no parking there ever:
the deaths as
after it might be said
"ordered," the one
the two old   55
songsters would not
live to see—
the death of
the young man,
who had possibly   60
alleviated
the death of
the oldest
vagrantly back he
might have thought   65
from vying culturally
with the Russian
Puritan Bear—

to vagary of
Bear hug and King
Charles losing his head—
and the other
a decade younger
never international
emissary
at least not
for his President,
aged in a suburb
dying maundering
the language—
American—impatient now
sometimes extreme clarity—
to hurrȳ
his compost
to the hill
his grave—
(distance
    a gastank)

he would
miss
living thru the
assassination

70

75

80

85

90

Stanley Kunitz (b. 1905)

Father and Son (1944)

Now in the suburbs and the falling light
I followed him, and now down sandy road
Whiter than bone-dust, through the sweet
Curdle of fields, where the plums
Dropped with their load of ripeness, one by one.
Mile after mile I followed, with skimming feet,
After the secret master of my blood,
Him, steeped in the odor of ponds, whose indomitable love
Kept me in chains. Strode years; stretched into bird;
Raced through the sleeping country where I was young,
The silence unrolling before me as I came,
The night nailed like an orange to my brow.

How should I tell him my fable and the fears,
How bridge the chasm in a casual tone,
Saying, "The house, the stucco one you built,
We lost. Sister married and went from home,
And nothing comes back, it's strange, from where she goes.

5

10

15

I lived on a hill that had too many rooms:
Light we could make, but not enough of warmth,
And when the light failed, I climbed under the hill.   20
The papers are delivered every day;
I am alone and never shed a tear."

At the water's edge, where the smothering ferns lifted
Their arms, "Father!" I cried, "Return! You know
The way. I'll wipe the mudstains from your clothes;   25
No trace, I promise, will remain. Instruct
Your son, whirling between two wars,
In the Gemara of your gentleness,
For I would be a child to those who mourn
And brother to the foundlings of the field   30
And friend of innocence and all bright eyes.
O teach me how to work and keep me kind."

Among the turtles and the lilies he turned to me
The white ignorant hollow of his face.

W. H. AUDEN (1907–1973)

As I Walked Out One Evening (1937)

As I walked out one evening,
  Walking down Bristol Street,
The crowds upon the pavement
  Were fields of harvest wheat.

And down by the brimming river   5
  I heard a lover sing
Under an arch of the railway:
  "Love has no ending.

"I'll love you, dear, I'll love you
  Till China and Africa meet,   10
And the river jumps over the mountain
  And the salmon sing in the street,

"I'll love you till the ocean
  Is folded and hung up to dry
And the seven stars go squawking   15
  Like geese about the sky.

The years shall run like rabbits,
  For in my arms I hold
The Flower of the Ages,
  And the first love of the world."   20

But all the clocks in the city
  Began to whirr and chime:
"O let not Time deceive you,
  You cannot conquer Time.

"In the burrows of the Nightmare   25
  Where Justice naked is,
Time watches from the shadow
  And coughs when you would kiss.

"In headaches and in worry
  Vaguely life leaks away,   30
And Time will have his fancy
  To-morrow or to-day.

"Into many a green valley
  Drifts the appalling snow;
Time breaks the threaded dances   35
  And the diver's brilliant bow.

"O plunge your hands in water,
  Plunge them in up to the wrist;
Stare, stare in the basin
  And wonder what you've missed.   40

"The glacier knocks in the cupboard,
  The desert sighs in the bed,
And the crack in the tea-cup opens
  A lane to the land of the dead.

"Where the beggars raffle the banknotes   45
  And the Giant is enchanting to Jack,
And the Lily-white Boy is a Roarer,
  And Jill goes down on her back.

"O look, look in the mirror,
  O look in your distress;   50
Life remains a blessing
  Although you cannot bless.

"O stand, stand at the window
  As the tears scald and start;
You shall love your crooked neighbour   55
  With your crooked heart."

It was late, late in the evening,
  The lovers they were gone;
The clocks had ceased their chiming,
  And the deep river ran on.   60

W. H. AUDEN (1907–1973)

Musée des Beaux Arts* (1940)

About suffering they were never wrong,
The Old Masters: how well they understood
Its human position; how it takes place
While someone else is eating or opening a window or just walking dully
     along;
How, when the aged are reverently, passionately waiting   5
For the miraculous birth, there always must be
Children who did not specially want it to happen, skating
On a pond at the edge of the wood:
They never forgot
That even the dreadful martyrdom must run its course   10
Anyhow in a corner, some untidy spot
Where the dogs go on with their doggy life and the torturer's horse
Scratches its innocent behind on a tree.

In Breughel's *Icarus,* for instance: how everything turns away
Quite leisurely from the disaster; the ploughman may   15
Have heard the splash, the forsaken cry,
But for him it was not an important failure; the sun shone
As it had to on the white legs disappearing into the green
Water; and the expensive delicate ship that must have seen
Something amazing, a boy falling out of the sky,   20
Had somewhere to get to and sailed calmly on.

DYLAN THOMAS (1914–1953)

Do Not Go Gentle into That Good Night (1952)

Do not go gentle into that good night,
Old age should burn and rave at close of day;
Rage, rage against the dying of the light.

Though wise men at their end know dark is right,
Because their words had forked no lightning they   5
Do not go gentle into that good night.

Good men, the last wave by, crying how bright
Their frail deeds might have danced in a green bay,
Rage, rage against the dying of the light.

Wild men who caught and sang the sun in flight,   10
And learn, too late, they grieved it on its way,
Do not go gentle into that good night.

---

* The painting *Landscape with the Fall of Icarus* by Pieter Brueghel the Elder, on which the poem is based, is in the Musées Royaux des Beaux-Arts in Brussels.

Grave men, near death, who see with blinding sight
Blind eyes could blaze like meteors and be gay,
Rage, rage against the dying of the light.   15

And you, my father, there on the sad height,
Curse, bless, me now with your fierce tears, I pray.
Do not go gentle into that good night.
Rage, rage against the dying of the light.

HENRY REED (1914–1986)

Naming of Parts (1946)

Today we have naming of parts. Yesterday,
We had daily cleaning. And tomorrow morning,
We shall have what to do after firing. But today,
Today we have naming of parts. Japonica
Glistens like coral in all of the neighbouring gardens,   5
    And today we have naming of parts.

This is the lower sling swivel. And this
Is the upper sling swivel, whose use you will see,
When you are given your slings. And this is the piling swivel,
Which in your case you have not got. The branches   10
Hold in the gardens their silent, eloquent gestures,
    Which in our case we have not got.

This is the safety-catch, which is always released
With an easy flick of the thumb. And please do not let me
See anyone using his finger. You can do it quite easy   15
If you have any strength in your thumb. The blossoms
Are fragile and motionless, never letting anyone see
    Any of them using their finger.

And this you can see is the bolt. The purpose of this
Is to open the breech, as you see. We can slide it   20
Rapidly backwards and forwards: we call this
Easing the spring. And rapidly backwards and forwards
The early bees are assaulting and fumbling the flowers:
    They call it easing the Spring.

They call it easing the Spring: it is perfectly easy   25
If you have any strength in your thumb: like the bolt,
And the breech, and the cocking-piece, and the point of balance,
Which in our case we have not got; and the almond-blossom
Silent in all of the gardens and the bees going backwards and forwards,
    For today we have naming of parts.   30

RANDALL JARRELL (1914–1965)

The Woman at the Washington Zoo (1960)

The saris go by me from the embassies.

Cloth from the moon. Cloth from another planet.
They look back at the leopard like the leopard.

And I. . . .
              this print of mine, that has kept its color   5
Alive through so many cleanings; this dull null
Navy I wear to work, and wear from work, and so
To my bed, so to my grave, with no
Complaints, no comment: neither from my chief,
The Deputy Chief Assistant, nor his chief—   10
Only I complain. . . . this serviceable
Body that no sunlight dyes, no hand suffuses
But, dome-shadowed, withering among columns,
Wavy beneath fountains—small, far-off, shining
In the eyes of animals, these beings trapped   15
As I am trapped but not, themselves, the trap,
Aging, but without knowledge of their age,
Kept safe here, knowing not of death, for death—
Oh, bars of my own body, open, open!

The world goes by my cage and never sees me.   20
And there come not to me, as come to these,
The wild beasts, sparrows pecking the llamas' grain,
Pigeons settling on the bears' bread, buzzards
Tearing the meat the flies have clouded. . . .
                         Vulture,   25
When you come for the white rat that the foxes left,
Wings that have shadowed me, and step to me as man:
The wild brother at whose feet the white wolves fawn,
To whose hand of power the great lioness
Stalks, purring. . . .   30
               You know what I was,
You see what I am: change me, change me!

JOHN BERRYMAN (1914–1972)

Henry's Confession (1964)

from The Dream Songs 76

Nothin very bad happen to me lately.
How you explain that?—I explain that, Mr Bones,
terms o' your bafflin odd sobriety.
Sober as man can get, no girls, no telephones,

what could happen bad to Mr Bones?   5
—*If* life is a handkerchief sandwich,

in a modesty of death I join my father
who dared so long agone leave me.
A bullet on a concrete stoop
close by a smothering southern sea   10
spreadeagled on an island, by my knee.
—You is from hunger, Mr Bones,

I offers you this handkerchief, now set
your left foot by my right foot,
shoulder to shoulder, all that jazz,   15
arm in arm, by the beautiful sea,
hum a little, Mr Bones.
—I saw nobody coming, so I went instead.

THOMAS MCGRATH (1916–1990)

All the Dead Soldiers (1982)

In the chill rains of the early winter I hear something—
A puling anger, a cold wind stiffened by flying bone—
Out of the north . . .
                           and remember, then, what's up there:
That ghost-bank: home: Amchitka:* boot hill. . . .   5

They must be very tired, those ghosts; no flesh sustains them
And the bones rust in the rain.
                           Reluctant to go into the earth
The skulls gleam: wet; the dog-tag forgets the name;
The statistics (wherein they were young) like their crosses, are weather-
      ing out.   10

They must be very tired.
                           But I see them riding home,
Nightly: crying weak lust and rage: to stand in the dark,
Forlorn in known rooms, unheard near familiar beds:
Where lie the aging women: who were so lovely: once.   15

ROBERT LOWELL (1917–1978)

Skunk Hour (1963)

for Elizabeth Bishop

Nautilus Island's hermit
heiress still lives through winter in her Spartan cottage;

* Aleutian island used for atomic bomb tests.

---

her sheep still graze above the sea.
Her son's a bishop. Her farmer
is first selectman in our village;   5
she's in her dotage.

Thirsting for
the hierarchic privacy
of Queen Victoria's century,
she buys up all   10
the eyesores facing her shore,
and lets them fall.

The season's ill—
we've lost our summer millionaire,
who seemed to leap from an L. L. Bean   15
catalogue. His nine-knot yawl
was auctioned off to lobstermen.
A red fox stain covers Blue Hill.

And now our fairy
decorator brightens his shop for fall;   20
his fishnet's filled with orange cork,
orange, his cobbler's bench and awl;
there is no money in his work,
he'd rather marry.

One dark night,   25
my Tudor Ford climbed the hill's skull;
I watched for love-cars. Lights turned down,
they lay together, hull to hull,
where the graveyard shelves on the town. . . .
My mind's not right.   30

A car radio bleats,
"Love, O careless Love. . . ." I hear
my ill-spirit sob in each blood cell,
as if my hand were at its throat. . . .
I myself am hell;   35
nobody's here—

only skunks, that search
in the moonlight for a bite to eat.
They march on their soles up Main Street:
white stripes, moonstruck eyes' red fire   40
under the chalk-dry and spar spire
of the Trinitarian Church.

I stand on top
of our back steps and breathe the rich air—
a mother skunk with her column of kittens swills the garbage pail.   45

She jabs her wedge-head in a cup
of sour cream, drops her ostrich tail,
and will not scare.

ROBERT DUNCAN (1919–1988)

The Torso (1968)

Passages 18

> Most beautiful!   the red-flowering eucalyptus,
> > the madrone, the yew

> > Is he . . .

> *So thou wouldst smile, and take me in thine arms*
> *The sight of London to my exiled eyes*   5
> *Is as Elysium to a new-come soul*

> > If he be Truth
> > I would dwell in the illusion of him

His hands unlocking from chambers of my male body

> > such an idea in man's image   10

> rising tides that sweep me towards him

> > . . . *homosexual?*

> > and at the treasure of his mouth

> > pour forth my soul

> > > his soul   commingling   15

> I thought a Being more than vast, His body leading
> > into Paradise,   his eyes
> > > quickening a fire in me,   a trembling

> > hieroglyph: At the root of the neck

> *the clavicle,* for the neck is the stem of the great artery   20
> > upward into his head that is beautiful

> > > At the rise of the pectoral muscle,

> *the nipples,* for the breasts are like sleeping fountains
> > of feeling in man, waiting above the beat of his heart,
> > shielding the rise and fall of his breath, to be   25
> > awakend

> > > At the axis of his mid hriff

> *the navel,* for in the pit of his stomach the chord from
> > which first he was fed has its temple

At the root of the groin   30

      the pubic hair, for the torso is the stem in which the man
         flowers forth and leads to the stamen of flesh in which
         his seed rises

a wave of need and desire over   taking me

                    cried out my name   35

        (This was long ago.   It was another life)

                            and said,

          What do you want of me?

I do not know, I said.   I have fallen in love.   He
         has brought me into heights and depths my heart   40
                would fear   without him.   His look

        pierces my side   •   fire eyes   •

      I have been waiting for you, he said:
                  I know what you desire

        you do not yet know   but through me   •   45

    And I am with you everywhere.   In your falling

I have fallen from a high place.   I have raised myself

        from darkness in your   rising

               wherever you are

        my hand in your hand   seeking   the locks, the keys   50

I am there.   Gathering me, you gather

      your Self   •

    For my Other is not a woman but a man

    the King upon whose bosom let me lie.

CHARLES BUKOWSKI (1920–1994)

my old man (1977)

16 years old
during the depression
I'd come home drunk
and all my clothing—
shorts, shirts, stockings—   5
suitcase, and pages of
short stories
would be thrown out on the
front lawn and about the
street.   10

my mother would be
waiting behind a tree:
"Henry, Henry, don't
go in . . . he'll
kill you, he's read   15
your stories . . ."

"I can whip his
ass . . ."

"Henry, please take
this . . . and   20
find yourself a room."

but it worried him
that I might not
finish high school
so I'd be back   25
again.

one evening he walked in
with the pages of
one of my short stories
(which I had never submitted   30
to him)
and he said, "this is
a great short story."
I said, "o.k.,"
and he handed it to me   35
and I read it.
it was a story about
a rich man
who had a fight with
his wife and had   40
gone out into the night
for a cup of coffee
and had observed
the waitress and the spoons
and forks and the   45
salt and pepper shakers
and the neon sign
in the window
and then had gone back
to his stable   50
to see and touch his
favorite horse
who then
kicked him in the head
and killed him.   55

somehow
the story held
meaning for him
though
when I had written it   60
I had no idea
of what I was
writing about.

so I told him,
"o.k., old man, you can   65
have it."
and he took it
and walked out
and closed the door.
I guess that's   70
as close
as we ever got.

RICHARD WILBUR (b. 1921)

Thyme Flowering among Rocks (1969)

This, if Japanese,
Would represent grey boulders
Walloped by rough seas

So that, here or there,
The balked water tossed its froth   5
Straight into the air.

Here, where things are what
They are, it is thyme blooming,
Rocks, and nothing but—

Having, nonetheless,   10
Many small leaves implicit,
A green countlessness.

Crouching down, peering
Into perplexed recesses,
You find a clearing   15

Occupied by sun
Where, along prone, rachitic
Branches, one by one,

Pale stems arise, squared
In the manner of *Mentha*,°   *plants of the mint genus*   20
The oblong leaves paired.

One branch, in ending,
Lifts a little and begets
A straight-ascending

Spike, whorled with fine blue   25
Or purple trumpets, banked in
The leaf-axils. You

Are lost now in dense
Fact, fact which one might have thought
Hidden from the sense,   30

Blinking at detail
Peppery as this fragrance,
Lost to proper scale

As, in the motion
Of striped fins, a bathysphere   35
Forgets the ocean.

It makes the craned head
Spin. Unfathomed thyme! The world's
A dream, Basho° said,   *early Japanese Haiku master*

Not because that dream's   40
A falsehood, but because it's
Truer than it seems.

JACK KEROUAC (1922–1969)

239th Chorus (1959)

Charley Parker Looked like Buddha
Charley Parker, who recently died
Laughing at a juggler on the TV
after weeks of strain and sickness,
was called the Perfect Musician.   5
And his expression on his face
Was as calm, beautiful, and profound
As the image of the Buddha
Represented in the East, the lidded eyes,
The expression that says "All is Well"   10
—This was what Charley Parker
Said when he played, All is Well.
You had the feeling of early-in-the-morning
Like a hermit's joy, or like
                    the perfect cry   15
Of some wild gang at a jam session
"Wail, Wop"—Charley burst
His lungs to reach the speed
Of what the speedsters wanted
And what they wanted   20
Was his Eternal Slowdown.
A great musician and a great
                    creator of forms
That ultimately find expression
In mores and what have you.   25

SHIRLEY KAUFMAN (b. 1923)

Nechama (1973)

They changed her name
to Nellie. All the girls.
To be American.
And cut her hair.

She couldn't give up   5
what she thought she lost.
Streets like ceiling cracks
she looked up watching
where the same boy bicycled always
to the gate of her Russian house.   10
She saw him tremble
in the steam over her tea
after the samovar was gone.
She was Anna Karenina*
married to somebody else.   15

        *

Oh she was beautiful. She could turn
into an egret with copper hair.
She could turn into a fig tree.
She could turn into a Siberian wolfhound.
She could turn into an opal   20
turning green. She could drown us
in the lake of her soft skin.

Rhythm of chopping garlic
motion as language in her wrists
warming her hands   25
rubbing it
over the leg of lamb.

        *

Leaving the kitchen she would cry
over pictures telling us
nothing new   30

till the small light by her bed
kept getting lost under the blanket
where she crawled looking
for something she forgot
or money in her old house   35

* The novel *Anna Karenina* (1877) by Leo Tolstoy deals with the title character's extramarital relationship.

under the hankies looking
for spare parts.

She swallowed what we brought
because we said to.

*

The rabbi knows 40
the 23rd psalm backwards
and he pretends he came for a wedding.

Do me a favor she still pleads
under the roses
begging for proof of faithfulness 45
or love. If I say yes
she might ask anything like
stay with me
or take me home.

*

It's my face staring 50
out of her picture
wrinkled and old
as a newborn infant) *paradox*
pushed there
ahead of myself 55

or memorizing lines
over and over in a soundproof room
until the smile is stuck there
and the lips stay frozen
like a hole in the ice ⌉ *simile* 60
where a child fell in. ⌋

DENISE LEVERTOV (b. 1923)

February Evening in New York (1959)

As the stores close, a winter light
 opens air to iris blue,
 glint of frost through the smoke
 grains of mica, salt of the sidewalk.
As the buildings close, released autonomous 5
 feet pattern the streets
 in hurry and stroll; balloon heads
 drift and dive above them; the bodies
 aren't really there.
As the lights brighten, as the sky darkens, 10
 a woman with crooked heels says to another woman

while they step along at a fair pace,
"You know, I'm telling you, what I love best
is life. I love life! Even if I ever get
to be old and wheezy—or limp! You know? 15
Limping along?—I'd still . . ." Out of hearing.
To the multiple disordered tones
   of gears changing, a dance
   to the compass points, out, four-way river.
   Prospect of sky 20
   wedged into avenues, left at the ends of streets,
   west sky, east sky: more life tonight! A range
   of open time at winter's outskirts.

ALAN DUGAN (b. 1923)

On Hurricane Jackson (1961)

Now his nose's bridge is broken, one eye
will not focus and the other is a stray;
trainers whisper in his mouth while one ear
listens to itself, clenched like a fist;
generally shadowboxing in a smoky room, 5
his mind hides like the aching boys
who lost a contest in the Panhellenic games
and had to take the back roads home,
but someone else, his perfect youth,
laureled in newsprint and dollar bills, 10
triumphs forever on the great white way
to the statistical Sparta of the champs.

RICHARD HUGO (1923–1982)

Driving Montana (1973)

The day is a woman who loves you. Open.
Deer drink close to the road and magpies
spray from your car. Miles from any town
your radio comes in strong, unlikely
Mozart from Belgrade, rock and roll 5
from Butte. Whatever the next number,
you want to hear it. Never has your Buick
found this forward a gear. Even
the tuna salad in Reedpoint is good.

Towns arrive ahead of imagined schedule. 10
Absorakee at one. Or arrive so late—
Silesia at nine—you recreate the day.
Where did you stop along the road
and have fun? Was there a runaway horse?
Did you park at that house, the one 15

alone in a void of grain, white with green
trim and red fence, where you know you lived
once? You remembered the ringing creek,
the soft brown forms of far off bison.
You must have stayed hours, then drove on.   20
In the motel you know you'd never seen it before.

Tomorrow will open again, the sky wide
as the mouth of a wild girl, friable
clouds you lose yourself to. You are lost
in miles of land without people, without   25
one fear of being found, in the dash
of rabbits, soar of antelope, swirl
merge and clatter of streams.

DANNIE ABSE (b. 1923)

Pathology of Colours (1968)

I know the colour rose, and it is lovely,
but not when it ripens in a tumour;
and healing greens, leaves and grass, so springlike,
in limbs that fester are not springlike.

I have seen red-blue tinged with hirsute mauve   5
in the plum-skin face of a suicide.
I have seen white, china white almost, stare
from behind the smashed windscreen of a car.

And the criminal, multi-coloured flash
of an H-bomb is no more beautiful   10
than an autopsy when the belly's opened—
to show cathedral windows never opened.

So in the single blessing of a rainbow,
in the bevelled edge of a sunlit mirror,
I have seen, visible, Death's artifact   15
like a soldier's ribbon on a tunic tacked.

DONALD JUSTICE (b. 1925)

Sonatina in Yellow (1973)

Du schnell vergehendes Daguerrotyp
In meinen langsamer vergehenden Händen.*
     —Rilke

The pages of the album,
As they are turned, turn yellow, a word,

* "You rapidly fading daguerrotype in my more slowly fading hands."

Once spoken, obsolete,
No longer what was meant. Say it.
The meanings come, or come back later, 5
Unobtrusive, taking their places.

Think of the past. Think of forgetting the past.
It was an exercise requiring further practice;
A difficult exercise, played through by someone else.
Overheard from another room, now, 10
It seems full of mistakes.
                              So the voice of your father,
Rising as from the next room still
With all the remote but true affection of the dead,
Repeats itself, insists, 15
Insisting you must listen, rises
In the familiar pattern of reproof
For some childish error, a nap disturbed,
Or vase, broken or overturned;
Rises and subsides. And you do listen. 20
Listen and forget. Practice forgetting.

Forgotten sunlight still
Blinds the eyes of faces in the album.
The faces fade, and there is only
A sort of meaning that comes back, 25
Or for the first time comes, but comes too late
To take the places of the faces.

                              Remember
The dead air of summer. Remember
The trees drawn up to their full height like fathers, 30
The underworld of shade you entered at their feet.
Enter the next room. Enter it quietly now,
Not to disturb your father sleeping there. *He stirs.*
Notice his clothes, how scrupulously clean,
Unwrinkled from the nap; his face, freckled with work, 35
Smoothed by a passing dream. The vase
Is not yet broken, the still young roses
Drink there from perpetual waters. *He rises, speaks . . .*

Repeat it now, no one was listening.
So your hand moves, moving across the keys, 40
And slowly the keys grow darker to the touch.

MAXINE KUMIN (b. 1925)

The Excrement Poem (1978)

It is done by us all, as God disposes, from
the least cast of worm to what must have been

in the case of the brontosaur, say, spoor
of considerable heft, something awesome.

We eat, we evacuate, survivors that we are. 5
I think these things each morning with shovel
and rake, drawing the risen brown buns
toward me, fresh from the horse oven, as it were,

or culling the alfalfa-green ones, expelled
in a state of ooze, through the sawdust bed 10
to take a serviceable form, as putty does,
so as to lift out entire from the stall.

And wheeling to it, storming up the slope,
I think of the angle of repose the manure
pile assumes, how sparrows come to pick 15
the redelivered grain, how inky-cap

coprinus mushrooms spring up in a downpour.
I think of what drops from us and must then
be moved to make way for the next and next.
However much we stain the world, spatter 20

it with our leavings, make stenches, defile
the great formal oceans with what leaks down,
trundling off today's last barrowful,
I honor shit for saying: We go on.

KENNETH KOCH (b. 1925)

The History of Jazz (1961)

1

The leaves of blue came drifting down.
In the corner Madeleine Reierbacher was reading *Lorna Doone.**
The bay's water helped to implement the structuring of the garden hose.
The envelope fell. Was it pink or was it red? Consult *Lorna Doone*.
There, voyager, you will find your answer. The savant grapeade stands 5
Remember Madeleine Reierbacher. Madeleine Reierbacher says,
"If you are happy, there is no one to keep you from being happy;
Don't let them!" Madeleine Reierbacher went into the racing car.
The racing car was orange and red. Madeleine Reierbacher drove to
 Beale Street.
There Maddy doffed her garments to get into some more comfortable
 clothes. 10
Jazz was already playing in Beale Street when Madeleine Reierbacher
 arrived there.
Madeleine Reierbacher picked up the yellow horn and began to play.

* Romance novel (1869) by Richard Doddridge Blackmore.

No one had ever heard anything comparable to the playing of Madeleine
  Reierbacher.
What a jazz musician! The pianist missed his beats because he was so
  excited.
The drummer stared out the window in ecstasy at the yellow wooden
  trees.   15
The orchestra played "September in the Rain," "Mugging," and "I'm Full
  of Love."
Madeleine Reierbacher rolled up her sleeves; she picked up her horn;
  she played "Blues in the Rain."
It was the best jazz anyone had ever heard. It was mentioned in the
  newspapers. St. Louis!
Madeleine Reierbacher became a celebrity. She played with Pesky
  Summerton and Muggsy Pierce.
Madeleine cut numerous disks. Her best waxings are "Alpha Beta and
  Gamma"   20
And "Wing Song." One day Madeleine was riding on a donkey
When she came to a yellow light; the yellow light did not change.
Madeleine kept hoping it would change to green or red. She said, "As
  long as you have confidence,
You need be afraid of nothing." Madeleine saw the red smokestacks, she
  looked at the thin trees,
And she regarded the railroad tracks. The yellow light was unchanging.
  Madeleine's donkey dropped dead   25
From his mortal load. Madeleine Reierbacher, when she fell to earth,
Picked up a blade of grass and began to play. "The Blues!" cried the
  workmen of the vicinity.
And they ran and came in great numbers to where Madeleine Reier-
  bacher was.
They saw her standing in that simple field beside the railroad track
Playing, and they saw that light changing to green and red, and they saw
  that donkey stand up   30
And rise into the sky; and Madeleine Reierbacher was like a clot of blue
In the midst of the blue of all that sky, and the young farmers screamed
In excitement, and the workmen dropped their heavy boards and stones
  in their excitement,
And they cried, "O Madeleine Reierbacher, play us the 'Lead Flint Blues'
  once again!"

O railroad stations, pennants, evenings, and lumberyards!   35
When will you ever bring us such a beautiful soloist again?
An argent strain shows on the reddish face of the sun.
Madeleine Reierbacher stands up and screams, "I am getting wet! You
  are all egotists!"
Her brain floats up into the lyric atmosphere of the sky.
We must figure out a way to keep our best musicians with us.   40
The finest we have always melt into the light blue sky!

In the middle of a concert, sometimes, they disappear, like anvils.
(The music comes down to us with sweet white hands on our shoulders.)
We stare up in surprise; and we hear Madeleine's best-known tune once
    again,
"If you ain't afraid of life, life can't be afraid for you."   45
Madeleine! Come back and sing to us!

2

Dick looked up from his blackboard.
Had he really written a history of the jazz age?
He stared at his television set; the technicolor jazz program was coming on.
The program that day was devoted to pictures of Madeleine Reierbacher   50
Playing her saxophone in the golden age of jazz.
Dick looked at his blackboard. It was a mass of green and orange lines.
Here and there a red chalk line interlaced with the others.
He stared attentively at the program.

It was a clear and blue white day. Amos said, "The calibration is fin-
    ished. Now there need be no more jazz."   55

In his mountain home old Lucas Dog laughed when he heard what
    Amos had said.
He smilingly picked up his yellow horn to play, but all that came out of
    it was steam.

FRANK O'HARA (1926–1966)

The Day Lady Died* (1964)

It is 12:20 in New York a Friday
three days after Bastille day, yes
it is 1959 and I go get a shoeshine
because I will get off the 4:19 in Easthampton
at 7:15 and then go straight to dinner   5
and I don't know the people who will feed me

I walk up the muggy street beginning to sun
and have a hamburger and a malted and buy
an ugly NEW WORLD WRITING to see what the poets
in Ghana are doing these days   10
                I go on to the bank
and Miss Stillwagon (first name Linda I once heard)
doesn't even look up my balance for once in her life
and in the GOLDEN GRIFFIN I get a little Verlaine†
for Patsy with drawings by Bonnard‡ although I do   15

* Jazz singer Billie Holiday.

† French poet.

‡ French impressionist painter.

think of Hesiod,* trans. Richmond Lattimore or
Brendan Behan's† new play or *Le Balcon* or *Les Nègres*
of Genet,‡ but I don't, I stick with Verlaine
after practically going to sleep with quandariness

and for Mike I just stroll into the PARK LANE   20
Liquor Store and ask for a bottle of Strega and
then I go back where I came from to 6th Avenue
and the tobacconist in the Ziegfeld Theatre and
casually ask for a carton of Gauloises and a carton
of Picayunes, and a NEW YORK POST with her face on it   25

and I am sweating a lot by now and thinking of
leaning on the john door in the 5 SPOT
while she whispered a song along the keyboard
to Mal Waldron and everyone and I stopped breathing

A. R. AMMONS (b. 1926)

The City Limits (1971)

When you consider the radiance, that it does not withhold
itself but pours its abundance without selection into every
nook and cranny not overhung or hidden; when you consider

that birds' bones make no awful noise against the light but
lie low in the light as in a high testimony; when you consider   5
the radiance, that it will look into the guiltiest

swervings of the weaving heart and bear itself upon them,
not flinching into disguise or darkening; when you consider
the abundance of such resource as illuminates the glow-blue

bodies and gold-skeined wings of flies swarming the dumped   10
guts of a natural slaughter or the coil of shit and in no
way winces from its storms of generosity; when you consider

that air or vacuum, snow or shale, squid or wolf, rose or lichen,
each is accepted into as much light as it will take, then
the heart moves roomier, the man stands and looks about, the   15

leaf does not increase itself above the grass, and the dark
work of the deepest cells is of a tune with May bushes
and fear lit by the breadth of such calmly turns to praise.

* Greek poet.
† Irish playwright.
‡French playwright and novelist.

ALLEN GINSBERG (b. 1926)

A Supermarket in California (1956)

What thoughts I have of you tonight, Walt Whitman, for I walked down the sidestreets under the trees with a headache self-conscious looking at the full moon.

In my hungry fatigue, and shopping for images, I went into the neon fruit supermarket, dreaming of your enumerations!

What peaches and what penumbras! Whole families shopping at night! Aisles full of husbands! Wives in the avocados, babies in the tomatoes!—and you, García Lorca,* what were you doing down by the watermelons?

I saw you, Walt Whitman, childless, lonely old grubber, poking among the meats in the refrigerator and eyeing the grocery boys.

I heard you asking questions of each: Who killed the pork chops? What price bananas? Are you my Angel?   5

I wandered in and out of the brilliant stacks of cans following you, and followed in my imagination by the store detective.

We strode down the open corridors together in our solitary fancy tasting artichokes, possessing every frozen delicacy, and never passing the cashier.

Where are we going, Walt Whitman? The doors close in an hour. Which way does your beard point tonight?

(I touch your book and dream of our odyssey in the supermarket and feel absurd.)

Will we walk all night through solitary streets? The trees add shade to shade, lights out in the houses, we'll both be lonely.   10

Will we stroll dreaming of the lost America of love past blue automobiles in driveways, home to our silent cottage?

Ah, dear father, graybeard, lonely old courage-teacher, what America did you have when Charon quit poling his ferry and you got out on a smoking bank and stood watching the boat disappear on the black waters of Lethe?

Berkeley, 1955

PAUL BLACKBURN (1926–1971)

Listening to Sonny Rollins† at the Five-Spot (1967)

THERE WILL be many other nights like

be standing here with someone, some

one

someone

---

* Spanish surrealist poet.

† Jazz saxophonist.

some-one

some

some

some

some

some

some

one

there will be other songs

a-nother fall, another—spring, but

there will never be a-noth, noth

anoth

noth

anoth-er

noth-er

noth-er

        Other lips that I may kiss,

but they won't thrill me like

          thrill me like

              like yours

used to

     dream a million dreams

but how can they come

when there

         never be

a-noth—

JAMES MERRILL (1926–1995)

The Pier: Under Pisces (1985)

The shallows, brighter,
Wetter than water,
Tepidly glitter with the fingerprint-
Obliterating feel of kerosene.

Each piling like a totem
Rises from rock bottom
Straight through the ceiling
Aswirl with suns, clear ones or pale bluegreen,

         5

And beyond! where bubbles burst,
Sphere of their worst dreams,
If dream is what they do,
These floozy fish—

Ceramic-lipped in filmy
Peekaboo blouses,
Fluorescent body
Stockings, hot stripes,

Swayed by the hypnotic ebb and flow
Of supermarket Muzak,
Bolero beat the undertow's
Pebble-filled gourds repeat;

Jailbait consumers of subliminal
Hints dropped from on high
In gobbets none
Eschews as minced kin;

Who, hooked themselves—bamboo diviner
Bent their way
Vigorously nodding
Encouragement—

Are one by one hauled kisswise, oh
Into some blinding hell
Policed by leathery ex-
Justices each

Minding his catch, if catch is what he can,
If mind is what one means—
The torn mouth
Stifled by newsprint, working still. If . . . if . . .

The little scales
Grow stiff. Dusk plugs her dryer in,
Buffs her nails, riffles through magazines,
While far and wide and deep

Rover the great sharkskin-suited criminals
And safe in this lit shrine
A boy sits. He'll be eight.
We've drunk our milk, we've eaten our stringbeans,

But left untasted on the plate
The fish. An eye, a broiled pearl, meeting mine,
I lift his fork . . .
The bite. The tug of fate.

10

15

20

25

30

35

40

45

HARRY HUMES (b. 1926)

The Great Wilno (1990)

Dressed in a silver skin-tight suit,
he'd come out of the red and yellow tent,
his cape rising behind him with each step,
and a beautiful young girl
in sequins holding his hand   5
in the night that arced
over the Pennsylvania mining town,
and walk to the flatbed truck
with its mounted black cannon
where the beautiful girl in tights   10
would take his cape and kiss him goodbye
as he climbed a ladder
and lowered himself into the muzzle,
waving once to us before sinking from view,
a large clock showing the seconds left   15
before the explosion.
Hardly a sound in the fairgrounds,
the bats in and out of the shadows,
and across the black creek,
a child crying.   20

And then the whump of it, the smoke,
and the Great Wilno flying out,
helmet and goggles filled with the blaze
of lights from two Ferris wheels
he'd sail over each night for a week,   25
free of us, somersaulting among the stars
high in the darkness over the valley,
until I'd imagine he'd never come down,
or land too far away to find his way back,
and so come to another town, become a clerk   30
in a grocery, marry, have children,
buy his own small store,
and once in a while on summer evenings
run his fingers over the powder burns
on both his arms and wonder.   35

But down he'd come to us
and to the girl in sequins
who would run to the net beyond the Ferris wheels,
down he'd come like a toy parachute
dropped from a Piper Cub,   40
and at the last minute roll over in air
to hit the net perfectly on the small of his back,
spring to his feet, wave to us again,

then do a rollover along the net's edge,
a backflip to the ground   45
and vanish with the beautiful girl,
while the rest of us turned home,
talking about Wilno and the girl,
about the red and yellow tent,
about the years ahead of us,   50
about what we were going to do.

W. S. MERWIN (b. 1927)

Yesterday (1983)

My friend says I was not a good son
you understand
I say yes I understand

he says I did not go
to see my parents very often you know   5
and I say yes I know

even when I was living in the same city he says
maybe I would go there once
a month or maybe even less
I say oh yes   10

he says the last time I went to see my father
I say the last time I saw my father

he says the last time I saw my father
he was asking me about my life
how I was making out and he   15
went into the next room
to get something to give me

oh I say
feeling again the cold
of my father's hand the last time   20

he says and my father turned
in the doorway and saw me
look at my wristwatch and he
said you know I would like you to stay
and talk with me   25

oh yes I say

but if you are busy he said
I don't want you to feel that you
have to
just because I'm here   30

I say nothing

he says my father
said maybe
you have important work you are doing
or maybe you should be seeing   35
somebody I don't want to keep you

I look out the window
my friend is older than I am
he says and I told my father it was so
and I got up and left him then   40
you know

though there was nowhere I had to go
and nothing I had to do

GALWAY KINNELL (b. 1927)

Saint Francis and the Sow (1980)

The bud
stands for all things,
even for those things that don't flower,
for everything flowers, from within, of self-blessing;
though sometimes it is necessary   5
to reteach a thing its loveliness,
to put a hand on its brow
of the flower
and retell it in words and in touch
it is lovely   10
until it flowers again from within, of self-blessing;
as Saint Francis
put his hand on the creased forehead
of the sow, and told her in words and in touch
blessings of earth on the sow, and the sow   15
began remembering all down her thick length,
from the earthen snout all the way
through the fodder and slops to the spiritual curl of the tail,
from the hard spininess spiked out from the spine
down through the great broken heart   20
to the sheer blue milken dreaminess spurting and shuddering
from the fourteen teats into the fourteen mouths sucking and
    blowing beneath them:
the long, perfect loveliness of sow.

MARTIN CARTER (b. 1927)

After One Year (1964)

After today, how shall I speak with you?
Those miseries I know you cultivate

are mine as well as yours, or do you think
the impartial bullock cares whose land is ploughed?

I know this city much as well as you do,   5
the ways leading to brothels and those dooms
dwelling in them, as in our lives they dwell.
So jail me quickly, clang the illiterate door
if freedom writes no happier alphabet.

Old hanging ground is still green playing field.   10
Smooth cemetery proud garden of tall flowers.
But in your secret gables real bats fly
mocking great dreams that give the soul no peace,
and everywhere wrong deeds are being done.

Rude citizen! think you I do not know   15
that love is stammered, hate is shouted out
in every human city in this world?
Men murder men, as men must murder men,
to build their shining governments of the damned.

JOHN ASHBERY (b. 1927)

One Coat of Paint (1987)

We will all have to just hang on for a while,
It seems, now. This could mean "early retirement"
For some, if only for an afternoon of pottering around
Buying shoelaces and the like. Or it could mean a spell
In some enchanter's cave, after several centuries of which   5
You wake up curiously refreshed, eager to get back
To the crossword puzzle, only no one knows your name
Or who you are, really, or cares much either. To seduce
A fact into becoming an object, a pleasing one, with some
Kind of esthetic quality, which would also add to the store   10
Of knowledge and even extend through several strata
Of history, like a pin through a cracked wrist bone,
Connecting these in such a dynamic way that one would be forced
To acknowledge a new kind of superiority without which the world
Could no longer conduct its business, even simple stuff like bringing 15
Water home from wells, coals to hearths, would of course be
An optimal form of it but in any case the thing's got to
Come into being, something has to happen, or all
We'll have left is disagreements, *désagréments,* to name a few.
O don't you see how necessary it is to be around,   20
To be ferried from here to that near, smiling shore
And back again into the arms of those that love us,
Not many, but of such infinite, superior sweetness
That their lie is for us and it becomes stained, encrusted,
Finally gilded in some exasperating way that turns it   25

To a truth plus something, delicate and dismal as a star,
Cautious as a drop of milk, so that they let us
Get away with it, some do at any rate?

PHILIP LEVINE (b. 1928)

What Work Is (1991)

We stand in the rain in a long line
waiting at Ford Highland Park. For work.
You know what work is—if you're
old enough to read this you know what
work is, although you may not do it.   5
Forget you. This is about waiting,
shifting from one foot to another.
Feeling the light rain falling like mist
into your hair, blurring your vision
until you think you see your own brother   10
ahead of you, maybe ten places.
You rub your glasses with your fingers,
and of course it's someone else's brother,
narrower across the shoulders than
yours but with the same sad slouch, the grin   15
that does not hide the stubbornness,
the sad refusal to give in to
rain, to the hours wasted waiting,
to the knowledge that somewhere ahead
a man is waiting who will say, "No,   20
we're not hiring today," for any
reason he wants. You love your brother,
now suddenly you can hardly stand
the love flooding you for your brother,
who's not beside you or behind or   25
ahead because he's home trying to
sleep off a miserable night shift
at Cadillac so he can get up
before noon to study his German.
Works eight hours a night so he can sing   30
Wagner, the opera you hate most,
the worst music ever invented.
How long has it been since you told him
you loved him, held his wide shoulders,
opened your eyes wide and said those words,   35
and maybe kissed his cheek? You've never
done something so simple, so obvious,
not because you're too young or too dumb,
not because you're jealous or even mean

or incapable of crying in   40
the presence of another man, no,
just because you don't know what work is.

CONRAD HILBERRY (b. 1928)

The Moon Seen as a Slice of Pineapple (1984)

Tonight an old man follows the narrow streets
turning and returning like a thought.
His hat down, his loose pants flapping,
he looks in at the light of a cantina,

then walks on, wind in a thin body of dust.   5
He has looked everywhere. Already his sons
are lost and now his daughter has slipped
away, the girl who wakened him like rain.

Five mongrels, bleached by the moon, circle him
and snarl, slouching like thieves. They take him   10
for a stranger, but he pries a stone from the street.
He has lived here longer than any of them.

He knows where she must be: in the gardens
of the rich, it rains every day. She sits
on the branch of a jacaranda, while a man   15
with perfect teeth, hardly younger than himself,

holds to her mouth a slice of pineapple.
"Eat," he says as the juice drips from his hand.
She eats and a black dog slides from the shadows
to lick the moonlight falling on her legs.   20

ANNE SEXTON (1928–1974)

Her Kind (1960)

I have gone out, a possessed witch,
haunting the black air, braver at night;
dreaming evil, I have done my hitch
over the plain houses, light by light:
lonely thing, twelve-fingered, out of mind.   5
A woman like that is not a woman, quite.
I have been her kind.

I have found the warm caves in the woods,
filled them with skillets, carvings, shelves,
closets, silks, innumerable goods;   10
fixed the suppers for the worms and the elves:
whining, rearranging the disaligned.

A woman like that is misunderstood.
I have been her kind.

I have ridden in your cart, driver, 15
waved my nude arms at villages going by,
learning the last bright routes, survivor
where your flames still bite my thigh
and my ribs crack where your wheels wind.
A woman like that is not ashamed to die. 20
I have been her kind.

DONALD HALL (b. 1928)

Names of Horses (1978)

All winter your brute shoulders strained against collars, padding
and steerhide over the ash hames, to haul
sledges of cordwood for drying through spring and summer,
for the Glenwood stove next winter, and for the simmering range.

In April you pulled cartloads of manure to spread on the fields, 5
dark manure of Holsteins, and knobs of your own clustered with oats.
All summer you mowed the grass in meadow and hayfield, the mowing
machine
clacketing beside you, while the sun walked high in the morning;

and after noon's heat, you pulled a clawed rake through the same acres,
gathering stacks, and dragged the wagon from stack to stack, 10
and the built hayrack back, up hill to the chaffy barn,
three loads of hay a day, hanging wide from the hayrack.

Sundays you trotted the two miles to church with the light load
of a leather quartertop buggy, and grazed in the sound of hymns.
Generation on generation, your neck rubbed the window sill 15
of the stall, smoothing the wood as the sea smooths glass.

When you were old and lame, when your shoulders hurt bending to graze,
one October the man who fed you and kept you, and harnessed you
every morning,
led you through corn stubble to sandy ground above Eagle Pond,
and dug a hole beside you where you stood shuddering in your skin, 20

and lay the shotgun's muzzle in the boneless hollow behind your ear,
and fired the slug into your brain, and felled you into your grave,
shoveling sand to cover you, setting goldenrod upright above you,
where by next summer a dent in the ground made your monument.

For a hundred and fifty years, in the pasture of dead horses, 25
roots of pine trees pushed through the pale curves of your ribs,
yellow blossoms flourished above you in autumn, and in winter
frost heaved your bones in the ground—old toilers, soil makers:

O Roger, Mackerel, Riley, Ned, Nellie, Chester, Lady Ghost.

ADRIENNE RICH (b. 1929)

Aunt Jennifer's Tigers (1951)

Aunt Jennifer's tigers prance across a screen,
Bright topaz denizens of a world of green.
They do not fear the men beneath the tree;
They pace in sleek chivalric certainty.

Aunt Jennifer's fingers fluttering through her wool   5
Find even the ivory needle hard to pull.
The massive weight of Uncle's wedding band
Sits heavily upon Aunt Jennifer's hand.

When Aunt is dead, her terrified hands will lie
Still ringed with ordeals she was mastered by.   10
The tigers in the panel that she made
Will go on prancing, proud and unafraid.

ADRIENNE RICH (b. 1929)

Diving into the Wreck (1973)

First having read the book of myths,
and loaded the camera,
and checked the edge of the knife-blade,
I put on
the body-armor of black rubber   5
the absurd flippers
the grave and awkward mask.
I am having to do this
not like Cousteau with his
assiduous team   10
aboard the sun-flooded schooner
but here alone.

There is a ladder.
The ladder is always there
hanging innocently   15
close to the side of the schooner.
We know what it is for,
we who have used it.
Otherwise
it's a piece of maritime floss   20
some sundry equipment.

I go down.
Rung after rung and still
the oxygen immerses me
the blue light   25
the clear atoms

of our human air.
I go down.
My flippers cripple me,
I crawl like an insect down the ladder   30
and there is no one
to tell me when the ocean
will begin.

First the air is blue and then
it is bluer and then green and then   35
black I am blacking out and yet
my mask is powerful
it pumps my blood with power
the sea is another story
the sea is not a question of power   40
I have to learn alone
to turn my body without force
in the deep element.

And now: it is easy to forget
what I came for   45
among so many who have always
lived here
swaying their crenellated fans
between the reefs
and besides   50
you breathe differently down here.

I came to explore the wreck.
The words are purposes.
The words are maps.
I came to see the damage that was done   55
and the treasures that prevail.
I stroke the beam of my lamp
slowly along the flank
of something more permanent
than fish or weed   60

the thing I came for:
the wreck and not the story of the wreck
the thing itself and not the myth
the drowned face always staring
toward the sun   65
the evidence of damage
worn by salt and sway into this threadbare beauty
the ribs of the disaster
curving their assertion
among the tentative haunters.   70

This is the place.
And I am here, the mermaid whose dark hair

streams black, the merman in his armored body
We circle silently
about the wreck
we dive into the hold.   75
I am she: I am he

whose drowned face sleeps with open eyes
whose breasts still bear the stress
whose silver, copper, vermeil cargo lies   80
obscurely inside barrels
half-wedged and left to rot
we are the half-destroyed instruments
that once held to a course
the water-eaten log   85
the fouled compass

We are, I am, you are
by cowardice or courage
the one who find our way
back to this scene   90
carrying a knife, a camera
a book of myths
in which
our names do not appear.

ADRIENNE RICH (b. 1929)

Rape (1973)

There is a cop who is both prowler and father:
he comes from your block, grew up with your brothers,
had certain ideals.
You hardly know him in his boots and silver badge,
on horseback, one hand touching his gun.   5

You hardly know him but you have to get to know him:
he has access to machinery that could kill you.
He and his stallion clop like warlords among the trash,
his ideals stand in the air, a frozen cloud
from between his unsmiling lips.   10

And so, when the time comes, you have to turn to him,
the maniac's sperm still greasing your thighs,
your mind whirling like crazy. You have to confess
to him, you are guilty of the crime
of having been forced.   15

And you see his blue eyes, the blue eyes of all the family
whom you used to know, grow narrow and glisten,
his hand types out the details
and he wants them all

but the hysteria in your voice pleases him best.   20

You hardly know him but now he thinks he knows you:
he has taken down your worst moment
on a machine and filed it in a file.
He knows, or thinks he knows, how much you imagined;
he knows, or thinks he knows, what you secretly wanted.   25

He has access to machinery that could get you put away;
and if, in the sickening light of the precinct,
and if, in the sickening light of the precinct,
your details sound like a portrait of your confessor,
will you swallow, will you deny them, will you lie your way home?   30

GARY SNYDER (b. 1930)

Hitch Haiku (1968)

They didn't hire him
            so he ate his lunch alone:
the noon whistle

                    *   *   *

Cats shut down
            deer thread through
men all eating lunch

                    *   *   *

Frying hotcakes in a dripping shelter
            Fu Manchu
Queets Indian Reservation in the rain

                    *   *   *

A truck went by
            three hours ago:
Smoke Creek desert

                    *   *   *

Jackrabbit eyes all night
   breakfast in Elko.

                    *   *   *

Old kanji hid by dirt
on skidroad Jap town walls
            down the hill
to the Wobbly hall

                              Seattle

                    *   *   *

Spray drips from the cargo-booms
a fresh-chipped winch
            spotted with red lead
young fir—
            soaking in summer rain

                    *   *   *

Over the Mindanao Deep

Scrap bass
        dumpt off the fantail
falling six miles

        *   *   *

[*The following two were written on classical
themes while traveling through Sappho, Washington.
The first is by Thomas L. Hoodlatch.*]

Moonlight on the burned-out temple—
        wooden horse shit.

Sunday dinner in Ithaca—
        the twang of a bowstring

        *   *   *

After weeks of watching the roof leak
        I fixed it tonight
by moving a single board

        *   *   *

*A freezing morning in October in the high
Sierra crossing Five Lakes Basin to the
Kaweahs with Bob Greensfelder and Claude Dalenburg*

Stray white mare
        neck rope dangling
forty miles from farms.

        *   *   *

Back from the Kaweahs

Sundown, Timber Gap
        —sat down—
           dark firs.
 dirty;   cold;
too tired to talk

        *   *   *

Cherry blossoms at Hood river
        rusty sand near Tucson
mudflats of Willapa Bay

        *   *   *

Pronghorn country

Steering into the sun
        glittering jewel-road
shattered obsidian

        *   *   *

The mountain walks over the water!
Rain down from the mountain!
        high bleat of a
cow elk
        over blackberries

A great freight truck
          lit like a town
through the dark stony desert
                    *   *   *

Drinking hot saké
                    toasting fish on coals
    the motorcycle
out   parked in the rain.
                    *   *   *

Switchback

turn, turn,
and again,   hard-
scrabble
steep travel a-
head.

DEREK WALCOTT (b. 1930)

Sea Grapes (1976)

That sail which leans on light,
tired of islands,
a schooner beating up the Caribbean

for home, could be Odysseus,*
home-bound on the Aegean;   5
that father and husband's

longing, under gnarled sour grapes, is
like the adulterer hearing Nausicaa's name
in every gull's outcry.

This brings nobody peace. The ancient war   10
between obsession and responsibility
will never finish and has been the same

for the sea-wanderer or the one on shore
now wriggling on his sandals to walk home,
since Troy sighed its last flame,   15

and the blind giant's boulder heaved the trough
from whose groundswell the great hexameters come

---

* For background, see p. 291. Princess Nausicaa (line 8) fell in love with Odysseus when he was carried by a storm to Phaiacia; he could have married her and stayed there, but he chose to go home. Odysseus blinded Polyphemos (line 16), a giant one-eyed Cyclops, who held him prisoner; as Odysseus escaped, Polyphemos threw great rocks in front of his boat to wash it back to shore. Homer's epic poem *The Odyssey* was written in Greek hexameter (see line 17).

to the conclusions of exhausted surf.
The classics can console. But not enough.

TED HUGHES (b. 1930)

Crow's First Lesson (1970)

God tried to teach Crow how to talk.
"Love," said God. "Say, Love."
Crow gaped, and the white shark crashed into the sea
And went rolling downwards, discovering its own depth.

"No, no," said God, "Say Love. Now try it. LOVE."   5
Crow gaped, and a bluefly, a tsetse, a mosquito
Zoomed out and down
To their sundry flesh-pots.

"A final try," said God. "Now, LOVE."
Crow convulsed, gaped, retched and   10
Man's bodiless prodigious head
Bulbed out onto the earth, with swivelling eyes,
Jabbering protest—

And Crow retched again, before God could stop him.
And woman's vulva dropped over man's neck and tightened.   15
The two struggled together on the grass.
God struggled to part them, cursed, wept—

Crow flew guiltily off.

JEROME ROTHENBERG (b. 1931)

B · R · M · Tz · V · H (1980)

a poem from memory for Matthew Rothenberg's thirteenth birthday celebrated as a "bar
mitzvah event" one month after the date three decades three years past my own

naming the day it comes
deep into March
Aquarius has shifted into Pisces
—Diane's time—
waters receded & warm days   5
hanging over San Diego
where never in my life I thought to end up
or thought to be here
standing in this western yard
to make bar mitzvah   10
as event—I stress—not
the ghost of ceremony
I recall from my own lost 13th year
middle of wartime & reports
first coming in that told   15

---

deaths of others curly-headed
cousins sacrificed
only their photos left to scan thru
later • "who is this?"
you asked   20
"a child" I answered
hair curled like your own
forget it
death's depressing after all
someone still dreams of   25
a universe   benign   & wakes
to stifled flesh
I wouldn't interrupt this day with
but wonder
how any sanity was possible   30
this century
o Matthew Matthew born once
in the glow of brother—Milton's—death
the mystery thus thrust
into our thoughts   35
—of light & dark
co-equals—
I was alone to greet you (as I hope
you will not be)
of those who shared the table   40
at our home back in the Bronx
by then I was
the one surviving
(as I knew it would be)
& thought: how could I   45
bring them to life for you
except the poems pictures
I began around
their deaths   your life
fathers mothers grandmothers   50
set there as titles
ancestors the imagination made
the shades all poetry
recalls back to Ulysses in the pit*
voice of David out of Sheol   55
orphic Jew my master
de profundis† I could see her wraith
—those mad poetic words!—
my mother enter in dark of

* See Homer, *Odyssey,* bk. 11.
† "Out of the depths"—opening words of Psalm 130.

restless sabbaths   60
she who would call us "sweet face"
too much love
has spoiled her
I could never
answer that or answer   65
my father's angers
disappointments of his life in dry goods
peddling peddling
the old books forsaken
he dropped off in sleep & told me   70
"strange that it takes so long to die"
& she "the whole town's talking"
mysteries of death
& life
fantastic faces all we know   75
we love
bar mitzvahs happening
on sabbaths that divide
the day that Jesus died
from Easter   80
—Esther of my mother's name—
when all the dead arise
in mind they sing
song that first ushered in your birth
a man child   son   85
grown old & beautiful
at last
"joy   joy
"praise   praise

GEOFFREY HILL (b. 1932)

In Memory of Jane Fraser (1959)

When snow like sheep lay in the fold
And winds went begging at each door,
And the far hills were blue with cold,
And a cold shroud lay on the moor,

She kept the siege. And every day   5
We watched her brooding over death
Like a strong bird above its prey.
The room filled with the kettle's breath.

Damp curtains glued against the pane
Sealed time away. Her body froze   10
As if to freeze us all, and chain
Creation to a stunned repose.

She died before the world could stir.
In March the ice unloosed the brook
And water ruffled the sun's hair.   15
Dead cones upon the alder shook.

SYLVIA PLATH (1932–1963)

Metaphors (1960)

I'm a riddle in nine syllables,
An elephant, a ponderous house,
A melon strolling on two tendrils.
O red fruit, ivory, fine timbers!
This loaf's big with its yeasty rising.   5
Money's new-minted in this fat purse.
I'm a means, a stage, a cow in calf.
I've eaten a bag of green apples,
Boarded the train there's no getting off.

CHRISTOPHER OKIGBO (1932–1967)

Elegy for Alto (1968)

(With drum accompaniment)

AND THE HORN may now paw the air howling goodbye . . .

For the Eagles are now in sight:
Shadows in the horizon—

THE ROBBERS are here in black sudden steps of showers, of caterpillars—

THE EAGLES have come again,   5
The eagles rain down on us—

POLITICIANS are back in giant hidden steps of howitzers, of detonators—

THE EAGLES descend on us,
Bayonets and cannons—

THE ROBBERS descend on us to strip us of our laughter, of our thunder— 10

THE EAGLES have chosen their game,
Taken our concubines—

POLITICIANS are here in this iron dance of mortars, of generators—

THE EAGLES are suddenly there,
New stars of iron dawn;   15

So let the horn paw the air howling goodbye . . .

O mother mother Earth, unbind me; let this be
    my last testament; let this be
The ram's hidden wish to the sword the sword's
    secret prayer to the scabbard—   20

THE ROBBERS are back in black hidden steps of detonators—

FOR BEYOND the blare of sirened afternoons, beyond
    the motorcades;
Beyond the voices and days, the echoing highways;
    beyond the latescence
Of our dissonant airs; through our curtained eyeballs,   25
    through our shuttered sleep,
Onto our forgotten selves, onto our broken images;
    beyond the barricades
Commandments and edicts, beyond the iron tables,
    beyond the elephant's   30
Legendary patience, beyond his inviolable bronze
    bust, beyond our crumbling towers—

BEYOND the iron path careering along the same beaten track—

THE GLIMPSE of a dream lies smouldering in a cave,
    together with the mortally wounded birds.   35
Earth, unbind me; let me be the prodigal; let this be
    the ram's ultimate prayer to the tether . . .

AN OLD STAR departs, leaves us here on the shore
Gazing heavenward for a new star approaching;
The new star appears, foreshadows its going   40
Before a going and coming that goes on forever . . .

ETHERIDGE KNIGHT (1933–1991)

Hard Rock Returns to Prison from the Hospital for the Criminal Insane (1968)

Hard Rock / was / "known not to take no shit
From nobody," and he had the scars to prove it:
Split purple lips, lumbed ears, welts above
His yellow eyes, and one long scar that cut
Across his temple and plowed through a thick   5
Canopy of kinky hair.

The WORD / was / that Hard Rock wasn't a mean nigger
Anymore, that the doctors had bored a hole in his head,
Cut out part of his brain, and shot electricity
Through the rest. When they brought Hard Rock back,   10
Handcuffed and chained, he was turned loose,

Like a freshly gelded stallion, to try his new status.
And we all waited and watched, like a herd of sheep,
To see if the WORD was true.

As we waited we wrapped ourselves in the cloak   15
Of his exploits: "Man, the last time, it took eight
Screws to put him in the Hole." "Yeah, remember when he
Smacked the captain with his dinner tray?" "He set
The record for time in the Hole—67 straight days!"
"Ol Hard Rock! man, that's one crazy nigger."   20
And then the jewel of a myth that Hard Rock had once bit
A screw on the thumb and poisoned him with syphilitic spit.

The testing came, to see if Hard Rock was really tame.
A hillbilly called him a black son of a bitch
And didn't lose his teeth, a screw who knew Hard Rock   25
From before shook him down and barked in his face.
And Hard Rock did *nothing*. Just grinned and looked silly,
His eyes empty like knot holes in a fence.

And even after we discovered that it took Hard Rock
Exactly 3 minutes to tell you his first name,   30
We told ourselves that he had just wised up,
Was being cool; but we could not fool ourselves for long,
And we turned away, our eyes on the ground. Crushed.
He had been our Destroyer, the doer of things
We dreamed of doing but could not bring ourselves to do,   35
The fears of years, like a biting whip,
Had cut deep bloody grooves
Across our backs.

Jim Barnes (b. 1933)

Return to La Plata, Missouri (1982)

The warping bandstand reminds you of the hard rage
you felt in the heart of the town the day you said goodbye
to the park, silver jet, and cicadas dead in the sage.

The town is basic red, although it browns. A cry
of murder, rape, or wrong will always bend the night   5
hard into the broken grass. You listen close for sighs

of lovers on the ground. The darkness gathers light
and throws it down: something glows that you cannot name,
something fierce, abstract, given time and space you might

on a journey leave behind, a stone to carve your fame   10
on, or a simple word like *love*. The sun is down
or always going down in La Plata, the same

sun. Same too the child's cry that turns the mother's frown
brittle as chalk or the town's face against the moon.
Same too the moan of dog and diesel circling the town   15

in an air so heavy with cloud that there is little room
for breath or moon. Strange: in a town so country, so
foreign, you never hear a song nor see a loom

pattern dark threads into a history you would know
and would not know. You think you see one silver star.   20
But the town offers only itself, and you must go.

KAMALA DAS (b. 1934)

In Love (1965)

Of what does the burning mouth
Of sun, burning in today's
Sky remind me . . . oh, yes, his
Mouth, and . . . his limbs like pale and
Carnivorous plants reaching   5
Out for me, and the sad lie
Of my unending lust. Where
Is room, excuse or even
Need for love, for, isn't each
Embrace a complete thing, a   10
Finished jigsaw, when mouth on
Mouth, I lie, ignoring my poor
Moody mind, while pleasure
With deliberate gaiety
Trumpets harshly into the   15
Silence of the room. . . . At noon
I watch the sleek crows flying
Like poison on wings—and at
Night, from behind the Burdwan
Road, the corpse-bearers cry "Bol   20
Hari Bol," a strange lacing
For moonless nights, while I walk
The verandah sleepless, a
Million questions awake in
Me, and all about him, and   25
This skin-communicated
Thing that I dare not yet in
His presence call our love.

Imamu Amiri Baraka (b. 1934)

The New World (1969)

The sun is folding, cars stall and rise
beyond the window. The workmen leave
the street to the bums and painters' wives
pushing their babies home. Those who realize
how fitful and indecent consciousness is   5
stare solemnly out on the emptying street.
The mourners and soft singers. The liars,
and seekers after ridiculous righteousness. All
my doubles, and friends, whose mistakes cannot
be duplicated by machines, and this is all of our   10
arrogance. Being broke or broken, dribbling
at the eyes. Wasted lyricists, and men
who have seen their dreams come true, only seconds
after they knew those dreams to be horrible conceits
and plastic fantasies of gesture and extension,   15
shoulders, hair and tongues distributing misinformation
about the nature of understanding. No one is that simple
or priggish, to be alone out of spite and grown strong
in its practice, mystics in two-pants suits. Our style,
and discipline, controlling the method of knowledge.   20
Beatniks, like Bohemians, go calmly out of style. And boys
are dying in Mexico, who did not get the word.
The lateness of their fabrication: mark their holes
with filthy needles. The lust of the world. This will not
be news. The simple damning lust,   25
                           float flat magic in low changing
                           evenings. Shiver your hands
                           in dance. Empty all of me for
                           knowing, and will the danger
                           of identification,   30

            Let me sit and go blind in my dreaming
            and be that dream in purpose and device.

            A fantasy of defeat, a strong strong man
            older, but no wiser than the defect of love.

Charles Wright (b. 1935)

Sitting at Night on the Front Porch (1977)

I'm here, on the dark porch, restyled in my mother's chair.
10:45 and no moon.
Below the house, car lights
Swing down, on the canyon floor, to the sea.

In this they resemble us,   5
Dropping like match flames through the great void
Under our feet.
In this they resemble her, burning and disappearing.

Everyone's gone
And I'm here, sizing the dark, saving my mother's seat.   10

MARGE PIERCY (b. 1936)

The Friend (1969)

We sat across the table.
he said, cut off your hands.
they are always poking at things.
they might touch me.
I said yes.   5

Food grew cold on the table.
he said, burn your body.
it is not clean and smells like sex.
it rubs my mind sore.
I said yes.   10

I love you, I said.
That's very nice, he said
I like to be loved,
that makes me happy.
Have you cut off your hands yet?   15

JAYNE CORTEZ (b. 1936)

Into This Time (1991)

(for Charles Mingus) *

Into this time
of steel feathers blowing from hearts
into this turquoise flame time in the mouth
into this sonic boom time in the conch
into this musty stone-fly time sinking into   5
the melancholy buttocks of dawn
sinking into lacerated whelps
into gun holsters
into breast bones
into a manganese field of uranium nozzles   10
into a nuclear tube full of drunk rodents
into the massive vein of one interval

* Innovative jazz bassist.

into one moment's hair plucked down into
the timeless droning fixed into
long pauses   15
fixed into a lash of ninety-eight minutes screeching into
the internal heat of an ice ball melting time into
a configuration of commas on strike
into a work force armed with a calendar of green wings
into a collection of nerves   20
into magnetic mucus
into tongueless shrines
into water pus of a silver volcano
into the black granite face of Morelos*
into the pigeon toed dance of Mingus   25
into a refuge of air bubbles
into a cylinder of snake whistles
into clusters of slow spiders
into spade fish skulls
into rosin coated shadows of women wrapped in live iguanas   30
into coins into crosses into St. Martin De Porres†
into the pain of this place changing pitches beneath
fingers swelling into
night shouts
into day trembles   35
into month of precious bloods flowing into
this fiesta of sadness year
into this city of eternal spring
into this solo
on the road of young bulls   40
on the street of lost children
on the avenue of dead warriors
on the frisky horse tail fuzz zooming
into ears of every madman
stomping into every new composition   45
everyday of the blues
penetrating into this time

This time of loose strings in low tones
pulling boulders of Olmec heads into the sun
into tight wires uncoiling from body of a strip teaser on the table   50
into half-tones wailing between snap and click
of two castanets smoking into
scales jumping from tips of sacrificial flints
into frogs yodeling across grieving cults
yodeling up into word stuffed smell of flamingo stew   55
into wind packed fuel of howling dog throats slit into

* José María Morelos, Mexican revolutionary leader (1765–1815).
† Seventeenth-century Peruvian saint.

this January flare of aluminum dust falling into
laminated stomach of a bass violin rubbed into red ashes
rubbed into the time sequence of
this time of salmonella leaking from eyeballs of a pope   60
into this lavender vomit time in the chest into
this time plumage of dried bats in the brain into
this wallowing time weed of invisible wakes on cassettes into
this off-beat time syncopation in a leopard skin suit
into this radiated protrusion of time in the desert into   65
this frozen cheek time of dead infants in the cellar
into this time flying with the rotten bottoms of used tuxedos
into this purple brown grey gold minus zero time trilling into
a lime stone crusted Yucatan belching
into fifty six medallions shaking   70
into armadillo drums thumping
into tambourines of fetishes rattling
into an oil slick of poverty symbols flapping
into flat-footed shuffle of two birds advancing
into back spine of luminous impulses tumbling   75
into metronomes of colossal lips ticking
into a double zigzag of callouses splitting
into foam of electric snow flashing into this time
of steel feathers blowing from hearts
into this turquoise flame time in the mouth into   80
this sonic boom time in the conch
into this musty stone fly time sinking into
the melancholy buttocks of dawn

NANCY WILLARD (b. 1936)

Saint Pumpkin (1982)

Somebody's in there.
Somebody's sealed himself up
in this round room,
this hassock upholstered in rind,
this padded cell.   5
He believes if nothing unbinds him
he'll live forever.

Like our first room
it is dark and crowded.
Hunger knows no tongue   10
to tell it.
Water is glad there.
In this room with two navels
somebody wants to be born again.

So I unlock the pumpkin. 15
I carve out the lid
from which the stem raises
a dry handle on a damp world.
Lifting, I pull away
wet webs, vines on which hang 20
the flat tears of the pumpkin,

like fingernails or the currency
of bats. How the seeds shine,
as if water had put out
hundreds of lanterns. 25
Hundreds of eyes in the windless wood
gaze peacefully past me,
hacking the thickets,

and now a white dew beads the blade.
Has the saint surrendered 30
himself to his beard?
Has his beard taken root in his cell?

Saint Pumpkin, pray for me,
because when I looked for you, I found nothing,
because unsealed and unkempt, your tomb rots, 35
because I gave you a false face
and a light of my own making.

C. K. WILLIAMS (b. 1936)

From My Window (1983)

Spring: the first morning when that one true block of sweet, laminar, complex scent arrives
from somewhere west and I keep coming to lean on the sill, glorying in the end of the wretched winter.
The scabby-barked sycamores ringing the empty lot across the way are budded—I hadn't noticed—
and the thick spikes of the unlikely urban crocuses have already broken the gritty soil.
Up the street, some surveyors with tripods are waving each other left and right the way they do. 5
A girl in a gym suit jogged by a while ago, some kids passed, playing hooky, I imagine,
and now the paraplegic Vietnam vet who lives in a half-converted warehouse down the block
and the friend who stays with him and seems to help him out come weaving towards me,

their battered wheelchair lurching uncertainly from one edge of the sidewalk to the other.

I know where they're going—to the "Legion": once, when I was putting something out, they stopped,　　　　10

both drunk that time, too, both reeking—it wasn't ten o'clock—and we chatted for a bit.

I don't know how they stay alive—on benefits most likely. I wonder if they're lovers?

They don't look it. Right now, in fact, they look a wreck, careening haphazardly along,

contriving, as they reach beneath me, to dip a wheel from the curb so that the chair skewers, teeters,

tips, and they both tumble, the one slowly, almost gracefully sliding in stages from his seat,　　　　15

his expression hardly marking it, the other staggering over him, spinning heavily down,

to lie on the asphalt, his mouth working, his feet shoving weakly and fruitlessly against the curb.

In the storefront office on the corner, Reed and Son, Real Estate, have come to see the show.

Gazing through the golden letters of their name, they're not, at least, thank god, laughing.

Now the buddy, grabbing at a hydrant, gets himself erect and stands there for a moment, panting.　　　　20

Now he has to lift the other one, who lies utterly still, a forearm shielding his eyes from the sun.

He hauls him partly upright, then hefts him almost all the way into the chair, but a dangling foot

catches a support-plate, jerking everything around so that he has to put him down,

set the chair to rights, and hoist him again and as he does he jerks the grimy jeans right off him.

No drawers, shrunken, blotchy thighs: under the thick, white coils of belly blubber,　　　　25

the poor, blunt pud, tiny, terrified, retracted, is almost invisible in the sparse genital hair,

then his friend pulls his pants up, he slumps wholly back as though he were, at last, to be let be,

and the friend leans against the cyclone fence, suddenly staring up at me as though he'd known,

all along, that I was watching and I can't help wondering if he knows that in the winter, too,

I watched, the night he went out to the lot and walked, paced rather, almost ran, for how many hours.　　　　30

It was snowing, the city in that holy silence, the last we have, when the storm takes hold,

and he was making patterns that I thought at first were circles, then
    realized made a figure eight,
what must have been to him a perfect symmetry but which, from where
    I was, shivered, bent,
and lay on its side: a warped, unclear infinity, slowly, as the snow came
    faster, going out.
Over and over again, his head lowered to the task, he slogged the path
    he'd blazed,   35
but the race was lost, his prints were filling faster than he made them
    now and I looked away,
up across the skeletal trees to the tall center city buildings, some, though
    it was midnight,
with all their offices still gleaming, their scarlet warning beacons signaling
    erratically
against the thickening flakes, their smoldering auras softening portions
    of the dim, milky sky.
In the morning, nothing: every trace of him effaced, all the field pure
    white,   40
its surface glittering, the dawn, glancing from its glaze, oblique, relent-
    less, unadorned.

KEKI N. DARUWALLA (b. 1937)

Pestilence (1970)

pairs of padded feet
            are behind me

astride me
              in front of me
the footpaths are black feet   5
converging on the town

brown shoulders   black shoulders
shoulders round as orbs
muscles smooth as river-stones
              glisten   10
till a dry wind scourges
the sweat from off their backs

they are palanquin-bearers of a different sort
on the string-beds they carry
no henna-smeared brides.   15
prone upon them are frail bodies
frozen bodies   delirious bodies
some drained of fever and sap
some moving   others supine
transfixed under the sun   20

the hospital-floors are marble-white

black bodies dirty them
nurses in white habits
unicef jeeps with white bonnets
doctors with white faces receive them   25
"who says they have cholera?
they are down with diarrhoea
who says it is cholera?
it is gastro-enteritis
who says they have cholera?"   30

the land's visage is unmarked
soot-brown   soot-green
            soot-grey
mongrels tail the ambulance
till dust and gasoline-fumes   35
choke them off

but memory like a crane-arm
unloads its ploughed-up rubble
ancient visitations is what one recalls
the sweep of black feet   40
            towards the ghats
dying villages
the land   surplus once again
as after a flood
migrations as only birds have known   45
forgotten cattle dying at the stakes
—someone left them untethered

this is miniature by contrast
but the image lingers
string-beds creaking   50
over padded feet
and when of a sudden
cholera turns to death
the feet keep up their padded progress
only the string-bed is exchanged   55
for a plank

CHARLES SIMIC (b. 1938)

Begotten of the Spleen (1980)

The Virgin Mother walked barefoot
among the land mines.
She carried an old man in her arms.
The dove on her shoulder

barked at the moon.
The earth was an old people's home.
Judas was the night nurse.
He kept emptying bedpans into river Jordan.

The old man had two stumps for legs.
He was on a dog-chain. St. Peter pushed a cart
loaded with flying carpets.
They weren't flying carpets.

They were bloody diapers.
It was a cock-fighting neighborhood.
The Magi stood on street corners
cleaning their nails with German bayonets.

The old man gave Mary Magdalena
a mirror. She lit a candle,
and hid in the outhouse. When she got thirsty,
she licked the mist off the glass.

That leaves Joseph. Poor Joseph.
He only had a cockroach
to load his bundles on.
Even when the lights came on she wouldn't run
into her hole.

And the lights came on:
The floodlights
in the guard towers.

MICHAEL S. HARPER (b. 1938)

Nightmare Begins Responsibility (1975)

I place these numbed wrists to the pane
watching white uniforms whisk over
him in the tube-kept
prison
fear what they will do in experiment
watch my gloved stickshifting gasolined hands
breathe *boxcar-information-please* infirmary tubes
distrusting white-pink mending paperthin
silkened end hairs, distrusting tubes
shrunk in his *trunk-skincapped*
shaven head, in thighs
distrusting-white-hands-picking-baboon-light
on this son who will not make his second night
of this wardstrewn intensive airpocket

where his father's asthmatic   15
hymns of *night-train,* train done gone
his mother can only know that he has flown
up into essential calm unseen corridor
going boxscarred home, *mamaborn, sweetsonchild*
gonedowntown into *researchtestingwarehousebatteryacid*   20
mama-son-done-gone/me telling her 'nother
train tonight, no music, no breathstroked
heartbeat in my infinite distrust of them:

and of my distrusting self
white-doctor-who-breathed-for-him-all-night   25
say it for two sons gone,
say nightmare, say it loud
panebreaking heartmadness:
nightmare begins responsibility.

GARY GILDNER (b. 1938)

The High-Class Bananas (1978)

The bananas down at the Safeway
were doing OK last week, just as
they'd been doing all along probably,
just lying around on the wood bench
waiting for folks to come by &   5
look over what they'd like sliced up
on their Grape Nuts in the morning,
or in their raspberry Jello at night,
or maybe what they'd go for after school, plain,
with a big glass of nice cold sweet milk   10
—to get away from questions like
"How many lights are now on in the 1st place?"
or that other devil, "The fountain pen
was invented 1 century and 1 year
after the balloon. In what year   15
was the fountain pen invented?"
No, nobody had a lot of grief
over the bananas down at the Safeway,
not the way they just lay there
waiting for you, wanting to make you feel good.   20
Then somebody, maybe somebody who *knew*
how many lights were now on in the 1st place,
got to thinking, Hey!
why don't we get a merry-go-round
down at the Safeway? A big red carousel   25
that makes a little pizzaz? a little hubba hubba?
& put the bananas on it! & stick some plastic

leaves on top! & some fuzzy monkeys!
& some palm trees! & everybody pushed up close
said Yeah! They said Yeah! Yeah!   30
& so now we got high-class bananas
going round & round down at the Safeway.
& you stand there, maybe scratching where it itches,
waiting for your bunch to come around.

SEAMUS HEANEY (b. 1939)

Digging (1966)

Between my finger and my thumb
The squat pen rests; snug as a gun.

Under my window, a clean rasping sound
When the spade sinks into gravelly ground:
My father, digging. I look down   5

Till his straining rump among the flowerbeds
Bends low, comes up twenty years away
Stooping in rhythm through potato drills
Where he was digging.

The coarse boot nestled on the lug, the shaft   10
Against the inside knee was levered firmly.
He rooted out tall tops, buried the bright edge deep
To scatter new potatoes that we picked
Loving their cool hardness in our hands.

By God, the old man could handle a spade.   15
Just like his old man.

My grandfather cut more turf in a day
Than any other man on Toner's bog.
Once I carried him milk in a bottle
Corked sloppily with paper. He straightened up   20
To drink it, then fell to right away
Nicking and slicing neatly, heaving sods
Over his shoulder, going down and down
For the good turf. Digging.

The cold smell of potato mould, the squelch and slap   25
Of soggy peat, the curt cuts of an edge
Through living roots awaken in my head.
But I've no spade to follow men like them.

Between my finger and my thumb
The squat pen rests.   30
I'll dig with it.

AL YOUNG (b. 1939)

A Dance for Ma Rainey (1969)

I'm going to be just like you, Ma
Rainey this monday morning
clouds puffing up out of my head
like those balloons
that float above the faces of white people   5
in the funnypapers

I'm going to hover in the corners
of the world, Ma
& sing from the bottom of hell
up to the tops of high heaven   10
& send out scratchless waves of yellow
& brown & that basic black honey
misery

I'm going to cry so sweet
& so low   15
& so dangerous,
Ma,
that the message is going to reach you
back in 1922
where you shimmer   20
snaggle-toothed
perfumed &
powdered
in your bauble beads

hair pressed & tied back   25
throbbing with that sick pain
I know
& hide so well
that pain that blues
jives the world with   30
aching to be heard
that downness
that bottomlessness
first felt by some stolen delta nigger
swamped under with redblooded american agony;   35
reduced to the sheer shit
of existence
that bred
& battered us all,
Ma,   40
the beautiful people
our beautiful brave black people

who no longer need to jazz
or sing to themselves in murderous vibrations
or play the veins of their strong tender arms   45
with needles
to prove we're still here

STEPHEN DOBYNS (b. 1941)

Black Dog, Red Dog (1984)

The boy waits on the top step, his hand on the door
to the screen porch. A green bike lies in the grass,
saddlebags stuffed with folded newspapers. The street
is lined with maples in full green of summer, white houses
set back from the road. The man whom the boy has come   5
to collect from shuffles onto the porch. As is his custom,
he wears a gray dress with flowers. Long gray hair
covers his shoulders, catches in a week's growth of beard.
The boy opens the door and glancing down he sees yellow
streaks of urine running down the man's legs, snaking   10
into the gray socks and loafers. For a year, the boy
has delivered the man's papers, mowed and raked his lawn.
He's even been inside the house which stinks of excrement
and garbage, with forgotten bags of groceries on tables:
rotten fruit, moldy bread, packages of unopened hamburger.   15
He would wait in the hall as the man counted out pennies
from a paper bag, adding five extra out of kindness.
The boy thinks of when the man's mother was alive.
He would sneak up to the house when the music began
and watch the man and his mother dance cheek to cheek   20
around the kitchen, slowly, hesitantly, as if each
thought the other could break as simply as a china plate.
The mother had been dead a week when a neighbor found her
and even then her son wouldn't let her go. The boy sat
on the curb watching the man hurl his fat body against   25
the immaculate state troopers who tried not to touch him
but only keep him from where men from the funeral home
carried out his mother wrapped in red blankets, smelling
like hamburger left for weeks on the umbrella stand.

Today as the boy waits on the top step watching the urine   30
trickle into the man's socks, he raises his head to see
the pale blue eyes fixed upon him with their wrinkles and
bags and zigzagging red lines. As he stares into them,
he begins to believe he is staring out of those eyes,
looking down at a thin blond boy on his front steps.   35
Then he lifts his head and still through the man's eyes
he sees the softness of late afternoon light on the street

where the man has spent his entire life, sees the green
of summer, white Victorian houses as through a white fog
so they shimmer and flicker before him. Looking past   40
the houses, past the first fields, he sees the reddening
sky of sunset, sees the land rushing west as if it wanted
to smash itself as completely as a cup thrown to the floor,
violently pursuing the sky with great spirals of red wind.

Abruptly the boy steps back. When he looks again into   45
the man's eyes, they appear bottomless and sad; and he
wants to touch his arm, say he's sorry about his mother,
sorry he's crazy, sorry he lets urine run down his leg
and wears a dress. Instead, he gives him his paper
and leaves. As he raises his bike, he looks out toward   50
red sky and darkening earth, and they seem poised
like two animals that have always hated each other,
each fiercely wanting to tear out the other's throat:
black dog, red dog—now more despairing, more resolved.

ROBERT HASS (b. 1941)

Late Spring (1989)

And then in mid-May the first morning of steady heat,

the morning, Leif says, when you wake up, put on shorts, and that's it for
the day,

when you pour coffee and walk outside, blinking in the sun.

Strawberries have appeared in the markets, and peaches will soon;

squid is so cheap in the fishstores you begin to consult Japanese and
Italian cookbooks for the various and ingenious ways of preparing *ika*
and *calamari;*

and because the light will enlarge your days, your dreams at night will
be as strange as the jars of octopus you saw once in a fisherman's boat
under the summer moon;

and after swimming, white wine; and the sharing of stories before dinner
is prolonged because the relations of the children in the neighborhood
have acquired village intensity and the stories take longer telling;

and there are the nights when the fog rolls in that nobody likes—hey,
fog, the Miwok* sang, who lived here first, you better go home, pelican is
beating your wife—

and after dark in the first cool hour, your children sleep so heavily in
their beds exhausted from play, it is a pleasure to watch them,

* Native American people formerly living in California.

Leif does not move a muscle as he lies there; no, wait; it is Luke who lies there in his eight-year-old body,

Leif is taller than you are and he isn't home; when he is, his feet will extend past the end of the mattress, and Kristin is at the corner in the dark, talking to neighborhood boys;

things change; there is no need for this dream-compelled narration; the rhythm will keep me awake, changing.

LYN HEJINIAN (b. 1941)

A Mask of Anger (1977)

he said I should try something harder
a mask of rage

says of snakes
says of broken glass
says of aged foundations   5
unconsolable wildness,
an imagination uncomforted,
says without comfort

where are the gods who support the event

crashed into the circle   10

took the blue out of the sky

walled the warbler; turned the walker

wrong and wrong

there's no song but what's said
felt it   15
and no thought but what's bitten

JAMES A. PERKINS (b. 1941)

Boundaries (1993)

for Harry D. Perkins, Jr. (1927–1993)

The doorways of public buildings smell
like the hands of my brother,
who smoked *Herbert-Tarytons*,
three packs a day,
then quit,   5
too late.

Fearing secondary smoke,
we've sent them out,
reefer-mad Christos,*

* Contemporary avant-garde artist.

who wrap our buildings   10
tight as cellophane
in the stench of nicotine.

This is the smell
that gets in your clothes
in bars and hotel lobbies   15
where lonely, unremarkable people
tell each other they're important.
This is the smell
you can never get out
of your car.   20

Now, as we approach that invisible barrier,
the odor smacks our senses
like the yellow-stained hand
of someone we miss.

RICHARD GARCIA (b. 1941)

Why I Left the Church (1992)

Maybe it was
because the only time
I hit a baseball
it smashed the neon cross
on the church across   5
the street. Even
twenty-five years later
when I saw Father Harris
I would wonder
if he knew it was me.   10
Maybe it was the demon-stoked
rotisseries of purgatory
where we would roast
hundreds of years
for the smallest of sins.   15
Or was it the day
I wore my space helmet
to catechism? Clear plastic
with a red and white
inflatable rim.   20
Sister Mary Bernadette
pointed toward the door
and said, "Out! Come back
when you're ready."

I rose from my chair 25
and kept rising
toward the ceiling
while the children
screamed and Sister
kept crossing herself. 30
The last she saw of me
was my shoes disappearing
through cracked plaster.
I rose into the sky and beyond.
It is a good thing 35
I am wearing my helmet,
I thought as I floated
and turned in the blackness
and brightness of outer space.
My body cold on one side and hot 40
on the other. It would
have been very quiet
if my blood had not been
rumbling in my ears so loud.
I remember thinking, 45
Maybe I will come back
when I'm ready.
But I won't tell
the other children
what it was like. 50
I'll have to make something up.

ELLEN BRYANT VOIGT (b. 1943)

The Farmer (1987)

In the still-blistering late afternoon,
like currying a horse the rake
circled the meadow, the cut grass ridging
behind it. This summer, if the weather held,
he'd risk a second harvest after years 5
of reinvesting, leaving fallow.
These fields were why he farmed—
he walked the fenceline like a man in love.
The animals were merely what he needed: cattle
and pigs; chickens for a while; a drayhorse, 10
saddle horses he was paid to pasture—
an endless stupid round
of animals, one of them always hungry, sick, lost,
calving or farrowing, or waiting slaughter.

When the field began dissolving in the dusk, 15
he carried feed down to the knoll,

its clump of pines, gate, trough, lick, chute
and two gray hives; leaned into the Jersey's side
as the galvanized bucket filled with milk;
released the cow and turned to the bees.   20
He'd taken honey before without protection.
This time, they could smell something
in his sweat—fatigue? impatience,
although he was a stubborn, patient man?
Suddenly, like flame, they were swarming over him.   25
He rolled in the dirt, manure and stiff hoof-prints,
started back up the path, rolled in the fresh hay—
refused to run, which would have pumped
the venom through him faster—passed the oaks
at the yard's edge, rolled in the yard, reached   30
the kitchen, and when he tore off his clothes
crushed bees dropped from him like scabs.

For a week he lay in the darkened bedroom.
The doctor stopped by twice a day—
the hundred stings "enough to kill an ox,   35
enough to kill a younger man." What saved him
were the years of smaller doses—
like minor disappointments,
instructive poison, something he could use.

MICHAEL ONDAATJE (b. 1943)

Biography (1979)

The dog scatters her body in sleep,
paws, finding no ground, whip at air,
the unseen eyeballs reel deep, within.
And waking—crouches,
tacked to humility all day,   5
children ride her, stretch
display the black purple lips,
pull hind legs to dance;
unaware that she
tore bulls apart, loosed   10
heads of partidges,
dreamt blood.

JAMES TATE (b. 1943)

The Wheelchair Butterfly (1969)

O sleepy city of reeling wheelchairs
where a mouse can commit suicide if he can

concentrate long enough
on the history book of rodents
in this underground town   5

of electrical wheelchairs!
The girl who is always pregnant and bruised
like a pear

rides her many-stickered bicycle
backward up the staircase   10
of the abandoned trolleybarn.

Yesterday was warm. Today a butterfly froze
in midair; and was plucked like a grape
by a child who swore he could take care

of it. O confident city where   15
the seeds of poppies pass for carfare,

where the ordinary hornets in a human's heart
may slumber and snore, where bifocals bulge

in an orange garage of daydreams,
we wait in our loose attics for a new season   20

as if for an ice-cream truck.
An Indian pony crosses the plains

whispering Sanskrit prayers to a crater of fleas.
Honeysuckle says: I thought I could swim.

The Mayor is urinating on the wrong side   25
of the street! A dandelion sends off sparks:
beware your hair is locked!

Beware the trumpet wants a glass of water!
Beware a velvet tabernacle!

Beware the Warden of Light has married   30
an old piece of string!

Nikki Giovanni (b. 1943)

Nikki-Rosa (1968)

childhood rememberances are always a drag
if you're Black
you always remember things like living in Woodlawn
with no inside toilet
and if you become famous or something   5
they never talk about how happy you were to have your mother
all to yourself and
how good the water felt when you got your bath from one of those
big tubs that folk in chicago barbecue in

and somehow when you talk about home   10
it never gets across how much you
understood their feelings
as the whole family attended meetings about Hollydale
and even though you remember
your biographers never understand   15
your father's pain as he sells his stock
and another dream goes
and though you're poor it isn't poverty that
concerns you
and though they fought a lot   20
it isn't your father's drinking that makes any difference
but only that everybody is together and you
and your sister have happy birthdays and very good christmasses
and I really hope no white person ever has cause to write about me
because they never understand Black love is Black wealth and they'll   25
probably talk about my hard childhood and never understand that
all the while I was quite happy

MICHAEL PALMER (b. 1943)

Fifth Prose (1988)

Because I'm writing about the snow not the sentence
Because there is a card—a visitor's card—and on that card
    there are words of ours arranged in a row

and on those words we have written house, we have written
    leave this house, we   5
have written be this house, the spiral of a house, channels
    through this house

and we have written The Provinces and The Reversal and
    something called the Human Poems
though we live in a valley on the Hill of Ghosts   10

Still for many days the rain will continue to fall
A voice will say Father I am burning

Father I've removed a stone from a wall, erased a picture from
    that wall, a picture of ships—cloud ships—pressing toward the sea

words only   15
taken limb by limb apart

Because we are not alive not alone
but ordinary extracts from the tablets

Hassan the Arab and his wife
who did vaulting and balancing   20

Coleman and Burgess, and Adele Newsome
pitched among the spectators one night

Lizzie Keys
and Fred who fell from the trapeze

into the sawdust   25
and wasn't hurt at all

and Jacob Hall the rope-dancer
Little Sandy and Sam Sault

Because there is a literal shore, a letter that's blood-red
Because in this dialect the eyes are crossed or quartz   30

seeing swimmer and seeing rock
statue then shadow

and here in the lake
first a razor then a fact

LOUISE GLÜCK
Gratitude (1975)

Do not think I am not grateful for your small
kindness to me.
I like small kindnesses.
In fact I actually prefer them to the more
substantial kindness, that is always eying you,   5
like a large animal on a rug,
until your whole life reduces
to nothing but waking up morning after morning
cramped, and the bright sun shining on its tusks.

CRAIG RAINE (b. 1944)
Dandelions (1979)

"and we should die of that roar which lies on the other side of silence"
      —George Eliot, *Middlemarch*

Dead dandelions, bald as drumsticks,
swaying by the roadside

like Hare Krishna pilgrims
bowing to the Juggernaut.

They have given up everything.   5
Gold gone and their silver gone,

humbled with dust, hollow,
their milky bodies tan

to the colour of annas.
The wind changes their identity: 10

slender Giacomettis, Doré's convicts,
Rodin's burghers of Calais

with five bowed heads
and the weight of serrated keys . . .

They wither into mystery, waiting   15
to find out why they are,

patiently, before nirvana
when the rain comes down like vitriol.

ROBERT MORGAN (b. 1944)

Mountain Bride (1979)

They say Revis found a flatrock
on the ridge just
perfect for a natural hearth,
and built his cabin with a stick

and clay chimney right over it.   5
On their wedding night he lit
the fireplace to dry away the mountain
chill of late spring, and flung on

applewood to dye
the room with molten color while   10
he and Martha that was a Parrish
warmed the sheets between the tick

stuffed with leaves and its feather
cover. Under that wide hearth
a nest of rattlers,   15
they'll knot a hundred together,

had wintered and were coming awake.
The warming rock
flushed them out early.
It was she   20

who wakened to their singing near
the embers and roused him to go look.
Before he reached the fire
more than a dozen struck

and he died yelling her to stay   25
on the big four-poster.
Her uncle coming up the hollow
with a gift bearham two days later

found her shivering there
marooned above a pool   30
of hungry snakes,
and the body beginning to swell.

ALICE WALKER (b. 1944)

"Good Night, Willie Lee, I'll See You in the Morning" (1979)

Looking down into my father's
dead face
for the last time
my mother said without
tears, without smiles   5
without regrets
but with *civility*
"Good night, Willie Lee, I'll see you
in the morning."
And it was then I knew that the healing   10
of all our wounds
is forgiveness
that permits a promise
of our return
at the end.

JACK MAPANJE (b. 1944)

From Florrie Abraham Witness, *December 1972* (1981)

There are times when their faith in gods
Really fascinates me. Take when the Anglican
Priest with all pomp and ceremony married
Abraham and Florrie, why didn't he realise
Abe and Florrie would eventually witness   5
The true Jehovah in his most pristine? And silly
Little Florrie, couldn't she foresee the run against
The only cards possible when she said her
"Yes, I do; for kids or for none?" And when
Florrie's mother dear, with all her Anglican   10
Limping love for her first and only daughter
Still intact, even when she thought she might
Still visit the prodigals notwithstanding, how
Couldn't she see that she too would be booted out
Landing carelessly bruised and in *Moçam-*   15
bique! The buggers! They surely deserve it;
They deserve such a good kick on their bottom.
I mean, there are times when their faith just
Fails me. Take today, when silly little Florrie
Should scribble a funny epistle on stupid roll—   20
And Love did you have to call it thus? I mean,
It sounds so strangely imprudent of . . . But . . .
Anyway: Darling Brother, only God of Abraham

Knows how we escaped the petrol and matches
Yet we are all in good hands. They give us   25
Free flour, beans free and their kind of salted
Meat and fish. We've even built a ten-by-ten yard
Little hospital for our dear selves. Only we
Haven't got any soap. But we'll manage and do not
Be anxious over us here dear Brother; Mummie   30
And the kids are all in good shape. They send
Their Christmas greetings. Read well and, oh, note:
Psalms! Where in London is the blooming Bible?

ANNE WALDMAN (b. 1945)

Bluehawk (1991; rev. 1996)

Homage to Thelonius Monk, 1917–1982

Monk's gone
      blown
those keys
   his
     alone   5
unlock
    a heart-mind
sway
  swipe those tears away
      Monk's gone   10
      Monk's gone
(pause)
       a minor chord
    asymmetry
    (accent on the "try")   15
  push limits
    all his own
    &
    music of the spheres
     (song the gong)   20
gone
Monk's gone
     old Buddha fingers gone
       bluehawk
          in the sky   25
   soars high

AI (b. 1947)

Why Can't I Leave You? (1972)

You stand behind the old black mare,
dressed as always in that red shirt,
stained from sweat, the crying of the armpits,
that will not stop for anything,
stroking her rump, while the barley goes unplanted.   5
I pick up my suitcase and set it down,
as I try to leave you again.
I smooth the hair back from your forehead.
I think with your laziness and the drought too,
you'll be needing my help more than ever.   10
You take my hands, I nod
and go to the house to unpack,
having found another reason to stay.

I undress, then put on my white lace slip
for you to take off, because you like that   15
and when you come in, you pull down the straps
and I unbutton your shirt.
I know we can't give each other any more
or any less than what we have.
There is safety in that, so much   20
that I can never get past the packing,
the begging you to please, if I can't make you happy,
come close between my thighs
and let me laugh for you from my second mouth.

SHELLY WAGNER (b. 1947)

Thirteenth Birthday (1994)

September 29, 1991.
He would have been thirteen today.
There will be no party for my teenager.
There is work to do in the yard.
I'll cut off the arms of ivy   5
reaching toward the river.
Their begging will not persuade
him to come back.
I'll prune dead roses,
lay them in circles   10
like memorial wreaths
on the grave-like mound of compost.
Using my heavy metal rake,
I'll comb pine needles
out of the lawn like tangles   15
out of wet hair. I'll pour

grass seed into a small blue cart,
walk back and forth slowly
as though strolling a baby carriage.
I'll turn on the sprinkler to soak the seeds,   20
stand back and watch it oscillate
back and forth by the bulkhead,
waving goodbye to sorrow.
That will encourage me to do what I must
in the attic—sort through the last   25
of his clothes. Over my head on the roof,
I know fall leaves are piling
one upon another like children at recess;
that I neither hear nor see them
does not mean they are not there.   30

WENDY ROSE (b. 1948)

Loo-Wit (1985)

The way they do
this old woman
no longer cares
what others think
but spits her black tobacco   5
any which way
stretching full length
from her bumpy bed.
Finally up
she sprinkles   10
ashes on the snow,
cold buttes
promising nothing
but the walk
of winter.   15
Centuries of cedar
have bound her
to earth,
huckleberry ropes
lay prickly   20
on her neck.
Around her
machinery growls,
snarls and ploughs
great patches   25
of her skin.
She crouches
in the north,
her trembling
the source   30

of dawn.
Light appears
with the shudder
of her slopes,
the movement   35
of her arm.
Blackberries unravel,
stones dislodge.
It's not as if
they weren't warned.   40

She was sleeping
but she heard
the boot scrape,
the creaking floor,
felt the pull of the blanket   45
from her thin shoulder.
With one free hand
she finds her weapons
and raises them high;
clearing the twigs   50
from her throat
she sings, she sings,
shaking the sky
like a blanket about her
Loo-Wit sings and sings and sings!   55

SEKOU SUNDIATA (b. 1948)

Blink Your Eyes (1995)

(Remembering Sterling A. Brown)

I was on my way to see my woman
but the Law said I was on my way
thru a red light red light red light
and if you saw my woman
you could understand,   5
I was just being a man
It wasn't about no light
it was about my ride
and if you saw my ride
you could dig that too, you dig?   10
Sunroof stereo radio black leather
bucket seats sit low you know,
the body's cool, but the tires are worn.
Ride when the hard time come, ride
when they're gone, in other words   15
the light was green.

I could wake up in the morning
without a warning
and my world could change:
blink your eyes.   20
All depends, all depends on the skin,
all depends on the skin you're living in.

Up to the window comes the Law
with his hand on his gun
what's up? what's happening?   25
I said I guess
that's when I really broke the law.
He said *a routine, step out the car*
a routine, assume the position.
Put your hands up in the air   30
you know the routine, like you just don't care.
License and registration.
Deep was the night and the light
from the North Star on the car door, deja vu
we've been through this before,   35
why did you stop me?
Somebody had to stop you.
I watch the news, you always lose.
You're unreliable, that's undeniable.
This is serious, you could be dangerous.   40

I could wake up in the morning
without a warning
and my world could change:
blink your eyes.
All depends, all depends on the skin,   45
all depends on the skin you're living in.

New York City, they got laws
can't no bruthas drive outdoors,
in certain neighborhoods, on particular streets
near and around certain types of people.   50
They got laws.
All depends, all depends on the skin,
all depends on the skin you're living in.

AGHA SHAHID ALI (b. 1949)

I Dream It Is Afternoon When
I Return to Delhi (1987)

At Purana Qila I am alone, waiting
for the bus to Daryaganj. I see it coming,

but my hands are empty.
"Jump on, jump on," someone shouts,
"I've saved this change for you   5
for years. Look!"
A hand opens, full of silver rupees.
"Jump on, jump on." The voice doesn't stop.
There's no one I know. A policeman,
handcuffs silver in his hands,   10
asks for my ticket.

I jump off the running bus,
sweat pouring from my hair.
I run past the Doll Museum, past
headlines on the Times of India   15
building, PRISONERS BLINDED IN A BIHAR
JAIL, HARIJAN VILLAGES BURNED BY LANDLORDS.
Panting, I stop in Daryaganj,
outside Golcha Cinema.

Sunil is there, lighting   20
a cigarette, smiling. I say,
"It must be ten years, you haven't changed,
it was your voice on the bus!"
He says, "The film is about to begin,
I've bought an extra ticket for you,"   25
and we rush inside:

Anarkali is being led away,
her earrings lying on the marble floor.
Any moment she'll be buried alive.
"But this is the end," I turn   30
toward Sunil. He is nowhere.
The usher taps my shoulder, says
my ticket is ten years old.

Once again my hands are empty.
I am waiting, alone, at Purana Qila.   35
Bus after empty bus is not stopping.
Suddenly, beggar women with children
are everywhere, offering
me money, weeping for me.

JAMES FENTON (b. 1949)

God, A Poem (1983)

A nasty surprise in a sandwich,
A drawing-pin caught in your sock,
The limpest of shakes from a hand which
You'd thought would be firm as a rock,

A serious mistake in a nightie,   5
A grave disappointment all round
Is all that you'll get from th'Almighty,
Is all that you'll get underground.

Oh he *said:* "If you lay off the crumpet
I'll see you alright in the end.   10
Just hang on until the last trumpet.*
Have faith in me, chum—I'm your friend."

But if you remind him, he'll tell you:
"I'm sorry, I must have been pissed—
Though your name rings a sort of a bell. You   15
Should have guessed that I do not exist.

"I didn't exist at Creation,
I didn't exist at the Flood,
And I won't be around for Salvation
To sort out the sheep from the cud—   20

"Or whatever the phrase is. The fact is
In soteriological terms
I'm a crude existential malpractice
And you are a diet of worms.†

"You're a nasty surprise in a sandwich.   25
You're a drawing-pin caught in my sock.
You're the limpest of shakes from a hand which
I'd have thought would be firm as a rock,

"You're a serious mistake in a nightie,
You're a grave disappointment all round—   30
That's all that you are," says th'Almighty,
"And that's all that you'll be underground."

VICTOR HERNÁNDEZ CRUZ (b. 1949)

Problems with Hurricanes (1991)

A campesino looked at the air
And told me:
With hurricanes it's not the wind
or the noise or the water.
I'll tell you he said: 5
it's the mangoes, avocados

---

* See 1 Corinthians, 15:52.

† Play on words: the Diet of Worms was a church council in Germany, 1521, at which Martin Luther was condemned as a heretic.

Green plantains and bananas
flying into town like projectiles.

How would your family
feel if they had to tell   10
The generations that you
got killed by a flying
Banana.

Death by drowning has honor
If the wind picked you up   15
and slammed you
Against a mountain boulder
This would not carry shame
But
to suffer a mango smashing   20
Your skull
or a plantain hitting your
Temple at 70 miles per hour
is the ultimate disgrace.

The campesino takes off his hat—   25
As a sign of respect
towards the fury of the wind
And says:
Don't worry about the noise
Don't worry about the water   30
Don't worry about the wind—

If you are going out
beware of mangoes
And all such beautiful
sweet things.   35

RAY A. YOUNG BEAR (b. 1950)

From the Spotted Night (1990)

In the blizzard
while chopping wood
the mystical whistler
beckons my attention.
Once there were longhouses   5
here. A village.
In the abrupt spring floods
swimmers retrieved our belief.
So their spirit remains.
From the spotted night   10
distant jets transform

into fireflies who float
towards me like incandescent
snowflakes.
The leather shirt   15
which is suspended
on a wire hanger
above the bed's headboard
is humanless; yet when one
stands outside the house,   20
the strenuous sounds
of dressers and boxes
being moved can be heard.
We believe someone wears
the shirt and rearranges   25
the heavy furniture,
although nothing
is actually changed.
Unlike the Plains Indian shirts
which repelled lead bullets,   30
ricocheting from them
in fiery sparks,
this shirt is the means;
this shirt *is* the bullet.

CHARLES BERNSTEIN (b. 1950)

Of Time and the Line (1984)

George Burns likes to insist that he always
takes the straight lines; the cigar in his mouth
is a way of leaving space between the
lines for a laugh. He weaves lines together
by means of a picaresque narrative;   5
not so Hennie Youngman, whose lines are strict-
ly paratactic. My father pushed a
line of ladies' dresses—not down the street
in a pushcart but upstairs in a fact'ry
office. My mother has been more concerned   10
with her hemline. Chairman Mao put forward
Maoist lines, but that's been abandoned (most-
ly) for the East-West line of malarkey
so popular in these parts. The prestige
of the iambic line has recently   15
suffered decline, since it's no longer so
clear who "I" am, much less who *you* are. When
making a line, better be double sure
what you're lining in & what you're lining
out & which side of the line you're on; the   20

world is made up so (Adam didn't so much
name as delineate). Every poem's got
a prosodic lining, some of which will
unzip for summer wear. The lines of an
imaginary are inscribed on the   25
social flesh by the knifepoint of history.
Nowadays, you can often spot a work
of poetry by whether it's in lines
or no; if it's in prose, there's a good chance
it's a poem. While there is no lesson in   30
the line more useful than that of the pick-
et line, the line that has caused the most ad-
versity is the bloodline. In Russia
everyone is worried about long lines;
back in the USA, it's strictly soup-   35
lines. "Take a chisel to write," but for an
actor a line's got to be cued. Or, as
they say in math, it takes two lines to make
an angle but only one lime to make
a Margarita.   40

CAROLYN FORCHÉ (b. 1950)

The Colonel (1978)

What you have heard is true. I was in his house. His wife carried a
tray of coffee and sugar. His daughter filed her nails, his son went
out for the night. There were daily papers, pet dogs, a pistol on the
cushion beside him. The moon swung bare on its black cord over the
house. On the television was a cop show. It was in English. Broken
bottles were embedded in the walls around the house to scoop the
kneecaps from a man's legs or cut his hands to lace. On the windows
there were gratings like those in liquor stores. We had dinner, rack
of lamb, good wine, a gold bell was on the table for calling the maid.
The maid brought green mangoes, salt, a type of bread. I was asked
how I enjoyed the country. There was a brief commercial in Spanish.
His wife took everything away. There was some talk then of how dif-
ficult it had become to govern. The parrot said hello on the terrace.
The colonel told it to shut up, and pushed himself from the table.
My friend said to me with his eyes: say nothing. The colonel re-
turned with a sack used to bring groceries home. He spilled many
human ears on the table. They were like dried peach halves. There is
no other way to say this. He took one of them in his hands, shook it
in our faces, dropped it into a water glass. It came alive there. I am
tired of fooling around he said. As for the rights of anyone, tell your
people they can go fuck themselves. He swept the ears to the floor
with his arm and held the last of his wine in the air. Something for

your poetry, no? he said. Some of the ears on the floor caught this scrap of his voice. Some of the ears on the floor were pressed to the ground.

JORIE GRAHAM (b. 1951)

Wanting a Child (1983)

How hard it is for the river here to re-enter
the sea, though it's most beautiful, of course, in the waste
of time where it's almost
turned back. Then
it's yoked,   5
trussed. . . . The river
has been everywhere, imagine, dividing, discerning,
cutting deep into the parent rock,
scouring and scouring
its own bed.   10
Nothing is whole
where it has been. Nothing
remains unsaid.
Sometimes I'll come this far from home
merely to dip my fingers in this glittering, archaic   15
sea that renders everything
identical, flesh
where mind and body
blur. The seagulls squeak, ill-fitting
hinges, the beach is thick   20
with shells. The tide
is always pulsing upward, inland, into the river's rapid
argument, pushing
with its insistent tragic waves—the living echo,
says my book, of some great storm far out at sea, too far   25
to be recalled by us
but transferred
whole onto this shore by waves, so that erosion
is its very face.

PAUL MULDOON (b. 1951)

Hedgehog (1973)

The snail moves like a
Hovercraft, held up by a
Rubber cushion of itself,
Sharing its secret

With the hedgehog. The hedgehog   5
Shares its secret with no one.

We say, Hedgehog, come out
Of yourself and we will love you.

We mean no harm. We want
Only to listen to what   10
You have to say. We want
Your answers to our questions.

The hedgehog gives nothing
Away, keeping itself to itself.
We wonder what a hedgehog   15
Has to hide, why it so distrusts.

We forget the god
Under this crown of thorns.
We forget that never again
Will a god trust in the world.   20

DAVID MURA (b. 1952)

The Natives (1984)

Several months after we lost our way,
they began to appear, their quiet eyes
assuring us, their small painted legs
scurrying beside us. By then our radio
had been gutted by fungus, our captain's cheek
stunned by a single bullet; our ammo vanished   5
the first night we discovered our maps were useless,
our compasses a lie. (The sun and stars
seemed to reel above us.) The second week
forced us on snakes, monkeys, lizards, and toads;   10
we ate them raw over wet smoking fires.
Waking one morning we found a river boat
loaded with bodies hanging in trees
like an ox on a sling, marking the stages
of flood. One of us thought he heard the whirr   15
of a chopper, but it was only the monsoon
drumming the leaves, soaking our skin so damp
you felt you could peel it back to scratch
the bones of your ankle. Gradually our names
fell from our mouths, never heard again.   20
Nights, faces glowing, we told stories of wolves,
and the jungle seemed colder, more a home.

And then we glimpsed them, like ghosts of children
darting through the trees, the curtain of rain;
we told each other nothing, hoping they'd vanish.   25

But one evening the leaves parted. Slowly
they emerged and took our hands, their striped
faces dripping, looking up in wonder
at our grizzled cheeks. Stumbling like gods
without powers, we carried on our backs 30
what they could not carry, the rusted grenades,
the ammoless rifles, barrels clotted with flies.
They waited years before they brought us
to their village, led us in circles till
time disappeared. Now, stone still, our feet 35
tangled with vines, we stand by their doorway
like soft-eyed virgins in the drilling rain:
the hair on our shoulders dangles and shines.

NAOMI SHIHAB NYE (b. 1952)

Catalogue Army (1986)

Something has happened to my name.
It now appears on catalogues
for towels and hiking equipment,
dresses spun in India,
hand-colored prints of parrots and eggs. 5
Fifty tulips are on their way
if I will open the door.
Dishrags from North Carolina
unstack themselves in the Smoky Mountains
and make a beeline for my sink. 10

I write a postcard to my cousin:
this is what it is like to live in America.
Individual tartlet pans congregate
in the kitchen, chiming my name.
Porcelain fruit boxes float above tables, 15
sterling silver ice cream cone holders
twirl upside down on the cat's dozing head.

For years I developed radar against malls.
So what is it that secretly applauds
this army of catalogues marching upon my house? 20
I could be in the bosom of poverty, still they arrive.
I could be dead, picked apart by vultures,
still they would tell me
what socks to wear in my climbing boots.

Stay true, catalogues, protect me 25
from the wasteland where whimsy and impulse

---

never camp.
Be my companion on this journey between dusts,
between vacancy and that smiling stare
that is citizen of every climate   30
but customer to nothing,
even air.

MARY RUEFLE (b. 1952)

The Derision of Christ in New England (1989)

Big fat moon
clearing the clothesline:
buffoon in a cheap red shirt,
he's knocked himself out
on a bottle of wine.   5
His wife's resigned to looking
like this, propped up in bed,
wads of Kleenex under her night table,
chicken feathers round the stump.
She sees things on TV.   10
How to stuff the little chicken
in French; its infantile figure,
naked and winged, flying off
before Madame can get the
vitals back in.   15
Sunday, before light, the clothes
start flapping.
All of the crows take flight.
She crosses herself,
and knows his scabby head   20
will be beating old sores
against the window tonight.

ALBERTO RÍOS (b. 1952)

*Mi Abuelo** (1982)

Where my grandfather is is in the ground
where you can hear the future
like an Indian with his ear at the tracks.
A pipe leads down to him so that sometimes
he whispers what will happen to a man   5
in town or how he will meet the best
dressed woman tomorrow and how the best
man at her wedding will chew the ground
next to her. Mi abuelo is the man

* My grandfather.

who speaks through all the mouths in my house.   10
An echo of me hitting the pipe sometimes
to stop him from saying *my hair is a*
sieve is the only other sound. It is a phrase
that among all others is the best,
he says, and *my hair is a sieve* is sometimes   15
repeated for hours out of the ground
when I let him, which is not often.
An abuelo should be much more than a man
like you! He stops then, and speaks: *I am a man*
who has served ants with the attitude   20
of a waiter, who has made each smile as only
an ant who is fat can, and they liked me best,
but there is nothing left. Yet I know he ground
green coffee beans as a child, and sometimes
he will talk about his wife, and sometimes   25
about when he was deaf and a man
cured him by mail and he heard groundhogs
talking, or about how he walked with a cane
he chewed on when he got hungry.
At best, mi abuelo is a liar.   30
I see an old picture of him at nani's with an
off-white yellow center mustache and sometimes
that's all I know for sure. He talks best
about these hills, *slowest waves,* and where this man
is going, and I'm convinced his hair is a sieve,   35
that his fever is cooled now underground.
Mi abuelo is an ordinary man.
I look down the pipe, sometimes, and see a
ripple-topped stream in its best suit, in the ground.

RICHARD JONES (b. 1953)

The Color of Grief (1991)

We drop petals
on the water
in his memory,

as if he
and the river   5
were one.

We talk
about him
while the flowers float away.

How lucky we are   10
he died
in the river behind our house,

where the ducks he loved
waddle up the lawn.
How much better   15

to remember him here,
where the river whispers
he's alive!

than at the grave,
where his five years   20
are carved in stone,

and the hardened earth
is silent,
and grief is green

and always edged   25
with dying flowers;
for we know grief

is blue, like the river,
which takes our flowers
when they are fresh   30

and carries them away.

LOUISE ERDRICH (b. 1954)

A Love Medicine (1984)

Still it is raining lightly
in Wahpeton. The pickup trucks
sizzle beneath the blue neon
bug traps of the dairy bar.

Theresa goes out in green halter and chains   5
that glitter at her throat.
This dragonfly, my sister,
she belongs more than I
to this night of rising water.

The Red River swells to take the bridge.   10
She laughs and leaves her man in his Dodge.
He shoves off to search her out.
He wears a long rut in the fog.

And later, at the crest of the flood,
when the pilings are jarred from their sockets   15
and pitch into the current,
she steps against the fistwork of a man.
She goes down in wet grass

and his boot plants its grin
among the arches of her face.   20

Now she feels her way home in the dark.
The white-violet bulbs of the streetlamps
are seething with insects,
and the trees lean down aching and empty.
The river slaps at the dike works, insistent.   25

I find her curled up in the roots of a cottonwood.
I find her stretched out in the park, where all night
the animals are turning in their cages.
I find her in a burnt-over ditch, in a field
that is gagging on rain,   30
sheets of rain sweep up down
to the river held tight against the bridge.

We see that now the moon is leavened and the water,
as deep as it will go,
stops rising. Where we wait for the night to take us   35
the rain ceases. *Sister, there is nothing*
I would not do.

LORNA DEE CERVANTES (b. 1954)

Freeway 280 (1981)

Las casitas° near the gray cannery,   *little houses*
nestled amid wild abrazos° of climbing roses   *bear hugs*
and man-high red geraniums
are gone now. The freeway conceals it
all beneath a raised scar.   5

But under the fake windsounds of the open lanes,
in the abandoned lots below, new grasses sprout,
wild mustard remembers, old gardens
come back stronger than they were,
trees have been left standing in their yards.   10
Albaricoqueros, cerezos, nogales* . . .
Viejitas° come here with paper bags to gather greens. *old women*
Espinaca, verdolagas, yerbabuena† . . .

I scramble over the wire fence
that would have kept me out.   15
Once, I wanted out, wanted the rigid lanes
to take me to a place without sun,

* Apricot, cherry, and walnut trees.

† Spinach, purslane, mint.

without the smell of tomatoes burning
on swing shift in the greasy summer air.

Maybe it's here
en los campos extraños de esta ciudad*
where I'll find it, that part of me
mown under
like a corpse
or a loose seed.

CORNELIUS EADY (b. 1954)

My Mother,
If She Had Won Free Dance Lessons (1985)

Would she have been a person
With a completely different outlook on life?
There are times when I visit
And find her settled on a chair
In our dilapidated house,
The neighborhood crazy lady
Doing what the neighborhood crazy lady is
        supposed to do,
Which is absolutely nothing

And I wonder as we talk our sympathetic talk,
Abandoned in easy dialogue,
I, the son of the crazy lady,
Who crosses easily into her point of view
As if yawning
Or taking off an overcoat.
Each time I visit
I walk back into our lives

And I wonder, like any child who wakes up one day
        to find themselves
Abandoned in a world larger than their
        Bad dreams,
I wonder as I see my mother sitting there,
Landed to the right-hand window in the living room,
Pausing from time to time in the endless loop
        of our dialogue
To peek for rascals through the
Venetian blinds,

I wonder a small thought.
I walk back into our lives.
Given the opportunity,

* In the strange fields of this city.

How would she have danced?
Would it have been as easily   30

As we talk to each other now,
The crazy lady
And the crazy lady's son,
As if we were old friends from opposite coasts
Picking up the thread of a long conversation,   35

Or two ballroom dancers
Who only know
One step?

What would have changed
If the phone had rung like a suitor,   40
If the invitation had arrived in the mail
Like Jesus, extending a hand?

MARILYN CHIN (b. 1955)

Turtle Soup (1987)

You go home one evening tired from work,
and your mother boils you turtle soup.
Twelve hours hunched over the hearth
(who knows what else is in that cauldron).

You say, "Ma, you've poached the symbol of long life;   5
that turtle lived four thousand years, swam
the Wei, up the Yellow, over the Yangtze.
Witnessed the Bronze Age, the High Tang,
grazed on splendid sericulture."
(So, she boils the life out of him.)   10

"All our ancestors have been fools.
Remember Uncle Wu who rode ten thousand miles
to kill a famous Manchu and ended up
with his head on a pole? Eat, child,
its liver will make you strong."   15

"Sometimes you're the life, sometimes the sacrifice."
Her sobbing is inconsolable.
So, you spread that gentle napkin
over your lap in decorous Pasadena.

Baby, some high priestess has got it wrong.   20
The golden decal on the green underbelly
says "Made in Hong Kong."

Is there nothing left but the shell
and humanity's strange inscriptions,
the songs, the rites, the oracles?   25

for Ben Huang

JIM DANIELS (b. 1956)

Hard Times in the Motor City (1985)

When Louie got married
somebody gave him
a broken bicycle for a present
in all sad seriousness.

Louie gave it back—   5
him and his new wife
traveling light—
a toaster and clock radio
heading south west east
wherever jobs might be.   10

                    *

Up and down the streets
men mow their lawns
do yardwork
many try to grow vegetables.

Some of the wives work now   15
behind counters at McDonald's
marking clothes at K-Mart
pulling in minimum wage
grocery money for another week.

Everybody's already had a garage sale.   20

                    *

In the bar
Steve talks about
the afternoon tv movie
about Elvis
about fighting   25
anyone.
He says he'll dig ditches
or clean shitholes
all he wants is a job.
He's got a wife, two kids.   30
He looks me hard in the eye:
"a man can always afford a drink."

                    *

Dennis, laid-off trucker
borrowed some money
took his rig to Florida   35
loaded up a truck full of pot
sells it out of his basement
to help make house payments.

Dennis sits on his porch
smoking up the profits   40
singing old rock and roll songs
his electric guitar plugged into the bushes.

                              *

An old man talks about the Great Depression:
"you don't see nobody jumpin' out of windows
around here."   45

But in the backyards of Detroit
Warren, Hazel Park, Center Line
men on their knees
pray over
their rotten tomatoes   50
their deformed carrots
their ragged, ragged lettuce.

LI-YOUNG LEE (b. 1957)

Eating Alone (1986)

I've pulled the last of the year's young onions.
The garden is bare now. The ground is cold,
brown and old. What is left of the day flames
in the maples at the corner of my
eye. I turn, a cardinal vanishes.   5
By the cellar door, I wash the onions,
then drink from the icy metal spigot.

Once, years back, I walked beside my father
among the windfall pears. I can't recall
our words. We may have strolled in silence. But   10
I still see him bend that way—left hand braced
on knee, creaky—to lift and hold to my
eye a rotten pear. In it, a hornet
spun crazily, glazed in slow, glistening juice.

It was my father I saw this morning   15
waving to me from the trees. I almost
called to him, until I came close enough
to see the shovel, leaning where I had
left it, in the flickering, deep green shade.

White rice steaming, almost done. Sweet green peas   20
fried in onions. Shrimp braised in sesame
oil and garlic. And my own loneliness.
What more could I, a young man, want.

TOM ANDREWS (b. 1961)

The Hemophiliac's Motorcycle (1994)

For the sin against the HOLY GHOST IS INGRATITUDE.
  —Christopher Smart, *Jubilate Agno**

May the Lord Jesus Christ bless the hemophiliac's motorcycle, the
  smell of knobby tires,

Bel-Ray oil mixed with gasoline, new brake and clutch cables and
  handlebar grips,

the whole bike smothered in WD40 (to prevent rust, and to make
  the bike shine),

may He divine that the complex smell that simplified my life was
  performing the work of the spirit,

a window into the net of gems, linkages below and behind the given
  material world,   5

my little corner of the world's danger and sweet risk, a hemophiliac
  dicing on motocross tracks

in Pennsylvania and Ohio and West Virginia each Sunday from April
  through November,

the raceway names to my mind then a perfect sensual music, Hidden
  Hills, Rocky Fork, Mt. Morris, Salt Creek,

and the tracks themselves part of that music, the double jumps and
  off-camber turns, whoop-de-doos and fifth-gear downhills,

and me with my jersey proclaiming my awkward faith—"Powered
  By Christ," it said above a silk-screened picture of a rider in a
  radical cross-up,   10

the bike flying sideways off a jump like a ramp, the rider leaning his
  whole body into a left-hand corner—

may He find His name glorified in such places and smells,

and in the people, Mike Bias, Charles Godby, Tracy Woods, David and
  Tommy Hill, Bill Schultz†—

their names and faces snowing down to me now as I look upward to
  the past—

---

* In 1756 Christopher Smart (1722–1771) was seized by an urge to pray publicly, kneeling in streets and parks of London and sometimes forcing passersby to kneel with him. He was placed in an institution, where he began pouring out innovative poetry, including *Jubilate Agno* (*Rejoice in the Lamb*), written from 1759 to 1763. It is, in part, a liturgy of worship, joining the material and spiritual universe in prayers of praise and thanksgiving. The most famous section is known as "My Cat Jeoffry."

† Motocross racers.

friends who taught me to look at the world luminously in front of
    my eyes,   15

to find for myself the right rhythm of wildness and precision, when
    to hold back and when to let go,

each of them with a style, a thumbprint, a way of tilting the bike this
    way or that out of a berm shot, or braking heavily into a corner,

may He hear a listening to the sure song of His will in those years,

for they flooded me with gratitude that His informing breath was
    breathed into me,

gratitude that His silence was the silence of all things, His presence
    palpable everywhere in His absence,   25

gratitude that the sun flashed on the Kanawha River, making it
    shimmer and wink,

gratitude that the river twisted like a wrist in its socket of
    bottomland, its water part of our speech

as my brother and I drifted in inner tubes fishing the Great
    White Carp,

gratitude that plump squirrels tight-walked telephone lines and
    trellises of honeysuckle vines

and swallows dove and banked through the limbs of sycamore trees,
    word-perfect and sun-stunned   30

in the middle of the afternoon, my infusion of factor VIII* sucked in
    and my brother's dialysis sucked in and out—

both of us bewildered by the body's deep swells and currents and
    eerie backwaters,

our eyes widening at the white bursts on the mountain ash, at
    earthworms inching into oil-rainbowed roads—

gratitude that the oak tops on the high hills beyond the lawns
    fingered the denim sky

as cicadas drilled a shrill voice into the roadside sumac
    and peppergrass,   35

gratitude that after a rain catbirds crowded the damp air, bees
    spiraling from one exploding blossom to another,

gratitude that at night the star clusters were like nun buoys moored
    to a second sky, where God made room for us all,

may He adore each moment alive in the whirring world,

as now sitting up in this hospital bed brings a bright gladness for the
    human body, membrane of web and dew

* Enzyme essential to blood clotting.

I want to hymn and abide by, splendor of tissue, splendor of cartilage
    and bone,   35

splendor of the taillike spine's desire to stretch as it fills with blood

after a mundane backward plunge on an iced sidewalk in Ann Arbor,

splendor of fibrinogen and cryoprecipitate, loosening the blood
    pooled in the stiffened joints

so I can sit up oh sit up in radiance, like speech after eight weeks
    of silence,

and listen for Him in the blood-rush and clairvoyance of the
    healing body,   40

in the sweet impersonal luck that keeps me now

from bleeding into the kidney or liver, or further into the spine,

listen for Him in the sound of my wife and my father weeping
    and rejoicing,

listen as my mother kneels down on the tiled floor like Christopher
    Smart

praying with strangers on a cobbled London street, kneels here in
    broad daylight   45

singing a "glorious hosanna from the den"

as nurses and orderlies and patients rolling their IV stands behind
    them like luggage

stall and stare into the room and smile finally and shuffle off, having
    heard God's great goodness lifted up

on my mother's tongue, each face transformed for a moment by
    ridicule

or sympathy before disappearing into the shunt-light of the hallway,   50

listen for Him in the snap and jerk of my roommate's curtain as he
    draws it open

to look and look at my singing mother and her silent choir

and to wink at me with an understanding that passeth peace, this
    kind, skeletal man

suffering from end-stage heart disease who loves science fiction
    and okra,

who on my first night here read aloud his grandson's bar mitzvah
    speech to me,   55

". . . In my haftorah portion, the Lord takes Ezekiel to a valley full
    of bones,

the Lord commands him to prophesy over the bones so they will
  become people . . . ,"

and solemnly recited the entire text of the candlelighting ceremony,

"I would like to light the first candle in memory of Grandma Ruth,
  for whom I was named,

I would like Grandma Dot and Grandpa Dan to come up and light
  the second candle,   60

I would like Aunt Mary Ann and my Albuquerque cousins Alanna
  and Susanna to come up and light the third candle . . . ,"

his voice rising steadily through the vinegary smell and brutal hush
  in the room,

may the Lord hear our listening, His word like matchlight cupped to
  a cigarette

the instant before the intake of breath, like the smoke clouds pooled
  in the lit tobacco

before flooding the lungs and bloodstream, filtering into pith
  and marrow,   65

may He see Himself again in the hemophiliac's motorcycle

on a certain Sunday in 1975—Hidden Hills Raceway, Gallipolis, Ohio,

a first moto holeshot and wire-to-wire win, a miraculously benign
  sideswipe early on in the second moto

bending the handlebars and front brake lever before the possessed
  rocketing up through the pack

to finish third after passing Brian Kloser on his tricked-out
  Suzuki RM125   70

midair over the grandstand double jump—

may His absence arrive like that again here in this hygienic room,

not with the rush of a peaked power band and big air over the jumps

but with the strange intuitive calm of that race, a stillness
  somehow poised

in the body even as it pounded and blasted and held its line across
  the washboard track,   75

may His silence plague us like that again,

may He bless our listening and our homely tongues.

APPENDIX A
Bibliography

RESOURCES FOR THE STUDY OF POETRY

Basic Reference Works

Serious students of literature should own *and use* the following basic reference works:

—A good desk dictionary (not just the small paperback kind)
—A good literary handbook—like
   Abrams, M. H., *A Glossary of Literary Terms* (Harcourt Brace Jovanovich paperback)
   Harmon, William, and C. Hugh Holman, *A Handbook to Literature* (Macmillan paperback)
   Frye, Northrop, et al., *The Harper Handbook to Literature* (Harper-Collins paperback)
—A Bible with a concordance
   The King James Version (1611) is valuable for the literature student because it is the one many authors knew and quoted from or alluded to
—A handbook to classical mythology—like
   Tripp, Edward, *The Meridian Handbook of Classical Mythology* (New American Library-Dutton)
   Bulfinch's *Mythology* or Edith Hamilton's *Mythology,* with an index

Students of literature should be familiar with the following works (locate them in the library—they will most likely be in the reference section—so you can find them easily when the need arises):

DICTIONARIES

Oxford English Dictionary (OED), ed. James A. H. Murray et al.
Dictionary of American English on Historical Principles (DAE), ed. William Craigie and J. R. Hulbert
Partridge, Eric, *A Dictionary of Slang and Unconventional English*

The English Dialect Dictionary
Dictionary of American Regional English

ENCYCLOPEDIAS

Encyclopaedia Britannica and *Encyclopedia Americana* (the 11th edition of the *Britannica,* 1910–11, is particularly useful for students of earlier British literature because of the depth of the entries and the excellent scholars who wrote them)
The Encyclopedia of Religion, ed. Mircea Eliade, and the older *Encyclopedia of Religion and Ethics,* ed. James Hastings
Encyclopedia of the Social Sciences, ed. Edwin Seligman and A. Johnson
Encyclopaedia Judaica and the older *Jewish Encyclopedia*
New Catholic Encyclopedia and the older *Catholic Encyclopedia*
The Encyclopedia of Philosophy, ed. Paul Edwards
An Encyclopedia of World History, William L. Langer
The [Princeton] Encyclopedia of Poetry and Poetics

BIOGRAPHY

Dictionary of National Biography (DNB), ed. Leslie Stephen and Sidney Lee—covers British citizens
Dictionary of American Biography (DAB), ed. Allen Johnson and Dumas Malone
Dictionary of Literary Biography (well over 100 volumes, 1978–   )
Contemporary Poets

LITERARY HISTORIES AND COMPANIONS

Baugh, Albert C., et al., *A Literary History of English*
Oxford History of English Literature, in many volumes, in progress
Spiller, Robert E., et al., *Literary History of the United States,* 4th ed.
The Oxford Companion to English Literature, 5th ed., ed. Margaret Drabble
The Oxford Companion to American Literature, 5th ed., ed. James D. Hart
The Oxford Companion to Classical Literature, ed. M. C. Howatson

POETRY INDEXES

Granger's Index to Poetry
Chicorel Index to Literature

ON ALLUSIONS

Smith, William, *A Smaller Classical Dictionary*
The Oxford Classical Dictionary
Young, Robert, *Analytical Concordance to the Bible*
Concordances to many American, British, continental, and classical authors are available.

BIBLIOGRAPHY (SEE PAGES 467–68)

MLA Bibliography of Books and Articles in the Modern Languages and Literature
Altick, Richard D., and Andrew Wright, *Selective Bibliography for the Study of English and American Literature,* 6th ed.

ADDITIONAL SOURCES: POETRY AND POETS

Poetry is available in a number of venues in addition to books (anthologies of poems, old and new, and collections of poems by individual poets). We encourage you to buy poetry collections, of course, and we hope you will take advantage of other opportunities for encountering contemporary poetry as well.

Poetry Magazines.   Many poets first publish their work in small literary magazines and larger-circulation magazines that include poetry. Hundreds of poetry magazines are published, from large publishers and poetry centers to small, specialized endeavors. Each magazine has its own identity, something that in itself can be interesting to explore.

For a convenient listing of many of these magazines and for descriptions of the types of poetry a magazine publishes see *The International Directory of Little Magazines and Small Presses* (Dustbooks) and *Poet's Market* (Writer's Digest Books). Both also provide guidance on submitting your own poetry for publication, should you be so inclined.

Poetry Readings.   Another way to encounter new poetry is to listen to poets read their work aloud. You can experience a variety of types of readings. At poetry slams, the audience members cheer, jeer, and pick winners from a number of readers. Performance poets fuse poetry with theatrical elements—everything from stand-up comedy to dance, music, and drama. At formal readings, poets mix anecdotes and contextual information with a reading of poems, often arranged in an engaging order. Open-mike readings invite anyone in the audience to come up and read his or her work. Other readings bring together a poet with musicians, dancers, artists, or prose writers.

Listening to poetry read in the poet's voice differs from reading the poem yourself and often adds to, opens up, or simply enriches what you experience as you read. Every poet has a reading style as well as a writing style; it can be interesting to discover the variety of ways poets read their works.

You can find out about local readings through the arts listings in your newspaper, from your library, from the literature creative writing programs at colleges and universities, or from events listings at bookstores, coffeehouses, art galleries, and other places where readings are held.

You (or your class) might want to organize a reading at your own campus or perhaps at a local café or bookstore.

A wide variety of audiotaped and videotaped readings, often including conversations with a poet, are also available. These give you the opportunity to listen at your convenience and offer you the chance to listen several times to a poem or a whole reading.

Poetry on the World Wide Web.   All sorts of poetry can be found on the Web, from individual home pages by aspiring writers to sophisticated sites organized by poetry centers, from poems just composed to collections of texts from classic works. Surfing will turn up an interesting and intriguing variety of poems and on-line forums for listening to and entering conversations about poetry.

You can just browse, using key words as specific as an author's name or as general as *contemporary poetry.* Or you can begin with a home page and follow the leads it provides. There is an *Approaching Poetry* home page http://www.smpcollege.com/smp_eng/schakel.html, which offers additional information, an on-line forum, and interconnections with other poetry web sites. Currently the most helpful starting point, in our estimation, is The Electronic Poetry Center at the State University of New York at Buffalo: http://wings.buffalo.edu/epc/

FURTHER READING ON CRITICAL APPROACHES

A great deal has been published on critical theory over the past few decades. This appendix can do no more than offer a few starting points. A convenient, helpful guide for proceeding further is Donald G. Marshall, *Contemporary Critical Theory: A Selective Bibliography* (New York: Modern Language Association of America, 1993). The lists below suggest introductions and surveys that supplement Chapters 11–14 in this book in clarifying the ideas of various theorists and the directions theory has taken. In addition to reading introductions and surveys, it would be helpful to begin reading works by theorists themselves—by Richards, Brooks, Iser, Derrida, Barthes, Fish, and so on, some of which are listed below as well.

INTRODUCTIONS TO CRITICAL THEORY

Eagleton, Terry. *Literary Theory: An Introduction.* Minneapolis: University of Minnesota Press, 1983.

Gibaldi, Joseph, ed. *Introduction to Scholarship in Modern Languages and Literatures.* New York: Modern Language Association of America, 1992.

* Greenblatt, Stephen, and Giles Gunn. *Redrawing the Boundaries: The Transformation of English and American Literary Studies.* New York: Modern Language Association of America, 1992.

Guerin, Wilfred L., et al. *A Handbook of Critical Approaches to Literature.* 2d ed. New York: Harper and Row, 1979.

* Leitch, Vincent B. *American Literary Criticism from the 30s to the 80s.* New York: Columbia University Press, 1988.

Payne, Michael, ed. *A Dictionary of Cultural and Critical Theory.* Oxford, England: Blackwell, 1996.

Selden, Raman. *A Reader's Guide to Contemporary Literary Theory.* Lexington: Kentucky University Press, 1985.

Walhout, Clarence, and Leland Ryken, eds. *Contemporary Literary Criticism: A Christian Appraisal.* Grand Rapids, Mich.: Eerdmans Publishing Company, 1991.

PSYCHOANALYTIC

* Elliott, Anthony. *Psychoanalytic Theory: An Introduction.* Oxford, England: Blackwell, 1994.

Freud, Sigmund. *Introductory Lectures on Psycho-Analysis.* Trans. Joan Riviere. London: Allen, 1922.

———. "The Relation of the Poet to Day-Dreaming." In *On Creativity and the Unconscious.* New York: Harper & Row, 1958. 44–54.

* Items marked with an asterisk are good places to start.

Gallop, Jane. *The Daughter's Seduction: Feminism and Psychoanalysis.* Ithaca, N.Y.: Cornell University Press, 1982.

* Hall, Calvin S. *A Primer of Freudian Psychology.* New York: New American Library, 1954.

Holland, Norman H. *Holland's Guide to Psychoanalytic Psychology and Literature-and-Psychology.* New York: Oxford University Press, 1990.

Trilling, Lionel. "Freud and Literature." *The Liberal Imagination: Essays on Literature and Society.* New York: Viking Press, 1951. 34–57.

Williams, Linda Ruth. *Critical Desire: Psychoanalysis and the Literary Subject.* London: Edward Arnold, 1995.

* Wright, Elizabeth. *Psychoanalytic Criticism: Theory in Practice.* London and New York: Methuen, 1984.

NEW CRITICISM

* Brooks, Cleanth. "The Formalist Critics." *Kenyon Review* 13 (1951): 72–81.
———. *The Well Wrought Urn: Studies in the Structure of Poetry.* New York: Harcourt, Brace and Company, 1947.

* Graff, Gerald. "What Was New Criticism?" *Literature Against Itself: Literary Ideas in Modern Society.* Chicago: University of Chicago Press, 1979. 129–49.

Handy, William J. *Kant and the Southern New Critics.* Austin: University of Texas Press, 1963.

Richards, I. A. *Practical Criticism: A Study of Literary Judgment.* London: Kegan, 1929.

Wellek, René. "The New Criticism: Pro and Contra." *Critical Inquiry* 4 (1978): 611–24.

ARCHETYPAL

Frye, Northrop. *Anatomy of Criticism: Four Essays.* Princeton, N.J.: Princeton University Press, 1957.

Jung, Carl. *The Essential Jung.* Ed. Anthony Storr. Princeton, N.J.: Princeton University Press, 1983.

STRUCTURALISM

Barthes, Roland. *A Barthes Reader.* Ed. Susan Sontag. New York: Hill, 1982.

* Culler, Jonathan. *Structuralist Poetics: Structuralism, Linguistics, and the Study of Literature.* London: Routledge, 1975.

Hawkes, Terence. *Structuralism and Semiotics.* Berkeley: University of California Press, 1977.

Jameson, Fredric. *The Prison-House of Language: A Critical Account of Structuralism and Russian Formalism.* Princeton, N.J.: Princeton University Press, 1972.

Scholes, Robert. *Structuralism in Literature: An Introduction.* New Haven, Conn.: Yale University Press, 1974.

DECONSTRUCTION

* Culler, Jonathan. *On Deconstruction: Theory and Criticism after Structuralism.* Ithaca, N.Y.: Cornell University Press, 1982.

de Man, Paul. "Semiology and Rhetoric." In *Allegories of Reading.* New Haven: Yale University Press, 1979. 3–19.

Derrida, Jacques. "Structure, Sign, and Play in the Discourse of the Human Sciences." In *The Languages of Criticism and the Sciences of Man: The Structuralist Controversy,* ed. Richard Macksey and Eugenio Donato. Baltimore: Johns Hopkins University Press, 1970, 247–72.

Leitch, Vincent B. *Deconstructive Criticism: An Advanced Introduction.* New York: Columbia University Press, 1980.

Norris, Christopher. *Derrida.* Cambridge, Mass.: Harvard University Press, 1987.

* Scholes, Robert. *Textual Power: Literary Theory and the Teaching of English.* New Haven: Yale University Press, 1985.

READER-RESPONSE

Beach, Richard. *A Teacher's Introduction to Reader-Response Theories.* Urbana, Ill.: National Council of Teachers of English, 1993.

Bleich, David. *Subjective Criticism.* Baltimore: Johns Hopkins University Press, 1978.

Fish, Stanley. *Is There a Text in This Class? The Authority of Interpretive Communities.* Cambridge, Mass.: Harvard University Press, 1980.

Freund, Elizabeth. *The Return of the Reader: Reader-Response Criticism.* London and New York: Methuen, 1987. 112–33.

Holland, Norman N. "UNITY IDENTITY TEXT SELF," *PMLA* 90 (1975): 813–22.

―――. *5 Readers Reading.* New Haven, Conn.: Yale University Press, 1975.

* Iser, Wolfgang. *The Implied Reader: Patterns of Communication in Prose Fiction from Bunyan to Beckett.* Baltimore: Johns Hopkins University Press, 1974.

―――. *The Act of Reading: A Theory of Aesthetic Response.* Baltimore: Johns Hopkins University Press, 1979.

* Suleiman, Susan R. "Introduction: Varieties of Audience-Oriented Criticism." In *The Reader in the Text: Essays on Audience and Interpretation.* Ed. Susan R. Suleiman and Inge Crosman. Princeton, N.J.: Princeton University Press, 1980), 3–45.

* Tompkins, Jane P. "An Introduction to Reader-Response Criticism." *Reader-Response Criticism: From Formalism to Post-Structuralism.* Baltimore: Johns Hopkins University Press, 1980.

Wilson, W. Daniel. "Readers in Texts." *PMLA* 96 (1981): 848–63.

CULTURAL

Grossman, Lawrence, Cary Nelson, and Paula A. Treichler, eds. *Cultural Studies.* New York: Routledge, 1992.

* McCormick, Kathleen. *The Culture of Reading and the Teaching of English.* New York: St. Martin's Press, 1994.

Miller, Jane. *Seductions: Studies and Readings in Culture.* Cambridge, Mass.: Harvard University Press, 1991.

NEW HISTORICISM

Foucault, Michel. *The Foucault Reader.* Ed. Paul Rabinow. New York: Pantheon, 1984.

Greenblatt, Stephen. *Renaissance Self-Fashioning: From More to Shakespeare.* Chicago: University of Chicago Press, 1980.

McGann, Jerome. *Historical Studies and Literary Criticism.* Madison: University of Wisconsin Press, 1985.

* Thomas, Brook. *The New Historicism and Other Old-Fashioned Topics.* Princeton, N.J.: Princeton University Press, 1991.

Veeser, H. Aram, ed. *The New Historicism.* New York: Routledge, 1989.

MARXIST

* Eagleton, Terry. *Marxism and Literary Criticism.* Berkeley: University of California Press, 1976.

Goldstein, Philip. *The Politics of Literary Theory: An Introduction to Marxist Criticism.* Gainesville: University of Florida Press, 1990.

Jameson, Fredric. *The Political Unconscious: Narrative as a Socially Symbolic Art.* Ithaca, N.Y.: Cornell University Press, 1981.

Marx, Karl, and Friedrich Engels. *Marx and Engels on Literature and Art: A Selection of Writings.* Ed. Lee Baxandall and Stefan Morawski. St. Louis: Telos, 1973.

Williams, Raymond. *Marxism and Literature.* Oxford, England: Oxford University Press, 1977.

FEMINIST

Beauvoir, Simone de. *The Second Sex.* Trans. H. M. Parshley. New York: Vintage, 1974. (*Le deuxième sexe.* 2 vols. Paris: Gallimard, 1949.)

Gilbert, Sandra M., and Susan Gubar. *The Madwoman in the Attic: The Woman Writer and the Nineteenth-Century Literary Imagination.* New Haven, Conn.: Yale University Press, 1979.

Kahn, Coppélia, and Gayle Greene, eds. *Making a Difference: Feminist Literary Criticism.* London: Methuen, 1985.

Ruthven, K. K. *Feminist Literary Studies: An Introduction.* Cambridge, England: Cambridge University Press, 1984.

* Showalter, Elaine. "Feminist Criticism in the Wilderness." In *The New Feminist Criticism: Essays on Women, Literature, and Theory.* Ed. Elaine Showalter. New York: Pantheon, 1985. 243–70.

Spivak, Gayatri Chakravorty. *In Other Worlds: Essays in Cultural Politics.* New York: Methuen, 1987.

GENDER

Abelove, Henry, Michèle Aina Barale, and David Halperin, eds. *The Lesbian and Gay Studies Reader.* New York: Routledge, 1993.

Chodorow, Nancy. *The Reproduction of Mothering: Psychoanalysis and the Sociology of Gender.* Berkeley: University of California Press, 1978.

* Haggerty, George E., and Bonnie Zimmerman, eds. *Professions of Desire: Lesbian and Gay Studies in Literature.* New York: Modern Language Association of America, 1995.

Sinfield, Alan. *Cultural Politics—Queer Reading.* Philadelphia: University of Pennsylvania Press, 1994.

CRITIQUES OF CONTEMPORARY TRENDS

This book explains theories of literature but does not attempt to evaluate them, except insofar as any theory critiques and responds to earlier approaches. Beyond such responses, some scholars have undertaken critiques of contemporary theoretical trends. These are not necessarily negative: often these work from a healthy appreciation of the contributions made by recent theorists, but raise questions about epistemological starting points or about philosophical implications.

In addition to the examples below, note that Walhout and Ryken's *Contemporary Literary Criticism* (listed on page 444 under Introductions to Critical Theory) provides critiques as well as sound summaries of a number of contemporary approaches.

Abrams, M. H. *Doing Things with Texts: Essays in Criticism and Critical Theory.* New York: Norton, 1989.

Bruns, Gerald L. *Inventions: Writing, Textuality, and Understanding in Literary History.* New Haven: Yale University Press, 1982.

Ellis, John M. *Against Deconstruction.* Princeton: Princeton University Press, 1989.

Steiner, George. *Real Presences.* Chicago: University of Chicago Press, 1989.

Responding on Paper

Writing is an excellent way of entering conversations about poems and poetry—conversations between the poems themselves, between poems and readers, between readers and other readers, and between ways of reading and other ways of reading.

I. WRITING IN THE MARGINS

One way of writing about poetry takes place around the poem itself. If you own the book you are using, try reading with a pencil or pen in hand. You can underscore lines or phrases or words you find striking; you might draw stars or put checks or brackets next to passages you want to go back to; you might write comments as you proceed through a poem ("powerful image," "stupid idea," "tone shifts"); you might enter into dialogue with the poem—raising questions, disagreeing with what is said, noting things that remind you of other poems by the same writer or by a different writer, jotting down possibilities for papers. Scribble all through it, if you like.

Writing in a book, this form of "engaged reading," is actually an ancient and honored tradition: reading the "marginalia" that famous people, from Shelley to Bach, wrote in their books can be interesting and informative. Poet Li-Young Lee tells in a video of discovering his father's Bible, a book Lee had never seen until after his father's death. He discovered there in the marginalia a man he had never known before. The margins were filled with overwhelming, fierce, penetrating questions that seemed out of character with the minister father Lee had known—always strong, confident, certain, sure about religious issues.

We don't mean just the kind of highlighting you do in your sociology book, or penciling in an outline of the major points, to help you with reviewing for the next exam. We mean talking back to the poem, complimenting it, wondering about things in it, raising questions or stating problems. We hope that you do (or have been doing) lots of writing in this book. Taking a short view, such jottings can be helpful for class participation. Taking a longer view, we hope you will want to return to some of these poems later, perhaps years later, to reread them and the notes you wrote about them. You may wonder who that person was who responded as you did; you might reacquaint yourself with who you were; or you might discover how much you have added to your experience with poetry since then.

Here—just to illustrate what we mean, not to prescribe how it should be done—is some writing in the margins done by one of our students, Kristin Knippenberg. She later used these notes to write a journal entry on the poem (see p. 452), which she could have used as the starting point for a paper.

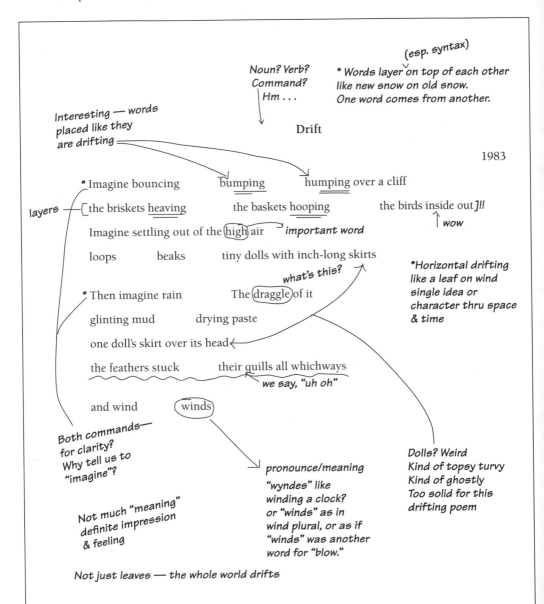

II. JOURNAL WRITING

Writing in a journal enables you to include not only brief jottings but also longer responses, developing your thoughts and feelings in greater detail. It's also a great place to store information, poems, related ideas, personal anecdotes, tangential insights—anything that might be connected to what you are studying or that can be extended from or associated with it.

Journals can be written primarily for yourself—like a diary, centered on your thinking and reading and even any daily events and activities that relate to your study. You can keep track of what you've read (characters' names or notes on specific elements, lines you want to remember, unusual uses of line, form, diction, or rhythm, things you were drawn to or put off by). You can treat a journal as an extension of the notes you take in class, reorganizing them, perhaps, and clarifying and expanding them (which can be a great help for reviewing later). A journal also provides a place where you can express ideas or feelings stimulated by what you read or by conversations with other people. Some people divide their journals into two columns, or use the left- and right-hand pages differently—one side for notes or information, the other side for reflections and observations.

If a journal is assigned for your course, or if keeping a journal simply appeals to you, buy a notebook and begin writing entries as responses to poems, chapters, discussions, and assignments connected with this course. The suggestions for writing at the ends of chapters may stimulate some ideas; your teacher will bring up some; you will think of others yourself. Try to be specific and precise about your ideas, observations, and reflections. And date each entry. Keeping a journal can help you trace your own development and growth in taste, judgment, attitudes, and so on. As mentioned before, it can be surprising, interesting, fun, and helpful to one day look back at who you were.

In some cases teachers assign journals as part of the writing to be done for a course. A benefit (or intention) of this is to illustrate the value of keeping a journal, so students may decide to continue them after the course is over. Instructors who include journals in their courses do so because journals can allow for immediate, reactive, personal, and flexible responses to reading. Often the writing itself emerges from a deeply intimate connection of the self with the poem. We tap into the part of ourselves that seeks to respond, record, and retain things that feel meaningful to us. Many writers keep notebooks/journals of quick impressions, reactions, lists of words, and so on, not just about what they read but about what they experience generally.

Doing a journal as a class assignment can change its nature to some degree, especially if the journal is handed in and read by the teacher. A personal journal is often private. An assigned journal may be less so. Assigned journals differ also in that some of the writing in them may be directed; that is, the teacher could ask you to focus on a specific topic in a given entry ("Discuss images in one of the poems assigned for today"). Teachers will not necessarily be looking for certain answers or interpretations. Rather, they will look for clear evidence that you have read the poems carefully; that you have made a thoughtful effort to engage with the material and to respond sensibly and sen-

"Drift" by Alberta Turner — This poem is pretty awesome. It's about everything and nothing. Every little word and phrase and sound & image contributes, nothing is Xtra or unnecessary. I never really stopped to think about drifting, in & of itself. Not many do — I suppose that's why she TELLS us to imagine. Usually when you think of drifting, you think of THINGS that actually do the drifting, or drifting as a contribution to a larger nature scene or some romantic autumn or winter day, you & your lover kissing in the woods. None of that in this poem. It's all very dreamlike. One has to wonder — is the poem about drifting, or is it actually doing the drifting? A bit of both? The words occur both as layers, one on top of the other, like snow, AND also as a single idea, merely twisting & turning & changing on a single path — like a leaf! OO-EE. Awesome how those words work out like that — "bumping, humping, heaving, hooping." Also are some ambiguous pivot words, that could mean different things. "Drift" — noun or verb or command? I hope it's a command — I'd love to be part of the drifting. If dolls can, I can. Another weird word is "winds" the last word in the poem. The sounds in the poem are all very soft & rounded, which is why it would be so interesting if that "winds" were pronounced like "winding a clock." That pronounciation has a couple o' teeth in it. It would be a wierd tonal shift, right smack at the end, almost ominously, so "drift" isn't so sweet & innocent anymore. OR, if you don't like weird tonal shifts, pronounce it like plural "winds", or as a funky new verb for "blow" or something. (New weird words — what the heck is draggle?) The poem gets almost scary towards the end with those dolls. They just sort of APPEAR in the poem, like poltergeists that fade in, fade out. Dolls are easy to play with, manipulate, if you will. But they add a strange heaviness and real/fakeness to the poem, as if they are the antagonist in a story, or some sort of proof that the equal and opposite from "drift" is just as true. Wonderfully haunting, halting.

sitively to its emotional, aesthetic, and intellectual dimensions; and that your comments are clear and specific. Above is a page from Kristin's journal on "Drift." Look for places where she carried over ideas from her marginal notations and elaborated on or changed them.

III. WRITING ESSAY EXAMINATION ANSWERS

An essay examination answer is a conversation between you and your teacher. Think of it as an opportunity to have your teacher's undivided attention. The essay answer is a one-on-one, student-with-teacher format.

It may help to think about essay exams from a teacher's point of view. A teacher often chooses to give an essay examination to see how well you can think through a problem. The object is not just to find out *what* you know. An essay question seeks to help you develop what you can do with what you know—to synthesize it, apply it, see it in relation to other things, and respond to its challenges.

Here are a few tips for writing essay answers:

1. Read the question carefully several times and make sure you understand what it asks you to do. It is crucial to understand what the question is

focusing on. If you need clarification, ask the teacher, rather than risk going at it wrong. If you are allowed to use your book in class, double-check with your teacher about whether and how you may use the marginalia you've jotted in it.

The St. Martin's Handbook suggests identifying two kinds of terms—*strategy* terms that describe the task, and *content* terms that indicate the scope and limits of the topic.

┌─ STRATEGY ─┐ ┌──────────────── CONTENT ──────────────┐
Discuss how figures contribute to tone in Ransom's "Bells for
└──────────────────────────────────────┘
John Whiteside's Daughter."

┌──────── STRATEGY ────────┐ ┌──────── CONTENT ────────
Compare and contrast rhythm and how it is controlled in Whitman's
                                 └──────────────────────────┘
"When Lilacs Last in the Dooryard Bloomed" and Pastan's "love poem."

It is important to have a clear sense of what the strategy terms used for discussing literature mean. Here are some common ones:

DISCUSS: Comment thoughtfully about a poem or poems, or features in it or them.

ANALYZE: Divide an idea or technique into its component elements.

COMPARE: Point out similarities between two or more works or features in a work or more than one work.

CONTRAST: Point out dissimilarities between two or more works or features in a work or more than one work.

COMPARE AND CONTRAST: Point out both similarities and dissimilarities between two or more works or features in a work or more than one work.

EXPLAIN: Make a topic clear and understandable by offering reasons, examples, and so on.

EXPLICATE: Explain a passage in detail, concentrating on language, style, textual interrelationships and how they shape and relate to content.[1]

2. You probably want to plunge right in, since time is limited and you feel under pressure. But pause to plan and organize before beginning to write. You will use your time better if you reflect briefly. Decide what you will *do* with the strategy you choose. Your answer should be more than just a list of comparisons and contrasts, for example; the list should add up to something, make a point. Jot that point down, as your "thesis," and state it clearly, at the beginning or the end of your answer. Sketch an outline of points that will clarify what you mean and will support and illustrate its validity.

3. Then start writing. The most efficient way to get moving is to state your central point immediately, repeating words from the question, in order to indicate that you are answering it directly, meeting it head-on. Keep your out-

---

[1] Adapted from Andrea Lunsford and Robert Connors, *The St. Martin's Handbook,* 3d ed. (New York: St. Martin's Press, 1995), 742–43.

line in mind, but don't stick to it slavishly. An exciting part of writing is that in the process of creating and thinking, you make discoveries, you get insights and ideas you didn't expect when you began. These often take off in new directions, may even be opposite to what you originally intended to say. When you're writing an essay, you revise in order to incorporate such discoveries in a unified way. But there's no time to revise essay answers. So, do you ignore the new insight and stick to the outline, or include it? We think it's better to include it—but you should explain that you're changing directions ("That's the way it looked to me at first, but as I examine the poem more closely I see something different in it"), not leave the teacher thinking you don't realize that what you are saying now doesn't fit with the way you started.

4. Start a new paragraph when you move to a new subpoint. This will make the answer clearer and easier to read. And don't write so fast that your handwriting becomes illegible—the best ideas in the world are of no use if the reader can't read them.

5. Try to leave yourself a couple of minutes to read through your answer. Be sure you have offered support (explanations, details, quotations) for each subpoint. Check spelling and grammar.

The sample answer on the following pages illustrates how one of our students handled an essay question on Theodore Roethke's "Root Cellar."

IV. WRITING SHORT PAPERS ABOUT POETRY

Another way of engaging in a conversation about poetry is to write a paper intended for a larger audience. In practice it may be read only by your teacher, but ideally others would read it too. In some classes students read each other's papers, to learn from each other, to help each other, and to create a sense that they are writing for an audience larger than one. Who is this audience? Anyone interested in the subject matter—at this stage that may be only the other students in your class; but later it may be the readership of a literary magazine or periodical.

Because the presumed audience for an essay is larger than the audience for journals or essay examination questions, your essay needs to follow conventions readers have come to expect. Here are some suggestions, growing out of those inherited traditions, for writing essays about poetry:

1. Be sure you are clear about what is expected of you. Double-check the assignment, and confirm with your teacher any questions about the expected length, form, subject matter, approach, format, and deadline.

2. If you choose your own topic, your marginal jottings and journal entries may be good places to start. Look through them for poems that engaged you—ones that intrigued you, or puzzled you, or opened up new perceptions, insights, or ideas. Topics that struggle with a problem, suggest ambiguous resolutions, or explore a difficulty often work well.

Anne Lucas

4. (20 minutes) Discuss (1) how the following poem
enables us to experience the scene with our senses and
(2) how it directs the way we respond to that scene.

emptiness—eerie   Root Cellar (1948)   _alliteration_

Nothing would sleep in that cellar, dank as a ditch,

More → Bulbs broke out of boxes hunting for chinks in the dark,
alliteration

→ Shoots dangled and drooped,

Lolling obscenely from mildewed crates, ←   _rhyme_

Hung down long yellow evil necks, like tropical snakes.

And what a (congress) of (stinks)!— _neat word_   _IMAGERY!_
                                                      Simile

→ Roots ripe as (old bait), _SMELL_

Pulpy stems, rank, silo-rich,

More → Leaf-mold, manure, lime, piled against slippery planks.
odors &
visions Nothing would give up life:

Even the [dirt] kept breathing a small breath.
    lifeless yet ———→ _alive_
                              —Theodore Roethke

The root cellar lives on. . . .

_Anne took time
to read the
poem carefully,
mark useful
details, and jot
notes as
reminders._

I. Experience the scene through our senses through
   descriptive terms, imagery, alliteration, simile,
   creative word choice.
      A. Imagery—sights!—words, alliteration, simile
      B. Smell—word choice, richness
II. All elements above direct the way we respond to
   the scene, create the image of the root cellar
   which we are drawn into, darkness, dankness,
   eeriness—yet it lives on—

_She took
time to write
a brief outline
for the essay
answer._

The "Root Cellar" by Theodore Roethke is rich with descriptive words, imagery, poetic devices such as alliteration and simile, and ~~clever~~ creative word choice. The combination of these ~~factors~~ elements enables the reader to experience the scene through his/her senses.

A wealth of imagery throughout the poem enables us to envision the root cellar. Words and phrases such as "mildewed crates" and "Leaf-mold, manure, lime, piled against slippery planks" create this image (lns 4 & 9). Alliteration is especially useful in adding to the richness of the images. The cellar is "dank as a ditch," while "bulbs broke out of boxes" and "Shoots dangled and drooped" (lns 1, 2, & 3). The author uses simile to present the shoots and their "long evil necks" which are "like tropical snakes" ~~(lns 5 &~~ (line 5). The use of ~~alliteration~~ word choice, alliteration, and simile all contribute to create a depth of visionary description.

The reader is invited to smell the intense odors of the root cellar. Again, word choice is used to create a scene with "Roots ripe as old bait," "Pulpy stems" which are "rank, silo-rich" (lns 7 & 8). Words such as "Leaf-mold, manure, lime" all contribute not only to the visual effect, but also to the sense smell of ~~small~~. Word choice enables the odors to rise from the root cellar and become part of the poem's overall effect.

elements   previously
All of the ~~poems~~ which I have described contribute to the way in which the reader responds to the poem. Roethke creates ~~are~~ a dark, dank, mysterious environment, rich in smells and sights. The word choice is one which ~~presents~~ produces an eerie sense, a ~~sense~~ feeling of darkness and depth. However, the root cellar is also a place ~~of~~ rich with life as the ~~final line~~ one line asserts "Nothing would give up life" (ln 10). In the last line, Roethke brings together this dark, perhaps seemingly lifeless "dirt" as it too kept "breathing a small breath" (ln 11). The poem has directed the reader to envision the root cellar and to realize the vitality and fullness of life which ~~lives~~ resides within the darkness.

Clear, specific statement of central point of the answer.

Specific examples to illustrate, with comments to tie them in to the main point.

Topic sentence for part 2 of the question.

Discussion of the reader's experience, tied in directly in the final sentence.

If you are given an unfamiliar poem to write about, or if you choose an unfamiliar one, use marginal writing and a journal entry to help get into the poem. Then look over what you've underlined or circled or marked with "?" or "*" or "!" Note what engaged you: images? figures? word choice? rhythm? line breaks? ideas? the arrangement? the ending? similarities to or differences from another poem(s)? Go through the poem again, circling or marking anything interesting that you hadn't seen before. Then look for connections, patterns, focuses, questions, or problems. Begin asking why: Why is the speaker's tone this way? Why does the poem end this way? Why is the diction mixed? Consider alternatives: ask how the poem's effect would change if it had used different metaphors, or been written with (or without) rhyme, or been written in third person instead of first.

3. This process generates ideas, which could lead you to an interesting subject area to work with. But it's important to remember that a key aspect of planning a paper involves narrowing and focusing that broad subject area to a clearly defined topic that can be explored in detail within the assigned length. Too large a topic for the length of the paper will be ineffective because it will skim rather than cover. Too limited a topic can leave you without enough to say to fill the needed pages. But how do you focus a broad topic? One way is to keep in mind the strategy words listed on page 453: you can focus your paper by means of the strategy you use in approaching the poem—by deciding to analyze, compare and/or contrast, explicate, and so on. Or you can focus by deciding to do only part of what you originally intended instead of all of it ("Imagery in 'Saint Pumpkin'" instead of "Nancy Willard's Use of Imagery"). Or you can limit yourself to a specific part of the broad topic ("Imagery in 'Saint Pumpkin'" can be narrowed to "Religious Imagery in 'Saint Pumpkin'"). Or, for longer poems, you can concentrate on one section instead of trying to cover the whole work ("Figures and Rhythm in the Last Five Stanzas of 'Cherrylog Road'"). Don't hesitate to ask your teacher if your topic seems right for the assigned length.

4. You've narrowed the topic. Now you need to develop what *you want to say* about that topic. This is where the *conversation* starts. Readers can know a poem for themselves. They can know the images. But what they don't yet know are your explanations, or interpretations, or observations, perceptions, or connections. As you think about what to say about your topic, try to focus it on a central idea, main point, key observation, or thesis. Your thesis might emerge, or develop, or even change as you write. In any case, an effective essay presents a clear focus (usually at the end of the first paragraph, because readers have become accustomed to looking for it there), which helps the reader know what to look for, what is being "developed."

5. It is often helpful to have an outline—a plan, an advance sketch of the steps the paper will take the reader through. Some students write out a detailed outline, even using Roman numerals, numbers, and letters as headings. Others jot down a list of subtopics. Still others have a plan clear in their heads. People work in different ways, and it's helpful to find what works best for you. For some, thinking ahead before beginning to write is essential for

the essay to have a focus and direction from the start. Others begin by "brain-storming" or freewriting. For them, it's the writing that gets them thinking. If you have found an outlining system useful in other courses, you might also use it here.

6. Once you have a focused topic, and at least a tentative direction, you can begin writing. Try starting with a bald, direct statement of your central point: "This paper will argue that 'Saint Pumpkin' is valuable to read because of its imaginative imagery, and because it also contains a deeper message that makes it worthwhile examining the poem closely." Such a sentence makes it clear to yourself what you need to do. When you get to the end of the paper, go back and develop a fuller introduction. Sometimes the last paragraph you write, one you planned as the conclusion, can suggest (or even become) a good introduction.

Writing, for most people, is like playing a sport or a musical instrument—to start doing it well, some warm-up is needed to get "in the flow," or "get the creative juices going." The key about starting is to START. Read the poem two or three times, so its words fill your mind. Do more underlining and annotating as you read. Then, make yourself put words down. Write anything that comes to mind about the topic, in any order, without stopping or editing or changing anything. Or try clustering. Write down each of your points. Then write any ideas that come to mind that can be associated with the points.

Many people find that it works best to write a first draft rapidly and get their ideas down, without worrying about neatness, grammar, or spelling. But others need to work more slowly, getting each sentence and each paragraph right before moving on to the next one. There is no single "right" process; find the one that suits you best.

7. The key part of a successful paper lies in developing your ideas. That means explaining your ideas so readers can understand them readily, and supporting them with information and quotations, giving your readers confidence that the points are well-grounded and worth considering.

Should you do library research on the poem or author? That depends on what the teacher prefers. For some subjects, teachers may prefer to see what you come up with on your own, and may discourage you from reading criticism by others. Other teachers may have different objectives and prefer such reading. If the assignment doesn't specify whether you should read critics or not, it's usually best to ask. (See pages 468–475 for more information on using research in a paper about poetry.)

A key issue in all academic work involves giving proper credit for anything taken from another source. If you do consult any books other than your course textbook and dictionaries, even if you do not quote directly from them, you must acknowledge these sources in notes or a bibliography. In fact, you should acknowledge any external assistance, like discussing the assigned poem with your former high school teacher or another student who is especially knowledgeable about the topic. Failure to do so, and thus presenting the ideas or work of others—intentionally or even unintentionally—as if they were your own, is plagiarism, a very serious academic offense.

How many quotations from the poem should you use? The answer requires good judgment, depending on specific situations. Quotations connect your explanations and interpretations strongly to the poem and show that they are firmly based. But if you find yourself in an alternating pattern—quotation, explanatory sentence, quotation, explanatory sentence, throughout a paragraph—you probably are overdoing quotations. Keep in mind that a reader goes to your paper to learn *your* approach and explanations and ideas. The poem can be read elsewhere, but your ideas can't be.

You need to make clear where quoted lines or phrases can be found. If you're writing on one poem from this book, it should be acceptable if you put the line number(s) in parentheses at the end of the quotation (see the sample paper on pages 464–468). If you have found a poem elsewhere, you will need a footnote or bibliographic entry (see section VI below) to inform the reader where the poem can be found; but specific passages can be identified by line numbers. If you include several poems in the paper, include a shortened title as well as a line number in the parenthetical reference if necessary to make the source clear.

Here are a few other guidelines for handling quotations and citations:

Titles of poems, short stories, and essays should be placed within quotation marks ("Saint Pumpkin").

Titles of books should be underlined or put in italics.

Quotation marks should always be placed outside commas and periods (." or ,") and inside semicolons (";). American punctuation conventions never put the period or comma outside quotation marks.

Always use double quotation marks (" "), except for a quotation within a quotation, which is indicated by single quotation marks (' ').

The end punctuation of a quotation may be dropped and replaced by punctuation appropriate to your sentence; thus, a period ending a line of poetry may be replaced with a comma if your sentence goes on. You should never have a (.",) or (,".) in a paper.

In all other respects, quotations must be precisely accurate, including original spelling, capitalization, and punctuation.

Ellipsis marks (. . .) are generally not needed at the beginning or end of a quotation, but are essential if words or punctuation marks are omitted within a quotation.

Indenting a quotation is the same as putting it within quotation marks. Put quotation marks around an indented passage only if it had quotation marks around it in the source.

When quoting more than one line of poetry without indenting, separate the lines with a slash (first line, / second line).

You need not—even should not—start a new paragraph after a quotation. A quoted passage should almost always be followed by an explanation of the point the quotation is illustrating, tying it in to the rest of the paper.

8. Once you finish a draft of the paper, revise it. This doesn't mean just correcting spelling and grammar errors: that's editing, the next step. The word *revision* derives from the Latin words for *look* and *again:* revising means taking another look at what you've written, examining it closely, thinking it through again, trying to improve it. It means making changes to improve the content, organization, and expression of your essay. It's hard to get a fresh look right after you finish writing—you are usually still too close to it to come up with different ways of explaining, or arranging, or expressing. Revision often works best if you can lay your essay aside for a day or two or even more before revising. Gaining some distance, stepping back a bit before approaching the paper again, generally is helpful. Budget your time so that you can work ahead. It also may help to have someone else read the paper, to check whether ideas and organization are clear and adequately supported. You may have done this in a composition class; it can often help in a literature class, too.

If you used a computer word-processing program for composing or typing your paper, we suggest that at least one revision (and the final proofreading and editing) be done from a printed copy. It can be helpful to see the sentences and paragraphs the way they will look on paper, in the finished product.

Revision is the key to good writing, for most people. And while it requires a good bit of work, that can also be liberating. It can ease your stress to realize that almost everyone needs to do this work in order to write well. You may not always have time to revise an essay several times. But try to. An old cliché says that good writing requires perspiration, not inspiration. Trite, yes, but true most of the time.

9. After revising your paper, you need to check for errors in spelling and grammar, and for any awkward expressions. If you use a computer for typing your paper, your word-processing package may include a program to check the spelling and perhaps one to check part of the grammar. If so, by all means use them.

A computer check, of course, doesn't free you from the need to read closely as well. The computer can tell you that it doesn't recognize *thier* and ask if you intended to write *their;* but it won't notice if you wrote *their* when you should have used *there.* Again, distance (coming back after a couple of days) can be helpful, because you may have become so familiar with your essay that it is hard to see what should be different. Some writers, when they proofread, start at the end and read backwards, as a way of looking at the words instead of getting caught up in the meaning. Again, having another person read your essay can sometimes be useful—if she or he is a good speller and an attentive reader.

• • •

To illustrate all this, compare a paper on Nancy Willard's "Saint Pumpkin" with the first steps in the writing process, beginning with writing in the margins and a journal entry:

Saint Pumpkin (1982)

Somebody's in there.
Somebody's sealed himself up
in this <u>round room</u>,
this <u>hassock upholstered in rind</u>,   *—yes!*
this (padded cell.)   5
He believes if nothing unbinds him
he'll <u>live</u> forever.   *immortality*

life/
death Like <u>our first room</u>   *(womb)*
it is dark and crowded.
Hunger knows no tongue   10
to tell it.
> (Water) is glad there.
In this room with two navels
somebody wants to be born <u>again</u>.   *?*

So I (unlock) the pumpkin.   15
I carve out the lid
from which the stem raises
> a dry handle on a (damp) world.
Lifting, I pull away
(wet) (webs), (vines) on which hang   20
> the (flat tears) of the pumpkin,

<u>like</u> fingernails or the currency
of bats. How the seeds shine,
> as if (water) had put out
> hundreds of <u>lanterns</u>.   25
> Hundreds of eyes in the (windless) (wood)
gaze peacefully past me,
(hacking) the <u>thickets</u>,   *ouch!*
> and now a white (dew) beads the (blade.)
Has the saint <u>surren</u>dered   *?*
himself to his beard?   30
Has his beard taken root in his cell?   *?*

   Saint Pumpkin(pray for me,)
   because when I looked for you, <u>I found nothing</u>,
   because unsealed and unkempt, your <u>tomb</u> <u>rots</u>,   *!*
   because <u>I</u> gave you <u>a false face</u>   35
   and a light of <u>my</u> own making.

Wow! What images — pumpkin seeds as tears, fingernails, bats' coins, eyes. And there's such <u>wetness</u> to it all . . .

This is about much more than carving Jack-O-Lanterns (which will never be the same again for me . . .) There's a jarring sadness to it — is Willard saying that we commit an atrocity each time we invade or alter the natural world? She makes the pumpkin seem human — or beyond that, nearly divine [or suggesting even a lowly pumpkin has a right to lie undisturbed in the garden? — almost a pantheistic notion —]

But nothing stays untouched in nature, ever. Pumpkins eventually rot, even if they believe that "if nothing unbinds them they'll live forever": so why shouldn't she use it, carve it, open it? And having done that, why is she so sorry, needing the pumpkin to pray for her?

Maybe the last 2 lines say it all: <u>I</u> gave <u>you</u> a false face & a light of <u>my</u> own making. Like forcing someone/thing to be other than its intended self, according to my dictates. So demeaning. [Why else would she put these 2 lines last? seems like they're there for emphasis]

This poem has plenty of ambiguities, sorta like life. Worth exploring more . . .

_(mystery)
1. "<u>somebody</u>" is secreted away in the enclosed rind
          — and wants to stay that way —
2. BUT also "wants to be born again"
          —born again = spiritual awakening?
          —<u>again</u> : why again? hmmm . . .
3. SO s/he unlocks it; and:
          sees the damp world inside,
          flat <u>tears</u> of the pumpkin
               —poem starts to feel sadder, now that
               pumpkin's been violated.
4. shining seeds (YES!), like lanterns extinguished
          [more sadness/loss]
     — seeds like eyes <u>gaze</u> <u>peacefully</u> beyond
          her hacking (ouch)
5. dew beading the blade
          — like blood on a razor-sharp knife (more pain)
          sadness for the surrendered saint, who's clinging, rooted,
          to the bottom of the pumpkin-cell
6. And now sorrow, apology needed for prayer from
          The Violated (forgiveness?)
               why?
                    — because she "found nothing"
                    — now the <u>tomb</u> (formerly <u>room</u>) will ROT
                    — <u>and</u> she gave it a false face and <u>her</u> (false?) light

"I had lots of thoughts about the poem spinning in my head and wanted to get them on paper, so I wrote a journal entry on the poem."

"The paper sort of organized itself — just followed the flow of the poem. But I did write out a sketchy outline of where my ideas were going."

After several drafts, proofreading, and editing, the paper was then formatted for printing in its final draft:

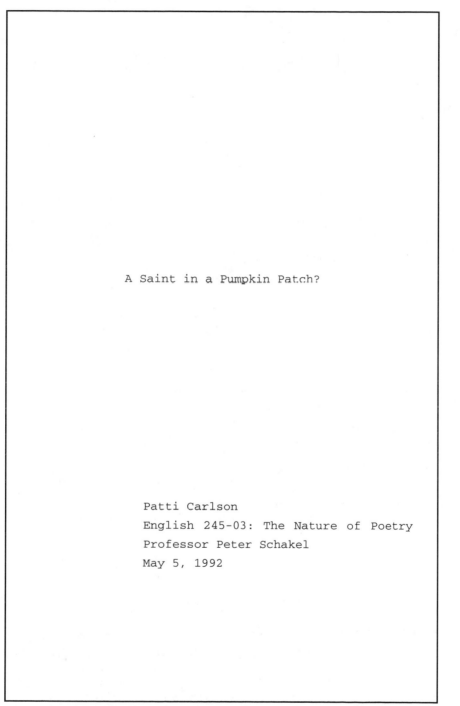

A Saint in a Pumpkin Patch?

Patti Carlson
English 245-03: The Nature of Poetry
Professor Peter Schakel
May 5, 1992

A poem about a pumpkin? A pumpkin that's a saint? Any poem about such an odd idea must have something important to say. And it does. Nancy Willard's poem "Saint Pumpkin" is pleasurable to experience not only because of its vivid images, but also because it holds a deeper message, making it worthy of contemplation and closer examination.

The peculiar juxtaposing of the words "Saint" and "Pumpkin" calls to mind two quite disparate elements and immediately captures the reader's sense of inquisi- tiveness and maybe even bewilderment. The poem begins with a sense of mystery, wonder, and contained (like a pumpkin) excitement: "Somebody's in there" (1). It's almost as if the speaker is whispering, eyes lit with questioning anticipation--could it be that there is a person hiding inside the pumpkin? The pumpkin itself is like a secret, enclosed room; and the poem uses variations of this metaphor to consider the possi- bilities. The pumpkin is described with alliteration as a "round room" (3), as a "hassock upholstered in rind"--a particularly cunning image (4), and--since it is tightly sealed--as a "padded cell" (5).

A simile is used in the next stanza as the poet compares this cell to "our first room" (8), the womb. She spends seven lines with this image, giving it major importance. The speaker muses about the nature of that "first room," where "it is dark and crowded" (9). Even though it is somewhat like an enclosed prison, it's a place free of anxiety and need. "Hunger knows no tongue / to tell it" (10-11) and "water is glad there" (12) are wonderfully fresh ways of saying the fetus neither eats nor drinks. And water, sometimes a symbol or archetype of danger, death, and mystery, "is <u>glad</u> there." Water is the

first element in which all of us float in our pre-birth
existence, and the poet personifies it by suggesting it
is "glad" when it nurtures a fetus.

"Saint Pumpkin" is about much more than carving
jack-o-lanterns for Halloween. It's also about birth and
death and infinity. The speaker's suspicion is that the
imaginary creature inhabiting the pumpkin longs for
immortality, just as we all do: "He believes if nothing
unbinds him / he'll live forever" (6-7). But before we
can become, we all must be born. And in this setting,
too, this "room with two navels / somebody wants to be
born again" (13-14). One might argue that the line could
have stood quite well without the last word. However, by
using the words "born again," the author taps into
another stream of thought, calling to mind the religious
usage of those terms, that of coming to know new life
through spiritual conversion.

At any rate, the "somebody" is still waiting: "So I
unlock the pumpkin" (15). These next two stanzas describe
with magically striking imagery what the speaker
experiences and discovers as she proceeds to "unlock"
(well-chosen word) the pumpkin and its mysteries. The
image of water is used again, when the "stem raises / a
dry handle on a damp world" (17-18), contrasting the
pumpkin with all its wet secrets to the dry, hostile
outside world. "Wet webs" (20--alliteration) fill the
inside of the pumpkin, and they are compared to "vines on
which hang / the flat tears of the pumpkin" (20-21). Here
water is mentioned once more, but this time in the form
of tears, hinting at sadness, now that the pumpkin's
precious interior has been exposed.

The poet uses three striking and lovely comparisons
at this point. Pumpkin seeds do look like "flat tears"
(21--why didn't I ever notice that before?!) or "like
fingernails" (22), or even like "the currency / of bats"
(22-23--simile) hanging upside down as they sparkle like

coins. The caesura in this line calls attention to the next important metaphor. The seeds look wet and "shine, / as if water had put out / hundreds of lanterns" (23-25). Water again! Only this time it has snuffed out all those tiny little lanterns in their secret hiding place--and we know it will never be the same again. The pumpkin has been invaded. Repeating "hundreds" in the next line gives emphasis to this sad awareness. Now the seeds are likened to "hundreds of eyes" (26) which, although they have been violated, continue to "gaze peacefully past me" (27). The pathos builds throughout the poem and seems to climax at this point. The placid, innocent pumpkin contrasts starkly with the speaker who is "hacking [ouch!] the thickets" (28). Also, in the previous line, the lonely "w" sound in "windless wood" (26) enhances the mood, and the archetypal image of woods, or forest, symbolizes danger, the unknown.

The next stanza is rather ambiguous, giving the poem just enough sense of mystery, which is in keeping with the theme of the unanswerable questions of life and death. "And now a wet dew beads the blade" (29) calls to mind the drawing of blood. The next line mentions the word "saint" for the first time, suggesting the purity and incorruption of this being who has just been defiled. But how or why has he "surrendered / himself to his beard" (30-31)? And why is "beard" repeated in the next line, where it has "taken root in his cell" (32)? Maybe the beard is a metaphor for the stringy vines inside the pumpkin, which drag out as the lid is pulled away, as if they were embedded in the bottom. "Surrendered" suggests that the saint sacrificed his beard, gave it up, in order to escape the invader of his cell. After all, the speaker finds only the beard, not the saint.

The form calls attention to the final five lines. Lines 1-28 are divided into four seven-line invented stanzas. Lines 29-32 seem to start a fifth stanza, but

suddenly it is broken off and the poem finishes with
five lines, not the expected three, and they are indented
to call attention to the change. Here the essence of the
poem is revealed. There's a great sense of remorse and
sorrow as the speaker pleads for forgiveness from "Saint
Pumpkin." She pleads for an intercessory prayer on her
behalf.

      Lines 34-36, all beginning with "because," emphasize
the speaker's sense of emptiness and sorrow. She prays
for forgiveness because "when I looked for you, I found
nothing" (34). Did she find nothing because nothing was
ever there? Apparently not, or she wouldn't still address
"Saint Pumpkin" as she does. She implies, rather, that
she caused the death of the saint by invading his cell.
Perhaps, unlike embryos, he would have "lived forever" if
she had not opened his cell. The womb paradoxically
becomes a "tomb." And now it's too late. "Unsealed and
unkempt," the "tomb [will surely] rot" (35), a strong and
terrible word. And, worst of all, the speaker is finally
responsible for not only the demise of the saint, but
also for giving it a "false face / and a light of my own
making" (36-37). Is there anything more demeaning than to
force one's own demands and alterations on another?

      All the elements in "Saint Pumpkin" work together to
make this a haunting and beautiful poem. It is written in
a free, unconventional form. The sound combinations are
smooth and graceful, making it readable and inviting
throughout. The use of both short and long lines
contributes to an irregular, somewhat halting rhythm and
keeps the poem interesting. In the first stanza a
pattern is set that quickly captures the reader's
attention. The three shortest lines--"in this round room"
(3), "this padded cell" (5), "he'll live for-ever" (7)--
give us a clue that this is not just a frivolous poem
filled with shallow sentiments; it begins to build
anticipation.

I'm sure I'll never again feel the same about
carving out a jack-o-lantern. And I greatly admire Nancy
Willard's ability to choose something as simple and
earthy as a pumpkin to marvel about the great mysteries
of life.

V. WRITING ESSAYS IN OTHER FORMATS

Essays can be developed in ways other than the standard explanation, analysis, or compare-and-contrast formats. Sometimes developing a paper as a letter—to a friend, or to the poet, or to the speaker in the poem, or as a reply to a question from a former English teacher, or as an answer to a hostile critic—can get ideas flowing. The letter form supplies a context and an audience you can write to. Sometimes, when you want to present both sides of an issue strongly or want to be more creative, you can develop a paper as a dialogue (as we did to open Chapter 2) or a debate, which enables you to imagine the characters participating, voicing their thoughts, as well as developing the ideas and positions you want to convey.

The alternative forms require the same preliminary steps: finding a topic, identifying a central point you want to develop, outlining the subpoints you will cover. For a mock letter, the outline will be much like that for a conventional essay. But for a dialogue or debate, an outline will likely become a plan for what the characters are like, what their opinions are, and what things they will talk about.

VI. WRITING A LITERARY RESEARCH PAPER

Another type of essay on literature you may be asked to write is the research paper. It extends the conversation about poetry further, including other critics. A research paper involves a dialogue with literary critics in addition to that with the poem and your reader.

1. The Nature of Research Papers

A research paper is a form of conventional essay, of the sort discussed in section IV above. As with other essays, the most important part is what *you* say in it, the development of *your* approach and ideas and interpretations. Like other essays, it needs to develop and support a thesis. The only difference is that, as you shape and develop and support your ideas, an additional resource is available: the words of other writers who have commented on the texts or authors you are working with.

As you carry out your research, it's usually best to read several books or articles that disagree with one another, or one that modifies what another has said. This can help you see what questions you might have raised or disagreed with. Another safeguard against uncritical acceptance of a critic's views is to develop your own response for your paper, sketching out a tentative central point, even doing a rough draft, before beginning to read what critics have written. If you start with the critics, their explanations may be so convincing, and you may be so impressed by them, that you won't be able to come up with ideas of your own. If you begin with your own ideas, what you read can confirm and help support your judgments, and suggest ways you can modify, or extend, or add to what you thought of.

2. Locating Critical Material and Creating a Working Bibliography

Each library search is unique and requires its own use of imagination and common sense—and, in many cases, help from a librarian. But there are some steps most literary searches will include. We will illustrate by searching for materials on Frost's " 'Out, Out—.' "

A library search almost always begins with the card catalog or on-line catalog, checking for books about the author you are dealing with. From the titles you find, select ones that seem likely to be helpful, and then check the books (using the table of contents or index, or skimming) to determine if they contain anything on your subject or poem. Those titles become the beginning of your working bibliography.

Next, find out if a bibliography or checklist of critical writings has been published for your author. One of the categories listed under Robert Frost in our on-line catalog was BIBLIOGRAPHY, and under it appeared:

```
------------------------------------------------------------------

Author:        Van Egmond, Peter.
Title:         The critical reception of Robert Frost: <an
               annotated bibliography of secondary
               comment>.
Published:     Boston, G. K. Hall, 1974.
SUBJECT HEADINGS (Library of Congress; use s=):
               Frost, Robert, 1874-1963--Bibliography.
------------------------------------------------------------------


------------------------------------------------------------------

Author:        Van Egmond, Peter.
Title:         Robert Frost : a reference guide, 1974-1990
Published:     Boston, Mass. : G. K. Hall, 1991
SUBJECT HEADINGS (Library of Congress; use s=):
               Frost, Robert, 1874-1963--Bibliography.
------------------------------------------------------------------
```

These two volumes list books and articles about Frost published between about 1915 and 1991. For those years, the necessary searching has been done for us.

A third kind of search is for articles in magazines, journals, and periodicals published later than the bibliography, and for recent books not included in your library's catalog. The best source for most authors and literary topics is the *MLA Bibliography of Books and Articles in the Modern Languages and Literature,* issued yearly and available on CD-ROM in some libraries. It is divided into sections by nationality and era (English literature 1500–1599, Scottish literature 1700–1799, etc.), with special topics listed and then authors listed under them. Frost is located in "American literature 1900–1999." Here is part of the Frost entry from the volume for 1993:

American literature/1900–1999

FROST, ROBERT (1874–1963)/*Poetry*/*"Grace Notes"*

Letters

[9754] Monteiro, George, ed. "Robert Frost: An Unpublished Letter and an Inscription in a Copy of *A Boy's Will.*" *N&Q.* 1993 Mar; 40[238](1):70-71. [Introd., 70. † Edition; inscription (1927).]

[9755] ———. "Three New Robert Frost Letters, an Inscription, and an Unrecorded Emendation." *PLL.* 1993 Winter; 29(1): 111-13. [Introd., 111; prev. unpub. material. † And inscription; emendation. Edition.]

Poetry

[9756] Bagby, George F. *Frost and the Book of Nature.* Knoxville: U of Tennessee P; 199. xv, 217 pp. ISBN 0-87049-805-3 (hbk.). [†Treatment of nature.]

[9757] Cornett, Michael E. "Robert Frost on *Listen America:* The Poet's Message to America in 1956." *PLL.* 1993 Fall; 29(4): 417-35. [† On *Listen America* as radio broadcast at University of North Carolina at Chapel Hill (1956).]

[9758] Cramer, Jeffrey S. "Forgotten Frost: A Study of the Uncollected and Unpublished Poetry of Robert Frost." *RFR.* 1993 Fall; 1-23. [Cont. from 92-1-9027.]

Some authors (especially contemporary or popular ones) may not be included in the *MLA Bibliography.* For those you should check in periodical indexes. In some libraries you can do CD-ROM or on-line searches of articles in journals and periodicals; if you cannot do this in your library (or to fill in what they don't cover), you can use printed indexes. From high school research projects or your freshman comp course, you are probably familiar with at least one index, the *Readers' Guide to Periodical Literature,* and know how to find it in your library. This may be helpful, especially for popular authors, but it will not be adequate for most college literary topics. Similar to the *Readers' Guide,* and located near it in the library, is the more specialized *Humanities Index,* which uses the same format but indexes journals that are more scholarly than those indexed by the *Readers' Guide.*

3. Indicating Sources

The method of citing sources for papers on literature preferred by most teachers is the "MLA style," described in detail in the *MLA Handbook for Writers of Research Papers* by Joseph Gibaldi, 4th ed. (New York: Modern Language Association of America, 1995). It is a simple, convenient system using a bibliography, and parenthetical references to it, for citations. Notes—either footnotes or endnotes—are used to supply comments or information that does not fit into the text of the paper, or cannot be handled adequately through parenthetical citation.

The heart of the system is the bibliography. The *MLA Handbook* recommends that it be a list of "Works Cited"—that is, containing only works referred to within the paper. In some cases, for a student paper, a "Bibliography of Works Consulted" might be preferred over "Works Cited" to indicate the range of research, if non-cited works are an important part of the context of the paper. Check with your teacher, if you think that might apply to your paper.

We will give instructions here for the most common items in literary study. For other sorts of items, consult the *MLA Handbook,* or *The St. Martin's Handbook* (Chapter 44), or another up-to-date composition textbook.

BOOK BY ONE AUTHOR

Oster, Judith. *Toward Robert Frost: The Reader and the Poet.* Athens: University of Georgia Press, 1992.

BOOK BY TWO AUTHORS

Brooks, Cleanth, and Robert Penn Warren. *Understanding Poetry.* 3rd ed. New York: Holt, Rinehart and Winston, 1960.

ESSAY IN A BOOK

Ross, Haj. "Robert Frost's 'Out, Out—': A Way In." *Crossing the Boundaries in Linguistics: Studies Presented to Manfred Bierwisch.* Ed. Wolfgang Klein and Willem Levelt. Dordrecht: Reidel, 1981. 265–82.

ARTICLE IN A SCHOLARLY JOURNAL (PAGINATED CONTINUOUSLY THROUGH THE YEAR)

Abel, Darel. " 'Unfriendly Nature' in the Poetry of Robert Frost." *Colby Library Quarterly* 17 (1981): 201–10.

ARTICLE IN A POPULAR MAGAZINE (EACH ISSUE PAGINATED SEPARATELY)

Howe, Irving. "Robert Frost: A Momentary Stay." *New Republic* 23 Mar. 1963: 23–28.

REPRINT OF AN ARTICLE IN A COLLECTION

Montgomery, Marion. "Robert Frost and His Use of Barriers: Man vs. Nature Toward God." *The South Atlantic Quarterly* 57 (1958): 339–53. Rpt. in *Robert Frost: A Collection of Critical Essays.* Ed. James M. Cox. Englewood Cliffs: Prentice-Hall, 1962. 138–58.

Parenthetical references in the text of the paper to items in the bibliography complete the system. After a quotation or a sentence using facts or ideas drawn from a specific source (wherever you would put a footnote), insert in parentheses the last name of the author and the page(s) being used—for example (Howe 25), or (Montgomery 152). If your bibliography includes two items by Irving Howe, the parenthetical citations will need a shortened title as well: (Howe, "Robert Frost" 25).

Here is a short research paper on " 'Out, Out—' ":

English 245
Professor Ridl
1 April 1993

Mountains and Meanings in Frost's " 'Out, Out--' "

How should one look upon those mountains? The
"five mountain ranges" in Robert Frost's " 'Out,
Out--,' " "one behind the other / Under the sunset
far into Vermont," have become central to an
interpretive debate about the poem. Two broad
views of the poem have emerged, one stressing the
importance of the mountains, the other not.
Neither side, however, has taken into account a
rarely mentioned biblical allusion[1] which can serve
as a bridge between the two interpretive camps.

In one view, the theme of the poem is the
"senselessness of the boy's accidental death"
(Marcus 79). Early readings of the poem stress in
it "the pathos and horror of the unreasonable and
unpredictable end that at any moment may come to
life" (Brooks and Warren 28) and "the ironic
symbolism of life unexpectedly and tragically
snuffed out like a candle" (Thompson 117).
Laurence Perrine expressed this position most
fully: Frost's "theme is the uncertainty and
unpredictability of life, which may be
accidentally ended at any moment, and the tragic
waste of human potentiality which takes place when
such premature deaths occur" (Perrine 108). There
is broad consensus that " 'Out, Out--' " is "by any
standards one of

[1] The only reference in print is by Rosendorff
and Freedman, who suggest that the allusion to
Psalm 121 is part of a pattern which establishes
the boy as a Christ figure.

Outline of the paper and indication of its central point

Parenthetical references give the author's name and the page on which the quoted words can be found

Quotations blended into the flow of the sentences

A quotation introduced more formally, using a colon

Footnote supplying pertinent information that did not fit in the body of the paper

Frost's grimmer poems" (Pritchard 154). None of these readings calls special attention to the mountains.

This approach was challenged in a response which found the mountains to be of great significance. Weldon Thornton argued that the poem, rather than illustrating the unpredictability of life, is in fact "a psychological drama played out between the boy and his family." Thornton said that the lines "And from there those that lifted eyes could count / Five mountain ranges" (4-5) differentiate the young and sensitive boy, forced to work unreasonably long hours rather than enjoy the beauty and freshness of nature, from his well-meaning but insensitive parents who find nothing in the mountains to tempt them. William S. Doxey supports Thornton's reading by noting that the jagged-tooth points of the mountains reflect the teeth of the saw: longing for the unattainable mountains, the boy "gives" his hand to the saw as a manifestation of his desire to escape the restraints placed upon him. And William J. Kelly completes their readings by arguing that the personification (or "animating," since it is given animal-like, not human, attributes) of the saw is crucial because it represents the danger of prematurely imposed responsibility from which the boy wishes to escape.

Transition to a contrasting way the poem has been approached

Perhaps the mountains do direct us toward a parent vs. child, dullness vs. sensitivity, responsibility vs. escape conflict within the poem; but they also direct us to the broader theme emphasized by Brooks and Warren and by Perrine. Frost, we are told, was "soaked in the King James version" of the Bible (Reichert 421). In that case, the phrase "lifted eyes . . . mountain ranges" might

Transition to the paper's central point, as it modifies and adds to previous readings

--2--

be not just an intertextual echoing, but a deliberate allusion to the opening lines of Psalm 121: "I will lift up mine eyes unto the hills, from whence cometh my help. My help cometh from the Lord, which made heaven and earth." The Psalmist conveys to his readers "the calm and comforting assurance of an unshaken trust" (Weiser 745). If the critics summmarized above are correct that the boy did desire to look up, it might be not only to appreciate the beauty of the mountains, but also from a sense of confidence in the Lord who made them.

In this poem's context, such confidence is deeply ironic. The boy is about to lose his hand, and then his life, through a complex but ultimately incomprehensible event. But according to the verses which follow in the Psalm, "He [God] will not suffer thy foot to be moved: he that keepeth thee will not slumber. . . . The Lord shall preserve thee from all evil . . . even for evermore." The God of the poem seems very different from that of the Psalmist. The unbiblical tone of Frost's biblical allusion provides powerful confirmation of the world-view Howard Mumford Jones finds in Frost, that "the universe is indifferent to man's fate . . . [and] it does no good to complain of cruelty and catastrophe" (Jones 140). It reinforces the Shakespearean allusion in the title, with Macbeth's sense of the brevity and insignificance of life.

The readings of Thornton, Doxey, and Kelly are not, as they contend, incompatible with those of Brooks and Warren or Perrine. If the poem contains psychological drama, it also stands as a scene in a cosmic drama. The limitations or mistakes of well-meaning parents and the subconscious conflicts of a dissatisfied boy take on fuller significance if they are seen

Summary and conclusion

--3--

within an overarching view of the tenuousness of human existence and the inscrutability of fate.

Works Cited

Brooks, Cleanth, Jr., and Robert Penn Warren. Understanding Poetry: An Anthology for College Students. New York: Henry Holt and Company, 1938.

Doxey, William S. "Frost's 'Out, Out--,'" The Explicator 29.8 (1971): item 70.

Jones, Howard Mumford. "The Cosmic Loneliness of Robert Frost." Belief and Disbelief in American Literature. Chicago: University of Chicago Press, 1967. 116-42.

Kelly, William J. "Frost's 'Out, Out--.' " The Explicator 38.3 (1980): 12-13.

Marcus, Mordecai. The Poems of Robert Frost: An Explication. Boston: G. K. Hall, 1991.

Perrine, Laurence. Sound and Sense. New York: Harcourt Brace, 1956.

Pritchard, William H. Frost: A Literary Life Reconsidered. New York: Oxford University Press, 1984.

Reichert, Victor E. "The Faith of Robert Frost." Frost: Centennial Essays. Jackson: University Press of Mississippi, 1973. 415-26.

Rosendorff, Valerie, and William Freedman. "Frost's 'Out, Out . . .,' " The Explicator 39.1 (1980): 10-11.

Thompson, Lawrance. Fire and Ice: The Art and Thought of Robert Frost. New York: Henry Holt and Company, 1942.

Thornton, Weldon. "Frost's 'OUT, OUT--.' " The Explicator 25.9 (1967): item 71.

Weiser, Artur. The Psalms. Philadelphia: Westminster Press, 1962.

--4--

APPENDIX C
Genre

Genre refers to the "kind" or "type" of a poem. In one sense, genre differentiates broad categories of form from one another, like drama, epic, lyric, novel, and short story. But in another sense those genres get divided into more specialized categories (drama is divided into comedy, tragedy, and tragicomedy, for example). Poetry, too, is subdivided into many genres.

Genre implies that groups of formal or technical characteristics exist among works of the same "kind" regardless of time or place of composition, author, or subject matter. Until about two hundred years ago, there was a tendency to assume that literary "kinds" had an ideal existence and obeyed "laws of kind," those laws being the criteria by which works could be judged. Poets, before the 1800s, as they prepared to write a poem, either began by deciding what kind of poem it would be, or saw its kind emerging as they worked on it. Poems were not only individual works but works of a traditional type—a sonnet, a litany, a chant, or an elegy. Because each type had a long history behind it, the poet felt she or he was entering that tradition—either taking part in it, continuing it, or extending it. Each type had features and characteristics that inspired, challenged, focused, and guided the poet's planning and imagination. Readers knew those poetic types, knew what features and characteristics to look for, and so were confidently expectant about the kind of experience they were entering.

Poetic types were arranged in a hierarchy, from those regarded as least important and respected, to most important—epigram, ballad, pastoral, lyric, elegy, ode, epic. The most important poetic genres are defined below, with titles of examples in this book:

>**epigram:** originally an inscription, especially an epitaph; in modern usage a short poem, usually polished and witty, with a surprising twist at the end. (For examples, see J. V. Cunningham, "Here Lies My Wife," p. 158, and Alexander Pope, "Epigram. Engraved on the Collar of a Dog Which I Gave to His Royal Highness," p. 306.)
>
>**ballad:** a poem that tells a story and was meant to be recited or sung; originally a folk art, transmitted orally from person to person and gener-

ation to generation. (See "Lord Randal" and "Sir Patrick Spens," pp. 295 and 296.)

pastoral: a poem (also called an eclogue, a bucolic, or an idyll) that expresses a city poet's nostalgic image of the simple, peaceful life of shepherds and other country folk in an idealized natural setting. (See Christopher Marlowe, "The Passionate Shepherd to His Love," p. 299.)

lyric: originally, a poem sung to the accompaniment of a lyre; now a short poem expressing the personal emotion and ideas of a single speaker. (See Ch. 1, pp. 13 and 16.)

elegy: in Greek and Roman literature, a serious, meditative poem written in "elegiac meter" (alternating hexameter and pentameter lines); since the 1600s usually a formal lament for the death of a particular person. (Famous examples include Milton's "Lycidas" and Tennyson's *In Memoriam*; in this book, see Walt Whitman's "When Lilacs Last in the Dooryard Bloomed," p. 133, and Geoffrey Hill's "In Memory of Jane Fraser," p. 387.)

ode: a long lyric poem, serious (often intellectual) in tone, elevated and dignified in style, dealing with a single theme. The ode is more complicated in form than other lyric poems generally. Some odes retain a formal division into strophe, antistrophe, and epode, which reflects the ode's origins in the chorus of Greek tragedy. (See Percy Bysshe Shelley, "Ode to the West Wind," p. 310; John Keats, "Ode to a Nightingale," p. 201, and "To Autumn," Ch. 4, p. 58.)

epic: a long narrative poem that celebrates the achievements of great heroes and heroines, often determining the fate of a tribe or nation, in formal language and an elevated style. (Examples include Homer's *Iliad* and *Odyssey*, Virgil's *Aeneid*, and John Milton's *Paradise Lost*.)

Around 1800, questions about the adequacy and value of genre distinctions began to arise. Reservations about genre have continued since then. The New Critics put very little emphasis on genre because their attention remains closely focused on individual poems, not on the groups or traditions poems fit into. Postmodern literary theories do not focus on genre because of genre study's emphasis on universal categories and criteria. Poets are still fascinated by traditional types, but readers do not come to twentieth-century poems with assured expectations, because the idea of shared intention is no longer as prevalent as it was in the past. To add to your ways of responding sympathetically to traditional poems, however, it can help to learn something about the traditions and to notice if and how a poem you are looking at relates to its tradition.

APPENDIX D

More on Scansion

In order to provide some further practice on scansion and appreciation of its value without overloading Chapter 9, we decided to offer an additional discussion in this appendix. It deals with a famous passage from Shakespeare's tragedy *Macbeth* (Act 5, scene 5, lines 19–28), the passage Robert Frost alluded to in the title of "'Out, Out—.'" It appears when Macbeth is near the end of his life. His evil deeds have been found out, his opponents are closing in on his castle, and he has been told that his wife has just committed suicide. Full of grief and despair, Macbeth utters a bleak assessment of human existence. Read the passage, then scan it yourself before looking at the way we did it:

> Tomorrow, and tomorrow, and tomorrow
> Creeps in this petty pace from day to day
> To the last syllable of recorded time,
> And all our yesterdays have lighted fools
> The way to dusty death. Out, out, brief candle!   5
> Life's but a walking shadow, a poor player
> That struts and frets his hour upon the stage
> And then is heard no more. It is a tale
> Told by an idiot, full of sound and fury,
> Signifying nothing.   10

Here is the way we would scan the lines, but it is important to realize that this is not *the one, correct* way to scan them. Differences in pronunciation and interpretation can lead to entirely acceptable differences in scansion of a poem. (Acceptable differences do not include mispronunciations—you may need to look up pronunciations, as well as definitions, of unfamiliar words in order to be fair both to the sound and to the meaning of a poem.)

> Tŏmór|rŏw, ańd | tŏmór|rŏw, ańd | tŏmór|rŏw
> Créeps ĭn | thĭs pét|tў páce | frŏm dáy | tŏ dáy
> Tŏ thĕ lást | sýllă|blĕ óf | rĕcórd|ĕd tíme,
> Ańd áll | oŭr yés|tĕrdáys | hăvĕ líght|ĕd fóols

Th̃e wáy | tŏ dúst|ў̆ deáth. | Oút, oút, | bríef cán|dl̃e!   5
Lífe's bŭt ă | wálkiñg | sh̃adŏw, | ă póor | pláyĕr
Th̃at strúts | añd fréts | h̃is hóur | ŭpón | th̃e stáge
Añd thén | iš heárd | nŏ móre. | Iĭ iś | ă tále
Tóld bў̆ ăn | ídĭoĭ, | fúll ŏf | soúnd añd | fúrў̆,
Śigñi|[fyiñg | nóthiñg.   10

The passage, like much of the poetry in Shakespeare's plays, is written in blank verse (unrhymed iambic pentameter). The first line is regular, except for the extra unstressed syllable at the end. That syllable, together with the two caesuras and the time it takes to say each of the "tomorrow"s, lengthens the line, and slows it down, so that rhythmically it creeps, the way Macbeth says life does. Stressing "and" twice adds to the sense of circularity and monotony Macbeth finds in life. The second line begins with one of the most common metric substitutions, an initial trochee instead of an iamb, which puts extra emphasis on the key word "creeps." That the rest of the line is regular echoes the steady, plodding pace by which life proceeds, and it sets up the irregular, unexpected anapest and trochee of the first half of line 3—to think of the very end, the final millisecond, of history (recorded time) is jolting, and the meter jolts us as well. After two irregular lines the expected, regular iambics return for the rest of line 3, all of line 4, and half of line 5, again suiting the steady, plodding pace by which Macbeth says people follow one another through life toward death, the past like a lantern lighting the way as people foolishly imitate what those before them have done.

    The rest of line 5 is irregular: two spondees and an extra unstressed syllable: "Oút, oút | bríef cán|dl̃e!" Although life may seem to plod, it is short; and Macbeth expresses the wish that his would end. The double stresses of the spondees, emphasized by the caesuras that make one linger, give strength to the words "Out, out," and another spondee plus the extra syllable and definite end stop make us dwell on "brief candle!" The rhythm, which had been slow but steady, becomes broken and forceful here and in the following line. Line 6 also is highly irregular and unusual—first a dactyl and two trochees, an unusual metrical combination, difficult to enunciate, just as its thought (that there is no reality, that life is empty and meaningless) is difficult for most people to accept. The rest of the line is made up of an iamb and a trochee. These too are difficult to say, because of the adjoining stressed syllables, and surprising, because a trochaic substitution at the end of a line is rare. That slow, contorted line, rhythmically, leads into a line and a half that are metrically regular, reestablishing the expected meter, and with its mostly monosyllabic words, full of stops and fricatives, seems almost drumlike, booming its assertions about the brevity and unreality of people's stage-play lives: "That STRUTS and FRETS his HOUR upON the STAGE / And THEN is HEARD no MORE."

    After the full-stop caesura, the iambs continue for two feet but the drum disappears with the lightly stressed "is." But these quieter, softer lines ("Iĭ iś | ă tále / Tóld bў̆ ăn | ídĭoĭ, | fúll ŏf | soúnd añd | fúrў̆, / Śigñi|fyiñg | nóthiñg") are perhaps even more intense than those before them, as they describe life as having no more shape and significance than the babblings of an insane person. The meter in lines 9 and 10—two dactyls and six trochees—is madly unusual, and amazingly effective. Emphasis on "tale / Told" is heightened by stressing both and linking them by alliteration. The two dactyls, "Told by an idiot," can only be read slowly, with difficulty, which places unmissable emphasis on "idiot." The dactyls and the six trochees following illustrate the anticlimactic potential of "falling meter," as with each foot we seem to sink lower than the one before. The length of the ninth line, with its two extra syllables, makes an idiot's tale seem not only chaotic but also almost endless. The unifying sounds of the last six feet (the alliteration and assonance linking "full" and "fury," the alliteration linking "sound" and "signifying") make them forceful; the rhythm, steady in line 9, becomes less steady in line 10 (the stress on "fy" is so light that one may hear "signifying") and almost fades away (to "nothing"). When you are watching *Macbeth*, you probably do not think about the fact that much of it is poetry and can be discussed for its figures, sounds, meter, and rhythm like the short poems we have been examining throughout this book. Even though you are not thinking about or realizing the presence of the poetry, however, it contributes in an important way to the intensity and emotional power of the play.

Biographical Sketches

This section provides brief biographical sketches of poets included in this book. The sketches are not intended to provide sufficient detail for doing the sort of biographical criticism described in Chapter 11; for such information, you should go to the library and consult the *Dictionary of Literary Biography*, *Contemporary Poets*, or one of the other sources listed in Appendix A. These sketches are intended to situate authors in a way that will let you begin to understand the historical, social, and cultural context from which they wrote.

Dannie Abse (b. 1923), born in Wales of Welsh-Jewish ancestry, has combined his poetry writing with a career as a practicing physician in London. In the 1950s, Abse led a movement toward sentiment, sympathy, and strong emotion in poetry at a time when the literary establishment valued the opposite qualities.

Ai (b. 1947) is of Native American, African, and Asian descent. She earned a B.A. in Oriental studies from the University of Arizona and an M.F.A. from the University of California at Irvine. Ai has taught at Wayne State University, George Mason University, and the University of Kentucky.

Agha Ahahid Ali (b. 1949) was originally from Kashmir. He has taught at the University of Massachusetts. In addition to publishing his own poetry, Ali has translated a selection of poems by the Urdu poet Faiz Ahmed Faiz and written a critical study, *T. S. Eliot as Editor*.

Alta (b. 1942) has published more than a dozen volumes of poetry and stories. In 1969 she founded Shameless Hussy Press, the first feminist publishing house in the United States. She recently founded Dancing Cane Productions, a video production company.

A. R. Ammons (b. 1926) was born in Whiteville, North Carolina. He earned a B.S. degree at Wake Forest College—though he was already writing poems—and later attended the University of California at Berkeley. After serving as a high school principal and an executive in industry, he taught at Cornell University.

Tom Andrews (b. 1961) was born and grew up in West Virginia. He graduated from Hope College and earned his M.F.A. at the University of Virginia. He has published three books of poems and edited collections of essays on William Stafford and Charles Wright. Currently, he teaches at Purdue University.

Matthew Arnold (1822–1888) was born in the small English village of Laleham, and raised at Rugby School, where his father was headmaster. He later attended Oxford University. In 1857, Arnold's poetry earned him the elected post of Professor of Poetry at Oxford, which he held for ten years, writing mostly literary criticism. He also worked for thirty-five years as an inspector of schools and made two lecture tours of the United States.

John Ashbery (b. 1927) grew up on a farm near Rochester, New York. He attended Harvard—

where Robert Bly, Adrienne Rich, Kenneth Koch, and Frank O'Hara were among his classmates—and then Columbia University. Ashbery studied in France for two years, and then stayed on, writing art criticism for the *International Herald Tribune, Art News,* and *Art International.* Returning to New York, he has taught, edited *Art News,* and written for *Newsweek.*

Margaret Atwood (b. 1939) was born in Ottawa and raised in parts of Ontario and Quebec. She studied at the University of Toronto, published her first book shortly afterward, and then took a master's degree at Harvard. Atwood has worked as a cashier, a waitress, a market analyst, and a teacher. She has written numerous books of poetry, short stories, novels, and criticism, and has edited an anthology of Canadian writers.

Wystan Hugh Auden (1907–1973) was born in York, England. He went to private school and then Oxford, where he began to write poetry. He supported himself by teaching and publishing, and wrote books based on his travels to Iceland, Spain, and China. He also wrote (with Chester Kallman) several librettos, including the one for Igor Stravinsky's *The Rake's Progress* (1951). He lived in the United States from 1939 until his death, and became a U.S. citizen in 1946.

Jimmy Santiago Baca (b. 1952), whose heritage is Chicano and Apache, was born in Sante Fe, New Mexico. He lived on the streets as a youth and was imprisoned for drug possession. In prison, he began reading poetry and writing—and publishing—his first poems. He lives outside Albuquerque in a hundred-year-old adobe house.

Imamu Amiri Baraka (b. 1934) was born Everett LeRoy Jones in Newark, New Jersey. He studied at Howard University, then served in the U.S. Air Force for two years. After graduate study at Columbia, he joined the underground art scene in New York. He wrote several plays, including *Dutchman* (1964) and *Slave Ship* (1967), and formed two theater groups in the Newark slums. He became increasingly involved in black politics and in relations between blacks and black Africa, and is known now by his Muslim name.

Jim Barnes (b. 1933), born in Oklahoma of Choctaw-Welsh-English heritage, worked ten years as a lumberjack. He earned a Ph.D. from the University of Arkansas and is a professor of comparative literature at Northeast Missouri State University. He has published several books of poetry and is editor of *The Chariton Review.*

Aphra Behn (1640?–1689) was born in East Kent of middle-class parents, and in her early twenties traveled to Surinam in the West Indies. When she returned to England, she married a London merchant, who died, probably of plague, the following year. In financial difficulty, Behn worked as a spy in Antwerp for King Charles II but was not paid, so she turned to writing. She first wrote plays, as well as verse, and then turned to the newly emerging genre of prose fiction, in which she is best known for *Oronoko.*

Hilaire Belloc (1870–1953) was born in France to an English mother and was educated in England, including at Balliol College, Oxford. He married an American woman from California and made his living by writing popular history, travel books, and religious, political, and social commentary. He is best known for his comic poems, collected in *The Bad Child's Book of Beasts* and *Cautionary Verses.*

Charles Bernstein (b. 1950) was born and raised in New York City, attended Harvard University, and now teaches at the State University of New York, Buffalo. He is a leading theorist of language poetry. He has published books of essays as well as more than eighteen books of his poetry.

John Berryman (1914–1972) was born John Smith in McAlester, Oklahoma. He took the name of his stepfather after his father's suicide. He attended a private school in Connecticut, Columbia College, and Clare College, Cambridge. Subsequently, he taught at Wayne State, Harvard, Princeton, and at the University of Minnesota. Berryman suffered from mental and emotional difficulties, and finally killed himself by jumping off a bridge in Minneapolis. His best-known work is the collection *The Dream Songs.*

John Betjeman (1906–1984) was the son of a successful businessman who encouraged his son's literary interests but was aghast that it might become a career. Betjeman was determined, however, and after studying at Oxford, he became a schoolteacher and a writer of travel guides and books on England. A spokesman for an old, pastoral England, he served as poet laureate of Great Britain from 1972 until his death.

Elizabeth Bishop (1911–1979), born in Worcester, Massachusetts, was raised in Nova Scotia by her grandparents after her father died and her mother was committed to an asylum. She attended Vassar College, intending to study medicine, but was encouraged by Marianne Moore to be a poet. Bishop traveled widely, then lived in Rio de Janeiro for almost twenty years. She served as Consultant in Poetry at the Library of Congress, 1949–50.*

Paul Blackburn (1926–1971) was raised by his grandmother in St. Albans, Vermont, and moved to New York City when he was 14 to live with his mother, poet Frances Frost. He attended the University of Wisconsin and wrote poetry influenced by Black Mountain poetics, Beat poetry, and other experimental movements.

William Blake (1757–1827) was born and lived in London. His only formal schooling was in art—he studied for a year at the Royal Academy and was apprenticed to an engraver. He worked as a professional engraver, doing commissions and illustrations, assisted by his wife, Catherine Boucher. Blake started writing poetry at the age of 11 and later engraved and hand-printed his own poems, in very small batches, with his own hand-colored illustrations. His early work showed a strong social conscience, and his later work turned increasingly mythic and prophetic.

Robert Bly (b. 1926) was born in Madison, Minnesota, and served in the navy during World War II. He then studied at St. Olaf's College for a year before going to Harvard. After college Bly lived in New York and in Norway, then returned to Minnesota, where he now lives in the small town of Moose Lake. He founded (with David Ray) American Writers Against the Vietnam War. In addition to his poetry, he has published a great deal of criticism and has translated widely, including works by Pablo Neruda, Rainer Maria Rilke, Tomas Tranströmer, and the 16th-century Indian Kabir.

Eavan Boland (b. 1944) was born in Dublin, Ireland, and lives there today. She is author of seven volumes of poetry and a collection of essays, and writes reviews regularly for the *Irish Times*.

Boland has taught at Trinity College, Dublin; University College, Dublin; and Bowdoin College; and has been a member of the International Writing Program at the University of Iowa.

Anne Bradstreet (1612?–1672), born in Northampton, England, was educated by tutoring and private reading, chiefly in religious writings and in the Bible. In 1628, she married Simon Bradstreet, a brilliant young Puritan educated at Cambridge. They were among the earliest settlers of the Massachusetts Bay colony, in 1630, and her father and husband were leading figures in its governance. She wrote regularly in both prose and verse throughout her busy and difficult years in Massachusetts.

Emily Brontë (1818–1848) was the fifth of six children, three of whom (Emily, Charlotte, and Anne) became famous novelists. She was brought up, like her siblings, by her aunt at Haworth Parsonage in Yorkshire, where her father was a clergyman. Emily was educated at home and spent the rest of her life there, near the wild Yorkshire moors she loved. Charlotte sent some of the sisters' poetry to be published, under pseudonyms, in 1846, but the venture was not successful and the Brontës then turned to writing novels. Emily wrote the famous *Wuthering Heights*.

Gwendolyn Brooks (b. 1917), born in Topeka, Kansas, was raised in Chicago and wrote her first poems at age seven. She began studying poetry at the Southside Community Art Center. Her second collection of poems, *Annie Allen,* published in 1949, earned the first Pulitzer Prize given to an African American poet. She served as Consultant in Poetry at the Library of Congress, 1985–86, and has worked in community programs and poetry workshops in Chicago to encourage young African-American writers.

Olga Broumas (b. 1949) was born in Hermoupolis, Greece, and emigrated to the United States in 1967. She studied at the University of Pennsylvania and the University of Oregon and has taught at the University of Oregon, the University of Idaho, and Boston University. Broumas founded the Freehand women writers' and photographers' community and now lives in Provincetown, Massachusetts.

* The first appointment of a Consultant in Poetry at the Library of Congress was made in 1937. The title was changed to Poet Laureate Consultant in Poetry in 1986. Appointments are for one year, beginning in September, and sometimes have been renewed for a second year.

Elizabeth Barrett Browning (1806–1861) was born in Durham, England, and studied with her brother's tutor. Her first book of poetry was published when she was 13, and she soon became the most famous woman poet in England. A riding accident at the age of 16 left her a semi-invalid in the house of her possessive father, who had forbidden any of his eleven children to get married. She and Robert Browning were forced to elope (she was 39 at the time) and lived in Florence, Italy, where she died fifteen years later.

Robert Browning (1812–1889) was born the son of a bank clerk in Camberwell, outside London. In 1845, when he was a struggling poet, he met Elizabeth Barrett, already well known as a poet. The two eloped the following year and lived and wrote in Italy, where Robert Browning wrote his greatest works. After Elizabeth died in 1861 Robert moved back to London and established his literary reputation through dramatic monologues.

Dennis Brutus (b. 1924) was born in Rhodesia (now Zimbabwe) and grew up in Cape Province, South Africa. He graduated from Fort Hare University College and became a teacher, but was banned both from teaching and from pursuing his university law studies because of his leadership in the campaign to exclude South Africa from Olympic competition as long as South Africa practiced apartheid in sports. Brutus was arrested and sentenced to eighteen months of hard labor; his *Letters to Martha* are poems about his experiences as a prisoner on Robben Island.

Charles Bukowski (1920–1994), born in Andernach, Germany, came to the United States at age three and lived in Los Angeles, working there for many years in the U.S. Postal Service. He published numerous books of poetry, in addition to novels and short stories reminiscent of Ernest Hemingway. His poetry was influenced by the Beat movement and is very popular in Europe.

Robert Burns (1759–1796) was born in Ayrshire in southwestern Scotland and worked on four unsuccessful farms there throughout his life, beginning with his father's. As a boy, when he was not working, he read literature, theology, politics, and philosophy. Besides writing poetry, Burns also collected and edited Scottish folk songs.

Thomas Campion (1567–1620) studied law and medicine and was both a composer and a poet. He is recognized as one of the finest writers of lyric poetry in English.

Thomas Carew (1595–1640) [pronounced *Carey*] was born into a well-to-do and influential family, studied at Merton College, Oxford, and the Middle Temple, and served in various minor governmental posts. Carew did not publish a great deal of poetry, but was recognized as one of the most painstaking poetic craftsmen and acute literary critics of his age.

Lewis Carroll (1832–1898) was born Charles Lutwidge Dodgson, in Daresbury in northwest England, and went to school at Rugby, then at Christ Church College at Oxford, where he remained the rest of his life. He was a lecturer and fellow in mathematics there and published some thirty pieces on mathematics and logic. He was a bachelor and amateur photographer and loved children. Carroll's famous *Alice* books were written, under his pseudonym, for the amusement of Alice Liddell, daughter of the Master of Christ Church.

Jo Carson (b. 1946) is a prize-winning playwright and performer who lives in Johnson City, Tennessee. In addition to writing plays and poetry, she also writes books for children, short stories, and essays, and maintains an ongoing romance with the internal combustion engine.

Martin Carter (b. 1927) was born in Guyana and is a former civil servant and diplomat. He is author of some half-dozen books of poetry.

Lorna Dee Cervantes (b. 1954) was born in San Francisco and grew up in San Jose. There she studied at San Jose City College and San Jose State University. She has been a member of the Chicana Theatre Group, worked at the Centro Cultural de la Gente, and founded Mango Publications, a small press that prints books and a literary journal.

Marilyn Chin (b. 1955) was born in Hong Kong. A first-generation Chinese American, she was raised in Portland, Oregon. She has been a translator for the International Writing Program at the University of Iowa. Chin cotranslated the *Selected Poems of Ai Qing* and currently teaches at San Diego State University.

Lucille Clifton (b. 1936) was born in Depew, New York, studied at Howard University, and graduated from the State University of New York at Fredonia. She has taught at several colleges—she is currently at St. Mary's College in Maryland—and worked in the Office of Education in Washington, D.C. In addition to her poetry, Clifton has also published memoirs and many children's books.

Arthur Hugh Clough (1819–1861) [rhymes with *rough*] was a friend of Matthew Arnold and shared Arnold's struggles with religious authority and belief. Clough became a fellow at Oxford, but relinquished his post when he gave up adherence to the doctrines of the Church of England. He held various educational positions during the remainder of his life. Clough's distinctive achievements are more evident in his book-length poems than in the shorter pieces usually included in anthologies.

Wanda Coleman (b. 1946) was born and raised in the Watts district of Los Angeles. Her poetry, influenced by the work of Charles Bukowski, deals directly with the problems of poverty and race. Coleman has published several books of fiction in addition to her many books of poetry.

Mary Elizabeth Coleridge (1861–1907) was the great-great-niece of Samuel Taylor Coleridge. Her father was a lawyer with an interest in literature, who entertained such writers as Tennyson and Browning. She was exceedingly well educated and widely read, traveled extensively, and for twelve years taught literature at a college for working women. She published several successful novels as well as stories and essays, but most of her poetry was not published until the year after her death.

Samuel Taylor Coleridge (1772–1834) was born in Devonshire and sent to school in London after his father's death. He entered Jesus College, Cambridge, in 1791, but dropped out twice without a degree. Coleridge and William Wordsworth published *Lyrical Ballads* together in 1798, initiating the Romantic movement in English poetry and establishing the reputations of both poets. After 1802, Coleridge became addicted to opium, a common treatment for physical discomfort and seizures. Subsequently, he and his wife were separated, his friendship with Wordsworth broke up, and his poetic output stopped. From 1816 to his death, Coleridge lived under constant medical supervision, but still managed to publish a journal and write several plays, pieces of criticism, and philosophical and religious treatises.

Jayne Cortez (b. 1936) was born in Arizona, grew up in the Watts section of Los Angeles, and now lives in New York City. She is the author of ten books and eight recordings of poetry. Cortez often performs her poetry with her jazz group, the Firespitters.

Stephen Crane (1871–1900) was born in Newark, New Jersey, and attended Lafayette College and Syracuse University. He then worked as a freelance journalist in New York City, where he published an admired collection of free-verse poems. As a reporter he covered the Spanish-American and Greco-Turkish wars. Crane's second and most famous novel, *The Red Badge of Courage,* was a resounding success.

Robert Creeley (b. 1926) was born in Arlington, Massachusetts, and attended Harvard but left without a degree. He then lived in France and Spain before joining the faculty of Black Mountain College in 1954. Creeley founded the *Black Mountain Review* and exerted considerable influence on Black Mountain poetics. A faculty member of the State University of New York at Buffalo, he was named poet laureate of New York in 1992.

Victor Hernández Cruz (b. 1949) was born in Puerto Rico and moved to the Lower East Side of New York when he was 6. He dropped out of high school in his senior year and founded the Last Harlem Gut Theatre. He published his first book of poems at the age of 19. Cruz now lives in both San Diego and Puerto Rico.

Countee Cullen (1903–1946), born the son of a Methodist minister in New York City, studied at New York University and Harvard. He was assistant editor of the black journal *Opportunity,* spent a year in Paris, and then worked as a teacher in the New York school system. His poetry was part of the Harlem Renaissance of the 1920s. Cullen also published an anthology of black poetry, *Caroling Dusk,* in 1927.

e. e. cummings (1894–1962) was born in Cambridge, Massachusetts, where his father was a Unitarian minister and a sociology lecturer at Harvard. Cummings graduated from Harvard and then served as an ambulance driver during World War I. *The Enormous Room* (1922) is an account of his confinement in a French prison camp during the war. Remaining in Paris after the war, he painted and wrote, publishing his first books of poetry in 1923. He traveled to Russia in the 1930s and died in Conway, New Hampshire, in 1962.

J. V. Cunningham (1911–1985), of Irish Catholic background, was born in Cumberland, Maryland, and raised in Montana and Denver. After attending Jesuit schools he studied at Stanford, earning a B.A., M.A., and Ph.D. Cunningham taught for nearly thirty years at Brandeis University. Besides poetry, he also wrote translations and critical studies.

Jim Daniels (b. 1956) was born in Detroit, where he, his brothers, his father, and his grandfather all worked in the auto industry. He graduated with a B.A. from Alma College in Michigan and earned his M.F.A. from Bowling Green University. Daniels presently lives in Pittsburgh, where he teaches at Carnegie-Mellon University.

Keki N. Daruwalla (b. 1937) was educated in Ludhiana, a city in India, and has a master's degree in English literature. He is a police officer as well as the author of several books of poems and a collection of short stories. He won the Shaitya Akademi (Indian Academy of Letters) Award in 1984.

Kamala Das (b. 1934) was born in Kerala, India. Her mother, Balamani Amma, is a well-known Malayali poet. Das was educated at home and at a Catholic boarding school. She writes in both Malaylam (short stories) and English (poetry). In addition to her poetry, she has written an autobiography, *My Story*, published in 1975.

Sir John Denham (1615–1669) fought, though not bravely, for the king during the English civil war, and afterward was subject to fits of insanity. He lived in an inherited house in Surrey near the Thames where a nearby hill provided the view that inspired his most famous poem.

James Dickey (b. 1923) was an All-Southern halfback in high school. He studied at Clemson College and Vanderbilt in between service as a fighter pilot in both World War II and the Korean War. He worked in advertising for six years in his native Atlanta, writing ads for Coca-Cola and poems in his spare time. Dickey has written several books of poems and served from 1966 to 1968 as Consultant in Poetry at the Library of Congress. He also published two novels, one of which, *Deliverance,* was made into a successful film.

Emily Dickinson (1830–1886) was born in Amherst, Massachusetts, and lived there her entire life, rarely leaving even on trips. She briefly attended a women's seminary in Massachusetts but became homesick and left before a year was out. Dickinson never married and became reclusive later in life, forgoing even the village routines she enjoyed. She published very few poems; most were written for herself or for inclusion in her many letters. A complete edition of her poems as originally written was not published until 1955.

Stephen Dobyns (b. 1941) is a professor of English at Syracuse University and teaches in the M.F.A. program at Warren Wilson College. He is the author of some eight volumes of poetry and fifteen novels.

John Donne (1572–1631) was born in London into a wealthy Catholic family. His brother and uncle were both imprisoned for their Catholic connections, and Donne was not allowed to take a university degree, although he studied at Oxford and Cambridge. He fought with Sir Walter Raleigh in two pirating strikes against Spain. He later took orders as an Anglican priest, after which his poetry became markedly less amorous and more religious in tone. Serving as Dean of St. Paul's in London during his last ten years of life, he was a famous and popular preacher.

H. D. [Hilda Doolittle] (1886–1961) was born in Bethlehem, Pennsylvania. She went to private schools in Philadelphia and then dropped out of Bryn Mawr after a year because of ill health. She moved to England, where an old friend (and brief fiancé), Ezra Pound, encouraged her to write and sent some of her poetry to a journal. H. D. became a leader of Pound's Imagist group, but later left it. In 1933–34 she visited Freud as a patient and later wrote *Tribute to Freud* (1956). Besides poetry, she also wrote novels and translated Greek.

Mark Doty (b. 1953) is the author of four collections of poetry and a memoir. He has taught at Sarah Lawrence College, Vermont College, and Goddard. Doty now lives in Provincetown, Massachusetts.

Rita Dove (b. 1952)—see pp. 204–5.

Alan Dugan (b. 1923) was born in Brooklyn, New York. He attended Queens College in Flushing, New York; served in the U.S. Air Force during World War II; and graduated from Mexico City College. Dugan has taught at Connecticut College, Sarah Lawrence College, the University of Colorado at Boulder, and other institutions.

Robert Duncan (1919–1988) was born in Oakland, California, and attended the University of California at Berkeley for two years in the 1930s. He returned there from 1948 to 1950, after a stint in the army and as editor of two literary magazines. He met Charles Olson in 1947 and taught at Black Mountain College in 1956. Influenced by a wide variety of poets, Duncan credited a long correspondence with Denise Levertov for helping him find a new poetics—a magical, mystical blend of the experimental with the traditional.

Cornelius Eady (b. 1954) was born and raised in Rochester, New York, and attended Monroe Community College and Empire State College. He teaches and directs The Poetry Center at the State University of New York at Stony Brook.

Russell Edson (b. 1935) is essentially self-taught in writing, has had little formal schooling, and maintains a keen interest in philosophy and argument. His father created the Andy Gump cartoon, popular in newspapers in the 1940s and 1950s. Edson currently lives in Connecticut.

Thomas Stearns Eliot (1888–1965) was born and raised in St. Louis. He went to prep school in Massachusetts and then to Harvard University, where he earned a master's degree in philosophy in 1910 and started his doctoral dissertation. Eliot studied at the Sorbonne in Paris, and then at Marburg, Germany, in 1914. The war forced him to move to Oxford, where he married and abandoned philosophy for poetry. After teaching and working in a bank, he became an editor at the famous publisher Faber & Faber, as well as for the journal *Criterion*. The dominant force in English poetry for several decades, Eliot became a British citizen and a member of the Church of England in 1927. He also wrote plays, essays, and a series of poems on cats that was turned into a famous musical.

Elizabeth I (1533–1603) was queen of England from 1558 to 1603. In addition to being a skillful politician and ruler, she was well-educated and read widely. She wrote extensively, mostly speeches and translations, but also composed a few original poems in the forms and manner typical of her time.

Anita Endrezze (b. 1952) was born of Yaqui and European ancestry. A watercolorist and illustrator, she is a member of Atlatl, a Native American arts service organization. In addition to her poetry, she has published a children's novel, *The Mountain and the Guardian Spirit*, as well as other novels, short stories, and nonfiction.

Louise Erdrich (b. 1954) was born in Minnesota, of a French-Chippewa mother and German-born father, and grew up near the Turtle Mountain Reservation in North Dakota. Her grandfather was tribal chief of the reservation. She was among the first women admitted to Dartmouth College, where she began writing, and earned degrees at Dartmouth and Johns Hopkins University.

Martín Espada (b. 1957) was born in Brooklyn, New York, and has an eclectic résumé: radio journalist in Nicaragua, welfare rights paralegal, advocate for mental patients, night desk clerk in a transient hotel, attendant in a primate nursery, groundskeeper at a minor league ballpark, bindery worker in a printing plant, and bouncer in a bar. Espada presently lives in Boston, where he is a lawyer for Su Clínica, a legal services program run by Suffolk University Law School.

Gavin Ewart (b. 1916) was born in London and educated at Cambridge, and has worked as a copy editor and freelance writer.

Kenneth Fearing (1902–1961) was born and grew up in Oak Park, Illinois. He attended the University of Illinois and the University of Wisconsin, then went to New York and devoted his life to poetry, living off an allowance from his mother and from the sale of his pulp fiction. Fearing has been referred to as the "chief poet of the American Depression." He was the author of seven novels and seven books of poetry.

James Fenton (b. 1949) was born in Lincoln, England, and educated at Oxford. He has been a writer for the *New Statesman* and the *Guardian,* and has worked as theater critic for the *London Sunday Times* and book reviewer for the *London Times.*

Lawrence Ferlinghetti (b. 1919) was born in Yonkers, New York, the son of an Italian immigrant father and a Portuguese mother. He earned degrees at the University of North Carolina, Columbia University (after naval service in World War II), and the Sorbonne. He settled in San Francisco and cofounded City Lights Books. Ferlinghetti is recognized as one of the leading figures in the San Francisco Renaissance.

Francis Fike (b. 1933) was born in New York. He was educated at Duke University, Union Theological Seminary, and Stanford University, where he studied under Ivor Winters. A professor of English at Hope College, Fike is a skilled epigrammatist and has published two chapbooks of poetry.

Anne Finch, Countess of Winchilsea [Anne Kingsmill] (1661–1720) was born into an aristocratic family and went to the court of Charles II at age 23 as a maid of honor (attendant) to the Duchess of York. She married a Gentleman of the Bedchamber, but they were both forcibly retired when James II was deposed. After two years, her husband inherited a title and an estate, where they lived in the Kentish countryside. From the safety of a private country house, she bravely published a volume of her poetry, despite the mockery that she received as an aristocratic woman writer.

Carolyn Forché (b. 1950) was born in Detroit, Michigan, and attended Michigan State University, where she studied both international relations and creative writing. She has worked for Amnesty International in El Salvador and as Beirut correspondent for National Public Radio. Forché's poetry often reflects her interest in international issues. She has taught creative writing at a number of colleges and universities.

Robert Francis (1901–1987) lived most of his life in a one-room house just outside Amherst, Massachusetts. He never held a job and lived a simple, quiet life, often on a three-figure income. Besides several volumes of poetry, Francis wrote an autobiography *(The Trouble with Francis),* a novel, and criticism.

Robert Frost (1874–1963) was born in San Francisco and lived there until he was 11. When his father died, the family moved to Massachusetts, where Frost did well in school, especially in the classics. Dropping out of both Dartmouth and Harvard, he went unrecognized as a poet until 1913, when he was first published in England, where he had moved with his wife and four chil-

dren. Upon returning to the United States, he quickly achieved success with more publications, followed by teaching positions at Amherst, honorary degrees, and an invitation to recite a poem at John F. Kennedy's inauguration. He was Consultant in Poetry at the Library of Congress for 1958–59.

Alice Fulton (b. 1952) was born in Troy, New York, and lived there for twenty-five years. She has published four books of poetry. Fulton currently teaches at the University of Michigan and lives in an old farmhouse outside Ann Arbor.

Richard Garcia (b. 1941) was born in San Francisco, a first-generation American (his mother was from Mexico, his father from Puerto Rico). In addition to his poetry, he is author of a bilingual children's book, *My Aunt Otilia's Spirits.* Garcia is also poet-in-residence at Children's Hospital in Los Angeles.

Gary Gildner (b. 1938) grew up in the Midwest and has published collections of poetry, short stories, nonfiction, and novels. He has been a Fulbright scholar and currently lives in Idaho.

Allen Ginsberg (b. 1926) was born in Newark, New Jersey, and graduated, after several suspensions, from Columbia in 1948. Several years later, Ginsberg left for San Francisco to join other poets of the Beat movement. His poem "Howl," the most famous poem of the movement, was published in 1956 by Lawrence Ferlinghetti's City Lights Books; the publicity of the ensuing censorship trial brought the Beats to national attention. Ginsberg was cofounder of the Jack Kerouac School of Disembodied Poetics at the Naropa Institute in Boulder, Colorado.

Nikki Giovanni (b. 1943) was born in Knoxville, Tennessee, and returned there after spending her childhood years in Cincinnati. She received her B.A. from Fisk University and studied writing at Columbia University's School of Fine Arts. She has received wide popular acclaim as a writer (having published nearly twenty books) and as a lecturer on literature and on racial and social issues. Giovanni is a professor of English at Virginia Polytechnic Institute and State University.

Louise Glück (b. 1943) was born in New York City and educated at Sarah Lawrence College and Columbia University. She has published five collections of poetry and taught at numerous universities. Glück presently lives in Vermont.

George Gordon, Lord Byron (1788–1824) was one of the great Romantic poets, although he is best known for his lighthearted and humorous verse, such as *Don Juan*. He was born in London and raised in Scotland, then studied at Harrow and Trinity College, Cambridge. He inherited the title of Sixth Baron Byron (with estate) at age 10. The last few years of his life were spent in Italy, and he died in Greece after joining the Greek forces in their war for independence.

Jorie Graham (b. 1951) was born in New York City and grew up in France and Italy. She was educated at the Sorbonne, New York University, Columbia University, and the University of Iowa. Author of six books of poems, she is on the permanent faculty of the University of Iowa Writers' Workshop. Graham makes her home in both the United States and France.

Donald Hall (b. 1928) was born and raised in Connecticut, studied at Harvard, Oxford, and Stanford, and has taught at the University of Michigan. Besides his poetry, he has written prose memoirs, children's books, and poetry textbooks, and has worked as an editor and critic. Hall now lives on his grandfather's farm in New Hampshire.

Thomas Hardy (1840–1928) was apprenticed at age 16 to an architect and spent most of the next twenty years restoring old churches. He had always had an interest in literature and started writing novels in his 30s, publishing over a dozen. In 1896 Hardy gave up prose and turned to poetry, writing until his death at age 88. He had a consistently bleak outlook on life and spent most of his life in his native Dorset, England.

Joy Harjo (b. 1951) was born in Tulsa, Oklahoma. Her mother was of Cherokee-French descent, and her father was Creek. She moved to the Southwest and began writing poetry in her early twenties. She then earned her B.A. at the University of New Mexico and her M.F.A. from the University of Iowa Writers' Workshop. Harjo has published several volumes of poetry and is professor of English at the University of New Mexico, Albuquerque.

Michael S. Harper (b. 1938) was born in Brooklyn, New York, and grew up surrounded by jazz

music. When his family moved to Los Angeles, he worked at all kinds of jobs, from the post office to professional football. He studied at the City College of Los Angeles, California State University at Los Angeles, and the University of Iowa Writers' Workshop. Harper is presently professor of English at Brown University.

Robert Hass (b. 1941), in addition to publishing several books of his own poems, has published a book of essays, has collaborated with Czeslaw Milosz on a translation of his poems, and has published a volume of translations of and commentary on haiku. Hass was appointed Poet Laureate Consultant in Poetry at the Library of Congress for 1995–96.

Robert Hayden (1913–1980) was born in Detroit, Michigan, and graduated from Wayne State University. After working for newspapers and on other projects, he studied under W. H. Auden at the University of Michigan. Hayden taught at Fisk University in then-segregated Nashville and at the University of Michigan, publishing poems and two anthologies of African-American poetry. He served as Consultant in Poetry at the Library of Congress from 1976–78.

Seamus Heaney (b. 1939) was born in County Derry, Northern Ireland, and educated at St. Columb's College and Queen's University, Belfast. He spends part of each year at Harvard University, where he is a professor, and part at his home in Dublin.

Anthony Hecht (b. 1923) was born in New York City. He graduated from Bard College; after World War II army service in Europe and Japan, he earned an M.A. at Columbia University. Hecht has taught at a number of universities and served as Consultant in Poetry at the Library of Congress from 1982 to 1984.

Lyn Hejinian (b. 1941) was born near San Francisco and educated at Harvard University. She is one of the leading language poets. Hejinian has published several books of poetry and autobiographical writing and, more recently, translations from Russian of the works of Arkadii Dragomoschenko.

Felicia Dorothea Hemans (1793–1835) was born in Liverpool, England, and grew up in Wales. She was educated at home, reading widely in romances and poetry, and published her first volume of poems when she was 14. She married in 1812 and continued to write voluminously as she raised five sons (her husband moved to Rome in 1818 and never returned). Hemans maintained a cordial friendship with Sir Walter Scott from the early 1820s until his death in 1832.

George Herbert (1593–1633) was the fifth son of an ancient and wealthy Welsh family. He studied at Cambridge, graduating with honors, and was elected public orator of the university. He served in Parliament for two years but fell out of political favor and instead joined the church, becoming rector of Bemerton near Salisbury. Herbert was a model Anglican priest and an inspiring preacher. All of his poetry, religious in nature, was published posthumously in 1633.

Mary (Sidney) Herbert, Countess of Pembroke (1562–1621) was an important literary patron and writer of the Elizabethan period. In addition to editorial work and translations, she wrote a number of original poems. She also contributed 107 poetic renderings of psalms to a series of 150 begun by her brother Sir Philip Sidney, each in a different stanzaic and metrical pattern.

Robert Herrick (1591–1674), the son of a well-to-do London goldsmith, was apprenticed to his uncle (also a goldsmith), studied at Cambridge, and then lived in London for nine years, where he hobnobbed with a group of poets that included Ben Jonson. Under familial pressure to do something substantive, Herrick became an Anglican priest. He was given the parish of Dean Prior, Devonshire—a rural place which at first he hated—and there he quietly wrote poetry about imagined mistresses and pagan rites.

Conrad Hilberry (b. 1928) grew up in Michigan. He earned his B.A. at Oberlin College and his M.A. and Ph.D. at the University of Wisconsin and teaches at Kalamazoo College. Hilberry has published four collections of poetry and has served as poetry editor of *Passages North* and the anthology *Poems from the Third Coast*.

Geoffrey Hill (b. 1932) is a major presence in contemporary British poetry. He was born in Bromsgrove, Worcestershire, England, and attended Keble College, Oxford. He is currently a faculty member at Cambridge University.

Linda Hogan (b. 1947), a Chickasaw poet, novelist, and essayist, teaches creative writing at the University of Colorado. She is active in wildlife rehabilitation.

Garrett Kaoru Hongo (b. 1951) was born in Volcano, Hawaii, grew up on Oahu and in Los Angeles, and did graduate work in Japanese language and literature at the University of Michigan. Hongo has published several collections of poetry and is director of the creative writing program at the University of Oregon.

Gerard Manley Hopkins (1844–1889) was born in London, the eldest of eight children. His father was a ship insurer who also wrote a book of poetry. Hopkins studied at Balliol College, Oxford, and after converting to Catholicism, taught in a school in Birmingham. In 1868 he became a Jesuit and burned all of his early poetry. He then worked as a priest and teacher in working-class London, Glasgow, and Merseyside, and later as professor of classics at University College, Dublin. Hopkins published little during his lifetime; his poems were not known until his friend Robert Bridges published them in 1918.

A. E. Housman (1859–1936) was born in Fockbury, Worcestershire. A promising student at Oxford, he failed his final exams (because of emotional turmoil caused by his suppressed homosexual love for a fellow student) and spent the next ten years feverishly studying and writing scholarly articles while working as a clerk at the patent office. Housman was rewarded with the chair of Latin at University College, London, and later at Cambridge. His scholarship, like his poetry, was meticulous, impersonal in tone, and limited in output.

Susan Howe (b. 1937), born in Boston to Irish-American parents, studied painting at the Boston Museum School of Fine Arts. Her painting moved toward collage and then toward performance art, which eventually led her to poetry. She has been an actor and a stage manager at Dublin's Gate Theatre. Howe is currently professor of poetics at the State University of New York, Buffalo.

Langston Hughes (1902–1967), born in Joplin, Missouri, attended Columbia University but dropped out in 1922. Working as a busboy in a hotel in Washington, D.C., he left some poems next to the plate of poet Vachel Lindsay, who was much impressed. Hughes graduated from Lincoln University in 1929, and subsequently became one of the leading writers of the Harlem

Renaissance. Besides writing poetry, lecturing, and teaching poetry in elementary schools, Hughes wrote novels, stories, plays, songs, children's books, essays, and memoirs.

Ted Hughes (b. 1930) was born in Mytholmroyd, Yorkshire, and studied English literature, archeology, and anthropology at Cambridge. He has published many varied books of poetry and in 1984 was appointed poet laureate of England. (See also pp. 183, 190–91.)

Richard Hugo (1923–1982) grew up in Washington State. After service in World War II, he returned to the University of Washington, where he took courses in poetry from Theodore Roethke and worked for Boeing Aircraft. Hugo taught at the University of Montana, where he directed the creative writing program, and later moved to the island of Skye off northern Scotland. He is author of *The Triggering Town,* an influential collection of essays on writing poetry.

Harry Humes (b. 1935) grew up in the coal mining country of Pennsylvania and earned degrees from Bloomsburg University and the University of North Carolina. In addition to publishing eight books of poetry, he has written a book of short stories. Humes teaches at Kutztown State (Pennsylvania) and edits the poetry magazine *Yarrow.*

Randall Jarrell (1914–1965) was born in Nashville, Tennessee, and served in the air force during World War II. He studied at Vanderbilt with John Crowe Ransom and taught at many colleges and universities. From 1956 to 1958 he served as Consultant in Poetry at the Library of Congress. Besides poetry, he wrote a satirical novel, several children's books, numerous poetry reviews—collected in *Poetry and the Age* (1953)—and a translation of Goethe's *Faust.*

Robinson Jeffers (1887–1962) was born in Pittsburgh and moved with his family to southern California in 1903. After graduating from Occidental College in 1906, and studying medicine, forestry, and literature, Jeffers concentrated on poetry. In 1914 he settled in Carmel, California, where he spent the rest of his life in Tor House, the home he built with stone quarried from the Pacific beach.

Richard Jones (b. 1953) was born in London, where his father was serving in the U.S. Air Force, and studied at the University of Virginia.

He has taught at Piedmont College and the University of Virginia, and presently teaches at De Paul University in Chicago. Besides several volumes of poetry, Jones has also published two works of critical essays and has been editor of *Poetry East* since 1979.

Ben Jonson (1572–1637) was born in London, the stepson of a bricklayer (his father died before he was born). He attended Westminster School and then joined the army. Jonson later worked as an actor and as a playwright of satiric plays such as *Everyman in His Humor* (in which Shakespeare acted the lead), *Volpone,* and *The Alchemist.* He was named poet laureate and was the idol of a generation of English writers, who dubbed themselves the Sons of Ben.

James Joyce (1882–1941) was born and educated in Dublin. He left Ireland in 1904 and for the rest of his life lived in self-imposed exile in Europe, where he wrote literature largely about his Irish heritage. A major figure in modern fiction (*Dubliners, Portrait of the Artist as a Young Man, Ulysses, Finnegan's Wake*), Joyce is also known for a small body of excellent poetry.

Donald Justice (b. 1925) was born in Miami and earned degrees at Miami University, the University of North Carolina, and the University of Iowa. He was a teacher in the University of Iowa Writers' Workshop and is now poet-in-residence at the University of Florida.

Shirley Kaufman (b. 1923) grew up in Seattle, Washington, lived in San Francisco for many years, and now makes her home in Jerusalem. Kaufman has published several books of poems and several volumes of translations of Hebrew poetry.

John Keats (1795–1821)—see p. 197–98.

Jack Kerouac (1922–1969) was born in Lowell, Massachusetts, of French-Canadian descent, and attended Columbia University. He became one of the leaders of the Beat movement, writing in the improvisatory style of jazz music. Though he is best known for his novel *On the Road,* his work as a poet and his writings about poetry are also influential.

Galway Kinnell (b. 1927) was born in Providence, Rhode Island, and attended Princeton University and Rochester University. He taught in Iran for a year and has since taught at more than twenty colleges and universities. In addition to many books of poetry, he has written a novel and done translations of French writers, notably François Villon and Yves Bonnefoy.

Carolyn Kizer (b. 1925) was born and raised in Spokane, Washington. She graduated from Sarah Lawrence College, then was a Fellow of the Chinese government in comparative literature at Columbia University and lived in Nationalist China for a year. She founded the poetry journal *Poetry Northwest* in 1959 and edited it until 1965. From 1966 to 1970 Kizer served as the first director of the literature program for the newly created National Endowment for the Arts.

Etheridge Knight (1933–1991) fought in the Korean War and became addicted to heroin after returning home. He was caught stealing to support his habit and did time in Indiana State Prison, where he began writing poetry. After being released he taught poetry at several different colleges.

Kenneth Koch (b. 1925) was born in Cincinnati and, after service in World War II, educated at Harvard and Columbia University. His work is strongly influenced by European surrealistic and avant-garde traditions. In addition to his poetry, Koch has written plays, criticism, and several influential books on teaching creative writing to children, young adults, and senior citizens.

Yusef Komunyakaa (b. 1947) was born and grew up in Bogalusa, Louisiana. He earned degrees at the University of Colorado, Colorado State University, and the University of California at Irvine. He served in Vietnam as a correspondent and editor of *The Southern Cross*. Among his awards is the Thomas Forcade Award for Literature and Art Dedicated to the Healing of Viet Nam in America. Komunyakaa currently teaches at Indiana University.

Ted Kooser (b. 1939), born in Ames, Iowa, was educated at Iowa State University and the University of Nebraska and taught high school in Madrid, Iowa. He presently lives near Garland, Nebraska, where he works as a life insurance executive and occasional lecturer at the University of Nebraska. Kooser is also the publisher of Windflower Press.

Richard Kostalanetz (b. 1940) was born in New York City and studied at Brown University, at Columbia University, and at King's College, London,

on a Fulbright fellowship. He has written radio plays and short stories as well as working in electronic music and experimental TV. His career has taken him to Israel and Berlin as an artist-in-residence. Kostalanetz's work is called visual poetry, and since the 1980s he has been combining video with his poems.

Maxine Kumin (b. 1925) was born in Philadelphia and received her B.A. and M.A. at Radcliffe College. She has taught at the University of Massachusetts, Columbia University, Brandeis, and Princeton. Kumin collaborated on poems and children's books with her friend Anne Sexton. She was Consultant in Poetry at the Library of Congress for 1981–82.

Stanley Kunitz (b. 1905) was born in Worcester, Massachusetts, and earned his B.A. and M.A. at Harvard University. His first two books of poetry attracted little attention, but after service in World War II he continued to write and taught at various places, including Bennington College and Columbia University. Kunitz served as Consultant in Poetry at the Library of Congress from 1974 to 1976.

Li-Young Lee (b. 1957) was born in Jakarta, Indonesia, to Chinese parents. His father, a former physician to Mao Tse-tung, was a political prisoner under Sukarno but escaped in 1959 with his family, settling in the United States five years later. Lee studied at the University of Pittsburgh, the University of Arizona, and the State University of New York at Brockport. In addition to several books of poetry, he has published a prose memoir, *The Winged Seed*.

Denise Levertov (b. 1923) was born in Ilford, Essex. Her mother was Welsh and her father was a Russian Jew who became an Anglican priest. She was educated at home and moved to the United States after marrying the American writer Mitchell Goodman. There she turned to free-verse poetry and became involved in the antiwar movement during the Vietnam era. A member, with Robert Creeley, of the Black Mountain group in North Carolina, Levertov has also taught at Stanford and Brandeis.

Philip Levine (b. 1928) was born in Detroit and has degrees from Wayne State University and the University of Iowa. His poetry has been influenced by Spanish-American surrealist poets. Levine has had a long career as a professor at California State University, Fresno.

Larry Levis (1946–1996) grew up on a farm near Fresno, California. He received a Ph.D. in modern letters from the University of Iowa. Levis published several collections of poetry and a collection of short fiction. He taught at the University of Utah and at Virginia Commonwealth University.

Dorothy Livesay (b. 1909) studied at the University of Toronto and at the Sorbonne in Paris. She worked as a social worker in Vancouver, a reporter for the *Toronto Daily Star,* a scriptwriter for the Canadian Broadcasting Corporation, an English specialist for UNESCO in Paris, an English teacher in northern Rhodesia, an editor of literary journals, and a lecturer at Canadian universities. Livesay has written prize-winning poetry for over six decades.

Audre Lorde (1934–1992) was born in New York City to parents who had emigrated from the West Indies. She attended Hunter College and Columbia University and then worked as a librarian and teacher. Lorde published several books of poetry, two volumes of essays, and an autobiographical novel, *Zami* (1980).

Richard Lovelace (1618–1657) was born into a prominent family in Kent, England, and went to Oxford, where his dashing appearance and wit made him a social and literary favorite. He fought in the English civil war on the royalist side and was imprisoned and exiled, fought in France against the Spanish and was again imprisoned on his return to England. After his release he spent ten years in poverty and isolation before his death.

Amy Lowell (1874–1925) was born in Brookline, Massachusetts, into a prominent and wealthy New England family that included the poet James Russell Lowell and that later produced Robert Lowell. After eight years of private schools she began the life of society activities, travel, and volunteer work that was expected of her. Lowell soon turned to writing, however, and joined the Imagist group that H. D., Richard Aldington, and Ezra Pound had formed.

Robert Lowell (1917–1978) was born in Boston into the same prominent New England family as Amy Lowell, his distant cousin. He attended Harvard and then Kenyon College, where he studied under John Crowe Ransom. At Louisiana State University he studied with Robert Penn Warren and Cleanth Brooks as well as Allen Tate. Lowell's reputation was established early, and after *Life Studies* (1959) he was America's foremost "confessional" poet. Lowell served as Consultant in Poetry at the Library of Congress for 1947–48. He was always politically engaged, from World War II through the Vietnam War, and suffered from manic depression.

Mina Loy (1882–1966) was born in London, England; lived in Paris during the 1920s and was involved in the avant-garde movement; became a U.S. citizen in 1946; and lived in Aspen, Colorado, from 1953 until her death. Although she published relatively little during her lifetime, her work was praised by such poets as Yvor Winters, Ezra Pound, and T. S. Eliot and deserved to be more widely known than it was. Loy was also an artist and received recognition for her painting and her lamp shade designs.

Edward Lueders (b. 1923) was born in Chicago and studied at Hanover College, and—after three years in the air force during World War II—Northwestern University and the University of New Mexico. He taught at several colleges and universities and is professor emeritus at the University of Utah.

Mekeel McBride (b. 1950) was born in Pittsburgh and attended Mills College and Indiana University. Author of several books of poems, she has taught at Harvard University, Wheaton College, and the University of New Hampshire.

Thomas McGrath (1916–1990) was born on a North Dakota farm and educated at the University of North Dakota, Louisiana State University, and New College, Oxford, where he was a Rhodes scholar. In addition to his poetry writing, McGrath worked as a documentary film scriptwriter, teacher (at colleges and universities in Maine, California, New York, North Dakota, and Minnesota), and labor organizer.

Medbh McGuckian (b. 1950) was born in Belfast, where she lives today. She has published several books of poetry and was the first woman to be named writer-in-residence at Queen's College.

Heather McHugh (b. 1948) was born in San Diego and grew up in Virginia. She is a graduate of Radcliffe College and the University of Denver. McHugh has published several volumes of poetry as well as translations. She has taught at a number of universities and is a member of the continuing-core faculty in the Warren Wilson College M.F.A. program for writers.

Claude McKay (1890–1948), the son of poor farm workers, was born in Sunny Ville, Jamaica. By 1912 he had assembled two books of poems that won a prize, enabling him to study in the United States. In 1914 he moved to Harlem and became one of the senior members of the Harlem Renaissance. After committing to communism and traveling to Moscow in 1922, he lived for some time in Europe and Morocco, writing fiction. McKay later converted to Roman Catholicism, repudiated communism, and returned to the United States. He died in Chicago.

Archibald MacLeish (1892–1982) was born in Glencoe, Illinois, and educated at Hotchkiss School, Yale, and Harvard Law School. During World War I, he served as an ambulance driver and captain of field artillery. After the war he worked as a lawyer in Boston and then moved to France to concentrate on poetry. MacLeish became more and more involved in political life prior to World War II, writing radio plays warning about fascism and the coming war. He later taught at Harvard and Amherst College.

Jack Mapanje (b. 1944) was born in southern Malawi to Yao and Nyanja parents. He was educated at Zomba Catholic Secondary School, the University of Malawi, and the University of London. He has taught at Chancellor College, University of Malawi. Following the second reprint of his first book of poems, *Of Chameleons and Gods,* Mapanje was imprisoned by the Malawian government, without trial or formal charges, for over three and a half years. He was released in May 1991, after protests from abroad, and now lives in England.

Christopher Marlowe (1564–1593) was born in Canterbury, the son of a shoemaker. He attended, with the help of scholarships, King's School, Canterbury, and Corpus Christi College, Cambridge. He became involved in secret political missions for the government. He thereafter wrote plays, the best of which is *Doctor Faustus,* and continued his double life. He died after being knifed in a tavern fight, reportedly over his bill, at the age of 29.

Andrew Marvell (1621–1678) was born in Hull, Yorkshire, and educated at Trinity College, Cambridge. After traveling in Europe, he worked as a tutor and as a secretary to John Milton and later became a member of Parliament for Hull. Marvell was known in his lifetime as a writer of satiric verse and prose, and his "serious" poetry was not published until after his death.

William Matthews (b. 1942) was born in Cincinnati, Ohio, and is a graduate of Yale and the University of North Carolina. He has taught at several colleges and universities and was co-founder and editor of Lillabulero Press and its magazine.

James Merrill (1926–1995) was born in New York City, son of Charles Merrill, founder of Merrill Lynch. He received his B.A. from Amherst College after service in World War II interrupted his education. He published more than two dozen books of poetry.

W. S. Merwin (b. 1927) was born in New York City and lived in New Jersey and Pennsylvania during his precollege years. He studied creative writing and foreign languages at Princeton University and became a translator, living mostly in England and France until 1968, when he returned to the United States. Merwin has translated Portuguese, Latin, Greek, Japanese, Spanish, and Chinese authors. He currently lives in Hawaii and is active in environmental issues.

Charlotte Mew (1870–1928) was born in London to a middle-class family and turned to writing when her father's death left the family penniless. Although a morally strict Victorian woman, she dressed in men's clothes and wrote some surprisingly sensual poetry. Mew's work had become forgotten by the time she ended her life by drinking a bottle of Lysol.

Josephine Miles (1911–1985) was born in Chicago but lived in California after the age of five. She studied at UCLA and at the University of California, Berkeley. Miles was a scholar as well as a poet and was a professor at Berkeley for much of her life.

Edna St. Vincent Millay (1892–1950) was born in Rockland, Maine, and was encouraged to write from an early age by her mother. She attended Vassar College and spent the Roaring Twenties in Greenwich Village acting, writing plays and composing prize-winning poetry, and living a bohemian lifestyle. Millay continued to write and take an active part in political affairs for several decades thereafter, despite a diminished literary reputation.

John Milton (1608–1674), son of a well-off London businessman, was educated at St. Paul's School and at home with private tutors. After graduating with a master's from Christ's College, Cambridge, he spent the next six years reading at home. Milton had written verse since university days, but broke off to write prose tracts in favor of Oliver Cromwell, for whom he worked as secretary. The strain of long hours of reading and writing for the revolutionary cause aggravated a genetic weakness and resulted in his total blindness around 1651. He wrote his most famous works, *Paradise Lost* (1667), *Paradise Regained* (1671), and *Samson Agonistes* (1671), by dictating them to his daughter.

Gary Miranda (b. 1938) was born in Bremerton, Washington, and grew up in the Pacific Northwest. In addition to two book-length collections of poetry, he has published a translation of Rilke's *Duino Elegies*. Miranda currently works full-time at the Kaiser Permanente Center for Health Research.

Marianne Moore (1887–1972) was born near St. Louis and grew up in Carlisle, Pennsylvania. After studying at Bryn Mawr College and Carlisle Commercial College, she taught at a government Indian school in Carlisle. Moore moved to Brooklyn, New York, where she worked in a girls' school and a library and spent a good deal of time watching the Dodgers. Later she was editor of *The Dial* for four years. Moore's innovative and eccentric poetry earned her many honors.

Robert Morgan (b. 1944) grew up on a small farm near Zirconia, North Carolina. He has published eight books of poetry and two works of fiction. He is professor of English at Cornell University.

Thylias Moss (b. 1954) was born in Cleveland, Ohio. She attended Syracuse University, received her B.A. from Oberlin College, and did graduate work at the University of New Hampshire. Her poetry conveys the variety of black experience in America. Moss has held a number of teaching positions and currently is a faculty member at the University of Michigan.

Julie Moulds (Rybicki) (b. 1962) received her B.A. from Hope College and her M.F.A. from

Western Michigan University. She is author of the libretto of an operetta, based on the Russian witch Babba Yaga, which was given its first performance in March 1996.

Lisel Mueller (b. 1924) came to the United States from Germany at age 15. She earned her B.A. at the University of Evansville, Indiana, and did graduate study at Indiana University. She has published several books of poetry and several translations, including the poems of Marie Luise Kaschnitz. Mueller was also a member of the faculty of Warren Wilson College.

Paul Muldoon (b. 1951) was born in County Armagh, Northern Ireland, and was educated at St. Patrick's College, Armagh, and Queen's University, Belfast. In addition to his writing, Muldoon has worked as a radio and television producer and as a teacher, including appointments at Cambridge and the University of East Anglia.

David Mura (b. 1952), a third-generation Japanese American, was born in Great Lakes, Illinois, and graduated from Grinnell College in Iowa; he did graduate work at the University of Minnesota and Vermont College. Mura is a poet, creative nonfiction writer, critic, playwright, and performance artist.

Lorine Niedecker (1903–1970) spent all but a few brief periods of her life on Blackhawk Island near Fort Atkinson, Wisconsin. She went to Beloit College for two years, then worked as a proofreader, as a librarian, and later as a cleaning worker in a hospital. Although her life was spent away from publishers and other writers, Niedecker corresponded with Louis Zukofsky through the 1930s and published poems in the avant-garde magazine *Origin*.

John Frederick Nims (b. 1913) was born in Muskegon, Michigan, and studied at Notre Dame and at the University of Chicago, where he earned a Ph.D. in comparative literature. He has taught poetry and given workshops in poetry at numerous colleges and universities. Additionally, he was editor of *Poetry* from 1978 to 1984. Besides many books of poetry, Nims has also written a poetry textbook and edited a poetry anthology.

Naomi Shihab Nye (b. 1952) was born to a Palestinian father and an American mother. She grew up in both the United States and

Jerusalem. Nye has worked as a writer-in-the-schools throughout the United States, has written several volumes of poetry and essays, and has edited international poetry anthologies. She has been a part of three Arts America tours in the Middle East and Asia. Nye is also a singer–songwriter.

Frank O'Hara (1926–1966) was born in Baltimore and grew up in Worcester, Massachusetts. After World War II, during which he served in the navy, he studied at Harvard and at the University of Michigan. He later settled in New York City. He worked at the Museum of Modern Art and was a close follower of the New York art scene, scribbling down poems in spare moments. O'Hara was killed in 1966 when he was hit by a dune buggy on Fire Island.

Christopher Okigbo (1932–1967) was born in eastern Nigeria to a family of Igbo Catholics. He attended local Catholic schools and the Government College, Umuabia, and then studied classics at University College, Ibadan. He worked for some time as a businessman and a teacher, then as a university librarian, and later as the Nigerian representative for Cambridge University Press. During the turmoil of postindependence and the army massacre of Igbos in 1966, Okigbo joined the Biafran army in its fight for independence. He served as a major and was killed in action defending the town of Nsukka.

Sharon Olds (b. 1942) was born in San Francisco and educated at Stanford and Columbia University. She lives in New York City and teaches creative writing at New York University and at Goldwater Hospital in New York, a public facility for physically disabled persons.

Mary Oliver (b. 1935) was born in Cleveland, Ohio, and educated at Ohio State University and Vassar College. A longtime resident of Provincetown, Massachusetts, Oliver is a member of the writing staff at the Fine Arts Work Center in Provincetown.

Michael Ondaatje (b. 1943) was born in Sri Lanka and lived there until age 11. He moved to England, where he attended Dulwich College, London; then to Canada, where he attended Bishop's College, Quebec, the University of Toronto, and Queen's University, Kingston, Ontario. In 1971 Ondaatje joined the faculty at Glendon College, York University, in Toronto.

Simon J. Ortiz (b. 1941), born in Albuquerque, New Mexico, was raised in the Acoma Pueblo community. He studied at Fort Lewis College, the University of New Mexico, and the University of Iowa, where he was a part of the International Writing Program. Ortiz has taught Native American literature and creative writing at San Diego State University, Navajo Community College, Marin College, the Institute for the Arts of the American Indian, and now at the University of New Mexico.

Wilfred Owen (1893–1918) was born in Oswestry, England, and went to school at Birkenhead Institute and Shrewsbury Technical School. He studied at London University but was forced to withdraw for financial reasons, after which he went to Dunsden, Oxfordshire, as a vicar's assistant. At Dunsden, Owen grew disaffected with the church and left to teach in France. He enlisted in the army in 1915 and six months later was hospitalized in Edinburgh, where he met Siegfried Sassoon, whose war poems had just been published. Owen was sent back to the front and was killed one week before the armistice.

Michael Palmer (b. 1943) was born in New York City and studied history and comparative literature at Harvard. Since 1969 he has lived in San Francisco. He has published numerous books of poetry, often identified with the language poetry movement, and has served on the faculty of poetics at the New College of California. Palmer has also done collaborative work with choreographer Margaret Jenkins.

Dorothy Parker (1893–1967) was born Dorothy Rothschild and grew up in Manhattan, where she attended a convent school and then a school in New Jersey. She worked briefly writing advertising slogans for *Vogue* ("Brevity is the soul of lingerie"), then as drama critic for *Vanity Fair*, and then as the "Constant Reader" columnist for *The New Yorker*. She tried to commit suicide in 1923 and had two rocky marriages, but her writing was consistently successful throughout her life.

Linda (Olenik) Pastan (b. 1932) was born in New York City and educated at Brandeis University and Radcliffe. She has published many books of poetry and has lectured at the Breadloaf Writers Conference in Vermont. Pastan presently lives in Potomac, Maryland.

James A. Perkins (b. 1941) teaches English and survival skills at Westminster College in Pennsylvania. In addition to his poems, he has published a collection of short stories and critical work on Robert Penn Warren and Kenneth Fearing. Perkins has also written art criticism and has coordinated shows by artists throughout the United States.

Marge Piercy (b. 1936) was born in working-class Detroit and studied at the University of Michigan and Northwestern University. She has published eight novels and eleven books of poetry.

Sylvia Plath (1932–1963)—see pp. 184, 188–191.

Alexander Pope (1688–1744) was born in London to a successful linen merchant and spent his childhood in the country, stunted by tuberculosis of the spine (his height never exceeded four and a half feet). Pope was also limited by his Catholicism, which prevented him from going to university, voting, or holding public office. He instead turned to writing and gained considerable fame for his satire *The Rape of the Lock* and his translations of Homer. Fame also brought ridicule and vehement attacks from critics holding different political views, and Pope struck back with nasty satires of his detractors. He later wrote ethical and philosophical verse.

Ezra Pound (1885–1972) was born in Idaho but grew up outside Philadelphia and began studying at the University of Pennsylvania at the age of 16. He was fired from a teaching job at Wabash College and left for Europe, where he lived for the next few decades in Venice and London. There, Pound founded several literary movements—including the Imagists and the Vorticists—and began his major work, the *Cantos*. During World War II he did radio broadcasts from Italy in support of Mussolini, for which he was indicted for treason in the United States. Judged mentally unfit for trial, he remained in an asylum in Washington, D.C., until 1958, when the charges were dropped. Pound spent his last years in Italy.

Craig Raine (b. 1944) was born in County Durham, England, and educated at Oxford. After graduation he lectured at Oxford and did editorial work at several magazines. In 1981 Raine became poetry editor at Faber & Faber Ltd.

George Ralph (b. 1934) was born in New Haven, Connecticut, grew up in New Jersey and Ohio, and attended Stanford University, Union Theological Seminary, Northwestern University, and Michigan State University. He is professor of theater at Hope College. Ralph has won numerous awards, in the United States and Japan, for his haiku and tankas.

Dudley Randall (b. 1914) was born in Washington, D.C., and has lived most of his life in Detroit. He worked for the Ford Motor Company and then for the U.S. Postal Service, and served in the South Pacific during World War II. He graduated from Wayne State University in Detroit in 1949 and then from the library school at the University of Michigan. In 1965 Randall established the Broadside Press, one of the most important publishers of modern black poetry. He has been poet-in-residence at the University of Detroit and has taught at the University of Michigan.

John Crowe Ransom (1888–1974) was born in Pulaski, Tennessee, the son of a southern preacher. He studied at Vanderbilt and then at Christ Church College, Oxford, on a Rhodes scholarship. He was a lieutenant in World War II and then taught at Vanderbilt, where he was a leader of the agrarian movement. Ransom later taught at Kenyon College and edited the *Kenyon Review*. Besides poetry, he also wrote criticism.

David Ray (b. 1932) was born in Sapulpa, Oklahoma, and earned his B.A. and M.A. from the University of Chicago. In addition to several volumes of poetry, he has published fiction and literary criticism and is presently completing a memoir. Ray has retired from a long teaching career to Tucson, Arizona, in order to write full-time.

Henry Reed (1914–1986) was born in Birmingham, Warwickshire, England, and was educated at the University of Birmingham, where his circle of friends included W. H. Auden and Louis MacNiece. His service in the British Army during World War II provided the basis for his famous *Lessons of the War* (three related poems, of which "Naming of Parts" is the first). In addition to his one early volume of poetry, Reed is well known in Britain for his many radio plays; he has also published translations and a book on the novel.

Adrienne Rich (b. 1929) was born in Baltimore, the elder daughter of a forceful Jewish intellectual who encouraged and critiqued her writing. While she was at Radcliffe College in 1951, W. H. Auden selected her book *A Change of World* for the Yale Younger Poets Award. She became involved in radical politics, especially in the opposition to the Vietnam War, and taught inner-city minority youth. She had felt a tension as she modeled her early poetry on male writers, and in the 1970s Rich became a feminist, freeing herself from her old models and becoming an influential figure in contemporary American literature. She currently lives in California and teaches at Stanford University.

Alberto Ríos (b. 1952) grew up in Nogales, Arizona, and earned two B.A.s—in English and psychology—and an M.F.A. at the University of Arizona. In addition to his books of poetry, he has published a collection of short stories. Ríos currently teaches creative writing at Arizona State University.

Edwin Arlington Robinson (1869–1935) was born in Head Tide, Maine, and grew up, and later set much of his poetry, in the equally provincial Maine town of Gardiner. After spending two years at Harvard, he worked on the New York subway while trying to get his poetry noticed. President Theodore Roosevelt noticed it and managed to get Robinson a sinecure job in the New York Custom House, which gave him time to write.

Theodore Roethke (1908–1963) was grandson of the chief forester to Bismarck in Prussia, and the son of a commercial greenhouse-operator in Saginaw, Michigan. Roethke graduated from the University of Michigan, studied at Harvard, and then taught at various places, finally at the University of Washington, where he gained a reputation as an exceptional teacher of poetry writing.

Wendy Rose (b. 1948), of Hopi and Miwok ancestry, is author of ten volumes of poetry and has taught American Indian studies at Berkeley and California State University, Fresno. Rose has also been coordinator of American Indian studies at Fresno City College.

Christina Rossetti (1830–1894), born in London into a literary family (her brother Dante Gabriel Rossetti was one of the Pre-Raphaelite group), began writing poetry at an early age. Ill health saved her from a career as a governess; instead she nursed her ailing father and worked at the St. Mary Magdalen Home for Fallen Women. Rossetti had a strong Anglican religiosity that led her to give up theater and opera and turn down two offers of marriage. She wrote six collections of poetry, including *Goblin Market*, as well as short stories, nursery rhymes, and religious essays.

Jerome Rothenberg (b. 1931) was born in New York City into a Polish-Jewish family and earned his degrees at City College of New York and the University of Michigan. He has been a leader in the study of "ethnopoetics," which examines the ethnic particularity of poetry. Rothenberg has pursued this interest through translating poetry from several languages, editing anthologies and journals, and incorporating elements from other cultures into his own poetry.

Mary Ruefle (b. 1952) grew up as a member of a military service family. She has published five collections of poetry and lives in Shaftsbury, Vermont.

Muriel Rukeyser (1913–1980) was born in New York and attended Vassar College, Harvard, and Columbia University. At Columbia she began publishing her poetry and involving herself in political activism, two vocations that she would continue to combine for the rest of her life. Rukeyser was a very influential poet for a new generation of women writers.

Vern Rutsala (b. 1934) was born in McCall, Idaho, and educated at Reed College and the University of Iowa. Author of a dozen books of poetry, he was for many years a professor of English at Lewis and Clark College.

Carl Sandburg (1878–1967) was born in Galesburg, Illinois, to Swedish emigrant working-class parents. He left school after the eighth grade; he entered college later, and did well as a writer, but did not take a degree. He traveled and worked at a variety of jobs, mostly in journalism, until he was able to support himself from his writing and lecturing (on Abraham Lincoln and his wife, Mary Todd Lincoln, as well as on poetry). Sandburg gave American poetry a needed direction and intensity through his hard-hitting, energetic, often politicized verse, more notable for its content than for its craft.

Cheryl Savageau (b. 1950) was born of Abenaki and French-Canadian ancestry. Author of several books of poetry, she lives in Worcester, Massachusetts, where for many years she has worked as a storyteller and writer-in-residence in Massachusetts schools. Savageau teaches at Holy Cross College and Clark University.

Anne Sexton (1928–1974) was born in Newton, Massachusetts, and dropped out of Garland Junior College to get married. After suffering a nervous breakdown as a housewife in Boston, she was encouraged to enroll in writing programs. Studying under Robert Lowell at Boston University, she was a fellow student of Sylvia Plath. Sexton's emotional problems continued, along with a growing addiction to alcohol and sedatives, and she committed suicide in 1974. In addition to her poetry, she wrote three children's books with Maxine Kumin.

William Shakespeare (1564–1616) was born in Stratford-upon-Avon, where his father was a glovemaker and bailiff, and he presumably went to grammar school there. He married Anne Hathaway in 1582, and sometime before 1592 he left for London to work as a playwright and actor. Shakespeare joined The Lord Chamberlain's Men (later the King's Men), an acting company for which he wrote thirty-five plays, before retiring to Stratford around 1612. Besides his plays, he also wrote 150 sonnets, probably in the 1590s, though they were not published until 1609.

Percy Bysshe Shelley (1792–1822) was expelled from Oxford in 1811 for writing a defense of atheism. His first wife, who was 16 (he 19), killed herself when he left her. He then married Mary Wollstonecraft (who wrote *Frankenstein*). Shelley wrote most of his best poems in Italy shortly before he died in a shipwreck.

Sir Philip Sidney (1554–1586), a well-rounded courtier in Elizabethan England—soldier, writer, patron, diplomat—was the author of a very important work of prose fiction (*The Arcadia*), a landmark essay in literary criticism (*The Defense of Poesy*), and a memorable sonnet cycle (*Astrophil and Stella*).

Leslie Marmon Silko (b. 1948) was born in Albuquerque of mixed Pueblo, Mexican, and white ancestry and grew up on a Laguna Pueblo reservation in New Mexico. She has written poetry, a collection of short prose pieces (*Storyteller*, 1981), and novels, including *Ceremony* (1977).

Charles Simic (b. 1938) was born in Belgrade and raised in Paris, Chicago, and New York City. He attended the University of Chicago and New York University, spent time in the army, and worked at various jobs. Simic has taught at the University of New Hampshire since 1974 and has published numerous volumes of poetry as well as translations of French, Russian, and Yugoslav poetry.

Edith Sitwell (1887–1964) was born into an aristocratic and literary family in late-Victorian England. Influenced by Baudelaire and the symbolists, T. S. Eliot's poetry, Stravinsky's music, and modern, abstract art, Sitwell introduced verbal and rhythmic innovations that contrasted sharply with then-current verse.

John Skelton (ca. 1460–1529) was the major poet of the first quarter of the sixteenth century. He was an influential figure at court and a clergyman of note. As a writer Skelton is best known for his "plain style" satires, often vituperative, written in short lines with a mixture of high and low poetic styles.

Gary Snyder (b. 1930) was born in San Francisco and grew up in Oregon and Washington. He studied anthropology at Reed College and Oriental languages at the University of California, Berkeley, where he became associated with the Beat movement; however, his poetry often deals with nature rather than the urban interests more typical of Beat poetry. Snyder is active in the environmental movement. He also spent a number of years in Japan devoting extensive study to Zen Buddhism.

Mary Ellen Solt (b. 1920) was born in Gilmore City, Iowa, and has been a pioneering theorist and poet of concrete poems. She has published half a dozen books in this style, as well as an important anthology (*Concrete Poetry: A World View*). As a critic, Solt has written about her friend William Carlos Williams.

Cathy Song (b. 1955) was born of part-Korean descent in Hawaii and lived in the small town of Wahiawa on Oahu. She left Hawaii for the East Coast, studying at Wellesley and then at Boston University. Song teaches creative writing at various mainland universities but continues to regard Hawaii as her home.

Gary Soto (b. 1952)—see p. 212.

Edmund Spenser (1552–1599), a contemporary of William Shakespeare, was the greatest nondramatic poet of his time. Best known for his romantic and national epic *The Faerie Queene*,

Spenser wrote poems of a number of other types as well, and was important as an experimenter and innovator in metrics and forms (as in his development of a special form of sonnet that bears his name).

William Stafford (1914–1995), born in Hutchinson, Kansas, studied at the University of Kansas and then at the University of Iowa. In between, he was a conscientious objector during World War II and worked in labor camps. In 1948 Stafford moved to Oregon, where he taught at Lewis and Clark College until he retired. He served as Consultant in Poetry at the Library of Congress, 1970–71, and was a very influential teacher of poetry.

Gertrude Stein (1874–1946) was born in Allegheny, Pennsylvania. After attending Radcliffe College, Harvard University, and Johns Hopkins Medical School, she moved to France in 1903 and became a central figure in the Parisian art world. She was an advocate of the avant garde; her salon became a gathering place for the "new moderns." What Henri Matisse and Pablo Picasso achieved in the visual arts, Stein attempted in her writing. Her theories were of interest to, and perhaps exerted influence on, such writers as Ernest Hemingway, F. Scott Fitzgerald, and James Joyce.

Gerald Stern (b. 1925) was born in Pittsburgh and studied at the University of Pittsburgh and Columbia University. He has taught at the Writers' Workshop at the University of Iowa. Stern came late to poetry; he was 46 when he published his first book. Since then he has published more than ten collections of poems.

Wallace Stevens (1879–1955) was born in Reading, Pennsylvania, and attended Harvard for three years. He tried journalism and then attended New York Law School, after which he worked as a legal consultant. He spent most of his life working as an executive for the Hartford Accident and Indemnity Company, spending his evenings writing some of the most imaginative and influential poetry of his time.

Mark Strand (b. 1934) was born on Prince Edward Island, Canada, and studied at Antioch College, Yale Art School, the University of Iowa, and in Italy. He has taught at the University of Iowa, Yale, Brandeis, Columbia University, the University of Brazil, and the University of Utah. He served as Poet Laureate Consultant in Poetry at the Library of Congress during the year 1990–91. In addition to poetry, Strand has published a collection of short stories and several volumes of translations.

Sekou Sundiata (b. 1948) was born and raised in Harlem. His work is deeply influenced by the music, poetry, and oral traditions of African-American culture. Sundiata teaches at the New School for Social Research.

May Swenson (1913–1989) was born in Logan, Utah, and studied at Utah State University. She worked as a reporter in Salt Lake City and then as an editor in New York City for the publisher New Directions. Swenson wrote numerous volumes of poetry, some of them directed at younger readers, as well as translations of Swedish poets.

Jonathan Swift (1667–1745) was born in Ireland of English parents and educated at Kilkenny College and Trinity College, Dublin. He worked in England for a decade as a private secretary and for another four years as a political writer, but spent the rest of his life in Ireland, as dean of St. Patrick's Cathedral in Dublin. Though best known for his satires in prose (such as *Gulliver's Travels* and "A Modest Proposal"), Swift's original ambition was to be a poet, and he wrote occasional verse throughout his life.

James Tate (b. 1943), a native of Kansas City, Missouri, studied at the University of Missouri and Kansas State College during his undergraduate years. He then earned his M.F.A. at the University of Iowa Writers' Workshop the same year (1967) that his first poetry collection, *The Lost Pilot,* was published. Tate has taught at Iowa, Berkeley, and Columbia University, and now teaches at the University of Massachusetts at Amherst.

Alfred, Lord Tennyson (1809–1892) was born in Somersby, Lincolnshire, England, and grew up there in the tense atmosphere of his bitter and alcoholic father's rectory. He went to Trinity College, Cambridge, but was forced to leave because of family and financial problems. His first poems, published in the early 1830s, received bad reviews, but his *In Memoriam,* an elegy to a Cambridge friend who died of a brain seizure, won him considerable acclaim. Sales of his poems soon allowed Lord Tennyson to buy a house in the country and live a quiet, comfortable life as a writer.

Dylan Thomas (1914–1953) was born in Swansea, Wales, and after grammar school became a journalist. He worked as a writer for the rest of his life, writing poetry, short stories, radio plays (*Under Milk Wood*), and film scripts. Thomas's work on radio and his lecture tours and poetry readings in the United States brought him fame and popularity. Alcoholism contributed to his early death in 1953.

Edward Thomas (1878–1917) was born in London and educated there and at Lincoln College, Oxford. He supported himself by writing book reviews and editing anthologies until the approach of World War I. Although he had not written poetry seriously before 1915, poems suddenly began to flow from him as he struggled with feelings about the war and about whether to enlist. Thomas entered the military and continued to write powerful war poems. He was killed in action in January 1917.

Jean Toomer (1894–1967) was born in Washington, D.C., of, according to him, mixed French, Dutch, Welsh, Negro, German, Jewish, and Indian blood. He taught for a few years in local schools in Sparta, Georgia, and published poems and stories in small magazines. Toomer's first published work, *Cane* (1923), was a central work of the Harlem Renaissance. He then experimented in communal living and studied the Russian mystic George Gurdjieff, but published very little, writing mostly for himself.

Quincy Troupe (b. 1943), was born in New York City and grew up in East St. Louis. He earned degrees from Grambling College and Los Angeles City College. He is a poet, journalist, editor, and teacher. In addition to poetry, he has published *Miles*, the autobiography of Miles Davis, and edited *James Baldwin: The Legacy*. Troupe taught creative writing for the Watts Writers' Movement from 1966 to 1968 and served as director of the Malcolm X Center in Los Angeles during the summers of 1969 and 1970. He has held a number of university appointments and now teaches at the University of California at San Diego.

Alberta Turner (b. 1919) was born in New York City, studied at Hunter College and Wellesley, and earned a Ph.D. at Ohio State. Turner began teaching at Cleveland State University in 1964 and published her first book of poems in 1971, when she departed from strict formal poetry and found a darker and freer form. She has also written several textbooks on writing poetry.

Lee Upton (b. 1953) was born in St. Johns, Michigan. She received a Ph.D. from the State University of New York at Binghamton and teaches at Lafayette College. Upton has published three collections of poetry as well as fiction and criticism.

Jean Valentine (b. 1934) was born in Chicago and raised in New York and Boston. She studied at Radcliffe under William Alfred. Valentine has taught poetry workshops at Barnard College, Swarthmore, Yale, and Hunter College and now teaches at Columbia University and Sarah Lawrence College. She lives in both the United States and Ireland.

Ellen Bryant Voigt (b. 1943) was born in Danville, Virginia, and studied at Converse College, South Carolina, and at the University of Iowa, where she earned an M.F.A. in music and literature. She has taught at Goddard College, where she founded the writing program, at M.I.T., and now at Warren Wilson College in North Carolina, where she is the director of the writing program. Voigt is a professional pianist and lives in Vermont.

Shelly Wagner (b. 1947) has worked as a social worker for foster-care children, in a home for unwed mothers, and as an interior designer. Her youngest son, Andrew, drowned in 1984. Five years later Wagner began writing the poems that resulted in her first collection, *The Andrew Poems*. She currently lives in Norfolk, Virginia.

Derek Walcott (b. 1930), born on the eastern Caribbean island of St. Lucia, moves between the African heritage of his family and the English cultural heritage of his reading and education. His early training was in painting, which like his poetry was influenced by his Methodist religious training. Walcott attended college at the University of the West Indies in Jamaica. He then moved to Trinidad, which continues to be his home although he spends much time in the United States and teaches at Boston College.

Anne Waldman (b. 1945) grew up in Greenwich Village and is associated with the bohemian poetics of the Lower East Side in New York and with "Beat poetics." She attended Bennington College. Waldman cofounded the literary magazine *Angel Hair* and for ten years directed the St. Marks Poetry Project in New York City. Waldman has been an advocate of performance poetry and oral poetics and with Allen Ginsberg is cofounder of the

Jack Kerouac School of Disembodied Poetics at the Naropa Institute in Boulder, Colorado. She now lives in both Boulder, Colorado, and New York City.

Alice Walker (b. 1944) was born in Georgia, daughter of a sharecropper. She attended Spelman College in Atlanta and Sarah Lawrence College in New York. She was active in the voter registration and welfare rights movements in the 1960s. Walker has published several volumes of poetry in addition to her numerous works of fiction (notably *The Color Purple*).

Edmund Waller (1606–1687) was born into a wealthy English family and attended Eton, Cambridge, and Lincoln's Inn. He was elected to Parliament and married a rich woman who died soon after, leaving him her money. He was later exiled for involvement in a Royalist plot. Waller's poems, first published while he was in exile, enjoyed great popularity. After the Restoration he again joined Parliament, where he remained for many years.

James Welch (b. 1940) was born in Browning, Montana. His father was a member of the Blackfoot tribe, his mother of the Gros Ventre tribe. He attended schools on the Blackfoot and Fort Belknap reservations and took a degree from the University of Montana, where he studied under Richard Hugo. Welch has written several novels as well as poetry, and has worked as a firefighter and Upward Bound counselor. He now makes his home on a farm outside Missoula, Montana.

Winifred Welles (1893–1939) was born in Norwichtown, Connecticut. In addition to writing several volumes of poetry, she was an important writer of children's literature.

Roberta Hill Whiteman (b. 1947), a member of the Oneida tribe, grew up around Oneida and Green Bay, Wisconsin. She earned a B.A. from the University of Wisconsin and an M.F.A. from the University of Montana. Her poems have appeared in many magazines and anthologies. Whiteman's first book, *Star Quilt*, was illustrated by her husband, Ernest Whiteman, an Arapaho artist.

Walt Whitman (1819–1892) was born in rural Long Island, the son of a farmer and carpenter. He attended school for only five years before he began work as an office boy. Although Whitman liked to portray himself as uncultured, he read widely in the King James Bible, Shakespeare, Homer, Dante, Aeschylus, and Sophocles. He worked for many years in the newspaper business and began writing poetry only in 1847. Whitman's use of free verse, influenced especially by music, and his wide-ranging subject matter were generally rejected in his own day but are now regarded as marking the beginning of modern American poetry.

Richard Wilbur (b. 1921) was born in New York City and grew up in rural New Jersey. He attended Amherst College and began writing poetry during World War II while fighting in Italy and France. Afterward, he studied at Harvard and then taught there and at Wellesley, Wesleyan University, and Smith. He was Poet Laureate Consultant in Poetry at the Library of Congress for 1987–88. Besides poetry Wilbur has also done translations, including celebrated versions of Molière and Racine.

Nancy Willard (b. 1936) is a Michigan native who earned her Ph.D. from the University of Michigan. After living in Oslo and Paris she now teaches at Vassar College. In addition to collections of poems and stories, Willard has written novels and more than a dozen children's books.

C. K. [Charles Kenneth] Williams (b. 1936) was born in Newark, New Jersey, and educated at Bucknell and the University of Pennsylvania. He has developed a poetry therapy program, has been a group therapist for adolescents, and has edited and written articles about both psychiatry and architecture, in addition to his many collections of poetry and translations. Williams has taught at several universities, including Columbia University, George Mason, and Princeton.

William Carlos Williams (1883–1963) was born in Rutherford, New Jersey, the son of an English emigrant and a mother of mixed Basque descent from Puerto Rico. At 14, he was sent to school in Geneva and Paris, and later went to high school in New York City. He graduated from medical school at the University of Pennsylvania, where he was friends with Ezra Pound and Hilda Doolittle. After an internship in New York, writing poems between seeing patients, Williams practiced general medicine in Rutherford (he was Allen Ginsberg's pediatrician). His first book of poems was published in 1909, and he subsequently published poems, novels, short stories, plays, criticism, and essays. Williams was a writer who exerted great influence on his own and later generations.

Ivor Winters (1900–1968) was a leader in formalist poetry and criticism. Born in Chicago, he spent his childhood in the West, but returned to Chicago for high school and a year at the University of Chicago, before moving to Santa Fe, New Mexico, to convalesce from tuberculosis. Winters began teaching at Stanford University in 1928, and remained there until his retirement in 1968.

William Wordsworth (1770–1850) was born and raised in the Lake District of England, and both his parents died by the time he was 13. He studied at Cambridge, toured Europe on foot, and lived in France for a year during the first part of the French Revolution. He returned to England, leaving behind a lover, Annette Vallon, and their daughter, Caroline, from whom he was soon cut off by war between England and France. Wordsworth met Samuel Taylor Coleridge, and in 1798 together they published *Lyrical Ballads*, the first great work of the English Romantic movement. In 1799 he and his sister moved to Grasmere, in the Lake District, where he married Mary Hutchinson, a childhood friend. In 1843 he was named poet laureate of England.

Charles Wright (b. 1935) was born in Pickwick, Tennessee, and grew up in Tennessee and North Carolina. He studied at Davidson College, served a four-year stint in Italy as a captain in the U.S. Army Intelligence Corps, and then resumed his education at the University of Iowa Writers' Workshop and at the University of Rome on a Fulbright fellowship. Wright taught at the University of California, Irvine, for almost twenty years and now teaches at the University of Virginia.

James Wright (1927–1980) grew up in Martin's Ferry, Ohio. His working-class background and the poverty he saw during the Depression stirred a sympathy for the poor and for outsiders of various sorts, which remained with him and infused the tone and content of his poetry. Wright studied under John Crowe Ransom at Kenyon College, which sent his early poetry in a formalist direction, and later under Theodore Roethke at the University of Washington.

Lady Mary Wroth (1587?–1651?), niece of Sir Philip Sidney and Mary Sidney Herbert, Countess of Pembroke, was one of the best and most prolific women writers of the English Renaissance and an important literary patron. As a poet she wrote 103 songs and sonnets that appeared in *Pamphilia to Amphilanthus*, the only known English sonnet sequence by a woman; seventy-four poems that appeared in her romance *The Countess of Montgomery's Urania*; and several other pieces.

Sir Thomas Wyatt the Elder (1503–1542) was born in Kent and educated at St. John's, Cambridge. He served Henry VIII in many capacities, including as ambassador to Spain and as a member of several missions to Italy and France. These travels introduced Wyatt to Italian writers of the High Renaissance, whose work he translated, thus introducing the sonnet form into English. He was arrested twice and charged with treason once, sent to the Tower of London, and acquitted in 1541.

John Yau (b. 1950) was born in Lynn, Massachusetts, a year after his parents emigrated from China. He was educated at Bard College and Brooklyn College, where he studied with John Ashbery. Yau currently lives in Brooklyn and writes art criticism for several magazines.

William Butler Yeats (1865–1939) was born in Dublin to an Anglo-Irish family. After abandoning art school, Yeats moved to London, where he was a member of the Theosophical Society and the Order of the Golden Dawn, two groups interested in Eastern occultism, as well as the Rhymers' Club. Back in Ireland, he became interested in Irish nationalist art, helping to found the Irish National Theatre and the famous Abbey Theatre. He again left for England but returned after the Easter Rising of 1916, refurbishing an old Norman tower at Ballylee in Galway. In 1922 Yeats became a senator of the new Irish Republic.

Al Young (b. 1939) was born in Ocean Springs, Mississippi, and lived for a decade in the South, then moved to Detroit, Michigan. He attended the University of Michigan and the University of California, Berkeley, and now lives in the San Francisco Bay area. Young has been a professional musician (guitarist and singer), disk jockey, medical photographer, and warehouseman, along with a number of other jobs, and has written poetry, fiction, essays, and filmscripts.

David Young (b. 1936) is professor of English at Oberlin College. He has published seven collections of poetry and several volumes of translations. He is coeditor of the literary magazine *Field,* of the *Field* Translation Series, and of the *Field* Contemporary Poetry Series. Young has written critical studies of Shakespeare and a book on William Butler Yeats.

Ray A. Young Bear (b. 1950) is a lifetime resident of the Mesquakie (Red Earth) Tribal Settlement near Tama, Iowa. A writer of poetry, fiction, and nonfiction, he has contributed to the study of contemporary Native American poetry for over two decades.

Paul Zimmer (b. 1934), born in Canton, Ohio, and educated at Kent State University, has founded poetry series at three university presses—Pittsburgh, Georgia, and Iowa. Zimmer has published eight book-length collections of poetry and currently lives both in Iowa City and on his farm in Wisconsin.

Louis Zukofsky (1904–1978), a lifelong friend of Ezra Pound and a ceaseless experimenter in poetry and theory, was a leading member of the "Objectivist" group, together with William Carlos Williams, Charles Reznikoff, George Oppen, and Carl Rakosi.

Acknowledgments

Dannie Abse. "Pathology of Colours." From *Collected Poems* by Dannie Abse. Copyright © 1977. Reprinted by permission of the University of Pittsburgh Press.

Ai. "Why Can't I Leave You?" From *Cruelty*. Copyright © 1973 by Ai. Reprinted by permission of Houghton Mifflin Company. All rights reserved.

Agha Shahid Ali. "I Dream it is Afternoon when I Return to Delhi." From *The Half-Inch Himalayas*. Copyright © 1987 by Agha Shahid Ali. Wesleyan University Press. Reprinted by permission of University Press of New England.

Alta. "Penus Envy." From *I Am Not A Practicing Angel*. Copyright © 1975 by Alta. Reprinted by permission of The Crossing Press, Freedom, CA 95019.

A. R. Ammons. "The City Limits." From *Collected Poems 1951–1971* by A. R. Ammons. Copyright © 1972 by A. R. Ammons. Reprinted with the permission of W.W. Norton and Company.

Tom Andrews. "The Hemophiliac's Motorcycle." Copyright © 1994 by Tom Andrews. Reprinted from *The Hemophiliac's Motorcycle* by permission of the University of Iowa Press.

John Ashbery. "One Coat of Paint." From *April Galleons* by John Ashbery. Copyright © 1984, 1985, 1986, 1987 by John Ashbery. Used by permission of Viking Penguin, a division of Penguin Books USA Inc.

Margaret Atwood. "Postcard." From *Selected Poems II: Poems Selected and New 1976–1986* by Margaret Atwood. Copyright © 1987 by Margaret Atwood. Reprinted by permission of Houghton Mifflin Company. All rights reserved. Copyright © Margaret Atwood 1990. Reprinted by permission of Oxford University Press Canada.

W. H. Auden. "As I Walked Out One Evening." From *W. H. Auden: Collected Poems* by W. H. Auden, edited by Edward Mendelson. Copyright © 1940 and renewed 1968 by W. H. Auden. Reprinted by permission of Random House, Inc. "The Quest" from *W. H. Auden: Collected Poems* by W. H. Auden, edited by Edward Mendelson. Copyright © 1941 and renewed 1969 by W. H. Auden. Reprinted by permission of Random House, Inc. "O Where Are You Going?" from *W. H. Auden: Collected Poems* by W. H. Auden, edited by Edward Mendelson. Copyright © 1934 and renewed 1962 by W. H. Auden. Reprinted by permission of Random House, Inc. "Musée des Beaux Arts," from *W. H. Auden: Collected Poems* by W. H. Auden, edited by Edward Mendelson. Copyright © 1940 and renewed 1968 by W. H. Auden. Reprinted by permission of Random House, Inc.

Jimmy Santiago Baca. "Family Ties." From *Black Mesa Poems*. Copyright © 1989 by Jimmy Santiago Baca. Reprinted by permission of New Directions Publishing Corp.

Amiri Baraka. "The New World." Copyright © 1979 by Amiri Baraka. Reprinted by permission of Sterling Lord Literistic, Inc.

Jim Barnes. "Return to La Plata, Missouri." From *The American Book of the Dead*. Copyright © 1982 by Jim Barnes. Used with the permission of the author and of the University of Illinois Press.

Hilaire Belloc. "On His Books" by Hilaire Belloc. From *Complete Verse*, Copyright © 1970. Reprinted by permission of the Peters Fraser & Dunlop Group Ltd.

Charles Bernstein. "Of Time and the Line." From *Rough Trades* (Los Angeles: Sun & Moon Press, 1991), pp. 42–43. Reprinted by permission of the publisher.

John Berryman. "Ball Poem" from *Short Poems* by John Berryman. Copyright © 1965 by John Berryman. Reprinted by permission of Farrar, Straus & Giroux, Inc. "Henry's Confession" from *The Dream Songs* by John Berryman. Copyright © 1969 by John Berryman. Reprinted by permission of Farrar, Straus and Giroux, Inc.

John Betjeman. "In Westminster Abbey." From *Collected Poems* by John Betjeman. Copyright © 1958. Reprinted by permission of John Murray (Publishers) Ltd.

Elizabeth Bishop. "Sestina." From *The Complete Poems 1927–1979* by Elizabeth Bishop. Copyright © 1979, 1983 by Alice Helen Methfessel. Reprinted by permission of Farrar, Straus & Giroux, Inc.

Paul Blackburn. "Listening to Sonny Rollins at the Five-Spot." From *The Collected Poems of Paul Blackburn*, edited by Edith Jarolim. Copyright © 1985 by Joan Blackburn. Reprinted by permission of Persea Books.

Robert Bly. "Driving to Town Late to Mail a Letter." From *Silence in the Snowy Fields*, Wesleyan University Press, 1962. Copyright 1962 by Robert Bly. Reprinted with his permission.

Eavan Boland. "The Pomegranate." From *In a Time of Violence* by Eavan Boland. Copyright © 1994 by Eavan Boland. Reprinted with the permission of W.W. Norton and Company, Inc.

Gwendolyn Brooks. "The Bean Eaters" and "We Real Cool." From *The Blacks* by Gwendolyn Brooks. Copyright © 1991 by Gwendolyn Brooks. Reprinted by permission of the author.

Olga Broumas. "Cinderella" from *Beginning with O*. Copyright © 1977 by Olga Broumas. Reprinted by permission of Yale University Press.

Dennis Brutus. "Nightsong: City." From *A Simple Lust: Selected Poems*. Copyright © 1973 by Dennis Brutus. Reprinted by permission of Hill and Wang, a division of Farrar, Straus & Giroux, Inc. and Heinemann Books (UK).

Charles Bukowski. "my old man." Copyright © 1977 by Charles Bukowski. Reprinted from *Love is a Dog from Hell: Poems 1974–1977* with permission of Black Sparrow Press.

Jo Carson. "I Cannot Remember All the Times." From *An Ear to the Ground: An Anthology of Contemporary American Poetry* by Harris & Aguero. Reprinted by permission of The University of Georgia Press.

Martin Carter. "After One Year." From *Selected Poems*. Copyright © Martin Carter. Demerara Publishers, Ltd. (Guyana). Reprinted by permission.

Lorna Dee Cervantes. "Freeway 280." Reprinted by permission of the publisher, *Latin American Literary Review*, Volume V, number 10 1977, Pittsburgh, Pennsylvania. "Poem for the Young White Man Who Asked Me How I, an Intelligent, Well-Read Person, Could Believe in the War Between the Races" from *Emplumada*, by Lorna Dee Cervantes, copyright © 1981 by Lorna Dee Cervantes. Reprinted by permission of the University of Pittsburgh Press.

Marilyn Chin. "Turtle Soup." From *The Phoenix Gone, The Terrace Empty* by Marilyn Chin. Copyright © 1994 by Marilyn Chin. Reprinted with permission from Milkweed Editions.

Lucille Clifton. "good times." Copyright © 1987 by Lucille Clifton. Reprinted from *Good Woman: Poems and a Memoir, 1969–1980*, by Lucille Clifton, with permission of BOA Editions, Ltd., 92 Park Ave., Brockport, NY 14420. "homage to my hips" reprinted by permission of Curtis Brown Ltd. Copyright © 1980 by the University of Massachusetts Press. First appeared in *two-headed woman*, published by The University of Massachusetts.

Wanda Coleman. "At the Jazz Club He Comes on a Ghost." Copyright © 1983 by Wanda Coleman. Reprinted from *Imagoes* with the permission of Black Sparrow Press.

Jayne Cortez. "Into This Time." From *The Jazz Poetry Anthology*, edited by Sacha Feinstein & Yusef Komunyakaa, Indiana University Press (1991). Copyright © 1996 by Jayne Cortez. Reprinted by permission of the author.

Robert Creeley. "Time." From *Collected Poems of Robert Creeley*, 1945–1975, copyright © 1983 by The Regents of the University of California. Reprinted by permission of the University of California Press.

Victor Hernandez Cruz. "Problems with Hurricanes." Originally appeared in *Red Beans* by Victor Hernandez Cruz, Coffee House Press, 1991. Copyright © 1991 by Victor Hernandez Cruz. Reprinted by permission of the author and Coffee House Press.

Countee Cullen. "Incident." From *Color* by Countee Cullen. Copyright © 1925 by Harper & Brothers; copyright renewed 1953 by Ida M. Cullen. Reprinted by permission of GRM Associates, Inc., Agents for the Estate of Ida M. Cullen.

e. e. cummings. "in Just—," and "Buffalo Bill's," are reprinted from *Complete Poems 1904–1962* by E. E. Cummings, edited by George J. Firmage. Copyright © 1923, 1926, 1944, 1951, 1954, 1972, 1991 by the Trustees for the E. E. Cummings Trust. Copyright © 1976, 1985 by George James Firmage. Reprinted by permission of Liveright Publishing Corporation.

J. V. Cunningham. "Here Lies My Wife." From *The Collected Poems and Epigrams of J.V. Cunningham*. Copyright © 1971 by J.V. Cunningham. Reprinted with the permission of Jessie Cunningham.

Jim Daniels. "Hard Times in the Motor City." From *Places/Everyone* by Jim Daniels. Winner of the 1985 Brittingham Prize in Poetry. Copyright © 1985 (Madison: The University of Wisconsin Press.) Reprinted by permission of The University of Wisconsin Press.

Keki Daruwalla. "Pestilence." From *Under Orion* by Keki Daruwalla (1975). Reprinted by permission.

Kamala Das. "In Love." From *The Best of Kamala Das* by Kamala Das. Published by Bodhi Publishing House, Kozhikode, Kerala, India (1991). Reprinted by permission of the author.

James Dickey. "Cherrylog Road." From *Helmets*. Copyright © 1964 by James Dickey, Wesleysan University Press by permission of University Press of New England.

Emily Dickinson. "I'm Nobody! Who Are You?," "There is No Frigate Like a Book," "I Heard a Fly Buzz," "I Like to See it Lap the Miles," and "Because I Could Not Stop for Death" reprinted by permission of the publishers and the Trustees of Amherst college from *The Poems of Emily Dickinson*, edited by Thomas H. Johnson. Cambridge, Mass.: The Belknap Press of Harvard University Press. Copyright © 1951, 1955, 1983 by the President and Fellows of Harvard College.

Stephen Dobyns. "Black Dog, Red Dog." From *Velocities* by Stephen Dobyns. Copyright © 1994 by Stephen Dobyns. Used by permission of Penguin, a division of Penguin Books USA Inc.

H. D. [Hilda Doolittle]. "Garden." From *Collected Poems, 1912–1944*. Copyright © 1982 by The Estate of Hilda Doolittle. Reprinted by permission of New Directions Publishing Corp.

Mark Doty. "Tiara." From *Bethlehem in Broad Daylight* by Mark Doty. Reprinted by permission of David R. Godine, Publisher, Inc. Copyright © 1991 by Mark Doty.

Rita Dove. "Silos." From *Grace Notes* by Rita Dove. Copyright © 1989 by Rita Dove. Reprinted with permission of the author and W. W. Norton and Company. "Adolescense–III," "Anti-Father," "The Event," "Jiving," "Courtship," "The Satisfaction Coal Company," "Weathering Out," "Sunday Greens." From *Selected Poems*. Pantheon/Vintage. Copyright © 1980, 1983, 1986, 1993 by Rita Dove. Reprinted by permission of the author.

Alan Dugan. "On Hurricane Jackson. From *New and Collected Poems* by Alan Dugan. Copyright © 1961, 1962, 1968, 1972, 1973, 1974, 1983 by Alan Dugan. First published by The Ecco Press in 1983. Reprinted by permission of the publisher.

Robert Duncan. "The Torso, Passage 18." From *Bending the Bow*. Copyright © 1968 by Robert Duncan. Reprinted by permission of New Directions Publishing Corp.

Cornelius Eady. "My Mother, If She Had Won Free Dance Lessons." From *Victims of the Latest Dance Craze*. Copyright © 1985 by Cornelius Eady. Reprinted by permission of the author.

Russell Edson. "The Fall." From *What a Man Can See*. Copyright © 1969 by Russell Edson. Reprinted by permission. "A Performance at Hog Theatre" from *The Intuitive Journey and Other Works*. Copyright © 1976 by Russell Edson. By permission of Georges Borchardt, Inc., agents for the author.

T. S. Eliot. "The Journey of the Magi," "Preludes," and "The Love Song of J. Alfred Prufrock" from *Complete Poems 1909–1962* by T. S. Eliot. Copyright 1936 by Harcourt Brace & Company; copyright © 1964, 1963 by T. S. Eliot. Reprinted by permission of the publisher.

Anita Endrezze. "The Girl Who Loved the Sky." From *Harper's Anthology of 20th Century Native American Poetry*, ed. by Duane Niatum. Copyright © 1988 and published by Harper SF, a division of HarperCollins Publishers.

Louise Erdrich. "A Love Medicine." From *Jacklight*. Copyright © 1984 by Louise Erdrich. Reprinted by permission of Henry Holt and Company, Inc.

Martín Espada. "The Saint Vincent de Paul Food Pantry Stomp." From Martín Espada's *Rebellion Is the Circle of a Lover's Hands / Rebelión es el giro de manos del amante* (Curbstone Press, 1990). Copyright © 1990 by Martín Espada. Reprinted with permission of Curbstone Press.

Gavin Ewart. "Psychoanalysis." Copyright © 1950, 1978 The New Yorker Magazine, Inc. Reprinted by permission. All rights reserved.

Kenneth Fearing. "Love, 20¢ the First Quarter Mile." From *New and Selected Poems 1936–1976* by Kenneth Fearing. Copyright © 1976 by Kenneth Fearing. Reprinted by permission of Indiana University Press.

James Fenton. "God, A Poem." Published in *Children in Exile*. Copyright © 1983 by James Fenton. Reprinted by permission of Sterling Lord Literistic, Inc.

Lawrence Ferlinghetti. "Constantly Risking Absurdity." From *A Coney Island of the Mind*. Copyright © 1958 by Lawrence Ferlinghetti. Reprinted by permission of New Directions Publishing Corp.

Francis Fike. "Doves." From *In the Same Rivers* by Francis Fike. Published by Robert L. Barth, Florence, Kentucky. Copyright © 1989 by Francis Fike. Reprinted by permission of the author.

Carolyn Forché. "The Colonel." From *The Country Between Us* by Carolyn Forche. Copyright © 1981 by Carolyn Forche. Originally appeared in *Women's International Resource Exchange*. Reprinted by permission of HarperCollins Publishers, Inc.

Robert Francis. "Silent Poem." From *Robert Francis: Collected Poems, 1936–1976* (Amherst: University of Massachusetts Press, 1976). Copyright © 1976 by Robert Francis. Reprinted by permission of The University of Massachusetts Press. "The Base Stealer." Originally titled "The Pitcher" from *The Orb Weaver*. Copyright © 1960 by Robert Francis (Wesleyan University Press). Reprinted by permission of University Press of New England.

Robert Frost. "After Apple Picking," "Fire and Ice," "Nothing Gold Can Stay," " 'Out, Out—,' " "The Road Not Taken," "Stopping by Woods on a Snowy Evening" from *The Poetry of Robert Frost*, edited by Edward Connery Lathem. Copyright 1923, © 1969 by Henry Holt and Company, Inc. Reprinted by permission of Henry Holt and Company, Inc.

Alice Fulton. "You Can't Rhumboogie in a Ball and Chain" from *Dance Script with Electric Ballerina* (University of Pennsylvania Press). Copyright © 1979, 1983, 1991, 1996 by Alice Fulton. Reprinted by permission of the author.

Richard Garcia. "Why I Left the Church." From *The Flying Garcias* by Richard Garcia. Copyright © 1993. Reprinted by permission of the University of Pittsburgh Press.

Gary Gildner. "The High Class Bananas." From *Blue Like the Heavens: New and Selected Poems* by Gary Gildner. Copyright © 1984. Reprinted by permission of the University of Pittsburgh Press.

Allen Ginsberg. "A Supermarket in California." From *Collected Poems 1947–1980* by Allen Ginsberg. Copyright © 1955 by Allen Ginsberg. Copyright renewed. Reprinted by permission of Harper-Collins Publishers Inc.

Nikki Giovanni. "Nikki-Rosa." From *Black Feelings, Black Talk, Black Judgment* by Nikki Giovanni. Copyright © 1970 by Nikki Giovanni. By permission of William Morrow and Company, Inc.

Louise Glück. "Love Poem." From *The House on Marshland* by Louise Glück. Copyright © 1971, 1972, 1973, 1974, 1975 by Louise Glück. First published by The Ecco Press in 1975. Reprinted by permission.

Jorie Graham. "Wanting A Child." From *Erosion*. Copyright © 1983. Reprinted by permission Princeton University Press.

Donald Hall. "Names of Horses." From *Old and New Poems*. Copyright © 1990 by Donald Hall. Reprinted by permission of Houghton Mifflin Company. All rights reserved. Originally published in *The New Yorker*.

Joy Harjo. "She Had Some Horses." From the book *She Had Some Horses*. Copyright © 1983 by Joy Harjo. Used by permission of the publisher, Thunder's Mouth Press.

Michael Harper. "Nightmare Begins Responsibility." From *Images of Kin: New and Selected Poems* by Michael S. Harper. Copyright © 1977 by Michael S. Harper. Used with permission of the author and the University of Illinois Press.

Robert Hass. "Late Spring." From *Human Wishes* by Robert Hass. Copyright © 1989 by Robert Hass. First published by The Ecco Press in 1989. Reprinted by permission.

Robert Hayden. "Those Winter Sundays" and "Bone-Flower Elegy." From *Collected Poems of Robert Hayden*, edited by Frederick Glaysher. Copyright © 1985 by Erma Hayden. Reprinted by permission of Liveright Publishing Corporation.

Seamus Heaney. "Digging" from *Poems, 1965–1975* by Seamus Heaney. Copyright © 1980 by Seamus Heaney. Reprinted by permission of Farrar, Straus & Giroux, Inc. and Faber and Faber Ltd.

Anthony Hecht. "Dover Bitch." From *Collected Earlier Poems* by Anthony Hecht. Copyright © 1990 by Anthony Hecht. Reprinted by permission of Alfred A. Knopf, Inc.

Lyn Hejinian. "A Mask of Anger." Copyright © by Lyn Hejinian. Reprinted by permission of the author and Burning Deck, 71 Elmgrove Avenue, Providence, R.I., 02906.

Conrad Hilberry. "The Moon Seen as a Slice of Pineapple." From *The Moon Seen as a Slice of Pineapple*. Copyright © 1984 by Conrad Hilberry. Reprinted by permission of The University of Georgia Press.

Geoffrey Hill. "In Memory of Jane Fraser." From *Collected Poems* by Geoffrey Hill. Copyright © 1985 by Geoffrey Hill. Reprinted by permission of Oxford University Press, Inc.

Linda Hogan. "The Rainy Season." Copyright © 1985 by Linda Hogan. Reprinted from *Seeing through the Sun*, by Linda Hogan (Amherst: University of Massachusetts Press, 1985). By permission of the publisher. "Workday." First appeared in *Savings* by Linda Hogan, Coffee House Press, 1988. Copyright © 1988 by Linda Hogan. Reprinted by permission of Coffee House Press.

Garrett Hongo. "Yellow Light." From *Yellow Light*. Copyright © 1982 by Garrett Karoru Hongo, Wesleyan University Press. By permission of University Press of New England.

Susan Howe. "Speeches at the Barriers." From *Defenestration of Prague, The Europe of Trusts* (Los Angeles: Sun & Moon Press, 1990), pp. 101–102. Copyright © 1990 by Susan Howe. Reprinted by permission of the publisher.

Langston Hughes. "The Negro Speaks of Rivers" and "Dream Variations" from *Selected Poems* by Langston Hughes. Copyright 1926 by Alfred A. Knopf, Inc. and renewed 1954 by Langston Hughes. Reprinted by permission of the publisher. "Dream Deferred" ("Harlem") from *The pan-*

ther and the Lash by Langston Hughes. Copyright 1951 by Langston Hughes. Reprinted by permission of Alfred A. Knopf, Inc. "Theme for English B" from *Collected Poems* by Langston Hughes. Copyright © 1994 by the Estate of Langston Hughes. Reprinted by permission of Alfred A. Knopf, Inc.

Ted Hughes. "Crow's First Lesson." From *Crow by Ted Hughes*. Copyright © 1971 by Ted Hughes. Reprinted by permission of HarperCollins Publishers, Inc. and Faber & Faber (UK).

Richard Hugo. "Driving Montana." Reprinted from *Making Certain It Goes On: The Collected Poems of Richard Hugo*. Copyright © 1984 by The Estate of Richard Hugo. Reprinted with permission of W. W. Norton & Company, Inc.

Harry Humes. "The Great Wilno." From *The Way Winter Works* by Harry Humes. Copyright © 1990. Reprinted by permission of The University of Arkansas.

Randall Jarrell. "The Woman at the Washington Zoo." From *The Complete Poems* by Randall Jarrell. Copyright © 1969 by Mrs. Randall Jarrell. Reprinted by permission of Farrar, Straus, & Giroux, Inc.

Robinson Jeffers. "Hurt Hawks." From *The Selected Poetry of Robinson Jeffers* by Robinson Jeffers. Copyright © 1928 and renewed 1956 by Robinson Jeffers. Reprinted by permission of Random House, Inc.

Richard Jones. "The Color of Grief." From *At Last We Enter Paradise*. Copyright © 1991 by Richard Jones. Reprinted by permission of Copper Canyon Press, PO Box 271, Port Townsend, WA 98368.

James Joyce. "On the Beach at Fontana." From *Poems and Shorter Writings* by James Joyce. Copyright © 1991 by The Estate of James Joyce. Reprinted by permission of The Estate of James Joyce.

Donald Justice. "Sonatina in Yellow." From *New and Selected Poems* by Donald Justice. Copyright © 1995 by Donald Justice. Reprinted by permission of Alfred A. Knopf, Inc.

Shirley Kaufman. "Nechama." From *Gold Country* by Shirley Kaufman, University of Pittsburgh Press. Copyright © 1973 by Shirley Kaufman. Reprinted by permission of the author.

Jack Kerouac. "239th Chorus." From *Mexico City Blues*. Copyright © 1959 by Jack Kerouac. Reprinted by permission of Sterling Lord Literistic, Inc.

Galway Kinnell. "St. Francis and the Sow." From *Mortal Acts, Mortal Words*. Copyright © 1980 by Galway Kinnell. Reprinted by permission of Houghton Mifflin Co. All rights reserved.

Carolyn Kizer. "Bitch." From *Mermaids in the Basement*. Copyright © 1984 by Carolyn Kizer. Reprinted by permission of Copper Canyon Press, PO Box 271, Port Townsend, WA 98368.

Etheridge Knight. "Hard Rock Returns to Prison from the Hospital for the Criminal Insane." From *The Essential Etheridge Knight* by Etheridge Knight. Copyright © 1986 by Etheridge Knight. Reprinted by permission of the University of Pittsburgh Press.

Kenneth Koch. "The History of Jazz." Copyright © 1962 by Kenneth Koch. Reprinted by permission of the author.

Yusef Komunyakaa. "Facing It." From *Neon Vernacular*, copyright © 1993 by Yusef Komunyakaa, Wesleyan University Press. By permission of University Press of New England.

Ted Kooser. "Flying at Night." From *One World At a Time* by Ted Kooser. Copyright © 1985 by Ted Kooser. Reprinted by permission of the University of Pittsburgh Press.

Richard Kostelanetz. "Disintegration." From *Wordworks: Poems New & Selected* by Richard Kostelanetz. Copyright © 1990, 1993 by Richard Kostelanetz. Published 1993 by BOA Editions, Ltd. Reprinted by permission of the author.

Maxine Kumin. "The Excrement Poem." From *Our Ground Time Here Will Be Brief: New and Selected Poems*. Copyright © 1982 by Maxine Kumin. From Selected Poems 1960–1990 by Maxine Kumin. Reprinted by permission of W.W. Norton & Company.

Stanley Kunitz. "Father and Son." From *The Poems of Stanley Kunitz 1928–1978*. Copyright © 1979 by Stanley Kunitz. Reprinted with the permission of W.W. Norton & Company, Inc.

Li-Young Lee. "Visions and Interpretations" and "Eating Alone." Copyright © 1986 by Li-Young Lee. Reprinted from *Rose* by Li-Young Lee, with the permission of BOA Editions, Ltd., 92 Park Ave., Brockport, NY 14420.

Denise Levertov. "February Evening in New York." From *Collected Earlier Poems 1940–1960*. Copyright © 1960, 1979 by Denise Levertov. Reprinted by permission of New Directions Publishing Corp.

Philip Levine. "What Work Is" from *What Work Is* by Philip Levine. Copyright © 1991 by Philip Levine. Reprinted by permission of Alfred A. Knopf, Inc.

Larry Levis. "The Poem You Asked For." From *Wrecking Crew* by Larry Levis, copyright © 1972 by Larry Levis. Reprinted by permission of University of Pittsburgh Press.

Dorothy Livesay. "Green Rain." From *The Self-Completing Tree: Selected Poems*, copyright © 1986 by Dorothy Livesay. Press Porcépic (Victoria, Canada). Reprinted by permission of the author.

Audre Lorde. "Coal." From *Undersong: Chosen Poems, Old and New* by Audre Lorde. Copyright © 1992, 1976, 1970, 1968 by Audre Lorde. Reprinted with the permission of W.W. Norton and Company, Inc.

Richard Lovelace. "To Lucasta, Going to the Wars." Copyright © Richard Lovelace. Reprinted by permission.

Robert Lowell. "Skunk Hour" from *Selected Poems* by Robert Lowell. Copyright © 1976 by Robert Lowell. Reprinted by permission of Farrar, Straus & Giroux, Inc.

Mina Loy. "The Widow's Jazz." From *The Last Lunar Baedeker*. Copyright © The Jargon Society. Reprinted by permission.

Edward Lueders. "Your Poem, Man..." from *Some Haystacks Don't Even Have Any Needle: And Other Complete Modern Poems*. Compiled by Stephen Dunning, Edward Lueders and Hugh Smith. Copyright © 1969 by Scott, Foresman and Company, Glenview, Illinois 60025. Reprinted by permission.

Mekeel McBride. "A Blessing." From *Going Under of the Evening Land*. Copyright © 1983 by Mekeel McBride. Reprinted by permission of the author and Carnegie Mellon University Press.

Thomas McGrath. "All the Dead Soldiers." From *Selected Poems 1938–1988*. Copyright © 1988 by Thomas McGrath. Reprinted by permission of Copper Canyon Press, PO Box 271, Port Townsend, WA 98368.

Medbh McGuckian. "Lighthouse with Dead Leaves." From *On Ballycastle Beach* by Medbh McGuckian. Reprinted with permission of Wake Forest University Press.

Heather McHugh. "What He Thought" and "Language Lesson 1976" from *Hinge & Sign*, copyright © 1994 by Heather McHugh, Wesleyan University Press. By permission of University Press of New England.

Claude McKay. "America." From Selected Poems of Claude McKay. Copyright © 1981 by the Estate of Claude McKay. Used by permission of The Archives of Claude McKay, Carl Cowl, Administrator.

Archibald MacLeish. "Ars Poetica." From *Collected Poems 1917–1982* by Archibald MacLeish. Copyright © 1985 by The Estate of Archibald MacLeish. Reprinted by permission of Houghton Mifflin Company. All rights reserved.

Jack Mapanje. "From *Florrie Abraham Witness*, December 1972," from *Of Chameleons and Gods* by Jack Mapanje. Reprinted by permission of Heinemann Publishers Ltd.

William Matthews. "Blues for John Coltrane, Dead at 41." From *Selected Poems and Translations*. Copyright © 1992 by William Matthews. Reprinted by permission of Houghton Mifflin Company. All rights reserved.

James Merrill. "The Pier: Under Pisces." From Selected Poems, 1946–1985 by James Merrill. Copyright © 1993 by James Merrill. Reprinted by permission of Alfred A. Knopf, Inc.

W. S. Merwin. "Yesterday." From *Opening the Hand* by W. S. Merwin. Copyright © 1983 by W. S. Merwin. Reprinted by permisson of Georges Borchardt, Inc.

Josephine Miles. "On Inhabiting an Orange." From *Collected Poems, 1930–83* by Josephine Miles. Copyright 1983 by Josephine Miles. Used with permission of the University of Illinois Press.

Edna St. Vincent Millay. "Wild Swans" by Edna St. Vincent Millay. From *Collected Poems*, Harper-Collins. Copyright 1921, 1948 by Edna St. Vincent Millay. Reprinted by permission of Elizabeth Barnett, literary executor.

Gary Miranda. "Love Poem" from *Grace Period*. Copyright © 1983 by Princeton University Press. Reprinted by permission of Princeton University Press.

Marianne Moore. "The Steeple-Jack." Copyright © 1951, 1970 by Marianne Moore; © renewed 1979 by Lawrence E. Brinn and Louise Crane, Executors of the Estate of Marianne Moore. From *The Complete Poems of Marianne Moore* by Marianne Moore. Used by permission of Viking Penguin, a division of Penguin Books USA Inc.

Robert Morgan. "Mountain Bride." From *Groundwork* (1979). Reprinted by permission of Gnomon Press.

Thylias Moss. "Sunrise Comes to Second Avenue." From *At Redbones*, Cleveland State University Poetry Center. Copyright © 1990 by Thylias Moss. Reprinted by permission of the author and the Cleveland State University Poetry Center.

Julie Moulds. "Wedding Iva" copyright © 1995 by Julie Moulds. First published in *The PrePress Awards Volume Two: Michigan Voices*. Reprinted by permission of the author.

Lisel Mueller. "The Deaf Dancing to Rock." From *Waving from Shore* by Lisel Mueller. Copyright © 1979, 1986, 1987, 1988, 1989 by Lisel Mueller. Reprinted by permission of Louisiana State University Press.

Paul Muldoon. "Hedgehog." From *Mules and Early Poems* by Paul Muldoon. Copyright © 1986 by Paul Muldoon. Reprinted with the permission of Wake Forest University Press and Faber and Faber Ltd.

David Mura. "The Natives." From *After We Lost Our Way* (E. P. Dutton) and first appeared in *The American Poetry Review*. Copyright 1989 by David Mura. Reprinted by permission of the author.

Jack Myers. "Why Don't You Ask Your Father?" From *Blindsided* by Jack Myers, copyright © 1993 by Jack Myers. Reprinted by permission of David R. Godine, Publisher, Inc.

Lorine Niedecker. "Will You Write Me a Christmas Poem?" From *From this Condensery: The Complete Writing of Lorine Niedecker*. Copyright © 1985 by the Estate of Lorine Niedecker. Reprinted by permission.

John Frederick Nims. "Love Poem." From *Selected Poems*. Copyright © 1982 by the University of Chicago. Reprinted by permission of The University of Chicago Press. All rights reserved.

Naomi Shihab Nye. "Catalogue Army." From *Words Under the Words: Selected Poems* by Naomi Shihab Nye; published by Far Corner Books, Portland, Oregon. Copyright © 1995 by Naomi Shihab Nye. Reprinted by permission.

Frank O'Hara. "The Day Lady Died." Copyright © 1964 by Frank O'Hara. Reprinted by permission of City Lights Books.

Christopher Okigbo. "Elegy for Alto." From *Collected Poems* by Christopher Okigbo. By permission Heinemann Publishers (Oxford) Limited.

Sharon Olds. "The Victims." From *The Dead and the Living* by Sharon Olds. Copyright © 1983 by Sharon Olds. Reprinted by permission of Alfred A. Knopf, Inc.

Mary Oliver. "Sleeping in the Forest." From *Twelve Moons* by Mary Oliver. Copyright © 1978 by Mary Oliver. First appeared in *The Ohio Review*. By permission of Little, Brown and Company.

Michael Ondaatje. "Biography." From *There's a Trick With a Knife I'm Learning to Do: Poems 1963–1978*. Copyright © 1979 by Michael Ondaatje. Reprinted by permission of Michael Ondaatje.

Simon J. Ortiz. "Speaking." Previously published in *Woven Stone*, University of Arizona Press, 1992. Copyright © 1992. Reprinted by permission of the author.

Wilfred Owen. "Dulce et Decorum Est." From *Poems of Wilfred Owen*. Copyright © 1963 by Chatto & Windus, Ltd. Reprinted by permission of New Directions Publishing Corp.

Michael Palmer "Fifth Prose." From *Sun*, North Point Press, 1988. Copyright © 1988 by Michael Palmer. Reprinted by permission of the author.

Dorothy Parker. "Résumé" by Dorothy Parker. Copyright 1926, 1928, renewed 1954, © 1956 by Dorothy Parker. From *The Portable Dorothy Parker* by Dorothy Parker, introduction by Brendan Gill. Used by permission of Viking Penguin, a division of Penguin Books USA Inc.

Linda Pastan. "love poem." From *The Imperfect Paradise: Poems by Linda Pastan*. Copyright © 1988 by Linda Pastan. Reprinted by permission of W.W. Norton & Company, Inc.

James A. Perkins. "Boundaries." Published for the first time by permission of James A. Perkins.

Marge Piercy. "The Friend" from *Circles on the Water* by Marge Piercy. Copyright © 1982 by Marge Piercy. Reprinted by permission of Alfred A. Knopf, Inc.

Sylvia Plath. "Daddy" and "Edge" from *Ariel* by Sylvia Plath. Copyright © 1963 by Ted Hughes. Copyright renewed. Reprinted by permission of HarperCollins Publishers, Inc. and Faber and Faber Ltd.; "Tulips" from *Ariel* by Sylvia Plath. Copyright © 1962 by Ted Hughes. Copyright renewed. Reprinted by permission of HarperCollins Publishers, Inc. and Faber and Faber Ltd.; "Nick and the Candlestick" from *The Collected Poems of Sylvia Plath*, edited by Ted Hughes. Copyright © 1966 by Ted Hughes. Copyright renewed. Reprinted by permission of Faber and Faber Ltd. "Metaphors" from *Crossing the Water* by Sylvia Plath. Copyright © 1960 by Ted Hughes. Copyright renewed. Reprinted by permission of HarperCollins Publishers, Inc. and Faber and Faber

Ltd. "The Colossus." From *The Colossus and Other Poems* by Sylvia Plath. Copyright © 1961 by Sylvia Plath. Reprinted by permission of Alfred A. Knopf, Inc. and Faber and Faber Ltd.

Ezra Pound. "In a Station of the Metro." From *Personae*. Copyright © 1926 by Ezra Pound. Reprinted by permission of New Directions Publishing Corp.

Craig Raine. "Dandelions". Copyright © 1979 by Craig Raine. From *A Martian Sends a Postcard Home* by Craig Raine (1979). Reprinted by permission of Oxford University Press.

George Ralph. "Darkness of the Rose" by George Ralph, first published in *The International Haiku Contest*, 1987; "Hanging from the Eaves" by George Ralph, first published in the *American Association of Haikuists Newsletter*, Spring 1986. Reprinted by permission of the author.

Dudley Randall. "Ballad of Birmingham." From *Cities Burning*. Copyright © 1968 by Dudley Randall. Reprinted by permission of Broadside Press.

John Crowe Ransom. "Bells for John Whiteside's Daughter." From *Selected Poems* by John Crowe Ransom. Copyright © 1924 by Alfred A. Knopf, Inc. and renewed 1952 by John Crowe Ransom. Reprinted by permission of the publisher.

David Ray. "Greens." From *X-Rays* by David Ray. Copyright © 1965 by Cornell University Press. Reprinted by permission of the author.

Henry Reed. "Naming of Parts." From *Collected Poems*, Copyright © 1991 by the Executors of Henry Reed's Estate. By permission of Oxford University Press.

Adrienne Rich. "Aunt Jennifer's Tigers," "Diving Into the Wreck" and "Rape." Reprinted from *The Fact of a Doorframe: Poems Selected and New, 1950–1984* by Adrienne Rich. By permission of the author and W.W. Norton & Company, Inc. Copyright © 1984 by Adrienne Rich. Copyright © 1975, 1978 by W.W. Norton & Company, Inc. Copyright © 1981 by Adrienne Rich.

Alberto Ríos. "Mi Abuelo." First printed in *Whispering to Fool the Wind* (Sheep Meadow Press) by Albert Rios. Copyright © 1982 by Albert Rios. Reprinted by permission of the author. "Fixing Tires." From *Teodoro Luna's Two Kisses* by Albert Rios. Copyright © 1990 by Albert Rios. Reprinted by permission of W.W. Norton & Company, Inc.

Edwin Arlington Robinson. "Richard Cory." From *The Children of the Night* by Edwin Arlington Robinson. (New York: Charles Scribner's Sons, 1897). Reprinted by permission of Simon & Schuster.

Theodore Roethke. "My Papa's Waltz." Copyright 1942 by Hearst Magazines, Inc. "Dolor" copyright 1943 by Modern Poetry Association, Inc. "Meditation at Oyster River" copyright © 1960 by Beatrice Roethke as administratrix of the estate of Theodore Roethke. From *The Collected Poems of Theodore Roethke* by Theodore Roethke. Used by permission of Doubleday, a division of Bantam Doubleday Dell Publishing Group, Inc.

Wendy Rose. "Loo-Wit." From *The Half-Breed Chronicles* (West End Press). Copyright © 1985 by Wendy Rose. Reprinted by permission.

Jerome Rothenburg. "B•R•M•Tz•V•H." From *Vienna Blook & Other Poems*. Copyright © 1980 by Jerome Rothenberg. Reprinted by permission of New Directions Publishing Corp.

Mary Ruefle. "The Derision of Christ in New England." From *The Adamant* by Mary Ruefle. Copyright © 1989 by Mary Ruefle. Reprinted by permission of the University of Iowa Press.

Muriel Rukeyser. "Rune." From *The Collected Poems of Muriel Rukeyser*, McGraw-Hill, New York, 1978. Copyright © 1976 by Muriel Rukeyser. By permission of William L. Rukeyser.

Vern Rutsala. "Furniture Factory." Copyright © Vera Rutsala. Reprinted by permission.

Carl Sandburg. "Grass." From *Cornhuskers* by Carl Sandburg. Copyright 1918 by Holt, Rinehart and Winston, Inc. and renewed 1946 by Carl Sandburg. Reprinted by permission of Harcourt Brace & Company.

Cheryl Savageau. "Bones—A City Poem." From *Home Country*. Copyright © 1992 by Cheryl Savageau. Reprinted by permission of Alice James Books.

Anne Sexton. "Her Kind." From *To Bedlam and Part Way Back*. Copyright © 1960 by Anne Sexton; renewed 1988 by Linda G. Sexton. Reprinted by permission of Houghton Mifflin Co. All rights reserved.

Leslie Marmon Silko. "Prayer to the Pacific". Copyright © 1981 by Leslie Marmon Silko. Reprinted from *Storyteller* by Leslie Marmon Silko, published by Seaver Books, New York, New York. By permission of the publisher.

Charles Simic. "Begotten of the Spleen." Copyright © 1980 by Charles Simic. Reprinted by courtesy of George Braziller, Inc.; "Everybody Knows the (Story about Me and Dr. Freud)." from *The World*

Doesn't End. Copyright © 1987 by Charles Simic. Reprinted by permission of Harcourt Brace & Company.

Edith Sitwell. "Lullaby." From *The Collected Poems of Edith Sitwell* by Edith Sitwell (Sinclair-Stevenson). Copyright © 1968 by Edith Sitwell. Reprinted by permission of David Higham Associates.

Gary Snyder. "Hitch Haiku." From *The Back Country*. Copyright © 1968 by Gary Snyder. Reprinted by permission of New Directions Publishing Corporation. "Riprap." From *Riprap and Cold Mountain Poems* by Gary Snyder. Copyright © 1965 by Gary Snyder. Reprinted by permission of Farrar, Straus & Giroux, Inc.

Mary Ellen Solt. "Forsythia." From *Flowers in Concrete* by Mary Ellen Solt. Published by Design Program, Department of Fine Arts, Typography: John Dearstyne. Indiana University, 1966. Reprinted by permission of the author.

Cathy Song. "Girl Powdering Her Neck." From *Picture Bride*. Copyright © 1983 by Cathy Song. Reprinted by permission of the publisher, Yale University Press.

Gary Soto. "The Morning They Shot Tony Lopez, Barber and Pusher Who Went Too Far, 1958," "The Elements of San Joaquin," "Field Poem," "Hoeing," "Harvest," "Summer," "History," "Mexicans Begin Jogging," "Envying the Children of San Francisco." From *New and Selected Poems* by Gary Soto. © 1996, published by Chronicle Books, San Francisco. Reprinted by permission of the author and Chronicle Books.

William Stafford. "Notice What This Poem is Not Doing." Copyright © 1980 The Estate of William Stafford. This poem first appeared in *Things That Happen Where There Aren't Any People* (BOA Editions, 1980). Reprinted by permission. "Traveling Through the Dark." Copyright © 1977 William Stafford from *Stories That Could Be True* (Harper & Row). Reprinted by permission of The Estate of William Stafford.

Gertrude Stein. "Susie Asado." From *Selected Writings of Gertrude Stein* by Gertrude Stein. Copyright © 1962 by Gertrude Stein. Reprinted by permission of Random House, Inc.

Gerald Stern. "The Dog." From *Leaving Another Kingdom: Selected Poems* by Gerald Stern. Copyright © 1990 by Gerald Stern. Reprinted by permission of HarperCollins Publishers, Inc.

Wallace Stevens. "Anecdote of the Jar." From *Collected Poems* by Wallace Stevens. Copyright 1923 and renewed 1951 by Wallace Stevens. "Final Soliloquy of the Interior Paramour" from *Collected Poems* by Wallace Stevens. Copyright 1951 by Wallace Stevens. Reprinted by permission of Alfred A. Knopf, Inc.

Mark Strand. "Eating Poetry." From *Selected Poems* by Mark Strand. Copyright © 1979, 1980 by Mark Strand. Reprinted by permission of Alfred A. Knopf, Inc.

Sekou Sundiata. "Blink Your Eyes." Copyright © 1995 Sekou Sundiata. Reprinted by permission.

May Swenson. "The Shape of Death." From *The Love Poems of May Swenson*. Copyright © 1991 by The Literary Estate of May Swenson. Reprinted by permission of Houghton Mifflin Co. All rights reserved.

James Tate. "End of a Semester." From *Absences: New Poems* by James Tate. Copyright © 1970 by James Tate. By permission Little, Brown and Company. "The Wheelchair Butterfly" from *Selected Poems*. Copyright © 1991 by James Tate, Wesleyan University Press by permission of University Press of New England.

Dylan Thomas. "Do Not Go Gentle into That Good Night," "The Hand that Signed the Paper" and "Fern Hill." From *The Poems of Dylan Thomas*. Copyright © 1939 by New Directions Publishing Corp. Reprinted by permission of New Directions Publishing Corp. and David Higham (U.K.).

Jean Toomer. "Face." From *Cane* by Jean Toomer. Copyright 1923 by Boni & Liveright, renewed 1951 by Jean Toomer. Reprinted by permission of Liveright Publishing Corporation.

Quincy Troupe. "Snake-Back Solo 2." From *Avalanche* (Minneapolis: Coffee House Press, 1996). Copyright © 1996 by Quincy Troupe. Used by permission of the author.

Alberta Turner. "Drift." From *A Belfry of Knees* by Alberta Turner. Copyright © 1983 The University of Alabama Press. Reprinted by permission of the University of Alabama Press.

Lee Upton. "Photographs." Copyright © 1984. From *The Invention of Kindness*, University of Alabama Press. By permission of Lee Upton.

Jean Valentine. "December 21st." From *The Messenger* by Jean Valentine. Copyright © 1979 by Jean Valentine. Reprinted by permission of Farrar, Straus, and Giroux, Inc.

Ellen Bryant Voigt. "The Farmer." From Ellen Bryant Voigt, *The Lotus Flowers*. Copyright © 1987 by Ellen Bryant Voigt. Reprinted with the permission of W.W. Norton & Company, Inc.

Shelly Wagner. "Thirteenth Birthday." From *The Andrew Poems*. Copyright © 1994 by Shelly Wagner. Reprinted by permission of the publisher, Texas Tech University Press.

Derek Walcott. "Sea Grapes." From *Collected Poems 1948–1984* by Derek Walcott. Copyright © 1986 by Derek Walcott. Reprinted by permission of Farrar, Straus and Giroux, Inc.

Anne Waldman. "Bluehawk." Copyright © 1984 by Anne Waldman. Reprinted by permission of the author.

Alice Walker. " 'Good Night, Willie Lee, I'll See You in the Morning.' " Copyright © 1975 by Alice Walker. From *Good Night, Willie Lee, I'll See You in the Morning* by Alice Walker. Used by permission of Doubleday, a division of Bantam Doubleday Dell Publishing Group, Inc.

James Welch. "Christmas Comes to Moccasin Flat." From *Riding the Earthboy 40* by James Welch, Harper & Row. Copyright 1971 by James Welch. Reprinted by permission of James Welch. All rights reserved.

Winifred Welles. "Cruciform." Copyright © 1938, 1966 by The New Yorker Magazine, Inc. Reprinted by permission. All rights reserved.

Roberta Hill Whiteman. "The White Land." From *Star Quilt* by Roberta Hill Whiteman copyright © 1984. Reprinted by permission of Holy Cow! Press (Duluth, Minnesota).

Richard Wilbur. "Thyme Flowering Among Rocks." From *Walking to Sleep: New Poems and Translations*, Copyright © 1968 by Richard Wilbur. Reprinted by permission of Harcourt Brace & Company. "Year's End." From *Ceremony and Other Poems*. Copyright 1949 and renewed 1977 by Richard Wilbur. Reprinted by permission of Harcourt Brace & Company.

Nancy Willard. "Questions My Son Asked Me, Answers I Never Gave Him." From *Household Tales of Moon and Water*. Copyright © 1978 by Nancy Willard. Reprinted by permission of Harcourt Brace & Company. "Saint Pumpkin." From *Household Tales of Moon and Water*. Copyright © 1980 by Nancy Willard. Reprinted by permission of Harcourt Brace & Company.

C. K. Williams. "From My Window." From *Poems 1963–1983* by C. K. Williams. Copyright © 1988 by C. K. Williams. Reprinted by permission of Farrar, Straus & Giroux, Inc.

William Carlos Williams. "The Red Wheelbarrow," "Spring and All," and "The Dance." From *Collected Poems: 1909–1939*, Volume 1. Copyright © 1938 by New Directions Publishing Corp. Reprinted by permission of New Directions Publishing Corp.

Yvor Winters. "At the San Francisco Airport" from *The Collected Poems of Yvor Winters* (Ohio University Press/Swallow Press, 1978). Reprinted with the permission of The Ohio University Press/Swallow Press, Athens.

Charles Wright. "Sitting at Night on the Front Porch." Copyright © Charles Wright. Wesleyan University Press by permission of University Press of New England.

James Wright. "Saint Judas" from *Saint Judas*, copyright © 1959 by James Wright. Wesleyan University by permission of University Press of New England.

John Yau. "Chinese Villanelle" copyright © 1989 by John Yau. Reprinted from *Radiant Silhouette: New & Selected Work 1974–1988* with the permission of Black Sparrow Press.

William Butler Yeats. "The Wild Swans at Coole," "The Second Coming," "Adam's Curse," "Among School Children." From *The Poems of W.B. Yeats: A New Edition*, edited by Richard J. Finneran. Copyright © 1924 by Macmillan Publishing Company. Renewed 1952 by Bertha Georgie Yeats. Reprinted by permission of Simon & Schuster.

Al Young. "A Dance for Ma Rainey." Copyright © Al Young. Reprinted by permission.

David Young. "The Portable Earth Lamp" from *The Planet on the Desk: Selected and New Poems 1960–1990*. Copyright © 1991 by David Young. Wesleyan University Press by permission of University Press of New England.

Ray A. Young Bear. "From the Spotted Night" from *The Invisible Musician*, copyright © 1990 by Ray A. Young Bear. Reprinted by permission of Holy Cow! Press.

Paul Zimmer. "The Eisenhower Years." From *Family Reunion: Selected and New Poems* by Paul Zimmer. Copyright © 1983 by Paul Zimmer. Reprinted by permission of the University of Pittsburgh Press.

Louis Zukofsky. Excerpt from "A" 15. From *"A,"* pp. 359–375. Copyright © 1978 by Louis Zukofsky. By permission of The Johns Hopkins University Press.

Other Credits:

Robert Frost: Letters (#9754, 9755); Poetry (#9756, 9757, 9758), p. 251. From MLA International Bibliography of Books and Articles on the Modern Languages and Literatures. Volume 1. © 1994 by The Modern Language Association of America. Reprinted by permission of The Modern Language Association of America.

Dictionary Credits:

"silo," "martial," "physical," "humor," "deck," "deconstruction." From Webster's College Dictionary, McGraw-Hill Edition. © 1991 Random House, Inc. Reproduced with permission of The McGraw-Hill Companies.

"humor." From The Oxford English Dictionary, 2e, volume VII (Hat-Intervacuum). © 1989 Oxford University Press: Prepared by J.A. Simpson and E.S.C. Weiner. Reprinted by permission of Oxford University Press.

"beneficial." From The Oxford English Dictionary, 2e, volume XI (Ow-Poisant). © 1989 Oxford University Press. Prepared by J.A. Simpson and E.S.C. Weiner. Reprinted by permission of Oxford University Press.

Index of Authors and Titles

Thomas, Edward, 501; Dark Forest, The, 120

Those Winter Sundays, 149

Thou Art As Tyrannous, So As Thou Art, 182–83

Though Ye Suppose, 40

Three Companions, The, 121, 124

Thyme Flowering among Rocks, 358–59

Tiara, 154, 262–63

To an Athlete Dying Young, 318–19

To Autumn, 58–59, 154, 477

To Daffodils, 161

To His Coy Mistress, 153, 231–32

To Lucasta, Going to the Wars, 93–94, 244

To My Dear and Loving Husband, 304

To See a World in a Grain of Sand, 122

To the Virgins, To Make Much of Time, 303

Toomer, Jean, 501; Face, 86, 154

Torso, The, 355–56

Traveling through the Dark, 17–18, 88, 89n, 90, 95, 154

Troupe, Quincy, 68, 501; Snake-Back Solo 2, 136–38, 155

Tulips, 193–94

Turner, Alberta, 501; Drift, 6, 450, 452

Turtle Soup, 433

239th Chorus, 359

Tyger, The, 306–7

Ulysses, 293, 313–14

Upton, Lee, 501; Photographs, 261–62

Valediction: Forbidding Mourning, A, 301–2

Valentine, Jean, 192, 501; December 21st, 256

Victims, The, 30

Visions and Interpretations, 153, 174–75

Voice, The, 147

Voigt, Ellen Bryant, 501; Farmer, The, 408–9

Wagner, Shelly, 501; Thirteenth Birthday, 416–17

Walcott, Derek, 501; Sea Grapes, 384–85

Waldman, Anne, 501–2; Bluehawk, 415

Walker, Alice, 502; "Good Night, Willie Lee, I'll See You in the Morning," 414

Waller, Edmund, 502; Song, 102–3

Wanting a Child, 425

Warren, Robert Penn, 142, 229, 280

We Real Cool, 156, 159

Weathering Out, 210–11

Wedding Iva, 83

Welch, James, 502; Christmas Comes to Moccasin Flat, 279–90

Wellek, René, 229

Welles, Winifred, 502; Cruciform, 104–5

Western Wind, 31

What He Thought, 9–11, 155, 247

What Work Is, 376–77

Wheelchair Butterfly, The, 155, 156, 409–10

When I Consider How My Light Is Spent, 154, 304

When I Have Fears That I May Cease to Be, 201

When I Heard the Learn'd Astronomer, 65

When I Was Fair and Young, 297–98

When Lilacs Last in the Dooryard Bloomed, 133–34, 155, 477

When My Love Swears That She Is Made of Truth, 93

When Thou Must Home, 300

White Land, The, 233

Whiteman, Roberta Hill, 502; White Land, The, 233

Whitman, Walt, 502; Song of Myself, 65; When I Heard the Learn'd Astronomer, 65; When Lilacs Last in the Dooryard Bloomed, 133–34, 155, 477

Why Can't I Leave You, 416

Why I Left the Church, 407–8

Widow's Jazz, The, 328–29

Wilbur, Richard, 95, 138, 502; Thyme Flowering among Rocks, 358–59; Year's End, 232

Wild Swans, 340–41

Wild Swans at Coole, The, 322–23

Will You Write Me A Christmas Poem?, 343–45

Willard, Nancy, 502; Questions My Son Asked Me, Answers I Never Gave Him, 4, 87, 153; Saint Pumpkin, 230, 395–96, 461–68

Williams, C. K., 502; From My Window, 396–98

Williams, William Carlos, 8, 502–3; Spring and All, 329–30; Red Wheelbarrow, The, 53, 90

Index of Terms

ideal reader, 226
image, 51
imagery, 51
implied author, 249
implied metaphor, 86
implied reader, 249
intended reader, 250
internal rhyme, 123
interpretive communities, 255
irony, 72
Italian sonnet, 163

juxtaposition, 156

line, 131, 158
litotes, 94
lyric, 16, 477

Marxist criticism, 274
masculine rhyme, 123n
metaphor, 84
meter, 138
metonymy, 88
monometer, 140

narrative, 16, 153
near rhyme, 123
New Criticism, 223
New Historicism, 272

octave, 163
ode, 177
onomatopoeia, 119
open form, 170
ottava rima, 162
overstatement, 94

paradox, 93
parallelism, 155
partial rhyme, 123
pastoral, 477
pause, 131
pentameter, 140
persona, 66, 227
personification, 87
Petrarchan sonnet, 163
poem, 28
poetry, 8
poststructuralism, 237
prose poem, 158
psychoanalytical criticism, 185, 233, 256
pun, 95

quatrain, 161

readers, 21, 27, 248
refrain, 125
rhyme, 122
rhyme royal, 162
rhyme scheme, 124
rhythm, 131
rising meter, 140n
run-on line, 131

sarcasm, 72
scansion, 140, 478
sestet, 163
sestina, 165
Shakespearean sonnet,
     163
shaped poem, 169
simile, 82
single rhyme, 123
situational irony, 73
slant rhyme, 123
sonnet, 163
sound, 118
speaker, 65, 227
Spenserian stanza,
     162
spondee, 140
sprung rhythm, 138n
stanza, 160
stress, 138
structuralism, 235
substitution, 139
syllabic verse, 138n
symbol, 102
synecdoche, 89

terza rima, 162
tetrameter, 140
text, 28, 222, 252
tone, 70
transferred epithet,
     92
trimeter, 140
trochaic meter, 139
trochee, 139

understatement, 94

verbal irony, 72
villanelle, 167
voice, 68